THE BOX

JEFF KISSELOFF

THE BOX

An Oral History

of Television,

1920–1961

● VIKING ●

VIKING
Published by the Penguin Group
Penguin Books USA Inc., 375 Hudson Street, New York, New York 10014, U.S.A.
Penguin Books Ltd, 27 Wrights Lane, London W8 5TZ, England
Penguin Books Australia Ltd, Ringwood, Victoria, Australia
Penguin Books Canada Ltd, 10 Alcorn Avenue, Toronto, Ontario, Canada M4V 3B2
Penguin Books (N.Z.) Ltd, 182–190 Wairau Road, Auckland 10, New Zealand

Penguin Books Ltd, Registered Offices: Harmondsworth, Middlesex, England

First published in 1995 by Viking Penguin, a division of Penguin Books USA Inc.

1   3   5   7   9   10   8   6   4   2

LIBRARY OF CONGRESS CATALOGING IN PUBLICATION DATA
Kisseloff, Jeff.
The box: an oral history of television, 1920–1961 / Jeff Kisseloff
p.   cm.
Includes bibliographical references and index.
ISBN 0-670-86470-6
1. Television broadcasting—United States—History.   2. Television
producers and directors—United States—Interviews.   3. Television actors
and actresses—United States—Interviews.   4. Television personalities—
United States—Interviews.   I. Title.
PN1992.3.U5K52   1995
791.45'0973—dc20   95-10720

This book is printed on acid-free paper.

(∞)

Printed in the United States of America
Set in Bembo
DESIGNED BY BRIAN MULLIGAN

To my parents,
for their love
and their twenty-one-inch Zenith color console

I would sit in that control room, and as it got closer to air you could feel everything going softer and quieter. In front of me would be the director and his associates and all the earphones, switches, and plugs. Outside that plate-glass window was the studio. You could see the sets for your play. Finally, the lighting people would beam the sets, and the actors would come in and take their places in their costumes, standing quietly, waiting. In that last minute before you went on the air, you would watch the sweep hand going around, and there would be absolute silence, nobody moving. Then suddenly, the sweep hand would hit the hour, and you would hear a crash of music, and the announcer saying, "Live from New York," and you knew that your little play was going out to fifty million people. And nowhere have I ever felt a thrill like that. I love the theater, but it beats opening night in the theater every time.

— *TAD MOSEL*

CONTENTS

BOOK TWO

INTRODUCTION

It says something about our society that Elvis Presley gets his face on a postage stamp while the memory of the man whose great invention beamed the swiveling pelvis into millions of American homes is relegated mostly to "Jeopardy!" questions.

Philo Farnsworth is not the only television pioneer consigned to the dustbin of the American psyche. This project was in its embryonic stage when Dan O'Connor, a retired NBC employee, offered to track down Robert Sarnoff, the former NBC president and son of the late David Sarnoff. The General, as he liked to be called, was a founder of RCA, NBC's parent company, and its guiding spirit for forty-two years. He is easily the most important figure in the history of telecommunications.

After a few phone stops around the NBC offices, Dan was transferred to the personnel department. He explained once again that he needed to reach Robert Sarnoff. A silence at the other end of the line prompted Dan. "You know who he is, don't you? He's the General's son."

There was another hesitation before the voice asked, "How do you spell Sarnoff?"

Dan never got the number, but he confirmed the sad fact that those who contributed so much to television's development have largely been forgotten. Few people know of Ted Smith, who built the first television station in New York City; or Fred Coe, who opened the curtain on television's Golden Age; or Alex Anderson, who gave us two of early television's most beloved cartoon characters, Crusader Rabbit and Bullwinkle Moose.

When Sid Caesar's name came up in a recent conversation with a friend of my own vintage, I could have identified the brilliant comedian as Julius's Jewish cousin and gotten the same disinterested shrug. The irony is that Sarnoff and the magnetic power of the device he helped develop and market so skillfully must take some of the blame for people who think "Dr. Quinn, Medicine Woman" provides them with all the history they need to know.

The comedian Red Buttons made a career out of moaning about how unappreciated he is. "Nobody ever gave me a dinner," he whines at the Friars' Club roasts. The same can be said for many of the people in this book who were never famous enough to be forgotten, so let this tome be their dinner, and to make it more interesting we'll even invite those we prefer to forget.

This is a memory book, not a fact book. I have tried to answer the basic question "What was it like?" by re-creating those years when men and women from many fields came together first to assemble the golden box and then to figure out what to do with it.

Who were these people? There was Captain William Crawford Eddy and his merry band of pirates at WBKB in Chicago who liberated a barber's chair to build their first elevated camera and used an empty pickle jar to complete their transmitter. There was Klaus Landsberg, KTLA's feisty genius, who gave the world Lawrence Welk and television's first live broadcast of an atomic bomb test. (Which was the more destructive force depends on your point of view.) There were the twin cameramen, Eugene and Charlie Jones, television's first foreign correspondents, dodging live bullets on the front lines in Korea; Sylvester "Pat" Weaver, the president of NBC who insisted that television could elevate as well as entertain; and Paul Draper, the effervescent dancer who had the courage to stand up to Senator Joseph McCarthy's allies, and for his efforts never worked in television again. There was also Charlie Vanda, who created a live daily western in a vacant lot in Philadelphia and made it work, even though the horses sometimes mistook the microphones for oats; and another Charlie—Douglas—who invented the laugh machine, and Gracie Allen, who didn't need one. Even they are only part of the story. Television had large subsets of heroes. Landsberg's atomic bomb broadcast succeeded because Joey Featherston camped on a bare, snowy mountaintop to make sure the network held together.

Over the course of some four hundred interviews, time and again I heard, "We didn't know what we were doing. We just made it up as we went along." How exciting it must have been to be there at television's beginning. These people really were explorers, trekking like Lewis and Clark through uncharted territory.

If anything united the early pioneers, it was an innate skepticism and curiosity that led them to question axioms and to search for solutions to complex problems. None of them entered television with the idea of making a killing. It was the possibility of combining sight with sound and making it work that fascinated them. Even now, their memories of those days are remarkable for their lack of cynicism. This really was a different time and these people were a different breed, brilliant and gentle but determined to make something good come from their work.

The book opens back in the years before radio came along, when the notion of sending voices through the air was still scoffed at. The scientists and the experimenters soon take up the story of the early days of radio. One cannot fully comprehend television's development without appreciating radio. When television finally came along, broadcasters had only their experiences in radio to guide them. Like a child in hand-me-down clothes, television inherited the best and worst that radio had to offer, from the Ed Wynns and Jack Bennys, who made millions of Americans laugh every week, to the blatant commercialism that drove the system. Television did it all, but radio did it first.

The witnesses' reminiscences then cover television's story through 1961, the year of Federal Communications Commission Chairman Newton Minow's "vast wasteland" speech, delivered the same month that a Congressional committee opened hearings into violence on television. The disturbing aspect of those hearings was not so much the violent programs as the cynical attitude of the three networks toward such programming, laid bare when the committee subpoenaed the networks' internal memoranda. The crass commercialism of CBS president Jim Aubrey's dictum that his shows contain "bosoms, broads, and fun" provides a natural counterpoint to the idealistic atmosphere that permeated Philo Farnsworth's television laboratory in the 1930s where, one visitor recalled, the dedicated staff looked gaunt from overwork and undereating.

The voices represent every aspect of the industry, from the scientists and technicians who created it to the producers, directors, writers, performers, cameramen, stage managers, stagehands, station managers, network executives, advertisers, and lawyers who ran it. Many of them spoke with genuine passion of their work, and most of them made the interviewing process a rewarding one. A few were unforgettable. The comedian Jack Carter, whose now-forgotten variety show on NBC closely rivaled the classic "Your Show of Shows" for laughs, stood for an hour and a half in the kitchen of his Beverly Hills home and turned our interview into a hilarious monologue on his life in show business. And for an old TV buff, how does it get any better than sitting with Morey Amsterdam in his video editing room, roaring at kinescopes of Amsterdam and Art Carney cutting up on his old DuMont show?

By the time my early afternoon interview with director Greg Garrison was over, we were sitting in darkness. His stories were so mesmerizing that we had neglected to turn on the lights when the sun went down. Unfortunately, most of what he told me couldn't be included here, only because this is not the Greg Garrison story. That deserves its own volume, and I hope he'll write it one day.

The greatest pleasures of this project came, however, from getting to know those who took part in the creation of television. That world is still alive to them, even in their eighties and nineties. While they expressed general dismay at the path their invention has taken, they also spoke with genuine pride in their achievements.

Some of those included here had already spent a lifetime talking to the press and had little more to gain by cooperating with me, but they did, sometimes with a raw honesty that amazed me. Rod Steiger's forthright self-criticism was astonishing. Albert Freedman, who was indicted in the quiz-show scandals, spoke openly about the subject, which still causes him great pain. Kim Hunter broke into tears talking about her efforts to remove herself from the blacklist.

Stockton Helffrich, the longtime NBC censor, does not appear often enough in these pages, simply because he was hard to place in specific areas, but nobody I spoke with surprised me more. Helffrich's work at NBC went much further than making sure dirty words weren't broadcast or that lacing was draped over Faye Emerson's decolletage. Helffrich worked hard to remove racial stereotypes and denigrating references to mentally handicapped people from scripts. For his efforts he received several awards from the American Mental Health Association.

Helffrich lobbied forcefully, but unsuccessfully, to keep "Amos 'n' Andy" off television, though he was more successful in keeping astrology advertising off the air. He worked hard to limit the violence in NBC's programming and did the best he could to promote truth in advertising on the network. For ten years, he published a weekly in-house report on the efforts of his office. I had a chance to read the reports, and they provide a consistently literate, witty, and sometimes quite critical commentary on NBC programming practices—too critical for his superiors at NBC who eventually put a stop to them.

As for the more mundane work of the censor, the blue pencilling of "objectionable material," Helffrich's views have evolved. "I used to argue about this with the ACLU. They took the position that there ought to be built into this thing self-obsolescence, that we should eventually cease to exist. As time went on I began to find my own views broadening, and I came to that conclusion myself at the end of my career: that even a little bit of censorship is bad." It is a remarkable statement from someone who has spent most of his adult career as a censor.

Other interviews were less thrilling. I literally fell asleep in the middle of one telephone interview, and I can still see Frank Stanton's face contorted in anger after I had the temerity to question his judgment regarding the CBS blacklist. Two former children's show hosts were shockingly rude. At least one of them could say he was drunk at the time. The other couldn't even use that as an excuse. The interviews with them were like walking into a bedroom and finding your favorite uncle having a good time with someone who is not your aunt.

On the other hand, there was Barbara Billingsley. If the woman who played June Cleaver had turned out to be more suited for the role of Alexis Carrington, there's no telling what this baby boomer would have done. No need to have worried. About a minute into our interview she began calling me "hon." Barbara Billingsley wasn't acting on "Leave It to Beaver." She is Mrs. Cleaver.

One could ask what a book whose time frame reaches only to the Kennedy administration would have to say in the age of tabloid TV and the information superhighway. The answer is that for all its glass and wire, television is a very human gizmo, a kind of electronic mirror, reflecting those who have developed it and we who have watched it over the years. The technology may change, but the way it changes doesn't. DuMont Television and Apple Computer were both born in garages, just forty years apart. This book is a celebration of creativity and persistence, human qualities that are valued in any era.

For better or worse, television programming has a lot to say about who we are or, at least, who network and advertising executives have thought we were. Those attitudes haven't changed much over the past fifty years. Tabloid TV is simply an extension of the hard-nosed attitude Don Hewitt brought to CBS News back in 1948. There really isn't anything on television now whose roots don't go back at least forty years. MTV? NBC was doing "Disc Magic" in 1946. This also extends to deceit. When the afternoon trash talk shows bring on guests whose stories are faked in order to stir up the ratings, they are just repeating what the producers of the rigged quiz shows were doing forty years ago.

Six years ago, I wrote a book about New York City that was also an oral history. I believed then that there was much to learn from listening to those who survived nearly a century of life's challenges. The same principle applies here. Pat Weaver proved that contrary to what H. L. Mencken said, sometimes you can underestimate the intelligence of the American people. Fred Coe showed that an atmosphere of creativity and a bedrock faith in talented writers could give rise to superb results. By sponsoring "CBS Reports," Peter Peterson of Bell & Howell courageously thumbed his nose at the accepted advertising theory that controversy is by its very nature dangerous to a company's bottom line.

Many of television's biggest success stories occurred because somebody was willing (or was persuaded) to take a chance. Nobody at CBS wanted to give Desi Arnaz the opportunity to play opposite his wife. Only after Lucille Ball insisted did they give him the chance to show that he was one of the best straight men television has ever seen. Irna Phillips had to personally foot the bill for the pilot of "The Guiding Light" because Procter & Gamble said soap operas would never work on television.

The people who tell these stories were interviewed (for the most part) separately over a four-and-a-half-year period. When threading the interviews together, I tried to imagine all of them (except the Mormon Farnsworths) bantering and trading war stories over beers at Hurley's bar. Remarkably, even the bitterest of their memories are laced with humor, and happy times are sometimes recalled with touching wistfulness.

Each of the chapters generated its own arclike storyline. If there is a link that connects them, it is this: money rules. He who has it wins. Farnsworth had the talent and the drive, but he didn't have the money, and he didn't win.

When money rules, as the writer Max Wilk points out, Gresham's Law applies: bad television pushes out good television. Maybe that's why Philo Farnsworth has been forgotten, and his electronic miracle largely reduced to one big home shopping network. Ironically, it violates the industry's own code, which says the bad guys are supposed to get it in the end. Maybe they still will. Until then, a tip of the hat to those whose talents at least sometimes turned that box of glass and wire into a magical window on the world.

They tell great stories, too.

BOOK ONE

SOMETHING
IN THE AIR

If Hollywood ever makes a movie about the invention of television, a suitable title might be *Three Hundred Men and a Baby*. Three hundred is, in fact, a conservative figure since it took nearly a century of research before Milton Berle could show up in your living room in drag.

However, in the crowded field of TV's fathers, one name—Philo Farnsworth—stands out. Farnsworth was skinny as a stick with blue eyes, brown hair, and principles. "Phil," as his friends called him, was a true genius. At thirteen, he was doing more advanced work on television theory in his attic with a pencil and paper than men three times his age were doing in their corporate research centers. He was all of twenty-one in 1927 when, with a staff consisting of his wife, Pem, his brother-in-law, and a few trusted associates, he produced the first all-electronic TV picture, years ahead of scientists at Bell, RCA, and GE. Certainly, it was one of the most remarkable scientific achievements of the century.

Farnsworth, of course, benefitted from earlier research. Television was pieced together like Lego blocks by scores of scientists over more than half a century. The parallel development of radio also made television possible. Wireless research produced the first vacuum tubes and transmitters, leading to the development of the first broadcasting techniques, all of which were later integrated into television. Early radio also lit the inquisitive fires of hundreds of young boys. Wide awake long past their bedtimes, they used sets cobbled together from oatmeal boxes and galena crystals to pick up distant stations from the ether. They would be the future engineers, inventors, and technicians, who went to work for RCA, Farnsworth, Philco, DuMont, and Baird.

The first efforts to create moving pictures took place in the 1820s. These early marvels had equally marvelous names—the Fantascope, the Phenakistiscope and the Zoetrope. They were made by imprinting drawings around the edges of a disk. When the disk spun and was seen through a viewer, the pictures appeared to be in continuous motion.

In the decades that followed, communication research branched off in new directions. Morse's telegraph made instantaneous cross-continental communication practical. Then, Alexander Graham Bell's telephone not only linked voices electronically, but also raised the possibility of bringing music and other forms of entertainment into the home.

In a cartoon for the magazine *Punch* in 1879, an artist named George DuMaurier took the idea even further. He depicted two people sitting by a fireplace in their home watching a sporting event on a screen above the mantel. DuMaurier may or may not have known that scientists had already taken their first steps toward making that impish suggestion a reality.

Back in 1858, Julius Plücker and Heinrich Geissler had designed a sealed glass tube that glowed when a current was applied to its electrodes. This was the first primitive vacuum tube which would eventually power early wireless and television systems. It was also the basis for the cathode ray tube, which provides our television pictures today.

In 1884, Paul Nipkow applied for a German patent for what later became known as the Nipkow Disk, which was a more advanced version of the old Phenakistiscope. In theory, a person or object is placed before a very bright light. The light from the subject would be passed though a spinning disk perforated with holes that would mechanically "scan" the subject and turn the image into electrical impulses. The transmitting disk was connected electronically with a receiver, whose disk inside spun at the exact same speed as the transmitting disk and would transform the electronic impulses back into the image of the person or object, which could then be seen on a small tube in front of the receiver. This simple *mechanical* system would be the basis for nearly all television research for the next fifty years until Farnsworth rendered it obsolete almost overnight in 1928 with his *all-electronic* system. His was a system that used no moving parts, such as a spinning disk, to create a picture. Instead, the scanning is done electronically by a tube. That is the way television operates today.

While Nipkow's invention was going through a series of refinements, startling advances were being made in wireless communication. In 1896, an Italian college student named Guglielmo Marconi created a small black box that generated radio waves, which could then ring a bell across his workroom. That was only the beginning. He immediately recognized the box's potential to bring about long distance wireless communications. At his mother's insistence, he packed up his black box and took it to England, hoping to find backing for his ideas. However, English customs officials took one look at the box, decided Marconi was an assassin, and smashed his invention to pieces.

Marconi was undeterred. He quickly rebuilt his box and convinced a group of British businessmen to form the British Marconi Company. The twenty-three-year-old inventor was now a twenty-three-year-old millionaire inventor.

In 1901, Marconi caused an international sensation when he transmitted a

Morse code "s" by radio wave from Cornwall, England, to Newfoundland. Soon, wireless communications became the rage on both sides of the Atlantic, and the race began to be the first to replace Morse's dots and dashes with voice transmission.

Reginald Fessenden had a plan to do it, but needed a high-powered generator that only General Electric could then build. The people at GE thought so little of the idea that they assigned the project to a low-level engineer, a Swedish immigrant named Ernst F. W. Alexanderson, the only one "crazy enough to try it," according to his colleagues.

Alexanderson was also smart enough to build it. On Christmas eve, 1906, using the newly developed Alexanderson Alternator, Fessenden sent out voice transmissions to ships at sea from his factory in Brant Rock, Massachusetts. That night, radio operators on the Atlantic accustomed to the usual blips on their wireless headphones were startled to hear the strains of a violin (Fessenden himself playing O Holy Night) and a voice reading a chapter from Luke.

With the transmission of voices a reality, the next step was to improve the process of receiving those voices. Up until then, the detecting device had been the sort of quartz crystal common to any backyard garden. It worked, but not always reliably. Almost by accident, an American inventor named Lee DeForest developed what he called the Audion tube while attempting to improve his radio receivers. Although DeForest received a patent for his tube, which broadcasting historian Erik Barnouw termed "a Pandora's tube of endless ramifications," he never really understood how it worked. Still, the Audion improved radio reception dramatically.

DeForest was quite a character. In 1902, he raced an automobile equipped with his wireless apparatus around the streets of New York to demonstrate radio's possibilities. He also rented out the Eiffel Tower one night to promote radio broadcasting. While others viewed wireless as a communications tool for ships at sea, it was DeForest, perhaps alone among early radio pioneers, who saw radio's potential as a broadcasting and entertainment medium. He produced a series of programs in New York featuring the singer Enrico Caruso. In 1909, his mother-in-law took to the air, demanding votes for women. In 1915, he began a regular schedule of programs from a transmitter in the Bronx. The next year, he was the first to broadcast election returns, albeit incorrectly, declaring Charles Evans Hughes the victor over Woodrow Wilson.

In 1909, Charles David Herrold began regular broadcasts in San Jose, California. His wife, Sybil, became the first female disc jockey when she borrowed hot records from a local record store to amuse the younger listeners.

Someone else also grasped radio's potential. In 1915, the American Marconi Company's young commercial manager, David Sarnoff, wrote a memo to his boss, proposing that radios be marketed and sold as home "music boxes." He even suggested that the radio would become a "household utility in the same sense as the piano or phonograph. The idea is to bring music into the house by wireless." Unfortunately for the Marconi Company, Sarnoff's ideas were too radical. The memo was filed away and forgotten—but not by Sarnoff who in later years enjoyed dusting it off whenever he felt people needed to be reminded of his prescience.

Memo or not, the twenty-four-year-old Sarnoff was already a rising star in the communications field. His was a classic bootstrap story. He was nine years old when his family arrived in America from Russia in 1900. They settled amidst dreadful poverty on the Lower East Side of New York. His father worked only sporadically, so it fell to young David to keep the family alive. Like many other immigrant children, he became a newsboy, but he separated himself from his peers by forming a group of investors to back him in a newsstand and hiring others to deliver his papers.

Newspapers instilled in him a love for the English language and journalism. Seeing himself as a future great American newspaper editor like his hero James Gordon Bennett of the *New York Herald*, Sarnoff at age fifteen walked over to the *Herald* office at Thirty-fifth and Broadway to seek a job. By mistake, he entered the ground floor office of the Commercial Cable Company and was immediately offered a job as a messenger boy for five dollars a week. Sarnoff accepted, and the communications industry would never be the same. Years later, his son Robert Sarnoff would say, "Imagine what would have happened had he turned left instead of right . . ."

Sarnoff loved the clatter of the telegraph keys. Soon he became a skilled operator. Within a year, the local Marconi branch hired him away. There, he got to meet the great inventor himself, and ran errands for him (including arranging flower deliveries to the married Marconi's many *inamoratas*). Eventually the two became close associates.

Sarnoff made it a point to work harder than anyone else and to learn everybody's business. One story has it that Sarnoff's co-workers would harass him by putting every bit of extra busywork on his desk. They stopped only when they realized he was doing all of it without complaint. He soon became Marconi's commercial manager, developing a better grasp of the company, its equipment, and the industry itself than anyone else at Marconi, including its president.

As Sarnoff climbed the Marconi ladder, events began unfolding in Washington and Schenectady, New York, that would determine not only his fate but that of radio and television, too. In 1919, the British Marconi Company made an offer to buy the worldwide rights to the Alexanderson Alternator, which was proving to be vital for transatlantic communication. Officials in Washington became alarmed by the prospect of a foreign company controlling international communications. A counterproposal was made to GE: the alternator would be placed with a newly created subsidiary of GE. The subsidiary would operate the U.S. end of international wireless circuits for both government and commercial traffic. As a further inducement, the Navy offered to turn over wireless patents it had received through wartime research. The government, in effect, was handing GE a private mint, its own monopoly instituted and supported by the United States.

Of course GE accepted. The new organization was called the Radio Corporation of America. RCA's chairman was Owen D. Young; its chief engineer Ernst Alexanderson; and its general manager twenty-eight-year-old David Sarnoff.

Within a few months, AT&T, Westinghouse, and United Fruit (which used wireless to coordinate work on its Central American plantations), bought major chunks of RCA shares and agreed to divvy up radio's future riches among themselves.

World War I had pushed radio research a long way. Technology and production advances now put the most modern equipment into the hands of thousands of amateurs. Scores of these "hams" set up their own stations powered by cheaper tubes and spark-coil transmitters, which only sounded slightly less irritating than a revving sports car. Soon, the airwaves crackled with hams gleefully talking back and forth like mutes suddenly given the gift of speech.

The most important of the amateur stations was set up in the Wilkinsburg, Pennsylvania, garage of Frank Conrad, a researcher for Westinghouse. Conrad built his first receiver to hear the time signals from the Naval Observatory at Arlington, Virginia, so he could settle a five-dollar bet on the accuracy of his twelve-dollar watch.

Soon he began regular broadcasts. Like Mrs. Herrold, Conrad also played records donated by a local store. It was a good deal for the store's owner, who found that the records played over Conrad's station enjoyed increased sales.

Conrad's station made history when a local department store mentioned it in an ad for wireless sets. A Westinghouse vice president named Harry P. Davis spotted the ad, and the proverbial light bulb blinked over his head: radio's greatest potential lay in the home! DeForest and Sarnoff may have realized it first, but it was Davis who followed through. He convinced Conrad to increase the power of his small transmitter and move it to the roof of the Westinghouse factory. Next, they applied for and received a commercial license, the first one granted by the government. KDKA's inaugural broadcast was on November 2, 1920, when it announced the returns of the Harding-Cox presidential race— and this time the winner was called correctly.

Within weeks, Westinghouse stations with powerful transmitters sprang up all over the country: WJZ in Newark, WBZ in Springfield, and KYW in Chicago. Other companies quickly followed suit. By the end of 1921, twenty-eight stations had been granted licenses. In the first seven months of 1922 some 430 more were issued. Licenses went to department stores, hotels, stockyards, farms, even laundries. A station in Washington, D.C., was granted to a local priest. Its call letters were WJSV, which stood for Will Jesus Save Virginia.

Watching these new developments from the sidelines was David Sarnoff. He toted out the old music box memo, and this time his bosses reluctantly agreed to back him, though only to the tune of $2,500. That was enough for Sarnoff.

The most hyped sporting event of the 1920s took place on July 2, 1921, when the barbarous heavyweight boxing champion Jack Dempsey fought a rather undernourished French light heavyweight named George Carpentier. The whole world was anxious to learn the results from Boyle's Thirty Acres in Jersey City where the fight took place. Sarnoff decided that RCA would provide them. In a historic radio "first" (and in violation of an agreement among RCA's partners), he arranged to broadcast the fight. He borrowed a huge transmitter and stationed it at a nearby Erie-Lackawanna Railroad shed. He then hired an announcer, Andrew White, one of his own employees and a boxing buff. However, while more than 300,000 people heard the broadcast, they couldn't hear White's breathless commentary. Networking technology didn't exist yet. Instead, White's words were relayed to an RCA technician at the railroad shed who reported the story into a microphone attached to the transmitter.

The show went off without a hitch, owing to the speed with which the Manassa Mauler dispatched the Orchid Man. Had the fight gone beyond four rounds, the only way anybody would have heard the story would have been by White shouting very loudly; the July heat had turned the transmitter into a molten mass that all but ceased to function at the same time Carpentier did.

Still, the fight generated tons of publicity, which was Sarnoff's intention. The company then installed a transmitter atop Aeolian Hall in New York and also absorbed Westinghouse's WJZ as its flagship station. The new stations sold lots of radios.

Sarnoff, who was now RCA's most important asset, wasn't through writing visionary memos. He correctly saw that the immediate future of radio was not in smaller local stations, but in a national network which, he wrote in 1922, would "entertain a nation" with high-quality programs of news, sports, and music. In the memo, he proposed a "National Broadcasting Company," which would be run by RCA.

AT&T hooked up a network of its own, using AT&T telephone lines to link stations around the country. Sarnoff now knew he had to move on his own network plan, but when he approached the phone company for permission to lease its lines, AT&T refused. Instead, Sarnoff was forced to use Western Union and Postal Telegraph lines which were poorly equipped to carry voice.

AT&T seemed determined to drive a wedge between itself and its partners. In 1925, it announced it would begin manufacturing receivers without paying a licensing fee to RCA. Things got even uglier when the head of AT&T, Walter Gifford, suggested that the disagreement could be solved if RCA got rid of its "Jewish" general manager. However, cooler heads prevailed, and RCA and AT&T began negotiations to settle the dispute. The result was a complete victory for Sarnoff. RCA got AT&T's radio network, including its flagship station,

WEAF. The phone company would not manufacture receivers. In return, RCA agreed to rent AT&T's phone lines, which it was willing to do all along.

Sarnoff's 1922 memo was now dusted off. In September 1926, RCA officially announced the formation of the National Broadcasting Company. NBC would be composed of two networks: WEAF would be the flagship station of the Red network and WJZ would be the flagship of its Blue (and slightly lesser quality) network. Legend has it the colors were derived from the colored markers used by the engineers on their network maps.

The rise of the national networks all but ended the hegemony of the local radio stations. The move was hastened by Herbert Hoover, who then headed the Federal Radio Commission. When Hoover granted AT&T a clear (long distance) channel, he did so at the expense of the smaller stations, which received limited assignments and were trampled upon by the larger stations.

"That opened the whole barn door and was one of the pivotal moments in American broadcasting," says television historian Erik Barnouw. "The government created a hierarchy when they began assigning channels. The big stations became big business, and the local stations were small entrepreneurs. It's amazing how readily that was accepted, despite the fact that it is a perversion of the idea that the air belongs to everyone.

"Since Hoover, the Federal Communications Commission [stepchild of the FRC] has not served the public; they have been serving the industry," Barnouw adds. "He made the right pronouncements about things being scandalous, and then he handed this plum over to AT&T. And he continued to feel that unhealthy tendencies would be purged by competition. It is a nice theory anyway."

As radio moved into young adulthood, television was still very much a toddler—but a growing one. The term was used for the first time in a paper on the subject given by Constantin Perskyi at the 1900 Paris Exhibition. However, much of the research centered on Teleautograph machines, which were primitive faxes.

In 1907, Boris Rosing, a physics professor at the St. Petersburg Institute of Technology, applied for a Russian patent for a television apparatus that for the first time departed from the Nipkow system, because the receiver would scan the picture electronically, without the moving disk. Rosing's research also introduced one of his students to TV's possibilities. This was Vladimir Zworykin, who would soon leave Russia and accept a post at Westinghouse in Pittsburgh.

The first working television apparatus was a mechanical system produced in 1910 by two Frenchmen, Georges Rignoux and A. Fournier. Reporters who saw the system said that it produced crude pictures of a series of alphabet letters, as well as images of a lead pencil and a bottle.

Meanwhile, in 1920, a Scottish inventor named John Logie Baird returned to Britain from South America where his plan to make a fortune manufacturing jams and preserves fell through when a swarm of insects devoured his profits.

When another idea to manufacture a special resin-based soap failed, Baird, who had always been a reader of scientific journals, began taking an interest in another wild scheme: television.

Working on an extremely limited budget, Baird managed to file for a patent in 1923 for a mechanical television system. Its receiver was a bank of lamps. Baird built an operating system in 1925. A few months later, an American inventor, Charles Francis Jenkins, reported that he, too, had mechanically produced a picture. Although both systems produced images of less than fifty scanning lines (the higher the number of lines the sharper the picture—today's pictures are 525 lines), at least the pictures were recognizable. Television really worked! Baird in particular produced a picture that differed from others in that it showed gradations of black and white. In that sense his was the first practical television system.

Despite his successes, Baird had a difficult time interesting others in television. At one point, he even knocked on the door of the British Marconi office to see if someone there might like to hear of his work. When the door was opened by a Marconi assistant, Baird inquired, "Are you interested in television?"

"Not in the slightest degree," the man said. "No interest whatsoever."

"It was," Baird later said, "as if I had asked if he was interested in brothels."

In 1926, Baird gave a demonstration to scientists from the prestigious Royal Institute. Baird's biographer, Sidney Moseley, wrote that the doubts of the senior scientists were not erased by the demonstration. In fact, they were only increased when one of the men got his long white beard caught in the spinning disk.

However, Baird's work did attract some interest. He was invited to set up a demonstration at Selfridge's Department Store in London, probably the first such public demonstration of any television system. A reporter who covered the demonstrations in the store's electrical department was intrigued by the jerry-built nature of Baird's equipment. He described several motors, which he said looked like electrical fans, a lot of electrical parts, and "a *Rich Mix* biscuit tin." While the television showed several simple pictures, the reporter said the inventor busied himself keeping little old ladies from tampering with the wiring.

Jenkins was a better salesman than Baird and had little difficulty attracting major investors. In 1927, he obtained the first experimental TV license issued in the United States, W3XK. While his station broadcast film shorts, he also set up a manufacturing plant in Jersey City. Jenkins sold several thousand receivers, but his programming simply wasn't sufficient to attract enough viewers, and he couldn't make enough money to cover his costs. Within a few years Jenkins declared bankruptcy and was out of the TV picture.

At least four other companies were actively involved in TV research. In Schenectady, GE's Ernst Alexanderson built a mechanical system and received experimental license W2XAD. In 1928, the station received gobs of publicity when it broadcast the first television drama, J. Hartley Manners's "The Queen's Messenger." In later years, Alexanderson enjoyed recalling the dubious responses to his early TV research. Once during a meeting in his living room he suddenly introduced a man who appeared on the small screen. The man greeted his friends from a house located in another part of town, but the others in the room refused to believe it. One guest even checked the back of the cabinet to see if the man wasn't somehow hiding inside.

At Bell Laboratories, a scientist named Herbert Ives headed a team that developed a mechanical system capable of a fifty-line picture. Ives even convinced Herbert Hoover, then running for president, to be televised. It didn't take much convincing, and Hoover became the first politician to walk a path that would become well-worn in the years to come.

In Boston and Chicago, Hollis Baird (no relation to J. L. Baird) and U. A. Sanabria were putting together successful mechanical systems and selling sets on the basis of limited broadcasts. Baird even climbed on the roof of his laboratory and aimed his cameras at Fenway Park across the street, televising baseball games nearly eight years before RCA claimed it had achieved this historic "first."

However, even before these inventors reported their first successes, their systems had been rendered obsolete when in January 1927, twenty-year-old Philo Farnsworth filed his historic patent for an all-electronic system which used guided electron beams that did away with a revolving disk. That Farnsworth succeeded in becoming anything other than a poor Utah farmer is amazing in itself. He began working to help support the family before he was in his teens. In high school, he worked so hard at part-time jobs that he had to limit his own study time to between two and four in the morning. Although his family was supportive, they had no money for college. Nevertheless, he managed to enroll at Brigham Young, but his college education ended midway through his freshman year with the sudden death of his father. To keep the family going, he worked as a radio installer, an electrician's trainee, and a janitor, without ever losing sight of his dream of perfecting a television system.

Farnsworth was not yet of legal age when he convinced several backers to give him enough money to set up a laboratory in San Francisco. This was no RCA or AT&T setup. The lab was a converted loft. His budget for both personal and professional expenses was less than two thousand dollars a month. The staff seemed to fluctuate between five and seven, depending on whether or not there was money to pay for an extra hand. Farnsworth's most trusted aide was his brother-in-law, Cliff Gardner, who became an expert glass blower by necessity, since the tubes they needed hadn't even been invented yet.

Despite the odds, Farnsworth promised his backers a picture within a year. It was a startling boast for any experienced group of scientists, but here was a youth with little formal education charting territory that the likes of Baird, Alexanderson, Zworykin, and Jenkins had yet to even approach. He would soon force the others to take notice. One of those who did was David Sarnoff, and before long the boy genius and the communications industry's boy wonder would find themselves on a collision course.

AGNES FARNSWORTH LINDSAY: From the beginning, there was a special thing about Philo. When Mother was ready to give birth, Father went to get the horse ready to go to the doctor. He had been a widower when he married Mother, and while he was in the barn, he had a feeling that his first wife was very close. He said that she was there to tell him that this child would be a very special person. He related that to Mother, and from that moment on they felt that there was a reason for this boy to come to the earth. And truly, he brought with him something that has changed the whole world.

From the time he was a little boy, Philo wanted to know what made things go. He would open up a watch to figure out how it ran. He was always thinking of ways that he could do things better.

ELMA "PEM" FARNSWORTH: He was six when he saw a gramophone and a telephone for the first time. His father told him they came from two inventors named Thomas Edison and Alexander Graham Bell. Philo decided right then that inventors were special people and that he would be an inventor one day.

Phil never had any experience with electricity until he was twelve and the family moved to his uncle's ranch in Idaho. The ranch had a large Delco farm generator, and this was just heaven to Phil. He soon learned all he could about electrons.

AGNES LINDSAY: Until then we only had kerosene lamps. What a miracle it was that you could just reach up and turn on a light! That engendered a lot of the dreams we all had. It was Phil's and my job to turn the handles on the washing machine. He fixed up a little motor and put it on our washing machine and made our first electric washer.

Walking up and down the long beet rows in Idaho, thinning beets, we would dream about all these things we were going to have. First was an inside bathroom. Then Philo told us that we would sit in our home and talk on the telephone and see the people we were talking to. He said we were going to see people from as far away as Salt Lake, maybe further. He didn't call it television at that time. It was just something where we would be able to see people at a great distance.

Gradually, he started thinking more and more substantively about what this television thing could do. Then he began drawing sketches about what it would be like. We thought his idea was wonderful. With his enthusiasm, we never questioned what he was telling us. It was just going to be.

* * *

HAROLD BEVERAGE: I grew up on a farm in North Haven, Maine, and I was fifteen years old when I built my first receiver in 1908. It was all handmade. It didn't have any tubes. I got the crystal from the floor in the high school. I could hear NAX, a Navy station down in Panama. Of course, it was all Morse code. There wasn't any voice transmission then.

BENJAMIN CLAPP: We never even imagined we could pick up voices with our radio. No one really thought of sound until after the first World War. And we never had the minutest thought of sending pictures over the air.

A friend and I built a little spark transmitter and receiver together when I was still a boy in school outside London. The neighbors didn't know why I was putting up wires in the garden. They thought radio was a joke. Somebody called me "The Mad Boy of Perley."

HAROLD BEVERAGE: My grandmother didn't believe that all the buzzing noise on my receiver meant much. One day I recorded a message that Mrs. Woodrow Wilson had died, and she didn't believe it. A few days later it was verified in the newspaper, and she said to me, "My goodness, that buzzing noise did mean something." And she gave me a five-dollar gold piece.

Then in 1912, I was at the University of Maine, and when the *Titanic* set sail, I copied the regular messages it was sending to Cape Race. That night, I hung up the phones and went to bed. The next morning I put the phones on, and I heard the *Carpathia* describing what had happened.

HERBERT IRVING: When I was in the Navy from 1917 until 1919, they sent me to radio school in the Philippines. Then I came back to the United States. I was on a ship anchored in Hampton Roads, Virginia, just prior to the armistice when I heard voices on the radio for the very first time. I was on duty that night, and I had dozed off. I could see myself being shot at sunrise, but I woke up to hear these submarine chasers talking to each other over the radio. They'd get on the air and say, "Hello, hello." That sure surprised me!

ARCH BROLLY: There was a man in San Jose named Charles Herrold. He had the first radio station out in this area. He took his power for his transmitter off the trolley system in San Jose. He was on the air with an old Edison phonograph and his own voice about once a week for an hour or two. All of us kids around here made our own radio sets so we could listen to his broadcasts.

CAPTAIN WILLIAM CRAWFORD "BILL" EDDY: When I was a teenager in Saratoga Springs, I think it was *Popular Mechanics* that had an article about how to build a radio receiver with a Quaker Oats carton, coil, and a hunk of coal. People came from all over town to listen to these fantastic voices through the air.

BENJAMIN CLAPP: It wasn't until after the First World War that I heard the first voices over the air. One day, I was listening in on my radio and I heard a voice come in and I answered him. It was an American named Sheldon Heap. That was the first two-way radio conversation ever made overseas.

HAROLD BEVERAGE: I made a couple trips on the steamship *George Washington* with a radio phone for the use of President Wilson. He was going back and forth to the peace conference at Versailles. Every day I made a test call to the Navy Department in Washington. One time this voice with a very special quality came over the air. I said, "To whom am I speaking?"

He said, "This is the Assistant Secretary of the Navy, Franklin Delano Roosevelt."

BILL EDDY, JR.: My grandfather was very close to Roosevelt at that time. That's how all the Eddy boys got into the Naval Academy. My grandmother died when my Dad was ten, and the boys were left to run and got into some trouble, so he sent them away to military school and then to the Naval Academy. Dad prided himself that he graduated from the Naval Academy with more cumulative demerits than any other person in its history.

BILL EDDY: After I graduated, I chose the submarine service because it had the fewest regulations. You wore a sweater and no uniform whatsoever. The freethinkers in the Navy were all in the submarines. Submarines were the gulag of the Navy, and that appealed to me no end.

I started losing my hearing as a kid and was deaf when I entered the Navy, but I had learned to read lips, so every time they put me through the audio tests, they said I had perfect hearing. With the great knowledge of the Navy I was assigned to be sound officer on the submarine. I couldn't hear the signals coming from the enemy submarines, so I went to Kresge's department store and bought some parts and devised an amplifier where the sound signals came out as a movement on a dial. By looking at the dial, I knew if we were on target for an enemy ship and could fire a torpedo. It worked very well, and our submarine was the only one that was scoring hits. Soon, so many people had these amplifiers and were scoring hits that the Navy Department heard about it, and they asked me to develop a model of this amplifier using the finest parts. I put it together and it didn't work. In desperation, I went out to Kresge's and bought these cheap tubes and transformers and put together the Eddy Amplifier and it worked. It became a very interesting patent because it only worked with Kresge parts. That was how I got into electronics.

HERBERT IRVING: I heard KDKA's first broadcast on November 2, 1920, when I was a civilian radio operator on an Army transport ship. In 1923, I got a job at KDKA as a technician. To save money, they had the operating technicians make all the local announcements and station breaks. I had a pretty good voice, so they asked me to do some announcing.

I had never heard the word "broadcast" as it pertained to radio until I came to KDKA. When I grew up out West, the farmers didn't have modern tools, and they would "broad cast" the wheat, barley, and rye seeds from the rear end of a wagon, throwing them out in all directions. A radio station does the same thing with radio waves.

Years later when KDKA moved its radio transmitter to Saxonberg, it went on higher power to a seven-hundred-foot vertical antenna. That summer was extremely dry, and the farmers in the area thought that the KDKA antenna might be the cause of it. Around the farms in the area, poor or broken metal connections on barn rain scuppers and downspouts at times caused small electric arcs and acted as crystal detectors, and they played music as one farmer was milking his cows. At the same time, his garden gate, which was also metal, picked up enough radio frequencies to become real warm.

I helped repair the poor connections, and I explained to him that the antenna had nothing to do with the weather, but the farmer said to me, "When your garden gate gets hot, and your barn plays music, you'll believe most anything."

W. GORDON SWAN: In September 1924, I went to work at WBZ, the Westinghouse station in Boston, as an announcer. I was still in school at the time, but that didn't cause any problems because they didn't go on the air till six o'clock at night, and we were off by ten or eleven o'clock.

THEODORE A. "TED" SMITH: Westinghouse was never very enthusiastic about radio. They sort of submitted to this work that Conrad had been doing in Pittsburgh. They were more interested in selling dynamos, generators, and instruments, things like that, so in Pittsburgh they sort of fenced off a little corner in the top floor of their factory for a studio. They had phonograph records, but once in a while a soprano would come in and sing—if she didn't charge anything.

W. GORDON SWAN: Our studio in Boston was in a building on the roof. You would take the elevator to the top floor, then go up a flight of stairs. The studio was a single room draped with monk's cloth to deaden the sound. It had a piano at the center of the room. At the far end was a microphone stand. At the right was the announcer's desk. Over his head in the corner was a loudspeaker so he could hear what was coming down the line from Springfield.

The engineer had a little room in one corner of the studio. He had to set up the program by guess and by God. If we had time, we had them do a brief run-through of their numbers to see if we had the balance good. Sometimes, we didn't even have time for that.

The engineer sat at a desk in one corner of the studio. The amplifier was powered by wet batteries, which were where would normally be the typewriter slide of the desk. If he didn't get in there early and open up the windows that we had, you would walk in that door and the acid from the batteries would cut your breath right out. There were a couple of times when a soprano who started to sing a song just quit.

TED SMITH: RCA eventually took over WJZ and moved it over to Aeolian Hall in New York. They had a famous announcer named Norman Brokenshire. They had a problem with him—he used to drink—but he was best when he was about half-lit. They had a special microphone made so he could lay down and be supine and talk while it was held over his head.

There was no air-conditioning in those days, and in the summertime, the studios got to be hot. Brokenshire would sometimes talk for hours. While he was on the air, he would shed all his clothes except for his underwear. Then he would lay down on the sofa and talk. That didn't cause any problems either until one day when Sarnoff had a group of foreign visitors in, and they discovered the great Norman Brokenshire laying there broadcasting in his underwear.

W. GORDON SWAN: I had to dress in a tuxedo every night. Our one hostess dressed in an evening gown. The idea was to show that radio was an important thing. It made us look very important, and the guests felt that they were important, having been asked to perform.

The station manager's secretary booked the guests. We had a hypnotist on who said he could hypnotize people over the air. The plan was he would go on the air in Springfield, and then get some people lined up in Boston that he could hypnotize. They got some Harvard students, but after he supposedly hypnotized them, we lost the line between Springfield and Boston. They had to get the line back so they could bring them back to.

We picked up the organ from the Capitol Theater. We had a mike backstage until two stagehands got too close to it and were telling dirty stories, so we had to set up in the dressing area. People called up after the show and asked about the end of the stories. Unfortunately, where we now set up was a toilet. That thing sounded like the end of the world when anybody flushed it, and it would happen right in the middle of a show.

TED SMITH: When I got involved with the radio network, RCA sent their signals by Western Union telegraph wire. RCA also had to maintain its own repeater stations, because Western Union knew about telegraph but not radio or telephone. There was a repeater station in Conchohocken, Pennsylvania, which was the only one used between Washington and New York. If a tube went out in that repeater, somebody put on their overcoat, got on the Pennsylvania Railroad, came to Philadelphia, bought a couple of tubes, took the bad one out, and put the new one in. In the meantime, the network didn't work.

Even when it did work, it was a terrible system because the telegraph wire was so bad. By the time you sent music from New York to Washington, it didn't sound like anything at all.

W. GORDON SWAN: The Western Union line ran along the Boston and Albany railroad tracks, and people had a habit of throwing baby carriages up on the wire, which didn't help at all. We would be in the middle of a program out of Boston and something would happen, and then Springfield would have to take it over.

STUDS TERKEL: I first heard radio in the rooming house, 1923. It was a crystal set. My father had an earphone and I had an earphone. You move around the wire and you don't know what the hell you'd get. Then you get something and you strike pay dirt. The two great names for me were Sen Kaney, the famous announcer, and Wendell Hall, "The Red-Headed Music Maker." He played the ukulele. "It ain't gonna rain no more. How in the heck are ya gonna wash your neck when it ain't gonna rain no more?"

I heard the Scopes trial on WGN in the summertime, and the death of Floyd Collins, who was stuck in the Sandstone Cave. I heard the auto racing from Indianapolis. A girl named Dorothy Koppel and I, both of us were the top kids in the class, and we were invited down to the basement gym to listen to the radio. We each had an earphone to hear Calvin Coolidge accept the presidency from a New Hampshire back porch.

In the summer of 1924, we were at Rosensweig's Resort, Workman's Circle. They had a huge ugly set. The kids were all playing outside. I listened to all 104 ballots at the Democratic convention. "[Loudly] Twenty-four for Alabama, twenty-four votes for Underwood."

LEE COOLEY: Radio was magic, and it grabbed me completely. In 1920 or 1921, we were living in a house on Coronado Terrace in Los Angeles. My brother and I slept on a back screen porch, and an uncle of mine gave us a crystal set, and we could hook the antenna into the screen. The station we could get best was only about ten blocks away from us. That was Aimee Semple McPherson's station, KFSG, K Foursquare Gospel. I listened every night to Aimee McPherson and to Dr. Black and the Silver Band and the whole come-to-Jesus bit that she did beautifully.

HERBERT IRVING: After NBC was organized, it changed everything. Radio jumped from nothing to millions of millions of dollars. Operators had to have a license and the station had to have a license. Of course, now, you have to be a millionaire to get a broadcasting license.

ERIK BARNOUW: When the formation of NBC was announced, Sarnoff didn't let out that the whole system was based on the sale of time on a national basis, because there had been quite a lot of uproar against the idea. A lot of people said this was a shocking way of using this great public service. Even Herbert Hoover said that. Instead, NBC announced that they were bringing important events before the public. They didn't go into the economics, except for some phrase that they would "always show discrimination," which is interesting.

When the commercials began, NBC insisted that there would only be indirect advertising. No prices would be mentioned, and nothing callous on the air. Then during the Depression, George Washington Hill of American Tobacco found that on the CBS network, he could say what he wanted to about his cigars: that they cost five cents and were not made with spit. "There is no spit in Cremo." That was the beginning of the kind of advertising we see today.

*   *   *

WILLIAM PARKER: I graduated from high school in '25. When I was at the University of Illinois, I worked for a couple of fellows who were making photoelectric cells for various experimenters, including Lee DeForest and U. A. Sanabria. They said, "Bill, as long as you live in Chicago, why don't you go see Sanabria? Maybe you can work with him over the summer."

Sanabria did not complete high school, but when he was a teenager, he talked William Randolph Hearst out of several thousand dollars to set him up a laboratory in the Hearst Building in Chicago.

When I first saw Sanabria he was just in his twenties. He had a very active mind and was a real inventor. His lab was two rooms about ten or twelve feet square. He demonstrated his television for me. You held your hand between the light and the drum and you could look at it on the scanner at the other side of the drum. You could just about distinguish your hand from a monkey wrench.

He gave me a little written test. I didn't pass, so I didn't work for him that summer. Instead, I spent the summer in Schenectady at General Electric. Ray Kell was working in Alexanderson's laboratory. Occasionally, they would do some broadcasting in the evening, no programs or anything, just to see if they could get a signal over the air.

EDITH ALEXANDERSON NORDLANDER: Daddy came to this country in 1903 when he was twenty-five. He went to see Edison himself to ask for a job. Edison offered him a job, but for fourteen dollars a week, and Daddy said it wasn't enough. Not only did he not get a job, but he also got his wallet swiped on the Brooklyn Bridge.

In the meantime he had read all about Charles Steinmetz's work at General Electric, so he came to Schenectady and went to Steinmetz's home. Steinmetz was a hunchback and had a long beard, and when he met Daddy, he was wearing a black bathing suit that came down to his knees. Daddy said he wasn't at all sure this was exactly human, but from that minute they got along beautifully, and he started to work for GE as a test man. He made many inventions for the company, but he only got a dollar from GE for each one. That was the company's policy.

BILL EDDY: RCA also paid a dollar a patent. When I was there, I didn't need the money, so I would paste the checks on the wall of my working space. I had a whole wall covered with RCA one dollar checks until the comptroller of RCA wondered why he couldn't balance his books. Then he found out about my wall. We tried to wet 'em down and get 'em off the wall, but it didn't work, so we finally destroyed the wall, dissolved the plaster, took the checks out, and balanced the books of RCA.

EDITH NORDLANDER: Daddy used to bring these men home from General Electric, and they experimented with television in our living room. Of course, there were no programs at the time. If we saw anything at all, it was usually a man at GE sitting around eating a chicken sandwich or something like that.

BENJAMIN CLAPP: In 1926, Baird gave a demonstration to the Royal Institution of a vague television picture. I had read about that, so I rang Baird up and told him I would like to come and see him.

On that first visit, I was received very undiplomatically. He wasn't really interested in talking about it because it was all very secret. He merely said, "Yes, I'm interested in television, but there's not much in it."

I went by there again. This time Baird was more cooperative. Then Baird asked me himself to come visit, and he asked me to work for him for eight pounds a week.

His laboratory had four rooms. One they used as an office. One was a little workshop with a bench where I worked. Then he had the little transmitter in a bigger room, divided into two so that nobody could see anything but the receiving disk at the other end of a long shaft. At the receiving end, you could see the picture through the lens. For the first few weeks, I wasn't allowed to see the transmitter because it was all so secret, but he realized that if he were going to make any use of me at all I would have to know all about it.

He was quite eccentric. One night he went to a restaurant with an engineer. He drew some diagrams on the tablecloth. The restaurant manager said, "Look, you've ruined my tablecloth."

"Never mind, I'll buy the tablecloth and take it with me so the engineer can have it." He gave it to the engineer and said, "I want to see how it works in the morning."

HAROLD BEVERAGE: Alexanderson was also very absentminded. You'd be talking to him, and all of a sudden he'd start talking in Swedish. You'd have to say, "Hold on, back to English."

EDITH NORDLANDER: Once he bumped into a telegraph pole, and just said, "Good morning," and walked away. Another time I met him at the corner of Erie and State, and he bowed to me. I finally said, "Daddy, hello!" He didn't know who I was.

TED SMITH: But he was also a brilliant scientist with a stable of some of the very, very finest research people at that time. His alternator was a great new invention for radio because it could send radio waves across the ocean. Then in the 1920s, he decided to develop television.

EDITH NORDLANDER: One day my mother invited these ladies to lunch because she wanted to show them how the TV worked. We turned on the set and nothing happened. We tried everything we could, but it wouldn't work. At that point, my father drove up in a taxi, and my mother said, "Thank goodness, here's the expert."

But Daddy said, "I have no idea." He couldn't cope with anything like that. He couldn't open a can of soup. Finally, mother and I saw that the set wasn't plugged in. We plugged it in, but the man on the screen was so still that everybody thought it was a photo. Then Daddy told him to wiggle his ears. He did, and then they believed it.

ERIK BARNOUW: My first awareness of television goes back to around 1927. My father was a professor at Columbia and was considered sort of a cultural consul. He was constantly being invited to one thing or another. One day he said to me, "I have an invitation. Maybe you want to go with me. This is a demonstration by AT&T of television. They want two people. I'm supposed to go to 195 Broadway. You have to go to the Western Electric Laboratory on West Street. Then we're going to talk to each other by television."

That sounded interesting. I hadn't been aware of television. I went down to this place on West Street. I was told to go into a little room and talk to my father. They were very emphatic, saying, "You can only use three minutes because it is very expensive."

So I went into this little booth, and my father's face appeared on this screen, looking absolutely ghastly. I remember the conversation vividly:

"It's amazing, isn't it?"

"Yeah, absolutely, amazing."

Then he said, "Are you going home for lunch?"

"Yes, I'm going home for lunch."

"I think I'll go to the Century Club. Will you tell Mother I won't be home for lunch?"

We had already had this conversation on the subway on the way down, but we simply couldn't think of anything else to say. Finally, I said, "Well, I suppose our time is probably up. We can only use three minutes."

"Yes, I guess so, but it is amazing."

"Yes."

I said good-bye and left the room, and the man said, "You only used a minute." He asked me what I thought of it. I said, "Oh, it's amazing. What are you going to do with it?" I didn't see any hope in it at all.

He said, "Well, we figure there will be a time when a man wants to cash a check in Minneapolis, and he's from New York, so they will ask him to step into this booth, and somebody from New York will identify him. It will be very useful that way." They weren't thinking about entertainment, but even as a two-way telephone, the picture was so poor, I didn't think it was worth anything at all.

BENJAMIN CLAPP: The first picture I saw on the screen was a very crude face of a ventriloquist's dummy. Baird had to use the dummy because the heat from the lamps was so bad, it was completely impossible to sit there for more than five minutes at a time.

When he first showed the picture to the Royal Society, he got a boy off the street and sat him there. When he went into the other room, there was nothing there, and he was terribly disappointed. He thought he was a failure. He went back and found out the boy had left. He was so hot, he couldn't stand it anymore.

One day, Baird said to me in his slow way of talking, "Mr. Clapp, will you go up to Glasgow and see if we can get a picture on land line?" It was about four hundred miles away. I went up there, and we experimented for about a week, and we did get this very, very crude, vague picture. It was seen by three eminent Glasgow citizens, who also couldn't understand the use of a little tiny thing like that.

Then one day he said to me, "Mr. Clapp, can you go to America?" We were going to try to send a picture across the ocean. I put the receiver I made in a big black box, which I called "experimental radio equipment" at Customs because I was afraid if I called it television equipment they would stop it.

I was met at the boat by a Mr. Robert Hart. He took me up to his home in Hartsdale, New York. We set up the equipment in his basement. It took about two months until we could receive a picture because we had to build much of the equipment and there were problems with the weather. Finally, one evening a picture of the dummy suddenly appeared. I was jumping for joy. It was then that we decided to call the press. We demonstrated it for them, and we got one-inch headlines all over the country.

Undoubtedly because of all the press coverage from my trip, the company reformed as Baird Television Development, Ltd. We raised altogether from public subscription over a million pounds. Baird soon moved to a much larger place above a motor engineering firm. We had a whole floor there with quite a lot of space, and by then we had two or three hundred employees.

TOM GOLDSMITH: My grandmother was almost stone deaf. She used one of those ear trumpets. I got into electronics when I tried to build an amplifier so she could hear better. In 1925, '26, I began to build amplifier tube radios. One day I picked up a signal at the end of the AM broadcast band. Through the Federal Radio Commission, I traced down what it was. It was television signals being sent by C. Francis Jenkins in Washington, D.C. He had a station there, and it was transmitting very crude pictures about the size of a postage stamp.

IRMA KROMAN: In 1929, a friend of mine said to me, "Would you like to work in television?" because I had done some acting.

"I don't know. What is television?"

He told me something about it, and I went over to Jersey City and met a Mr. Replogle and was hired as the program director at the Jenkins Television Corporation. No one knew what they were doing. They had the eighth floor of an empty factory building. On the roof was a shack in which they had their broadcasting stuff. It was the beginning of everything.

ARTHUR "ART" HUNGERFORD: While I was in MIT, a fellow in Boston named Hollis Baird had a television with quite a large revolving disk machine. We had a receiver in our fraternity. The only way we could keep it in sync with the transmitter was by taking a pencil eraser and holding it against our disk so it would be the same speed as the disk in Hollis's studio. We would send one of our brothers over there, and the rest of us watch our machine to see if we could see him, but all we ever saw was really shadow.

DONALD GLEN FINK: When we sent Art over to the station to be televised, and he came back, we said, "We knew that you were a man and not a dog because you were smoking." The smoke came out very clearly. It is an interesting thing that smoke is the one thing that always looks good on television.

IRMA KROMAN: Jenkins also made television sets and sold 'em, but people didn't buy too many of 'em because there wasn't much to see. Mostly you would get somebody to stand in front of there and talk or read or just make faces. When you looked at the picture on the tube, the background was bright red, and the figures were black, and there was no delineation whatsoever. I remember Mickey Mouse's figure with the ears standing up. That was all you could see.

LOYD SIGMON: I did some work for Hollis Baird. We usually went on the air in the evening hours with somebody reading a book or talking. We were right in back of Fenway Park, and we used to get up on the roof and try to pick up a baseball game. I guess you can say they were the first games ever shown on TV.

IRMA KROMAN: I was supposed to put out programs for a certain number of hours a day, but the whole thing was so tenuous I never knew what we were going to have that day. I might interview people, like Ruth Etting, "Ten Cents a Dance," or Lee DeForest, who used to visit the studio. If I couldn't think of something to do, I would put on a movie. If I didn't have a new one, I played the same ones over. Who was gonna look? I never got any complaints about it. There weren't that many people watching.

WILLIAM PARKER: In the fall of 1929, I was assigned to design and build television equipment for the use of W9XAP, that was the *Chicago Daily News* station. It later became WMAQ. For the first time, multiple cameras were to be used to facilitate instantaneous scene changes required for programming. The equipment was on a rigid metal stand, but you could tilt the mirror on the camera to direct the scanning field around.

For our grand opening we had Bill Hay, of "Amos 'n' Andy" fame. We had sets out at the various Sears & Roebuck's stores around the Chicago area, but it was a complete disaster, because that night the atmospheric conditions made the picture so terrible.

Still, that fall, we broadcast the election returns. We just scribbled the results on a piece of paper and stuck 'em up on the wall. In January 1931, we broadcast the play "The Maker of Dreams" with Ireene Wicker and Vinton Hayworth. We had a little bit of scenery. People could move around within their limits of six or eight feet.

I thought television would be entertainment with educational possibilities. Sanabria also thought it would be used for education and entertainment, but he believed he would make money selling sets, not in broadcasting. Later on he did go into business making television receivers. He built quite a few of them and sold them around the Chicago area.

BENJAMIN CLAPP: The BBC granted us their first television license. It was called 2TV. We began to send out our own programs over BBC after midnight. We had to pay the BBC five pounds for each half hour's transmission. The shows usually consisted of someone sitting in front of a transmitter singing, or Cyril Smith, the one-armed piano player.

There were a few hundred amateurs who had receivers by then. They built their sets themselves. Plessey eventually made what they called the Tin Lizzy Televisor. It was a tin box with a flat front and a flat top. At the back of the box was the circle raised up where the disk was. A few thousand of those were manufactured.

TED SMITH: I went to RCA for twenty-five dollars a week, which was a large amount of money in 1925. RCA was a very small company then, with a total sales of less than fifty million dollars a year. We were simply a sales agency for GE and Westinghouse receivers, plus the transoceanic communications business which was out in Long Island. We also did research on communications. That was Beverage. The only other facility we had was the Technical and Test operation where I worked, which wasn't very big.

There was no talk at RCA about television then. This was such an early stage of development of the whole field of electronics, that we had all kinds of other things to work on. For example, we developed the first radio receiver capable of operating from an AC source.

Nobody except Zworykin at Westinghouse and Farnsworth were doing any work on electronic TV. I didn't know of Zworykin's work. Even Westinghouse didn't think it was worth anything. I didn't read anything about Farnsworth. Then in 1927, Alexanderson invited Sarnoff up to see his mechanical system. I went up with him and saw it. They had a little studio where they had produced these elementary programs. We weren't that impressed with the system itself. When we were riding home, Sarnoff said, "It's a great advance, but we can't sell it."

But when he went back and thought about it, he realized that sooner or later RCA and GE might not be following the same path, and that television could supplant radio and that we ought to be in on this thing. His concept of being successful was that you had to be first, and if you were first you could make all kinds of money.

I got appointed as the person to do it. I was given four things to do. First, I was to build a television station in New York. Second, I was to devise a system which would transmit the picture and sound on the same channel. The third was to improve the picture as much as I could. The fourth thing was later. Sarnoff had gotten the idea that the future of television was the showing of pictures in theaters, so I was to develop a system that would produce a picture in a standard motion picture theater. I didn't think it would work so I didn't want to do it, but he insisted.

PEM FARNSWORTH: Phil had read about mechanical television, but he felt that the mechanical disks were not only clumsy but possibly dangerous to operate at the speeds they'd have to be run. He figured he could train electrons to do what the mechanical system was doing. That was just after World War I when he was thirteen.

The summer after he turned fourteen he was on a harrow when he had a vision about television. He had read that you could manipulate electrons in a vacuum, and he had been thinking about how to make these electrons cover a picture. At one point he turned and saw all the fine lines on the field he had gone over with the harrow, and he said to himself, "I can just magnetically deflect those electrons across the screen in the same way you plow a field, line after line." That's the way he did it, and that's the way it is done today.

AGNES LINDSAY: He made himself a lab in a little attic in our home in Idaho. He would set the alarm and be up at two o'clock in the morning and have maybe four hours of precious time to study by himself.

PEM FARNSWORTH: When Philo entered his first year of high school, he wanted to sign up for chemistry, but the teacher, Justin Tolman, said, "You can't handle that. That's a senior subject." Philo asked if he could sit in on chemistry. Mr. Tolman said it wouldn't do any harm. He figured Philo would lose interest quickly. Within two weeks, Mr. Tolman realized Phil was getting the subject better than a lot of his students.

One day, Mr. Tolman happened to go by the study hall, and he saw that Philo had covered the blackboard with equations. He was explaining Einstein's theory of relativity to the class.

When Philo was fifteen, he explained his theories about television to Mr. Tolman and drew him a picture of his "image dissector" camera tube. Mr. Tolman told him, "I don't understand all that you told me, but I'm sure if you keep working on it, you'll get it."

Eventually, Phil lost contact with Mr. Tolman. In 1936 during the patent interference with RCA, our patent attorney found Mr. Tolman in Salt Lake. He went out to take his deposition, and Mr. Tolman was able to describe what Philo had drawn for him. It proved to RCA that Phil had made this invention at that time.

AGNES LINDSAY: Pem and I met the day we both entered Provo High School. One day when we were sophomores, we were home for lunch when Phil came in. He was taken immediately.

PEM FARNSWORTH: He had very deep blue eyes with a twinkle in them. He was charming, but I was only a sophomore in high school. I couldn't think of anything romantic with him. But my brother played the trombone. I played the piano. When Phil found out, he came over with his violin, and we got better acquainted.

He had been going with a young lady and I guess he was talking to her about marriage, but when he told her about his ideas for television, she said, "I would never marry a dreamer. The man that I marry has got to be going somewhere." That turned him off cold about revealing his plans.

He was even careful about what he would say to me about television. Then one day we went on a horseback ride up Provo Canyon to a place called Bridal Veil Falls. We came over a high cliff, and there was a huge rock in the center that parted the stream in two and created misty falls that resembled a bridal veil. It was actually very romantic. When he first told me, it was a fairy tale. I had a hard time understanding it, but I had such faith in Phil that if he said he could fly to the moon, I would have believed him.

He talked a lot about what television would do. He foresaw everything that was going to happen. He saw that television would allow people to learn about each other. He felt that if you could learn how other people live, world problems would be settled around the conference table instead of bloody battlefields. He thought that everyone in the world could be educated through television, and that it could also be used for entertainment and sporting and news events.

I remember asking him, "How are you going to get the signal over the ocean?"

He said, "We'll get it there. We'll have to replay it with captive balloons," which is the same concept as the space satellite.

Phil was at Brigham Young when he got a job on the community chest campaign, which brought him in contact with George Everson and Les Gorrell, who had come from California to organize the drive. Phil had also become close with my brother Cliff. It was Cliff who told Gorrell that Phil had some really good ideas that they should hear about. Cliff knew Phil's reticence about talking about it, but he felt that perhaps this would be the one chance he might have. At least people from California had different ideas from Utah people. Phil had approached a number of people in Utah about funding his ideas, but no one could understand it. They thought Phil was just a crazy kid.

Phil was apprehensive because his idea wasn't patented and these Californians were strangers, but he realized it was a chance, and they agreed to set him up in California with six thousand dollars.

By this time Phil and I had become engaged, and when he got his backing, he said, "I don't want to go without Pem."

Then he called me and said, "Can you be married in three days?"

George loaned Phil his Chandler roadster to come down to Provo for the wedding, and the night Phil had to return the car he was gone a long time, but they had a lot to talk about. George and Les were putting their faith in this young boy they had known for just a couple of months, but I really think that they had an ulterior motive: I think they were trying to keep us apart.

When Phil finally came back that night, he said, "I have to tell you, there's another woman in my life, and her name is television. I want you to work with me, because it's the only way we'll have much time together."

After we were married, we spent three months in Hollywood while George Everson tried to get more backing up in San Francisco. My brother Cliff came to live with us. He took a lesson in glassblowing from the head of the glassblowing department at U.C. Berkeley. Very quickly, he could do things that no one else had done before, and it was Cliff who made the first workable television tubes.

Phil was doing a lot of experiments on a dining room table. When George and Les would bring friends in to see, he would shut the blinds. When they'd go, we would open the blinds. This was during Prohibition, and I guess it looked very suspicious because one day two very large policemen came to the door. One of them said, "We've had a report that you're operating a still here."

I said, "Just a minute, I'll go get my husband."

George had been in the back winding deflection coils and had his hands all covered with shellac. He beat a retreat out the back door because he didn't want to be caught in that situation, but two more big policemen came and said, "Oh, no you don't buddy."

Phil invited them in and explained what we were doing. Then the ones who came in from the front called the ones in back and said, "It's okay, they don't have a still. It's something crazy they call vision or something."

TED SMITH: Soon after we began working on television at RCA, we used a Kerr cell to generate light for the television picture. One problem with it was if there was the slightest amount of moisture in the liquid the thing would just go up in smoke. We finally found out that the only way we could dry out the Kerr cell was with absolute alcohol: 240 proof.

But this was during Prohibition, so we had to file an application with the Department of Alcohol in downtown New York. We needed about a quart a month. It took a while before we finally got permission to get some. They were terribly suspicious, thinking what the hell are we going to do with all this stuff in the laboratory? Each time we notified them we needed some alcohol, they would send an armored truck up, with guards, and deliver one quart to the laboratory on 242nd Street.

After the lab closed up, we had some left over. I think my boss would take it home, mix it with some flavoring, and make liquor.

PEM FARNSWORTH: At the end of the summer, George Everson got additional backing from this financial group in San Francisco, so we moved up there. We found a space about thirty by thirty, and out of that Phil made a laboratory.

Cliff, Phil, and I were the only three working on the project. Phil told the backers, "If you'll give me twenty-five thousand dollars, in a year I'll have a picture for you." Phil knew he could do it, but I think he felt more pressure than he let on.

They agreed he would get a thousand dollars a month. Out of that, we had a personal budget of two hundred dollars a month. Food was forty-five dollars and transportation was forty dollars. Cliff lived with us and paid something like twenty-five dollars a month on the rent. We had enough to eat. We had a nice place to live. We had no money for movies or entertainment or anything like that, but we made out all right.

We felt very fortunate to have what we had. Our biggest fortune was having Phil, who was nineteen. I was eighteen. I felt like I was a kid, but Phil looked and acted much older than his age. In fact, when George Everson found out he wasn't even old enough to sign a legal document yet, he was surprised.

Very few people thought Phil could do it. He spoke to the heads of the electrical departments at Berkeley and Stanford. Both gave him the same advice he was given at BYU: "You are just attempting the impossible." Well, he knew he could do it, so he didn't listen to them, but Phil needed help so badly that I learned to do a lot of things. They taught me how to use the precision welder. I made components to go in the tubes. I did his drawings in his books from his sketches. There were tense moments, but Phil's attitude was, "Well, if one way doesn't work, I'll invent a way around it," and that's what he did.

AGNES LINDSAY: I went to San Francisco in June of 1927 after I graduated from high school. Eventually, the whole family moved out to San Francisco into Phil's house at 3208 Lyons Street. Instead of going to college, I got a job with the telephone company, and I was the family breadwinner for several years.

We were very much a part of the ups and downs. Cliff would work for days getting a tube ready, and then it would break. There were so many discouraging times. There were times when he didn't have money. That first summer, I've never eaten so many beans in my whole life.

PEM FARNSWORTH: On August 30, 1927, he got a fuzzy image of a horizontal line—or so he thought, but he was afraid it was just interference, so he took it all apart and tried it again on September 7, 1927.

That morning we went over to the lab around eight as usual. Phil said, "Will you go in and finish making drawings of the sketches I left on my desk, and we'll call you when we're ready." They did. Cliff was in the next room at the transmitter with a picture of a line on a slide. Phil called to him and said, "Turn it at right angles, Cliff." They could see the line move, so they knew they had it.

There was stunned silence in the room for a little bit because we couldn't believe what we were seeing. We were all exhilarated. Phil was outwardly fairly calm, but he was also very, very excited. There was no celebration. It was just get back to work, "We need a two-dimensional picture before we can show the backer."

They did one thing, though. Les Gorrell used to come in and slap Phil on the back and say, "Hi, Phil, you got the damn thing to work yet?" So, George and Phil concocted a wire to send to Les that said, "The damn thing works."

AGNES LINDSAY: That was the way we all felt: the damn thing worked. We were living the dreams we had in the beet fields. And there it was, the most exciting thing in the whole world. It makes my heart beat faster now.

TED SMITH: I built our mechanical station, W2XBS, in 1928. An engineer came up with the idea of focusing on something in motion instead of still pictures, so we got this little figure of Felix the Cat and let it run around on the phonograph for hours at a time. There may have been twenty-five receivers around New York who could have seen Felix the Cat dancing on a turntable.

In 1930, we demonstrated the system for Sarnoff in a theater on West Fifty-eighth Street. We were able to generate a six-foot picture in the theater, and it was black and white, which you could get with a Kerr cell as opposed to the salmon color you got from the neon tube. Still, the outcome of the demonstration was we took all the equipment down, threw it away, and left. He could see there wasn't enough resolution to go to a movie where you had to have a sharp resolution on the screen. After talking with Zworykin, he knew that there was no future in the mechanical system.

ART HUNGERFORD: A scanning disk machine has a built-in end to it. The more lines you have, the smaller the holes have to be, and it's harder to get light through, so there comes a point of diminishing returns. The most it could get was 240 lines.

WILLIAM PARKER: In 1933, we built mechanical equipment for a number of different places in Canada, but somehow or other we never got paid for that. We got paid in Eskimo Pie stock because they were the ones who were bankrolling us. I still have a lot of Eskimo Pie stock that's not worth anything.

WMAQ, which I built personally with my own two hands, was purchased by RCA in 1933. That was the end of my mechanical television career. Sanabria was working on large screen television. He had the Chicago Bridge and Iron Company build a great big television about ten or twelve feet square, and he demonstrated it all around the country.

I went to Philadelphia and got a job at Philco. Four of five of RCA's key engineers also joined the company. In September 1934, I saw my first electronic TV picture in the factory. It was quite an improvement over Sanabria's mechanical picture.

LOYD SIGMON: Hollis Baird tried to sell stock to keep the place going, but it finally folded. I drove all night to Germantown in Pennsylvania. By then Farnsworth had moved there. He showed me his TV picture, and I just flipped. I said, "Boy, this is it." It was no comparison to ours.

He wanted me to join him. I went to his lab, and it was pitiful. These poor guys were wearing suits that looked like they had been moth-eaten. These guys were so dedicated but they were starving. I thought about it, and I went back to Farnsworth, and I said, "I'm gonna get married, and I better stay with my job."

Hollis and I tried to build a tube like Farnsworth's, but we never could. Still, it was great being a young man and seeing the possibilities, not knowing what would happen.

ERIK BARNOUW: The inventors who built mechanical systems, Baird, Alexanderson, and Jenkins, got people excited about the possibilities of television, getting them to accept the idea that it was inevitable in spite of the fact that it was so obviously unsatisfactory at that time. That was their importance.

PEM FARNSWORTH: One day, we saw something that looked like smoke coming on the picture tube. It turned out that Cliff had tried to step in front of the viewing area but the lights were too hot. Instead, he blew some smoke past the viewing area, and that was the first two-dimensional picture we saw.

Then we started sending still pictures and cartoons. We had the first Mickey Mouse Disney film, *Steamboat Willie*. We also had short bits of film from Hollywood that we did experiments with. We made a loop of Mary Pickford combing her hair in *The Taming of the Shrew*.

She came to the lab. United Artists had gotten a little concerned about what television might do to their business, so Mary Pickford, Douglas Fairbanks, and Robert Fairbanks, who was Douglas's brother and business manager, and the producer Joseph Schenck all came to take a look.

We had had a good picture before then, but something happened, and it wasn't nearly as good as it had been, so they went home not very worried.

We didn't show the backers anything until 1928. By then we were showing geometrical forms. One of the backers was a man by the name of James J. Fagan. Whenever he saw George Everson, he would say, "When are we gonna see some money in Phil's gadget?" So when they came in May 1928, Phil was ready for them.

That day, he called to Phil, "Farnsworth, when are we gonna see some money in this gadget?" As an answer, Phil put in a slide with a dollar sign on it and showed it to him on the television.

THE RACE IS JOINED

"There are liars, damn liars, goddamn liars, and patent experts," Ernst Alexanderson once complained to Harold Beverage in the wake of yet another patent fight. Indeed, patent battles consumed most of those who ventured forth with new ideas in the electronics industry. The most aggressive fighters were those with the deepest pockets to pay for high-priced legal talent, and in the late 1920s, the deepest pockets and longest arms belonged to RCA. In 1924, sales from RCA radio receivers passed $50 million. Two years later, RCA reached a patent licensing agreement with other radio manufacturers that gave the company five percent of their sales, which added $506 million to its coffers.

Under Sarnoff's direction, RCA's patent attorneys were among the busiest in the field. The company aggressively pursued anyone it believed was infringing upon its manifest destiny, which apparently covered the entire electronics field. RCA was also the defendant in numerous suits brought by those who felt RCA's long limbs were reaching too far. That included an angry claim by the inventor Edwin Armstrong, RCA's single largest stockholder, against his former friend Sarnoff for infringing on his patent for FM broadcasting. But the biggest threat to RCA's patent empire was coming from the loft in San Francisco where Phil Farnsworth and his small crew had confounded the industry by producing the first all-electronic television picture.

Sarnoff respected Farnsworth—even liked him, he claimed later—but business was business, and he set out to teach the young Mormon a lesson. He moved quickly on two fronts. First, he pushed RCA's own television research ahead at full speed. Second, he instructed his lawyers to do whatever was necessary to stop Farnsworth, knowing that Farnsworth's small operation couldn't hold up under the financial crunch of a full-court legal press. Where he miscalculated badly, however, was in measuring Farnsworth's determination.

Meanwhile, RCA's own research team would prove to be enormously successful, thanks largely to the blank check Vladimir Zworykin received from

Sarnoff. Arriving in the United States in 1919, Zworykin went to work at Westinghouse, where he continued the television research he had begun under Boris Rosing at the University of St. Petersburg. However, Westinghouse remained skeptical of Zworykin's work—and for good reason. Although he filed for a patent on his all-electronic camera, the iconoscope, in 1923, the thing just didn't work very well. A demonstration for Westinghouse executives in which they saw only the haziest of pictures left them shaking their heads in bewilderment. They were more interested in refrigerators anyway.

The government altered his fate in 1930 when the Justice Department filed an anti-trust action against RCA, Westinghouse, AT&T, and GE to dissolve the monopoly it had created only eleven years earlier. As a result, GE and Westinghouse agreed to divorce themselves from RCA (AT&T had already split) and end their TV research. Zworykin, who had been encouraged by Sarnoff at a 1929 meeting, happily moved to RCA's new research center in Camden, New Jersey. He quickly organized a team of some sixty researchers. Much of their work centered on improving Zworykin's iconoscope TV camera, which used an electronic "storage" system that required less light on a subject than Farnsworth's image dissector to produce a picture. On the other hand, the image dissector, being a simpler camera, produced sharper pictures, although it required so much light that its subjects were virtually baked in order to get those pictures.

In England, like Harold Lloyd dangling from a huge clock, Baird was still clinging tenaciously to his mechanical system. To his credit he had improved his picture to 240 lines. In 1936, however, the BBC decided to match Baird's apparatus against an all-electronic system produced by British Marconi that surpassed even RCA's in the sharpness of its resolution. The test was intended to take a year, but Marconi's superiority was apparent from the start. Baird was devastated. The man who had produced the first working television system faded from the TV scene, although he would contribute vital work on radar during World War II.

While RCA feverishly worked to improve its camera as well as the rest of its TV system, Farnsworth was granted a patent on his entire electronic television system. It was the first such patent granted. Unfortunately for him, the FCC refused at the time to issue commercial TV licenses. Without the possibility of income from programming, there was little incentive for broadcasters to set up stations, and without any stations, there were no manufacturers interested in taking licenses from Farnsworth (and risking RCA's wrath) to build sets. Farnsworth could only hope that further research advances would pressure the FCC to relent. In the meantime, he entered into a working agreement with Philco, one of the nation's top radio manufacturers, to move his laboratory to the company's headquarters in Philadelphia.

Before Farnsworth headed east, he was visited by both Zworykin and Sarnoff. Sarnoff stated publicly that Farnsworth was no threat to RCA even though he knew that wasn't true. RCA stepped up its anti-Farnsworth campaign. Philco secretaries were suddenly courted by RCA flunkies. RCA employees harassed Farnsworth during his public lectures. Finally, by claiming that Zworykin should be credited with inventing all-electronic television, due to his 1923 patent application, RCA goaded Farnsworth into filing an expensive patent clarification suit. That was the opening bell of the heavyweight championship of patent fights, an electronic paternity suit to settle once and for all who was the father of television.

PEM FARNSWORTH: Although we got a picture within a year, the backers said they were in the banking business, not the television business, and they kept saying, "This is going to take a pile of money as tall as the tallest building in town."

A couple of times, the backers just closed the lab and locked Phil out. Sometimes, Phil and his men had to take in outside work to keep going. They were about to set up a lab in my basement when George Everson decided to go public with it, so there was a press conference on September 2, 1928. The press people were so excited about this Horatio Alger story. Here was a farm boy who came out here with almost nothing and produced electronic television when all the other companies couldn't do it. Finally in 1929, the company was reorganized, and Phil got a percentage of the stock.

TED SMITH: In the early 1930s, Sarnoff began putting about a million dollars a year into television. The stockholders had complete confidence in him. They were mostly Russian Jews like he was, and they believed in him.

Under Sarnoff, RCA was a marvelous company to work for. It was very loose-jointed with very few rules or regulations. There was a great freedom for people to make decisions down the line, and there was very little pressure on people for what they did. They let you try, and if you failed, you weren't necessarily out in the cold. The emphasis Sarnoff put on research and development was unusual. Of course, he believed that all sorts of goodies would come out of it.

ROBERT SARNOFF: He wasn't a trained engineer or physicist, but he had an innate understanding of electronics, and a great respect for scientists. He loved them, and he loved talking with them in their language.

LES FLORY: Sarnoff always told the story about his first meeting with Zworykin when Zworykin was trying to convince him to put money into television research. Sarnoff asked Zworykin, "How much do you think it will take?"

Zworykin said, "Oh, maybe a hundred thousand."

And Sarnoff would say laughing, "After we invested a hundred million, then we got someplace."

LOREN JONES: Zworykin had interesting ideas about inventing in general. When he said that the iconoscope was a thousand times more sensitive than the image dissector, he said it didn't pay to invent things that aren't many times better than what came before, that any minor improvement is not worth very much. He had other interests besides television. He had 114 patents. He developed a computer for medical purposes because he thought computers could help doctors diagnose diseases. I remember him saying that a computer is not going to have a hangover one day or a bad memory. Today, of course, doctors use them all the time, so Zworykin was on the right track.

He learned about acupuncture long before Nixon's trip to China. He worked with General Motors on an automatic automobile. The idea was to bury some wires in the roadway and have them control the direction of the car, which would also prevent collisions. I rode in the car on a test track. It worked just fine, but it wasn't practical because of the cost of wiring the roadways. Still, it was Zworykin as usual being thirty to forty years ahead of his time.

The very first remote-control TV receivers that I ever saw, maybe the first in the country, were Zworykin's. He used a telephone-like dial on a small box equipped with a transmitter, and he could dial the receiver and get the station he wanted. He had a volume control on it, too. He was a good scientist, maybe not in Einstein's depth, but he deserves credit. He was really a promoter, and a very effective one.

TED SMITH: Most great scientists were promoters.

LOREN JONES: Yes. Speaking of Einstein, when Zworykin lived in Princeton, he and Einstein were neighbors. Zworykin had a dog named Rex, and they used to say it must be a very intelligent dog because it ran around with Einstein's dog.

*   *   *

TED SMITH: Unlike radio, in television, things had to fit together. Every receiver must be capable of picking up every transmitter. The picture must have enough resolution to fool your eyes into thinking you are seeing more detail than there really is. You also have to have enough pictures in a second to give you motion and not flicker. All of this requires a great deal of coordination, because if you don't have the things that will work together, it won't work at all.

RCA spent more time and more money on a system that would hang together. This was the phase in which RCA did one of the most remarkable things that has ever been done. Sarnoff put up the money for a complete test system, including not only the receivers, but also the transmitters and a complete broadcasting studio. Eventually, they solved all the problems that needed to be overcome. In that sense, television was really invented by RCA, because you had to have it all fit together in a lock-and-key type of thing, and RCA's system did.

LES FLORY: When I joined RCA in 1930, I went into television research because it was something that was totally new and important. We weren't working towards a means of broadcasting Milton Berle. We were interested in the technical part of it. If anything, we looked at it more as an extension of your vision, putting a camera where you couldn't put your eyes, where it was too dangerous, like into a hot furnace.

There were about twenty people working in television at RCA, ten in the research group and ten designing equipment. Zworykin headed up the research department. I liked Zworykin very much, but he was an impatient person. He wanted everything done instantly. Sarnoff and Zworykin were always of the same mind in that they wanted to get things done faster than we could do 'em.

PEM FARNSWORTH: In 1930, Zworykin came out to San Francisco to see Phil's work. Our backers hoped to sell a license to Westinghouse or have them buy it. They thought Zworykin was still employed there, but he had already been hired by RCA. He said later that the patent attorneys for RCA had asked him to come out.

The backers told Phil to show Dr. Zworykin the whole thing, which he did. When Zworykin saw it, he said, "Beautiful, I wish I had invented it myself." This came back to haunt him during the patent interference case. Zworykin also asked Cliff if he could watch him make a tube. When he saw Cliff's work, Zworykin said, "My man said that was impossible."

LINCOLN FARNSWORTH: My brother Carl was in the lab in 1930 when Zworykin and Sarnoff came out together to see what the kid had. They had already made up their mind they were going to find some way of claiming prior conception. On the way out, he heard Sarnoff telling Zworykin, "It's our job to collect royalties; we don't *pay* royalties."

At that time, their receiver tube was all electronic, but they didn't have a transmitter tube. They went to work on it with the ideas they took from Phil.

LES FLORY: We knew about his work and had contacts with him. He was a real genius, but his camera lacked sensitivity. We came up with the iconoscope camera tube, which needed about one one-hundredth of the light that Farnsworth's dissector took. The image dissector gave quite a good picture, but for commercial television pickup, the iconoscope was definitely a better tube.

My job mostly involved making the internal parts of the tubes. Everything was done by hand, so it could take several days to make just one experimental tube. We had numerous moments when we got a new idea and we made a tube that worked. That was exciting, but the other ninety-nine of them didn't work, and they weren't so exciting. That's research. You learn as much from things that don't work as you do from things that do work.

By '32, with the iconoscope, we were ahead of Farnsworth. We began to poke our camera out the window at a street corner and watch cars go by. If it was a bright day, we had a good picture.

LOREN JONES: Once, as the engineers had the camera aimed out the window, a building across the street caught fire. The cameramen called the fire department, and the picture showed the whole thing. That was our first news broadcast.

I was in the Empire State Building when RCA put up the transmitter. I spent a lot of time at the top of the tower. There was a trapdoor by which you could get out to the top, and we had to put an antenna up there.

TED SMITH: It was quite a feeling to go through that trapdoor and find yourself on top of the world. You couldn't see the rest of the building because the sides sloped down. You were suspended in space on a six-foot-diameter surface of slippery stainless steel metal with four rickety iron posts and a chain around that kept you from going down.

LOREN JONES: You're talking to a world champion here. I flew a paper airplane from the top of the Empire State Building. I followed it with binoculars, and it landed in Brooklyn.

TED SMITH: That used to be a favorite pastime of the engineers. They had club called the Top Notchers. To be a member, you had to fly your paper airplane from the Empire State Building either to Brooklyn or New Jersey. There was a metal circle about six feet in diameter on the top. Going through it was a rod about half an inch in diameter with a cross on top. The Top Notchers had to climb that rod and touch the weather vane atop that cross, which was about twelve feet up. I got as far as the crossbar and then couldn't go any farther. I didn't have the nerve.

Joe Chambers was the engineer at WNW in Cincinnati. He did a number of rash things as a flier and he wanted to try it. When he got to the top, he made one dive for the thin metal pole in the center, grabbed it, and was too scared to even look around. He said later, "If you ever get back there, you'll find my fingerprints in the iron."

*   *   *

PEM FARNSWORTH: In 1931, we moved to Philadelphia to set up a research laboratory and an experimental TV station for Philco.

TED SMITH: Philco had a camera at the University of Pennsylvania swimming pool. They would just keep the camera running to test their transmission. Our people would tune it in occasionally to test their own equipment. Merril Trainor called them one day and said, "You know your camera at the swimming pool? Do you know some men are swimming without bathing suits?"

PEM FARNSWORTH: Phil was fired by Philco because RCA told them, "If you do business with Farnsworth you can't do business with RCA." RCA held the licenses on the radio business where Philco was making a lot of money, so they had no choice.

This was typical of RCA. While we were at Philco, RCA tried to get information from our secretaries by plying them with drinks. RCA also had a "get around Farnsworth" department. They would hire the best young engineers they could find. If they couldn't get around Farnsworth they were let go. We found out because a lot of these people came to us for jobs.

Phil avoided writing papers and giving talks because he knew that these people who had lots of money and lots of engineers would try to take his work and run with it. When he did do lectures, he would use slides to describe what he was talking about. The front of the lecture hall would always be lined with people with cameras. Afterward, they would file a patent on the things they heard Phil talk about. It was harassment action more than anything else. After we left Philco, Phil decided to stay in the East. He set up a new company called Farnsworth Television Co.

ARCH BROLLY: They took a little plot of land just outside of Philadelphia in Chestnut Hill and built on that a small development laboratory from a truck garage. I came East and went to work in the laboratory. They also built a little studio with lots of equipment. Every once in a while something would be broadcast, but it could only be seen by people who came to the laboratory and went upstairs to watch the receivers. That's where Bill Eddy came into the picture.

BILL EDDY: In 1934, the Navy finally tripped me up by changing to an electronic system of measuring hearing. I was sent to the Brooklyn Navy Yard for retirement. That fall, I was driving to Washington when I ran into a snowstorm and got iced up in Philadelphia. With nothing to do that afternoon, I looked in the phone book to see if I could find this boy Farnsworth whom I had read about.

Luckily, Phil was listed. I went out to see him, outlining my own interests in the field. Then he outlined what he was doing. By the time he was halfway through, I was enthralled. By midnight that night, after we had completely exhausted each other, I said, "Phil, I'd like to go to work for you."

He said, "Fine, Bill, I'd like to have you, but I can only give you thirty-five-dollars a week."

I called my wife, and she thought if that was what I wanted to do it was okay with her, so I joined this small group of people who were trying to send pictures through the air. Besides Phil and Pem, there was Mabel Bernstein, his secretary; Arch Brolly, the chief engineer; Cliff Gardner and the two Rutherford boys; plus Joe Spallone, the janitor. That was the whole crew. Arch was the only graduate engineer. The rest of us were starry-eyed technicians.

One of our major problems was the insensitivity of the camera tube. I was assigned to investigate the problem of lighting, makeup, and miniature staging, which would be required in the future of television.

We had to develop a system of lighting that could be controlled from backstage. Since we were live, we couldn't stop the action and adjust the lights. I built an eight-by-ten-foot house on the studio floor, lined it with lights on the inside, and got one of the girls to sit in front of the holes on the side of the box in which we stuck the camera tube. We turned the lights on until her hair began to smoke, and we knew that was the limit. Her hair was the key to the whole thing.

Our cameras were red sensitive: red lipstick, red rouge, or pink rouge came out pure white, which destroyed all details on the face, so we resorted to black lipstick, black eye shadow, and black rouge, which made for quite a beautiful person.

All this time, we knew nothing about what was going on at RCA. They were able to keep their work under wraps because they had all the financing to do a major program of development. Meanwhile, we, with five thousand dollars a year development fees, were forced to make every move we made very obvious to the public in the hopes of getting new investors and new money.

If we didn't have money, we didn't get paid. Phil would sometimes give us fifteen dollars, or twenty dollars and a couple shares of stock. A stock that had no real value at all. To eat, we'd go to the Italian market in South Philadelphia and buy a gunnysack of week-old bread for one dollar. Bread, and rabbits that I raised on our farm in Philadelphia, constituted my family's menu.

Still, there was no lack of enthusiasm. We were either naive or crazy. If morale dropped, Phil would get up on his platform and start spouting his ideas, and we were back in battery again. He was a world class promoter and P.R. man.

PEM FARNSWORTH: In 1934, we gave the first major public demonstration of Phil's system at the Franklin Institute in Philadelphia. The screen was about a foot square set in a fifty-seat auditorium. There were long lines to get in. We had to change audiences every fifteen minutes to take care of the crowds.

BILL EDDY: We had one camera at that time. That was on the roof, and we had one receiver, which we put in the auditorium. Our program matter was primarily the traffic flowing down the parkway, which you could see from the roof, or the skyline of Philadelphia. Both of them actually entranced the audience.

PEM FARNSWORTH: We also had ventriloquists, puppet shows, and trained animal shows. We set up a ring and invited little urchins to come and box a few rounds.

LINCOLN FARNSWORTH: I never thought of it this way, but I guess we were the first TV producers. One of the scientists at the Franklin Institute was W. F. G. Swann, a doctor. He was also a very good cellist. He had a Stradivarius, which started to burn up under the bright lights. We tried to get him to stop, but he wouldn't. Luckily, all that burned up was a little shellac.

BILL EDDY: One of the biggest stories to come out of that was when we happened to focus on the moon, and we got an absolutely perfect picture of a full moon. That also got Phil to come up with the idea of using his tubes for an electronic telescope.

PEM FARNSWORTH: Around 1934, we learned that RCA was claiming that Zworykin was the originator of television. Therefore, we couldn't sell licenses under Phil's patents because people said, "What about RCA?" So we went to the patent office and said, "We have to have a clarification on this."

Zworykin had filed for a patent on a camera tube in 1923. He didn't know how he was going to build it, but he wanted to get control. Well, the plans he filed were not workable, and he wasn't issued a patent, but RCA hired Zworykin, thinking that they could control television the way they controlled radio to the point that nobody could build anything without a license from RCA. When they finally got their tube to work, they claimed they had a right to the patent based on the 1923 application.

BILL EDDY: They sued Farnsworth for patent infringement. It all went to court. In the end, whoever would win was going to be the kingpin of television.

LINCOLN FARNSWORTH: That lawsuit! That's why we all got so damned angry at RCA. I am still angry with a man like General Sarnoff. They tried to steal the whole damn thing. Phil had to spend money on patent lawyers to prove that it was his idea, and it was money he didn't really have.

BILL EDDY: In the end, the patent office had awarded these two very important patents to Farnsworth. When the papers were dropped off at the laboratory, everybody went into raptures. It was amazing what it did for our stock and what it did for the morale of the group.

PEM FARNSWORTH: The end result was that Phil held the six basic patents for television. Without them, no television system could function, even today. RCA had to take a license under Farnsworth's patent. The whole industry had to and they did, but RCA was the last, in 1938. The agreement was pretty close to what we were asking, and Phil was pleased. It was the first time that RCA had ever had to pay royalties to anyone. Our patent attorney was there when the deal was signed, and the RCA attorney had tears in his eyes.

DONALD GLEN FINK: Still, RCA clearly won the battle for a television camera that had memory, which was the iconoscope. The use of memory was absolutely essential if you were going to get a practical camera that could be used in ordinary outdoor light and ordinary movie studio light.

As to who was the inventor of electronic television, that's a different matter. I think Farnsworth should clearly be given the credit, and I'm not sure that he does get it.

ERIK BARNOUW: Farnsworth is certainly the father of electronic television. Zworykin had the vision, but he couldn't figure out how to do it. It was Farnsworth who helped complete the package. That infuriated Sarnoff because he thought he had assembled all the best people in his laboratory. They had been ordered to get the job done. That was typical of Sarnoff. Later, when he was trying to block the FCC from okaying the CBS color system, he told the FCC, "One year from now, we will be able to demonstrate to you a system that is completely compatible with present black and white sets. I will have it for you in a year." And he did.

But this kid out there put together the first electronic television. Sarnoff and Zworykin thought they didn't need him, but they did. It is absolutely mind-boggling what Farnsworth accomplished. And it came just at the time when everybody was assuming that from now on inventions are going to be something in corporate laboratories, but it continues to happen the way it did with Farnsworth.

ARCH BROLLY: In 1937, Farnsworth was really having difficulties in maintaining the laboratory, so they just closed the place. We were all out out of jobs. Bill Eddy went to RCA. I went scouring around clear up to Boston looking for a job. Finally, I was welcomed back at Philco.

PEM FARNSWORTH: The Farnsworth Television Corporation operated an experimental station in Philadelphia from 1936 until the end of 1938. We applied for a commercial license, but RCA wasn't ready so they lobbied against us. When our last appeal was turned down, Phil realized that everything had been going into research and decided to go into manufacturing. They bought the Capehart plant in Fort Wayne, Indiana. They produced radios and radio phonograph combinations under the Farnsworth name, and when commercial television did come they produced televisions.

AGNES FARNSWORTH LINDSAY: It was around 1935 that I saw the beginning of the change in my brother. I didn't realize it because he was still very productive. At meals, instead of chattering away about what was going on like he used to, he was withdrawn. He would get these ideas and he couldn't turn his mind off. You go to bed and you usually want to sleep to restore your mental capacities and your body. He would be working on a problem, and he couldn't turn it off. He would work on it while he was sleeping. He paid a heavy toll for this brilliance.

PEM FARNSWORTH: Baird brought Phil over to England because he wanted to get in on the electronic scene. While Phil and I were in Europe, it became obvious to us that there was going to be a war. Phil said, "You know, we're not going to get commercial television until after all this is settled, and we might be in for a long haul."

The problem was patents go into public domain after seventeen years. He worried that we wouldn't have commercial television until his patents were about to expire, which is what happened.

Phil wanted the patent money, yes, but to finance his research. There were so many things he wanted to work on. He had invented the Isolette, the baby incubator, and the gastroscope. These were things he felt he owed to humanity, and he never took any money for these things.

When he realized that his work hadn't gone to anything, he had a nervous breakdown. He had given practically his life's blood to television. He had done a superhuman job. Having to worry about finances all the time had just taken all his will, and he was so physically exhausted.

For a while, he wouldn't even allow the word television to be used in our home. When the *Encyclopedia Americana* asked him to do the article on television, he just threw the letter in the wastebasket. I was very very worried that we might lose him altogether.

Still, he never stopped thinking about what he could do to make the world better for people. He had made a tube which he called an electron amplifier. While testing it, he saw a strange light. He finally realized it was fusion. He thought it might provide a clue to taming atomic power. Phil was even approached to go to Chicago during the war to work on the Manhattan Project, but he said he wasn't interested in building an atomic bomb. He thought fusion could be used to eliminate pollution and help save the planet. That's what he was working on up until the day he died in 1971.

TV COMES TO
30 ROCK

Studio 3H at Rockefeller Center was a radio studio until 1933 when its doors were suddenly locked to all but a few NBC employees. Teams of carpenters and electricians were allowed inside. They were followed by stagehands carrying crates filled with strange equipment, and engineers and technicians who presumably knew what to do with the stuff. Something big was going on, but few knew just what. Then in 1936, NBC threw open the doors, revealing a full-fledged television studio. At twenty by fifty feet it was not very large. Camera movements were limited, and the low ceilings meant the hot lights were dangerously close to the performers and crew.

That year, NBC's inaugural broadcast was aired exclusively for RCA licensees. The show opened with an introduction by radio commentator Betty Goodwin, an attractive, personable brunette. She was selected to host the show at the last minute when the veteran radio announcer, George Hicks, walked off the set, disgusted with the chaos in the studio. Ms. Goodwin introduced a number of acts, including the cabaret singer Hildegarde, comedian Ed Wynn, members of the Rockettes, and a coterie of RCA executives eager to get their own mugs on the air. The twenty-minute show was followed by a press demonstration in November.

The New Yorker, for one, took a dim view (literally) of those proceedings, reporting that faces looked like they were mounted on watered silk. "President Roosevelt's face not only came and went," the reporter wrote, "it came and went *under water.*" There was still work to be done, but make no mistake about it, television was on its way.

BETTY GOODWIN BAKER: I was a feature writer with the *Seattle Times* until I was fired the morning after I eloped with Bernie Goodwin. They had a rule during the Depression that they fired anybody who had other means of support, so in January 1934, we decided I would go to New York and forage for work. I had letters to the head of NBC and Henry Luce at *Time*.

In New York, I was terribly disillusioned with Luce because he only offered me twenty-five dollars a week. Also, it wasn't in fashion, which I wanted to do.

He sent me to Edna Woolman Chase at *Vogue*. Here was this enormous gray-haired stern-faced woman, who had scared her own daughter to death, and I decided I didn't want to spend another five minutes with this woman who looked just like Queen Mary.

Then I went to see the president of NBC. By then I didn't care what he offered me, I would have swept out the place, but being an old newspaperwoman I was hired as an assistant to Abe Schecter, who was their head of news.

RAY FORREST: I started at NBC when I was twenty in the mailroom. Then a friend got me a job as a page for fifteen dollars a week. A stint as a page was obligatory if you wanted to advance, even if you wanted to be a producer or director. You might spend a few months in "guest relations." From there you worked your way into other categories. The whole idea was that you got to know the company, and you would find your niche in the business.

Then I became a guide. That was fun. You hung around the locker room with fifteen or twenty other guys—Dave Garroway was one of them when I was there—and waited for your turn to lead a tour. You would take people into a radio studio and do sound effects for them. There were coconut shells that did clippity-clops or crinkly cellophane for fire. Another studio had a bunch of cathode ray tubes with the green lines. A tourist could sing or talk and watch these waves being made by his voice. One guide loved to stand there singing and watching his own voice. That was Dick Haymes.

BETTY GOODWIN: There were a lot of sustaining [unsponsored] shows on the air, and they gradually began to ask me to do some of them. They sent me to places like the opening of the horse show or the opera. For anything that Mr. Sarnoff felt was important, there would be an announcer.

RAY FORREST: Guides could also participate in an announcer's class. Radio announcers were supposed to be very stentorian with beautiful pear-shaped tones. You had to get up and read. The idea was to write intros and then try to sound understandable. A lot of the scripts were introducing dance bands like Glenn Miller's. Mainly, we learned about what to do in a pinch, like when the thing dies on you and you get into "Due to circumstances beyond our control, we are unable to continue."

The course was about six months. If you graduated and were considered capable, you could then do menial announcer's work on your own time. There were about forty senior announcers for the Red and Blue networks. Each show had its own announcer. There were an awful lot of soaps, and the real hotshot announcers would introduce the shows and make a bundle doing the commercials for them. They would also do remotes like sports events.

BETTY GOODWIN: Ben Grauer was always used for the opera. He would present the social personalities, and I would describe what they were wearing. The listeners thought that stuff was incredibly glamorous. One particular night, Ben announced, "This is Marjorie Merriwether Post." I then said that she was wearing some beautiful carved green beads around her neck, and she hissed at me, "Carved *emeralds,* you dope!" I had never seen emeralds that large. They were the size of pheasant eggs.

RAY FORREST: I had volunteered to do all the station breaks, including signing on the station at six o'clock in the morning. We weren't on during the night in those days. Fortunately, I lived nearby. I could get up at a quarter to six, put on some clothes, run like hell across the parking lot, go up to the studio, and sign on the station with, "This is WJZ, authorized by the Federal Communications Commission to transmit on a frequency of so and so and so. We now begin our broadcast day." Then we would play "The Star-Spangled Banner" and go into programming.

I would work from six o'clock in the morning until five o'clock in the afternoon, except for grabbing a sandwich, doing all these standbys. I got so tired listening to soaps all afternoon. Then at five o'clock I would report for my guide duty till twelve-thirty, one o'clock.

After six months, I heard that there was an opening for a junior announcer for a hundred and twenty bucks a month—big deal. I auditioned for the job before Pat Kelly, a tough old Irishman who was head of the announcers. Pat told someone else, "This other guy's better, but Ray's been knocking the crap out of himself. He isn't any good, and he doesn't know what he's doing. He's got a lousy voice, but I can't give it to anybody else." That's how I got the job.

My real name is Feuerstein. My very first show as an announcer was a thing called "Neighbor Nell" with Nellie Revell, a nice old lady who did homilies. The first time I introduced the show, she said, "Thank you Ray Feu . . . Feu . . . Feur . . . Fire . . . Feur, what the hell is it?"

After the show, she said, "If you're going to work with me, you're gonna have to change that to something I can say."

I thought I could change it to Firestone, which is the correct translation and would have been easy enough to do, but then I thought, "If I ever get anywhere being an announcer, I'll never get a tire commercial."

Then I remembered that before I led my tours, the head guide would say, "Ladies and gentlemen, I would like to introduce your guide Ray Forrester." That sounded pretty good, but all the announcers had nice short names so it became Forrest.

* * *

ART HUNGERFORD: I joined RCA in 1933. Studio 3H activated as a television studio a year later, but it was all locked up and we couldn't get in there. Three of us decided that the world didn't know enough about television, so we decided to call ourselves the Television Research Institute. We read all the British magazine stories about TV and typed up stories about it. We put them in a newsletter which we sent out to advertising agencies for free. We had proposed to do this for NBC, but they said they wanted to keep it quiet. We knew we would get caught sooner or later, but we wanted to do it anyway. After eight months, we got a call from the vice president in charge of sales at NBC. We knew the jig was up then. What had happened was one of the sheets got into the hands of Mr. Sarnoff from Young and Rubicam. They had called him up and said, "David, what is this thing? It sounds like it's coming out of your shop."

He told us, "If you guys want to be in television that much, we better put you in it if you just promise to give up the magazine."

He then turned us over to Jimmy James, who asked us to think about television and write reports. For instance, we would ask ourselves, "How are we going to measure our audience?" Since we pretty much knew at the beginning where all the sets were, it was practical to send out cards to each of the viewers.

It was always assumed that TV would be supported by advertisers, so we were asked to think about how we should deal with the advertisers and how to introduce the system to them and make them experiment with commercials.

BETTY GOODWIN: In 1936, I was sent to the Democratic and Republican conventions. Mostly, I escorted Dorothy Thompson, who had signed on to be a commentator. CBS had Clare Luce, and these two were rivals. Dorothy used to say, "Oh, Clare Luce, she just climbed up by her bra straps."

She was married to Sinclair Lewis then. He was in Italy, and he would send her a wire every morning, saying how much he loved her. Dorothy was not wildly enraptured with Sinclair. Every night she would tell me, "Oh, Betty, I haven't answered this. You better go down and send lover boy a message."

"What should I tell him?"

"Oh, just like he sends in the morning."

The convention was the maddest kind of escapade. The engineers were working out of hotel bathrooms. We had to put up with all kinds of inconveniences, so it wasn't surprising that right after the convention Mr. Sarnoff gathered us together to tell us about some crazy new scheme. He figured the kind of people who lived through a convention were the people he wanted involved.

We were sitting in this congratulatory meeting when Doc Morton says, "You'll be working with the RCA engineers, and we're going to be able very soon to make public our achievements in television."

We said, "In what?"

"Television, it's just like radio except with pictures."

Then they ushered us into this horrible studio that had been closed off. It was a huge room full of more machines, more engineers, more lights, more chalk marks on floors, it was completely unlike anything we had ever seen. It was like some mad Hollywood studio. The cameras were these huge big black dinosaurs on wheels. They had people screaming from the control room. We were just bug-eyed by the whole thing.

They were planning this inaugural show for RCA license holders with Grace and Eddie Albert, Jean Sablon, Hildegarde, and a fashion show segment. Of course, the main thing was David Sarnoff announcing that television would be open to the public for the '39 World's Fair. I was supposed to assemble the fashion show, and go on to introduce the fashion models and tell what they were wearing.

ART HUNGERFORD: The whole show was only twenty minutes or so. I ran the mike boom for the show.

BETTY GOODWIN: I had to find out what the engineers needed for the fashions. They said nothing on your face would show unless you wore chalk white and black makeup, so all the clothes had to be sharp black or white.

We had hired Eddie Senz, a Hollywood makeup man, to do our makeup. He said to me, "Oh, the eyebrows are terrible," and he plucked my eyebrows out. I haven't had any since. Then he smeared chalk-white clown makeup all over my face and gave me brown eyebrows and lips. I didn't care. It was all so much fun.

In the meantime, the engineers would call me on the intercom by the hour to come down to the studio so they could test the cameras. You had to stand where the chalk marks were, and the second that red light went on, you were on.

ART HUNGERFORD: Betty would do that so often the engineers used to call her "The Human Test Pattern."

BETTY GOODWIN: The lights were so hot. Finally, I said, "Look, I can't do this, I'm getting blisters on my cheeks." I got them a mannequin I named Miss Patience. We gave her a whole wardrobe, and she did their testing.

She was my real contribution to television. They could experiment with all different shades of makeup on her without having her burn up under those lights.

George Hicks was the announcer picked to introduce General Sarnoff at the beginning of the show. He was chosen rather than Ben Grauer because Hicks was blond and tall, and Ben was short and dark. Poor George. Every day, they kept changing his script. Finally, he blew his stack and said, "This is just driving me crazy."

Not only did George bow out, but so did Ben Grauer and all of the well-known personalities. They wouldn't touch television with a ten-foot pole. In radio, they simply had to read what the advertising agency gave them. For this, they had to prepare for hours and hours, and they weren't making any money from it, because there were no commercials. I didn't complain, because I had always done ad-libbing, so I was given the job of announcing the show and introducing Mr. Sarnoff.

ART HUNGERFORD: After the introduction, there was a Pathé newsreel. Then we decided there should be some drama, so we had James Barton from *Tobacco Road* sit on a stool and do part of that. Then Ed Wynn and Graham McNamee did their bits. Wynn wasn't funny. He was a radio comedian who just didn't know what to do on television. Plus, we had a thousand foot-candles of light on him. That was a lot of heat.

We had the Pickens Sisters. We wanted to put the Rockettes in, but there were 120 of them. Russell Market from Radio City Music Hall looked the studio over and said we could fit three.

BETTY GOODWIN: The day of the show, Bonwit's sent over a black gown with a wide red cummerbund. On the screen, the cummerbund made the woman look like she had been sawed in half and had a missing middle. The people who watched it on television thought it was funny as hell.

ART HUNGERFORD: That first show was more or less a secret. The first show we did for the press was in November 1936. Hildegarde was on it. She was beautiful and talented, and we all loved her. She was a Milwaukee girl who wasn't getting anywhere. Then somebody sent her to France and she started the "Darling, je vous aime beaucoup," and she became very famous.

HILDEGARDE: Before I went on, they told me I had to wear black lipstick and, of course, mascara. I was hideous. The lights were so hot that my mascara fell down my cheeks. The cameraman crawled under the camera and gave me a napkin to blot out the smears. They didn't stop the cameras, and I just made believe it was part of my act. I'm famous for a hanky, so when it came to sweating I was pretty lucky, because I was always dabbing anyway.

BETTY GOODWIN: With that press show, RCA television came out of the closet. Now we could talk about it, and we didn't have to sneak into 3H as if we were going into a speakeasy. Of course, all hell broke loose. All of these stories about me came out. I was on the cover of *Scribner's*. *American* magazine did a feature. NBC even sent me to audition for the role of Scarlett O'Hara in *Gone with the Wind*.

The company immediately started planning more demonstrations. Mostly, they were Mr. Sarnoff and Grover Whalen talking about the World's Fair, and

I would introduce them. We just did these shows on call. We did so many that, after a while, we didn't even know who we were doing them for. We just knew it was for people on the fifty-second floor, who were looking at us through those crazy sets with the mirrors. We were just meat on the hook down below.

They debuted commercial television at the World's Fair. I had already left NBC by then. Women don't have to face this today, but there was a time when you made a definite choice, and we were told that if you wanted a child, you better have one before thirty. I was twenty-nine.

I didn't have to resign, but I said, "If you think that the television announcer of NBC is going to go up and down those elevators with a bulging stomach, you're crazy."

After the fair opened, everybody who took the NBC tour could go before a television camera and look at each other. At the exhibit, they also had Felix the Cat, and they would have Betty Goodwin on the first official television broadcast with David Sarnoff and Grover Whalen.

GIANT STEPS

It is 1940. You've just returned from seeing the exciting RCA exhibit at the New York World's Fair, and you've decided to be a pioneer. RCA and DuMont are selling television sets for $395. That is more than a month's salary for most Americans, but the idea of having a window on the world in your living room (even if it does come with freeloading neighbors) is irresistible.

Once you've mortgaged your home for a ten-inch black-and-white set, you send in a postcard to RCA to let them know you are now an official television viewer. In return, RCA sends you a postcard each week listing their programming schedule on their experimental TV station, W2XBS. RCA does this for every person who owns a set in the New York area. In 1940, there are about 2,500 of them.

The week of February 26 is fairly typical of what you can expect to enjoy on W2XBS. The week begins on Wednesday with a film short at 3:30 called "Little Miss Cowboy." It is followed by another movie—fifty minutes long—"Today We Build." Both films are typical 1940 TV-movie fare. The major film studios refuse to allow their films to be used on TV. Already, they are worried about potential competition from the small screen, so the station can offer only C movies from the most minor studios.

When "Today We Build" is over, you face two and a quarter hours of test pattern. You can tune in DuMont's station, but chances are that in the late afternoon the only advantage to DuMont's W2XWV is better music over their test pattern.

The news comes on at 6:45. Finally, you can see what newscaster Lowell Thomas looks like. The program is only fifteen minutes long, but by then you'll be tired of looking at him. This is a one-camera simulcast of Thomas's radio broadcast, so the script can't be changed to include pictures. Remember, there are 100 million people listening in, while only 2,500 can watch Thomas. He knows that, too, and some nights he doesn't bother to appear in the TV studio and does his radio broadcasts from his home. On those occasions, Ray Forrest will sit in at the studio and do the news. To most people who own a TV in the New York area, Ray is "the Television Man," W2XBS's only regular announcer. He is good-looking, friendly, and remarkably informal, compared to the stentorian announcers who fill the radio waves. Ray's manner is as comfortable as an old easy chair. He is the first of a long line of TV personalities to realize that this is one the secrets of success in the new medium.

After the news, it's back to the test pattern, but this time you might catch something on DuMont. Dennis James's sports show has been running, and he might have an interesting personality on with him. If not, it's back to 2XBS for the evening's big event—intercollegiate basketball from Madison Square Garden, a doubleheader featuring Fordham vs. Pittsburgh and NYU vs. Georgetown. If you don't want to miss any action, you might want to take care of business before the games begin. Unlike radio, which often sandwiches a little bit of programming between commercials, there are no planned interruptions. That doesn't mean there won't be any unplanned ones. Breakdowns in transmission are frequent. All kinds of things can go wrong between the Garden and the Empire State Building transmitter, and often all of them do, leaving the TV viewer literally in the dark.

The games, like all remotes, are picked up by two linked buses, a common sight around Manhattan since 1937. Called the Mobile Unit, the double bus is actually a studio and transmitter. It beams the signals from the broadcast location to the Empire State Building where they are transmitted to your TV set. Once the game is over at 11:15 or so—there is always an "or so" with programming scheduling; shows rarely begin or end on time—that's it for the evening.

For the rest of the week, you can look forward to wrestling from Ridgewood Grove arena on Thursday; "Burn 'Em Up Barnes," a film serial, on Friday. Also on Friday, if you are home between 4:20 and 4:30, you will be able to catch Thomas J. Watson receiving a plaque at the San Francisco Fair. Saturday has a feature film called "Little Red School House," starring Dickie Moore and Ann Doran, and a studio art show, "Art for Art's Sake," which will teach you all about the works of the great masters. It is usually the lowest-rated show on the 2XBS schedule.

Sunday is the big night. There's hockey at Madison Square Garden, with the Rovers facing off against Valley Field of Quebec. Then at 8:30 will be the best reason other than status or wrestling to have a TV: NBC presents from Radio City, Robert Henderson's production of "When We Are Married," a comedy currently playing at the Lyceum Theatre. Live theater is a W2XBS staple.

Considering the new medium's limitations, the range of live performances on the station is remarkable. There are also dancers like Buck & Bubbles, Paul Draper, and Hanya Holm. The comedienne Imogene Coca performs live, as does the satirical group called the Revuers, with Judy Holliday, Betty Comden, and Adolph Green, accompanied by a young pianist named Lenny Bernstein.

*   *   *

RCA opened its regular service on April 30, 1939. That historic telecast from the New York World's Fair featured an address by President Franklin Roosevelt and a presidential speech by David Sarnoff.

"Now we add radio sight to sound," said Sarnoff. "It is with a feeling of humbleness that I come to this moment of announcing the birth in this country of a new art so important in its implications that it is bound to affect all society. It is an art which shines like a torch of hope in a troubled world. It is a creative force which we must learn to utilize for the benefit of all mankind."

The other president for his part nearly stopped the show—literally. His car ran over the TV cable, but much to everyone's relief the transmission was uninterrupted.

Over the next year, this new art form began probing its own boundaries. There were programs of live interviews, parades, and even a broadcast from a plane circling around New York City. There were sports and lecture programs, including one show called "Microvivarium," depicting "the great battles between the uncounted hordes of bacilli in an ordinary drop of drinking water."

Ever so slowly a regular programming schedule began to evolve. Young, talented theatrical directors were brought in. They experimented with more sophisticated camera techniques and new programming ideas to take advantage of the new medium. The newcomers were often at odds with RCA's older radio directors, who were now only reluctantly in television, where the absence of commercials meant there was less money to be made on the side. Men like the legendary Warren Wade (some say the inspiration for Howdy Doody's Mr. Bluster) brought little visual sense to the new visual medium, and fought hard to impose a "radio with eyes" sensibility on television.

This disagreement went beyond the intellectual realm of Sarnoff, a "hardware man," who despite paying homage to "honing the new art form" had little interest in programming. Instead, such decisions were left in the hands of John Royal, the vice president in charge of television, and his subordinates Thomas Hutchinson and Alfred Morton, who had cut their teeth in radio during its earliest years.

The lack of young, innovative programming talent would eventually cost NBC, but not for a few years. In the meantime, RCA reveled in its long list of "firsts." There was the first entire baseball game shown on television, a Columbia–Princeton matchup at Baker Field, which NBC covered using only a single camera. On August 26, 1939, RCA used two cameras to broadcast its first major league game between the Cincinnati Reds and the Brooklyn Dodgers. At the mike was a young redhead, Red Barber. The hard-pressed announcer worked without a monitor. He had to watch the cameras and guess where they were pointed. Barber wasn't paid for his efforts, either. As a matter of fact, the game *cost* him when he asked RCA's programming chief Doc Morton for a souvenir of the historic broadcast. "He sent me an engraved silver box as Television's First Sports Announcer," Barber recalled, "and with it a bill for thirty-five dollars."

W2XBS also aired the earliest quiz shows, "Paul Wing's Spelling Bee" and a version of charades called "Play the Game," emceed by a college professor named Harvey Zorbaugh. The show's featured players were Zorbaugh's wife Geraldine and a group of their friends.

RCA also aired the first cooking shows. The earliest efforts featured salad recipes because the lights made it too hot to do any real cooking. In 1940, the station was the first to televise the Democratic and Republican conventions with Ray Forrest handling both the anchoring and interviewing chores.

In 1939, Sarnoff declared that by the end of the year, RCA would sell a hundred thousand sets. Despite the station's many triumphs, few people were willing to part with $2,400 (in 1991 dollars) for a TV set, and only three thousand sets were sold. Price was an issue but not the only one. An even bigger problem was the lack of relay facilities. In New York City only those within sight of the Empire State Building antenna could pick up the broadcasts. There were stations on the air in other cities like Los Angeles and Chicago, but their schedules were sporadic and they had no networking capabilities either. For most Americans, an RCA TRK-12 would have been nothing more than an expensive piece of furniture.

To make matters worse, two major radio manufacturers, Zenith and Philco, were succeeding in convincing the FCC and the public that commercial TV was not ready yet—largely because they weren't ready yet. The arguments between RCA and its competitors had a long history. For years Sarnoff considered the smaller electronic companies to be "bloated parasites who feasted on the products of RCA research." In return, Zenith's Eugene McDonald called Sarnoff a "monopolistic predator who played scheming Russian [a euphemism for Jewish] tricks to enforce RCA's illegal clutch on the industry."

Both Philco and Zenith were involved in TV research, but were also wary of television's potential to cut into profitable radio sales. Moreover, they were worried that when television did come, RCA would dominate the market. A delay in FCC approval would give them a few more years of uninhibited radio sales and also close the TV gap with RCA.

Sarnoff, of course, believed that television was ready, and if RCA was to dominate the market, so be it. The company had sunk more than ten million dollars into television research and now deserved to enjoy the fruits of its labors.

In the end, Philco and Zenith were no match for Sarnoff and RCA. A Sarnoff decision in 1938 to push ahead and market receivers without FCC approval forced the other manufacturers to come to an agreement with RCA on broadcast standards, the final roadblock to FCC approval of commercial television. The issue of standards was a crucial one that centered on the number of picture lines to be transmitted by every licensed TV station so that every set manufactured in the United States would be capable of receiving every broadcast TV signal.

An agreement on 525 lines was reached in early 1941. Quickly, the FCC announced it would grant the first commercial TV licenses. The big day was July 1, 1941, when W2XBS became the first TV station to end its experimental status. It was now WNBT with the right to broadcast advertising messages to pay for its programming.

The historic moment was announced on the air by Ray Forrest. Standing before the camera that July 1, 1941, he told New York's now five thousand viewers, "Tonight is the night we have been waiting for since we first started our program five years ago. We are proud to have you, our partners, through this experimental period with us tonight as we present our first ever performance under our new commercial license. . . ."

In other words, Sarnoff's "new art which shines like a torch" would now be polished by the likes of Ivory Soap.

RAY FORREST: In 1939, the television station was regularly calling up Pat Kelly to say, "We need a guy to do a variety show," or, "We need a guy to go to LaGuardia." Pat would then have to take one of his announcers and send him over to the television station, which loused up his schedule. Finally, Pat said, "Why don't you hire your own announcer? I got six junior announcers, and you can have 'em for a hundred and twenty bucks a month, and you can keep 'em."

We had an audition, and much to my delight, I won. I was their boy from the fall of '39 until I went to the Army in 1942. Everything that was put on the air I introduced. Right after the test pattern came the full face of whoever was signing the station on—in this case myself—in a tuxedo because it was evening and we were a high-class station. I had to have all my shirts tinted bright blue. That way they would look nice and white on the TV. I would say, "By authority of the Federal Communications Commission this is W2XBS, and we now begin our broadcast evening."

NOEL JORDAN: I came to NBC television in 1937 as a property man, even though I didn't know my ass from page eight about television.

EDWARD PADULA: Most of us weren't quite sure what we were doing or why. I joined NBC in 1938, fresh from the graduate school of drama at Yale where I had co-produced the American premiere of T. S. Eliot's *Murder in the Cathedral*. That caused quite a stir and brought me to the attention of

John F. Royal at NBC. They were looking for young, fresh, promising guys to get into a production unit.

I was hired for a hundred and twenty-five dollars a week. Coming out of school, it was a bonanza. I felt like a pioneer. In a sense we all were. I was carried away with the promise of TV. I realized then and I realize today that the power of television, the immediacy, exists nowhere else. Television is probably the most thrilling thing to come along since the beating of the first drum.

LENORE JENSEN: I was a radio actress doing serial shows in Chicago during radio's heyday when I married Joe Conn and we moved to New York. I wanted to be part of television, because he was in it as a cameraman.

I once heard a fellow say, "A control room is very much like being in the cockpit of a B-25 bomber." My husband told me that originally, the director with his microphone and his earphones was talking to each cameraman and the mike boom man, but in the excitement, everyone gets very tense, and pretty soon he's cursing the cameramen who are getting madder and madder and madder. The engineers all objected, so it was decided they would have a technical director—CBS calls them switchers—who would interpret and translate what the director says in more polite terms.

ART HUNGERFORD: My job was to provide all the film that NBC used. We didn't have a very good choice of movies because all the studios were down on us. Monogram and Republic helped, so did another studio named Chesterfield. Once in a while I would get a Disney. None of the films were very good. We had a lot of Hoot Gibson. We also got a lot of commercial movies from places like General Motors.

The theaters put pressure on producers of films not to help us. They would say to MGM, "If you start giving your pictures to television we won't allow your pictures in our theaters." In those days, the movie theaters were controlled by powerful chains, and they could call the tunes.

I went to see Spiro Skouras, the head of Twentieth Century Fox, to try to get their films. After I told him my story, he grabbed the phone and told his secretary to call Ralph Austrian, who was a big shot at RCA. He got on the wire, and Mr. Skouras said, "I've got some very enterprising young man here from your office who wants my films. What's going on?"

I was thrown out of the office. I thought I was fired. When I got back and called Mr. Austrian, he just said, "Well, you tried. I won't tell on you."

I finally got a decent film with Leslie Howard called *The Scarlet Pimpernel*. It had big reels that went twenty minutes. I was home watching it and all of a sudden the thing was over in forty minutes. The projectionist had put the third reel on instead of the second; the one decent film I had and the damn projectionist blew it.

NOEL JORDAN: The engineers were as important as the program people. There was a whole spirit of curiosity. We used to go out after shows or sometimes between the rehearsals and get a bite and talk about television, and try to think about what it was about, how it should be handled, and new kinds of options it might offer. There was a great deal of exploring and fantasizing about programs. There was a relationship between the engineers and the programming people that never existed in radio, and the engineers were very creative guys and full of ideas.

BILL EDDY: Sometimes we became a little bit obstreperous. One time, when an actor reached into a wall safe to take out the family jewels, we handed him a hot banana, and that caused a little bit of disruption.

EDWARD PADULA: The guys on the floor were tough. They thought I was a little crazy and arty. They would call me "Alfred Lunt." I demanded movement, to dolly in and get closeups and get a sense of rhythm. I was proud of my cutting. I knew how to grab a shot in what Bresson used to call the "obligatory moment." You'd see something on three screens and you'd say, "Take three! Take one! Take two!" They would say, "What the hell are you doing? We can't keep up with you."

George Balanchine befriended me early in my career. I asked him if he would let us have one or two of his dancers. His prima ballerina Tanaquel LeClerq and Moncion danced the *pas de deux* on television probably for the first time in the history of the medium. I learned how to shoot them, how to cut from hands to feet to body and torso and yet encompass the whole figure whenever the movement was full. I experimented a lot. Most of the people were wonderful about it, but there was resistance from Tom Hutchinson. He would say I couldn't do this or that. Here was a brand-new medium, and I would say, "Why not?"

When we did The Revuers, Leonard Bernstein played piano. If Lenny got carried away on the keyboard, I would say, "Shoot his hands!" Sometimes it was distracting, sometimes it was indulgent.

Generally people like Katherine Dunham or Hanya Holm were willing to experiment with television. One day I asked this young dancer on Broadway to create something. I could only pay him thirty-five dollars, but he agreed, and he appeared many times. That was Gene Kelly. He designed dances for the medium that ultimately led to *Singin' in the Rain.*

I got into montage, and we also superimposed images when Tom would let us alone. Bill Eddy was fabulous at playing with light. We did Vaseline shots and water shots, or we put gauze or netting over the lens just for effect.

RAY FORREST: Bill Eddy was brilliant. He devised the lighting for the studio. He and Reinald Werrenrath created a system of banked bird's-eye lamps, which were all on swivels and run by pulleys. It was amazing how he could move around on the narrow scaffolding. He had been very well equipped for that from working on submarines.

REINALD WERRENRATH: There were four different sets of light you had to provide: key light, which is the strongest light; fill light to fill shadows; back light to bring out highlights in hair and shoulder and separate them from the background; and background light to wash out shadows that people might cast on the background. All that light could really burn you.

We did a play called "A Game of Chess" in which a man is killed by drinking a poisoned glass of wine. What happened was the glass of wine had been sitting under the hot lights for about five minutes and had reached the boiling point. When he drank it on live television, he probably gave the most vivid and truthful death scene I've ever seen.

RAY FORREST: For hours after you stared into the camera you had spots in your eyes because those things were so strong. We would get people who wanted to get their feet wet for these afternoon variety shows. One of them was Dinah Shore. I got through introducing her, and she started singing when suddenly we realized there was something terrible going on.

ART HUNGERFORD: I was the stage manager, and I could see she was in trouble. She looked like she was going to faint. I tried to signal her to see if she wanted us to get her off. She somehow wiggled back that she could make it. It turned out that the lights had melted her mascara into her eyelashes and it had gone into her eyes.

RAY FORREST: Because of the heat, you got wringing wet in like five minutes.

LENORE JENSEN: The number-one requirement for appearing on television was your ability to keep your eyes open. You wanted to blink all of the time. My husband wore a sun helmet it was so hot.

RAY FORREST: When I arrived all the cameras were painted black, and all you had to do was put your hand on one and you would get a blister. Finally, somebody got the bright idea of painting them aluminum to reflect the light.

REINALD WERRENRATH: The producers were always looking for anything they could get. They would come in and say, "Bill, I need this . . ." And he would say, "Well, we'll work on it," and we'd come up with it. We were always improvising. We made trees out of sponges. We took sawdust and sprinkled it on a board and painted it green to make grass.

BILL EDDY: Miniature staging became highly important because we couldn't take this equipment outdoors. For instance, for "Jane Eyre," we had to burn down a castle. Well, we couldn't go do that on a remote, we had to burn a miniature. I used asthma powder to get a good cloud of smoke. Unfortunately, the air-conditioning system picked it up and spread it through the building, which didn't make me too popular with the management.

REINALD WERRENRATH: Walter O'Hara and I worked as a team for Bill. One show we did had a lot of special effects. One of them was an inkwell that tipped over mysteriously and left a blot, but during the show, it didn't work correctly. As Walter reached in to fix it, they cut to it when they shouldn't have, and there was this arm reaching out. The people who were watching thought it was part of the show. After that, the show became known as "The Hairy Arm."

BILL EDDY: We spent a great deal of our time wearing sandwich boards with test patterns on them to see what the camera could do with an image that moved back and forth across the screen. One night, I was walking back and forth, and I changed my sandwich board to one saying, "David Sarnoff is unfair to television technicians." I started to parade with this in front of the camera, not knowing that this was the one time Sarnoff would turn on his receiver while he was trying to demonstrate it to his bigshot investors.

NOEL JORDAN: Everybody worked sixty to eighty hours a week. They had a first-aid room with a couple of cots. We would sleep there at night. We felt pretty cocky about being in the forefront of something new. We didn't know what the hell it was, but we were too damned busy to dwell on it.

ART HUNGERFORD: The daily routine was interesting. We spent all day rehearsing. Then we would do a dress. Then we would go down to the basement of the RCA building and have oyster stew because we were all so nervous we couldn't eat a real dinner. Then we would come back and do the show, and then go back down and really eat and enjoy it. There was a lot of strain. You wanted to do it with as few mistakes as possible. One guy called these shows that didn't have much rehearsal "the Feenamint Follies," after the laxative. The tension was just terrible.

RAY FORREST: We were trying our equipment out to see what we could do with it, where it would work, how far we could get with it. We interviewed clowns at the Barnum and Bailey circus. We did every conceivable kind of remote. We went to LaGuardia airport which had just opened and interviewed the chefs and the flight attendants.

NOEL JORDAN: They tried to fill time with all kinds of crap. They had a guy come on with his coin collection. I was stage managing one of these clambakes, and ten minutes before this show the director Tony Bunzman was so bored he said, "I'm not going to do this. You direct the show." It was pretty terrifying, but he helped me out of trouble, and that's how I became a director.

EDWARD PADULA: Thelma Prescott was the first woman director/producer, and she did women's programs, but Tom Hutchinson really ignored her. I told him, "You can't let her go into the studio without letting her go through the indoctrination." He said, "Then do it yourself." I became her Pygmalion, and I married her in 1942.

The character of characters was Warren Wade. He was a big, fat radio theater actor, the personification of Barnum, blowing his own horn all the time. As directors, he and I were poles apart. He would do all this terrible vaudevillian stuff. One day I said, "You put on all those cheap dog acts and people jumping through hoops. I don't care how low you go, but it has to be high art. We'll do burlesque and really show you how it can be done well," so I convinced Gypsy Rose Lee to come in and do a strip on camera, but with great art. That put Warren in his place.

*   *   *

ERIK BARNOUW: In those years, I was at NBC as script director, and the programming people were taking all the categories of programming that existed on radio, and they were trying them one by one: drama, cooking, news, etc., and particularly advertising.

RAY FORREST: We talked Lowell Thomas into doing his radio news show as a simulcast out of Studio 3H. I had already learned that if you didn't put Pan-Cake makeup on, you looked terrible. Lowell had a very heavy beard. He was also a very macho guy. He had been with Lawrence of Arabia, and he had been in Tibet, so, when I said to him, "Lowell, you're going to have to put makeup on," he said [with pear-shaped tones], "Makeup? Not me."

"Lowell, you're gonna look like hell."

He went on without it, but someone said something to him, and the next week he agreed to use makeup. He wouldn't touch it, though. It was much too effeminate for him, so I became his makeup man.

Then every so often he would say, "I'm doing my show from Pawling." That meant he couldn't do the TV part of the simulcast, so I got the job of anchoring the TV news. I did it mostly by going up to the newsroom and tearing the copy off the teletype.

*   *   *

ART HUNGERFORD: Our budget on most of our plays was about three thousand dollars. That was out of pocket, covering talent and scenery and stuff. Doing live shows was less expensive than film, which has to be edited and scored. Besides, whatever television had at that time was spontaneity. So we were live as much as we could.

EDWARD PADULA: Gertrude Lawrence did "Susan and God" for virtually no payment. I would take our monologuist Sue Read to Saks Fifth Avenue to borrow clothes because everything had to be free. I would literally have to beg. It was like whoring. I would say, "I'm doing a program for NBC, but we don't have any money."

"Forget it."

Finally, I learned to give them credit at the end of the show in exchange for use of the dress.

NOEL JORDAN: The whole key to everything was that it was live. As a result, you got performances that you couldn't get on a movie set, but also it was panic for the actors. It was just terrible. Seasoned actors would turn ashen white.

RAY FORREST: Every once in a while you would get mike fright. Suddenly, everything disappears from your mind, and you don't know where you are, but somehow you work through it and hopefully it doesn't happen again.

Once, everybody thought it would be great to get this newsreel narrator to help me out on a boxing show. We went over to Madison Square Garden and got into the announcing cage. After the first round, I said, "And now it's a special privilege to present a man you know very well from the 'Review of the News,' and here he is." I looked at him, and nothing was coming out. He never did say a word that whole night.

NOEL JORDAN: For the most part they were (a) scared, (b) curious because they were doing something different, and (c) wondered why the hell they ever got themselves into a mess like that.

RAY FORREST: The radio guys were all very formal, very serious. Despite my tuxedo, I realized that this was not my way of talking. I just had an easygoing style. As a result, since I was the only guy on all the time, everybody thought they knew me, and they did. I got letters along the lines of, "If you're ever down here, drop in and have dinner with us." It was always very personal. People would even call me to say they were driving into New York City and to ask for directions to the Bronx.

I never thought I ever did anything to warrant that kind of recognition. Sometimes, it was embarrassing. There was an Automat right around the corner. Because I didn't have much money, that's where I ate. I would be having dinner, and people would stare at me. I thought I had spaghetti all over myself until it dawned on me that they had a set.

By the time the war began we had a viewership of five thousand to six thousand sets. We knew that from the cards we sent out. Each viewer got a tri-fold card every week, listing the programs that we were going to do for the week. On the third fold was an automatic judging card—poor, fair, good, excellent. They would check them off, send it back, and we had automatic ratings.

ART HUNGERFORD: The whole rating system was based on those postcards. It was interesting. They would do a play and it wouldn't get as good a rating as my two-hundred-dollar film. We had a lot of fun with that.

EDWARD PADULA: One of the shows I did was "Sunday Evening Supper" with Elsie de Wolfe, who was later known as Lady Mendl. She was a famous woman back then. She said, "I'll do it if you send a limousine for me," so every Sunday night I would send a limousine for her at the St. Regis, and she would invite her regular group, who were very café society, people like Sir Charles and Brenda Frazier, the kind of people she normally had over for her Sunday evening suppers, which we recreated in 3H. We had the table, the glassware, the china, the linens, all of which were sort of advertising for the companies that supplied them. Companies also gave us wines and champagnes.

Each week, a different chef from a famous restaurant would cook and give his recipes. Elsie would preside with her white gloves and jewelry and her blue hair and present her friends and guests. It was awful under those lights, but Elsie never complained. I don't think she allowed herself to sweat.

NOEL JORDAN: I remember that show. There were all these people in tuxedos. One time the chef was supposed to shake the salad in one of these wire baskets, but the top came off and he threw the salad into the lady's face.

RAY FORREST: With our mobile units we did boxing from Ridgewood Grove arena and wrestling from Jamaica Arena. The first time I got sent to do a hockey match was also the first hockey game I had ever seen. I had no idea what was going on, and it was a total fiasco. We also did the races from Belmont and Aqueduct. Clem McCarthy would call them. If Clem was away, Jack McCarthy used to call the races. Jack was a good race caller, except Jack was "undependable" and would occasionally not show up. Sure enough, I was there one day when Jack wasn't there and I was told I would have to do it. All I had were Clem's long glasses, which would let you see maybe one horse or half a horse on the other side of the track if you were lucky. They said to me, "Just do it."

I got about as far as the first turn and that was it. I just said into the mike, "I don't know where they are. I can't find them." And I never found them again the whole way around except at the end when I found out which horse had won.

In 1940, we did the Republican convention from Philadelphia. I think twelve people from RCA did the convention. Today, there would be five hundred. We all stayed in the Warwick Hotel in Philadelphia. It was the first network show. It went from Philly to New York to Schenectady.

We had three cameras there, and I did everything, like all these guys do today, except I was the only one. We didn't have any reporters on the floor. There was just me with a printed schedule of who was going to talk. When it got quiet on the floor, I would go downstairs, and interview anybody who was available. Of course there were no fancy sets. We tallied the votes for the nomination on a big piece of cardboard that was leaning against the back of a chair.

ART HUNGERFORD: Soon after the convention, the FCC shut us down. They told us that the standards weren't satisfactory. That's where Fink came in.

DONALD GLEN FINK: By 1940, the FCC knew we had to have a single standard for the number of lines in a television picture. All the companies wanted that, but they wanted it to be theirs not the others'. The FCC said it would not make that decision; the industry would have to make it.

Along came Doc Baker of GE, whose company didn't have a big stake one way or the other, but he was so well known and such a strong figure that he was able to convince people in RCA, DuMont, Zenith, and Philco that they should pull together and do things right or they weren't going to make any money. That convinced everybody. That's how the National Television System Committee was formed.

That year, I published a book called *Principles of Television Engineering*, which turned out to be the first technologically accurate treatment in book form of the state of television. It became a sort of bible. That was how I got into the NTSC.

The biggest decision we made was to establish the number of lines. RCA had 441 lines. Philco and DuMont wanted a higher number of lines, with DuMont looking for something like 650. Baker asked me to come up with a recommendation that would bridge this gap. We were on the phone when he challenged me to come up with a number, and I suggested 525. Everybody agreed, and that's the number we have today. Without the agreement we could have had a mess like they had in Europe where Britain had a 625 system and the French had 819, and they couldn't pick up each other's programs.

TOM GOLDSMITH: From 1939 to 1941, NBC had Channel Four in New York and Philco had Channel Three in Philadelphia. The FCC decided to use Channel Four in Philadelphia and Three in New York for mobile radio units in police and fire departments. I pointed out that if those cruisers used their radios outside their territory, they would squirrel up the TV pictures.

To prevent that, I suggested that they give the television people the clear channels two through six and take Channel One and assign it to the mobile radio police and fire departments. They did. That's why there's no Channel One on any television sets.

RAY FORREST: Everybody was thrilled to death on July 4, 1941, when we became commercial and went from W2XBS to WNBT, because now the station could make a little bit of money. That included me, even if it was just twelve dollars and fifty cents a commercial, which it often was. The first television commercial I did was for Adam Hats. I had to wear the hat. I didn't get any money for it, but I got to keep the hat. Once we went commercial, we did the same stuff we had always done, except that we would have these occasional announcements.

LENORE JENSEN: The absolute first commercial was my idea of the best commercial I have ever seen. All it was was the face of a Bulova watch. It had a sweep second hand. They would focus on it for one minute while they played the *Minute Waltz*.

I did tons of commercials. I did one for Waring Blender. When you turned on the blender, it sounded like an earthquake. They said, "Oh, God, that's a terrible noise."

I said, "Why not play a record when I throw the switch? The record I picked out was "I'm Looking Over a Four Leaf Clover," because that's the way the blender was shaped. There was just one problem: after seeing the commercial, a lot of people went to the store and asked for the blender that played music.

EDWARD PADULA: I had a passion for the medium, but I felt alone in this group. Suddenly, with sponsors, segments of time became important, not the whole show. I didn't allow commercials in the middle of my shows, and I was able to get away with it. I just said, "This is the program. It starts here and ends there. There's no break in the middle."

I just wanted to be left alone. If someone wanted to present a commercial at the beginning or the end of the show that was great, but after a while, I couldn't get away with it.

In 1941, the William Morris office got me a contract with Paramount Pictures and I left. I didn't fit in with NBC anymore. I was reaching for something. I wasn't quite sure what, but it wasn't what they were looking for. When I would bring in two dancers, they would say, "What's that gonna sell?"

RAY FORREST: On December 7, I was standing by on a broadcast of a film, *Millionaire Playboy* with Harry Richman, when somebody opened the door and said, "You better go over to the newsroom. I think we're in the war." The word came down from the newsroom that Pearl Harbor had been attacked. I was the guy who ran to the newsroom, got the copy, broke into the film, and announced the war on television. My first thought was, "Here I go." I was in the reserves, so I knew I was going to go in soon, and I did. When I came back after the war, everything was different.

DUMONT (THE RISE)

Allen Balcom DuMont's basement garage was an unlikely source of electronic miracles, but no more so than Philo Farnsworth's loft, John Logie Baird's garret, or Steve Jobs's garage, for that matter. In fact, so many great strides have been made in such improbable venues that even today's byte-oriented pioneers still might want to consider unused closet space for inspiration before hustling off to the great corporate laboratories.

In the case of Allen DuMont, his Upper Montclair, New Jersey, garage produced a modern electronics version of the biblical Hanukkah story. That ancient tale found the Hebrews partying hearty for eight days in a light miraculously provided by a single drop of oil. In the DuMont version, he and his three assistants were able to produce a picture tube that would last one thousand hours, ten times longer than the standard, thus springing television from the laboratories and into the home.

Within a few years, he went into television manufacturing and into network broadcasting. The excellent DuMont receiver was the first all-electronic set on the market, quite an achievement in itself considering the head start enjoyed by both Farnsworth and RCA.

Television's first self-made millionaire was born on January 29, 1901, in Brooklyn. His father was an executive with the Waterbury Clock Company, makers of the Ingersoll watch, a dollar timepiece known for its extraordinary accuracy. Young Allen and his two brothers all contracted polio as children. Then eleven years old, Allen was confined to bed for nine months. His father bought him a crystal set to keep him occupied. By the time he was able to leave his bedroom, the young man had taught himself enough about radio to build his own receiver-transmitter.

He graduated from Rensselaer Polytechnical Institute with an engineering degree in 1924 and went to work for Westinghouse where he modernized their radio tube manufacturing machinery. He went on to do the same thing for Lee

DeForest, the legendary radio inventor. While employed at DeForest, DuMont came across the television equipment that had formerly belonged to Charles Francis Jenkins. DeForest had purchased the equipment after Jenkins's television business went bust in the Depression. Curious about television, DuMont began experimenting with the Jenkins machine but realized quickly that Jenkins's Nipkow system was doomed.

He approached DeForest about investing in an all-electronic system, but the elder DeForest, once a pioneer himself, refused. So there was his young prodigy at the crossroads age of thirty ready to make his move in life. Although he was so cautious he wore suspenders and a belt at the same time, and he had a wife and child to support, he left the security of a fifteen-thousand-dollar-a-year job in the depths of the Depression to set up shop in his garage.

When he opened for business, DuMont could count one thousand dollars in capital, some secondhand manufacturing equipment, and three assistants, two of whom were part-time. The third was a full-time apprentice machinist, whom he paid ten dollars a week. However, he also had an unsurpassed knowledge of tube making and knew that if television was ever to become commercially viable, the cathode ray tube had to be improved dramatically. So far no one else had succeeded in doing it.

Very quickly he started increasing the life of the tubes. That first year he even sold two of them. His business grossed seventy dollars. By 1933, the company did twelve thousand dollars' worth of business, mostly selling tubes for use as oscillographs, invaluable laboratory diagnostic equipment. That year the company finally moved out of the garage and into a building in town. By 1935, they were incorporated as Allen B. DuMont Laboratories. The next year, after adding Dr. Thomas T. Goldsmith, a brilliant young engineer, to his staff (the DuMont station WTTG was named for him), he made his first moves into practical television research.

While business was solid, DuMont still did not have the capital to compete with Farnsworth or RCA. The problem appeared to be solved when he negotiated a stock deal with Paramount Pictures. With Paramount's cash, DuMont not only began manufacturing and marketing his own sets, but also went into broadcasting. He received a license for an experimental station W2XVT in February, 1939. The fifty-watt station operated out of the Passaic factory from twelve midnight to nine A.M. That spring, he was granted a permit for another station, W2XWV at 515 Madison Avenue, in New York City. It later became WABD, the flagship station of the DuMont network. It went on the air that spring. The kid from Brooklyn was about to go big time.

DR. THOMAS T. "TOM" GOLDSMITH: I was born in Greenville, South Carolina. In high school I won a chemistry prize and got a two-volume life of Thomas Alva Edison. I read those and said, "Gee, I think I'm gonna go work for that guy," but he up and died on me before I got through college.

I went through college at Furman University. When I came out, because of the Depression I could hardly get a job pumping gasoline at a gas station with a college degree! I decided I would take the two hundred fifty bucks that I saved being a newspaper courier boy for the *Greenville News* in South Carolina and chootle off and go to graduate school.

In 1934, I published a paper on cathode ray oscillographs while I was at Cornell University. Then in the summer of 1936, I was working on my thesis with Dr. Bedell, and I went with him to visit his sister in Montclair. The next morning, he said, "Let's go up the street to visit Allen DuMont."

I got to talking to Allen about his cathode ray tube, and he said, "Oh, you know something about oscillographs? You can start working for me."

I joined Allen that November, as the fourteenth employee of the company. I was the director of research, but whatever came along I worked on. We had to do whatever we could to stay solvent.

BRUCE DUMONT: I am the youngest of three brothers. We were raised in Brooklyn. All three of us had polio at the same time. My brother Donald and I threw it off in a couple of days, but Al was in bed for nine months. While he was in bed, he got a book by Jenkins. That's what got him interested in radio.

Al graduated from Rensselaer in 1924 and went to work at Westinghouse. He was there when he ran into Lee DeForest. DeForest was quite a guy. He had about seven wives. Later, when I worked with him in Passaic, he used to say, "I have to keep inventing things just to keep the alimony going."

TOM GOLDSMITH: Allen got started in television with Lee, who hired Allen to automate his manufacturing process. After Jenkins went bankrupt, DeForest bought his mechanical television equipment and moved it to Passaic, New Jersey. Allen worked with him on that, but finally he told Lee that cathode ray tubes were the only way to make television work. He said, "If you're going to go on with that mechanical system, fine, but I'm gonna start my own business, improve cathode ray tubes for television."

BRUCE DUMONT: He left DeForest and went on his own with his brother-in-law, Al Steadman, who was a chemist. I used to see them working on it down in the cellar. There was also John Hinck, who was his first employee. He was handy making welds.

TOM GOLDSMITH: Then there were four of them. Stan Cook was the glass blower. They got the fluorescent chemicals for the cathode ray tubes not from any supplier, but by going up to the zinc mines in New Jersey, collecting rocks in a bag, and lugging them back to Allen's basement.

In the early days, you were lucky to get a hundred hours out of a cathode ray tube. They worked out a process where they could make tubes that lasted. So that now, I can turn on a television set that was built twenty years ago and it still works. Television could not have been possible without it.

By the time Allen hired me, the laboratory was in two places, Allen's basement and three converted hat stores in Upper Montclair. My lab was just a workbench and some equipment in the corner of the lab. I didn't have any assistant. I was it.

My first assignment for DuMont was to set up a television system in the laboratory. By March or April 1937, we were getting pictures. We generated pictures right there in the laboratory by taking a tube and printing on it a picture of Claudette Colbert in black ink on an aluminum background. We'd scan that and use it as a test pattern.

BRUCE DUMONT: One of the things Al invented was the electronic eye tuner. He made twenty thousand dollars out of that.

TOM GOLDSMITH: It was enough for us to move out of our little hat stores and buy the Anna Meyers Pure Pickle Works in Passaic with six thousand square feet on each floor. The basement was relegated to me for research. We used to put a TV camera out the window to see what the weather was like.

We were up to around thirty-five people at the end of 1938 and there were three of us working on television. By 1941, when we stopped because of the war, we had maybe twenty-five people making them. Eventually, we built about two million sets all told at DuMont Laboratories.

Our first sets, like the Model 180, had a snap-switch tuner which selected four different channels. There were only three in New York, so we had a spare. The set cost $325, and while it didn't have the automatic features that the current TV sets have, it produced some very nice black-and-white pictures. There were eight knobs on the front of the set, a volume control, picture contrast, and tuning knobs. People wouldn't know how to tune those knobs or they'd let their kids get to 'em, and they'd turn 'em all out of adjustment, so they wouldn't get a picture for a while. So I made the sales department make a cardboard insert with slots to go over the knobs that would tell 'em how to turn 'em.

During the World's Fair, we had about five of those 180 sets and the 183 console model. One of them was in the Crosley exhibit. We had to go out there every day, turn on those sets, and see that they behaved. If one gave up, I would put it in the car, take it back to the plant, fix it, and bring it back.

BRUCE DUMONT: After I saw the opening of the World's Fair in 1939 on television at Al's house, I decided to join the business, and I began selling televisions. We decided that the bars were a good place to start. I would put a TV in the trunk of my Ford and I'd go around to north Jersey and Hoboken.

On the corners in these towns would be four bars, and we would say, "Look, you got the same beer as the next guy. If you have a television they'll come in here." We had a hard time, because we couldn't really demonstrate them. The problem was, there wasn't really any programming on. Still, we sold a few hundred sets.

TOM GOLDSMITH: Our sets were the only ones on the market at the start. We beat RCA to the market by a few weeks. We put Mark Lajoy in charge of selling television sets to the radio stores. He'd go around to a store and say, "We've got television. How about signing up to be a dealer for DuMont." They were tickled to death to get 'em, because it was great publicity. They'd have a television set on display and sell radio sets instead. They'd advertise, "Come see DuMont television in our store." They'd only have two sets, because we hadn't produced very many of 'em.

People could see the experimental transmissions from NBC, CBS, and DuMont. We had two studios: one in New York and one in New Jersey. The studio in New Jersey was in the pickle factory building. We were on the air in early 1938 in New Jersey and early 1939 in New York. DuMont mostly had movies and stills. Most of the early stuff was just experimental transmissions to show the FCC what television was all about.

BRUCE DUMONT: To sell our televisions, we had one hour of wrestling a week. Al had an engineer named Lou Sposa. One day Lou told me he had a brother who was in radio. He asked me if I would speak to Al about him, and I did.

DENNIS JAMES: I started in radio in 1938 as a kid just out of St. Peter's College in Jersey City. They hired me as a disk jockey. Frank Sinatra and I started there at the same time. The station manager at WAAT was Italian, but one day he said to me, "Why don't you change your name? I don't want any Italian names on the station."

I said, "My old man will kill me."

"I don't care. Change your name or you're fired."

I said, "What about Sinatra?"

"He's got talent."

My brother Lou said, "Why don't you take your first two names?" My first name was Demi, which came from Demitriou, my father's name. And he came up with the idea of Dennis James.

TOM GOLDSMITH: Our studio in New York was at 515 Madison Avenue. We had an antenna atop the building. RCA had the Empire State Building. The next tallest building was the Chrysler Building, and CBS had a corner on that one. DuMont picked the 515 building which was not surrounded by taller buildings.

HELEN GOLDSMITH: Our first son was born in March 1939. I was in the hospital two weeks. Tom brought the boy and the television set in the house the same day. All the neighbors came in to see the baby but they were more interested in television even if all they saw was a test pattern.

DENNIS JAMES: One of the first things I did for DuMont was a fifteen-minute show called "Dennis James' Sports Parade." I would interview a sports luminary for five minutes and then partake of the sport. If it was a wrestler, I wrestled. If it was a boxer I boxed him. If it was a fencer I fenced him. I wrestled a guy named Bibber McCoy. He put me in a choke hold and I was out unconscious on the air. They slapped me around, and when I came to I was all disheveled, but I completed the show.

I also did a show called "Television Roof." Because I was in radio as well, I would say to guys like Frank Sinatra and the Pied Pipers, "Nobody is gonna see you anyhow, if you come on with me, I'll play your stuff on radio." That was the incentive. Sinatra wouldn't do it, but the Pied Pipers did.

TOM GOLDSMITH: We had the bandleader Fred Waring, but only a few of his Pennsylvanians because we couldn't get them all in that small room.

About this time, we negotiated a deal with Paramount. They paid us $55,000 for 55,000 shares of B stock in DuMont. Paramount paid that much money in cash, which was useful to expand our business. Allen and I had talked it over, and we said, "We'll get Paramount in here, because we in the technical field know about electronics, but they are in the program field. They know the public and have a big backlog of movies. The combination of DuMont and Paramount ought to make a great go in building a network of television."

I was a scientist. Allen DuMont was a scientist. We were rookies in Wall Street. We didn't know the jargon. Had I known what was going to happen, I would never have agreed to it.

CBS OPENS ITS EYE

RCA and CBS may have been arch radio rivals, but when it came to television research, RCA's blazing lights had already melted dozens of performers by the time CBS's technicians began laying their first camera cables. As a manufacturer of television sets unlike CBS, RCA had much more of a stake in getting programs on the air, but the real reason for RCA's head start was the difference in the fundamental makeup of William S. Paley and David Sarnoff.

Sarnoff, who was Paley's elder by ten years, was a visionary when it came to technology. It was Sarnoff who first saw radio's possibilities and brought his dreams to fruition by altering RCA's corporate structure. Now, he was mobilizing RCA's resources to make television a reality against considerable opposition inside and outside the company.

Paley was one of the naysayers. He had little interest in pioneering. He was content to let Sarnoff take the lead and draft him like a bike racer before scooting ahead in the end. Actually, Paley did much the same with talent. While RCA developed stars, such as Jack Benny and Red Skelton, Paley waited until they were popular and then plucked them one by one off the RCA roster.

While Sarnoff believed from the start that TV would revolutionize home life, Paley publicly suggested that TV's métier would be in the theater. "Man is a social creature; he likes to rub shoulders with his fellows," he said, adding, "Perfections in the projection of motion pictures will play a large part in making television applicable to theater, rather than home, presentation."

Only after RCA made real strides in television development did Paley make his move, and even then with ambivalence. As CBS was building its studio and transmitter, its executives were sent down to Washington in a vain effort to convince the FCC to delay TV's arrival. Why? Since the FCC only permitted experimental licenses, broadcast companies could not recoup expenses by selling commercials. Therefore the only income available from television came in the sale of sets, which only RCA and DuMont were manufacturing. CBS, with no manufacturing arm, only saw money going into broadcasting and no profits coming out.

Paley never was a risk taker. Even his entry into the broadcasting business was a reluctant one. That story begins in 1927 when a theatrical agent named Arthur Judson created a network of second-line radio stations called United Independent Broadcasters to compete with NBC and make sure his artists were represented on radio. It was a struggle from the start for Judson and his partners, a salesman named George Coats and the radio announcer J. Andrew White. The next year, the nearly bankrupt network merged with the Columbia Phonograph Company to form the Columbia Phonograph Broadcasting System, a long name for a still-fledgling company whose books were kept in the head of its chief accountant, the future announcing star Ted Husing.

After absorbing huge losses, Columbia bowed out. With the company about to collapse, Coats began looking for new investors. He approached Leon and Isaac Levy, the owners of the network's flagship station WCAU. The fact that WCAU was the network's biggest prize was an indication of the kind of uphill battle it was facing. Leon was a dentist, who as Paley's biographer Sally Bedell Smith wrote, "divided his time between filling teeth in the mornings and programming the station in the afternoons."

According to Smith, the partners were on the verge of closing shop when Vitaphone, the makers of the first talking movies, agreed to advertise on the network. For the time being, that kept the grim reaper at bay. Then it was suggested that Leon Levy's brother-in-law, Sam Paley, a wealthy cigar maker, buy the network for his son Bill.

In the fashion of the day, Paley owned a time slot on CAU and called his musical show "La Palina Boy," to market his number-one cigar, La Palina. Neither the cigar nor the woman on the cigar band hailed from Cuba. Palina was a derivation of Paley, and the supposedly Hispanic woman on the band was actually Sam's wife, Blanche. When Sam told Bill about his plans to buy the network, the twenty-six-year-old Paley replied, "I don't want anything to do with this pipsqueak radio network, this phony chain."

Bill found, however, that he enjoyed the glamour of producing a radio show, and he had a change of heart. In 1928, he put up his own money and bought control of the company. For all his reluctance, he was a quick study. In short order, he made several business decisions that put CBS on solid footing. He developed an affiliation agreement which was more attractive than the deal offered by NBC. It brought many new stations into the fold. CBS had had nineteen stations in the network when Paley took over. By 1935, there were ninety-seven. He also displayed a nearly unerring program sense, signing on a number of talented young performers, including Morton Downey, Bing Crosby, Kate Smith, Burns and Allen, and Fred Allen, then raided NBC for more established stars, among them Al Jolson and Nelson Eddy.

Unlike Sarnoff, who resisted sharing authority, Paley hired a number of very capable people and leaned on them for guidance. There was Edward Bernays, the country's foremost public relations expert, who Paley hired to refine CBS's corporate image. Bernays in turn suggested Paley hire Ed Klauber, a *New York Times* editor, as his right-hand man. Klauber was the kind of tough-minded administrator that the somewhat reticent Paley needed. Klauber was so tough he soon fired Bernays. Klauber also hired Paul White, a veteran newspaper reporter, and together they forged the journalistic standards that made CBS's news division the finest broadcast news operation in the world.

Another Klauber find was Paul Kesten, who came from the advertising agency Lennen & Mitchell to direct CBS's promotions department. Kesten, who was so fastidious he polished the soles of his shoes, in turn hired Frank Stanton, who would work his way up from the marketing department to become Paley's second in command. Kesten was nicknamed "vice president for the future," because of his interest in TV. In 1935, Kesten read an article on television by a young Hungarian inventor, Peter Goldmark, and hired him to set up CBS's first electronic system.

CBS already had a Nipkow system that was in occasional operation. The company inaugurated the service on July 21, 1931, with a forty-five-minute variety show starring Ted Husing as the emcee, with performances by Kate Smith, the Boswell Sisters, and George Gershwin. In 1933, the station was dismantled. Paley was content to wait until NBC perfected their electronic system.

Soon after NBC aired its first show in 1936, Kesten was instructed to build an antenna that would be "bigger and better" than NBC's. Since NBC had the Empire State Building, Goldmark chose the city's number-two skyscraper, the Chrysler Building, which had one added benefit according to one former CBS employee, the john in the upper spires afforded the user the most spectacular views in the city.

Paley brought in a distinct outsider to program his new station. Gilbert Seldes, the New York critic, was best known for his book, *The Seven Lively Arts*, a critical look at popular culture. Seldes had written an article for the *Atlantic Monthly* in May 1937, called "The Errors of Television." In it, Seldes laid out a plan for television in the coming years, saying the medium needed an experimental period to find its way. At the same time, he wrote, popular entertainment was the surest road for success, a notion that appealed to Paley.

Again looking to top NBC, Paley told Goldmark he wanted the biggest TV studios in New York. CBS's real estate people found a suitable location in the area above the waiting room in Grand Central Station. Goldmark later wrote, "I measured the studio's dimensions carefully and drew up the design, and when I was finished, while I couldn't claim victory on height, I could happily report, after checking on RCA, that CBS had the largest television studio in the world—a fact that may have delighted Paley and for a moment made me feel a significant part of show business. . . . The urge to beat RCA and its ruler, David Sarnoff, was such an overriding force at CBS that it actually began to shape the direction of my own career."

That quest would meet with disastrous results for Goldmark and CBS. In 1940, Goldmark found himself enthralled by *Gone with the Wind*, the first color movie he had ever seen. With Kesten's approval he began experimenting with a color-TV system based on the old Nipkow disk. CBS eventually sunk millions into the project, which, because of its incompatibility with black-and-white receivers, was doomed virtually from the start.

Meanwhile, in late 1939, CBS began a limited closed-circuit programming schedule. The veteran Broadway director Worthington Miner was brought in to assist Seldes. The two of them had different views about TV from their NBC counterparts, whose roots lay deep in radio and vaudeville. Both Seldes and Miner believed that television was a unique medium whose potential could not be developed fully without a whole new set of production and technical guidelines. They hired a small but devoted staff, whose talent and youthful aggressiveness created a crackling atmosphere of excitement and experimentation, undoubtedly aided by the small budgets and the low expectations placed on them from above.

RUDY BRETZ: Before I joined CBS in 1938, I was in a department store on Madison Avenue when I saw television for the first time. I wrote about it in my diary:

> *Well, finally I saw a television program. I must confess I am most unimpressed. It was the noon hour broadcast. First a bunch of movies, then a studio presentation, a woman interviewing a hat manufacturer about current styles, and a news commentator with his face shown on the screen as he read his news. If I had lots of money to spare, I wouldn't buy a television set. I wouldn't want to even look at it if I had it, if this is all it's gonna be.*
>
> *. . . What does television got that radio and film haven't got? Whatever it is, that is what television programs must be built on. I think it is a sense of immediacy, a feeling of seeing something happen as it happens. The first real success of television will be not art, but as informal reporting of events as they take place.*

JOHN HOLLYWOOD: I went to CBS in 1936 as an engineer on Peter Goldmark's staff. We were not broadcasting yet, but we did give demonstrations on the fourth floor of Grand Central Terminal. During one demonstration, we showed a film on coffee making in Brazil. Our jack-of-all-trades, Bill Young, set up a percolating pot of coffee in a place that would feed into the air-conditioning system. And the visitors were quite impressed by the film. They said, "You can almost smell the coffee!"

MARIAN SELDES: When I was twelve I would just run down to Grand Central from the Dalton School. I would walk through that glass-enclosed walkway two or three stories up into this magical world.

BOB BENDICK: I had never been in a space as big as that studio. It was a little frightening. The studio was one big open room with big glass windows and a high, vaulted ceiling. There were cables all over and a huge grid of water-cooled lights. Too often during a program, the lights would begin to leak, you would hear the constant drip, drip, drip.

EDWARD ANHALT: And when the trains came in and out of the station, you could see it on the tube. Goldmark tried to fix it by cushioning the equipment, but he never really cured it.

I was working for Pathé News in 1938, '39, when I met Worthington Miner at a party. He had just been hired by CBS. He and I went out and started to bar-hop, and the next thing I know I was working at CBS. Everybody did everything there. I worked the cameras. I directed a show. I wrote. Whatever was going on, we did.

BOB BENDICK: There were three cameras in the studio. Mine was mobile. With the early cameras, the cameraman saw the image upside down and in reverse. We had to learn that if we saw something going to the left, we had to pan to the right. When you took your eye away from the finder the world began to look upside down.

RUDY BRETZ: I got to the point where I could see things quite well upside down. At restaurants, I could read the menu of a guy sitting opposite me without much trouble.

JIM LEAMAN: I was hired as a producer/director. When I came on, Seldes told me he wanted television to be a window on the world. He didn't think television was going to get anywhere unless it could get out of the studio.

RUDY BRETZ: We thought that by making it very informal, even if there were mistakes (which would be terrible in a film), they would add to the immediacy of it by keeping the audience aware that the damn thing was happening at the time they were watching it. *Variety* called it "Take It Easy Television," which was a pretty good description.

Seldes was a delight. He would come up with great little aphorisms, which we would repeat like, "Don't forget you are working in a postage stamp art," which was true.

BOB BENDICK: We were aware of the potential of this thing, and we were enthusiastic about learning how to use it. What was a closeup in television? What does a cut mean? No one cared about getting a program off and on on time. We didn't think that was possible anyway, and no one thought of it from a commercial point of view.

RUDY BRETZ: Even if we had a commercial license, there was not a big enough audience to be able to sell commercials. They could only see a long period of throwing money down the drain. As a result, Seldes spent a lot of time developing programs which were really not programs, but things to put onto the picture tube that wouldn't cost anything.

BOB BENDICK: We went out to Jones Beach to film the waves, and we played music to it.

EDWARD ANHALT: Their mortal fear was that NBC would be able to get color out of the Zworykin electronic television.

RUDY BRETZ: Because CBS was behind in the technology, they were anxious for Dr. Goldmark to develop color TV. At first they wouldn't talk about it. Then in 1940, I was sent out with a still camera to take a lot of color pictures. I asked them, "Why, are we going into color television?"

Goldmark said, "Oh, no, we just want to see how colors respond on the black-and-white system."

JIM LEAMAN: When we did see it, though, it was marvelous. We were invited to the sixth floor of 485 Madison where Goldmark had his lab. He pointed his camera out the window down at the intersection. At that moment, a Macy's truck went by with that big red star, and a woman in a yellow dress stepped off the curb. Well, we cheered. It was beautiful!

Soon after that, we rented a racetrack in Maryland, and Eddie Anhalt and I went there with a crew. We hired jockeys, and we recruited spectators, and we staged a race and shot it in color.

EDWARD ANHALT: CBS realized that the real money in television was at that point in equipment, like sets, so they first tried to acquire the manufacturing capacity. When that failed they tried to stop RCA by sabotaging television. Peter Goldmark and I went down to Washington with Peter's equipment and the test film I shot. We showed it to the FCC and the Senate committee and said that it was foolish to approve black-and-white television broadcasting when here was color. Of course, it was a foolish kind of color because Peter's mechanical system didn't work so well. At one point in the hearings, someone moved the TV set and the wheel inside the TV went right through the set and up to the ceiling.

Also, you had to be be looking directly at the set or maybe at a ten-degree angle away from it, because as you moved out of that line the color broke up. During the hearings, one senator asked Goldmark, "When I shake my hand in front of my eyes, the color breaks up. What can we do about it?"

And Goldmark answered, "Don't shake your hand in front of your eyes." It didn't work, but they made a run at it.

*   *   *

RUDY BRETZ: In the studio, Miner and Seldes were very competitive. Whatever Seldes did, Miner wanted to do it differently.

CARL BEIER: They didn't like each other. Seldes used to make remarks about the memos that Tony kept grinding out. It seemed a little ridiculous because you could talk to anybody walking by the office door. Seldes thought they were asinine as well as pompous. They were filled with things like how many watts of light you had to have, or he would pontificate on lenses.

PETER MINER: That was the difference between Tony and Gil. Tony had tremendous ideas about the mechanics of doing this. His role was to work out by experimenting in the studio how he thought this medium should be done. He essentially invented the way we shoot television.

BOB BENDICK: Tony knew that TV wasn't an extension of the movies, that it had to be interpreted in a different way. In the home, you got up, walked around, and had a hot dog, which was different from theater or movies. He wanted to find out how you overcome these things or how to use them to your advantage. For example, we learned to do more closeups, that with wide shots you lost much of the information.

PETER MINER: He cut to reaction shots. He also used lenses and shots to make the studios look big, getting it to look like Rome.

CARL BEIER: Seldes was definitely the man in programming. Gil personally brought in Anya Anders. We had Alexandra Danileva and Leonid Massin and we had Markova and Boland from the real ballet world. I brought in Eugene Loring and "Billy the Kid," with Aaron Copland.

Vice President Henry Wallace was set to appear on one of Seldes's panel shows. Gil called me on the phone and said, "Henry Wallace is here. [Whispering] He's nervous as a cat. Can you take him downstairs and get him a drink or something and tell him he's gonna be all right?"

There was no secret service or anything. We just went down to the Oyster Bar and had a drink. He was a very nice, pleasant man. Mostly, I said to him he must have been in tougher cabinet meetings, that he should just ignore the cameras and talk to the other people. Here I was twenty-one years old, just out of Princeton and having a drink with the vice president of the United States. Actually, I was much more impressed with having met Argentinita and Aaron Copland.

We had Eddie Condon's jazz group, and people like Pee Wee Russell. I saw them shooting up before air.

Seldes wanted to do a museum show. He schmoozed around with Francis Henry Taylor, of the Metropolitan. Taylor did not want to run it by his trustees, and Seldes didn't want to run it by CBS, so the two of them worked out this deal whereby the museum truck would pull up by the back of the Metropolitan at midnight. They would take whatever artworks we were having on that week's show, put them in the truck, and bring them up to the studio. We would use them that next day on two shows in the afternoon and the evening. The following midnight it would all be loaded back onto the truck and taken back up to the museum, and nobody asked any questions. That's what it was like to be in the early days of television.

✳︎   ✳︎   ✳︎

JIM LEAMAN: Every afternoon we were obliged to go to the twenty-second floor at 485 Madison and watch what NBC was doing.

RUDY BRETZ: We would go down there and watch wrestling. Imagine that. And with great interest! They even sent us to a wrestling match to observe how the cameras were placed.

JIM LEAMAN: NBC would announce a show, and we would put a similar show together and have the fun of seeing how it matched up with what they did. They did "The Monkey's Paw," so we did it.

NBC published a program schedule every week and mailed them out to people who requested them. We got on their mailing list. That way we knew where their big truck was gonna be, and we could follow it. They went to Madison Square Garden, and we went too. We'd go up close and look at the cameras and their huge cables.

When they did their inaugural broadcast from the World's Fair, we were there. I saw Roosevelt make his speech, but to tell you the truth he wasn't nearly as fascinating as seeing what kind of cable systems NBC was using in its mobile unit.

EDWARD ANHALT: Seldes sent me to the World's Fair with a hand-held 16-millimeter Eastman camera to cover anything that looked interesting. There was an African village, and the people appeared to be naked. There was a lot of excitement about that. I also spent a lot of time at the Billy Rose Aquacade because the girls were pretty, but I spent most of my time at the Ford Motor Company because they had a free bar for newspaper people.

JIM LEAMAN: Oh, yeah, we all took advantage of those things. There was an exhibit that we went back to a lot even though we couldn't get it on television—the Salvador Dali exhibit. It was females underwater, and their costumes concealed all of their bodies except the relevant parts. Then there was Billy Rose's nude ranch. We photographed that, too.

EDWARD ANHALT: Some of the pieces were edited and put together as part of a news presentation from time to time, because that was one thing we were concerned about: how to handle news. I used to keep this little camera with me all the time, and I just happened to be at a bank when the Esposito Brothers hit it. I photographed all the shooting and the guys being arrested. Then I ran to the studio, and we had it on the air that night.

When I heard that the *Normandie* was burning, I went down there before the cops closed off the area. I gave a kid a couple of bucks for a white Red Cross costume and I got on the boat, but I couldn't get off because I would have gotten caught with the film. It started to turn over very slowly. I had to keep changing my position and climb up the wall until it was on its side and stable, then I got off with the film. At that point I was arrested, not by the police, but by the Naval Intelligence people. They grabbed the film, so we weren't able to show it until several days later when we got it back censored.

Seldes was trying to get television into the news by doing things the news never got around to doing. Then, if it became controversial, naturally they would mention that it was CBS television. I was assigned to dive into the Hudson in a diving suit with a camera to photograph an area of Dyckman Street that was pouring sewage into the river. There were rats crawling all over me, but we got a lot of stuff.

Seldes was a real visionary. I don't think anybody was doing news with his format. Cutting in with film was his concept. He used maps and models. He said that just having somebody standing there to talk to the audience wasn't the way to handle it because a visual medium should be visually interesting.

* * *

RUDY BRETZ: In July 1941, when TV went commercial, that changed the atmosphere a lot. There were suddenly more pressures on you. Now we had to fill four hours a day with programs five days a week.

EDWARD ANHALT: We had no money to fill those four hours, so we got very innovative. I remember just sticking a camera out the window of Grand Central Terminal and following girls on the street, which was surprisingly erotic to the degree that the FCC made us stop it.

RUDY BRETZ: RCA used to do that, but just to get some light on the camera. We pointed it out the window and said, "Let's do a story about a pedestrian." And we actually did a ten-minute show called "The Pedestrian." The idea was to find out what made him tick. We even created a drawing that showed a cross section of a pedestrian's brain. [Laughs.]

It became the essence of television. You saw all those people walking down there and the melody of the traffic and everything. That was fascinating. Have you ever seen a camera obscura? There is one in a park in Santa Monica. You can go inside the building and watch people outside walking by. People stand there for hours and watch. That was the thing about television. It was real. It was two-dimensional.

BOB BENDICK: Because most of our shows were live and real time, you could use that to create suspense. That's an element in TV we have mostly lost, because now we are using television mostly to transport tape or film. The intensity of live TV could be great fun.

EDWARD ANHALT: There was another side to that. The pressure on us was tremendous. Some of us drank a lot in those days, so we were sort of anesthetized; drinking in the daytime, which very few people do now. Tony and I used to go to the Oyster Bar every day for lunch, and we always had two martinis in the middle of the day, so that made life easier.

RUDY BRETZ: One of the regular live shows we did was badminton.

BOB BENDICK: Badminton was the great sporting event, because we only worked in the studio, and badminton lent itself to a studio sports operation. The biggest problem was when the shuttlecocks went toward the lights, because back then if you focused the cameras on a bright light it knocked you off the air.

EDWARD ANHALT: We also got government films or commercial films from places like General Motors. We once got a film from the Bureau of Mines, which I put on the air without checking it first. There was a bar across the street on Vanderbilt Avenue where I used to go. After I put the film on, the bartender called me on the phone. "Have you looked at your monitor?"

I said, "No, I have them turned off." I turned the monitor up, and there's a lady lying on her back stark naked, exercising her legs. I looked at the can, and the label said, "Post-Natal Exercise." Why it came from the Bureau of Mines I don't know.

Then he said, "Look out the window." I looked out and there were five hundred people watching. With that the phone rang. It was the FCC. Then it was "Due to circumstances beyond our control . . ."

There were always funny things happening. We had a variety show called "Men at Work." An announcer would say, "And now the magician." They would cut away and the guy would be sitting there having coffee, or people would come with pet animals that couldn't be controlled. We finally stopped that after Fred Allen brought an eagle into the studio, and the eagle got away. That was a very famous broadcast in which Allen described the flight of the eagle as it shit on everybody.

MARIAN SELDES: We had a house in Croton Falls, New York, called Strawberry Hill. One Sunday morning, my father had a rather bad cold, and this extremely active man was sitting in bed. I brought him the papers and coffee, and the phone rang, and I saw my father suddenly transformed. At first, I heard him give a lot of instructions. Then, we all got in the car and went down to the train station and off my father went. Pearl Harbor had been bombed, and my father galvanized this small group of people into a news organization, and they aired the first news special.

RUDY BRETZ: Our newsman Dick Hubbell had the idea that we ought to put a camera on top of the Chrysler Building, where the transmitter was, so that we could show the action if the Japanese came and bombed New York. We didn't do it.

EDWARD ANHALT: I had to go in the Army. I was in there for six years, and I never came back to CBS. We suffered a lot of casualties during the war. Eleven or twelve people from CBS were killed. A lot of them became combat cameramen, and the death rate for combat camera people was very high. I was supposed to be a combat cameraman, but I wormed my way out of it when I found out what the casualty rate was.

RUDY BRETZ: It was sad to see everybody go. We were all close. We had a routine where each member of the staff would give a party for the whole staff. Eddie Anhalt gave his at a roller-skating rink. Someone else had one at a burlesque theater in New Jersey. After the war we had more people, more programs. Being a larger group it wasn't the same.

Before we all split up, we had a going-away party. We played musical chairs. Our announcer, Giles O'Connor, won. The prize was an iconoscope tube. Giles took it home and put it on his mantel. The months went by, and CBS was still trying to keep something going, but they couldn't get any more iconoscope tubes. Then they remembered this one that Giles had won. They called him up and asked him if he still had it, and they offered him five hundred dollars for it. That was a fortune in those days. He agreed, and CBS was able to stay on the air for a while longer.

CAPTAIN BILL EDDY
AND THE STORY
OF WBKB

At six feet seven inches tall, the legendary Captain William Crawford Eddy was a giant in the burgeoning TV industry, in both a literal and figurative sense. Eddy was too skinny to be called Bunyanesque, but he was probably as close as one could get in a world where the hero is the one who in the end always gets the patent. Eddy had over a hundred of them.

In 1939, the ex-submarine commander was hired away from RCA to set up and operate W9XBK, the experimental television station owned by Balaban & Katz, a Chicago-based movie-theater chain, which pioneered the use of air-conditioning in its ornate movie palaces. The marriage of the free-thinking Eddy and the bottom liners at B & K would last about a decade. During his tenure, W9XBK (later WBKB) along with KTLA in Los Angeles were the most influential independent stations in the country. Eddy was the creator of the puppet show "Kukla, Fran & Ollie." He also was the first to put Marlin Perkins of "Wild Kingdom" fame on the air. With the encouragement of Cubs' owner Phil Wrigley (who enjoyed TV coverage of his club because it meant he didn't have to go to the park himself), he literally wrote the book on how baseball should be done on television.

When Eddy took over the station, he had no radio or TV network to supply programming, and he had no manufacturing facility to offer up the latest technology. All he could hope for was the continued generosity of Balaban & Katz. Fortunately, their air-cooled movie houses were often packed. The company was co-owned by Paramount Pictures, and the TV station's start-up costs of sixty thousand dollars were less than the price of one of Paramount's B movies, so the investment wasn't much of a risk.

B & K and Paramount faced more serious problems, which prompted their interest in television in the first place. Paramount's founder, Adolph Zukor, like his fellow movie moguls, not only produced movies but also controlled their distribution in part by buying up theater chains around the country. At its peak, Paramount controlled some two thousand theaters.

The monopolistic practices of the big studios in general and specifically the cozy relationship between Paramount and Balaban & Katz eventually came to the attention of the Justice Department. A series of antitrust suits were initiated, which took more than a decade to settle. As the cases wound their way through the lower courts, Barney Balaban, who along with his brother, A.J., and Sam Katz, ran Balaban & Katz, realized that in the anti-monopolist New Deal era, they weren't going to win. It was time to look for alternative sources of revenue. Paul Raibourn, an M.I.T. graduate who worked for Barney, convinced the partners to apply for a TV license.

However, owning a TV license in 1939 didn't mean that Balaban & Katz knew what to do with it. For that, B & K needed Eddy, who knew as much about TV broadcasting as anyone else did in those days. But Eddy was no company man. Even as a youth in Saratoga Springs, New York, he displayed a rebellious, but inventive, genius. Thrilled by the exploits of the barnstorming pilots who worked Saratoga, he decided to build his own airplane. After the plane's engine blew up the woodshed and nearly took the house with it, he was sent packing to military school.

From there, he was enrolled at Annapolis where he built a small radio transmitter to warn his fellow students of surprise inspections. While serving in the Navy's submarine corps, he is said to have installed China's first flush toilet. But Eddy was no clown. His Eddy Amplifier was a sonar detection device that was much more accurate than anything the Navy employed. He was also a professional cartoonist, whose annual calendars for the Honeywell Corporation were printed in the millions.

With Farnsworth and later at RCA, Eddy virtually invented television lighting. He also pioneered the use of miniature sets for TV and created some of TV's first special effects, at times with unanticipated results. His former co-workers still chuckle at one Eddy idea that went awry on live TV. For a drama set on the high seas, Eddy put several model ships in a tank of water. To darken the water, Eddy bought a clutch of turtles, dabbed paint on their shells, and let them flap around in the water to spread the paint around. All went swimmingly until one of them picked the wrong moment to come up for air, and a closeup of a turtle looming over the model boat inadvertently turned the drama into a prequel of *Jaws*.

When Eddy joined Balaban & Katz and moved into the fourth floor of 190 North State Street, there were less than fifty TV sets in the Chicago area and no guarantees that there would ever be sixty. Eddy's chief engineer was Arch Brolly, an associate at Farnsworth. He also brought Reinald Werrenrath with him from New York. The rest of his staff he filled out from the Chicago area. The young staff of merry pirates were devoted to their leader, although Eddy must have taken some getting used to. Quite deaf, he had a habit of turning off his hearing aid when he became bored during meetings. To disguise his hearing loss, he invented a pipe that acted as a hearing aid by conducting sound through his teeth.

"Inventing came naturally," Eddy said years later. "Generally, the easiest way to do a job was to invent a new way of doing it, so that's what we did."

BILL EDDY: I was very happy with NBC, so I gave Paramount a price they could not accept and then set sail on my boat for New London. By the time I got there, they had sent a telegram saying my offer had been accepted. We built a studio on the top floor of the State Lake Building. I had brought a transmitter and a few receivers with me in the compartment of my Century. Reinald Werrenrath came out with me, and I hired about five boys, Jim Leahy, Bill Kusack, Dick Shapiro, Stan Osterlund, and of course Arch Brolly. That was the entire staff.

WILLIAM PETER "BILL" KUSACK: I was working for RCA Victor, which was the service company for RCA. I was a young engineer at the time. I got all the crud that no one else wanted to do—like television. The big operators were in theater sound and radio broadcasting. I got PA systems in churches. I also repaired RCA's TRK-12 television receivers. We had about ten of them in Chicago. I used to service those with the instruction book in my lap. If I needed more help, I would call Camden, where the sets were built, but we kept the sets goin'. One day, I read in the paper that Balaban & Katz was going to build a TV station. I told my boss, "We've got enough headaches with these ten receivers. Now, they're gonna import more of them."

He told me to go over there and see what these jokers were doing, so I went over to the State Lake building and met them. Once Bill found out I was servicing TV sets, which was a rare person in town, he talked me into giving up my job at RCA for the standard salary which he offered everybody, thirty-five dollars a week.

DICK SHAPIRO: Bill Kusack and I were working at RCA together. He called me up and said, "If you want to get into this stuff, you better run over," so I did. After five minutes, Bill Eddy said, "When can you start working?"

BILL KUSACK: We not only worked together, but we shared our spare time and our pleasure together, and we all had a great liking for Bill. He was the "Skipper" to us.

ARCH BROLLY: Our first transmitter was a little thing about a yard wide and seven feet high with all vacuum tubes. Bill, with his ingenuity, said, "Let's get a windmill tower and stick it on the roof. You design an antenna, and we'll put it up there and run this thing." So we did!

At first, we put audio signals on it, and we got a portable receiver together and went out and measured the signal around Chicago to see how far it would reach.

REINALD WERRENRATH: We got a panel truck and named it "Mobile Unit Number One" as a joke because there was no number two. Bill put some equipment inside and a collapsible antenna on the roof. Then he said to me, "You're gonna be the one to rig the antenna." We drove the truck around the outskirts of Chicago, and we'd run up the antenna, take a signal strength reading, run it down, go a few blocks, and run it up again and take another reading. My running in and out of the truck to do this took so much time that he said, "Why don't you just stay up on top?" It was a cold night, and I nearly froze to death. It was one of those cases where I found myself wondering how I ever got myself into this.

ARCH BROLLY: We also had to build our own cameras, and you couldn't go out and buy camera-mounting equipment, so Bill Eddy got the idea of taking a lift from a barber's chair and attaching a little motor to it, and we put the camera on that.

BILL KUSACK: Before we got the test pattern on the air, people would call up and say, "Hey, we just got a TV set but we don't see anything on Channel Four." We'd say, "Okay, keep the set on, and we'll turn on the transmitter." And we did that.

Zenith had a station and was already on the air at that time on Wednesday nights. They had one film which they showed every time they were on the air. It was called "Elephant Boy."

REINALD WERRENRATH: We were on every day for an hour or two. I did all the programming before the war. We did a lot of "man in the street" shows, because we could send an announcer down and let him go for an hour or more. That made life much easier for us.

The idea was to stay on the air as long as we could to develop an audience. We always thought there were four hundred sets, but that may have been a little optimistic.

BILL KUSACK: We used to ride the elevated into work, and if we saw a new antenna on a roof we would get all excited.

BILL EDDY: If Sally Rand was at the theater across the street, I could bring her in, set her in front of the camera, and we had an hour's program, but it was all hit and miss. We had no real audience to worry about, and there was no printed schedule.

BILL KUSACK: Whenever you got a call to have a meeting in Bill's office, you knew you were either in trouble or he had a bright idea. If he was puffing on his pipe something fierce with a pixie smile, all excited, that meant he had some wild idea. Once, that wild idea turned out to be a remote. He says, "We're gonna do remotes."

"We don't have remote cameras."

"We'll build a remote camera."

So we built a camera with a big lens. We told Beldon Cable we needed fifty feet of cable. When it arrived, it was about three inches in diameter, and fifty feet of that was a bloody ton. There weren't any connectors for a cable like that, so we hard-wired the camera to the cable. That meant whenever we moved the camera, one guy had to take the lens off, because the lens weighed as much as the camera. Somebody grabbed the camera, and two or three guys would try to carry the cable, which didn't coil very well. We looked like we were feeding a python at the zoo.

ARCH BROLLY: Our first remote broadcast was from a parking lot out at the lakefront in Chicago. We went out there with a little van we rigged up. We put the camera on top of the van and showed some neighborhood scenes. While we were there, a colored man came around, a street performer. His trick was to eat light bulbs. I introduced him as an itinerant street performer, and he chewed up a light bulb for our viewing audience.

*   *   *

BILL EDDY: I was in Michigan City on December 7, 1941, when I heard the news. I caught the four o'clock train to Washington. I went to the Navy Department and said, "We're gonna need radar in this war, and nobody knows anything about it. I've got a staff and a facility in Chicago that we can convert, and I'm sure Paramount will be glad to give it to you if you want to use it."

Without further recourse to Paramount Pictures, they accepted my offer of all the assets of BKB, and I returned to Chicago to set up the school. We estimated that they would have to train 135 radar technicians. We ended up training 86,000 and still not meeting our quota, but the school became a very, very large operation with classes held all over the country.

ARCH BROLLY: About a year into the war, the FCC notified all holders of experimental licenses that if they went on the air for four hours a week their licenses would be extended for the duration of the war.

The old transmitter was no good anymore, so Paramount ordered a transmitter to be built for us by a small firm in New York. They got started on it, but then they got a government contract, and work on our transmitter came to a halt. We decided to finish it ourselves. The problem was that parts were hard to find, so I spent two or three days canvassing the surplus and junk stores around Manhattan, looking for parts. Then my engineer and technician associates and I worked nights and Sundays putting it together, and we got on the air in time to satisfy the FCC. One typical problem was finding a water-cooling system receptacle. Then I remembered what we used in the old Farnsworth lab in San Francisco. We found a ten-gallon pickle jar, and it worked fine.

*   *   *

LEW GOMAVITZ: Before World War II, I was in New York, working as an assistant stage manager at a nightclub. The war came and I enlisted in the Navy. Because of my background, they had me doing shows for the enlisted men. Then they shipped me to Bill Eddy's place as a radio technician. While I was there, I spent half of my time at the television station, helping them out. If somebody wasn't on a camera I'd get on a camera. I did everything but run a record player for audio.

Eventually, I became the studio manager. I hired the help. Nobody wanted to work for twenty-five, thirty-five dollars a week. That's how Esther Rajeski, Rae Stewart, and Felice Kerrigan came aboard.

BILL EDDY, JR.: Pop always surrounded himself with women, and when he had the authority to hire, he hired them. His teams after the war were usually fifty percent women. They used to joke about his covey of girls, but they did the job.

FELICE KERRIGAN ELIAS: During the war, there were seven women who worked there. We called ourselves the WATC girls, the Women's Auxiliary Television Corps. We pushed cameras. We rode the microphones. We did the console work. We did everything.

LEW GOMAVITZ: These women were tough. During one show, Esther Rajeski put her foot in the power, and it knocked her across the studio floor. I said, "Esther, are you all right?"

"Yes, I'm all right."

"Then get the hell back on the camera."

FELICE ELIAS: I started as a dolly pusher. The dolly was the size of a dining-room table. Lew would say into your earphones, "Camera two, dolly in," and you would move it to a certain chalk mark on the floor. For $17.25 a week, it was hard work. I didn't know we were getting half the pay the men were getting, but people would do anything for Bill. I adored him.

They needed material to put on the air, so I wrote a couple of scripts for them. One of them was a murder mystery set in a saloon. At one point, the victim is standing at the bar, and he orders a bottle of liquor that turns out to be poison.

We didn't have any bottles of liquor, but I remembered there were some bottles in the darkroom that resembled liquor bottles. I found one that had formaldehyde in it. I made one of those old-fashioned liquor labels with "XXX" and a skull and crossbones which I put on the bottle. During the show, I was sitting in the control room, and when he picked up the bottle I said to myself, "God, Felice, you didn't empty the bottle! He really is drinking formaldehyde!"

The actor's last words before he collapsed on the floor were, "Hey, guys, I'm not kidding!" They rushed him to a hospital, and fortunately he lived. I didn't know what to do. I ran into the ladies' room and hid. When all the commotion died down, I went back to the control room, and Bill was there. I said, "My God, Captain Eddy, you won't believe it."

He said, "Did you have something to do with that? Just go home and don't say a word."

The next day, the headline in the *Chicago Tribune* said, REALISM HITS WBKB. Fortunately, my name wasn't mentioned.

LEW GOMAVITZ: We also had Hugh Downs and Mike Wallace doing shows.

HUGH DOWNS: I didn't know what I was going to do until the Depression. After one year of college, my dad suggested rather pointedly that I get a job. I pounded the pavement, but I couldn't find anything.

Then one day I was coming home after buying a jug of milk, when I passed by the local radio station. I went in and put the jug down, but a receptionist said they had auditions on Tuesday. I was getting ready to go when the program director appeared in the doorway. He said they were losing the one announcer they had. I read for him, and he said, "That was very bad, but great oaks from little acorns grow," and he hired me.

When I told my father, he told me to continue looking for a job for another week, and if I didn't find it then go to work for the station. As far as he was concerned I never found a job.

In 1945, I did a fifteen-minute newscast on WBKB. It was fifteen minutes with a camera on me. When the lights went on, the place was heating up so much that the sweat was dripping off my chin onto my paper. I sweated right through my jacket. I thought, "That's good, it'll keep the jacket from catching fire."

Television was fascinating, but I didn't do any more of it for another four years. You'd get five bucks for doing a television program, and who needed that. I kind of hoped television would go away. I thought it was a fad like 3-D movies. Mike Wallace didn't really take it seriously either. It's a sad commentary on our prophetic abilities.

LEW GOMAVITZ: I remember when he was a big shot in Chicago on radio, and I wanted him to do TV. Mike said to me, "Gomi, I can't do the show. Look at my pocked face. Who in the hell would want to look at it?"

"Mike, nobody sees your face. We'll put a little makeup on, and nobody will pay any attention to you."

MIKE WALLACE: I was sensitive about my skin. I figured I would look bad, but no one ever said anything about it.

When I got out of the Navy after the war, BKB called me. I made one appearance, and I figured I was dead in television because I couldn't take the brutal lights.

STERLING "RED" QUINLAN: I got out of the Navy in '45. I tried to write the great American novel and fell on my ass, so I got a job writing continuity for a radio station. Then I began hearing about this great new adventure called television and WBKB, which had just gotten its commercial license. Soon, there were signs all over the bars, WE HAVE TELEVISION.

"What the hell is television?"

"Pictures. You watch a test pattern with music on and wait for wrestling to come up."

I knew right then that that's what I wanted to get into. One night, I walked right into BKB. There was no security. I told the switchboard operator, "I just went to a saloon and saw television, and now I'd like to meet somebody in it."

She sent me down the hallway. I opened the door, and there was a bunch of people sitting around waiting for the wrestling to start. I had to go back a few times until I finally ran into Bill Ryan, who was in charge of the crew. He agreed to give me a job for thirty-five dollars a week. We would paint sets and move scenery. You did anything that anyone told you to do. There were no unions.

After six months, I got a big offer to go into the engineering crew, and I ran the record turntables. It was such free-form. The movies would usually be cowboy shoot-'em-ups. When the guy shot an Indian, I'd put in machine-gun sounds to see if anybody would phone. Nobody called. Nobody gave a shit. If the announcer, John Dunham, was a little stoned, he would sign on with, "This is WBKB, Constantinople, Turkey," just to see if anybody would call in. Nobody did.

Anybody could come down and audition. We had quartets, dancers, ukulele players, people mouthing words to Frank Sinatra, you name it. If they were any good we'd put 'em on between wrestling bouts. One night, I was in the control room when this quartet was on the air. The phone rang, and it was the Twelfth Street police station. Some guy says, "You got those singers on there? Keep 'em singin'. The guy on the right is wanted for burglary." We kept 'em on for another fifteen minutes until the police came and put the guy in jail. That was early television.

BILL KUSACK: Bill's biggest problems were with the bean counters who wanted to bomb the television group because they were losing money. We had to sell John Balaban and Barney Balaban that this was the thing, so he tried to get anything that was spectacular, like baseball and wrestling.

BILL EDDY: Phil Wrigley thought that television might increase the audience for baseball. He wanted a system that would better describe baseball to housewives, and he asked me to go to spring training and try to work out a system for televising baseball. We experimented with everything from buried cameras on the third-base side which players continually slammed into, to aerial cameras and cameras in back of the catcher. In the end, I wrote a manual on how to televise baseball, which is still in use today. In return, he gave me the rights to the Cubs for two years at no cost.

DICK SHAPIRO: We had a right-angle prism on the lens, so we could look into the dugout while they thought the camera was shooting out on the field. There were a couple of women who sat in back of the cameraman. He would swing the camera around so it would look south but it was actually shooting right into their crotches. Our transmitter would send these pictures of the women on Channel Thirteen to the guys in the control room before we went on the air. We found out later that people were tuning in Channel Thirteen and watching. The cameraman got his, though. One day a foul careened off the dugout right into his privates. They had to rush him down to the locker room and pack him in ice.

*　*　*

BILL KUSACK: One day, Werr and I went to see Fred Kohler, who was promoting wrestling at the Rainbow Arena, about putting wrestling on TV. We said, "We can't pay ya anything, we just wanna try it." He decided there was no harm in it, so he agreed. The arena was so empty when we first went in, there was an echo in the place. But the first night we started broadcasting some guy in a TV-repair place put a receiver in his window. They had to call the police because he was afraid the crowd outside his window would shatter the glass.

We had to put about five hundred foot-candles of light on the ring. People in the first three or four rows were wearing sunglasses. The sweat poured off the wrestlers, but they didn't complain. People were asking for their autographs for the first time in their lives, and in the meantime Kohler is building bleachers like mad. One day he said to me, "Bill, you know, all my wrestlers look black on TV."

I said, "That's easy to explain. It's the white mat you got on the ring. The electrons are redistributing in our tube, and it makes them look black."

He said, "How are we gonna get 'em back white?"

"Dye the mat some color."

So the next week he has that mat dyed green. That first night, there are hardly any falls. Or if there was a fall, it only lasted a short time. I grabbed one of the wrestlers, and I asked him, "What's the matter? There were no falls tonight."

He says, "You can fry an egg on that mat."

It was the infrared being soaked up by that darker mat.

DICK SHAPIRO: We also went to the track and put the five o'clock race on the air. We would be out there all day, practicing and sending in races. A couple of stagehands saw the picture come in, and they would send a guy to call their bookie, because the bookies back then got their information fifteen minutes later. The guy would make a big bet, clean up, and get out. Bill Eddy found out and made them cut it out real quick.

ARCH BROLLY: Bill was so imaginative and inventive. He could think of shows galore. He initiated "Kukla, Fran & Ollie."

LEW GOMAVITZ: Once they decided to do a kids' show with Burr, he came down to a meeting with Bill. At the meeting, Burr said he would like to have someone work with him in front of the stage. He said he wanted it to be a woman. I said to Bill, "The person who would be ideal for this would be Fran Allison." I had worked with her on Don McNeill's charades show.

Burr said, "I've done some shows with her at the Great Lakes Naval Station."

Well, she came down the next day, and we sat down and worked out a program for an hour's show. On that first show, Beulah Zachary was the director, and I was the producer. When Burr got on that Monday, he didn't follow notes or anything. We did it catch as catch can. It was really a wild thing for one hour. At the end of that one hour, Beulah said, "You direct and I'll produce." For the rest of the history of that show it was always ad-libbed.

DICK SHAPIRO: Burr was a very serious guy. He had a certain mysticism about the puppets. Sometimes, I would walk by the set in the dark studio, Kukla would be on the stage, and he would watch me walk by. I did what I had to do and then walked back, and the puppet would still be following me. Pretty soon it would say, "Hello, Dick," and I would answer it.

LEW GOMAVITZ: Burr had met a ballerina named Tamara Toumanova. When she appeared in Chicago, she invited him backstage. He brought a puppet in a little paper bag to give to her. In the dressing room, he took it out of the bag, and he put it on her shoulder, and she said, "Oh, a *kukla.*" *Kukla* in Russian means "doll."

Well, Burr didn't have the heart to give it to her. He took the puppet back and called it Kukla. In those days Kukla had a little round head made of cloth and a button nose, with a little red dress. The head was not much larger than a tennis ball.

In the beginning, Burr would bring Kukla and Ollie to the studio in a paper sack, and he traveled by El. Later, the puppets had their own leather cases, and Burr traveled by limousine. In the beginning, he only had Kukla and Ollie. Then he made Buelah Witch. Beulah Zachary loved it because she was a witch. She protected Burr and was tough as hell.

Burr also made Cecil Bill, the "tu tui man," who was named after Bill Ryan, who was on BKB's production crew. Bill talked like that. You couldn't understand the guy. Colonel Crackie was named after an RCA salesperson that Burr met in Bermuda. Fletcher Rabbit was Burr's mailman.

RED QUINLAN: With "Kukla, Fran & Ollie," finally, there was something for Mama to watch besides wrestling, and she said, "Okay, Daddy, let's spend a few hundred bucks for a TV." That was the first broadening of the demographic profile where the viewers were not just men going to the saloons to watch it.

ARCH BROLLY: Another show we started was with Marlin Perkins, who was the director of the Lincoln Park Zoo.

BILL EDDY: Perkins would arrive with boa constrictors and all sorts of wild animals which he would let loose in my office to attract my attention while he went on with this spiel about this "Zoo Parade" that he was going to put on. In desperation, I had to hire him to keep clear of all his animals.

BILL KUSACK: He would come to the studio with his animals in a bag. One day, he reaches into the bag and pulls out these snakes. In seconds, the place was empty. It was just Marlin Perkins alone in the studio.

BILL EDDY: We tried interesting Marshall Fields and Commonwealth Edison and all the other companies in advertising, but they said, "You get a big audience and we'll buy some time on your station."

We did it with subterfuge. We'd go to a bar in Michigan City and put a receiver in. Then we started calling up various bars around the city, asking "Do you have television?"

They said, "No."

We said, "Oh, we're sorry, we know the Indy has one up the street," so we'd send a salesman out and sell a receiver to that man. From then on, we multiplied the receivers in Michigan City very fast, and we were able to use it as a guinea pig as to what the future market might be.

ARCH BROLLY: That was also when Bill discovered that women's wrestling had become popular in and around Michigan City. It was lawful in Indiana, but not in Illinois, so he arranged for remote pickups, and that became quite a hit in Chicago.

BILL EDDY: I figured one of the big programs we could put on would be the Notre Dame football games. Arch and I decided that since we could transfer the signals by microwave from Chicago to Michigan City we could also transfer them to Rolling Prairie and from Rolling Prairie down into the stadium at Notre Dame. So we put all the publicity out that we were going to televise the games beginning a certain day. We had never seen a picture out of South Bend at that time, but the publicity sold a lot of sets.

BILL KUSACK: I built the whole microwave system between South Bend and Chicago. We put one relay tower in Bill Eddy's backyard in Michigan City, but then we found out there was no geodesic survey of the land elevation between Michigan City and South Bend. You need that to develop a line of sight and figure out how you're gonna build your towers, so I took a road map and drew a straight line between Michigan City and South Bend and walked the twenty-odd miles. Before I would cross certain fields, I would get the farmers' permission. They were all very suspicious that we were gonna be prospecting for oil. When the first tower was built at a place called New Carlisle, it looked like an oil derrick for sure, and the property around it went sky high.

In the meantime, I read that Bell Labs had done some tests across Long Island Sound and said that microwave was not very practical for transmitting over water, and at one point we had to go over forty miles of water. But Bill said, "We're gonna go over the water." Now I was sure we were gonna lay a real egg.

BILL EDDY: About ten o'clock in the morning the day of the game, I pressed the button and nothing happened. Eleven o'clock the same day, same thing. The game was not scheduled until one-thirty. In the meantime, I developed a world-class migraine. Then came time for the game, the opening whistle. Arch pressed the button, and in came Rolling Prairie, Michigan City, and Chicago. There is a God.

BILL KUSACK: The guy ran back the opening kickoff one hundred yards for a touchdown. You couldn't have done it any better if you cued it.

LEW GOMAVITZ: Even though AT&T called it "Eddy's Folly," the fact was that Bill's relay to South Bend was a great success, but it was very expensive and John Balaban wasn't in favor of his money being spent like that. Still, Bill spent it anyhow. He never cared about money. He was like the great theatrical directors. They spent as much as they needed for a super end product.

BILL EDDY: It was hit or miss when I was there. That's what caused John Balaban lots of worries. Paramount had spent sixteen million dollars developing BKB; John was the type who wanted to get a return on it yesterday. All we were interested in was spending money. We were having more fun building and testing the equipment than we were in making it pay off.

BILL KUSACK: Some of us in engineering looked at programming as a necessary evil. The test pattern gave us more information.

BILL EDDY, JR.: My father also couldn't understand the movie industry people who were moving into the television business. These were people who had a strictly turnstile mentality. He thought these people were used-car salesmen. These weren't people with vision, these were people who had grown up in the environment of big movie theaters with organs, sixteen million 60-watt light bulbs, chasers, and doing everything they could do to bring people in and sell them tickets. It just became so dichotomous to my father's own personal business mind, and he decided that he was fed up with it.

RED QUINLAN: Barney Balaban also got a little fed up with the costs of running that station. Bill, with his fantastic ability to sell ideas, may have gotten them enthused about breaking even sooner than the station was able to, and they decided that he wasn't gonna be able to do it.

BILL KUSACK: The company was losing money, but right after that particular time, a baboon could have run the company because television just took off. Bill always had a lot of faith in the future of television. I once went with him to a meeting with Paramount. He pleaded with them to buy more stations. He named the cities, but they turned him down. If they had listened to him, they would have made a bundle.

RED QUINLAN: Bill was called up to a showdown meeting with John Balaban up in Wisconsin. When he came back, there was a very sudden announcement that Bill Eddy was gone. The next thing I knew, a big tall guy named John Mitchell, a theater manager from South Bend, came in and announced that he was the manager. Around the station was just shock and sadness.

LEW GOMAVITZ: We were all very angry. Bill's departure didn't set well with Burr. "Kukla, Fran & Ollie" moved to the NBC station soon after Bill's departure.

BILL EDDY: I was only a little bit of a small potato. When you try to isolate and give anybody credit for anything as big as television, it's just foolish because it is the result of many, many people and many years of research by unknowns.

RED QUINLAN: Bill built the third station in the country at a time when there was no network, no film, and it was all from scratch.

BILL KUSACK: I call the present TV group "appliance operators." If anything goes wrong, they call the plant and have it fixed. We had to build everything, and when something broke down we had to fix it ourselves, and it always surprised everyone whenever they came to the station, and they saw how young we were. Except for Bill and Arch, we were all in our early twenties.

RED QUINLAN: WBKB's success was all Bill. I was heartbroken when he left. He was the most innovative and the most unusual guy I ever met in broadcasting. I was glad just to polish his shoes.

OVER HERE
AND THERE

Like Lucky Strike Green, television also went to war after Pearl Harbor. One by one, personnel shortages forced the stations to shut down with only DuMont remaining on the air.

While the studios were dark, the laboratory candles burned bright. From the RCA labs in Camden, New Jersey, to Baird's factory in England, TV researchers, who only a few months before were striving for sharper black-and-white pictures, were turning the same cathode ray tubes into instruments of war. The intensified research effort produced huge jumps in television technology, which brought TV into the modern era when the war was over.

Over 550 electronic companies supplied goods for the military. GE, Bell Labs, and RCA were all in involved in the war effort. Much of RCA's work revolved around television. Les Flory, one of RCA's earliest TV researchers, found himself working on infrared imaging tubes, which would be used for night viewing. "We put small tubes in binoculars which were attached to a helmet. You could put that on your head and use it for driving at night with infrared lights," he said. "We also made something called a Sniperscope. It was a monocular device on an infra-tube with a rifle and also an infrared light. You would illuminate a target with an infrared light and you could see it through your telescope, and whoever you were focusing on couldn't see the light at all."

One of the biggest projects involving television was the torpedo bomb, an idea Zworykin proposed in 1934 in a paper he called "Flying Torpedo with an Electric Eye." Although the torpedo bomb was used effectively during the war, the project probably had a greater impact on television itself when scientists realized that a tube superior to the iconoscope was necessary in order for the bomb to work. RCA's lab developed the Image Orthicon, a much more sensitive tube than the iconoscope. Since it required less light, it deserves full credit for finally making television practical.

Radar, with the cathode ray tube as its main component, was a natural outgrowth of television research. Baird in particular was very active in this area. His mine detectors cleared the way for Montgomery's troops in North Africa.

While the scientists worked their miracles, production staffs emptied as more and more men went into the service. DuMont was able to keep its station on the air only by persuading some of its factory workers to travel to Manhattan at night to work the cameras and run the station.

A number of television veterans signed on with the motion picture units of the Air Force and Army Signal Corps where their production experience was put to use in the making of propaganda films. It could be glamorous work when the corporal sitting across the luncheon table was William Holden.

The two chieftains of RCA and CBS were personally involved in the war effort. David Sarnoff, who had been a lieutenant colonel in the Signal Corps reserve since 1924, was activated in 1944 and sent overseas to organize the massive communications lines needed for D-Day. For his efforts, he was appointed Brigadier General, a title whose use he did little to discourage after his return to civilian life.

William Paley undoubtedly took note of Sarnoff's military status and secured a position with the Office of War Information. He was later attached to the OWI's Psychological Warfare Department working principally to organize broadcasts in the wake of the D-Day invasion. By all accounts he did excellent work, but he complained that he was only a colonel.

LENORE JENSEN: One day in 1940, on the first floor of Radio City I saw all these mannequins dressed in military uniforms. I went right upstairs to Warren Wade, and I said, "I can do a program where I interview people dressed in military uniforms about what they're doing to prepare for war."

He said "Great! Here's fifty dollars, go out and prepare it." After that first show, they asked me to do one on civil defense. When Pearl Harbor came, NBC got the idea from my series that they could train air-raid wardens with television. First, they borrowed as many of the three thousand sets as were then extant in New York City, and put them in precinct houses. People who were going to be air-raid wardens had to watch these twenty-minute programs. A warden would call on a couple. I played the wife. The warden would say, "I would like to tell you how to behave during a bombing," and we would ask questions. We did that seven times a day for seven weeks.

FRAN BUSS BUCH: Almost all the programming at CBS was aimed at the war effort. I did a series of programs about Red Cross First Aid. We used to call them Old Blood and Boredom.

CARL BEIER: In the Army, this personnel man went through my file, and since he couldn't punch in television on the IBM card, he punched in motion pictures, which was the closest thing. When the First Motion Picture Unit in Hollywood was looking for people, my card popped up.

I didn't know what the orders were for. I took a bus and a trolley to what turned out to be the Hal Roach Studios. I walked up to the guard gate and handed in my sealed orders. Inside with his feet up reading a book was Alan Ladd. He sent me to the adjutant. I walked around the corner. There was this big handsome guy feeding the fish in the pool that was used to film the *Our Gang* comedies. That was George Montgomery.

He directed me up a flight of stairs. There, the sergeant, who was Harold Hecht, told me to go on in. I stood in the door. The adjutant was wearing cavalry jodhpurs and riding boots. He was sitting there with his feet on the desk reading the *Hollywood Reporter*. When he finished his article, the paper came down, and there was Ronald Reagan.

Officially, Reagan was the adjutant to the commanding officer, who was Paul Mance, the stunt flyer, who practically never came in. As far as I could see Hecht ran the outfit like Radar O'Reilly in "M★A★S★H."

RAY FORREST: I was put in the training film business at Fort Monmouth and also in Long Island City and with the Signal Corps Photographic Center. We had a whole bunch of Hollywood brass out there as well as actors.

Once, we needed a tough young officer to demonstrate a 37-millimeter cannon. We got—much to his disgust—Dan Dailey. He had been in charge of an infantry company in the South Pacific. He was really very proud of his accomplishments. Suddenly, he was to report to a studio in Long Island City, and he was absolutely livid. When he showed up he hated everybody. He was a first looie, and all cameramen and grips were sergeants and corporals. He'd get teed off at them and make them dig foxholes. They were really grumbling, "That son of a gun, he's never gonna work in Hollywood again." They'd see to it.

CARL BEIER: Reagan would go out to Warner Brothers to have his hair cut. Their boot maker made his boots, and he'd go to the Warner's ranch to ride. He'd also go to the PX up in the valley to get steaks for himself and Jane Wyman. He narrated a series of films I did. He never bothered to memorize his lines. Holden was there, so was Joe Cotten who was 4F, and Clark Gable, who kept trying to get himself killed after Carole Lombard was killed. He was angry because he really wanted to go down. He was volunteering for the most dangerous missions, but they wouldn't put him on them.

RAY FORREST: We had also Herb Brodkin, Forrest Tucker, Herbie Anderson, who played Dennis the Menace's father. They knew I had been in television, but they were only vaguely interested in it. They thought it was just a toy.

LENORE JENSEN: I did the air raid warden shows until the end of '42. Then the Navy asked all the NBC engineers to join the Naval Reserve. My husband was sent to Western Oklahoma in the Dust Bowl. He worked on the drone airplane bomb.

TED SMITH: Loren Jones and I were responsible for that project. We persuaded the Navy that TV would be useful to them. One of the contracts we got was to build a small plywood plane without a motor, which could be hooked onto an airplane. There was a television camera mounted on this thing which could be controlled from the ground. The point was to put a charge with explosives in it and smash it by remote control against an enemy target.

LOREN JONES: This was Zworykin's idea. He was the first person to, in effect, propose that he could change the course of a missile after it left the gun barrel. We had a company build a small plane with an eight-foot wingspread to carry a TV camera and a parachute. We heard about this place called Muroc Dry Lake out in California. Now it's called Edwards Air Force Base, a tremendous dry area and absolutely flat. We took the thing out there to test it. We had two planes. On the first attempt, the thing tumbled out of control like a falling leaf and cracked into pieces. We were able to control the second one better, but we never could get them to drop with any real control.

JACK BURRELL: Before the war, I operated the RCA Mobile TV Unit. Then I went to Oklahoma with Joe Conn and some of the other fellows. Joe was my right-hand man on the drone project. We redesigned the camera tubes to make them work better. Then we put them in these big four-motored planes along with a pilot and copilot who were supposed to bail out after they got up, and then the control plane was supposed to take over.

In the South Pacific, they were a complete success. They were used to bomb the Japanese caves on Chock Island. We had about fifty percent hits, and we didn't lose a man, but the planes were also to be used against the German submarine pens in Europe, and there is a terrible story. The head of the program was also a pilot named Bud Wiley. His co-pilot was Joe Kennedy, Jr., and they were killed when their plane exploded in midair.

I have a very dear friend named Ernie Olson, who warned Kennedy that the pin on the bomb was unsafe, but Kennedy said, "I just can't believe the Navy would do anything that was desperately bad."

LOREN JONES: The bombs they are using today are based on Zworykin's original idea. You saw them in the Gulf War.

TED SMITH: When the project began, they knew the iconoscope wasn't sensitive enough. That's when Albert Rose, Paul Wymer, and Harold Law of

RCA developed the Image Orthicon, which was something like a hundred times more sensitive than the iconoscope.

PAUL WYMER: Actually, the first orthicon camera tube was developed around '38 or '39. Then Al brought Harold Law and me in to work with him. We worked on it continuously throughout the whole war. The objective was the TV-guided torpedo, but the Image Orthicon ended up being used in television from 1946 until about 1965 or 1970. There aren't many devices that have a useful period of twenty-five years. They actually called it the "Atomic Bomb of Television" because it made television a feasible thing.

TED SMITH: That's right. The iconoscope produced a very poor picture, and it took an operator adjusting something like fifteen knobs to get it right. The orthicon at first didn't have the resolution of the iconoscope but because it was more sensitive, it didn't require that tremendous light that was needed to get a picture from the iconoscope. In the long run television could not have operated under those hot lights.

OTIS FREEMAN: In 1944, Tom Goldsmith hired me at DuMont. One thing they did was send me over to a press conference at NBC where they introduced that Image Orthicon. There was a bunch of receivers in the room. They kept lowering the lights in the room until it got dark. In the middle of the room was a camera and a stool. When the lights went out, a girl slipped in and sat on that stool. A guy struck a match, and I swear there was a picture of the girl on those TV screens. It was the most wonderful thing I had ever seen.

TED SMITH: After the Image Orthicon was developed I had to make the decision. Are we going to build commercial equipment with iconoscopes or use the Image Orthicon? We couldn't afford to do both. The NBC technicians wanted to use the iconoscope because they weren't familiar with the Image Orthicon. Still, I made the decision to go with the Image Orthicon. Even if it didn't have the resolution of the iconoscope, I thought it would be improved.

PAUL WYMER: Sometimes, I look at television and say, "My God, what have you done?" But we didn't do it for that. If a problem exists, and you solve it, the results can be used in a lot of different ways. That was the case with our camera.

OTIS FREEMAN: During the war, DuMont's experimental station in New York City, W2XWB, was on the air about two or three hours a night twice a week. They used equipment that was put in there before the war. They just kept repairing that stuff.

RUDY BRETZ: I had been transferred to radio. The CBS television studio was closed, but Tony Miner sometimes used the control room to broadcast film.

LETTER FROM WORTHINGTON MINER TO HIS STAFF, CHRISTMAS, 1943:

Another year is drawing to an end, and a new one is about to start. To many of you, it will be hard to picture the gloomy emptiness of the shop. On Thursday and Friday evenings when we go on the air, one small, shielded pilot light stands in the studio, directed toward an announcer's script. The rest is towering shadows. . . . Inside the control room, we grind out long out-dated features, with the faces of out-dated stars abounding.

. . . This charnel mask is not, however, a completely valid picture of what goes on. For six months now, there has been, beneath the surface, a rising groundswell of interest in television. When luncheons, given by advertising clubs, the American Television Society, marketing associations, etc., advertise the topic, television, they find their doors stampeded with eager listeners, many of whom have to be turned away. Gil Seldes went to a lunch the other day, at which 300 people were turned back at the door. Radio Daily, which a year ago devoted about two inches in a month to television, runs now about two articles a day.

Most important of all, the electronic laboratories scattered all across the country have turned out a lot of stuff that is liable to make our 1941 system look like a patchwork of high hopes and spittle. . . . On every side, people are announcing new and revolutionary discoveries, practically guaranteeing a thousand-line-three-color-television-set in every pot. Don't be surprised if you hear reports in the near future that Butch LaGuardia has said, "What this country needs is a new five-cent kinescope."

Seriously though, the old girl isn't dead yet, and this is to let all of you know that Seldes and Miner,—old, fat, and forty,—are working overtime to try to make it a better toy for all of us to play with after the shooting's done. That would seem the least we can do.

HEINO RIPP: I was at RCA in their development group in New York. After a while, they reopened the film studio, 5F, and began showing some movies. The live studio, 3H, was just a storage room. Then they started 3H and a few times we would fire the gear up for test patterns and demos.

TED SMITH: One day, a fellow from Washington State came in and said he wanted to buy one of these TV cameras and portable equipment. We said, "We're sorry, but the only ones we're making are for the Army and the Navy."

He said, "We have a much higher priority than the Army and the Navy."

That was a jolt. Merril Trainor went out there to install the equipment. He came back shaking his head and said, "This was the damndest place I've ever been to in my life. It must be very, very secret." It turned out they were using the equipment to monitor the atomic bomb explosion in New Mexico.

RUDY BRETZ: In 1940, the BBC was actually in the middle of a program when a bomb cut the current. They were off the rest of that evening, and they were never on again until the end of the war. When they went back on after the war, they got the same announcer they had before, the same cast, the same script, and they said, "As we were saying when we were rudely interrupted."

RAY FORREST: I was still in uniform when I went to visit NBC, and they said, "We'd love you to host a variety show. We can show everybody that you're still alive." I did. Soon after that I was discharged from the Army and I went back on staff.

LETTER FROM WORTHINGTON MINER TO HIS STAFF, JULY 26, 1944

. . . *It was agreed that we would attempt, in the face of a grim situation indeed, to open the studio May 1 with one evening of live programs. For your information and, we hope, interested information, there wasn't much left of our erstwhile staff. One person only proved available to us,—Frannie Buss. 79% of all the male members of CBS Television as of January 1, 1942, were in the armed services. . . .*

And so, a very new, very untried, untested, and totally fledgling staff was accumulated. Presumably, technical rehearsals were to begin on April 1. But, as it turned out, we had only one stagehand available at that time . . . only one camera was working (and that not all the time), Frannie Buss was in the hospital and unable to come back until the middle of the month, one of the directors was still under contract to shortwave, CBS General Files still occupied the entire outer part of the studio, there were no officers, no furniture, no telephones, "no nothin'."

Somehow or other we got on the air on Friday, May 5,—no one yet has figured out exactly how. The program that evening truly dripped with nostalgia. We had news, music, an interview program called "They Were There," and closed with the quiz. It wasn't too bad, and actually a lot smoother in most ways than the opening in 1941.

But the net result was that every trade paper in town came out and took us for an unmerciful sleighride. . . . The boys compared us to the picture at the Roxy and the latest Norman Corwin Opus 57 on radio, and in that company they allowed as how we stank. And, in that company, we did. By the following Wednesday morning, everybody realized that whatever we got away with in 1941 and '42, we were never going to get away with it again.

NOW IT'S FOR REAL

By late 1944, Studio 3G in Rockefeller Center was a dark, forsaken place. Only the dustballs were dancing before the unplugged NBC cameras. While as entertainment that was only slightly inferior to much of what was on the air before Pearl Harbor, upstairs RCA executives were confident that peace would bring with it television's long awaited breakthrough.

Was it ready? Well, we already know the answer, but it's a mistake to assume that television would have automatically taken hold as quickly as it did. The truth was most people were quite content with their radios. You didn't have to see Jack Benny to laugh at his miserly ways. Indeed, Benny's Maxwell auto would always be a lot more amusing coughing and spitting across the cerebellum than it would be on the TV screen. While there was curiosity about television, there was no great demand for it. That's why God invented copywriters.

An RCA ad in the fall issue of *Televiser* magazine crowed that postwar viewers would "tour the world via television," and that "almost the entire American population should share in the variety of entertainment now concentrated only in large cities . . . drama, musical shows, opera, ballet." The ad also promised that television would provide jobs for returning soldiers and—for potential advertisers—"millions will be kept busy supplying products that television can *demonstrate* in millions of homes at one time."

RCA was not alone on the hustings. An enthusiastic DuMont copywriter proved that with all the wartime shortages, exclamatory type wasn't one of them:

> *Coming! Television: the greatest show on earth! Glamorous musicals and the stage's most brilliant dramas! Boxing and ballgames, races and wrestling! Parades, movie premieres and political conventions . . . running bumper to bumper in the most magnificent pageant ever dreamed!*

Journalists took a more cautious view. In a three-part series for the *Saturday Evening Post* entitled "Television: Boom or Bubble?," Alva Johnston noted:

Television is the greatest of all fields for prophets. They see the new medium putting a stadium, amusement park, theater, university and charm school in every home. . . . One cheerleader of television has promised the nation millions of identical dinners of gorgeous cookery, all presided over by one world-famous chef. . . . Another enthusiast has committed himself to having a Poiret dress the nation while an Escoffier feeds it. The greatest authorities on etiquette—dowager duchesses and possibly queen mothers—are to demonstrate what to do with olive pits after eating the olives, how to snub an upstart and whether to lead off with the right foot or left foot in entering a drawing room.

. . . One television executive has predicted that the new art will provide millions of new jobs in America.

But for every prophet there is a counter-prophet. There are brainy men in the industry who say that television will be an all-around disappointment and will be staggering along ten years from now about as it is today.

In 1944, the *Rotarian* waded in with a debate among industry heavyweights on the topic of "Is Television Ready?" The answer was a resounding yes from RCA and DuMont whose factories were ready to roll, and a Bronx cheer from the gang at CBS and Zenith, whose weren't.

Televison's arrival also created a series of political and technical disputes that would have left Solomon scratching his head. Any one of them could have sent television back to the laboratory for another ten years. That they didn't is attributable to the great democratic force known as the consumer. Four years of pent-up spending urges had created an unprecedented demand for new products by the war's end. Guided by the P.R. pens at RCA and DuMont, the glass-eyed wonder was more than another gleaming appliance in the local hardware-store window, it was the chance to own a piece of the American dream, "a miracle of engineering skill which one day will bring the world to the home," declared David Sarnoff, even if a grand duchess would never teach anyone the proper way to dispose of an olive pit (under your seat).

RCA and DuMont were anxious to start cashing in on years of costly research. CBS, however, presented a formidable roadblock. The argument between them was, as many are, over money. RCA and DuMont were about to rake it in, and Mr. Paley wasn't. As the war ended, the assembly lines at RCA and DuMont were poised to roll. Those dollars would be used to dominate the broadcast industry.

Paley and CBS President Frank Stanton saw salvation in their own labs, where Peter Goldmark had developed a system for color television, which, under the right circumstances, was capable of producing extraordinarily vivid pictures. If CBS could convince the FCC that color—and particularly the CBS color system—would soon be ready, the FCC might delay black-and-white broadcasting. This would not only prevent the others from getting the upper hand, but would also give CBS the time to set up its own factories.

RCA and DuMont, of course, demurred. They had spent millions developing black-and-white television, and, as RCA was quick to point out, the CBS system was not yet workable. While color and the battle for TV dominance was the real issue before the FCC, the legal arguments were actually fought over a much narrower question: the area on the broadcast spectrum that would be used for television broadcasting. The CBS system required UHF frequencies while RCA wanted broadcasting to remain at VHF, the area set for TV broadcasting before the war. The decision was in the hands of the FCC. It came in May, 1945. With some adjustment, television would be broadcast along pre-war channels. It was a defeat for CBS, albeit a temporary one, for the color fight would be joined another day. In a way, it was also a defeat for the consumer, because fewer channels were available on the VHF band, which meant fewer viewing options. That wouldn't be rectified for decades, when UHF and cable television would become widely available.

Nevertheless, the assembly lines could now be manned, and the dust blown off the camera lenses in 3G. If the people were indeed ready for television, it was now time to get television ready for the people. Uncle Miltie would be visiting soon.

RUDY BRETZ: I covered the ships carrying the GI's home from Europe as a cameraman. That was thrilling. The first ship was the *Normandie,* and it was loaded with GI's. It was still dark when we went out beyond the harbor to meet them with a couple of boats loaded with mothers and with girls. It was this foggy morning, and we began to hear it before we saw it loom up out of the fog. The guys were yelling, and there were all these white and black condoms floating off the ship in great numbers. It was fabulous.

MAX WILK: In New York after the war, I did a one-shot television show at NBC called "Home on the Range." It was Vincent Sardi demonstrating a recipe for some Broadway people. That's the kind of ideas you had in those days. To me, television was a toy. It was a way to make money. Suddenly you're making three or four hundred bucks and somebody says they're gonna give you a contract. All the guys I knew were doing it. Fred Coe, I knew from Yale. Perry Lafferty and George Schaefer were from Yale. If you came from Yale Drama School you had automatic entree, because hardly anybody knew anything about TV.

RALPH LEVY: I was a theater major at Yale. In 1946, CBS had an opening for an assistant director. I applied, and somebody at CBS asked me about my background. I said, "I used to direct theater at a summer camp."

They said, "Well, that's more experience than anybody else has," so I got the job. One of my jobs was to tell the announcer the time and to frame the camera on the clock, at which point he said, "It is six-thirty, Bulova watch time." I was congratulated because I suggested he say, "This is the correct Bulova watch time," because people could see the time on the screen. You see, they still weren't thinking in terms of television.

FRANKLIN HELLER: After the war, I was the resident director of the Bucks County Playhouse, which was one of the top theaters in America, but I wasn't making any money. Then one day I had lunch with a press agent named Sol Jacobson, and he called Jerry Danzig at CBS. Jerry said, "Send him right over. He's just the kind of fellow we need."

I met Jerry, but he said his boss Charlie Underhill did the hiring. Couldn't I come in tomorrow?

That night I went to see my mother. I was already getting gray hair, and she said, "You can't go in there looking like that," and she rubbed some stuff in my hair that darkened it. The next day I went to see Underhill. He was two years younger than I and his hair was absolutely white. He hired me that day, and I stopped putting that stuff in my hair. A few days later, someone at CBS said to me, "You're a legend around here. You're only here a week and your hair got gray."

BOB BENDICK: I returned to CBS in early '46. The place began to expand and subdivide quickly. I was now director of news and special events and religion and sports and everything else. Tony's operation became the entertainment one, and the two didn't have too much to do with each other.

Gil and Tony and Len Hole, all believed that this was a new medium, and they wanted to explore what its impact could be, but Paley decided we would follow radio's path with commercial programming. A lot of us were disappointed, especially Seldes.

Larry Lowman came in. He was in with Paley. They also brought in Jack Van Volkenburg for sales. He was strictly a commercial guy. He changed a lot of the aura around CBS television. It was no longer a medium that was great fun to experiment with. Now, we had to tighten down. Programs had to be fifteen minutes and thirty minutes and sixty minutes, and they had to have commercial possibilities. It was now, "What is going to appeal to the masses?" and, "How do we sell the most commercials?"

RAY FORREST: NBC was now very much more a business rather than the close-knit family we were before the war. I was no longer the sole guy. There were now a couple of other announcers. Back then, I shifted scenery if I had to. Now, I couldn't bring a prop into the building. It had to be left out in the street, and some union guy would bring it in.

DICK SMITH: I became interested in makeup in 1938 when I was a senior in prep school and I saw *The Hunchback of Notre Dame* with Charles Laughton. Even then, I was always doodling in my textbooks, turning Louis Pasteur into a monster with horns.

I was going to be a dentist, but at Yale, I bought this book called *Paint, Powder and Makeup*. One Saturday night, I made myself up as Spencer Tracy as Mr. Hyde and I scared a guy down the hall. Eventually, I went through all the old Universal film monsters, and every Saturday night we'd go around scaring people in my dorm. Soon the war was on, and I figured I was going to be killed. I decided to hell with being a dentist. If I survived, I would try to be a makeup artist.

I was hired by NBC after I got out of the Army. One of my first jobs was to pencil in hair on James Beard's scalp. It's like penciling eyebrows. You pencil long thin strokes. Television wasn't sharp enough to pick them up as pencil strokes.

When I began at NBC, Fred Coe was still an assistant director. He shared an office with Eddie Sobol and Ernie Colling. My office space was the bottom drawer in Fred's desk.

NOEL JORDAN: I got out of the Army in November 1945, and was hired back as the night operations supervisor. Then I went into the mobile unit. We did boxing and wrestling but what we really prided ourselves on were our "firsts." We did the first show on a submarine; and the first show from an aircraft carrier. We thought that was very exciting, but the shows themselves were probably as dull as dishwater.

We did the first pickup from the House of Representatives. The only incident was an engineer dropped an eight-inch lens off the balcony. It just missed killing a congressman. After that we chained the lenses to the cameras.

HARRY COYLE: At DuMont in those days, to do something extra special was to stay on the air. If we did an hour-and-a-half show and we lost the show for just a half hour, that was a victory. Forget losing *a* camera, this was where all you saw was a slide because *all* the cameras were out. Even when they were working they weren't that good. In the first remotes when you put the picture on the air, you didn't see the edges, all you saw was a little circle. That was Dr. Cyclops, the first remote camera.

The transformers in the remote trucks were burning up all the time. The engineers would go out there with their soldering irons trying to get them back. The trucks were always dark. I didn't have a suit that didn't have a burn in it from putting my coat down on a red-hot soldering iron.

NOEL JORDAN: The RCA truck was terribly confined. You practically got two elbows in your stomach for three hours. There were four of us in a space that wasn't eight feet by eight feet, and you had all those monitors, but for a young kid it was exciting.

HARRY COYLE: It was very common to hear during a remote, "We lost the West Coast somewhere over the Rockies." In one World Series, we lost the lake goin' up to Minnesota because some kid was sitting up on a hill with a .22 shooting out the microwave.

TED BERGMANN: DuMont did boxing and wrestling from the Jamaica arena. Our transmitter was on the roof of the arena, but after a while our chief engineer said, "I can't figure it out. Every week we have to put more power into the transmitter."

One of the engineers traced the signal and found that when it passed over Forest Hills it was within thirty feet of the ground, so he drove over there and found they were building an apartment house. As the framing went up, the signal got more interfered with. The question came up, "Do we rent a floor of the building and open up all the windows and send the signal through?"

Tom Goldsmith came up with a very bright idea. Behind the arena was the railroad station. He mounted a sheet of polished metal on top of the station. He turned his transmitter around and shot it at the sheet of metal which acted as a mirror and bounced it back out to 515 Madison. Now, the signal was two hundred feet off the ground, and the building didn't cause us any more problems.

CHRIS WITTING: NBC's signal came off the Empire State Building. DuMont's signal and CBS's signal came off lower buildings, which created shadows on the picture. The fiction grew under NBC's sponsorship that the only people who knew anything about the business was NBC. "You could tell just by looking at our picture."

Under the rules of the FCC, we could not force NBC to share the space up there, but we had a very smart lawyer, who had one failing: he was a drinker. I was about to fire him when he said to me, "Wait. I've just determined how we could get on top of the Empire State Building."

He said, "We'll tell Dave Sarnoff that we're taking the second highest building in New York where we can get a clear signal. He'll have to give us that because under the FCC rules if you can't get the tallest building, you can go on to the next highest building. He can't turn us down."

I said, "So what."

"Well, that building is the RCA Building. And to prevent any airplanes from running into it, we'll tell him we're gonna run the DuMont name down the front of the building on the top."

Three weeks later we were told they would let us share the space on the Empire State Building, and that's how we all were able to improve our signals.

*   *   *

RUDY BRETZ: Directors were always under tension. It didn't seem to bother me very much, but other people had nervous breakdowns. There was one director who vomited all over the keyboard and switching system, screaming, "Help me. Help me. Save me."

Terrible things happened from the strain, and it wasn't only the directors. There was a set designer at NBC who went berserk and started slashing the scenery with an axe.

RALPH LEVY: A movie director couldn't have worked in the control room. Once, I got a call saying that Frank Capra was interested in doing television. Could he follow me through a day and sit with me in the control room? I said I would be honored.

He sat through a rehearsal, we did the show live. I didn't use a script, and control rooms can be pretty confusing. I was just talking for a half an hour, cuing all the cameras, the sound, and God knows what. Capra was sitting behind me. Then, as he left, he turned around and he said, "Mr. Levy?"

"Yes, sir?"

"Are you out of your fucking mind?" He walked out of the building never to be seen again.

RUDY BRETZ: Producers were also under a lot of stress. As the producer, you might have two weeks from the time a script was accepted to the time where you got it on the air. You had to get the sets ready, the music, hire the actors, put the rehearsals together, and then get it into the studio. There were dozens of things that you had to watch over, and in the meantime you are working on other shows, too.

You were in charge of 150 people in the studio. Any one of them could make a mistake and ruin your program, and it would be your fault, but you can't possibly tell 150 people what to do. So much depends on everybody knowing what they were doing and doing *beyond* what they were told to do. And if something went wrong, you knew you wouldn't have another chance because you were live. You swore the day before you weren't going to do this ever again. Then, most of the time it came off and it felt so great, and you said, "Well, when does the next thing start?" [Laughs.]

One constant problem was the tension between the engineers and the program people. Among union workers, the loyalty was first to the union, then to the company. When I had a union job at CBS I felt the same way. Since we were protected by the union, we didn't have to be cooperative and we weren't. I was shocked by my own behavior, but that was the way it was. When the program guys were in a rush to get a show edited, that wasn't our concern. We were just doing our jobs. They would say, "Hey, hurry up a little."

And someone would go, "Sure, we'll hurry every chance we'll get."

HEINO RIPP: I was in the union. Many times I would come in at seven o'clock in the morning, and I wouldn't leave until the late news was over at eleven-thirty at night. I would do everything that was on the air that day. It just never stopped. I couldn't even get a lunch. It was finally put into the contract that after the fifth hour you had to have lunch. I was doing so much work from seven o'clock in the morning on, I was even making transitions in my sleep and in my sleep I never made it.

RUDY BRETZ: The contract protected the workers, but it also created problems. The stagehands' union was very jealous of their rights. They wouldn't let anybody touch anything. There was a case where a group of people were going to do a Ping-Pong demonstration. They brought in this Ping-Pong table with their own station wagon, but when they carried it across the sidewalk, it was not acceptable because it hadn't been brought in by a union crew, so they had to take it away and transfer it to a union truck, and then a couple of hours later the stagehands would take it across the sidewalk.

STEWART MACGREGORY: [Sarcastically] I could talk about a couple of actors. I worked on one show with Robert Montgomery. He was a pain in the ass from the motion picture industry. We did a show where there was to be a rain effect from these tanks put up over the set. There was a fellow up on a ladder with a nozzle and a hose to wet Montgomery down. During the dress rehearsal, the sprocket noise from the projector was bleeding out of the booth into the studio and was being picked up by the overhead microphone.

The director said, "What the heck is that noise?"

Montgomery said, "That's the special effects man."

The special effects man said, "No, it's not, it's the projectionist."

On the West Coast, they use the term "special effects" as everything. The guy who was special effects didn't want to be blamed for the thing, but it happened four times in a row. Montgomery kept saying, "It's the special effects man," and the special effects man kept saying, "No, it's the projectionist."

Now, they're gonna rehearse with the rain, so the projectionist is running the film, and they give him the cue, and the special effects man starts the water, and he soaks Montgomery who hadn't been informed that they were gonna do it, and Montgomery again says, "What was that?"

And the guy on the ladder says, *"That's* the special effects man."

RUDY BRETZ: In 1949, I visited TV stations across the country while I was researching a book. I visited a station in Syracuse where they didn't separate the engineers and the program people. That seemed to me to be such a wise way to go about it. There was a big difference in the attitude of the people. They were much more involved. Instead of working first for the union and second for the company, they were looking to do a good job.

In New York you often had a problem when engineers ran the cameras. You were always beating your head against the wall trying to get an engineer to frame a picture pleasantly. He doesn't know about principles of composition. The better cameraman knows what makes a good shot and will get a hold of a closeup quickly without the director having to tell him. They work together without having to talk to a large extent. It's important because a good cameraman could make quite a difference in a television show.

OTIS FREEMAN: Two things I never did but once in my life. One was umpire a Little League game and two was run a TV camera. They both gave me such a hard time. I was on a camera once—at DuMont during the war. We were at Ebbets Field, and they were short a man, so there I was behind a camera when this guy started tellin' me what to do, "You'll pan the camera this way and that way," and I didn't know what the hell he was talking about. Then he called me a dumb son of a bitch and I . . . well, I tell you in my whole career I never operated another camera.

DON HASTINGS: At DuMont, Wally Ferris did something that nobody else could do if they practiced for a month. When Jackie Gleason would say, "Away we go," he moved down a runway, and Wally would dolly in with an eight-inch lens and no zoom and stay in focus by pushing the camera while running his arm down the lens. That was an art.

WALLY FERRIS: I really practiced. I would put a match cover on the wall and take a very difficult lens, a long focal lens, and I would dolly in focusing. The focus handle was a little spinning wheel, and I would run the focus up my arm until I got it right. The technical aspects of the job really weren't technical, it was more physical, and I was a good athlete.

The Gleason shot came about accidentally. I was on the side camera, and he would do his monologue downstage and walk to the camera on the right. Then he would say, "On the show today is so and so, and away we go." As he leaned forward with those banjo eyes, I instinctively went to meet him, and all of a sudden I'm in on his eyeballs, and then I came back and followed him right into the wings. They said, "From now on it's in." It became a trademark, and it give me a reputation.

BOB BENDICK: A big holdup in the early days was the musician's union. They didn't allow any live music or a lot of movies with background music on the air. That precluded a lot of movies from being shown.

GIL FATES: The ban created an interesting problem. We would go to Madison Square Garden to do the rodeos or whatever, but we could only take the picture from there, not the sound, because we couldn't let any of the music come through, so they used to put me in a booth in the studio in Grand Central, and I would have to talk over the program. Then we put in crowd noise and other sounds. Otherwise it would have been a very dead picture.

CHARLES POLACHEK: I was in charge of the record library at CBS. From their sound effects collection, we would add everything we could think of, the horses' hooves in the rodeo, the cheering of the crowd. We had radio soundmen working the sound effects. They even would do the punches in the boxing matches. They knew how to do anything.

BOB BENDICK: The Petrillo agreement in '49 allowed us to use live music. Immediately, NBC announced that Toscanini would play live on television that Saturday night. CBS then decided that it could not allow NBC to go on with the first live major musical program, so we got hold of Eugene Ormandy and arranged to pick up his Saturday afternoon concert live from Philadelphia. A local director was going to direct it, and as the director of special events I was there, even though I don't know very much about music. Charlie Polachek, who did know music, was there, too.

We went over in the morning to set up the cameras. The local director was all set by one-thirty. Ormandy walks in at two, straight up, and this director has his watch out. There's much applause. Ormandy picks up his baton and bows to the audience. This guy still has his watch out. We poke the guy, and we tell him, "You've got to cut to a closeup," but the guy was frozen, absolutely petrified, so we pushed him out of the chair. I got in, and directed the thing. Not knowing music, I hadn't the vaguest idea when the bassoons were going to go. Whenever he could, Charlie, who was sitting there with the musical score on his lap, would say, "Bassoons, bassoons, go," so CBS put on this horrible pickup, but we were first.

*　　*　　*

PETER LEVATHES: In June 1946, I was at Twentieth Century Fox. I made arrangements to microwave the second Louis-Conn fight from Philadelphia into a theater on Broadway. We did the fight just to illustrate the advances that were being made in this miracle of television. Fox was also interested in large-screen television. That was another reason why it was done, to demonstrate the magic of the large screen.

We had a full house, over three thousand people. Within minutes after it started, we had ringside conditions. I couldn't believe the excitement. People were screaming as if they were at the fight. When it was over, our researchers polled them. One question we asked was, "What impressed you with this experience tonight?"

"The third round."

I waited for someone to say, "Hey, how the hell did you get this from Philadelphia to Broadway?"

We could have brought it by carrier pigeon, and they wouldn't have cared less. I never forgot that. After that, when people would talk to me about technicalities, about large screen, small screen, I wanted to talk program.

IRA SKUTCH: There were three thousand sets in New York in 1945. At NBC, we were broadcasting three or four nights a week, filling time with whatever would work and was cheap. Walter Law worked in the sales department. He was a philatelist. We used to put him on with his stamp collection.

Sunday night was NBC's big night. We had "Face to Face" with Steve Dunne and Bob Dunne. Steve would describe somebody in another room in the studio, and Bob would draw that person based on the description. Then they would bring the guy down, and he would stand next to the picture. At the end of the show, they would face the camera and say, "I'm Bob."

"I'm Steve."

"And we're Dunne!"

Then at eight o'clock we did a Broadway play. *The First Year* and *Blithe Spirit* were two shows we did. There were no time restrictions and no commercials, so everything ran when it ran. Nobody even timed anything.

We also did variety shows. Ray Forrest would host some of them. Others wouldn't even have a host. They would just go from one act to another. We had Rosie the Bear, who used to eat cigarette butts out of ashtrays. She would dance with her owner and pee down his leg.

GIL FATES: CBS did a fascinating show called "What's It Worth?" It could still be done today. Everybody has something in their attic that was given to them by an uncle who used to be a seafaring man. A few days before the show, people would come to the office, and an appraiser named Sigmund Rothschild would sit there and look at what they brought in. If Sig saw something interesting, he would tell them to come back to the studio without telling them what it was worth. He would appraise it on the air. You can imagine the excitement when he would say, "It's worth five thousand dollars!"

It was great. Actually, the only problem was that every time the camera did a closeup on Sig's hands I used to cringe, because his fingernails were always dirty. I always had to take him aside and tell him to clean out his nails.

IRA SKUTCH: One night in 1947 we opened the station early. John Royal wanted us to audition Kyle McDonnell because he had just seen her in *Make Mine Manhattan*. She did two songs. We aired it so Royal could watch her at home. Then we went back to test pattern.

He liked the audition, and he put her on a show called "For Your Pleasure," and she became the first real television star, which didn't really mean much. Basically, she got some local publicity and local column items, and of course recognition among the people who had television sets.

HENRY MORGAN: I had no interest in television until I thought, "Maybe I better get into this." I thought up a fifteen-minute across-the-board show of sketches and things, and Bob Sarnoff stared at the floor when I told him about this and said, "Okay, go ahead and do that," without ever lifting his head.

I had no idea what I'd have to go through to do this every day, coming up with stuff, doing the rehearsal. There were no prompters. You had to memorize, and I had never been too good at that. It never occurred to me that acting would be a problem. It turned out to be a Mexican standoff because they didn't know what to do with the cameras either.

It would have been easier had I started doing some work at eleven o'clock in the morning like a normal person. We went on at three. At one o'clock I said, "I better think of something." There was a harpist. Every time he was on, I would get a hard-boiled egg and slice it through the strings of the harp. He didn't think it was funny the first time, but fortunately he got used to it. It didn't matter. There was no studio audience, and the show lasted only six weeks, so I don't know if any human being every saw it.

IRA SKUTCH: Daytime television didn't really start until 1947 when the Swift Home Service Club came on at noon on Fridays. They opened the station with that. Then they closed the station until Friday night. Lee Cooley was the producer.

LEE COOLEY: NBC let us know at McCann-Erickson [a leading advertising agency] that if we would come in and program, they would reserve that time for us in perpetuity. They were desperate for us to come in. They virtually met us down in front of 30 Rockefeller with a red carpet.

Swift wanted a show that would be slanted toward women who did the shopping, cooked the food, and took care of the home. Nobody knew what would make a television show work in those days. Our research department took the ten leading women's magazines and analyzed all the editorial material in them. They came back with the contents of a typical show that would appeal to women: cooking, interior decoration, child care, recreation, education, and things of that sort.

Then I went to the Swift stockyards in Chicago. Shortly before lunch we had a meeting. When we finished our presentation, I couldn't tell whether or not they liked it. Then their number-two man, Ollie Jones, turned to his assistant and said, "Has Lee ever been through the killing floors?"

He had this funny look on his face.

I said, "Not really."

He said, "Let's go to lunch and we'll talk about what Lee has told us. In the meantime, show Lee the operation."

He took me to the noisiest and the bloodiest of all places, where they slaughtered the pigs. When you entered, the first thing you saw was a stretcher on the wall and a first-aid case and a telephone in case somebody fainted. It was not a pretty sight. These big Polish killers were standing on white tile floors with drains for the blood after they cut the carotid arteries on the hogs. I saw the pigs and heard 'em screaming. Their hind legs were chained together and pulled up on a conveyor belt. They knew what was gonna happen to them.

We walked on through the whole business and then got downstairs again. Jones said to his assistant, "How did Lee enjoy the operation?"

He said to him, "Sir, we have a real country boy on our hands here."

They were testing me. It only took about ten minutes more of hemming and hawing to sign the deal. I guess if I had fainted, they would have laughed like hell but gone ahead anyway.

The first program was called the "Swift Home Service Club." It was a half-hour show with Tex McCrary and Jinx Falkenburg as the hosts. We proved with the Home Service Club that daytime television would work. Swift was pleased not so much with the sales results because the market was so limited, but that they could show the product and demonstrate it while talking about it.

IRA SKUTCH: In 1946, Eddie Sobol directed another landmark program called "The Hour Glass." It was an hour show and was booked by J. Walter Thompson. It was the first big sponsored variety show on NBC, the forerunner of "The Ed Sullivan Show," but it didn't have Ed Sullivan. It had a minor movie star named Helen Parrish as the hostess. She was very good.

DICK SMITH: They had Bert Lahr doing the old woodchopper's act from burlesque. It was hilarious. He had a toupee that was truly a rug. It must have been stuck on only in the center of his scalp, because during the skit the toupee would rotate madly in one direction or the other.

They had a little fake tree, and he would sing this song, that went something like, "When the sun comes up, I chop, chop, chop." Every time he said, "Chop, chop, chop," he would swing this axe in mime at this little tree, and the prop man on the other side would throw kindling at him. In rehearsal he said, "Don't be afraid of hitting me. Throw it right at me." Well, they loved that, so they threw these handfuls at him, and he was ducking and weaving, and the toupee was rotating. It was hysterical.

IRA SKUTCH: "The Hour Glass" was a big deal. It was a network show, and it was completely agency produced, and it had commercials. That's why it was so important: it showed that there was money coming in. J. Walter Thompson was happy with the show, and so they brought in the Kraft Theater, which was the first big, live dramatic anthology.

AL DURANTE: They had a new product they were bringing out called Cheez Whiz. There were discussions about how to introduce it, and the decision was made to try a dramatic show. That's why the Kraft Theater came about.

*   *   *

MAX WILK: In October of '48, I got a call from Marc Daniels. He said, "Listen, I got a job doing television. Do you know how to write for television?"

"Yeah, as a matter of fact," and I told him about "Home on the Range."

So Marc said, "Then you know how to write for television.

"We're going to do a television show called 'The Ford Television Theatre.' We're gonna be live, and we're gonna put on a Broadway show for one hour at CBS, and by the way, you're gonna get paid."

I think he said two hundred dollars. The first show was "Joy to the World" with Alfred Drake and Janet Blair. We literally took the play as it had been done on Broadway and cut it down to fifty-five minutes. Then we rehearsed for six or seven days and on the eighth day we camera blocked. On the ninth and tenth days we did dress, and on the eleventh day we did the show. The way you worked was insane. You would get a studio for three hours and you do a show, and your crew would finish and be out the door and the next crew would walk in and take over the booth immediately. It was tension, tension, tension, all the way. When you put the show on, you sat there and you prayed that it would work, because you had no control on a live show.

While this is going, in comes Ralph Levy. He says, "You and George Axelrod come and do a television show." Then we get Dick Lewine and Ted Fedder and Al Selden, and the director is Barry Wood. We do a show called "The 54th Street Revue," three original sketches and four or five original musical numbers a week. A week! The dance team was Bob Fosse and Mary Jane Miles.

Pressure. "Go home and rewrite this whole scene." Every day we were fixing problems. We used to do what I would call, "wall writing." We would be backstage, and the comic would say, "We need two lines here," or the producer would say, "We're under three minutes," so you would take a piece of paper and put it on the wall, and we would write the stuff and hand it to him to do, and he would say, "Okay, I'll do that."

RALPH LEVY: During that show, Harry Ackerman came to see me work and decided to take me out to the Coast. He said they were going to open up a West Coast spot for emanation of shows that would be done by kinescope. The first show they were doing was "The Ed Wynn Show." Then I did George Burns and Jack Benny.

CBS wanted to go out there for the talent. People like Benny and Burns wouldn't give up their lives out there to do a show. I enjoyed the possibility. Hollywood is a town where you are fine if someone asks you to come out. If you want to go out and try to get into this, that's no way to go to Los Angeles.

*   *   *

BUDDY ARNOLD: I wrote a lot of Milton Berle's nightclub routines. He was also on radio for the Texas Company. One day in 1948 the Kudner Agency, which handled the show, said, "We're thinking of putting a show on television. Have you got any ideas?"

This was like three weeks before going on the air. Milton said, "I got no ideas. Get a few acts together and I'll introduce them just like I do in nightclubs."

There were two tryout shows in June. They wanted to see what the audience reaction would be before they committed to a season. The first show was introduced by a lady in a white smock named Betty Alexander. She just stood there and held up a can of Marfak and said, "We welcome you to a new program put on by the Texas Company, and this is their product, Marfak." She spoke about it for thirty seconds and then introduced Milton.

The next morning he called me and said, "Did you see it last night? The way the damn show opened was ridiculous. We gotta think of something else."

So Woody Kling and I met with Milton the next afternoon. I said, "Why don't we make it a singing opening?" They had a lot of jingles on radio at the time. I said, "Let's have a bunch of guys singing about the product and about you and introduce you."

One word led to another, and it was built to four guys at a service station who would sing a song. Milton said, "Can you have it done by next Tuesday?"

I said, "We'll not only do that, we'll cast it and rehearse it so it will be ready."

By Thursday night Woody and I wrote what is now the Texaco song. The lyrics are Woody's and mine. It is very intricately written with triple rhymes all the way. It was purely a plug for Texaco, so there is no mention of Milton in it. The music is mine, except the second section, which is Liszt's Hungarian Rhapsody no. 2.

For four or five years, it was the number-one sponsor-identification theme melody on radio and TV. It's still recognized today. When we edited the song down to size, we had to cut out about fifty percent of what was written. It originally had a big ending to it. Then they would make an announcement about some product they were featuring, and they would say, "Remember to be back next week [sings] to the best friend your car has ever had."

AARON RUBEN: Nat Hiken and I were writing Milton's radio show, but it never occurred to me to ask if I could work on the TV show. TV was like a trackless forest. Nobody realized what was about to happen until Milton burst forth.

That he was first was one reason for his success, but also, let's face it, the man was funny. He had one of the funniest, if not *the* funniest nightclub acts ever. You put that on TV and suddenly hundreds of thousands of people who have never seen him in a club are laughing their heads off. Until then, nobody really realized what a gigantic entertainment medium this was about to be or could be.

Pretty soon people were saying, "What the hell? Why should I pay money to go to a theater when I can see all this on television?" Milton and Sid Caesar were suddenly doing these marvelous one-hour shows. As a result, the tradition of the great Broadway revues, *Lend an Ear* and *Call Me Mister*, ceased to be and radio became a thing you listened to in your car.

OSCAR KATZ: Paley was a very itchy guy. He wanted things fast, and if NBC had something, he wanted it, too. When NBC put on specials, Paley wanted specials. When Berle came on, he wanted something to compete against him.

PETER MINER: My father was program manager by then. He knew Berle was gonna burn out, and when Paley told him to come up with an alternative to Berle, my father knew just what he needed: a variety show with a nonperforming emcee as host. The idea was the acts would change, and all the talent should do is introduce the acts. That way he wouldn't burn out.

He sat my mother and me down in front of the set to watch the Harvest Moon balls at Madison Square Garden. He was always looking to steal talent from anywhere and here was Ed Sullivan, hosting the balls and getting all the top stars.

JOSEPH CATES: Ed Sullivan was the Ziegfeld of our era. He didn't have a personality, but he didn't need one. He got the acts, and to get the acts you have to understand the country and the times. He did, and he was better at it than anybody else.

He also changed routining. In vaudeville, you start with an opening act and build to the closing. Ed said, "It's television. You think people are gonna wait to see what you got at the end? This isn't vaudeville. People flip that knob," so he front-loaded. He would start with Elvis Presley and the Beatles, and he would say, "They'll be back later in the program." Then he'd bury the weak acts in the back.

He knew that a variety show meant novelties. He worked even harder to get a balloon act than he did to get a star, because he knew the public tuned in for the novelty. He also recognized the contemporary nature of TV. If a guy pitched a no-hit game, he had him there in the audience to introduce.

JACK CARTER: The exposure you got from being on Sullivan was unbeatable, but Sullivan was vicious. Sullivan was crazed. That veneer of being [slips into a perfect Sullivan imitation] very holier-than-thou. "Hi there, the nuns are out here, and the priests are my dear friends. These nice youngsters . . ." But when you got into the dressing room after your run-through, he called you in [again, as Sullivan]: "What kind of fucking shit is that?! You do that shit on my fucking show. You asshole. Fuck you with that shit. How dare you come in here with that cock-sucking shit. I don't need that fucking shit. Don't do that cock-sucking shit on my show. Balls! That's bullshit. You're doing fucking shit. Now, take that out. You can't do that." It was hysterical.

Many a time, I was waiting to go on, and he forgot it was me next. They go [whispers], "Jack Carter."

"Oh, is he here? Is he in town? We never knew he would make it. His plane was late—Jackie Carter."

I'd come out, "Ed, I've been here three years. You saw me at the dress this afternoon," and he'd get furious.

JERRY DANZIG: In the beginning, people said, "God, he is so stiff." We thought he would get better and become more relaxed over time. What really happened was people began to imitate him, which indicated that he was being accepted, and he developed an ability to laugh at himself.

MADELYN PUGH DAVIS: In 1948, Bob Carroll, Jr., and I were staff writers at the CBS Radio Pacific network. By then, CBS had decided to do its own shows instead of having them created by the advertising agencies. They did "Our Miss Brooks" and "My Friend Irma." One week, Bob and I were were assigned to Lucy's radio show, "My Favorite Husband."

When CBS told Lucy they wanted her to go into television, we knew she would be wonderful because she was so physical. The trouble was that CBS wanted to go in with the radio cast, which had Richard Denning as her husband. Lucy said no. She wanted to go into television with Desi. She was doing movies and radio. He was doing bands at night. She would get up at five o'clock when he was just coming in. They wanted to see each other.

OSCAR KATZ: Hubbell Robinson, the head of CBS programming, said nobody will believe that Lucy, an all-American girl, could be married to a Cuban. He said, "No, no, not that Cuban, the country won't understand what the hell he's saying." He also didn't believe that Desi could act. "He's just a bandleader."

MADELYN DAVIS: To prove that he could play her husband, Bob and I wrote a bit for them to take on the road with a stage show. We had never worked with Desi before, and we were thrilled. He was a charming man and he turned out to be a pretty good actor. Together they were a big hit.

Jess Oppenheimer and Bob and I wrote the pilot. The only problem was she was pregnant at the time. We covered it up by putting her in a bathrobe that was as big as the Ritz. There wasn't any discussion about that. You just didn't have pregnant women on television.

RALPH LEVY: I directed the pilot. I didn't think it was so great, but that day you would have thought we had just won the war. The pilot was the talk of the town. Their agent and Desi came up to the house and offered me ten percent of the show to stay with them, and I turned it down. I was doing Benny and Burns and I was very happy.

MADELYN DAVIS: Someone said they've got to have neighbors because everybody has neighbors. I had neighbors named Mertz when I was kid, so we gave them neighbors named Mertz.

Then CBS said, "Of course, you'll do the show from New York," because the biggest audience was in New York, and they didn't want them to have to see kinescopes, which were terrible. This was before the coaxial cable went from coast to coast, but Lucy and Desi wanted to stay in California. Desi figured it would cost another five thousand dollars an episode to put it on film. He said they would absorb it if they could own the shows. CBS didn't care who owned the shows. In those days, they didn't rerun shows because the kinescopes were so bad. Lucy and Desi ended up making a fortune. From that they built Desilu Studios.

Then CBS said, "You can't do film in front of a live audience. It won't work." When they make movies, they stop and do the closeups and then start again. Here, they couldn't do that because the audience would be there until four o'clock in the morning. They had to figure out how to film the show in one shot, so there was a meeting at Lucy and Desi's ranch with the technical people, and they worked out this complicated formula for filming a comedy before a live audience with multiple cameras that has been the standard ever since.

MILTON DELUGG: I had come to New York to do a nighttime show with Abe Burrows called "Breakfast with Burrows." The joke was he got up late. It wasn't much of a joke, and the show only lasted thirteen weeks. I was about to go back to the coast when I got a call, "NBC wants to do a show live at eleven o'clock at night called 'Broadway Open House.' Do you want to stick around?"

There was nothing on TV at eleven o'clock except "The Star-Spangled Banner," but I thought why not. We did a pilot with a fellow named Creesh as the host. Then he suddenly died. The show went on with a different host each night. Everybody you can think of tried that show, and then they found Jerry Lester.

ALICE LESTER: One night, as Jerry and I were getting ready to go to a movie, Pat Weaver called and asked Jerry if he could do the show that night. Jinx Falkenburg and Tex McCrary had just hosted it, and it was a pretty sad show. Tex was rather dull.

That night he did anything that came to his mind. He wrecked the place. He jumped up and down on the couch like a monkey. He poked fun at the cameraman. He kidded everybody in the audience and kidded the show. He just had himself a good time.

After the show we rushed out to go to a movie when a page stopped us in the elevator, saying Pat wanted to talk to Jerry. He said the switchboard had lit up with a million calls. The next day they made a deal for Jerry to do the show, alternating with Morey Amsterdam.

MOREY AMSTERDAM: He did it one night, and I did it the next night. It wasn't like the late-night shows now where they have guests. It was like a little stock company stuck together with spit.

ALICE LESTER: The kids who went to work on the show were friends of ours. The Mello Larks were living in our building. We had met Dagmar in St. Louis. Then, when we got back to New York, we ran into her on the street, and she said, "Oh, boy, can I use the work. If you don't give me any lines, maybe I can have a couple of walk-ons."

MOREY AMSTERDAM: Most of the time she just sat there with big tits. People had never seen anything like that on television.

ALICE LESTER: She always was trying to show 'em, and they were tryin' to cover 'em up.

MILTON DELUGG: The big joke was, I said to Jerry, "This is gonna be our new girl singer."

Jerry says, "How does she sing?"

"Who cares?"

MOREY AMSTERDAM: I wrote her a routine where she'd play a dumb dame, kind of a Gracie Allen. She would say, "My father owned a grape-fruit farm in California."

I would say, "I can understand why."

The toughest part was getting a studio audience from eleven to twelve at night. I went down to the Greyhound Bus Company. They had all these tours of New York, and I said, "As you go around in the nighttime, ask the people in the buses if they would like to see a television show." Well, television was so new at that time, they all wanted to see it. That's where we got our studio audience.

MILTON DELUGG: Jerry left the show after a year or so because he wanted to be on by himself like Jack Benny. They tried Jack Leonard after Jerry. That didn't last. Then we did a show called "Seven at Eleven," me, Buddy Hackett, George DeWitt, but that didn't work either. Finally, they picked Steve Allen, and he did make it, and they called that version of it "The Tonight Show."

＊　＊　＊

MAX WILK: My agent said I would have to go to the Coast, but I didn't want to. The kind of television they did in California was where they gave you a shot of a fireplace, and a man sitting beside it, turning the pages of a book and saying, "I will tell you a wonderful story," and they dramatized something in the public domain. It was shit.

In New York you were writing a play or a book. You can be on Bleecker Street doing anything you want, and nobody can say boo because, they say, "He's got talent. It's gonna happen." Or he says, "I'm gonna make it." You could struggle in New York.

Yeah, you did crap in New York, "Martin Kane, Private Eye," "Rocky King,

Inside Detective." Look at the DuMont list. It's hilarious. Cheap writing has always been with us, but in New York if you wanted to write a little better than cheap writing you still had room to do it. That was the difference.

MARIAN SELDES: In a way I can understand it, but when television became this money-making machine, it lost people like my father. I don't think he ever was a company man. He couldn't toady to anybody or manipulate people. He had imagination, enthusiasm, and a willingness to give talented people a chance. He gave other people confidence. That was his gift.

He saw television as what people now regret that it isn't. He saw it as a teaching and cultural tool. He wasn't a fool. He loved Jack Benny and Fred Allen. He knew you can't put on stuff that doesn't succeed. We're not talking about someone in the clouds. He was realistic, but not in the sense of (a) his own career and (b) the commercial world. I think he dreaded what he knew was coming, but he knew it had to come, but as for himself, he didn't have it in him to compete politically with people like Tony Miner and remain a part of it.

SETS FOR SALE

"'Bout coupla monts ago business started gettin' stinkin'. We was losin' money, but fast. I gotta do somethin' to goose da place up. Now I'm a sport lover, see. So I figure maybe dese guys is goin' to hockey games or fights, an' I say, why not bring hockey or fights here, so guys can see sports and drink atta same time. So I buy dese gadgets. Slump in business stopped."
—Chicago saloonkeeper Al Schlossberg as quoted in Time, 1947

Sometime after VJ Day Americans were treated to the odd sight of their rooftops sprouting metal antlers. This phenomenon was not the bizarre result of radiation clouds wafting over the country. Such germination was usually preceded by the appearance of an RCA service truck on the block. The driver generally received the same hearty welcome that the local hero got upon his safe return from overseas. Television had finally arrived, and life in the home, around the country and around the world was about to be changed forever.

Modern sets had actually been on sale since 1939 when DuMont and RCA marketed their first all-electronic receivers. However, at prices ranging from $199.50 to $625 there were few takers, especially given the inferior programming available. Five months after they first put the sets on the market, RCA had sold only four hundred of them. Even when the company lowered their top price to $395, there was little interest. Had researchers, however, been paying attention to those pioneer families, they would have observed some surprising behavioral patterns that would be played out many thousand times over in the years to come.

The select few almost overnight altered their eating and sleeping schedules to accommodate viewing hours. Evening hours previously reserved for family conversation were now devoted to the set, which required two senses instead of radio's one. It also demanded quiet attention—except when conversation concerned what was on the screen.

The doorbell got a lot of exercise, and chairs had to be set up theater-style in the living room to accommodate neighbors who suddenly found reasons to drop by in the evening. The author's grandfather was a New York television dealer and had a set installed in his home just before the war. "We were the first ones in the area to have it. Everybody came to look at it. Even if all they saw was a test pattern with no sound, they would sit there and watch," recalls his daughter.

"During the war they had lectures on for the air-raid wardens, and once a week my folks invited the air-raid wardens to come into the house. They used to sit there and smoke and put their cigarettes out on the floor. They thought they were in a movie theater. My mother was hysterical."

Although relatively few sets were sold before the war, a Gallup poll taken in 1939 indicated that some four million Americans said they would buy a television if it was available to them. After the war, that number was reached with surprising swiftness. In 1946, the first RCA 630TS sets, the Model T of television, began rolling off the assembly lines to be sold mostly to bars in New York, Chicago, Los Angeles, and the four other cities that had TV stations. By the end of the year, ten thousand sets had been sold at $385 apiece. Within a year 250,000 sets made by dozens of manufacturers were sold nationwide. By 1950, over seven million sets were in circulation.

For RCA, David Sarnoff's theories of being first with the most paid off handsomely. Four-fifths of the sets sold the first year of mass production were manufactured by RCA. The company's number-two man was a marketing expert named Frank Folsom. Folsom instituted a policy offering a service contract with every set sold. To back it up, RCA hired and trained two thousand technicians to install and repair television sets, which not only kept the sets running but was also a remarkable public relations ploy for RCA, which had not been known for its service before then.

At the same time, RCA engaged in virtual warfare with its dealers, who were purple with rage over the company's allotment policy. When demand for the new sets far outstripped supply, RCA not only rationed its TVs carefully, but also forced a dealer to buy the company's less popular products if it had any hope of getting the 630. The situation lasted about a year before the seesaw tipped the other way. As more and more companies entered the market and set production increased some 500 percent over the previous year, RCA's market share dropped. Now the company was forced to fight for shelf space and regain the loyalty of dealers with long memories.

Nobody benefited more than the consumer. On New York City's Cortlandt Street, which in earlier years was known as "Radio Row," a customer could wander from one TV store to another, pitting the shopkeepers against each other until he left the last store with a TV at a price not far above wholesale. He was now a bona fide postwar neighborhood hero, only the metal was on his roof, not on his chest.

●   ●   ●

IRVING NEEDLE: I'm an old record man. I used to be with Columbia Records, Mercury, Decca, MGM Records. We all moved around. After the war, I went to Bruno New York, the distributor for RCA. I was the wholesaler. Back then, everybody got their televisions from Cortlandt Street. There were dozens of stores there. Leonard Radio, Vim, Davega. Hines and Bollet. I dealt with all those guys.

BOB ELLIOTT: Sam Alessi and I opened our own store in 1940. Before that I worked in a lot of places on Cortlandt Street starting in 1928.

JERRY FISHMAN: I worked for Elliott and Alessi and for Sam Coyne. There were maybe fifty stores. People came from all over to get the best deals, no matter what it was. If it was for a goddamned nickel battery, he was lookin' to pay four cents.

Most of the people who operated on Cortlandt Street were mom and pop shopkeepers without much capital. If that store cost a hundred dollars a day, no matter what, that hundred dollars had to come in. The most important thing was to make the nut. If you had to take a five-dollar bill or a ten-dollar bill for something, you did it. That hundred dollars had to come. That was the way the whole street operated.

The good table model TVs went for about $375 retail. That set cost roughly $175. On Cortlandt Street, you could buy it for $250, but the best price depended on how bad the day was. If it was a slow day, you could buy it for practically nothing.

The door was always open, no matter how cold it was, because people liked to walk into an open doorway. And no matter how cold it was outside, you had to stand outside along the window, and when somebody approached you had to start talking to him and entice him into the store and try to sell him something.

BOB ELLIOTT: The salesmen had a lousy habit. If they thought a customer was chiseling them, when he was walking out of the store, they used to spit on the back of his jacket, so if he went in the next store he would be marked. That was called "marking the noodge."

JERRY FISHMAN: Or throw snot on him. I heard of that. I never did it.

IRVING NEEDLE: Those customers were called "the toothpick brigade." Lunchtime, a guy would come in, just ate, toothpick in the mouth, used to walk around the stores. Nobody ever waited on 'im. They knew right away he was not a buyer. He was a looker.

BOB ELLIOTT: The pipe brigade! Anybody come in the store with a pipe, you lost 'im like they had cancer. They were just killing time on their lunch hour.

The dealers were also shrewd. We had another phrase, "*shtup* the seller." To get back at the people that used to chisel them they fix the radios so they would only get half the stations. They wanted the customer to come back and exchange it. Then you hit 'em on the head and got a nice price for another set.

We weren't selling television until 1945. That projection set they had before then, that was crap. The picture stunk. Philco had one too. It really started up right after the war when RCA came out with a seven-inch set and a ten-inch. DuMont came out with a twelve-inch set. We sold that when we moved to Newark. Philco had a ten-inch. The RCA 630 was one of the best sets they ever made. Then after a while they built a set that you had to have a fire insurance policy.

JACK SIEGRIST: DuMont made the best sets. I worked in their marketing division. I also worked for Admiral, Motorola, and Philco. For one thing, the DuMont cabinets were superb, and everything that we put in that chassis was absolutely top grade. We could only spend so much for the material, but when in doubt we always put in the good stuff and raised the price. On the line, if a little decal or a frame was out of alignment by a whisker, the line would stop and they would call me and ask if I would accept it. "No, fix it." At Philco I bent a little.

I remember something interesting about the manufacturing at Philco. We had girls for about an eighth of a mile assembling sets. One time, there were defects, and they traced it back to one woman. In winding coils, the women weren't allowed to do it when they were menstruating because we found that some acid would exude from their fingertips, and it would ruin the transformers. You can imagine the foreman on the line trying to keep track of who was menstruating. The routine was to ask her to see the nurse. There was one story about a woman who went to see the nurse, and the nurse asked her, "Are you menstruating?"

She said, "No, I'm winding coils on the fourth floor."

JERRY FISHMAN: The RCA 630 chassis was the biggest selling set of its day. Admiral, Philco, Motorola, and Crosley, used the same circuit. They just put it in different cabinets, but if you were to ask ten people to make their pick, nine of them would pick RCA. But if a dealer wanted a hot RCA product, he had to buy the rest of their line. You couldn't say, "I won't take this."

They'd say, "Nope, you gotta take the rest of the crap too."

BOB ELLIOTT: You had to buy those 45 r.p.m. record players from them. They wouldn't move, so you threw 'em down the basement. RCA dumped 'em on everybody. It was the same with Admiral. "If you want to buy the TV, you have to buy our white goods [kitchen appliances] too." They had you by the nuts.

IRVING NEEDLE: The service contracts were our salvation. They were a bonanza for us because we didn't get returns on the sets. The less problem you had the better the reputation.

We trained the serviceman. They had only two chassis to work on, so it wasn't too difficult. Sets were sold in the beginning with one hundred percent service contracts. The retail salesman made a commission on the service contract. Sometimes nothing happened to the set. Then it was all profit, but you scared the hell out of the consumer. You said, "Look, if it doesn't work, who are you gonna go to? I wouldn't give it to an Admiral serviceman. He doesn't know the set. I wouldn't give it to a DuMont serviceman," which wasn't true because they both had the same RCA chassis. Look, I can't say it, but I'll say it, most dealers they're crooks. They're tryin' to make whatever they can.

JACK SIEGRIST: In those days, if you had a television you were the big entertainer on the block. Those poles on the roofs were quite a status symbol. Some people put them up even though they didn't have television, just to achieve the status.

TED BERGMANN: I was a salesman for the DuMont network. We found that the largest concentration of television receivers was on the Lower East Side. The Italians liked the idea of an appliance that brought the family closer together. They were the first ethnic group to embrace television.

The biggest occupational group buying television was cab drivers. They would get home after driving a cab around, and all they wanted to do was put up their feet and stay home, so they bought television sets even though there wasn't much to look at.

LEONARD FAUPEL: The taverns were the first to get TV. That was a major thing because the people couldn't afford it at home. I worked for Ballantine Beer. After the war, the taverns were really having a hard time because people thought in terms of building up the home, not hanging out at taverns. The taverns were very much interested in a vehicle that would get people into their places again. Television was ideal.

OTIS FREEMAN: If a TV set went out in the bar, the people would just go across the street to the next bar, and the bar would lose its customers. He'd look in the Yellow Pages and wouldn't find any TV servicemen. They didn't have any, so he would call the station. If I was there, sometimes I would hop in a cab and run up and fix his TV set. Usually, I would just have to turn a knob. They didn't know how to do it or they were afraid of them.

JAMES MCMANUS: This bar has been here [at the corner of Nineteenth Street and Sixth Avenue in New York City] since 1937. After the war, people were going to bars that had TVs, so I wanted to get one. My father didn't. He figured at a bar people talk. They meet somebody, and the next time they come in they look to see if he's here, and he says, "Have a drink with me." With television, people drink while they're watchin'. The conversation is dead.

He may have been right, but I thought it would be good for business, so early one afternoon I went to an appliance store and bought a TV without my father's knowledge. I bought it with the condition that it be installed and playin' the right way before my father came in, which was about six o'clock at night. They got the TV in, but it wasn't workin' too good, so they got hold of the two RCA servicemen. They said we should try to get permission to run an antenna from the high-rise next door.

As we were doing this, there was a man in the men's room cleanin' Cosmoline off his hands in the sink. I gave him a can of Ajax and a rag, and said [sternly], "When you finish cleanin' your hands, clean the sink, and when you're finished, I want to check it to make sure it's properly cleaned."

He came out, and it was clean. Anyway, then I went next door to ask permission to put an antenna up, and the doorman tells me to go see his boss, Mr. Riley. He sends me to this guy who has his back to me. I tap him on the shoulder and say, "Pardon me, I'm from next door."

He said, "Oh, hello, Jimmy, how are ya?" This was the man in the men's room. I figured he would just say no. I explained what I wanted to do, and he said sure, so the RCA man went up, and he strung the wire, and the TV was fine. My father came in and looked at the TV and said, "Oh, that's nice."

There I was breaking my chops.

It brought in business, and Pop didn't object. He liked to watch Lawrence Welk on Sunday night. You better not drop a pin on the floor. You had to be quiet so he could enjoy the music.

MEL GOLDBERG: I was head of research at DuMont. We found that television grew in the same way most new inventions grew. You have prime movers. They are technological, and they buy a set. People all around them come to look at it, and then they buy one. You had that all over. Mostly, younger people bought it first.

WILLARD LEVITAS: After the war, the thing to do in Newark was to go downtown to L. Bamburger and R. H. Macy to see all the new things that were coming out. In the radio department was a roped-off area where they had a TV set, and all these people were standing around watching this little football game and you could see it so clearly.

My brother was a dentist. We would go to the fights together, and we heard about them being on TV, but you couldn't get a set. They were that much in demand. One of his patients was a salesman from the local radio-TV appliance place. While this guy's mouth was open, my brother said to him, "How about getting me a set?"

You know, it was "yeah, yeah, yeah, yeah." Finally, he got a call one day, "but you better come down and get it quickly," so we drove down, paid him $475 and loaded it in the car.

RCA had to install it. We didn't know how to do it. They plugged it in and put the antenna on the roof and aimed it at the Empire State Building. There was a test pattern on all day long, and he would tune it in to the test pattern. For forty-five dollars a year, you got a service guarantee. You needed it. The sets had vacuum tubes and they blew.

HARRY DUBIN: Of course when I got my TV, I was the fair-haired boy on the block. When there was a big fight, everybody called, "Can I come up for a few minutes?"

WILLARD LEVITAS: You would see the RCA truck parked on the street and everyone would say, "They've got a TV." Then, when Berle came on, the streets would literally be deserted. There would be a crowd in front of every store that had a TV in the window. Every house with a TV, there would be a crowd. You didn't invite, but you couldn't say no. They would all come in and sit around and watch the pictures and eat.

HARRY DUBIN: My living room was jammed. I lined up seats like a theater, maybe thirty of them, and everybody was glued to this little picture. It was more the phenomenon of a telecast, because the picture wasn't all that great.

WILLARD LEVITAS: The first show we saw was from one of the tire companies, "How to Make a Tire," with Brandon DeWilde's father as the narrator. We were very excited to see that.

E. LAWRENCE DECKINGER: Soon after the war, I did a survey of TV owners for a television research conference at Ohio State. So many of them told me it was the greatest thing that ever happened to them, to have this miracle in their living room. Nowadays people take it for granted, but back then people sat there in awe. Many of them were already constructing their lives around the daytime and evening programs. I realized it was going to change the lives of Americans.

RON DUBIN: It was such a novelty. People were always commenting on what was said and what they saw. There was as much conversation coming from outside the set as there was coming from the set. Nowadays, people are rather passive when they watch TV. Then, it was a much more active involvement.

HARRY DUBIN: To give you an idea of how few sets there were right after the war, we watched "Cash & Carry" with Dennis James. He had a barrel, and the TV audience could guess what was underneath it from these clues he gave you. Like he would say, "I'll throw you a line," and it was a fishing pole. The moment I had an idea, I rushed right over to the phone and called and you'd get them directly. The phone was never busy, and I'd make a big five dollars. I won almost every other week. After I kept guessing this thing, Dennis James called me up and invited me down to the studio and introduced me on the air.

JERRY FISHMAN: For a while, there weren't enough sets to go around. All you had to do was have it. There were enough customers for everybody. Then, by 1947, the dealers had all the sets they wanted because there were so many companies on the market. It was up to you to try to sell what you were overloaded in or what you got a better deal on.

JACK SIEGRIST: Home Demo. Our retailers would offer to come out and put a set of your choice in your home. Then they would come around to pick it up on Tuesday nights when Uncle Miltie was on, and the kids would hang on to the legs of the delivery man and everything, "No, no, no." So the old man would buy it. That was a great way of selling sets.

We would also work night and day before the big football games or during the World Series, and we would advertise specials where we would have it in your home almost like Domino Pizza in thirty minutes.

IRVING NEEDLE: Once the others started making enough sets, RCA had to kiss the dealer's ass instead of their kissing ours.

JERRY FISHMAN: There were some sets I would make more money on than RCA. Admiral might be an extra five dollars or they might have a promotion, like a trip to Vegas if you sold enough sets. Some company was always running a gimmick. If Admiral was offering us a trip, I tried to sell that set. If Philco was, I tried to sell theirs.

IRVING NEEDLE: Before you got a trip, you bought merchandise against the trip. Philco used to have a meeting on a boat going across the ocean. They'd get all the dealers on the boat, take their orders, and then tell the radioman, "No messages going back to the office," because otherwise every dealer would go up there and cancel his order.

JACK SIEGRIST: We'd take dealers on free trips. Some of them would want us to pimp for them. I remember telling my boss, "This son of a bitch wants me to get him a girl. I'm not gonna do it," so he said he would take care of it. What he did I don't know.

IRVING NEEDLE: There was a story about GE. Hotpoint had a meeting in New York. There was plenty of stuff [prostitutes] floating around. They made the mistake of transporting them to Jersey, and all these executives got fired. They got caught. All the dealers that were there fortunately got off, but that was really a fiasco.

The dealer would say, "Hey, what do you have up here besides food?" You take him over to your sales manager and let him take care of it. It was all paid for. Most guys didn't want to get laid. They wanted a blow job. They never got it at home. It was a new experience for them.

I once walked into a room without knocking, and there is this guy sitting on the couch with his pants down around his knees with some broad giving him a blow job. He said, "Hey, you're next." Everybody did it.

* * *

BOB ELLIOTT: My partner got a little too smart, so we had a terrible argument, and he wanted out. He took Cortlandt Street and I took Newark. He was only in business a very short while. He forgot my value to the store. I went out of business in 1955. Newark had been one of the finest shopping places in the country, but it died. It not only died, it dropped dead.

JERRY FISHMAN: I left in the fifties. It was starting to be thrown down for the World Trade Center. Leonard's Vim, Hines and Bollet. They don't exist anymore. The street doesn't even exist.

BOB ELLIOTT: They all went bankrupt. Nobody cared for the future. They all wanted to grab it right away. I'll tell ya, if you wanna curse anybody, let 'im go into the appliance and TV business. The customer cuts you down to the bone, but like a schmo we didn't want to lose the business. Instead of like a shoe store. Did you ever go to a shoe store and tell him you don't wanna pay the tax? You ever tell him you want shoelaces for nothin'? You ever tell him you want polish for nothin'? He'd tell ya to get lost. Shoes are at least a forty-percent markup. You know what my fondest wish was? To have a shoe store.

Any schmuck can open up a TV store, and most of them are underfinanced, so they gotta find dollars, and the manufacturer doesn't give a shit. You think you can tell these appliance guys to hold a price? We were friendly, but we'd cut each other's throat. Friends my eye. Business is business. Like you say, "Friends to the end."

"Lend me ten dollars."

"This is the end."

THE SPORTS SECTION

There isn't a better symbol of televised sports in their postwar infancy than Gorgeous George, the caped grappler with the peroxide do, of whom Red Smith once wrote unenthusiastically, "Groucho Marx is prettier than he, Sonny Tufts a more gifted actor, Connie Mack a better rassler, Happy Chandler funnier, and the Princeton Triangle Club has far superior female impersonators."

Maybe so, but George and his hairpins sold more television sets than Milton Berle ever did. The reason was simple: before the network technology was a reality, television stations had to fend for themselves in terms of finding programming that would get people to buy sets. The best shows were those which were cheap, occupied a big chunk of the schedule and appealed to the crowds in bars, ("videots" to Smith) where most television sets were located since they were still too expensive for the home. What went better with beer nuts than wrestling?

Actually, boxing had traditionally rung the opening bell for the mass media. In 1894, Jim Corbett kayoed Pet Courtenay in front of Thomas Edison's first movie cameras. Radio's first nationwide hookup featured the 1921 Dempsey-Carpentier match. In 1946, fight fans filled theaters in Washington, Schenectady, New York, and Philadelphia to watch Joe Louis defend his title against Billy Conn, and then again in 1947 against Jersey Joe Walcott.

Boxing would continue to be a popular attraction for television, but wrestling seemed to have a special appeal for programmers, maybe because women seemed to enjoy it as much as men did, and the fact that—kids, if you are reading this, please skip ahead to the next paragraph—the bouts could be controlled, which meant that the shows would not play havoc with the evening schedule.

Sports had been a staple for television programming since Hollis Baird first climbed up to his roof and aimed his camera across the street into Fenway Park. In 1939, when NBC broadcast its first baseball games, cameras were allowed into the park, but not with open arms. Surrendering even a few seats to an upstart, freeloading, television operation was still a losing proposition to a team owner. That changed dramatically in 1946 when television regained its commercial status. Now, sponsors were opening their checkbooks in exchange for TV rights, and most teams were only too willing to accommodate the equipment in return.

However, while the cash was welcome, some worried that it was a Faustian bargain. A fan no longer had to buy a ticket to see a match. He could see it in his living room for free. What would happen if the rights' fees failed to cover the decline in gate receipts? Boxing was one case where those fears were justified. For years, the sport was fed by a wellspring of small clubs around the country. After the war, boxing shows from the clubs were on the schedule almost every night of the week. Attendance soon dwindled below the break-even mark. One by one the clubs shut their doors forever, and the sport hasn't been the same since. Certainly, baby-booming and Messrs. Berle and Caesar also played a role in the clubs' demise, but there is no question that overexposure decimated the sport.

On the other hand, television transformed professional football teams from mom and pop operations into multi-million-dollar corporations. In the last decade, the combination of television and clever marketing has shot professional basketball into stratospheric popularity. Nor is television any longer a mere observer. In the late October chill, World Series games are played at night for prime-time audiences. The Super Bowl is delayed three hours to accommodate all the advertisers on the pregame show, and children grow up worshipping peroxide-coiffed wrestlers whose continued employment hinges on their ability to grunt and groan on cue. *Plus ça change . . .*

HARRY COYLE: Sports put TV over the barrel. DuMont had three nights of wrestling and two nights of boxing a week. We were almost the ESPN of that day. In 1947, we did every Yankees game. That year I directed the first World Series on TV. It helped put television over the hump, that, the Army-Navy game and the Louis-Walcott fight even though it only went to seven stations.

JACK JACOBSON: In 1948, I was hired as a cameraman at WGN in Chicago four days before the station went on the air. There was still no coaxial cable, so we relied on local programming. Sports, film, and kids' shows were the tripod the station was built on. Wrigley didn't charge rights fees, so with the Cubs we could cheaply fill three or four hours in the afternoon when we had nothing else.

Even when the cable came in from New York, sports were great counterprogramming. We must have done twenty remotes a week between boxing, wrestling, the Cubs and the White Sox, soccer, the Zephyrs, the Bears, high school sports. Wherever there was an event in Chicago, we covered it. We even did a six-day bike race.

BOB BENDICK: Sports has the greatest spontaneous quality and the most thrilling climaxes of any programming, much more so than dramatic shows or movies where the endings are often known. Nothing shows off television's ability to bring live action into the living room better than sports. That's why CBS did so much sports after the war. Also, sports were easy to pick up. There were no rehearsals, and we knew that TV was mostly in bars, where you had a male-oriented audience.

JACK JACOBSON: Most of the sponsors were male-oriented: beer, cigarettes, automobiles. Also, all our sponsorship was all local. Every car shop in Chicago was on television.

LEONARD FAUPEL: Of course, sports and the beer crowd are the most natural combination in the world. When Ballantine bought the rights to the Yankees the tavern business was the prime reason for our going into it. We made signs to put in the windows, WATCH THE GAMES HERE.

TOM VILLANTE: I was with BBD&O when the Brooklyn Dodgers' TV and radio rights were owned exclusively by our client, Schaefer Beer. In 1952, they sold half of that to another client of ours, the American Tobacco Company, which made Lucky Strike cigarettes.

In those days, the ad agencies played a very important role in the sports picture. They negotiated the rights, produced the broadcast and telecast, hired the talent, selected the flagship TV and radio station, developed the regional network, took care of the billing. In our case, I ended up doing all these things for the Dodgers.

Walter O'Malley was a very shrewd marketer. He knew that television would be a tremendous selling tool for baseball, and that someday it would generate huge revenues, but he and Branch Rickey wanted to protect the gate. To them, the gate was the single most important revenue source. Back in the early days of radio, they thought that broadcasting home games on radio would hurt the gate. They found out it didn't. Then they felt for sure that televising the home games would hurt the gate. That was the bugaboo, and it's still prevalent today. They felt the ideal way to go was to black out the home games and do the road games, which would not hurt the gate, while the road games would serve as a terrific promotional tool for the next home stand.

JACK JACOBSON: Wrigley always felt that the more exposure baseball got the better it was. Bill Veeck, who owned the White Sox, was a pussycat, but he felt that televising some of the home games could hurt attendance. They would let us televise a limited number of games, fifty percent of two-thirds, while the Cubs let us televise all of them. There is no question in my mind that the initial television exposure helped make the Cubs what they are in Chicago today. Kids grew up in Chicago knowing the Cubs were on television. If you were walking down the street and you walked by a bar or a window of some-place selling television, they always had a ball game on and it was the Cubs.

TOM VILLANTE: Rights were determined by sitting down with the owner, and he would say, "You're gonna cost me X number of seats," and you multiply that X number of times and you arrive at a rights number. It wasn't an add-on, it was a replacement.

The rights we paid to O'Malley were peanuts. Our first year we may have paid $200,000 for television and radio. Our last year, in 1957, we paid $600,000 for 125 TV games and all the radio games and the regional network. It was a tremendous buy.

BOB BENDICK: In the beginning, we were still small change. CBS would beg the Dodgers to allow us to put a camera behind first base. "But that will take three seats out of operation."

HARRY COYLE: There was no sense in complaining, because TV didn't generate any money. Yankee Stadium, they were the worst bastards. The first year, we didn't have a control room. We had to work out of a cage with a canvas over our head. We complained and complained, so they gave us space on the third deck between an elevator shaft and a men's room. Now, in double-headers, everybody lined up to go to the john. Some of 'em couldn't wait, and we noticed streams of water—not really water—coming under the door.

HEINO RIPP: After being in the studio, I wanted a taste of the field. One rainy day we went to Madison Square Garden. We had to crawl up these filthy holes to set up the cables. When it was over and we took them down, everything was wet. Dogs had crapped all over the cable, and I was filthy. Boxing crowds were cuckoo to begin with, and I just said, "I'm going back to the studio."

ALVIN "BUD" COLE: I was on the remote crew, and in the begin-ning when there were still only a few sets in New York, married guys would go to the fights with their girlfriends, and sometimes the wives would watch TV at their friends' and see their husbands. The husbands would call and threaten us. We had to announce that you are in a public place and you might be seen.

SAM LAINE: I was working at CBS radio in 1946 when Dennis James came by to do a commercial. He mentioned that he was gonna be doing his first fight that evening for DuMont. We started talking about fights, at which I had a background, and he asked me to come with him. I picked up a pair of binoc-ulars and we went out to Ebbets Field. The ring was over the pitcher's mound, and we had to work from the upper grandstands, a considerable distance away. They had one camera, which was in back of us, and one lens, the Cyclops. We had no monitor, so we had no idea what was being shown, except that at the end of each round, I waved to one corner or the other so the camera would pan to that corner.

DENNIS JAMES: I had never seen wrestling, so before I covered my first bouts, I bought Frank Gotch's wrestling book and during the match if I saw a hold, I would look it up and then say, "That's a hammerlock!"

SAM LAINE: Dennis built up the TV audience through wrestling. We even got letters complaining that Milton Berle was in conflict with our matches.

DENNIS JAMES: This is how I did it. I figured if I tried to tell these guys in the bars what a step-over toehold was, they would resent me and say, "Who the hell is he?" So I would tell it to "Mother." And if Mother was watching, she would say, "John, is that a hammerlock?" And John would say, "Of course," and I would make him a hero. Also, in those days, there was only one set in the home, so I had to interest Mother in sports or that house was in trouble and the guy could never watch. It worked, because wrestling really became a ladies' sport.

HARRY MARKSON: When I ran the Garden's boxing department, we had the Friday Night Fights. Television revolutionized boxing because it introduced the sport into thousands of homes where it had been completely unknown. If there was a controversial decision I would be swamped with mail calling me every kind of name you can think of. Many of these complaints come from women.

NOEL JORDAN: We had a problem with wrestling when we went network, because then we had to get on and off the air on time. I mentioned this to the promotor, and he said, "Don't worry. Tell me when you want the matches to end, and we'll end them."

ED STASHEFF: I produced a special on an eclipse for WPIX in New York with a special camera on the roof of the *Daily News* building. Then somebody discovered that that same night they had a contract to cover wrestling at St. Nicholas Arena. What to do? The sales manager and I went out to the arena, and the owner said, "You have to be on the air those whole two hours?"

"No, we need about two minutes when the eclipse starts, two minutes when the sun is completely obliterated, then two minutes at the end."

"You can tell just when that's gonna be?"

"Oh, we can give it to you in the split second."

"You write those times out for me, and I'll guarantee ya, every time you need the cameras, a bout will end."

He was as good as his word. We had an assistant director at ringside cue the referee, and the good guy pinned the bad guy right on time.

SAM MUNCHNICK: I started promoting fights in St. Louis in 1932. I had Jimmy Londos, Ed "Strangler" Lewis, Joe Stecher, and Lou Thesz. Some of those matches used to last two or three hours. I saw Lewis wrestle Stecher at the St. Louis Coliseum. The first fall was two hours and seventeen minutes.

LOU THESZ: It was very dull unless you were a wrestling student. You couldn't do that on television.

SAM MUNCHNICK: After TV came in there was a lot of showmanship, because that's what the people wanted. They also had to have time limits.

LOU THESZ: I started wrestling in '36. I'm from the old school. Right after World War II, the Gorgeous George thing came in. A lot of the serious aspects of wrestling were watered down to the point where they're doing things my grandmother can do, but they said, "This is what is making money."

SAM MUNCHNICK: I didn't mind Gorgeous George because he could wrestle. His real name was George Wagner, but when he wrestled as George Wagner he wasn't a drawing card. Then he came up with Gorgeous George, and television made him a star.

LOU THESZ: He got a lot of what we call in the business "heat," a big response from the women. After that, a lot of guys took it upon themselves to come up with some kind of gimmick, like Farmer Jones, who would enter the ring with his pig. I wouldn't wrestle on the same card with girl wrestlers or midgets or when some idiot brought in a bear, because then you are guilty by association, although I did train a kid who wrestled a bear in Tennessee and kicked the hell out of that bear. He was booked with that bear about a week later. The bear saw that kid coming into the ring, and it left. The bear remembered him.

DENNIS JAMES: When I went to my first wrestling match, I said, "I can't play this straight." Yet, I had to find some happy medium so that the wrestlers wouldn't hate my guts, so I added sound effects. If a guy was twisting another guy's leg, I had a crackle bone that I would twist. If he pulled on his trunks, I would tear a window shade. I got hold of a slide whistle when they went up and down. I did one whole wrestling match in rhyme: "They're out of the ring, but now they're back, and when they do, two heads will crack."

SAM LAINE: There were a few wrestlers who struck up a friendship with Dennis, but most of them felt he was ridiculing them. Still, a lot of them realized that because of the publicity he was making them money.

There were the Garibaldis, who were a family of wrestlers. Gino Garibaldi was 240 pounds of solid rock. He was from the old school who stayed with wrestling when it became show business. He resented Dennis very much until one night when Gino's son was taken to the hospital with the possibility of polio. Dennis went on the air to ask the public to say a prayer for the boy. From that point on, he could do no wrong as far as Gino was concerned.

BOB DOYLE: I used to do wrestling all over New York. Oh, I hated it, wrestling and the Roller Derby. In Roller Derby nobody cared who won. It was just the action, but nobody had ever ever seen anything like Roller Derby before.

KEN NYDELL: Leo Seltzer owned the Roller Derby. He hired me to do the announcing. In the summer of '49, he and I went to New York to get Roller Derby started on TV. CBS agreed to broadcast it from the armory on Twenty-fourth Street. The armory was nearly empty the first night. The cameramen had no idea how to follow it. It was really funny. I would say, "There goes Tuffy Bruzhoon over the rail, ladies and gentlemen. The cameramen don't have it for you, but don't blame them, because the action is so terrific you'll have to be here in person to see it. Call Judson 6-4646 for reservations."

The phone started ringing twenty minutes after we were on. The game ended at eleven. At three o'clock in the morning we were sold out. We were there for seventeen days, and we sold out every night.

RUSS MASSRO: I started skating with them right when TV started. It was utterly fantastic. Girls would literally corner me and try to tear my clothes off me. We booked the Garden for our playoffs and we had the largest crowd ever in there for the month of May. I think we had 21,000 people.

MEL ALLEN: In 1937, CBS offered me a job as a staff announcer, but they said they would appreciate it if I thought of some other last name. My name was Israel. They said, "Not that there's anything wrong with the name, but it's a little too all-inclusive. It includes all the tribes."

My parents were against it, but I didn't think I was gonna be with CBS for long, I was going to be a lawyer, so I thought of a name to take, and I used Allen, which was my father's middle name. I ended up staying. I did quiz shows and soap operas. If there was a second sports event, they would assign me to that. When I came out of the Army in 1946, I asked CBS for permission to do free-lancing. I did the Notre Dame games at DuMont, but primarily I worked at NBC, and I eventually became their top sports announcer.

The first baseball games we did on television were simulcasts. You had to adjust by taking a little off your radio report so you wouldn't be overtalking for television, the idea being that the people can see what is going on, and you're describing what they're already seeing.

JACK BRICKHOUSE: In those days, of the 10,000 sets in Cook County, probably 9,500 of them were in bars. In the beginning, we took the position, "Let the picture do the work. Don't talk too much." However, because of the noise level in the bars, they weren't getting much information from the audio part of the television. They turned on the radio—to watch the picture and listen to the radio broadcast, so we started to talk more.

Then as sets started to go into the homes, we got mail saying, "Don't talk so much," so we reduced it. We also had to learn to watch the monitor. There's no substitute for the human eye, but if you describe too many things that don't appear in the picture, you'll antagonize your audience.

MEL ALLEN: I used to check in with other announcers. "What would you rather do, radio or TV?"

"Oh, hell, I'd rather do radio." The reason being that when you're doing radio, your eyes are moving all the time. A lot of people think nothing is going on in baseball between pitches when everything in the world is going on. A shortstop after a pitch adjusts his position to the count. A smart infielder won't give his position away. He'll walk around to the edge of the grass and with his back to the plate, maybe take a blade of grass and chew on it. Then he gets set for the next pitch, but this time he might be two steps to his left. You bring something like that to your description in radio, but you can't do that in TV. If the camera is on one part of the field, and you see somebody jumping up in the dugout waving a fielder over, by the time you get word to the director and have the cameraman point the camera to that spot, it's all over.

You were constantly distracted. You'd be in the middle of a description, and you'd suddenly hear the director say, "After this pitch, we're gonna take a shot of some cheesecake up in the left-field stands."

TOM VILLANTE: Red Barber recognized early on that unlike radio, TV was under the director's control, so what he did was build two miniature replicas of the ballpark, with little lights at the various positions on the field. One of these was in the broadcasting booth and the other in the director's booth, so if he wanted a shot of the bullpen, he would flick a little switch and a light would go on in the bullpen in the director's room, and he knew that Red wanted a shot of the bullpen. That way Red got back some of the control of the picture and the flow of the game.

HARRY COYLE: Put yourself in the stands. Where are the best seats in the house? Behind home plate, so that's where your main camera should be. Baseball is the toughest sport going. Football and basketball are obvious. You know they're either gonna run or pass, and it's obvious when they're gonna pass. What can happen? An interception, maybe a fumble. The majority of your action is right there. Basketball just goes up and down.

In baseball, you don't know where the hell the ball is gonna go. We play percentages. If a right-hander is up it should go to left field or center. The ball is travelin' at what, ninety miles an hour? We checked it one time, a hit to third base and the throw to first took about two and a half seconds. In that time you might have to click twice.

JACK JACOBSON: In 1951, I directed a Little League game at Thillins Stadium. We couldn't get a behind-the-plate shot because it had a real low screen. The field was so small that if you went between third base and home plate there would be so much panning everyone would get dizzy, so I walked around out in center field, and I saw the pitcher pitching batting practice. I took a framer out with me and said, "Let's try a camera here."

That was the first center-field shot ever done. The next day we put it in at Wrigley Field. About two or three years later, NBC started using it on their Game of the Week, and it's been a standard shot for baseball ever since.

NOEL JORDAN: When we first covered the Giants' games at the Polo Grounds for Chesterfield, Lucky Strike bought up all the billboards around the outfield, so everytime you panned up you had ads for the opposition. The first game that season, I got this roar through my headset. "What the hell are you doing showing those signs? Don't you know who our sponsor is?"

I tried to evade the signs, but there was no way you could do it when a ball was hit to the outfield.

HARRY COYLE: It was the same thing with the Dodgers. Gillette screamed that at Ebbets Field there was a Gems sign in right field. We couldn't do anything about it.

There were also a lot of discussions with Happy Chandler about what they would not like you to show. Spitting, players grabbing their crotches, or making gestures out of the dugout was a terrible thing in the early days. They didn't want us to look into the dugout, because they didn't know what we would pick up.

I said, "Why worry about shooting in the dugout? At Yankee Stadium if there are 75,000 people there, 35,000 can see in each dugout. What about them?" In those days, there were more people in the stadium than there were watching TV.

BOB DOYLE: After I moved to ABC in 1948, Bob Kintner made a deal to do the Major League Game of the Week. Every week we would go to, say, Chicago, use the local baseball crew and put [former pitching great] Dizzy Dean's voice on instead of the local announcer. Diz was a great guy. I thought I knew baseball until I met him. I loved to listen to him describe what was gonna happen next and get it right.

We used to get hundreds of letters from teachers. "You can't say 'slud into third base' or 'he flang the ball.' " Dizzy could speak better English than you or me, but he knew it made him distinctive. He was self-educated and extremely bright.

Diz didn't like to fly. We went everywhere by train. When his wife stayed at home, she would give me his money and say, "Only pay for his dinner, and don't let him have a drink."

He wasn't a drunk, but he'd look at me and wink and say, "I won't, honey." Then he'd walk into the bar car and stand up and say, "Who wants to buy Ol' Diz a drink?" And every guy in the bar would buy Ol' Diz a drink.

Dizzy did the commercials for Falstaff Beer. He always ad-libbed them. He'd say, "Me and my wife was having our beer last night. I thought about how wonderful Falstaff is. The taste, oh, boy, let me tell you."

He was marvelous. He put Falstaff on the map with those commercials. The president of Falstaff told me that Dizzy had built him three or four new breweries.

He did something that broke me up for years afterwards. At one point, a little guy about five feet three came to be the coordinator of the commercials, and we had to go to Detroit. This time we had to fly. A limousine met us at the airport. This guy immediately started nagging Dizzy, "You gotta read this." He just kept saying it. It was about a thirty-mile ride from the airport to the hotel. After about four or five miles, Dizzy had had enough. He reached over and tapped the driver on the shoulder, and said, "Will you stop here, Pardnuh?"

We were out there in nowhere. He grabbed this little guy, opened the door, put him out in the street, shut the door, and said to the driver, "Move on."

LEONARD FAUPEL: Ballantine was responsible for putting preseason games on TV. The Yankees never considered it until we suggested it to them. "You mean you're gonna bring the game up from Florida?"

"Yeah, we'd love to."

We wanted to lengthen the season, knowing that it was a tremendous selling tool. Bringing in a baseball game in March from Florida had quite an effect on the public.

TV also made Ballantine in the greater New York area. Of the three major breweries in the area, Schaefer, Rheingold, and Ballantine, we were third. To be able to tell tavern owners, "We are bringing you the Yankee baseball games for your television and your patrons," was a tremendous incentive to put our beer in or to favor it. Soon, we were number one in the East.

MEL ALLEN: Toward the end of the game, the Ballantine people would bring up a bottle and an opener and set it alongside. When the game was over you would say, "While we recap the game for you, how about joinin' me in a bottle of Ballantine?"

You'd ad-lib a brief commercial, uncap the bottle, and pour the beer into a glass (I had to practice how to pour it to get a reasonably proper head) and take a sip. Soon, the other beer companies started doin' the same thing, because that was your best commercial.

The idea of sipping a beer came to me while I was watching a Bette Davis movie. She was constantly smoking, and during her movies, people would be walking into the lobby to light up. It was auto-suggestion. In our case, a guy would say, "Gee, I'll go upstairs and get a bottle of beer."

It worked beautifully, but a couple of years later, the Women's Christian Temperance Movement went to Washington and caused them to stop it because kids were watching. After that, you'd bring it up to your mouth, and they would cut away. Then they would cut back as I was putting it back down after I had poured out so much of it. It was too enticing the other way.

LEONARD FAUPEL: After that, you had the famous rule that you had to show lights between the lips and the beverage. Television is a very powerful medium, and the impact per person when Mel would take a sip was incredible, but the breweries went along with the rule because this wasn't long after Prohibition, and they knew they were vulnerable.

We had another innovation at Ballantine: letting the foam cascade over the side, which gave it terrific appetite appeal.

WES KENNEY: I worked for Harry Coyle sometimes. They used to put Alka-Seltzer in the beer to make it foam.

TOM VILLANTE: There were no taboos against cigarette smoking. You could light up a cigarette, and there were no problems showing the announcer puffing or exhaling.

SAM LAINE: Dennis would always refer to me as "my bald-headed friend." He did the commercials, except one night the producer said I would have to do it because Dennis was late. It was for Troll Hair Control. Everything we did was ad-lib, so I got on and said, "Hey, don't laugh. If I had used Troll I wouldn't look like this."

ROGER MUIR: I did the famous push-push, click-click commercial for Gillette when the blade wouldn't open. This was a big introduction of this new razor during the Friday Night Fights. Bob Stanton was Mr. Sports Commentator at NBC. He gets on the air, and push, pull, click-click, and the goddamned thing didn't work. He's struggling with it, and I've got the agency people right over my shoulder and they're dying. It made the front page of *The New York Times*. I thought we would lose the account, but it wasn't our fault, but Gillette got too much mileage out of it to fire us.

WES KENNEY: One night, I was sitting home watching the Melrose Games. Nobody had ever cleared fifteen feet in the pole vault, and this was the big event. DuMont was covering it live. Cornelius Warmerdam just missed. He threw his pole down and sat down on the runway.

"Well, Mr. Warmerdam will be ready for his second attempt in a few minutes. In the meanwhile we'll go back to the studio," and they went into a commercial. When they came out of the commercial, Madison Square Garden was in bedlam. The minute they cut away, Warmerdam had run up, grabbed his pole, taken off down the runway, and cleared fifteen feet. Harry told me that just before he jumped, they were arguing with the agency man. "We should come back."

"No, no, he won't make it."

Well, of course, they didn't come back and he made it.

Harry has never lived that down. When he used to do the football games out here, I would sneak in the back of the truck and say, "Then there were the Melrose Games of 1950," and I would hear this voice go, "Get that son of a bitch Wes Kenney out of the truck."

*　　*　　*

LEONARD FAUPEL: Because of heavy sponsorship by the breweries and their willingness to invest in it, I think it brought a lot of innovations in sports coverage.

HARRY COYLE: The zoomar lens, color, and the instant replay were the three biggest innovations.

OTIS FREEMAN: We started the instant replay at WPIX around 1959. One day I was standing in the tape room when Mel Allen said about one play, "Wouldn't it be great if we could see that again?" I picked up the phone and called our director, Jack Murphy, and said, "You know, we have that on tape. We could rewind the tape and play it again," and that's the way instant replay started.

HARRY COYLE: Overall, televised sports really changed around 1952 when we went nationwide for the first time. Until then, the equipment was so unstable you spent most of your time thinking about keeping the show on the air, but then the equipment improved so you could think about programming.

Tom Gallery of DuMont signed the first contract with the NFL for DuMont. That deal made football. Those games were very popular on Saturday night. I directed the '58 championship game. I was at NBC by then. It changed things too, but the greatest thing that ever happened to football was the Heidi game [a crucial 1968 game between the New York Jets and the Oakland Raiders that was interrupted on the air so the network could show the film *Heidi*, generating huge protests]. It proved to the networks and the advertising people that people were watching. Up to that point the AFL was a lame-duck operation.

JACK JACOBSON: With the success of pro football, the networks moved into college football and pro basketball. And after the coaxial cable, the networks began paying big rights fees and the sponsors began really paying for commercials. That's when things really changed. We were no longer just covering the games, we were a part of them.

TOM VILLANTE: Because of the Dodgers, Schaefer had this tremendous identification. Then in 1958, the Dodgers left for L.A.

Budweiser and Miller and Schlitz were all local beers. The smartest thing they ever did was call themselves "premium" beers. The reason they called themselves that was they had to charge more because the beer had to be shipped.

But when the Dodgers went west, there were still no national beers, so there was a big void for Schaefer, which had all of this money for a TV budget but no Dodgers. I suggested to Rudy Schaefer that if we don't have the Dodgers, there were a lot of sports out there to be had that had not been seen on TV or were seen very infrequently. We could put them all together on a regional network and give them an umbrella and call it "The Schaefer Circle of Sports."

We bought a lot of these different sporting events, racing, jai alai, major league players playing golf. That show did very very well. That show was the forerunner for ABC's "Wide World of Sports," which Roone Arledge did soon after that. When Roone came in that's when the story changed and sports became really big business.

HARRY MARKSON: We started getting a better class of viewer. Instead of calling me a dirty rat, people were writing me letters saying I was an incorrigible reprobate.

TV GOES NATIONWIDE

Richard Nixon claimed he was tested by six crises in the early stages of his political career. Colby Lewis usually reached six by noon. As it was, the young director at WTMJ in Milwaukee was ready for the men in the white coats after three months on the losing end of a Herculean battle with the electronic Hydra, live TV. This was not the way it was supposed to be in the exciting new world of television, but in 1948, there were dozens of Colby Lewises at local stations that were springing up across the country, battered young television warriors, with fingernails chewed down to the nub, living on Maalox and coffee.

The reason for so much heartache was that network links between New York and the rest of the country were—with the exception of some connections between New York, Washington, and Schenectady—nonexistent. That left station managers to their own devices when it came to programming their stations. They did use kinescopes—films of New York television shows, which were received by mail, but kinescopes were usually of such poor quality that viewers often preferred the cheaper, local programming. There was plenty of that. Start-up costs were generally so high that there was little left in the budget for programming. That, and a paucity of both on- and off-camera talent combined to make ulcers the number one health hazard among station executives. At least Lewis was warned, as he ruefully noted in a letter that April to his mentor Rudy Bretz.

> By now with some 13 weeks of television directing behind me, I appreciate the wisdom of many of the opinions you declared to our class at the workshop. For instance I recall you stressing the question: What are you going to do when the film breaks, the camera busts, etc.? By now I've encountered many such emergencies—not so much because of equipment failure as because of human error: the fashion model who forgets her purse, which you realize as the announcer begins to describe it, the light stand a floor man left right in the middle of your opening shot; the camera-boom dolly that by being six inches out of place, prevents you from dollying in to a tight closeup on an actor to cover his companion's leaving the table to get to another set, etc., etc., etc.

Good professional talent is scarce in Milwaukee. The more skillful entertainers are busy in nightclubs and won't come for the small fees I can offer them. If they are comedians, their patter is too risqué for television.

There's insufficient rehearsal time. Besides [his five regular shows], *I catch assignments on the control desk for films and remotes. I have to cast all my live shows (and talent searching takes a lot of time), hunt up music, plan sets, write whatever script is necessary. Result: about fifty-five or sixty-hour week that's worn me down.*

I also miss an opportunity to achieve perfection. Everything is so compromised by lack of time to plan and do things right . . . and anyway, Milwaukeeans don't like the aesthetic—at least most of them don't. Their favorite radio shows are polkas and hillbilly ballads. Our audience is sharply divided between the barroom trade on one hand and well-to-do ladies on the other; and on Man About Town [one of his shows] *I soon discovered that one man's bear is another's poison.*

At least I've learned a lot. I'm used to the complexity, know what to expect of lenses and cameramen, am beginning to be able to give orders, watch script and pictures and even think at the same time. It's a perverse, exhausting, but fascinating, business.

Milwaukee was no different from Seattle, Los Angeles, Boston, or Buffalo when it came to the conundrum that plagued nearly every station trying to keep afloat in the days before the growing network of coaxial cable reached their city from New York, bringing with it big-time programming and advertising manna: people won't buy TV sets if there are no quality programs; advertisers won't pay for quality programming if there is no audience; station owners can't put on quality programs without advertising money.

To break the cycle, programmers had to put *something* on the air besides a test pattern in the hope that at least the novelty of TV would raise circulation. Unfortunately, while anyone with a few dollars and some back issues of *Popular Science* could put a radio station on the air, television start-up costs were in the seven figures before the cameras were even turned on. That left a program manager with a budget only slightly larger than the average adolescent's allowance.

Typical was WLWT in Cincinnati. When Saul Carson of *The New Republic* visited the station, he found that its owners had spent some $1.5 million on the latest television gear to air $1.50 worth of programming:

. . . WLWT's showing recalls one that took place a little more than two years ago in New York when the DuMont firm opened a brand-new, beautifully equipped studio. The pièce de résistance *of the premiere was a series of corny acts and amateurish singing that would not pass muster at a grammar school graduation.*

If a programmer was lucky, his city had a baseball team; real lucky, a wrestling arena. The grunt-and-groan game was a sure bet to attract viewers. Some stations were more successful than others. While some simply aired test patterns or waited for fuzzy kinescopes to be sent by mail from New York, others showed remarkable ingenuity. WRGB in Schenectady carried a variety of live programs as early as 1943. Their schedule included a hoedown, a revival meeting, a professional circus, a bridge tournament, and grand opera. WBZ in Boston, New England's first television station, carried a very strong local lineup, especially in news coverage. Philadelphia's WFIL and New York City's WPIX also aired ground-breaking prime-time newscasts. PIX, owned by *The New York Daily News*, often scooped the local NBC and CBS stations, and in 1951 scored a beat on the networks with its coverage of the Kefauver anti-crime hearings.

WPTZ in Philadelphia, which was owned and operated by Philco, primarily to sell Philco sets, suffered the typical birth pangs of a local station but benefitted from an early connection to the NBC network. Still, WPTZ had one asset that no network could match, the most inventive comedian ever to develop at a local station—Ernie Kovacs, who in 1950 burst onto the screen with the kind of unhinged mischief that made the "Today" show's chimp J. Fred Muggs seemed dignified by comparison.

Network TV, however, offered fame and fortune, for Kovacs and many other talented performers. While they looked toward New York, the coaxial cable spread west, and by 1951 could wrap its copper fingers around every television station from coast to coast. Now, "I Love Lucy" could be broadcast instantaneously in New York, Omaha, and Detroit. Was there a station manager in the country who didn't prefer the latest hijinks of the Ricardos and the Mertzes to the amateurish offerings from a local dance troupe? Surprisingly, Lewis, for all his troubles, was ambivalent.

"It's my guess that 'Man About Town' will be replaced by a feature movie, since better features seem available," Lewis continued in his letter to Bretz. "Along about October, we expect to be hooked in on a Midwest network, which by January will be joined to the Atlantic coast. What happens to the local direction staff I don't know."

What happened to Lewis was mirrored around the country. Improved programs arrived in the mail or by cable from New York. These were no longer two-bit productions, but sophisticated newscasts (including coverage of all three political conventions) and expensive variety shows such as "Texaco Star Theater" and Ed Sullivan's "Toast of the Town." The shows attracted both national and local advertising, and the local stations began turning the corner.

Lewis, for one, had had enough, though. He went back to school, earned his Ph.D. in communications, then spent the rest of his career teaching. The local talent that remained on the air was, for the most part, pushed aside to daytime or late-night, and quite naturally so, for few on the local level could match the brilliance of a Sid Caesar or an Ed Murrow. On the other hand, something was lost when the juggernaut blew in from the East—the local flavor, a showcase for home-grown talent. WTMJ's programming may not have been great, but it was theirs. Ernie Kovacs was great, because he was given a chance to be great. When the "Today" show took over his time period, he moved on, and a slot for the next Kovacs was lost forever. Who knows how much we are the poorer for it.

GREG GARRISON: What was it like? IT WAS SUCH GREAT FUN! SUCH WONDERFUL PEOPLE! SUCH NON-BULLSHIT! Such no fucking newspapers to pick up on Wednesday to say our ratings were 7, 12, 102. You didn't know whether you were getting picked up or not. Sometimes you didn't know whether your check was coming in, but we all generally liked and cared for one another.

HERBERT HORTON: We worked for $18.75 a week, and we could work for as many days and hours as we wanted to, as long as it was over a hundred, and it was a very bright spot in all our lives.

SYLVESTER L. "PAT" WEAVER: In 1932, I was working for KHJ radio in Los Angeles. One day, I went up on the roof to see if the sun was out. I couldn't believe my eyes when I saw this little movie machine. Harry Lubcke explained that there were two television sets in Los Angeles, and the programs were all old movies, and old movies in '32 were old movies.

HARRY LUBCKE: I got into television before there was a television. In 1928, I gave a talk at the Institute of Radio Engineers in San Francisco. When I finished speaking, Philo Farnsworth approached me and asked if I would be interested in working for him. While I was at Farnsworth, I heard Don Lee was interested in television. He had a network of radio stations. I went to see him, and the next day I was hired.

We began building a television system at Seventh and Bixel, where the KHJ studios were above Mr. Lee's Cadillac agency. It took a few months to get a picture on our apparatus. Meanwhile, we applied for a TV license. They assigned us W6XAO. W means North America. Six means the sixth district. The X meant experimental.

Starting on December 23, 1931, we went on the air one night a week from six to seven. After a while, we were on the air eighteen hours a week every day and every Sunday, and soon there were about three hundred sets in the area.

LEE COOLEY: In 1937, I got a job as a news editor and announcer at KHJ. There was a room right next to the announcer's booth. The sign on the door said NO ADMITTANCE. Of course, a reporter would never take that sign seriously. I opened the door and walked into W6XAO.

There was Harry, and maybe two or three other engineers. Harry was one of those wonderful dreamers like Lee DeForest. He saw no limitations at all. His only limitation was money, but Don Lee was an innovator in those days, and he was generous.

TV SCHEDULE FOR W6XAO, JUNE 13, 1940

8:00 Sign on
8:02 Film—cartoon
8:08 W. H. Mehring (acro)
8:14 Judy Lynn (song)
8:17 Jerry Linton (play)
8:27 Jack Miller (song)
8:30 Neal (interview)
8:35 Film (war news)
8:43 Buddy Swan & Marcella Wisman (mono's)
8:51 Jane Jones Trio (song)
8:55 Tanchuk Play
9:07 Film—two reel
9:37 Sign off

LEE COOLEY: We had the Sons of the Pioneers do a show for us. The were all Okies who knew horses and were also damn good musicians. One of them was a guitar player named Len Slye. Len came to me one day and said, "Hey, Lee, I hope I can miss rehearsal tomorrow." He said he had a very important appointment at one of the studios. At the next rehearsal I asked him how he made out, and he said [in a Western accent], "Well, Ah think ah made out all rahght. They're talkin' about takin' me into pictures, but they wanna change mah name."

I said, "What do they want to call ya?"

He said, "They wanna call me Roy Rogers."

ARCH BROLLY: In 1940, both Philco and NBC broadcast the political convention from Philadelphia. Somehow or other NBC had gotten a special telephone line up to New York to broadcast the convention, but Philco decided to set up a special relay from Convention Hall to the plant. I was appointed to build the relay transmitter. During the convention I sat with my fingers crossed in a hut on the roof of Convention Hall watching the transmitter while my compatriots ran the cameras on the convention floor.

HERBERT HORTON: I was hired by Philco a few months after the convention. There were still less than five hundred television sets in Philadelphia, but we knew it was gonna be really big. When it became commercial in 1941, a bunch of us went out and drank all the beer we could. Our world was now without end.

At that time, there was a radio-wave network between Schenectady, New York City, Philadelphia, and Washington. My first job was to go to the University of Pennsylvania. They had a shack on a rooftop there. I was to call the station at a certain hour, and they would tell me when to turn this antenna around so we could get pictures from New York instead of from Washington. What they didn't tell me was that sometimes I had to go up there in a blinding rainstorm with all the thunder and lightning. They would ask me, "Is it lightning there?"

"Yeah." I was expecting them to say, "Don't go out."

Instead they said, "Grab it and move it *real quick.*"

We were on five or six hours a day. Some of our programming came from New York, but we also did our own news, like films and wrestling. We signed on the evening's broadcast ourselves. When it was my turn, I'd put on a clean shirt and tie, focus the camera a little bit ahead of the drape, and run around in front of it and say, "This is W3XE your Philco television station," and so on, "This evening's program will begin with a newscast." Then I would run around and point the camera at a newscaster.

HARRY LUBCKE: We were really flexing our muscles come December 1941. After Pearl Harbor the technical help went to war. We worked for the military on overtime and on regular time we put on the television station once a week and then slowly expanded with various wartime programs. By the end of the war, we had really blossomed quite a way.

*   *   *

TED SMITH: Right after the war, David Sarnoff called a series of monthly meetings in Washington to discuss all the things that would be necessary to establish a working commercial television system. Engineers from RCA's home instrument department reported on the status of manufacturing. The tube people reported on what tubes were available. NBC talked about their plans for programs. I reported on transmitting equipment. Our lawyers discussed their plans to get the FCC's permission to begin their efforts to get AT&T to move on the coaxial cable.

These meetings were crucial because everything had to hang together. For example, you couldn't install transmitting equipment without any receivers. You couldn't build receivers without tubes. The stations that Sarnoff was pushing to put in transmitting equipment couldn't really afford to do their own programming. They needed to hook up with the network.

The meetings went from seven o'clock Saturday night to three in the morning on a monthly basis until Sarnoff got the answers he needed and the plans for television were put into motion. Our ultimate goal, of course, was to sell receivers and tubes. To do that we had to set up TV stations. There were already stations in New York, Philadelphia, Chicago, Los Angeles, and Schenectady, but no place else. To get it going as quickly as possible, several of us traveled around the United States in 1946 to try to persuade radio people to get television licenses.

We went to all our newspaper customers, because they owned a lot of radio stations. We went to the *Buffalo Evening News*, to the *Chicago Tribune*, the newspaper-owned stations in Omaha and Denver, Dallas, Nashville, and back to Philadelphia. They had all made a lot of money in broadcasting, and they were all favorable.

TOM GOLDSMITH: RCA had an interesting technique in dealing with them. Take an affiliate, let's say in Columbus, Ohio. When TV started, RCA would tell that station, "Hey, we're startin' in television now. Get yourself a TV license and we'll feed programs to you. If you don't, we'll cut your AM-FM affiliation off." That was some serious pressure, and most of them ante'd up if they wanted to keep their money rolling in.

TED SMITH: There is something to that. NBC was desperate to get enough stations on the air so that you could have national programs, so they would say, "If you don't set up a TV station, we'll look for another outlet."

BILL SWARTLEY: Plenty of stations wanted to get into it but were scared stiff of the coast. There was a question of how fast the network could be delivered, according to where your city was. In our case, at WBZ in Boston we were fortunate because the link was completed before we hit the air, so we were assured of whatever network service there was at the time. That wasn't always true in other cities.

MAXIE SOLOMON: I was a time salesman in radio before I moved to TV. Everywhere I went in Philadelphia, people said, "You should have stayed in radio because this television thing is only a flash in the pan."

TED SMITH: On our trip, we also saw the heads of Fox, Paramount, and MGM. We tried to convince them that television was the coming thing, but with the exception of Paramount, they all said, "Who is going to look at a little picture like that when they can go to a theater and see something on the big screen?"

PETER LEVATHES: In 1947, Fox bought a station in St. Louis, but the home office showed little interest in it. I made applications for stations in San Francisco, Los Angeles, Boston, and Washington, but the board withdrew its support. They said television was not their business. Actually, they didn't want to upset the theater owners, who were well organized and very powerful. The licenses would have cost us $50,000 apiece. Soon, those stations were worth many times more than the whole company was worth.

TED SMITH: I started planning for TV back in 1938. As I saw the situation, stations would not be making money for a few years. They would need programming that would be cheap but interesting. I told the RCA engineers, "Develop portable equipment that a small station in Albuquerque can take to baseball and football games," which everybody would want to see, even if they were high school games.

We developed a cheap low-power transmitter and a specially equipped projector to show movies. We also sold them trucks with power supplies and generators to transport all the gear. We gave them a catalogue that had everything a TV station could want, tripods to mount cameras, lenses, towers, and antennas that went on top of the towers. The whole package only cost about $100,000, and that would get you on the air. We also set up a school to train their technicians. It worked very well. We actually couldn't manufacture the equipment fast enough because the demand was so high.

BILL SWARTLEY: In each department one man was given the responsibility of learning all he could about television in that category. An assistant in the program department was sent to NBC to learn programming. In engineering, a radio expert was sent to RCA's school to learn about transmitters. Westinghouse had its own building and construction department. With them we built a studio that would house Arthur Fiedler and his orchestra.

RUDY BRETZ: When I visited TV stations around the country, I always knew I was approaching the studio when I came across scenery in the hallway. That was because most of the stations were owned by radio people who were not used to worrying about scenery. Even CBS in Grand Central Station was the same way. After a show, the sets were ruthlessly taken out and destroyed.

There were exceptions. A Fort Worth station had their studio designed to fit a herd of cattle. That's Texas for you. They planned to have real cattle auctions on the air.

BILL BODE: At WCAU in Philadelphia, the assholes that built our studios put slots in the ceiling so we could fly the flats up to the second floor. That lasted twenty minutes. Who has time to put hooks and chains on and fly things up and down? The director was yelling, "Get the goddamn set into the goddamn studio now!" It was bullshit, so we just stored them in the halls.

The sound deadening didn't work. When you put a live orchestra in you could hear right through the walls into the other studios. He also didn't believe in windows. The place was a cave. One of the announcers found himself saying the sun was shining when it was raining. He refused to renew his contract until they built him a window so he see what the weather was.

Frank Lloyd Wright came in to do a show. His only comment was the architect must have had very good kidneys, because the rest rooms were seven thousand miles from the studio.

MAXIE SOLOMON: I was with WFIL in Philadelphia when the station opened. The studio was maybe twelve by fifteen. Up the hall was a dentist. When we first put the cameras on wheels, if we had to pull the camera into the hall for a longer shot, people couldn't get through to the dentist. They would say, "What are you doing here?"

"We're doing television."

"What the hell is that?"

JACK STECK: We generally did an hour and a half at night, starting at six o'clock. We just did whatever we could think of. We had no schedule. We found eleven installments of a serial called "Ramar of the Jungle." We played each one eighty-five times by actual count. The odd thing was, they grew in the ratings each time. The kids loved knowing the lion was going to jump out at a certain moment and the guy would hit him with a lance.

That was all due to the general manager, Roger Clipp, who was a martinet, very Wharton School–oriented. I operated programs at one half the budget of any other station in town and was competitive. Clipp's reasoning was, "Anybody can be a genius with a million dollars. Your job is to be a genius without it."

TED SMITH: Before the network was delivered, some stations began to fail. This was the old chicken and egg problem. The whole system nearly went under. They were running out of funds, and they worried that it wouldn't amount to anything. Then, in 1947, there was a meeting of the National Association of Broadcasters in Atlantic City. There was a lot of talk about getting out of television, but Sarnoff gave a very inspiring speech. He said, "I haven't ever broken my promise to you. I told you you can make money on this, and you will. You can buy it cheaply now or spend a lot more money later."

BILL SWARTLEY: That was a very important speech. There's no question he got it moving when a lot of broadcasters were dragging their feet. He assured them that television had a great future, and he was right.

TED SMITH: This was a year before Berle came along. There was no question Sarnoff saved it.

BILL SWARTLEY: We knew we would be in the red for some time. Our first rate card was $50 an announcement and $250 for an hour. We couldn't charge any more because we only had five thousand sets when we got the air. The advertisers didn't buy circulation, though; they bought to be first on and for prestige. Shawmut Bank bought up almost anything. We hoped to be in the black in three years. We actually earned it back in a year and a half.

LENORE JENSEN: My husband Joe came out west after the *Los Angeles Times* promised they would build the finest TV station possible. Everybody who applies for a license claims that, but the *Times* was very anxious to have a first-rate station.

We officially went on the air on January 1, 1949, with the Rose Parade. By then, the *Times* had sold half the station to CBS, and all the noble ideas were being changed. It was no longer going to be an independent station. That broke Joe's heart, but he stayed on as chief engineer.

You can imagine how nervous everybody was before the parade began. Then at five minutes to nine, bang! They lose their picture. "What's the matter?"

Some guy with a popcorn machine had plugged into the same house where we were getting our power, and it blew a fuse. They said, "Make him stop."

"He paid twenty-five dollars to the people to get the power."

"Collect twenty-five dollars and buy popcorn."

They got it back with just seconds to spare.

MARGE GREENE: I went to a party, and the hostess had this tiny television. Nobody cared about the party. The TV was the party. We sat and watched the kids' show. Who cared what it was, we wanted to see radio with pictures. After that I decided television was where it was going to be. I quit my advertising job, marched over to WPTZ, and told them I could act and write. They asked me to write a Westinghouse commercial. I guess I did a good job because they gave me another one and another.

Then I said I wanted to act in these commercials. Well, my first one was for—say it fast—the Gerard Trust Corn Exchange Bank. I was the wife. My only line was "Well, if it works the way you say it does, let's go down tomorrow morning and open up an account at the Gerard Trust Corn Exchange Bank."

We rehearsed at the end of the studio. Then we waited for our cue. The second guest on the show was a piano player, who came in carrying extra shirts. Then he sat down and beat the hell out of this piano. I couldn't believe a human being acted like this. There was perspiration flying all over. After he was finished, they cut away to the commercial, and he ripped his clothes off down to his shorts! That was Johnny Ray, and he knocked every line out of my head. I said, "Oh, if it works like you say it does, let's go down tomorrow and open up a bank, the Gerard Crust Chorn Exchange Bank."

The bank was furious. I was fired, and I didn't act again on TV for a long time.

BOB DOYLE: Most of us who were around then are so thankful that Milton Berle didn't start selling television sets until 1948. In Washington, we did shows you wouldn't believe. The wife of the station's vice president was a Junior Leaguer. She talked him into an hour show put on by the League. They taught you how to sew. Oh, God, what a disaster, but it stayed on for a year. A lot of crap stayed on for a year.

JIM LEAMAN: We were really desperate for programming at KFI in Los Angeles. We had an idiot savant who came on. Someone would take a dollar bill out of his pocket and flash it, and he could tell you the serial numbers, or we would flash a page from the Bible in front of him, and he could tell you every word on both pages.

MARGE GREENE: PTZ found a puppeteer named Lee Dexter. He sold them a show called "Nixie the Pixie." They needed a "Nixie the Pixie" script, and I got the job.

Lee was a wild man. He worked with his wife behind the booth. It was her job to put puppets on his hands at the right time, but she would miss cues and he'd beat the hell out of her backstage. He would scream at her, and she would throw the puppet at him. He would yell at her again, and she would hit him over the head. Once a shoe came out of the booth toward the camera. If they had turned the booth around the ratings would have gone through the roof.

LENORE JENSEN: I did a cooking show on KFI. I couldn't cook, but they had a colored lady who was a wonderful cook mix everything. Monty Margetts couldn't cook either, and she was always having things happen on her show. People watched it because she was so funny.

MONTY MARGETTS: I was the only child of English parents. They traveled a good bit. We always lived in apartments and hotels, so I knew nothing about cooking. I became an actress and like a damn fool got married, and I still knew nothing about cooking. That didn't cause the divorce. Other things did.

One day a friend of mine at KFI called me and said, "Monty, can you cook?"

I said, "Is this a switch on the casting couch?"

"No, smart-ass. We want to try out some commercials. We've had a home economist doing a show, but they're so deadly dull. Would you like to try it?"

One of the commercials was for Iris Canned Peaches, so I went to the library and read everything I could about peaches. On the air, I launched forth about peaches. They said, "That probably set the *Encyclopaedia Britannica* back a few years."

Naturally, I had trouble with the can opener and sort of a comedy show was born. The upshot was, they said, "Will you do Monday through Friday, a half an hour. We've got commercials waiting for you from guys who have been watching you."

One of them was for a tuna company. My daughter remarked under my window to her little neighbor, "Mary Louise, my mother used to be a Shakespearean actress. Now she sells fish on television." That has been my accolade in life.

The show was called "Monty Margetts." They tried to call it "The Cook's Corner," but I said, "You can't call it that because there's no cook here." I'm not a dizzy dame, I'm just interested in a hell of a lot more things than cooking, and I made no secret about it. I always did my best, but nobody knew at the end of the show whether it was going to come out, least of all me. I went through a time trying to run out a Jell-O mold. That ran for ten days before I finally made it.

I had a friend I would phone in desperation. Once I asked her, "For God's sake, Helen, what does marinate mean?"

She said, "How could you live so long and learn so little?"

All sorts of things would happen. One day, I was trying to make a simple white cake before the show, and I had never made a cake in my life. It said to beat it well. I knew nothing about electric mixers, so there I was hand-beating it when an electrician came by to change a bulb. All this carbon came floating down into the batter. When he got down I hissed, "Look at that! What am I going to do?"

"Tell them it's raisins."

On the show, when I brought it out of the oven, it hadn't raised very much. I said, "Well, that's the saddest-looking cake I've ever seen, but those *are* raisins." The crew ate it anyway. They ate anything.

PRESTON STOVER: I was a cameraman at PTZ. One night they brought in a guest chef for a cooking show. He started scrambled eggs in a pan and got distracted. Suddenly, the eggs were about to burn. A stagehand ran to a workbench, picked up a can of motor oil, squirted it into the pan, and gave the eggs a quick stir. Nobody saw this except the crew. The chef took the eggs out, and the guests ate them. Nobody ever said a word.

MONTY MARGETTS: I had a sponsor that made pasta. They brought out a deep thing with a built-in colander. You boiled the pasta, then lifted out this colander to drain it. I thought this was something great.

I felt brave, so I made a sauce. I took this thing with the spaghetti in it to the sink and lifted up the colander to drain it. Then I said, "Now you toss in the sauce." I poured it over the pasta while it was still in the colander, and it all went through into the sink! Of course, my director knew goodamn well what was going to happen. He brought the camera in for a closeup.

People would write in and say, "My dear, I remember when I was first married and this happened. Try this," and I would read these different things on the air. I also got letters from people who were aghast that I would lick my fingers and things like that. I read them on the air, too. I said, "It hadn't occurred to me that I was doing anything wrong. I'm awfully sorry." Then I got letters like, "Monty, pay no attention. Tell that person to take a long walk off a short bridge."

I gave up the show after five years. By then, I was actually learning, and I couldn't have gone on being amusing much longer. I wouldn't say I got good at it. My husband, poor soul, he used to say he lived dangerously.

＊　＊　＊

GREG GARRISON: When I was a kid growing up I was a runner for the Fiaschetti Mob in Chicago. They would give me a paper bag and a dollar and say [gruffly], "Take the bag down to Thirty-fourth and Austin Street. Don't look in the bag, and take money for the trolley car before you go. You don't need no transfers."

My father was a mechanical engineer. Son of a bitch was a genius. He designed printing machines, and he had patents all over the world. For that he made a dollar a year; one of the truly great men who ever lived was my father. Hardly a week ever goes by that I don't think about him for three minutes.

He said to me one day after I got out of the Army, "I want you to come to Philadelphia Monday morning. Wear a shirt and a tie and jacket. If you don't have one buy one." My father never talked to me like that. My father had no neck, but he never touched me. My mother used to beat the shit out of me.

He told me to go see Roger Clipp. He said, "You're going to work for his television station."

"Gee, Pop . . ."

"Nine o'clock, sharp. Be there."

The station was owned by the *Philadelphia Inquirer.* My father helped design the world's largest rotogravure plant for Triangle Publications, which owned the *Inquirer*, WFIL, the *Daily Racing Form*, *TV Guide*.

Mr. Clipp sent me to see the guy in charge of the studio. After I introduced myself, he said, "Who the fuck sent ya?"

"Roger Clipp."

"Oh yeah? He never called me."

He calls, and he says, "Okay, fine, thank you." Then he says to me, "All right, here's your schedule. I want you here eight every morning. First, clean out all the wastepaper baskets. Next, go around to all the men's rooms and ladies' rooms and clean them up. I want everything done by nine. Then you work the switchboard."

He hated my guts. That's what I did for two weeks. They didn't have light stanchions. I would be standing there like a Polack holding lights. He'd go by and go [slaps himself in the belly], "Hold 'em up higher." I did that for another three weeks, and I loved it.

Three or four weeks later was Easter Sunday. The director got sick. They call me and they say, "You do it." Even before high school, I worked nightclubs around Chicago, developing pictures of the customers. I knew cameras. I knew lenses. I was taking movies when I was twelve years old, so I felt comfortable right away, and from that day on I was a director.

HERB HORTON: Greg was a natural. He had the attitude, which was the only one you could have, "You're very lucky I'm working here." He was a ballsy guy. That's why he could handle Berle, and all these people. Nobody could shake Greg.

In those days, FIL was a business in every respect, and the business was selling air time, however we did it. The sales department ran the station. Still, I liked

Maxie Solomon. Maxie was the prototype time salesman. He was the only person I've ever known who could walk down the boardwalk in Atlantic City with his wife on one arm and his girlfriend on the other.

MAXIE SOLOMON: I was only only five one and a half, and everybody called me the "Big Doctor." I had fun. One night a guy said to me, "There's only one good spot, Tuesday night right before Berle."

I said, "I'll give you that spot if you could buy it."

"I'll take it." He calls me the next morning. "My spot wasn't on."

I said, "Yes, it was. It was on my station."

"But you don't carry Berle."

I said, "I never said we carried Berle, but your spot was on immediately preceding Berle." He wasn't angry. I put it down as a no-charge.

At FIL, we were always a poor third, so when the clients wanted to talk ratings, I would tell them jokes. When I got through with the jokes they forgot what they asked me.

One day Roger Clipp told me that CAU and PTZ are tied for first place. I said, "Let's promote that. If they are both in first, it's the first time we're ever in second place!"

GREG GARRISON: Paul Mowry showed up one day from ABC, and he said, "You want to go to work for us?"

"Sure."

He said, "You can go to New York or Chicago." I picked Chicago because it was going to be six months to a year before the outlet in New York got going, and Chicago was really rolling. I learned my trade there. Fifteen years ago, I had four series on the air at the same time, and I directed and produced all four of them. I was able to do that because of my experience in Chicago. I was directing between thirty-five and forty shows a week. I did the news, sports, an hour variety show. I also did "Super Circus," which was the big show on the schedule. Mike Wallace was the announcer. I worked with Mike in radio before the war. I was a kid then, and he was like a big brother to me.

MIKE WALLACE: I knew Greg before the war, long before he came out to Chicago the second time. He was a kid named Harvin Ginsberg. He was my copyboy on "The Air Edition of the *Chicago Sun*." He was just this dirty-nailed teenager, a really good kid, willing to work but utterly unschooled. After a while, he departed for the Army. As far as we knew he had been captured by the Germans, and he was in a stalag and he had died.

GREG GARRISON: The war is over. I'm in New York, Philadelphia, and now Chicago. I come up with an idea for a show called "Standby for Crime." The guy who plays Inspector Webb can't memorize his lines. He once fucks up a show so badly that at the end I take the card that reads "produced and directed by Greg Garrison" and rip it up. He's fired. The next day, I call some- one and say, "Listen, find Mike Wallace and a few other people for an audition."

I go out and I buy a baseball hat as a disguise. I get a cigar, stick it in my mouth. I never smoked a cigar in my life. I'm sitting there as Mike walks in along with everybody else. [He mimes their slow recognition of each other.] We stood up, and we cried, and nobody knew why.

He got the job. Then I got him a job as a commercial announcer on "Super Circus." He didn't want to be ringmaster because that was a schmuck job.

One day I'm looking at *Billboard* magazine, and I see TOM KATZ AND HIS FIVE BABY ELEPHANTS CLOSE IN ST. LOUIS ON MAY 6TH AND ARE OPENING UP AT THE MILWAUKEE SHOWGROUNDS ON MAY 15TH. They gotta go through Chicago. "Mr. Katz, how do you do, my name is Garrison. I'm with WENR. We have 'Super Circus,' the television show."

[In a very, very gruff monotone] "What the fuck is this 'Super Coicus' tele- vision show. Whattayou? Whattayou kiddin' me, what coicus? What, you gotta coicus on television? You're hoitin' my fuckin' livelihood. Is that what ya tryin' to tell me? Ya gonna put a fuckin' circus up?"

"No, sir, we're just trying to get . . ." Anyway, to cut around the bullshit, I booked the act. At rehearsal, he's standin' in the wings of the Civic Opera House. He's wearing a big rubber glove, and he's standin' behind the elephants and he's goin' into each one and *Pushhhht* [makes the motion of extending his arm and pulling it back five times]. I'm watching this, and I don't dare say, "What the fuck are ya doin'? You gettin' ya fuckin' nuts off goin' through an el- ephant's ass?"

The assistant says to me, "He cleans 'em out so they don't do anything on stage."

"Fine." [Screams] I'M NOT SMART ENOUGH TO SAY, "WHY DOESN'T HE DO IT RIGHT BEFORE THE SHOW?" I'M ASSUMING HE'S GONNA DO IT BEFORE THE SHOW, RIGHT?

We start the show live, *boom, bing, da, da, bing, bing.* A lion, a tiger, an acro- batic team, "And now, ladies and gentlemen, here is Mary Hartline and the Super Circus Orchestra." Mary Hartline is a girl about twenty-four years old who has the biggest pair of tits on a white girl I have ever seen [extends his arms]. Unbelievable, and a dingbat, but she married some of the richest men in America, five husbands.

We decided that she should follow the elephants, so out come the elephants, and they go *badabib badabing badabing badabing. Bang!* One elephant starts to take a crap. And when one elephant starts to take a crap, on cue, five baby elephants start crapping and pissing all over the fucking ring.

"AND NOW, LADIES AND GENTLEMEN, MARY HARTLINE." Out she comes, and she's leading the whole fucking orchestra right through the shit. She falls right on her ass. She gets up, and she's covered.

MIKE WALLACE: The smell of elephant shit was heavy in the hall. Now the doors open and the kids come running down and they begin to smell it themselves, and nobody wants to sit in the first ten rows.

Greg goes out to shovel the shit. Now, instead of being eighteen inches deep, the shit is a mere nine inches deep, and I have to do a Peter Pan Peanut Butter commercial. I'm not on camera, although the boy is. I say, "Watch little Tommy as he spreads Peter Pan Crunchy Peanut Butter on that piece of bread. Watch as he bites into that luscious Peter Pan Peanut Butter." The kid bites into it, smells the shit, and begins to cry.

GREG GARRISON: Mike yells, "Jesus Christ!" With this, the kid turns and runs across the stage, falls in the elephant shit, and starts bawling again.

KARL WEGER: Murphy's Law was invented to describe what was going on them. We just took it for granted because it happened so regularly.

HERB HORTON: When Israel became a state, FIL sent a camera crew up to Boston to shoot a freighter that was sailing under the Israeli flag. We got a recording of the "Boston Cadre March" to use over the picture. The whole thing was beautiful until they cut to the shot of the flag as it went up the mast, and the music changed to eight bars of "Onward Christian Soldiers."

Shortly after that, we made arrangements with the Catholic Congress to pick up their annual convention at Convention Hall. As soon as they booked it, my boss said, "Look, after this Israeli thing, I want you to do this, but I want it flawless."

They gave me the name of a priest who would help out. We went over how it worked. Then he said, "By the way, the whole ceremony is in Latin. Do you understand it?"

"Me, a Methodist? We gotta sit down and talk."

I told him that he would have to tell me what was coming up so I could punch up the right buttons. Well, we did the show. For an hour and a half it went perfectly. We got the nuns with their hands crossed on the Bibles. It was splendid. Then Cardinal Doherty came in, and my helpful priest says, "It's very important that every time the Cardinal crosses himself, we get a picture of it."

"Okay. Just punch me on the arm when he's gonna do it, and I'll punch up Camera One."

Great. He punches me on the arm. I take the shot. The priest says, "Watch, the Cardinal is gonna cross himself." Bump, I punch up Camera One. This goes on for ten minutes and everything is beautiful. He says, "Can you get closer?"

So we flip the lenses, and I get a real headshot of the Cardinal. Now, I start having fun with my friend, because I am beating him to the punch. When I see the Cardinal's hand come up, I punch the picture up. Now, I see his hand come up, and I punch it up, and I am mesmerized because this time the Cardinal takes his right finger and puts it up his nose. He takes out a couple of boogies and flicks them with his finger. Finally, I call to Camera Three, but he is laying on the floor hysterical. My priest friend is muttering something. He's got his beads out.

When we get off the air, I walk out to the truck, and there is the priest standing there in utter shock. His hair is standing on end, and he is in full sweat. He grabs me by the arm, and he says, "Herb, we're gonna go talk to the Cardinal, and you're going to tell him how this happened."

We had a room set up for all the dignitaries to watch the program. We go in, and there are all the priests standing there mimicking the Cardinal, who is standing in front of them laughing! He says, "Well, that just shows you I am human."

I spoke to Clipp after the show, and he said, "That was great. I've gotten so many calls from the church. They say they finally got something on the old man."

RUDY BRETZ: The most interesting program experiment was done on WCAU in Philadelphia. It was a daily western, live, half an hour five days a week. It was called "Action in the Afternoon." I went down there and watched them do it.

The station was on the outskirts of town. They had a big lot out back where they built a replica of this town. The interior shots were done in the studio. It was the same cast each day. If they didn't like an actor, they would eliminate him from the script by shooting him.

BILL BODE: Charlie Vanda created that show. He ran WCAU. He was forever going to New York to pitch more shows. In those days, the local stations fed many programs to the network, which was a gargantuan thing that required a lot of product. At one point, WCAU fed nine network shows a week.

One day he was up there pitching three or four other shows. They didn't like them, and they said, "What else have you got?"

He didn't have anything, so on the spot he came up with this idea for a live outdoor western set in a town called Huberle after [CBS executives] Hubbell Robinson and Harry Ommerlee. He *knew* how to sell. They said, "Okay, feed us a pilot."

We had three or four weeks to get the pilot together. Our whole budget was $6,900 a week. This was for five shows. Under that kind of pressure, the writers were going to their old script trunks for their old plots. We were up to midnight sharpening up the scenes. Sometimes, we would literally have runners taking pages from the writers to the mimeograph machine. Once I simply rewrote *Macbeth*, and it worked fine, great plot.

JAMES HIRSCHFELD: I was an assistant director on the show. Outside the studio, there was nothing on Cityline Avenue besides CAU, so we could shoot the exteriors and just get trees in the background.

BILL BODE: There was a natural creek, and in the parking lot they put mockups of the bar, the jail, and the newspaper office.

JOHN ZACHERLE: They got horses from a local riding academy. We did the chases live. The lot was at least a hundred yards long. You could do a chase that disappeared up into the hills.

BILL BODE: You never knew with the horses, though. At the end of one episode when the baddies had ridden out of town, our hero went to the sheriff and said, "Where did they go?"

He said, "Thataway."

Jack jumped on his horse to race after them, but the horse *walked* out of town.

JOHN ZACHERLE: Occasionally, the camera would pick up an airplane passing overhead or a bus would be seen through the trees. It kind of ruined the illusion of being in 1884.

I started out as an extra on the show. Eventually, I got some starring roles. Sometimes we played more than one role on a show. You'd do a scene, put on a beard, and you were somebody else.

JAMES HIRSCHFELD: Sound was the biggest problem. The mikes had to be hidden in the hitching posts along the street. You had to walk over to the hitching post to do a scene.

JOHN ZACHERLE: They were also in tree stumps. Sometimes, a mike would go out and you would have to run and die in another place. They would tell you, "Don't die here! Die over there!"

BILL BODE: Once, there was a horrendous sound over the air. We couldn't figure it out until we saw a horse biting one of the microphones at a hitching post.

JAMES HIRSCHFELD: We did a hanging scene which got scary when the actor nearly got hung. We had to cut away and quickly cut him down. You shouldn't hang somebody on live TV because you can't get off.

BILL BODE: We all lost five years of our lives working on the show. Between casting, scripting, staging, it was almost impossible to do. We weren't that good for the first six months. We were damn good the last six months.

DOC LIVINGSTON: We were all learning. At KFI, it was like the studio was on fire. You didn't mind working long hours. You woke up in the morning, and you were ready to go to work. Each of us had three or four shows every day. The high creativity was unrestricted by the accountants and lawyers who came later.

BUD COLE: While we didn't have the budgets of some of the New York shows, we were in some cases better than the shows that were on the network, but our stuff never saw the light of day. When you did a local show in New York, the execs saw them, but they didn't see the shows that were being done out here.

One day this tall, European-looking guy walks into my office. He says his name is Renzo Cesano and he's got this act called "The Continental," which he had done on the radio up in San Francisco. He played a romantic foreigner who talks to his girlfriend. The gimmick is you never see the girl. She's the camera. All you see is The Continental making love to the camera.

I knew right away it was a big fucking idea. This was the first true television show; it took advantage of what television really was instead of the warmed-over crap they had on the air. I ran down to my boss, and I said, "He'll either be the biggest fuckin' thing that ever happened on television or he'll be the biggest bomb. I personally think it'll be the former."

The secret to the show was the illusion. The woman at home thinks that when he opens that door and says, "Come in, darling," and the camera goes in, and he lights her cigarette and hands her a glass of champagne, that broad is sittin' at home thinking that he's with her and he's gonna lay her.

The show generated tons of publicity. Durante, Berle, every one of them did him or had him on as a guest. Letters poured in from love-starved women. I still have one from a truck driver that says

> *Dear Continental, I used to come off the road, having been gone 48 hours or a week. I kick off my shoes, sit around in my underwear and have a couple of beers and wait for my wife to fix dinner. Now, I have to wear a shirt and tie. We have to have the goddamned candlelight and champagne. You've ruined my life.*

BILL SWARTLEY: In the early days you had to create a lot of programming because it wasn't coming down the line. Different stations approach that in different ways. Westinghouse stations traditionally did a lot of local programming and got a lot of awards for it. Still, when we got those network shows, which were usually of superior quality, we were glad to have them, and we found another outlet for our programming.

RUDY BRETZ: Much of the local programming was an effort to strike a common denominator. They had to make it salable, but forget that baloney about television being an art form. That didn't interest anybody who was in charge. I was interested, but I wasn't in charge.

The FCC would specify that the stations had to do a certain amount of public service broadcasting. The stations would put it on in the middle of the night or anyplace they felt it would do the least harm, because they were sure it was going to lose audience, and in most cases it probably did.

CAL JONES: We were very proud of a show at PTZ called "Telerama." It was kind of a low-budget "60 Minutes." We went behind the scenes to watch how they got the *Philadelphia Inquirer* out from midnight to three A. M. We photographed a peace meeting between youth gangs. I found out about it from Frank Rizzo, who was a twenty-six-year-old police inspector. He used to tip me off to everything that was going on in town.

ED STASHEFF: At WPIX, we had a show called "Television Chapel." We did different religious services each Sunday. PIX poured money into the show after they had trouble getting their license. The *Daily News* owned the station, and their editorial writer, John O'Donnell, was probably the most bigoted editorial writer journalism has ever known. The American Jewish Congress and the Anti-Defamation League fought the *News* getting a TV license. The FCC granted it, but only for a year, not three, and they had to prove that far from being anti-semitic, they would provide the most ecumenical religious programming you ever saw.

They leaned over backwards. They made no secret of why they did it. Then, at the end of their first year, they got their three-year license, and the budget for our programming went from $80,000 to $40,000.

CAL JONES: If you look at the most prosperous television station in any market, I guarantee you that that guy was number one on public service. For Westinghouse stations, your budget was never penalized for any dollar you spent on public service because they believed public service was good business. All the Westinghouse stations, Boston and Philadelphia, were king of the hill because of their public service attitude.

RUDY BRETZ: There were very few local dramatic productions. You need a day in a studio for each show, and hell, they've got sixteen other shows to do that one day.

BILL SWARTLEY: We found out early in the game that a whole lot of live drama was not gonna pay off. A sponsor would much rather go for star value of a movie when movies became available. The very first film package was the Alexander Korda package. Shawmut Bank immediately agreed to sponsor it. We dropped a popular local variety show called "Swan Boat" when the films were made available. We lost some audience for a while, but film eventually brought in more audience than we had had.

BILL BODE: Charlie Vanda, always out for the buck, knew of these two photographers who went to Africa and filmed these fantastic animal battles, lions fighting tigers, stuff like that. Charlie made a deal for their unedited footage, from which we discovered that those animals never fought each other willingly. They'd catch them and throw them into a pit they couldn't get out of, horrible stuff.

By editing those films and splicing in our own inserts, Charlie created a show called "The Adventurer." We shot outside from the ground up so all you saw were trees and sky. Then we put an actor named Piggy Barnes in this adventurer's uniform with a pith helmet, and he went on these "adventures." He would push through the trees and say things like "Ny eeria nieeria acumba," which he supposedly picked up from the natives. Then as he pointed, we would cut to the films.

After that we began getting free films from everywhere. One was about tuna fishing. We cut out everything but the fishing. I put Piggy in a mockup of a boat, and we shot up at him fishing. When he didn't fight enough with the fish, I grabbed the line and fought the son of a bitch. I made him reel me in. Then I would run like hell and take the line away from him.

JACK STECK: Bob Horn was a disk jockey who we hired to do a television show at WFIL. He just played these musical film shorts, and it wasn't drawing. At the same time, two local deejays were on PEN radio, playing records, but they would also invite kids in the afternoon to come and watch the show. Finally they said, "'Why don't you kids dance while we're doing this?"

Horn picked the idea up and brought it to us. We were a few blocks from two Catholic schools. We deliberately put this show on after their classes, and we told them they could come dance on TV. They flocked over, and the show was a hit from the beginning. The record industry loved it. Their acts could appear on the show, and they gladly lip-synched to the records. We had to do it that way. Otherwise, we would have had to hire a band.

Then Horn got involved with some of the kids on the show, and we had to fire him. He wasn't entirely to blame, and I felt sorry for him. For the next six months we did it with Tony Mammorelli, but the station manager hated Italians, so we had a meeting. Roger Clipp asked our production manager, "Who should get the show?" Now, I auditioned Dick Clark, and had used him on radio for a while. The production managed suggested Dick, and that was it.

A couple of years later, ABC was looking for a cheap show to put on in the afternoons. Dick went over to New York and sold them the idea. They just changed the title from "Bandstand" to "American Bandstand."

Horn ended up working at an Austin radio station under the names Charles Adams. Then a tourist going through town recognized him and called the station and they fired him. He died very shortly thereafter. He didn't have a dime.

*   *   *

HAROLD PANNEPACKER: We always had hangers-on, kids who wanted to be in the business. There was one kid who spent so much time in our studios everybody thought he worked there. One day we hired somebody new. He said to the boss, "Why would you hire somebody else? I'm here, and I want a job."

We said, "We thought you worked here." That kid was Andy McKay.

JACK KENNEDY: Ernie Kovacs was a big talent, but he had Andy who was a genius at figuring out ludicrous situations for him. Andy was more Kovacs than Kovacs. When Ernie would fill the glass and the glass would slide back and forth, that was Andy. He lived for gimmicks and prop shtick. He'd spend hours rooting around prop closets and trunks to come up with sight gags.

ANDY MCKAY: In January 1950, Ernie came in to audition as host of a fashion show called "Pick Your Ideal." The others that came in were radio people in three-button suits. Ernie was dressed in a barrel held up by suspenders. He had no clothes on except his shorts. He broke us up.

He did that show, and then he did a cooking show called "Deadline for Dinner." It was a straight show, but Ernie played it anything but straight. The cook was a regular chef named Albert Mathis. It was a tossup who was funnier, Kovacs or Mathis. Sometimes, they forgot what was being cooked.

But the best show Ernie ever did was "Three to Get Ready." It was on Monday through Friday from seven-thirty to nine in the morning.

CAL JONES: I did the first "Three to Get Ready" and then Joe Behar did the show. The idea was "turn on Channel Three and get ready to go to work." It turned into a vehicle for Ernie.

ANDY MCKAY: The set was a mish-mash of stuff from other shows. There was a piece of a mansion, a piece of farmland, a moon painted on a flat. Ernie sat at desk with all this behind him, and he would give the weather, time, news, and do bits. Norman Brooks would do the news in front of an ordinary flat. If Norman said it was raining, Ernie would climb up on a ladder behind the flat and drop water on Norman's head.

He would talk to the cameraman or the mike boom operator. He'd go inside the control room and play with the buttons or pull out a deck of cards and play with the director—during the show! The cameramen had no choice but to follow him. The director was usually at a loss trying to outguess Ernie, "What's he gonna do next?" It was all ad-lib.

TRIGVE LUND: There was absolutely no rehearsal. He walked in about ten minutes prior to the show, sat down and started talking. When I stage-managed, he would say, "Hey, Trigger, what are ya doin' tonight?" And I would get out and talk to him for a while. For this doughnut commercial, a guy would deliver fresh doughnuts every morning. He would just come onto the set with them, and Ernie would take one, offer me a doughnut and ask me if I liked them.

Sometimes he would show up late. Once, we started without him and we were wondering where he was. We kept calling his apartment, thinking he was asleep. We did about fifteen minutes of the show, and then he strolls in and says, "Hey, you guys did a pretty good job. I was home watching."

JOE BEHAR: He was constantly late. We would yell at him, but it didn't do any good. One day to embarrass him I took a zoom lens and pointed it out the window, and we took a shot of him coming up the street to show everybody that it was two minutes after seven and he was just showing up. That became such a big hit that we started to do stuff like that on purpose.

ANDY MCKAY: We did all kinds of bits out in the street. The problem was we couldn't get a mike out there, so we held up large cards with the dialogue written on them like silent movies.

KARL WEGER: Ernie would come up the street with a big papier-mâché version of the RCA Victor dog. Sometimes, he put it down beside a fire hydrant. He paid the driver of a horse-drawn trash wagon to allow him to drive it.

JOE BEHAR: They were excavating the parking lot, and this was sort of an ethnic slur, we dressed up someone as a Chinaman, and he came out of the hole. In theory they were digging so far, they dug all the way to China.

CAL JONES: We dressed Ernie in a gorilla suit and let him run into restaurants with this suit on. We were adventurous kids having fun, and we were encouraged to do different things. I never saw that happen in New York when they got him up there. They didn't know what to do with him.

KARL WEGER: Ostensibly, I was lightning the show, but I did a little bit of everything. I had a Crosley station wagon, which was smaller than an Austin. One day, Ernie looked at it and said, "How many people can you get in that?"

I said, "Two in the front and maybe one in the back."

"What happens if you take the seats out except for the driver's seat?"

"I don't know. Why?"

"I'd like to get six or eight people in that."

We did it. I dressed as a chauffeur. Ernie was in the back with six others dressed up formally like ambassadors with sashes across their chests. We drove into the lot. Andy rolled out a red carpet. I got out, went around, and opened the door, and one by one these guys got out and lined up alongside the car. Finally, Ernie came out puffing his cigar.

JACK KENNEDY: Edie [Adams] added a lot to the show. He would trash her act when she sang, people falling off the piano benches, things like that, but she learned to deal with this clown, and she was very good for him.

ANDY MCKAY: Ernie once put out a plea on the air, "We've got a fifteen dollar a week budget. We're very low on props. Anything around the house you don't want, send it in." Immediately, the lobby was filled with all sorts of bric-a-brac, fishing poles, old clothing, hats, canes. A lady sent a life-sized doll that Ernie dubbed "Gertrude." She became our mascot.

TRIG LUND: Gertrude had a terrible life. He would throw her up into the rafters or onto the light bridge. Sometimes he would climb up to the catwalk with her and toss her off while the soundman would throw in a scream or a flushing toilet.

ANDY MCKAY: I had a wagon where I kept all the props. One of them was a dead fish that had been mounted. I took it off the mounting board, and if I thought Ernie was going long, I would throw the fish at him.

We were always going to the thrift shops or the Salvation Army to look for props. I picked up the Percy Dovetonsils glasses for a dime in a novelty shop. I just thought, "These will be great for Ernie." A poet named Ted Malone was the inspiration for Percy Dovetonsils. He had a radio show called "Between the Bookends." Percy's hairdo was suggested by a man named Mr. John, who designed ladies' hats.

KARL WEGER: I was playing around on my own when I developed the "Image Inverter."

ANDY MCKAY: Karl Weger was very inventive. He took out the ends of a Campbell's Soup can and put in a couple of mirrors at an angle. Then he attached this gizmo onto a three-inch camera lens. By turning it you would invert the picture. We could actually rotate Ernie upside down.

ANDY MCKAY: With that we had Ernie vacuum the ceiling. That inverted lens was really the precursor of the tilted table routines that Ernie later made famous in New York and Hollywood.

JOE BEHAR: That show was complete insanity, but it got such big ratings, they didn't care what we did.

ANDY MCKAY: Philadelphia did not carry the "Today" show because we were on the air the same time.

CAL JONES: I came over to the Architects' Building one morning. Pat Weaver was sitting in the lobby. He was there to read the riot act to the station manager. "Get that son of a bitch off the air and take the 'Today' show. The whole future of the show is riding on your clearing Philadelphia," and we had to do it. I'm sure they threatened to take away our affiliation.

MARGE GREENE: Ernie's morning show was very successful, but he didn't have to pay attention to the practicalities and time factors because he had two full hours, and it wasn't network. He could take twenty minutes to build a horse if he wanted.

It was Cal Jones who came to me and said, "We're creating a show for him on the network, and I would like you to be part of it as an actress." I said sure. Ernie always denied any part in creating the format for "Kovacs on the Corner." People wrote that it was the worst thing that happened to Ernie when these executives who didn't know anything foisted the Fred Allen format on him. Let me tell you, you didn't push anything on Ernie. He did what he wanted to do.

The idea was that he would emerge from the door, and everything would happen on the block. When the show hit the air, it was a horror. There was no continuity to it. Ernie had a wonderful imagination, but he was a punster. A pun lasts for twenty seconds. This was a thirty-minute show. They called a big meeting in New York. Then I got a call to meet with Cal Jones. He said, "Marge, Ernie's not the writer anymore. We think you can pull this show off."

Come Monday morning there was a big meeting, Ernie and Edie, myself, Cal, and a few others. Ernie walked in, eyes down, didn't say a word. He had already been told. Cal announced that I was now the writer of the show, and everybody looked down. We didn't know what to say. Then he said, "All right, Marge, why don't you pass around the scripts."

Ernie took the script and ripped it into a hundred pieces and threw it up in the air. We all sat there in complete shock. Cal said, "Ernie, may I see you outside for a moment?"

They went out, and they came back, and he said, "Okay, Marge, will you give Ernie another script?"

CAL JONES: I told Ernie, "We've got a whole new set of responsibilities. It's not 'Three to Get Ready.' If we do it right, everybody's gonna benefit, mostly you," but it was like pulling teeth. He was paranoid about trusting other people's creative ability. There was also an "I know better" attitude.

MARGE GREENE: From that moment on, there was absolute hatred for me. I became a nonperson to Ernie and Edie. The scripts were handed to them, and I can still hear him say, "Just lay it over there. I'll look at it when I'm ready."

The word was "unprofessional." He wouldn't rehearse. When he had to work with me he played it, but he didn't give me anything. After a while he wouldn't even act. In one bit I was supposed to blow up his closet to get to his money box. I had grease all over me. Now, Ernie knew what would happen, but he still wore one of his expensive suits. After the explosion, I grabbed his suit. He went out of character. He pushed me, and said, "Get away, look at my suit." He just walked off. We had to go to music. No one could believe such unprofessional behavior.

CAL JONES: The station manager finally said, "We're not gonna renew his contract." Actually, his exact words were, "You can fuck Sears and Roebuck only once."

There was another thing that really screwed Ernie with all of us. We were missing some things from our desks. Also, papers were looked at and files were opened. We alerted the security people. When it happened again, we asked the guard who had been upstairs the night before, and he said, "Mr. Kovacs."

Ernie did not have an office in our building. We decided he had been looking for memoranda that would confirm his suspicions that everybody was out to get him. He was paid off before the conclusion of his contract. The show was over. We tried to build a stable situation on an unstable star, and you just couldn't do it.

MARGE GREENE: I had to come up with a script for the last show. I decided to say we're all going on vacation. I joked to Ernie on the air about the Scotch being very frugal. I said, "I'm goin' somewhere, Ernie, but I'm not payin' a penny."

I explained how my friends were going to nail me in a coffin and put me aboard the ship. Then a balsa-wood coffin was wheeled in. I got in. He closed the lid, and he had a hammer and a few nails. We didn't know it, but he had a bunch of nails in his pocket, and he starts pounding them in. He was supposed to put three in around the edges, but he is pounding, and the nails are coming in all around me. He wouldn't stop. He went insane! I started to scream because I realized something was wrong. Cal started yelling, "My God, he's gonna kill her. The nails are going to go through her face."

Then I thought, "That son of a bitch," and I stopped screaming. Now, he wondered, "Did I hit her?"

They never finished the show. It went off the air while he was screaming at me, "Have a good time in Scotland," and pounding nails into the coffin.

Cal was screaming, "Is she dead? Get her to say something."

I didn't say anything. Ernie panicked. He yelled, "Are you all right in there?" I wouldn't answer. Cal and the others came down to the floor. Ernie realized he went too far. I jumped out of there, and grabbed him around the neck. Cal pulled me away. My husband was coming out of the control room to knock Ernie through the scenery, but somebody held him back.

Ernie later said that he took a hammer and destroyed the set, but that's not true. They would have killed him. Everybody thought he had gone off his marbles, and they just hated him for what he did. There was a big party afterward at Johnnie's bar. Ernie and Edie came, but nobody sat with them. They ate and left.

＊   ＊   ＊

GREG GARRISON: When I was in Chicago, two guys would come by the studio. One was a little guy from New York, who wore a funny hairpiece. Another one was Fred Allen. They would ask me why I did what I did. I tried to explain while I sat and looked into Fred Allen's eyes, and I would go, "Yes, Fred," because he kept saying, "Please call me Fred." Inside I'm going, IT'S FRED ALLEN AND HE'S TALKING TO ME. I CAN'T STAND IT, AND HE'S CALLING ME GREG; GOD, POP, WHERE ARE YOU? CAN YOU HEAR THIS! "Yes, Fred, that's very interesting."

Then I get a call from Pat Weaver. He says to me, "When's your day off?"

"Thursday."

"Can you fly to New York and meet me in my office at NBC on Thursday afternoon?"

"*Babababababa.* Okay."

I was making three hundred bucks a week. I had to borrow the money for my ticket. I fly to New York. I go up to his office. He puts his arm around me and he gives me a hug. I say to myself, "Jesus Christ, what a nice man. He's chairman of the board of NBC. He runs the world, and he's patting me on the head."

He says, "We're going up the street, here. C'mon."

We got downstairs and get into a limousine, which is a block long. I never sat in a limousine in my life. We go to the City Center building, take the elevator up to the fifth floor, go inside into an office, and there's this little man that's been coming to Chicago, and he stands up and he says, "Hello, son, I'm glad you're going to do our show."

"What show?"

Weaver said, "I haven't told him yet."

The man was Max Liebman, and the show was "Show of Shows."

MARGE GREENE: When Lucy came on, someone decided PTZ ought to have a show like that in the afternoon, so I created a five-day-a-week domestic show called "Marge and Fred." We were an average couple with a dog who lived in an apartment.

We didn't have time to rehearse or memorize lines, so we never used a script. There was never one word written. DuMont fell in love with the show and took me to New York and it was a big success for them.

BOB DOYLE: Harry Truman helped me an awful lot. I put him on television the first time he ever went on, at the Mayflower in Washington in 1947. People were sitting before a long table. Margaret was there, sitting way down below the salt. She fell asleep, and the whole crew wanted me to get a shot of it on TV.

I said, "Nah, it's not fair. She wasn't elected to anything." I'd be fired for that today. About ten days later, Truman's secretary called me, "The boss wants to see you."

"What have I done?"

"Just go in to see him."

I walked in, and the president said, "I want to thank you."

Phew. "For what?" I didn't know what he was talking about.

"You didn't take a picture of my baby."

I laughed and said, "No, I didn't think I should."

He said thank you again. A few weeks later, Sig Mickelson, who was the vice president of CBS News, asked me, "What have you done? It's been intimated to us that whenever the president goes on it would be okay with him if you were the director."

I never told him why.

BILL BODE: In the late fifties, the business moved from New York to Hollywood when they went to film. As soon as Hollywood could produce the stuff—and reruns came in with films—they just locked us out of the network.

CAL JONES: PTZ became an O & O [network-owned and -operated station], which are somewhat sterile when it comes to programming innovation. They're all stepping stones for people going into the network, and you don't go onto the network by people risking capital on local programming. That would piss them off.

TRIG LUND: I hated to leave Philadelphia, but when Ernie decided to go to New York, it took me five minutes to give him an answer. I had a little old Mercury car, and I filled it up with all of our props. Andy and I drove up in front of CBS on Madison Avenue. Here we were, our first time in New York and in this old heap full of garbage. The doorman comes up with this long coat and big hat, and he says, "Whattya doin' here?"

"We're movin' in. We're with the Ernie Kovacs show."

"Who zat?"

Finally, he let us up. We unloaded all this crazy stuff, things like Gertrude. They couldn't believe it.

ANDY MCKAY: You have to get New York out of your system. If you don't go to New York, you're going nowhere. I tagged along with the right guy. I knew Ernie had it. He always tried to outdo himself with fresh material. I used to say, "Ernie, why don't you give Edie another vocal or give Eddie [Hatrack] some time on the piano to stretch the material?"

He would put his two hands on my shoulder and say, "Nothing in moderation, my boy, nothing in moderation."

It is very rare that you come across a person like that. He was somehow destined to do what he did do. He always lived according to tomorrow, never today. That was Ernie. When we first got to CBS we went up to the ninth floor. He opens the window and he hollers down below, "New York, I ain't afraid of you."

KTLA:
PROMISE FULFILLED

There was a company, Hoffman Television, which built TV sets in the early days. They came to KTLA with a commercial about the "easy tuning" Hoffman Television. Easy tuning was the switch from channel to channel. Klaus refused to accept the commercial because, he says, "People aren't ever going to change from Channel Five. I'm not gonna carry the commercial."

—BILL WELSH

In 1939, Klaus Landsberg was a rising star in Allen B. DuMont's New Jersey stables when Paramount offered him the same advice that Horace Greeley proffered five score years before. It had to do with following the setting sun.

One wonders about the fate of Greeley's young charge, but of Landsberg one need only switch on Los Angeles's Channel Five to find KTLA, the country's greatest independent station and a monument to the skill, brilliance, and sheer audacity of a German immigrant who literally gave his life to the new medium.

For Landsberg, the journey west began in 1937 when he was twenty-one and fled Germany rather than turn over a radar patent to the Third Reich. Landsberg arrived in America in 1938. He worked briefly for Philo Farnsworth before moving on to RCA in New York and then to DuMont. At the time, Paramount was buying into television with the idea of promoting its films. The company not only co-owned the DuMont station but also had TV licenses in Chicago and Los Angeles. Bill Eddy, given the choice of running either of the two, took the former. That left KTLA for Landsberg.

The station began operating experimentally as W6XYZ in 1941. It went commercial with its new KTLA call letters on January 22, 1947. The gala opening was hosted by Bob Hope, who was so nervous he flubbed his lines even though he was reading them off a script. Since there was no network service to the coast, the station had to rely on Landsberg's own programming sense to attract viewers. That he succeeded beyond anyone's expectations is not only a tribute to him, but also to the notion that through creative local programming and public service, an independent station could compete commercially and artistically with the networks.

During Landsberg's tenure, it wasn't unusual for KTLA to carry eight of the top ten programs in the ratings. Even after the coaxial cable finally touched both coasts in 1951, KTLA had twenty-two of the top twenty-seven shows in the Tele-Que ratings.

KTLA flourished because Landsberg promoted local talent. He liked upbeat musical variety shows, and since his viewers agreed with him, he gave them their fill. There was Ina Ray Hutton and Her All-Girl Orchestra, Harry Owens and his Royal Hawaiians, Spade Cooley's Western Swing show, and Lawrence Welk. To every show he attached a host who was also local favorite, so it wasn't just wrestling, it was Dick Lane and wrestling or Dick Lane hosting Roller Derby. Who cared if ninety-nine percent of the country never heard of Dick Lane, the people of Los Angeles had, and they loved him.

He also had an eye for odder fare, whether it was Bob Clampett's puppet show "Time for Beany" or Bud Stefan's "Yer Ole Buddy," an often hilarious guide to the machinations of a television studio. Landsberg, an Olympic-level skater, also produced the first and only weekly variety show on ice—"Frosty Frolics." The organist Korla Pandit was another curiosity. Pandit, a native of India, never spoke a word during any of his nine hundred shows. Instead, he would play the organ wearing a jeweled turban, while superimposed clouds floated behind his head.

Landsberg really left his mark in news coverage. "The most outstanding of the contributions that television can be expected to make to further democracy . . . will be its unique usefulness as a means of public information," he said.

This wasn't just lip service. It was Landsberg's desire that when breaking news occurred in Los Angeles, viewers would automatically turn to Channel Five for the story. They did, starting on April 27, 1949, when a four-and-a-half-year-old girl named Kathy Fiscus fell some 237 feet into a large pipe near her home in San Marino. Landsberg immediately ordered his remote crews out to the site. There, Stan Chambers and Bill Welsh broadcast uninterrupted for twenty-seven and a half hours straight until the girl's lifeless body was brought to the surface. Los Angeles television was never the same again. No longer was it considered merely an entertainment tool. More than anything, the Kathy Fiscus tragedy demonstrated television's powerful ability to captivate and unite a community around a news story.

Another event also demonstrated Landsberg's amazing zeal. On April 22, 1952, the Atomic Energy Commission exploded an atomic bomb at its Nevada testing site. Only three weeks before, Landsberg had sought and received permission to telecast the blast live. To do that, he and his crew needed to set up a 275-mile relay through the desert and over the treacherous Charleston Mountains, a process the Bell Telephone company said would take six to eight months. When the connection was made, they had one chance to get it right;

there were no second takes with atomic explosions. It did work, and the broadcast was one of the most stunning achievements in television history.

What is even more remarkable is that Landsberg was putting in twenty-two-hour days to get the telecast ready while being treated for cancer. Over the next four years, his health was buttressed only by his obstinate nature. He was often driven by ambulance to work, and then back to the hospital when shooting was completed. His body finally gave out in 1956. He was forty.

In 1958, the station bought the nation's first telecopter. A flying remote was a natural in a traffic-choked city, but it was during the Watts riots that its coverage earned the station a Peabody Award. In 1992, with Stan Chambers aboard, the copter captured some of the fiercest riot footage in the wake of the Rodney King verdict. Thirty-six years after his death, Landsberg's spirit still permeated the station. Los Angelinos should be grateful.

EDDIE RESNICK: Klaus's first studio was the size of a big living room. It was just off the Paramount lot. He only had himself and two kids out of school. He hired me to push the cameras.

We had a list of about 150 people who had hand-built TV sets in the city. We would go on at four o'clock with an Indian-head test pattern, and all four of us would get on the phones. "How is the pattern?"

"Well, it's a big goose egg."

Klaus sat on the telephone by the transmitter, twiddling dials and fartin' around with the thing. Then, when enough people by eight o'clock or eight-thirty said, "Well, it's not a bad goose egg," he'd say, "Okay, we'll go on with the show," so we went on with a one-hour show of newspaper comics on slides and this guy sitting at a desk reading news from off a teletype machine. At the end of the hour, we would get on the phones again, "Hey, how did you like the goddamn show? Pretty good wasn't it?" We fiddled around that way for a year.

On my second Thursday, someone didn't show up just before we were about to go on the air, so Klaus said, "Get on that camera and point it. Don't touch nothin' except the handle, and if you break anything I'll break every bone in your body."

So I got on the second week I was there, and never got off.

BUD COLE: When I was offered a job with Klaus, I asked around, because he had worked at NBC when he first came over from Germany. They said he was a good engineer, but he was also a real son of a bitch. He turned out to be worse than that. He really brutalized guys. I got along with Klaus because he was a coward. I was a pretty big guy, and he knew not to fuck around with me. Still, I'll hand it to him. He did everything. We did mobile unit shows up the yang-yang. There wasn't anything in town that we didn't cover.

STAN CHAMBERS: Bud Stefan and I came to KTLA from USC in 1947. There was a lot of delightful chaos. That's one reason why I fell in love with television. Shortly before I went to work there, the studio was moved into a great big old garage. Eery so often, someone would open one of the service doors and walk right into the set while a show was going on.

BUD STEFAN: After Stan was hired, I went down there and kept bugging them with show ideas. Finally, I was hired for forty cents an hour as a dolly pusher. I was frightened to death of Klaus. He was very stern, with his German accent, and just not likable.

He used me unbelievably financially. At one point I wrote, and produced, and starred in "Yer Ole Buddy" every week. I wrote, produced, and directed "Fantastick Studios, Ink." I wrote and directed "Sandy Dreams." I did another little show called "Flickers Snickers," in which I narrated old silent movies over music. He also made me write for "Frosty Frolics," which was the toughest dialogue I ever did, because it was all mime. I was also doing regular directing for all shows. Still, it never dawned on me to go to another station. There was a tremendous feeling of camaraderie at KTLA. We all lived and worked together. We all got off at midnight. What else are you going to do?

BILL WELSH: Klaus once asked me, "What do people say about me?"

"That you're great technically, and you're great on programs."

"I want to be a programmer, not a technician."

BUD STEFAN: He was. Just look at Lawrence Welk. Klaus had Lawrence before anybody. Klaus believed in that show, and to this day that son of a bitch is still big in syndication.

BILL WELSH: Welk owes all his multi-million dollars to Klaus. He was playing dances at a ballroom over in Ocean Park when Klaus found him. Klaus had a great feel for what people would watch on television, whether it was Spade Cooley or Harry Owens or Ina Ray Hutton and her All-Girl Band.

BUD STEFAN: Because of Klaus we were number one all those years. To me, the number-one reason was familiarity. Everybody got to know the people at KTLA, and they wrote us letters, like "Dear Buddy," "Dear Stan." You were just a friend. The other stations were not like that. Also, we didn't look professional. Lawrence Welk wasn't a very good show, but people liked him even with his mistakes. Spade Cooley for years beat Milton Berle, even though it was a lousy show, but they loved him. I don't know why. He was a terrible guy. He actually murdered his wife.

Also KTLA had the best signal and picture. You tuned in KTLA, and your TV looked good. The others didn't.

STAN CHAMBERS: KHJ's signal was a problem because they were on Mount Lee, which isn't very high. Klaus put our transmitter on Mount Wilson, six thousand feet up. He always wanted to have that perfect picture. He was always tuning the transmitter, which would take hours and hours.

JOHNNY POLICH: Even after he went home at night, he would tell them to put the test pattern on after sign-off, and Klaus would call Mount Wilson and tune the transmitter from his house.

BUD STEFAN: He was on the phone all the time. I don't know how Stan and the others did it, because when they were on camera, Klaus was talking to them on their headsets chewing them out.

Dick DeMille was a director at KTLA. He hated Klaus as much as Bud Cole did. He could do a perfect audio imitation of Klaus. He would call you on the phone and yell at you for ten minutes, and you had no idea it wasn't Klaus.

EDDIE RESNICK: You had to follow his directions to the nth degree. One time, he says, "Dolly in." I go in until I'm about to knock over a background flat and I stop. After the show, he says, "I didn't tell you to stop." I told him what happened. He said, "I don't give a shit. You do what I say."

The next time he said "Dolly in," I dollied in until I knocked a flat over. He says, "What the hell did you do that for?"

I said, "You told me not to stop until you said so."

BUD STEFAN: Klaus was also a great counterprogrammer. He would start a movie at one minute to eight. The networks couldn't do that. By the time a network show came on, we had 'em.

STAN CHAMBERS: One of the first on-camera shows I did was "Meet Me in Hollywood," a man-on-the-street interview at Hollywood and Vine. Bill Welsh and I did it together.

BILL WELSH: People came from all over Southern California to get on camera. Marie Windsor showed up to plug a picture she was in. There was also a guy named Fred Mellenger, who gave away "clocked stockings." He became Frederick's of Hollywood. That show was his first real exposure.

STAN CHAMBERS: The musical shows were the great formula that Klaus had. He liked bright, ethnic music, a Hawaiian show with Harry Owens or a German oom-pah-pah band. They were all successful because they were happy and live.

BUD COLE: I was the one who saw Spade Cooley down in Santa Monica and told Klaus it would make a hell of a television show. I was also intrigued because here was Klaus, this banty rooster Nazi-type, and Spade, who was a heavy drinker and who would fight at the drop of a hat. I thought, "All I've got to do is introduce these two guys, and they'll destroy each other." Talk about lessons in human nature. It was love at first sight!

JOHNNY POLICH: Spade was tough. Once, he hired a piano guy, but the guy didn't sound good in rehearsal. He reminded Spade that he had a contract to play, so Spade put him in the men's room and made him play there.

STAN CHAMBERS: Central Chevrolet sponsored a segment of "The Spade Cooley Show." The segment was done by Dick Lane, who had this great voice. He was really L.A. television's first big star. There would be a thousand-plus people for the dance. When the music stopped everybody would start talking, and people couldn't hear Dick do the commercial, so Dick would bang the car with his hand. One night, he hit the car so hard, the fender fell off. From that night on, banging the fenders became his trademark.

JOHNNY POLICH: Actually, he bent the hood. He would hit it and say, "This car goes for eight hundred dollars." This time he bent it. "You can have this one for seven hundred dollars!"

Just before another show, I unbolted the fender and put the jack under the wheel and took all the lug nuts off, so when he hit it the whole car fell apart.

BUD STEFAN: After some of those shows I would go out in the alley and throw up because of miscues.

STAN CHAMBERS: Bud was a tremendous hit. His "Yer Ole Buddy" was really the first local comedy show.

BUD STEFAN: It was really a rip-off of Robert Benchley. Stan and I used to love staying after midnight answering calls from viewers who would have questions about television, like, "Where do you put the film in the cameras?" So I came up with this idea to do a show where I would make up questions about television and then answer them. I would sit at a desk and talk, and on purpose I would get hopelessly lost in my explanations.

Soon, we started to make fun of other shows. One of them was a show I did, "Sandy Dreams," which was about a little girl who dreams of faraway places, and then other kids act out her dreams. Well, I would be the one who daydreams, and I needed a girl who would be so sexy that every time I started to fall asleep I would dream of her in any role, whether it was Little Miss Muffet or Little Red Riding Hood. In that case, Joe Flynn, as my grandma, would slap my face and wake me up.

I asked a friend at William Morris to get me a girl who was so sexy that you couldn't forget her once you've seen her.

He sent down Marilyn Monroe. This was her first TV appearance.

She came in with no makeup and a loosely fitting dress. I was so disappointed, because she didn't look that good. We walked through the script, and then she disappeared into the makeup room. We went on at seven-fifteen. At seven o'clock, I knocked on the door and said, "Marilyn, we're on in fifteen minutes."

She said [whispering], "Okay."

She came out of that dressing room not five minutes before we went on the air, and my God, she had on a strapless yellow dress. Her hair was done, lots of false eyelashes, and the crew just went wild. She was absolutely transformed.

She was so sexy that everything we said on the show was taken wrong. Joe was saying things like "If you pricked your finger . . ." I looked up at one point, and I saw Klaus shaking his fist at me. After the show, he threw Marilyn out, and he threw Joe off the station. He, of course, went to glory as Captain Binghamton on "McHale's Navy."

STAN CHAMBERS: Klaus was very particular about what went on the air. He would also get very upset if a skater on "Frosty Frolics" had too much showing. He would literally go out onto the ice and put lace around her or have her change the costume. "Frosty Frolics" was a brilliant idea. Who could think that you could put an hour of musical comedy on ice every week? It was incredible.

BUD STEFAN: Klaus wasn't always that smart. I had known Liberace, and I took him to see Landsberg, but Klaus said, "Who wants to look at a piano player for fifteen minutes," so he went to KLAC and became a big hit.

STAN CHAMBERS: Klaus always wanted to get the cameras out of the studio into the community to show what was going on. One show was called "Fun on the Beach." That was typical Landsberg. He was doing "Bandstand Review" on Sundays at the Aragon Ballroom on a pier at Ocean Park. He had the crew there for eight hours, but he only needed them for three hours to do the show, so Klaus said, "I'll do another show on the beach."

Kids would come down to play running games and swimming games. The budget may have been seventy-five dollars with twenty-five dollars left over, and when we were through we took the cameras right back up on the pier for our evening show. We would go to the Pacific Auditorium for a basketball game or to a horse show. We would go to community events like the Fish Fry in Costa Mesa. People remember those fish fries to this day.

He had no problem with interrupting the regular schedule to cover a special news event. In fact, he wanted to. It was smart, because when events of that magnitude hit the area, everybody knew they could tune to Channel Five to find out what was happening. Other stations did that too, but we were the first.

BILL WELSH: I was at home one Saturday morning when Klaus called me and said this little girl had fallen down a well. He said, "I think we ought to televise it."

STAN CHAMBERS: Kathy Fiscus was playing hide-and-go-seek with her cousins on a Friday night when she fell down the well in her neighborhood. I was emceeing a luncheon at the Biltmore Hotel on Saturday when the phone rang. The headwaiter picked it up, and I saw him come toward me out of the perimeter of my eye. Klaus was calling to say I should head out to the site.

When I got out there, our remote equipment was already there getting ready to go. KTTV was there too.

EDDIE RESNICK: We expected to be back in an hour or two, but we stayed on for thirty hours. We just focused on the hole and the guys trying to reach her by digging a hole right next to her. It was dramatic as hell.

STAN CHAMBERS: Bill would do something for twenty minutes, and when he was talked out, he would sent it over to me for twenty minutes.

BILL WELSH: No television station ever operated for thirty straight hours. They would go on for four or five hours and shut down. Klaus said, "I don't know how long we can stay on the air. The transmitter might melt down, but we'll go till it does." It never melted down. They discovered that a television transmitter is much better if it is left operating all the time.

STAN CHAMBERS: At no time did we even make an attempt to talk to the Fiscus family. We didn't even give it a thought. I'd probably get fired for that today. Right off the top, the mother was talking to her, hearing her cry on Friday night for an hour or so, and that was the last they heard her. As it got dark on Saturday, the early optimism faded, and then they ran into a series of problems. The hole they were digging started to sag. They had to stop and build a parallel hole. Then they hit rock. The guys went in with picks and shovels to break the rocks up. They got through that and then they hit mud.

Finally, they sent the family doctor down in a parachute harness, and he obviously found out she was dead, but we didn't know that until later. Still, at that point, everyone got very grim, and you knew the news wasn't very good.

BILL WELSH: When it was over, the sheriff came up to me, and he said, "Bill, the Fiscus family lives a block up the street." They were watching on television until it got so depressing they turned it off. "They don't know what's happened, and somebody has got to tell 'em, and I'd sure appreciate it if you would do it."

So I walked up the street to the Fiscus house, got the family together in the living room, and said, "I'm here to tell you that Kathy is just not coming home." It was a pretty grim finish to the whole thing.

STAN CHAMBERS: I remember sitting in the truck, saying to myself, "Who in the world is watching this at three o'clock in the morning?" Little did we know.

BILL WELSH: Around that time, I said it was getting cold and we were not prepared for it. A friend of mine got in his car and drove thirty miles, to bring us two topcoats. That's when I realized we had an audience.

EDDIE RESNICK: Every store that was selling TVs had this on in the windows, and there were crowds outside watching. Every set in the city was tuned to the sight until the city practically shut down.

STAN CHAMBERS: It was a real surprise to learn how much attention it got. We had been on for almost two years, and nobody said anything about those shows. The Kathy Fiscus story was the turning point for television in Los Angeles. Until then, television was just a plaything. It was just something to watch, but here people lived through the moment. They were a part of the scene. To this day, I'll meet two or three people a week who will recall the Kathy Fiscus story.

BILL WELSH: Now, television not only made you laugh, it had a heart and soul. If you can be pleased with a tragedy, I think Klaus was satisfied that television had done its job the way he believed it could.

STAN CHAMBERS: The story had an impact on my life in a different way. I used to date my wife's sister when I was at USC. She was at her parents' ranch the weekend of the telecast. While they were watching it, her mother said, "Maurice, Beverly should meet some nice young man like this," and Marie said, "I know Stan, we were at SC together."

"Well, you ought to call and have him over for dinner." She did, and I met Bev and we were married five weeks later.

✳ ✳ ✳

BUD COLE: I saw Klaus mistreat people so badly. I remember saying to myself, "You son of a bitch, when I go, I'm gonna fuck you good." Finally, NBC asked me to come back. When I told Klaus he got chalk white. Nobody did this to him. He did this to other people. "You can't do that!"

I said, "You know, Klaus, this is a wonderful country. We can work for somebody until you really don't want to anymore, and then you can say, 'Fuck you, I'm leaving.' That's what I'm telling you." After that he respected the shit out of me. He even congratulated me after I won an Emmy.

I went to KNBT, which was coming on the air. They said, "We're gonna get all these big network shows, and Klaus is gonna be nothing."

But the network was a hindrance in Los Angeles, because the local programs were the whole show. I warned them, "You're not just gonna come in here with big names. That station has almost a personal relationship with everybody in this town. It's gonna be a hell of a fight, and you better be on your toes." And I was right.

STAN CHAMBERS: We did so many ambitious things. We always used microwaves whenever we went long distances, while the others used telephone facilities. The microwaves were easier because you didn't have to deal with the phone company's bureaucracy. When the Marines went to Korea and when they returned, we were down at the harbor for five, six, seven hours straight. It was very emotional and very powerful. Klaus set up the microwave system by himself.

JOHNNY POLICH: Some of the crew would get together on Sunday mornings at Klaus's house. We would have a nice lunch and talk about what we were gonna do. One Sunday he said, "Jesus, I went to Las Vegas, and they want the networks to cover the A-bomb test, but the telephone company can't supply video [a picture by telephone line] for six months to one year."

Klaus told Paramount he could do it himself with five or six transmitters, and sell the video to the networks. They told him to go ahead, and the networks agreed to pay the expenses. It was a terrific gamble. We had three weeks to set up a relay between Las Vegas and L.A. that the telephone company said could take a year. We had a transmitter which could go that distance, but we hadn't used it before, so we didn't know if it was gonna work. If he failed, we were stuck with all the expenses.

We had to set up four relay points from mountaintop to mountaintop. The first thing he did was call up the fellows on Mount Wilson and say, "Why don't you fellows go up to Mount Wrightwood and see if we can get a picture from Wrightwood to Mount Wilson." They took a transmitter up on a ski lift. We were at Klaus's house that day when they called us from Mount Wilson to say they had the signal. Klaus had them cut into a program so he could see it. It was fine.

Then Klaus drove by himself to the desert. He came back and said that the best place to get the signal to Wrightwood would be Clark Mountain. Clark Mountain is four thousand feet.

JOE FEATHERSTON: I was sent up to Clark Mountain. We called it Mount X because we were afraid once the others figured out where we were they would try to set up their own relay.

JOHNNY POLICH: Klaus called the P.R. guy for the Atomic Commission. He said, "Gee, we can't get our equipment to the top of the mountain."

The guy found two helicopters in Buffalo and had them flown out in a bomber, so we took our transmitter and drove to the foot of Clark Mountain. The helicopters come flying in about fifty feet above the ground. Klaus says, "If you can fly up the mountain and find a place at the point it will be perfect."

About an hour later the pilot came back and said, "Klaus, there's not a place to put down. Everything is razor-backed, staight up and straight down."

"How about on the right-hand side of the highway?" Klaus went up with him, and that was perfect. We took our transmitter, a generator I rented from a U-Haul place and an eight-foot dish that they tied to a rope on the side of the helicopter and flew it up the mountain.

JOE FEATHERSTON: After they flew the equipment up there, we had to climb the mountain. We had five-gallon cans of gas in our packs to keep the generator going. It was really tough up there. Lightning would strike quite often, and there was this very shale-like, loose rock. You would climb two steps and fall back one. Finally, we set it up, and we turned on the transmitter, and the guys at Wrightwood saw us.

After that we had to go up and down the mountain with gasoline cans. We did that hike, a mile and a half, every day. We took sandwiches, and the copter would bring in warm soup every once in a while. It was very cold, and the privy was a straight drop—a thousand feet down. There were plenty of times when we thought, "What are we doing up here?"

We had to make sure the dish was lined up perfectly. It kept shifting because at the top of the mountain the wind was very strong, and we had no anchor point to keep things in place.

JOHNNY POLICH: Now we have two points set up. From there we went to Mount Charleston, which was the point for all transmissions from Las Vegas. They have a good line of sight to the place where they are exploding the bomb. We could drive to the top of Mount Charleston in our truck. That was easy. From there, the signal went to the top of a building at Frenchman's Flat in Yucca Valley. So now we have it all set up from Yucca Flat to Charleston to Clark, to Wrightwood to Mount Wilson.

All this time Klaus is sleeping maybe two hours a day. A few days before the blast, there was a snowstorm at Wrightwood and we lost the picture. As the snow was melting, they had to keep moving the disk to make sure it was in line.

EDDIE RESNICK: There was a parade on in Las Vegas the day before the blast, and typical of Klaus, as long as we were there, he had us shoot it. When we needed some rest, he sent us to a room in the hotel—one room for eight or ten of us.

Early the next morning we left for Frenchman's Flat to set up the cameras. We had a twenty-four-inch lens. An atomic blast is like shooting the sun. You burn the camera, so we put six black filters on the lens. We were also issued goggles so dark you could barely see the sun, and we waited.

JOHNNY POLICH: Now we also had a camera up at Mount Charleston in case something happened to our two cameras at the site or the transmitter. Well, about fifteen minutes before the bomb was supposed to be dropped the gas runs out of the generator that is powering the transmitter. Holy God. Klaus was flipping like crazy, "What the hell we ran out of gas, for Chrissake?"

We put in a couple of gallons and got the thing started, but by the time the cameras were turned on again, they weren't ready when the bomb went off, so the blast was shown from the cameras on Mount Charleston.

All this was done without any advance publicity. There was a food show on KTLA. Thirty seconds before the blast, we cut the food show off the air and just went on.

The blast was scary. As soon as it exploded you could feel the heat on your neck, instantly. As soon as I felt the heat I turned around to take a look at it, but you could not look, it was brighter than the sun, and it was white, not yellow.

EDDIE RESNICK: It was the most gorgeous piece of fireworks I will ever see in my life. The streamers of light and fire coming down, all the colors of the rainbow. God, it was a pretty thing, but destructive as hell.

JOHNNY POLICH: I figured the truck would shake like hell, too, so I took some rope and tied it down against four big rocks. There was a kid was on top of this truck. He died of cancer, never smoked, never drank Coca-Cola. He had the healthiest body you ever saw in your life. His name was Jerry Westfall.

They told us that providing the wind keeps going away from you we were okay. If the wind shifted, we were supposed to get in the car and get the hell out of there. The next year, we televised two bombs. Of the guys that were there, three died of cancer. Two of them were young guys.

Klaus already had cancer. He was a heavy smoker. It started in his throat. Then he found a brownish mole the size of a nickel on his belt line. I told him to go to the doctor. He wouldn't at first, but finally he had a doctor cut it out. We were doing a "Frosty Frolics," and after the show he went to the telephone and called the doctor. The doctor told him it was malignant.

He lived five years; had seven operations.

STAN CHAMBERS: The station was his life to the end. I even brought a client to his house to complete a sale about three weeks before he died. He had lost a lot of weight, and he was in his bathrobe, but we talked about it, and that program lasted for another ten or fifteen years.

JOHNNY POLICH: I spoke to Klaus the day before he died. The next day we were doing "The Fisherman's Fiesta" from San Pedro. He said to me, "John, they can take a knife and cut off my arms and legs and everything. Just leave my head." He had a lot of pain, but he said he would see us tomorrow at the fiesta.

STAN CHAMBERS: When I arrived at the parade, I was told Klaus had died. Even though I knew it was going to happen, I couldn't believe it.

I think the station had already started to slip. Sales were good and ratings were good, but we just didn't dominate. Once the live cable came, that was the topper. We lost the advantage of going up against old kinescopes. We had live shows against us. Although "City at Night," Lawrence Welk, and Spade Cooley were right up there until the late fifties, we weren't able to re-create the early era and keep it as fresh and new and exciting.

BUD STEFAN: We slipped because the other stations had far better programming. My other little show, "Fantastick Studios, Ink.," was on at six-thirty Saturday night. Out came "Your Show of Shows." That blew us away. You know, the Model T Ford was great in its day, but the Cadillacs came out and knocked 'em out.

STAN CHAMBERS: We still went after news. Right after Klaus died, John Silva came along with our Telecopter. When the Watts riots happened in '65, we were the only ones up there.

BUD STEFAN: Even today, if there is a fire or a flood in L.A., people turn to KTLA first, because they know KTLA will wipe out the whole night's programming to cover that fire. The networks can't afford to do it. Still, Klaus could not have survived in the network period. Klaus was a man of his time. You could say that about a lot of people. Maybe Henry Ford couldn't cut it today for all I know, but he sure did it for his time.

THE CHICAGO
SCHOOL

I wasn't sure what television was going to be, but I knew what it could be and should be—different from any other communications medium, and I wanted to explore it to the nth degree. I wanted to innovate like crazy and blaze trails.

—TED MILLS

Jules Herbuveaux was a trumpet player by training, which didn't exactly qualify him to head up a TV station. On the other hand, in 1948 it didn't disqualify him either.

Herbuveaux may not have recognized the difference between a wipe and a dissolve, but he did know that a band was only as good as its sidemen, and in his young crew at Chicago's WNBQ, he had the wisdom to surround himself with some of the best (and hungriest) young talent in the business.

"TV is the most honest thing in the world," said Herbuveaux in 1951, "and there's no fakery in it. Be honest. Put on a good show, and the camera will take care of the rest."

Under Herbuveaux's guidance, the station earned a hallowed reputation for its charming puckish programs. These little gems such as "Studs' Place," "Garroway at Large," and "Kukla, Fran & Ollie," demonstrated that television is often at its best when it is at its most intimate and that big budgets are as dispensable as suntan oil in the Arctic when creative people are given the freedom to create.

WNBQ was already Chicago's fourth TV station when it debuted from the Merchandise Mart on January 7, 1949. Its first network offering was "Kukla, Fran & Ollie," a pickup from crosstown rival, WBKB. Within two years, the station was supplying half of NBC's network schedule. Most of those programs originated in the office of Ted Mills, the station's program director and a relative television veteran with three years under his belt when he signed on. It was Mills who assembled the staff, mostly recent college graduates with no experience in the medium. All Mills could offer them was low pay and long hours, as well as a blank programming slate with a mandate to fill it as creatively and cheaply as possible (with an emphasis on the latter). The need for thrift no doubt led to the "Chicago style" of television, whose hallmarks were intimacy, informality, and creativity born out of necessity. "The Chicago shows are making an effort to do something," said Fred Allen in 1950. "They're short on money, short on talent, and long on inventiveness."

Allen got two out of three right. The station had talent to burn. The young staff's inspiration was Paul Rhymer, the creator of the daffy radio serial, "Vic and Sade." Rhymer's influence could be seen on nearly all the station's successful offerings. His protégé, Charlie Andrews, was the creative force behind "Garroway at Large," a more-or-less variety show that virtually invented the visual pun. For example, after a performance by a harmonica quartet, Garroway appeared on camera gnawing an ear of corn.

The unique conceit of "Garroway at Large" was to include the viewing audience in the show's wink at show business. When a group of dancers ended their routine by diving into a swimming pool, Garroway suddenly appeared on camera and hopped in too, only to bounce back out. He then called in the overhead camera, so the viewers could see a pile of mattresses and an abashed group of hoofers huddling under the wooden set.

Nobody seemed to enjoy the mischief more than the show's amiable host. He could give a deadpan lecture about constructing eleven-foot poles "for touching people you wouldn't touch with ten-foot poles," while behind his thick lenses, his eyes literally sparkled in merriment. The thirty-seven-year-old former deejay was an unusual television star. He was low-key, and he radiated intelligence. Off-camera he had more interests than a troop of Eagle Scouts. *Newsweek* described him as an "an amateur mechanic, gem cutter, tile setter, photographer, bird fancier, cabinet maker and bibliophile."

Andrews struck gold again when he devised a format that showcased the personality of Studs Terkel, a veteran actor and radio personality who, one imagines, was a warm, crusty figure the day of his birth. "Studs' Place" was remarkable in that it had no script. The weekly show was set in a bar, where Terkel and his mates, folk singer Win Stracke, actress Beverly Younger, and pianist and racetrack habitué Chet Roble, improvised for half an hour from an outline by Andrews that was anywhere from two paragraphs to two pages in length. The characters they played were so real that they caused visitors to the city to wander the streets, searching for Studs' Place to enjoy the good fellowship and a home-cooked meal.

Improvisation was also the hallmark of "Kukla, Fran & Ollie," a Peabody-Award winner for children's programming in 1950, even though the show's fans were mostly among the shaving set. WNBQ produced a number of honored children's shows—"Mr. Wizard," "Ding Dong School," and "Zoo Parade"— that moved on to the network. Creativity also extended to the news department, whose "Five Star Final" not only featured outstanding local journalists but for entertainment purposes also threw in a pianist, Herbie Mintz, and the remarkable talents of Dorsey Connors, who earned national renown for her ability to transform a coat hanger into just about anything.

The Chicago school peaked in the early fifties. There was just too much ambition on the staff for a local station to hold. At the same time, network programmers were more interested in big shows that attracted larger advertisers. Most of the crew departed for New York, where they became key contributors to television's "Golden Age." As early as 1950, *Newsweek* reported that Garroway was headed for New York. Little did the magazine know that NBC president Pat Weaver was cooking up something called the "Today" show for him.

As for the rest, Andrews followed Garroway to the Big Apple, where he enjoyed a long successful career not only with "Today" but also as a writer for Sid Caesar and as producer of "The Arthur Godfrey Show" and "Candid Camera." The station's young directors seemed to be everywhere on the dial. Norman Felton produced and directed "Robert Montgomery Presents." Daniel Petrie's work was featured on "The U.S. Steel Hour" and "Playhouse 90." Bill Hobin directed the comedy classic, "Your Show of Shows." Bob Banner became one of the medium's busiest producers, while Ted Mills and Ben Park joined Weaver's executive staff at NBC.

Only Studs Terkel never found another niche on TV. After Joe McCarthy's minions turned the lights out on "Studs' Place" and cut short a promising television career, Terkel took up reporting. His series of oral history books set the standard for those who have followed in his footsteps.

By 1959, Chicago didn't have a single offering on the network schedule. Herbuveaux continued as head of NBC's central division until that unit was finally shut down in 1962. The Chicago School, whose doors were opened by Captain Bill Eddy in 1940, was closed for good. The kids had all graduated.

BOB BANNER: It's funny to hear people talk about the "Chicago style." When we were there doing it, we never thought about it. We were just trying to do the best we could with what we knew about television, and most of us didn't know anything.

STUDS TERKEL: Chicago was like a frontier town when it came to television. "Studs' Place" was a Chicago show. It could not have been done in New York. New York was so uptight. "You've got to be it! You've got to be big! You've got to score!"

CHARLIE ANDREWS: New York was the great museums, the great opera, the great everything. California was the golden land where you sat in the sun and created great big fuckin' movies. Chicago was the Second City. It made us work harder and take chances.

STUDS TERKEL: The city itself was different. Chicago was not the center of money. Chicago was the gypsy taverns on North Avenue and the South Side blues places. It was blue collar, farm equipment, steel, packing houses. We had Chicago jazz, Bud Freeman and Jimmy McPartland, and the writers. H. L. Mencken said, "You can't discuss American literature unless you discuss the Chicago palatinate," Dreiser, Norris, Sandburg, and Farrell.

People come to Chicago from the middle of the country, from the deep South, from farm country in Minnesota. Charlie Andrews came from Fond du Lac, Wisconsin. Fran Allison came from Waterloo, Iowa. I came from Sheboygan, Wisconsin. Everybody who came reflected that.

CHARLIE ANDREWS: I was raised in Fond du Lac, Wisconsin, by my grandparents. My grandfather was a railroad worker. He loved radio, and he loved books. I loved radio. After supper, we would go into the living room and read and listen to the radio. That's all we ever did during the winter months. I listened to all the jazz bands and the usual "Fibber McGee and Molly," and Fred Allen, but the show that I loved the most was "Vic and Sade." "Vic and Sade" was a continuing story, but it wasn't a soap opera. It was just episodes in the lives of these people "in a little house halfway up on the next block."

"Vic and Sade" had a magic. Everything about it was totally charming. Paul Rhymer wrote it. He didn't tell jokes. He just had great characters like "Richigan Sishigan from Fishigan, Michigan." He talked about one girl, "who was the most beautiful girl ever to drown in Miller's Pond." Vic told a story about one fellow, who worked for forty years for the railroad. He rode a bicycle to work. It had a wire basket on the handlebars to carry his lunch. Every day he would take home a small piece of the locomotive in his lunchbox. After forty years, he assembled an eight-wheel-drive locomotive in his backyard.

God, all I wanted to be was a radio writer. Later, when I went to Chicago, I wanted to meet Paul so badly. When I finally did, we went for a drink. We laughed at the same things. We became very close friends for years. He was a sweet funny man.

NORMAN FELTON: I went to see Paul about doing "Vic and Sade" on television. When I arrived at his apartment, I rang the bell, and there was no answer. The door was ajar. I opened it, and he was spread-eagled on the ground. For a second I was scared, but he was just being Paul Rhymer.

He would do crazy things. When he traveled the country, he would send postcards, saying, "I'm locked in the toilet in Grand Central Station. Get me out."

STUDS TERKEL: In 1944, I got a radio job, playing folk songs and old opera records, jazz. I called the show "The Wax Museum," a pun, wax museum and old records. I did takeoffs on the opera. Longshot Silvester, a tout who loved opera, was my character. After Louis' "West End Blues" or Woody doing "Do Re Mi," I'd slip in an old scratchy Columbia record of Emma Calvé, 1915, doing a great habañera, but before that I'd tell the story of Carmen through Longshot, "It's about a tomato who loves not too wisely but too often." Or Longshot would do Tristan. "He takes that magic potion and, 'Isolde, Isolde, I smolder and smolder.'"

CHARLIE ANDREWS: In those days, radio stations had girl singers on staff. At NBC there was Carolyn Gilbert. When fifteen minutes during the daytime wasn't sold, the word would go out, "Carolyn, you're doing fifteen minutes a day for the next three weeks," and all of the sudden on the radio would be "Carolyn Gilbert Time" with Hugh Downs as the announcer. I wrote some scripts for Carolyn on speculation. Jules Herbuveaux liked them, and he agreed to pay me seven dollars a script. Then he gave me other shows.

By then, I had heard Garroway on the radio. Dave was a staff announcer with a great voice and a very relaxed delivery. He had the "11:60 Club" between midnight and one o'clock in the morning. Dave would play records and tell little stories. I contacted him and said, "I've got a lot of stuff I think you could use."

We immediately hit it off. I was the only writer who really ever matched Dave. I designed "Garroway at Large," and later I came to New York with Dave for the "Today" show. He was the best man at my wedding and my best friend through all of those years.

TED MILLS: I got into show business by writing propaganda films with Frank Capra's unit during World War II. Then I took a job with NBC television. Two years later, I received an offer from WGN to put that station on the air, and the opportunity to be station manager and program manager was too good to pass up.

Unfortunately, I was working for Colonel McCormick and a guy named Schreiber, who ruled the station with an iron fist. I developed such a loathing for Schreiber that I went to Jules Herbuveaux. He said, "Why don't you come and work for me?"

I said, "I'll come over if I can have my head."

He said, "You know, Ted, I like to play golf," so I said okay, and I was totally on my own.

CHARLIE ANDREWS: Jules was a great guy. He had been a trumpet player, so he came out of the entertainment side as against the administrative side. He was the one who found Paul. Jules was also a great champion of Burr Tillstrom.

REINALD WERRENRATH: He didn't try to dictate what was done. He just tried to get the creative people to do a creative job. NBC was where I had begun, and when they started up out here I applied and was the second producer hired by Jules for the TV station. Norman Felton was the first.

TED MILLS: I put most of the staff together. There was Norman, who was later head of MGM Television, Dan Petrie, Ben Park, Bill Hobin, and Bob

Banner. They were talented with great ideas, and not one of them had any real experience in television. I just felt they would be explorers.

BOB BANNER: I was teaching at Northwestern University in the theater department. The dean of the department said to me one day in 1948, "You are the junior member of the faculty. Why don't you learn about television so we could teach it here?"

I got an intern job at WBKB. I also applied to WNBQ, but I never heard from them. Then just before Christmas, I came home late one night, and the phone was ringing. I picked it up and a voice said, "Congratulations, you have been accepted to work at WNBQ."

They wanted me to come down that night. I said, "Tonight?"

"Yes, right now."

I got there around nine o'clock, and they said, "You're going to work as a general helper but to do specifically stage managing, and you're stage managing a show tomorrow evening."

This was a Christmas show from the Great Lakes Naval Training Center in Chicago. The other person helping on the stage was Duane Bogie, who later became the chief executive for "Hallmark Hall of Fame." I introduced myself, and he said, "Have you worked at NBC?"

"No, I just got the job last night."

He had been working in the mailroom. I said, "Duane, what are we supposed to do?"

"Don't you worry, nobody else knows what they're doing either, so we'll be fine."

It seemed that the show ran nineteen hours. It probably ran an hour and a half. I suspect we showed more stagehands than we showed performers.

BEN PARK: One day when I was in radio I went to a party at which Burr Tillstrom was one of the guests. He asked me, "Do you ever see 'Kukla, Fran & Ollie'?"

I said no, I didn't have a television.

"Well, you ought to see it some time."

He was very cheerful and charming about the whole thing, so I went to a bar across from our office, and I watched an episode, and I was wiped out. I said, "Wow!"

I called Burr up, and told him I had seen it. He said, "Why don't you come over and sit in with me and the kids?"—the kids meaning the puppets. I did, and it was mind-boggling to watch the show from backstage. Ted Mills had already made a couple of overtures to me, but after I had seen "Kukla," I called him up and said, "I'm coming." It was that simple. Dan Petrie came in about the same time as I did. He was a wonderful assistant, because he actually knew something about television.

DAN PETRIE: I was teaching at Creighton University when I went to see Ted. I jokingly—but seriously—got down on my knees in his office, and I said, "You've got to give me a job."

He didn't have anything, but when I got back to Omaha, there was a message that he had called. Norman Felton had gotten an offer to do the Robert Montgomery show, and so a place had opened up. I was back two or three days later. I was supposed to be a floor manager, but that Saturday night Ted really riled over one of the shows, and he turned to me in back of the control room, "Well, kid, do you think you're ready to fly?"

Naturally, I couldn't say, "Oh, no," so I said, "Oh, yes."

"Next week, you're doing this fuckin' thing."

BOB BANNER: If you could read your name and spell it you could direct. They said they were going to train us, but training us meant walking us through the studios, and saying, "That's what it is and here's what you do. Here's a little dissolve thing, and here's the show you're going to do."

The first show I directed in the studio was a fifteen-minute program called "Gone But Not Forgotten." It was simple, just a singer, a piano player, and an announcer. I would sit in the control room and look at it. Then I would run downstairs to the floor and tell 'em where to stand, and then I would run back upstairs. After about a week, the technical director said, "Did you know that if you pressed this little button here, you can talk to the people in the studio?"

I thought, "My God, that's gonna save all our lives. I'm so exhausted from running up and down the stairs."

*   *   *

DAN PETRIE: My wife and I first heard Garroway on radio in '46 or '47. His theme song was "Gonna Take a Sentimental Journey." He would talk in that tone [softly], "Hi, Tiger," just like he's talking to a woman, and oh, man, we loved him.

LYNWOOD KING: He was very esoteric and very big with the Northwestern University crowd, but it took a Charlie Andrews to give him that twinkle in the eye. Not that Dave was humorless, he wasn't, and he was brilliant.

CHARLIE ANDREWS: He loved working on his car. Just before air time, the announcer would say to me, "Charlie, for Chrissakes, go get Dave." I'd get in a cab and go to Huron Street where Dave would be under a car, his overalls all covered with grease. I'd bring him to the studio still in his overalls.

LYNWOOD KING: NBC in Chicago had one of the most gorgeous staff orchestras in the world, but by the late forties they weren't doing much, and Jules figured since they were being paid, they would find a way to make use of them.

BOB BANNER: We decided to do a variety show. For the host, I said to Ted, "You know the darling of Northwestern is the radio announcer that's on late night, the crazy guy who talks to a mouse in the studio," and it was Dave.

TED MILLS: The first thing we put on the air was an absolute monstrosity called "Contrast."

CHARLIE ANDREWS: After two shows, Dave said, "These are so awful I can't do this anymore. Let's bring Charlie in and have him work on it."

Ted wanted to do a show with an audience, but on the radio, Dave would lean close to the microphone, lower his voice, and talk. It was very personal, and he had a big following so I said, "Do it in a studio so Dave won't have to face an audience. Let him talk to the camera."

We told Dave, "You are only talking to one person. The camera is your friend." Dave did that better than anyone, except Godfrey. Milton Berle was funny, man, but his show was television trying to be theater. We believed the Garroway show should be pure television—in other words, do what the camera indicates you should do rather than try to make the camera sit in the theater and look at a stage. That was partly why we decided to show the equipment on camera. There's nothing bad about a camera. If it takes pictures, take pictures of a camera.

BILL HOBIN: The camera would follow Dave walking from one set to the next one with the studio walls and the stagehands in the background.

LYNWOOD KING: I was stage manager for a few months. On the first show, Garroway started wandering all over the set, and the camera cables got so mixed up they looked like rows of knitting. It got so you couldn't get from Set A to Set B without panning across the man on the boom. "Well," Garroway said, "you just go ahead and do that." He just wandered by and said, "Hi, Bob," to the boom man and Bob said, "Hi, Dave," and that became the show.

TED MILLS: We used to pan the camera up and catch the stagehand shaking snow.

LYNWOOD KING: On the first show, Carolyn Gilbert sang a sad song called "The Black Coffee Blues." When she was done, Dave walked into the set and gave her a bottle of milk. That was another of those Charlie Andrews things. After that, they would say, "What's the milk bottle for this number?" In other words, "What's the kicker?"

For "By the Light of the Silvery Moon," the set was a barbershop with the moon shining through the window. At the end of the song, Dave came in with the moon as if it were a lollipop.

BILL HOBIN: We never had a script. We knew the musical numbers, and for the connecting talk, Charlie would just type out, "Dave talks to so-and-so and crosses to this set."

LYNWOOD KING: Charlie came up with great visual tricks. One of them people ask about to this day. Cliff Norton was a baseball pitcher and Garroway a catcher. When Cliff threw the ball it did all sorts of loops and curves. What we did was have two stagehands out of camera range on either side, and the ball was on a very fine piano wire that allowed it to behave that way.

There was another one where Les Paul and Mary Ford came out to do the show. Garroway just stood there and said, "I bet you didn't know I could play the guitar." Then the camera cut to these hands going wild over the guitar strings. Of course, they were Les Paul's hands, while Garroway would give that little twinkle when the camera was on him.

CHARLIE ANDREWS: I wrote little stories that could be danced out. One of them our choreographer, Edie Barstow, loved. A boy and a girl go to the beach. They change into bathing suits, leaving their glasses behind. Their world is a beautiful blur, and the camera goes blurry. They meet and they talk and they dance and they throw the ball back and forth, and they fall in love. They agree to meet at the bus stop and go home together, so they go get dressed and put their glasses on, and now they don't recognize each other, so they leave, two lonely people.

BOB BANNER: They made us say at the end of the show, "This program came to you from Chicago."

I asked, "Why do we have to say that? The shows from New York don't say, this program came from there."

"Because you are remote. New York is television." We got so annoyed, we said, "Let's do something about that."

So we did something that was considered to be very fancy. We said, "This program came to you from Chicago, which is at the bottom of Lake Michigan," and we got an aquarium and had the camera shoot through the fish tank with Dave Garroway on the other side.

New York said, "Don't add clauses to that. Just say, 'Came to you from Chicago.'" Well, we were determined. The next week we said, "This program came to you from Chicago, which is thirty-five miles southeast of the birthplace of Pat O'Brien."

LYNWOOD KING: Or "This program came to you from Chicago," and Dave would take an axe and cut a piece of cable on the floor and the picture went kaplooey.

CHARLIE ANDREWS: "This program came to you from Chicago, the friendly city," and when Dave turned around there was a knife in his back.

BOB BANNER: New York got progressively more annoyed at this, but we kept doing it. Around Thanksgiving, we had Dave standing there with a turkey, and he said, "This turkey came to you from Chicago." By then, they were terribly annoyed.

It was those kinds of things that made the show instantly recognized and critiqued as being special and good. One critic wrote, "A breath of fresh air blew out of windy Chicago. . . ."

CHARLIE ANDREWS: I was never so happy working. We had no interference, not from the advertisers, and not from Jules Herbuveaux. It wasn't like now where you have meetings about everything. We just met with Bill Hobin and Ted and David and I and Edie Barstow, the choreographer. Mostly we had lunch, and Billy would say, "Gee, I want to do a dance number with this."

I would say, "Well, you know how we could get into that? If you can use an umbrella, then we could do this."

"Yeah, we could use an umbrella."

They would change my mind or I would change their minds. Then at the end, we would have an agreement on what to do.

TED MILLS: This would happen all the time: the night before the show, we had to build scenery, but Charlie says, "I don't got one, sorry. Let's just cancel this one. I can't figure it out." Then at eleven o'clock, "Suppose . . ." And it would be brilliant.

CHARLIE ANDREWS: Sometimes it came easy; sometimes it came hard, but you always had to get there. I later wrote for the Sid Caesar show. There, if someone came up with an idea and you said immediately, "Let's use it," you were accused of being a "pilgrim," an early settler. If you finish too far ahead of time, you're being a pilgrim. My wife used to irritate the shit out of me. She'd say, "Here you are worried again. Why didn't you do it yesterday, then you could have gone to the movies tonight?" She didn't understand that you do it when your heart tells you it has to be done.

Who knows where an idea comes from. If you're struggling with an idea, the best thing to do is look at pictures or go to the movies. Go wherever there are things to look at. It doesn't do you any good to look at a wall, because then you've only got your head to work with.

I think the creative process is a negative process. It's a process of elimination. If you are writing about chickens, you read everything to read about chickens. You go to a museum and look at all the paintings of chickens. You go to a chicken movie and listen to chicken music. Then you sit at the typewriter and say, "Now, let's see, this is no good. I can't use this. This has nothing to do with it." Finally, you get down to about two things that are usable, and you say, "I'm gonna go with this one."

I got an idea for a routine when I was in a dentist's chair. I'm sitting there, and the light comes into you like this, and this machine comes right into your face. Back at my office, I called Bill Hobin, and we worked on it together.

On the show, Dave walks by a little flat that says DENTIST. He says, "I think you people need to have your teeth fixed." He walks into the door, and there is Cliff Norton. "Okay, sit down." He takes a napkin and goes up to the lens, looks at it and says, "Let's see what we have here." He takes a probe and brings it right up to the lens. We scratched an ice pick on a piece of slate so it would squeak. Then, he takes the drill, and we have an exaggerated sound. While he puts the drill just under the lens, another guy holds a fireworks sparkler under the lens. Well, it was funny, man, and it came from my trip to the dentist.

Sometimes, it was the cameramen came up with the ideas. Bob Haley loved that camera. He would say, "Hey, look what happens when I do this." There might be vertical lines on the screen, and we would say, "Hey, do that and we'll have a jail scene."

One time he came in with a glass building brick. He had one of the guys hold it up to the lens, and we could see something like one hundred images. The following week we had a number with Betty Chappel about twins. We said, "Hey, bring that in to rehearsal, and let's see what we can do with it."

BILL HOBIN: New York couldn't figure out how we got this "image multiplier," and we wouldn't tell them. Finally, they demanded that we tell them, so we just mailed them the brick.

CHARLIE ANDREWS: Our first advertiser was Congoleum Nairn. They left us alone, and we never had any trouble with them. Then the show moved to New York in 1951, and we did a season for Pontiac. At the end of the season, Mr. Pontiac said, "Fellas, I just love your show, but why doesn't Dave tell a few jokes?"

I said, "Gee, Mr. Pontiac, we've developed a style that Dave is comfortable with, and besides, it's very hard to do jokes without an audience."

He said, "You've put your finger on it. We need an audience."

And we were doomed. I've learned since that the people you have to answer to in television don't trust the audience at all. If you had a guy like Garroway who was just amusing, never funny, they were never sure. "How do you know people are amused?"

They always needed those guffaws. That's why they put in laughter in all the shows. It limited Garroway greatly, and I'm sure it hurt Paul Rhymer on television. Paul's stuff never had punch lines. I liked that. It made me chuckle rather than laugh out loud. It was warmer, sweeter, and had more character. I wanted to write like that.

*   *   *

BOB BANNER: I was still teaching at Northwestern when someone at NBC asked me to stage manage a puppet show. I was ashamed. I was in the "theattah" department at Northwestern. It was "Kukla, Fran & Ollie." When I got there, they explained that most of the show was ad-lib. Then they said, "What are we going to do today?"

I thought, Jesus, three hours before they go on the air, and they're deciding what they are going to do? They obviously don't know about the theater, music and art.

They said to me, "What did you do the last day or so?" I said I had seen *La Bohème* at the Met. "Great, let's do a parody of *La Bohème*."

I thought, What do these puppeteers know about *La Bohème*? I said, "Would you like me to go to the music library and get some music?"

"No," whereupon Jack Fascinato started to play. Fran said, "I want to sing Mimi's theme at the end of Act Two."

They never went to get any music. They made it all up, and I was astonished. They had so many subtleties, and it was funny and so understandable for the public, and to do a parody of *La Bohème* is tougher than doing the real *La Bohème*.

Of course, "Kukla, Fran & Ollie" became an instant hit. Then at Northwestern, when I said, "Do you know what show I'm working on? 'Kukla, Fran & Ollie,' " that was a big thing. [Laughs.]

LEW GOMAVITZ: Burr knew every opera. He had seen every ballet. When we had the singer Gladys Swarthout on, she did *Carmen,* and Kukla sang right along with her.

LYNWOOD KING: When their stage manager left, Burr knew I was a fan, and he asked me to take the job. I took it even though I was directing all sorts of things. That's how much I enjoyed it.

LEW GOMAVITZ: They began working on each show about two in the afternoon. Over coffee, Fran might say, "Guess what happened to me today?" Before you knew it, that would be a story line. Sometimes, if they hadn't jelled the music or the story, the meeting would go right up to airtime. When I got into the control room I had an idea of what it might be, but even then, it might start as a show about a fire and end up being about Harry Truman.

Fran had to keep up with Burr, but she was like an Artesian well. Kukla never knew what Fran was gonna say, either.

LYNWOOD KING: She was funnier than they were lots of times. She would break Burr up. Sometimes, I would hear him giggling over the microphone.

LEW GOMAVITZ: Marlin Perkins came on with a skunk which was supposed to have been deskunked. For some reason, the skunk got uncontrollable and bit Marlin on the hand. Fran laughed and ran off the stage just before the skunk sprayed the entire place. You can't imagine the stench. Meanwhile, the cameraman was laughing so hard, the camera was moving up and down. You would have thought there was an earthquake.

Finally, Perkins left and Kukla came up on the stage after a lapse of about two dead minutes. He had this little mop in his hand. He started mopping the stage and he looked out at the audience and said, "It happens in the best of families."

LYNWOOD KING: The only thing that Burr insisted on was that you treated the "kids" as if they were absolutely real.

LEW GOMAVITZ: We all looked at them as individuals. Kukla was Kukla. Burr would have fits when someone called Ollie an alligator. Ollie was, and is, a dragon. We had a stage manager do that on the air. That was his last show.

HUGH DOWNS: I replaced the first announcer after they found him backstage poking his arm into Ollie. That was a no-no. And anybody who said, "Hey, Burr, hold up Kukla a second," would be dismissed. No one ever addressed the puppets as Burr.

LYNWOOD KING: Over the intercom, I would tell Kukla or Ollie to do this or that. After the show, we would play our own kinescopes, and Burr would say, "Did you see what Kukla did?"

HUGH DOWNS: One show started going very differently from the way it had been planned. Colonel Crackie was talking about his high-school graduation. He went on and on and on. After the show, Burr said, "I couldn't get the Colonel to shut up!"

STUDS TERKEL: I was doing a radio show called "Briefcase," and I said to Burr's manager, Beulah Zachary, "Burr could come on with Madame Oglepuss to talk about opera, and I would do Fran Allison's role."

It was the most amazing experience. I was absolutely mesmerized. I would say, "Madame Oglepuss. I'm so delighted."

"Oh, dear boy. I'm so glad you like the opera, Studs." She was great. After it finishes, Burr, Bev Younger, and I go the bar downstairs. I say to Burr, "How did you like the show?"

Not a word.

In the middle of my second drink, Bev goes, "Ask him how Madame Oglepuss liked it."

"How did Madame Oglepuss like it?"

[Loudly] "She loved it. Fantastic." Unbelievable, Burr became this person. They were real to Burr.

HUGH DOWNS: Burr had kind of a multiple schizoid approach to these people. The character speaking would make errors, but Burr never crossed a voice. I thought that kind of error was just impossible to avoid until I saw him do a show at the old Actors' Club. This was mind-boggling. Burr had been drinking, and when he brought Ollie out, Ollie was pretty drunk. Kukla came on and was cold sober. With clear disapproval and without any slurring of words, he said, "Don't come to me with your big head tomorrow complaining about a headache." Burr was not sober! I said, "My, God, this is spooky."

LYNWOOD KING: Once it got on the networks, the show really caught fire. It appealed to show-biz folks. Tallulah Bankhead became a big fan, and Gertrude Lawrence, Shirley Booth, Lena Horne. One day, I asked Burr "Who's that upstairs?"

"Oh, that's that new actor, Brando." He was still growing the beard to do *Viva Zapata!*

LEW GOMAVITZ: Delores Dragon was named after Tallulah Bankhead's niece. Tallulah was a great, great fan of the show. In fact, when we took the show on the road, General Sarnoff gave her carte blanche to use the NBC lines to call us wherever we happened to be. One year, she called us every single night. We were in New York, and naturally she wouldn't miss one of the shows. One night she forgot what she was doing. She said, "My God," and she threw on her mink coat and jumped into a cab to the theater. She came in about two minutes before air. There wasn't a seat left in the theater, so Burr had her sit down right in front of the stage on the deck in her mink coat. During the show, Kukla said, "Talu, aren't you a wee bit warm with your coat on?"

"Yeah, but I can't take it off."

Kukla says, "Why not?"

She opened up her coat, and she didn't have a stitch on.

LYNWOOD KING: Burr never played to children. You don't build an entire half hour around "Talullah Bankhead called you yesterday," and call it a children's show. Even though he won awards, he used to really get red in the face and say, "This is not a kids' show." It wasn't. It was way too sophisticated for kids. Burr always did just what he wanted to do. You didn't tell Burr anything.

Everybody was saying what a genius Burr was, but the show got inbred. A half hour about Tallulah was too show-bizzy. My favorite show would be about Fran's shopping in Glockenspiel's or Buelah Witch buzzing the UN, things like that.

Eventually, NBC did up and drop him. ABC picked him up, but the show was never again as prestigious, and frankly it had lost some of its charm. Every show runs its course no matter how good it is, and "Kukla" had been on five days a week for five years.

STUDS TERKEL: Burr was the genius of television. At his funeral, I talked about Burr's world. In the world today it's every man for himself. The Kuklapolitan world is a tender world in which people behave decently toward one another. That was the world Burr created. In the midst of high technology, it was no-technology, just a guy with his hands and little pieces of cloth.

* * *

BEN PARK: "Hawkins Falls" pursued the whimsical tradition of "Vic and Sade."

LYNWOOD KING: Hawkins Falls was a small town, population 6,200. Belinda Catherwood was the richest lady in town. At one point she got bees in her attic. That would be the whole plot.

Philip Lord played the judge, and Butler Manville, who had to be eighty years old then, was the town clerk. He was wonderful. One day I went into his dressing room and he had lines all over his face. I said, "What are you doing?"

"I'm putting on my age."

He was an ancient, ancient guy, who would wear celluloid cuffs. He would write his lines on those cuffs, so when you saw him staring fixedly at his hands, he would be reading his lines.

One day we had finished dress rehearsal, and we were short, and there was a scene with Butler eating a sandwich, and I said to him, "We're short. See if you can do something."

He said all right. Well, when we got to that scene, he took out his sandwich from a brown paper bag. He looked at this sandwich. Then he opened the desk drawer, fumbled around, and pulled out a pair of shears, and he very meticulously trimmed the lettuce around the four sides of his sandwich. It was totally delightful and so fascinating I forgot we were on the air for a minute. It was things like that that no writer could write.

HUGH DOWNS: Frank Dane was the male lead until he got so overbearing. He once so humiliated Ben Park and the writer Bill Barrett in front of everybody, my toes curled up in my shoes. He said something like, "I was an established actor when you guys were in knee pants. Don't tell me . . ." and "If you don't meet my demands you won't see me on the set tomorrow."

He put on his hat and stormed out, and after an awkward silence, Ben looked at Bill and one of them said, "Let's kill him," and they did. They wrote him out.

BEN PARK: We sent him off in an airplane, and it crashed, but then Bill found it very hard to keep on writing Bernardine as a widow, so we resurrected him a year and a half later [laughs], only it was his twin brother. Frank had been chastised to stay on the ball from then on.

LYNWOOD KING: It started as an hour show. Then it went to a half hour and then fifteen minutes. By then it was really a soap opera. We felt very sad about that, but there was nothing we could do.

BEN PARK: The good side of being an O & O in the days before the accounting guys got in was we could call up and say, "We want to do something," and they would say, "Do it." On the other hand, we were constantly saying, "They don't know how good we are. They don't know how hard we're working out here." The network's decisions about our shows were pretty arbitrary. If they wanted to take something off they took it off. If they wanted to put it in, they put it in, and that was it.

LYNWOOD KING: Because we were an O & O, we had to carry the entire network lineup from New York. My first year, the entire Sunday-night schedule came from New York. I'd be about the only person in the station. My job was to take about three hours worth of film, splice in the blanks for station breaks, and roll it. I also had to cut "Hopalong Cassidy" from an hour and twenty minutes to fifty minutes to fit them into an hour and make way for commercials. The other fellow I worked with sometimes just whacked off the first twenty minutes of the film. I tried to be a little more sophisticated. I tried to cut out just the mushy love stuff.

BEN PARK: We originated "Ding Dong School," which was one of the few shows that was a friendly educator of children.

REINALD WERRENRATH: My five-year-old son named the show. I showed him the school bell that we were using as the signature of the show, and he said, "Ding dong," and that gave us the name of the program.

BEN PARK: It was the first show with the announced intention of introducing children to a full world of ideas, in terms of stories, experiences, and doing things.

I did a series of shows designed to bring the outside world into the home. "Down on the Farm" was a series of live visits to a working farm. We also did "Portrait of America" because I had this notion of looking into real people's lives. The first show was about a family that has an interracial marriage in it.

LYNWOOD KING: "Coffee And" starring Hugh Downs was another local show. It was a variety show that later became "The Bunch" on the network. Hugh was great fun. We did little things to take advantage of who he was. One of the best things we ever did was coming up with the *Concerto for Kazoo and Orchestra*. We had the NBC orchestra in their tuxedos performing a very complicated arrangement. Hugh stood there and played the kazoo all the way through.

People like Hugh became stars because of the public's acceptance. They think he's a nice man. It was the same thing with Arthur Godfrey, except Hugh really is a nice man. Godfrey was the biggest son of a bitch in the world.

HUGH DOWNS: The nature of my job is to get that spotlight directed someplace else. I'm comfortable with that, and if people are comfortable with me, I'm very grateful.

I used to think I was terrible because I don't sing or dance. I thought I didn't belong in the business, but if you take a really blockbuster talent like Frank Sinatra, he wouldn't dare go on the air on television once a month. He would burn out in a year, so in a way the less talent you have or deploy the less chance you have of overexposure. That may be why I have been on network television more than anybody in the world.

* * *

NORMAN FELTON: I had known Studs from his radio shows. I wanted to find some way to do a show with him. While he was playing *Death of a Salesman* in Detroit I said to him, "When you're through with the show, we'll figure out something." We talked about it, and out of that eventually came "Studs' Place."

CHARLIE ANDREWS: His show originally was a showcase for Carolyn Gilbert, who wanted to be on television, so we designed a show with her playing piano in a bar. We needed a guy behind the bar, and Studs was perfect for that. The problem was after the first show it was obvious who was going to be the star. Studs came off naturally. Meanwhile, Carolyn realized she was better on radio than she was on television.

STUDS TERKEL: It was easy from the beginning. I had done radio, and I had a way of talking as though to one person. When we put together the cast, Charlie said, "We need a waitress." We were watching a show called "The Clocks." In "The Clocks" was this actress, Bev Younger. She was good, so we went to Bev and asked her to play the waitress. She said, "Where's the script?"

"There isn't gonna be any."

"I'm leavin', good-bye."

But we got her. She was fantastic. She broke the stereotype of the waitress. Hitherto the waitress in the movies was the Brooklynese gum-chewing type. She had a kind of mother wit. We used our real names, but Beverly wasn't the right name. She suggested Grace. There was a slight touch of that intimation.

After Bev, in comes Win Stracke, my old friend from the Labor Theater.

CHARLIE ANDREWS: Win had played Lenny, the idiot guy in *Of Mice and Men*. I fell in love with him from the minute I met him. He just radiated this sweet shyness that you see occasionally in big men.

STUDS TERKEL: Win played the self-educated hobo. He was actually a very cultured guy. He attended Lake Forest College, but he also traveled with some of the hoboes when he was young. He sang on picket lines, but he could sing anything.

So we got the waitress, the handyman Win, who—and this again is my credo—is a self-educated laborer. The fourth regular was Chet Roble. Charlie knew I liked jazz. He says, "There's a guy at Helsing's Lounge, where Georgie Gobel is performing. This guy is the house pianist," and it's Chet.

Chet invented the piano bar. He knew the hep world. He had a language all his own. We called it "Roblasian." "Here comes Joe Loot," he's got lots of money. Or, "Here comes Joe Dames," the guy was a ladies' man.

In my case, I was the entrepreneur who didn't know what the hell he was doing. As a generosity, people come, but he is not very good as far as business was concerned. John Crosby loved the show. He wrote, "These are people you think it's real, you know it's not real, but they're people you learn to care for."

The end was a credit, "Dialogue by the cast." We had visitors on the set, and they'd ask, "Are you guys having conversation or is it part of the script."

"Oh, it's the script." They couldn't tell. Neither could the cast sometimes. [Laughs.]

CHARLIE ANDREWS: I'd write up a two- or three-page outline. "Studs had a fight with his wife. He doesn't want to buy her a refrigerator." Then we'd meet on the balcony of the Civic Opera Building and rehearse. I'd say, "Studs is upset because he just had a fight with his wife. What are you fighting about, Studs?"

Studs would say, "Last week, she wanted to go visit with her folks, and I didn't want to go."

"Well, tell me about that."

So he would say this and that. "Tell that to Grace."

He would fall into the character, "Grace, my wife . . ."

Then I would say, "Grace, what's your position on this?"

"He was wrong. He should have never . . ."

"Tell him that, Grace. Now, Chet, can you put in your two cents?"

"Well, my attitude is people should never get married."

"Good, say that."

And at the end of a day, we'd have a half-hour show.

STUDS TERKEL: We never played down to the audience. One show was about cigarettes being bad, long before there was anything about it. A guy comes in puffing on a cigar. I say, "Oh, God, I love cigars. I am Ulysses passing the Isle of Circe. Tie me to the mast."

NBC said, "You can't do that. They won't know what the heck you're talking about."

"They'll get the idea. Goddamn, we gotta do it." That was my whole point. People will get it.

People were never put down. The stories were about little aspects of their lives. It was built on character. There was no audience and no canned laughter. Charlie or I would have ideas.

CHARLIE ANDREWS: One time I was moving and I had trouble with a sofa, so now we had a show about getting a sofa stuck in the doorway.

STUDS TERKEL: Charlie came in with a penknife, and he says, "How about a show about an old con game?" These two old guys come in with their frayed collars. It's obvious they are down on their luck. I give them a cup of coffee, and they get into a big argument. It's fake! They may have done this fifty years ago. They're trying to sucker me into buying this knife.

"You telling me what that knife is worth?"

"Are you kidding me? How dare you?"

Then one of the great lines: "And where do *you* play piano?" That's an old-time phrase for "Who the hell do you think you are?" He's accusing him of playing piano at a sporting house.

So I walk over and ask them what the problem is. One of them says, "He says this knife is only worth a hundred dollars."

I say, "I tell you what. I'll give you guys two great meals."

"Deal."

In real life, I'm a sucker for any beggar on the street. Mike Royko did a column about me once. There was a great huge black kid on the streets. Mike called him "The Weeper." One day Mike and I are together and The Weeper stops me. He's starting to cry, so I give him a buck. He starts crying, "But my little brother." So I give him another. "And my mother." I wound up giving him four or five bucks.

Mike says to me, "You fell for The Weeper!"

"You forget, Mike. You forget the performance. How much do you pay to see Olivier or Alfred Lunt?"

It was this principle with the two old boys. They don't know that I know it's an act. At the end, I buy it from them. I give them two big meals. I slip them both a sawbuck apiece. Bev and Win, they think I was taken, but I said, "No, I wasn't. They were wonderful. Did you ever see a performance like that?"

CHARLIE ANDREWS: They relied on their lives. Studs was never much out of character. He was Studs Terkel, a James T. Farrell character. Studs's tastes are so catholic. He knows a little about everything and has a firm position on everything.

Chet was a barroom pianist, and that's all he was. He liked horse-racing and football scores. Beverly was the only real pro actor. She had a small town background to fall back on, which she knew how to do. Win was a folk singer. He'd have a fight with the cook, and say to Studs, "They're wasting food out there, Studs, and like the song says," and he'd sing a folk song about not wasting food. That would give us a breather.

LYNWOOD KING: People thought there really was a Studs' Place where we poked our cameras in and overheard what was going on.

STUDS TERKEL: For twenty years, women would look out the windows of their buses, "What happened to Studs' Place?" Or waitresses. Bev wore a union button, of course. "What the hell you lettin' him talk to you that way for?" It was real to them. When we had guests, we used their actual names. Phil Lord, the old actor, we called him Mr. Lord.

HUGH DOWNS: As *Time* magazine put it, "Phil Lord, a crusty old actor, is played by Phil Lord, a crusty old actor." I went on as myself, too.

STUDS TERKEL: That one with Phil was a nice one. A famous actor is coming through, and this old battered actor who hangs around the restaurant proudly says he was his teacher once. He says, "I left a message for him to come here. He'll come."

We call up his agent who says he never heard of Phil Lord. We ask him to ask his client. I called back, and he says, "He never heard of him," so what are we going to say to Phil Lord? We say the guy wanted so much to see you, but he's been stricken, and we make up a message to read to Phil, how much he respects and admires him and how he'll never forget him.

DAN PETRIE: I admired Studs because he would often dare to look bad, to be the villain, to supply the conflict. In a show about opera, he intimates that the masses don't understand it, but the point he wanted to make was that Win and Chet and Grace would instinctively be attuned to those beautiful masterpieces.

STUDS TERKEL: I wanted to show every aspect of the human being, so sometimes I played a shit. Charlie came in one day with a bottle of cognac. He got the idea of having this German actor play the bar's janitor. His daughter is getting married. "We gotta give her a gift."

In the meantime, this bottle of cognac is standing behind the bar. It's too valuable to touch, but Bev says, "Let's give her that."

"Are you crazy? You can't touch that. It's up there for show." But then Win sings this old German drinking song, and I realize, "What's it for?" We give her the gift. We open it and do a toast. The theme is very simple: you live, for Chrissake.

LYNWOOD KING: "Studs' Place" had the first pregnant woman on television, Eloise Kummer, a local actress. They worked it into the plot. She felt faint and wandered into Studs' Place. In those days, you didn't even use the word "pregnant," and they had to wait on clearance to use her.

STUDS TERKEL: Eloise was very pregnant and very beautiful. She had a little girl in her belly who turned out to be a Miss USA. Her name was Amanda Jones. Amanda used to say, "I was in show business before I was born."

We did a show about deaf people. Bev's husband Les Podewell played this deaf guy who loves this woman who is also deaf. It's also comic about how hearing people react to them. I would say [loudly], "How do you feel about things?"

Then they dance. Win had a way. He came up with the song "Spanish Is a Loving Tongue," a very beautiful song. They touched the strings of his guitar, and somehow they dance without hearing. That show won some award.

BEN PARK: Win played a character in "Hawkins Falls" until NBC blacklisted him. They said, "You've got to get Stracke off the show. The sponsor won't have him." It was one of those soul-searching problems. What are you gonna do? Are you gonna pull the show and put everybody out of work? Win became the sacrificial bait. It still doesn't make me happy.

STUDS TERKEL: I signed all kinds of petitions. I'd emcee programs for Soviet-American friendship during the war, or anti–Jim Crow and anti–poll tax. I'm not in *Red Channels,* which I attribute to New York parochialism.

Chicago had its own McCarthy, a guy named Ed Clamage. Ed was the head of the Americanism Committee of the Legion. He was a fat clown figure, but people were scared. He would say he would get the Legion after them. He didn't have any Legion. It was a one-man thing, but he had some clowns, and the climate was with him.

One day, Ted Mills gets a call, and he says, "Oh, shit." It's a guy from New York named [Fred] Wile. He's Pat Weaver's assistant. Ted says to me, "You've been called a Red. They've got your name on a lot of things."

There's a meeting in Chicago, and some NBC guy says, "Our suggestion is, say you were duped."

I knew communists had signed those petitions too, but I was being cute. I said, "I don't know if they were communists or not, but what's that got to do with price control? Suppose they came out against cancer. Should I come out for cancer?"

Finally, he said, "Look, you've got to stand up and be counted."

I stood up. He didn't think that was funny, but I refused to say I was duped, and they knocked me off the air.

DAN PETRIE: When that happened, we were up to our hips in letters in Studs's living room.

TED MILLS: Most of them were addressed to "Studs' Place, Chicago." They believed there really was such a place.

STUDS TERKEL: The span of the letters was quite remarkable, the embossed stationery of an old dowager or an actual scrubwoman who signed it with an X. Her daughter wrote the letter. I got one from an old man in Cleveland. He wrote, "I'm a Dutchman, and the show gives me a feeling of what we call *hein weh,* homesickness. You may or may not have heard I was a ballplayer with the Indians. My name is Bill Wambsganss."

I wrote back, "My God, you're the guy who pulled the triple play in the World Series!" Bill Wambsganss!

*   *   *

BEN PARK: When I was doing "Hawkins Falls," I would get in at eight A.M., and I would be there until midnight. That's when we went out and drank and talked shows. We talked shows all the time. We knew we were doing something that was so vibrant, so integrated with our time. We never went on vacations. Who wanted to go on vacation? We didn't want to miss out on what was going on. Life was a vacation.

Then New York began filling the network schedule with its own shows, and our shows were locked out. Somewhat begrudgingly they felt that the stuff we were doing was often very good. I think Chicago gave Pat Weaver trouble. While he had a lot of respect for what we had done, his other half, which he got from the advertising agency, told him that what sells are big smashing shows. Those weren't our shows.

BILL HOBIN: The "Garroway" show got a "Look" award, and we all went to New York for that. There was a big party at the Stork Club. Max Liebman introduced himself to me, and he took me over to the bar to meet Sid Caesar and Imogene Coca. Then he said, "We'd like you to do 'Show of Shows.' "

I had just decided that "Garroway" was my love, and I didn't particularly care about "Show of Shows" at that time. Then "Garroway" was canceled, and Max again offered me the job. This time I took it.

LYNWOOD KING: In 1955, I knew that Chicago as a network-originating point had had it. We all wanted to be network. I was asked to direct "Don McNeill's Breakfast Club," and I took it.

TED MILLS: I left in '51. Coca-Cola wanted to pay me a lot of money to do the "Kostelanetz" show, and I wanted to get into the big time in New York or on the Coast.

CHARLIE ANDREWS: New York was big time, and we all wanted to conquer the world. I went with Dave to do the "Today" show. Then I wrote for Sid Caesar. That was heavyweight stuff. It was all I could do to hang on. I wasn't the fair-haired boy anymore.

But it wasn't that we disappeared after Chicago. Bob Banner has been a top producer. Billy Hobin was a top-dog director. Edie Barstow was going great until she died. In a small way what we did opened up what you can do in a studio.

STUDS TERKEL: One night, Dave and I were in the urinal on the nineteenth floor of the Merchandise Mart. He says to me, "They love me. General Sarnoff called me."

I said, "Dave, you are very popular. You've got a very good program, and you're not hurting NBC at all. They love you because you're very valuable to them. Protect that, Dave."

He says, "Oh, they're wonderful people."

Twenty years later, Dave is out completely. There's a reunion of old men. Dave, Charlie, Cliff Norton. At dinner, Dave says to me, "You were right."

CHARLIE ANDREWS: I became a producer. I did the Emmys and Miss USA, Miss Universe, and they were damn good shows. Of course I wanted to write a novel, paint a great picture, write a great opera, and write an epic poem. A friend of mine wrote a poem, and the last line was, "He wanted more to have written than to write." That's how I feel. I would love to have written a great novel, but that takes a long time. You gotta know how to spell all those words.

It was wonderful that I drifted into this business and had some success and got those paychecks. When I was growing up I couldn't have imagined a better life. I wasn't ashamed of writing commercial stuff. I never thought of myself as an artist. I was a good craftsman, a damn good craftsman, better than most.

STUDS TERKEL: We did "Studs' Place" locally for Manor House Coffee. Then they dropped us. The last show, we lost our lease on Studs' Place, and we're leaving. I said, "You guys go on." Chet plinks the piano, bangs it shut, and leaves. Win strums the guitar and puts it on the wall. Then Bev does one last wash of a glass and takes her apron off, puts it neatly away, blows the candle out in the bottle we have, and gives the place that last look.

I just go, "Ahhhh, okay." I wipe some dust off the wall, turn out the light, and leave. You see the empty stage. [Laughs.] We milked that to the end. The letters came! "How dare you break their lease!" That was great. All along our attitude had been, "We'll show those guys." It felt good when the New York critics paid tribute to Chicago. It was exciting to be seen all over the country. It was one of the most exhilarating times of my life.

DUMONT (THE FALL)

When we last saw the folks at DuMont, an infusion of greenbacks from Paramount Pictures had enabled them to set up a manufacturing plant for DuMont television sets and broadcast facilities for its two experimental stations, W2XVT in Passaic and W2XWV in New York City. The future was as rosy as a black-and-white picture could be.

It didn't work out that way. In September 1955, the DuMont network, which at its peak consisted of three owned and operated stations and over 175 affiliates, shut down. Three years later, the corporation was reconstituted as the Metropolitan Broadcasting Corporation because management feared that the stigma of the DuMont name would only lead to more failures. Allen DuMont then resigned from the company that was born in his own garage. Seven years later, at sixty-four, he was dead. Today, he is largely forgotten except by those who recall his excellent TV sets, innovative programming, and, among those who worked for him, the joy of competing against the big boys and very nearly pulling it off.

Actually, television history is littered with the detritus of small companies who "nearly" overcame the odds. The fact is that once the industry was established, no matter how creative the programming or how inventive the technology, without a mountain of cash the little guy never really had a chance. You can sit at the card table with the big three, but they deal, and from a marked deck supplied by the federal government. In 1955, Allen DuMont was only the latest to be sent home with a wallet picked cleaner than zebra bones at a buzzards' picnic.

Yet in only the narrowest sense was DuMont a failure. His contributions to the field are still being felt today. DuMont's long-life cathode ray tube made broadcasting possible. He put the first modern sets on the market and was manufacturing twenty-inch sets when the rest of the industry was selling postage-stamp–size TV screens.

The DuMont network had more firsts than Adam. It produced the first live network broadcast, between New York and Washington, the first regularly scheduled children's show, "The Small Fry Club" with Big Brother Bob Emery; it introduced the first daytime schedule. It was the first to regularly broadcast pro football. It was on DuMont's "Cavalcade of Stars" that Ralph Kramden first threatened to send Alice to the moon.

DuMont's programming was often a triumph of brains over budget. Few kids noticed or cared that Captain Video's opticom scillometer was put together with assorted parts from Wanamaker's automotive department. "Monodrama Theater," a monologue in front of a curtain, was one of television's first late-night hits, and Bishop Fulton Sheen and a blackboard gave Milton Berle a run for his money in the early 1950s. DuMont was also a temporary home for Ernie Kovacs, still fondly remembered for guaranteeing the accuracy of a harpoonist, whose missile then mistook the control-room window for Moby Dick.

So what happened? Well, if the broadcasting field was a series of high hurdles, the DuMont Corporation was Danny DeVito. The FCC didn't help matters any by handing down a series of rulings that eventually crippled DuMont. The most critical was the "Sixth Report" issued in 1952, which decided on station allocations around the country. The "Sixth Report" allowed as many as four stations in only seven cities around the country, while smaller cities got only two or three stations. Most of those stations affiliated with NBC, CBS, or ABC, with whom they had had long relationships going back to radio. DuMont, which never had a radio network, was effectively blocked from those markets.

"If there had been four VHF outlets in the top markets," said Dr. Hyman Goldin of the FCC in a 1960 interview, "there's no question [that] DuMont would have lived and would have eventually turned the corner in terms of profitability. I have no doubt in my mind of that at all."

But it didn't happen. DuMont did have some affiliates in the larger cities, and those stations were committed to carrying DuMont programs. However, in the smaller cities, where there was no DuMont affiliate, it was left to the network's sales representatives to try and convince the local station to "clear" (air) DuMont's programs to fill out their broadcast schedules. But even when the salesmen succeeded and a station cleared a DuMont show, the program would often air after prime time when viewership was low. Fewer outlets and limited prime time access around the country for its programs meant huge financial losses for the network. And while CBS and NBC could rely on radio income to subsidize their TV networks, DuMont's only other income came from the sale of its TV sets, which was not enough to make up the deficit.

NBC and CBS permanently entered the black in 1951, but DuMont's losses were over a million dollars and mounting. Programming suffered, and while the staff down at the Wanamaker's studio did their best, they could no longer compete with the slicker productions offered by the larger networks. "Rocky King, Inside Detective" may have been a charming little show, but it wasn't much against the likes of the "Philco Playhouse."

The company's fate was sealed in 1953 when the FCC approved the merger of United Paramount Theatres with the ABC network. The infusion of $30 million into ABC, which had been considering a merger with DuMont, meant that DuMont was now fourth, and very definitely last in the industry hierarchy.

DuMont's other problems were internal. Paramount Pictures' cash put DuMont in business, but Barney Balaban and Paul Raibourn soon shut off the spigot. Under FCC rules, a company was allowed to own a maximum of five stations. Because Paramount was a half owner of DuMont and also owned two other stations, the FCC denied DuMont permission to purchase two more stations to go along with the three it already owned. The FCC ruled despite the fact that a Paramount station—KTLA—refused to clear any DuMont programs.

The company's top-level management also made some disastrous moves, the worst being the sale of its successful Pittsburgh station, WDTV, to Westinghouse in January 1955. That severed the last bastion of profitablity from the network. Within nine months, the DuMont network was gone. Perhaps not coincidentally, that same year CBS brought in its big-money quiz shows, while ABC began to make waves with violence and gore. The pioneering spirit may still have been still celebrated—but only in TV westerns. The little network that could, could no more.

TED BERGMANN: I worked for NBC before the war as a staff announcer. I went back after the war, but three months later they gave me my notice. They said they had fulfilled their obligations to me under the GI Bill of Rights. They had hired many people during the war, and they were the ones they wanted to keep.

I was fired the day my first son was born. I was desperate, so I answered an ad in *The New York Times* for a time salesman. I had never sold anything in my life. It turned out to be for DuMont. I was hired for a $150-a-week drawing account. Instead of a salary, you got a commission of ten percent of any time you sold, and our commissions would be charged against $150 a week. At the end of the first year, I owed the company about six thousand dollars. That's how much time I was able to sell.

CHRIS WITTING: After the war, I became the managing director of WABD in New York and WTTG in Washington. That was the first television network. We used to bring a fifteen-minute news show in from Washington at seven o'clock, "Walter Compton and the News."

LES AIRRES, JR.: The DuMont station in Washington was named WTTG in honor of Tom Goldsmith. The station was located in the Harrington Hotel, which was a salesman's hotel. The transmitter was on the top floor, and you could see a lot of things going on through the windows. That went through your mind, so once when our announcer didn't show up and I was called on to do a station break, I announced it as, "located in the Whorington Hotel." I didn't do any more announcing for a long time.

CHRIS WITTING: In New York, we were operating out of the studio on Madison Avenue. We needed a larger one, so we moved into a huge space at Wanamaker's department store.

DON HASTINGS: There was no security whatsoever. Someone could walk in and say, "What's going on here?" And we'd say, "We're on the air."

JACK RAYEL: Wanamaker had a tremendous auditorium with a huge balcony all around the edge, and you could sit at the railing and look down on the studio and watch.

STAN EPSTEIN: Richard Hayes and Peggy Ann Gornish used to make love up there. We used to call her "Peggy Ann Gornished."

JACK RAYEL: You could sit up in the balcony and look down and see the shows that were on the air and others preparing to go on. The sets for each show were cheek and jowl, arranged around the walls of the studio. Mary Kay and Johnny did a kind of soap opera. Right next to them in another cubicle was something called "The Record Shop." The host would talk about popular records. Next to that was the set for Wendy Barrie's talk show.

CHUCK TRANUM: The station didn't have a regular announcer. They did all of their station breaks by "electrical transcriptions." I was then doing guest relations at DuMont. I asked the station manager if I could do the station breaks live. I had never done anything like that in my life. We did a test, and I was sweating, and I could hardly get the words out, but he couldn't care less. "That sounds all right, Chuck," so I became DuMont's first staff announcer, "This is WABD, New York's window on the world."

JACK RAYEL: Jim Caddigan was in charge of programming. I became his assistant. Much of what went on DuMont was his. I used to sit in his office, and it was incredible to meet the people who wanted to come into television. The agents Ted Ashley and Aaron Steiner. Bill Todman and Mark Goodson came in a lot. These guys were all just beginning in television.

It was my job to screen all the new program ideas. Some of everything came in, personality shows, dramas. A columnist for a trade paper convinced Jim that his wife could do a fashion show. Once the show was on, we were bombarded with requests to put it on a better slot. We had the post office examine the letters, and it turned out they had faked all of them.

LARRY MENKIN: I was at WMCA in New York when a friend told me that the DuMont network was looking for people. I got in to see Caddigan who said he needed program ideas.

LEE POLK: Larry and Charlie Spear were partners and very prolific writers of mystery shows. If you were in trouble and had to get something out, nobody could turn it out faster. That was important in live television where you had to cover hours and try to maintain an audience against three networks. To have an innovator like Ernie Kovacs or a comedian like Gleason were the kinds of things we aspired to, but the meat of the schedule were the shows like Larry's. Caddigan would say to him, "We gotta fill some time," and Larry would think for a second and say, "Got it."

LARRY MENKIN: I started out working for a guy who sold radio scripts around the country. He hired me to do a western series, but after a while, even I began to get tired. He said, "You stay here until you finish four scripts. I'm gonna lock the door. If you have to go to the bathroom, knock, but that's all. You have to learn the biggest thing in this business is put it on paper and get it finished." I did. He was the greatest teacher I ever had.

Charlie Spear had been a news reporter, so he was very fast too. It was kind of an ESP between us. One week, I'd write the outline and then he would write the script. The next week we'd switch. One week we did a script, and then the next week we did the same script again. Chris Witting said, "Larry, are you guys running out of gas?"

He was the only one who noticed. The directors didn't give a shit. We asked Chris if he wanted us to do an extra one. He said, "No, both of them got big ratings."

JACK RAYEL: I became the daytime program manager in '48. We went on the air at seven o'clock. Caddigan ran a highly inventive schedule, considering that he was doing it with spit and ceiling wax. We began with an exercise program. Then we had news. There was also "Morning Chapel," "Your Television Babysitter," and others one after another right into the evening.

Every day at noon, I did a half-hour show called "Man on the Street" outside the Madison Avenue studio. I wore a pack on my back, and they put the camera in the window. I would walk from the corner up a block to the corner opposite CBS and down. I had regular visitors like Tuffy Bruzhoon, the Roller Derby queen. We never lacked for people to talk with.

Then one day Caddigan asked, "What would happen if we put a camera in the window at five o'clock in the afternoon and just looked at New York?" We tried it, and we showed some great sunsets, while I talked about New York in the afternoon.

WES KENNEY: We were all trained to direct on "Morning Chapel" because it was so simple. Within five weeks, I was doing about seven shows a day.

LEE POLK: I don't know when I had time to have kids. The schedule was continuous, "Okay, what's next?"

PAT FAY: I was directing like fifteen shows a day. One time I came in and they said, "You're directing the show."

"When?"

"It's already on."

WES KENNEY: You'd walk down the hall, and they would pull you in to do anything. You'd have thirty seconds to set the cameras and go for the next show. You had no rehearsal, no preparation or anything.

LARRY MENKIN: Charlie and I were very busy. Every week for a year and a half we did "Rocky King, Inside Detective." We also had "Captain Video" in the beginning, "Hands of Murder," and "The Plainclothesman," where the camera was the detective. You never saw his face.

LEE POLK: "Hands of Murder" was one of the shows where the title would change but it was really the same show.

PAT FAY: Every time we had a new sponsor, it went from "Hands of Murder" to "Hands of Destiny" to "Hands of Mystery."

LARRY MENKIN: A lot of the plots were the same. You can do the homicidal maniac and the girl a thousand times. He wants to kill girls, and the detective finds out. Who will get there first, the detective or the maniac? One week the killer works in a beauty parlor, maybe the next week a record library, or maybe he's a cutter in the garment industry with one of those big knives.

A timid guy gets angry at the world. He dreams that he kills all these people. When he wakes up he finds out he did kill all these people. Now he's a fugitive. I did that one three times.

I also created two cheapo soap operas called "One Man's Experience" and "One Woman's Experience." I hated them. I walked out of the studio one day. Somebody said, "C'mon back, it's not that bad."

"Yes, it is."

Then I was talking to an actor named Marty Koslick. He says, "Use the best stories. I'll do *Crime and Punishment*. Someone else can do Shakespeare." So we started "Monodrama Theater." There were no sets. It was a combination of monologue and narration.

LEE POLK: It was a fifteen-minute show. The same actor, Steve Elliott, for example, would do *Moby-Dick* as a monologue for a week. All he'd have to work with was a telescope. The camera would move up and down and be the ocean. It was a great actors' showcase. Koslick did several of them. He was a Method actor. He'd still be getting in the mood while we were throwing him cues to start. "We're on the air!" The stage manager had to crawl over, grab his leg, and turn him around.

The show wasn't bad. Those who put down the early days of television are putting down the technical aspects of it. To them that's more important than seeing something that touches you, but some of the things I saw were better than some of the multimillion-dollar productions you see today.

"Monodrama Theater" was the kind of low-budget show we had to do. The other networks could spend on their shows, while we were always cutting back. To save money on furniture, a guy would reach off-camera for, let's say, a decanter, and instead of having a cabinet there, a stagehand would simply hand it to him. Or they would take a flat from one show, drape it with venetian blinds and use it for another show.

LARRY MENKIN: We didn't have a lot of space for those shows, so for the chases we would show a sequence of very tight shots and intercut them: the cop chasing the guy, the guy looking around, the girl trying to run, the guy coming closer. We just used the three cameras and cut from one to another.

WES KENNEY: We cheated a lot with the chases. One Sunday when Wanamaker's was closed, I used the freight elevator for a shot. We just followed the feet into the elevator. That way the cameras wouldn't pick up the fact that they were running through Wanamaker's piano department.

Once, we had a chase on the fire escape outside the Ambassador Theater. Nobody thought to get clearance from the police because we weren't going out on the street. We were on the fire escape and the first thing you know we had a street full of police out on Ninth Street.

LEE POLK: A cop took out his gun. It took somebody diving in to save Karns. "It's a television show!"

Actually, imagination was the order of the day. "Magic Cottage" was a live show for kids. Pat Meikle would stand at the easel and draw a leprechaun. Then she would say, "We're going to have our friend visit us today." She would say some magic words, and the leprechaun would be standing there. For years, I was stopped by people, asking, "How did they do that?"

That was Hal Cooper's imagination. We also did rear-screen projection on that show.

HAL COOPER: We invented things all the time. We had a "magic" vase, that had "cracked" and lost its magic, and we needed somebody to say the magic words to make the cracks disappear. We had an artist draw all the cracks on the vase in dark red—this was in black and white. Then, when the time came we flipped a red filter in front of the camera and all the cracks disappeared.

There were a lot of other things. We needed to pan up a set to see a mouse in a clock. We were using a huge lens, and it was too cumbersome to pan up that far, but my cameraman strapped himself to the camera and said, "I can do it, watch." By using all his weight he did it. Everybody was trying things like that in those days.

LARRY WHITE: I directed "The Plainclothesman," which used the subjective camera as part of the concept. If he got something in his eye we made the camera blink by flicking it on and off. If he got hit, we would spin the camera up, and quickly out and into focus, or the guy would just wobble the camera.

WES KENNEY: Shows like "Magic Cottage" and Chuck Tranum's "Manhattan Spotlight" weren't rehearsed. You would just wing 'em. Of course all kinds of things happened. One day, a baby elephant was going to appear on "Manhattan Spotlight." Meanwhile, "Captain Video" was on the air. Suddenly, the elephant started trumpeting. The trainer gave him a jab, and he trumpeted again. On the air, Captain Video stood up and said, "What the hell is that?"

And the Ranger said, "I don't know, Captain, but get down, it could be dangerous!"

✳   ✳   ✳

TED BERGMANN: I put together the deal that gave birth to "Cavalcade of Stars," which starred Jack Carter, then Jerry Lester, and ultimately was the show Jackie Gleason did on DuMont. It worked so well that we sold a second hour called "Cavalcade of Bands" that ran simultaneously on another night.

JOSEPH CATES: Jack Carter was an enormous hit, but he was hired away by NBC and Jerry Lester took over. An agent got me a job as an assistant to the producer, Milton Douglas, who spent most of his time playing tennis or gin rummy.

Jerry stayed on until he got fired. What happened was he came out to do a monologue. He tells a joke. It doesn't work. He tells another joke. It doesn't work. He says, "You know what I think of the writer of that? *Thppt.*" He spits. "That's too good for him, *thhpt thhhp thpt.*"

Two days later, the president of the drug chain which owned the show said to Milton, quite properly, "Look, we don't interfere with how you do the show, but spitting on the runway is not appropriate."

At the next rehearsal, Milton said to Jerry, "A couple of guys took offense. You shouldn't spit."

Jerry said, "Sure, okay." Comes the show. Jerry does his monologue. He says, "You know, last week I told a joke. It didn't work. I said, 'You know what I think of the writer?' " He spat on the stage. "Then I wanted to make it clear, so I went *thpt thpt thpt.* I was criticized for it. I was told it was not appropriate for me to go, *thpt.* You know what I think of the people who told me that? *Thpt thpt thpt.*"

He was fired the next day. We signed Peter Donald to replace him, but he backed out. Benny Piermont knew Jackie Gleason from his nightclub days, and Jackie was available. We were desperate, and we took a chance on Gleason for $750 a week.

TED BERGMANN: As far as we were concerned, Gleason might have been a thirteen-week host if he didn't work out. A week before he started, I met him backstage at the Adelphi Theater. At that point, he was a tall, slim, good-looking man with black hair and a kind of map-of-Ireland face. He took my hand, and said, "Mr. Bergmann, I just want you to know that this is a great opportunity and I appreciate it. I'm gonna work my ass off, and we're gonna make a real dent with the show."

I didn't see him again until about six weeks later when the show was a big hit. I went backstage to his dressing room. He was sitting there staring at himself in the mirror. I tapped on the door, which was open, and he looked up at me in the mirror and said [contemptuously], "What the fuck do you want?"

JOSEPH CATES: Coleman Jacoby and Arnie Rosen wrote the first year for us. They created every character Gleason ever did with the sole exception of the Honeymooners.

COLEMAN JACOBY: They had a lot of trouble in the beginning with Gleason. They didn't know what to do with him, so Arnie and I started inventing. Our first sketch was a Reggie Van Gleason sketch. We wrote up a contract where we owned the characters we created. Unfortunately, when it came time to sue him, which we did, because he used those characters forever, we didn't get a quarter. The contract Arnie drew up was no damn good.

Gleason had no input into our work. His input was in his very good performance of the things we wrote.

JOE CATES: Art Carney was hired the second week of the show. Jacoby and Rosen had this sketch, a takeoff on Seagram's "Man of Distinction" ads. They needed a fey—you didn't say fag—photographer. I said, "Who will play the photographer?"

Either Arnie or Coleman said, "How about Art Carney?"

MOREY AMSTERDAM: One day I was auditioning people to play the waiter on my radio show. A guy walks into the theater. He picks up the script. He looks at it and then he starts to walk off. I said, "Hey, whatsa matter? Don't ya like the script?"

The theater is dark. He's looking. He can't see where we are. He says, "I guess it's all right, but I don't do comedy. I'm the heavy on 'Gangbusters.'"

"As long as you're here, read it."

Well, he read, and the guy broke me up. I wanted to hire him. Irving Mansfield looked at me, and he said, "This isn't television. They can't see that he's funny."

"They can hear it. If he don't work out, we'll get another waiter."

Well, he started working with me. That guy could play piano. He could dance. He could sing. He could do any goddamn thing, and it was the first comedy Art Carney ever did.

JOE CATES: I asked Irving Mansfield if I could use Art. He said okay, so Art shows up for rehearsal. Gleason walks in, and he says, "Who's gonna play the photographer?"

"A guy named Art Carney."

"Who is he, pal?"

"He's on Morey Amsterdam's show." So Jack walks over and says, "Hiya, pal," and that's how they met.

Everyone liked Art. He was brilliantly funny, but there were all sorts of Irish factors. Art would get drunk every six weeks, and Jackie would take care of him. It was a very odd relationship. If Art had been a slightly different personality it would have been Laurel and Hardy, Gleason and Carney.

I didn't like Jackie for many good reasons, but unlike performers like Ethel Merman, where if a smaller part stopped the show, the song was cut or she got it, Jackie welcomed it. He had confidence. He loved it. Art always said Jackie gave him stage. After that first show together, Jackie said, "Hey, pal, get him for next week. He's gold."

I said, "Jackie, the stuff's not written."

"We'll write for him." He was not threatened by him. He's maybe the only performer I met in forty-odd years who wasn't threatened by a fantastic talent. That's the nicest thing I can say about Jackie.

COLEMAN JACOBY: Almost everything Jackie did, even the way he crossed legs, I invented. All of the characters sprang into existence the first two months. Reggie was the first. Joe the Bartender was a steal from Art Duffy's Tavern. The Poor Soul started out as The Bachelor.

I directed the sketches. Gleason was a very apt pupil. He could move like Chaplin, and he never changed anything when it worked. After we left, Gleason reduced them all either to pantomime or they were almost identical to each other week to week. The aim was to do away with the necessity of learning a sketch. He did that with all of his sketches, except the Honeymooners, which were all scripted.

JOE CATES: The Honeymooners started the second year of "Cavalcade" when Joe Bigelow and Harry Crane were the writers. Even the truth of that has never been told. Jackie had a friend, Lew Parker, a vaudevillian. Lew had just spent the summer touring with his wife, doing Phil Rapp's Bickersons sketch. Gleason promised Lew he would put it on the show, so we rented the sketch from Phil Rapp. The Bickersons were characters on radio played by Don Ameche and Frances Langford, a husband and wife who bickered. We did the sketch, and at a meeting two days later, Jackie said, "We could steal that. It's perfect for me."

I said, "Jackie, let it rest for two or three weeks. If we do it again next week, Phil Rapp will sue the hell out of us."

"Don't be an idiot, Joe. After we're through switching, nobody will recognize it. I'll be a bus driver in Brooklyn. Art will be the guy who lives upstairs. He's a sewer worker," and that's how it grew.

I knew an actor named Ralph Bell, who was married to Pert Kelton, a funny Irish biddy of a lady who played the trombone. I got her to play Alice. I called Joyce Randolph to play Art's wife. It was no big significance. It was just a sketch.

We didn't have a set designer yet, so I designed the original set. I went across to the builder after Jackie had said, "I want a center entrance with a window so I can yell upstairs to Art. Put the kitchen here and the entrance to the bedroom here." I didn't let them decorate it. I was brought up in the Bronx during the Depression. I know what a grim set looks like, and they stayed with it all those years.

HARRY CRANE: I love Joe, but the Bickersons had nothing to do with it at all. I said to Jackie after the fourth or fifth week I was with him, "You need more characters." I even wrote an idea to do a sketch called "The Beast When the Honeymoon Is Over" about a bus driver and his wife, who fought all the time. That was my mother and father. I wrote about my life. I saw these people every day when I was growing up, fighting and scratching for their lives, and the arguments. There were no surgeons living in my building. When they could get a job, they worked as pressers in the hat factories and in the dress houses.

For the set, I just described my apartment, the three rooms. The kitchen was painted green. It looked like I lived inside a mailbox.

Jackie didn't want to do it. He said, "There's no bits. There's no action. They're talkin'."

"But the whole world knows this."

For weeks I begged him to do the sketch. Finally, five weeks later, he agreed to give it a shot. Well, the fuckin' switchboard was flooded with calls. When I went up to the dressing room after the show, I said, "What'd I tell ya."

He says, "We gotta do one of these every month."

"No, we'll do it every week."

COLEMAN JACOBY: Nat Hiken always said that what made "The Honeymooners" great was that it was the only show where you see the real Gleason. All that anguish and the bellowing and the bullying and the pipe dreams, that was really part of Gleason's early life. That's what made contact with millions of people. That plus one other thing—Carney, who gave it a note of originality, and who took the edge off the brutal aspect of it.

We quit after the first year. He became impossible to work for as he got bigger and bigger. He copped a plea with every sketch, so if it fell through he was off the hook. He'd say, "You've got nothing there, pal," but I would jam it through and tell him to try it. Then, after it worked, he would come over to the table and say, "Did it again, pal."

JOE CATES: At the start of the second year, Gleason, who was always in debt, needed money. He said, "If you will give me thirty thousand dollars, I'll sign up for an additional three years." Well, it was obvious to Milton Douglas and Ed Kletter, who was with Whelan, what to do, but they didn't have the money. It was DuMont's key show, so they went to Jim Caddigan for the money, but he said, "I have better plans for this money." He bought a dramatic hour starring Joseph Schildkraut. That was how wonderful Caddigan's instincts were about show business. Jackie finished out the year, sifted through his offers, and went with CBS.

*   *   *

TED BERGMANN: One of the most interesting sponsorships I was involved with was Bishop Sheen. We put him opposite Milton Berle because it was a dead time period and we wanted the cheapest programming possible. We decided that one week we would have a rabbi, one week a priest, one week a Protestant minister. Bishop Sheen was the priest. Early on we noticed that when he was on, the ratings blossomed, but at the end of the season we canceled the shows. When we told the archdiocese, they said, "If we got a sponsor, would you keep it on?"

I said, "You're talking our language. Sure."

About a month later, they said they had a sponsor, Admiral. They thought this was the way it was done. You selected the sponsor instead of the other way around. They wanted me to go see the head of the company, Ross Siragusa, which I did. When he asked me why I was there, I said, "Cardinal Spellman's office said you would sponsor Bishop Sheen."

"He's crazy. I can't sponsor a Catholic bishop on TV. All of my distributors are Jewish. They would be madder than hell."

"I don't think so. The Bishop has a large Jewish following. Ask your distributors."

So he had his secretary call Moe Ginsburg in Atlanta, Joe Cohen in Minneapolis, et cetera. I was sitting there when the phone calls started coming in. "Sam, I'm thinking about sponsoring Bishop Sheen for DuMont. What do you think? You do? The whole family? Really? I'll be darned. Thanks a lot."

He got consent from all of them, and we negotiated the deal.

WERNER MICHEL: Bishop Sheen ad-libbed the show except the last two minutes. When we gave him a signal for the last two minutes, he very elegantly got into his prepared script. He was wonderful. The first week, the announcer did a typical warm-up, a little cleaner than usual. Sheen was standing in the wings listening. Afterward, he said to me, "I can do better," so he did his own warm-up.

STAN EPSTEIN: He looked so intense, but he was funny.

DON HASTINGS: One time he said he was in Philadelphia trying to find the Coliseum where he was going to give a speech. He said, "I stopped a kid to ask him where the Coliseum was." The kid asked him what he was gonna do there.

"I'm gonna give a speech on how to get to heaven."

Then the kid said, "You can't even find the Coliseum."

ROY SHARP: Bishop Sheen appeared on more stations on the network than any other show. I think he had 215 clearances.

In 1950, I got a job at DuMont as the assistant to the traffic manager, George Faust. We cleared stations for shows such as "Cavalcade of Stars" and "Cavalcade of Bands," which were powerhouses. The company's ace in the hole was that they owned the only station in Pittsburgh, so when they wanted clearances in Boston, they could put the arm on NBC and CBS. NBC got one hour in Pittsburgh and DuMont would get maybe six hours on the NBC station in Boston. The reason that "Studio One" was on Monday night at ten o'clock was that that was the only time we would give it live clearance in Pittsburgh. Westinghouse, the sponsor, wouldn't take it on a delay in their home market.

TED BERGMANN: Pittsburgh was terrific. It had a gross income of six million dollars and a net of four million dollars. It supported the network.

When Chris Witting went to Westinghouse, he recommended that Don McGannon be given the job as head of the broadcast division and managing director of the network. Then I got a call from Dr. DuMont, inviting me to lunch. I met him at the Upper Montclair Country Club, and he said, "Chris has recommended that Don McGannon replace him, but Don has only been in the company a couple of years. You've been here a while, and I'd like you to replace Chris."

I said, "Doc, I'm not sure that's a good idea. I'm Jewish."

"What's that got to do with it?"

"Doc, there is no Jewish network president, and there's a good reason for that."

"I never heard of such a thing. Why is that so?"

"Most of your big advertising agencies do not hire Jews. The blue-chip advertisers are notoriously anti-Semitic. Procter & Gamble, Lever Brothers, Colgate don't hire Jews, and they don't want to deal with Jews. The networks have invariably had non-Jews as their presidents, non-Jews."

He pointed out that both Sarnoff and Paley were Jewish, but I said, "That's different. None of them on the line, operating the networks, are Jews."

He thought for a minute. Then he said, "If anybody doesn't want to give us their business because you're Jewish, I don't want their business."

From that day onward, I worked my ass off for him. He was very naive in these areas. He was a scientist, but he was a very gentle man and a very kind man. He allowed me to do whatever I wanted to do, but the thing I hated the most was I wasn't able to pull it off for him. It just couldn't work.

WERNER MICHEL: DuMont was a wonderful engineer, but he was the most naive man I ever knew in the business. The board of DuMont included him, a polio victim, Admiral Paton, who had one arm, and there was another guy with one eye. Everybody had a deficiency. We had a meeting, and Paton sat next to me, and he told me with a straight face that he had these little boats, and he would sit in the bathtub and play with them. You could make a television series out of that group.

ART ELLIOT: It was a pretty strange group at the top. They were a little like the Iraqi army general corps. Too bad, because DuMont had some excellent technical people and a lot of dedicated people who worked very hard.

TED BERGMANN: A transmitter salesman named Don Stewart was in charge of the Pittsburgh station. He had no broadcasting experience at all. Stewart was strange. A guy named Matty Fox, who had once been president of Universal Pictures, called me one day after Don had gone up to see him. He said Stewart had gone into Fox's office and threw himself on the floor, prostrating himself at his feet begging for his films.

LES AIRRES: Stewart's idea of ethics left something to be desired. He set up a mail-order business on the side, and he sold time on the station to that business at rates nobody else got. Also, he and his wife would come in after hours and go through your waste basket to see what you had thrown away. If paper wasn't used on both sides, it was back on your desk the next morning. And God forbid you let a paper clip get in the basket. That would be back, too, with a note, "These things cost money."

ART ELLIOT: Their lawyer, Ed McCrossin, was an awful drunk who would disappear for days until someone would go out and find him. The guy who ran the network, Mort Loewi, with his white hair and thousand-dollar suits, would return from lunch with a couple of ladies in tow. They would be about twenty-three years old with their skirts up to their butts. They'd go into his office, the door would close, and that would be all afternoon.

Les Airres's father was also a piece of work. He was the most ill-tempered guy I ever knew, and he was the guy who would clear the stations for the DuMont sports stuff. My God, the language, "You fuckin' son of a bitch, I'll come down and tear your gizzard out."

You never knew where you stood in the company. These guys would go out, get tight at lunch, then come in and fire two or three people. For Chrissakes, every Friday afternoon was like hitting Omaha beach.

DuMont himself didn't understand broadcasting. He wasn't a leader. He didn't know how to talk with the spear carriers, and he ran the place like a grocery store. He'd go away on a three-week trip, and all the paychecks would have to be held up until he got back.

WERNER MICHEL: I was then quasi–program director but my title was executive producer. Ted Bergmann and I decided to co-create a complete network schedule. Up to that point, it was just a little here, a little there. Ted and I put a schedule together, seven nights from eight to ten, and we brought it to Dr. DuMont and said, "This is the year to do it if we want to be the third network. Let's do it before ABC."

He phumped around for days. Finally, he said, "We can't afford it." He said we could use only one show—"The Stranger"—which was a terrible show. I know. I invented it.

ART ELLIOT: I went with DuMont in February 1949. My job was booking the orders for shows from stations around the country. Tom Gallery was the head of sales. He was a great big exuberant guy who had been with the Yankees, and who had been married to Zasu Pitts, but he didn't give us any leadership. When I began selling shows, Tom Gallery never accompanied me on a call. His assistant never accompanied me. It was always just me. I remember sitting in the waiting room at the biggest agencies in New York, ready to make a presentation and out would come six or seven CBS people, including Frank Stanton and Jack Van Volkenburg. Pat Weaver would accompany his people.

I also think the agencies didn't trust Tom. We had the Notre Dame games, which were sponsored by Chevrolet. At our Pittsburgh station, when they cut away for a commercial, up came a spot for a local Ford dealership. The guy who ran the account said to Tom, "How can you do that? That was promised to Chevrolet."

Actually, that was that peckerhead who ran the station, Don Stewart. His answer was tough shit. He made more money selling it locally—ten times the amount—than he could with the network commercials. The Doctor didn't do squat about it.

TED BERGMANN: We had "The Amateur Hour" on a network of about twenty-six stations until NBC decided they wanted it. They went out and put pressure on the NBC stations that were carrying us by saying, "Hey, we have a show we want you to carry at seven o'clock on Sunday," which was when we had "The Amateur Hour." "If you want to maintain your affiliation agreement with us, you'll clear it," so we'd lose them. Then NBC went to the ad agency, Lennen & Newell, and said, "Hey, why are you keeping 'The Amateur Hour' on DuMont? You're gonna lose all your stations. Bring it to NBC."

ART ELLIOT: When the agencies originated shows, generally DuMont got the leftovers, the stuff they couldn't clear elsewhere, because of our clearance record.

ROY SHARP: NBC and CBS had many more affiliates than we did. This all stemmed from the fact that they started with radio networks. The Doc didn't, and in those days the radio stations that went into TV kept their same affiliation. In Charlotte, for instance, there were two stations. They were affiliated with NBC and CBS. We were able to feed them one program, maybe Saturday-night wrestling. We did get clearances at NBC and CBS affiliates on "Captain Video," which ran Monday through Friday, seven o'clock, because they didn't have any network shows on that time.

ART ELLIOT: Clearing stations was the key, especially since in so many cities there was only one station in town. There was a lot of pressure on the guys who were on the road, trying to convince a station to clear one of our programs. If they couldn't clear a show they'd go home at night, and their blood pressure would be about 195.

At DuMont we could generally count on clearing WFIL in Philadelphia. We had WABD in New York. DuMont also owned Washington and Pittsburgh, and we had a close relationship with WGN in Chicago. There were three or four other stations that had bought DuMont equipment and part of the deal was you could write off some of these things if you became an affiliate. Cincinnati WCPO was an example of that. Erie, Pennsylvania, the guy never paid for any of his equipment but cleared all of DuMont's shows.

We didn't have a lot of stations, but we had a lot more than ABC did. If we had been differently financed and differently managed at the top, I don't think there's any doubt that we would have survived. The only reason ABC survived was they had been in the radio business, and they got the Paramount backing.

ROY SHARP: We hit our peak in 1950 when we were on even footing with the other networks, but little by little we lost the edge. NBC and Columbia were boosting their schedules, which left less time for our shows. Soon, we couldn't clear our regular shows. Of course, they had Ed Sullivan and Sid Caesar, and we had Arthur Murray or "Life Begins at 80." Then, when we lost Jackie Gleason, that was a real blow.

ART ELLIOT: I left DuMont because when Paramount bought ABC, the writing was on the wall. Everything was going one way, and DuMont was going the other way. I heard about a job that opened up at CBS in spot sales and I got it.

DuMont had an opportunity to really move, but it was run by a bunch of chemists. What they should have done was hire somebody to front the company who was a national name. But the old man didn't think that way. William Paley could swing out of his office and see anybody in the world. We didn't have anyone like that.

TOM GOLDSMITH: A major factor in our decline had to do with the number of channels allocated by the FCC. Allocations depended on the size of the city and its financial ability to support one or two or three stations. The setup on the VHF channels did not allow enough stations in some of the intermediate-size cities; in New York seven stations sure, Los Angeles, seven, in Philadelphia, four stations, but in the other cities, maybe they only had three allocated channels, well, NBC, CBS, and ABC snapped them up, and DuMont didn't have a chance.

TED BERGMANN: There weren't enough VHF stations out there to maintain four networks. There could have been enough stations if the FCC had supported the development of UHF stations, but it didn't. We lobbied hard for that, but we lost.

We tried to operate a UHF station ourselves. It was down in Kansas City. We literally paid a buck for it, but it still wasn't a bargain. It had no audience. The *Kansas City Star* owned the VHF station, and when the UHF station began, the paper ran a campaign saying, "Don't put a TV antenna on your roof, it will ruin the beauty of our city, and you don't need one to look at our station," which was true, but you couldn't look at our UHF without an antenna, and with no outdoor antennas in Kansas City there was nobody looking at our station.

It cost us a quarter of a million to shut it down. It proved that UHF couldn't compete with VHF. It wasn't until five years later that Congress said, "Every set manufactured in the United States must have UHF capability."

TOM GOLDSMITH: Paramount was our biggest problem. When Paramount bought into DuMont, they bought 55,000 shares of class B DuMont stock and the veto right to approve and disapprove any further financing. Well, if I had read that fine print and knew what it meant, I would have tried to stop it. As early as 1939, we realized that their objective in buying into DuMont was to destroy us as a threat to their box office.

TED BERGMANN: Paul Raibourn was Paramount's ax man. He was executive vice president of Paramount, and he sat on the board of DuMont. He was the one who gave Dr. DuMont all the trouble. He worked for Barney Balaban who was an awful man. Barney looked like a racetrack tout. He used to wear a pink shirt with a green-and-red tie. I used to look at him and say, "This man is head of Paramount Pictures?"

They would block everything, and we could never figure out why. They didn't want television to develop. They were constantly angry. It was the weirdest syndrome I've ever run into. Every time DuMont went to borrow money to expand the company, the potential lender would call Paramount, and they would inevitably kibosh it. "Lend money to that idiot, you've got to be crazy. He's a mad scientist." All kinds of things like that.

TOM GOLDSMITH: The FCC had ruled that a network could own only five stations. Then, because the FCC said we were co-owners, when Paramount set up their own stations in Chicago and Los Angeles, we were prevented from setting up additional stations of our own besides Washington, New York, and Pittsburgh. That killed our expansion in the network business.

TED BERGMANN: The three stations were each showing increasing profits every year. But we sold the Pittsburgh station in 1955 for $9.75 million. It was the highest price ever paid for a station to that date. On the other hand, we lost a lot of potential income when we sold it.

Finally, DuMont needed cash very badly, and Doc decided we should get out of the network business. One day I got a phone call from Doc, saying that Leonard Goldenson wanted to have dinner with us. This was about a year after he had taken over ABC. At dinner, Goldenson said we were knocking each other's ears off by lowering our prices and competing for advertisers, affiliates, and time periods.

"What do you think of merging our two networks. Then we could successfully compete with NBC and CBS. We'll take over all your network commitments. We'll pay you five million dollars, and we'll keep the name of the network ABC-DuMont for at least five years, which will give you the advertising for your television sets."

We said we'd talk about it. As we left, Doc asked me what I thought. I said, "Salvation day is here."

Doc told me to work it out. I did. Then Doc called a meeting of the DuMont board where I presented the idea. When I was done, Paul Raibourn said no way. "Any asset of this corporation that is worth five million dollars to Leonard Goldenson is worth a hell of a lot more than that. We're not going to risk a stockholders' suit and let you sell it off."

Instead, they proposed we bring in a consulting firm to examine the network. We paid them a couple-hundred thousand dollars. They worked for three months and came out with a report that was almost verbatim from the reports I had been giving the board of directors about the future of the DuMont network. They said that it couldn't make it.

Meanwhile, the deal with ABC evaporated. The odd thing was that Doc had enough votes on the board to overcome the Paramount people, but he didn't exercise that power. When we finally decided to close down the network, I was sitting with Doc at dinner at his house one night, and I asked him, "Why, when you and I both knew the deal was so good and would have taken us off the hook, why didn't you force it through?"

He said, "After that board meeting, I got a phone call from Paul Raibourn. He said the reason you were pushing the deal was that Leonard Goldenson had promised you the presidency of the new network. He said, 'Bergmann is selling you down the river.'"

I said, "Doc, why didn't you pick up the phone and call me? I never had one conversation with Goldenson except when you were there. That subject never came up."

He said, "I didn't want to embarrass you."

At the next stockholders' meeting, one of the stockholders got up and asked, "Why didn't the ABC merger go through?"

Doc got up and said, "Why don't you ask them?" And he pointed to the three Paramount people. Raibourn refused to answer.

TOM GOLDSMITH: In 1955, DuMont Laboratories was spun off into the DuMont Broadcasting Corporation. At the point of the spin-off, Paramount had muddied the waters so much they were able to buy up a disproportionate amount of shares, so Barney said to Allen, "I will take over DuMont Broadcasting Corporation and run that and show you how it can be done and make good money." He said the stigma of the DuMont name was why it wasn't doing well, and he changed the name to the Metropolitan Broadcast Company.

Dr. DuMont then said, "If you don't have enough respect for my name, I'm no longer going to be on your board of directors." So he withdrew and sold his stock. We finally got out altogether by selling our receiver business to the Emerson Company. Of course, Barney ran the broadcasting business into the ground. Then he sold it to a company that later became Metromedia.

TED BERGMANN: When all of this was going on, I remember sitting in Doc's study in his house, just the two of us. It was all coming apart at that point. We were having a drink before dinner, and he started to sob and said, "I can't let them take my company away from me. I can't let them do this." Then he recovered his composure, but they did take it from him.

BOOK TWO

THE GOLDEN AGE

"We used to have a saying, 'Our successes were historic, and our failures were numerous.'"

—PERRY LAFFERTY

After several years of honest endeavor to compile an oral history of television, one learns to cast a jaundiced eye (or ear) upon claims to have been "first." Inevitably, when a person asserts that he lit the first tube, another will insist his had already long been glowing. When a writer states that he tapped out the first sitcom, another swears that not only was his first, but the other guy stole his jokes. Listen, let Adam swear his toes were the first to tread in the Garden of Eden and someone else will come forward to claim his footprints were already in the sand when Adam ventured forth.

Having said that, one can claim with reasonable assurance that "The Queen's Messenger," airing on September 11, 1928, was indeed the first drama ever to grace the television screen. There will now be a short pause for the telephone to ring from some Baird-ite informing your reporter that the Englishman actually aired a play sometime in 1927.

Well, since no such call arrives, we can go forward. "The Queen's Messenger" also provoked the first critical review. "The pictures are about the size of a postal card and are sometimes blurred and confused," wrote Orrin Dunlap in *The New York Times*.

Ten years later, when NBC inaugurated its television service, dramatic productions were a mainstay of the schedule. Dozens of plays were performed with varying degrees of success, degrees being the operative word as the heat from the lighting equipment transformed the stage into a giant wok, and the actors into stir-fry. Clearly, until the technology improved, Broadway had little to fear from the upstart medium.

The postwar introduction of the Image Orthicon camera tube changed all that, well, dramatically. Its increased sensitivity meant that the technicians could relegate any further cooking on the air to the likes of James Beard.

Nearly as important was the arrival at RCA in 1945 of thirty-one-year-old Fred Coe, fresh from a little theater in Columbia, South Carolina. Coe was the Golden Age's El Cid, except he was very much alive when he inspired his troops. As director, Coe was one of the first to recognize television's unique ability to enhance drama through innovative camera techniques, but his influence was most widely felt as a producer of the "Philco/Goodyear Playhouse" where he assembled and nurtured an all-star team of television talent.

Coe conceived the anthology show as a vehicle for boiled-down live productions of Hollywood movies. By turning down that proposal, the studios unintentionally launched the careers of dozens of young writers, as Coe was forced to turn to them for original material. These playwrights—Paddy Chayefsky, Horton Foote (whose "A Trip to Bountiful" was originally done for Philco), Tad Mosel, J. P. Miller, Summer Locke Elliott, and Robert Alan Aurthur, among others, came from nowhere to do stunning work. Mosel, who went on to win the Pulitzer Prize for his *All the Way Home*, was an airline clerk and Miller, the author of "Days of Wine and Roses," an air-conditioning salesman when they were discovered by Coe. Chayefsky was writing radio dramas when he signed on with Philco. His play "Marty," performed in May 1953, was perhaps the most influential production of the entire era.

Television's status as a cultural slum district also brought it some of the finest young acting talent of the day. Aspiring actors had long been flocking to New York City with dreams of making it on Broadway. Of those who arrived after the war, few considered a career in television. However, established actors claimed the choice theatrical roles. When they tut-tutted TV because of its low pay and the distasteful notion of acting in between sales pitches, television quickly became an attractive alternative for the newcomers, especially when anthology series began offering up some of the meatiest parts in town.

Rod Steiger, Kim Stanley, Paul Newman, Joanne Woodward, Richard Kiley, and Jack Lemmon were just a few of the rising young stars who lit up the small screen with scorching performances. Suddenly, televised drama was a threat to the Great White Way, always offering a free ticket and good seats. While its productions ran the gamut from lavish to spare, the closeup camera work, expert direction, and the sheer adrenaline of the young stars often made for an evening of theater that was close or even superior to the live stage.

Kraft was the first major sponsor to commit to live drama. "The Kraft Television Theatre" had a shelf life nearly as long as its cheeses. The show premiered on NBC in 1947 and lasted eleven and a half years, presenting some 650 plays of varying quality. While much of their material was of a Velveeta-ish nature, Kraft did produce Rod Serling's "Patterns," a landmark production of the Golden Age, as well as "A Night to Remember," George Roy Hill's technical marvel about the sinking of the *Titanic*, with a record-setting cast of 107. NBC was also home to another big budget anthology, "Robert Montgomery Presents," which often featured Hollywood stars cajoled into making their television debuts.

CBS's first sponsored anthology was the "Ford Theatre," produced by the advertising agency, Kenyon & Eckhardt. "Studio One" was a different matter. Owned by CBS, it was created and produced by Worthington Miner. Miner was a veteran Broadway director when he joined CBS in 1939, and, in the intervening years, the CBS staff, under his direction, virtually wrote the book on television camera techniques. In its early days, "Studio One" offered mostly adaptations of classic literature before moving on to original fare when Felix Jackson took over the reins in 1953.

"Studio One" premiered on November 7, 1948, with a mystery, "The Storm," starring Margaret Sullavan and Dean Jagger. The broadcast ended with the viewing audience still very much bewildered as to the story's denouement. In an interview years later, Miner disingenuously insisted, "I deliberately went out of my way to do a show that would cause talk. The show had no ending. It left you in doubt. It was a revolution in techniques, in the mood lighting, in the use of the camera."

However, Werner Michel, who oversaw the production for CBS, recently put a different spin on the matter. "The payoff was a handkerchief. That's how the detective accused the murderer, but they put the wrong camera on and you couldn't see the handkerchief. Nobody could figure the story out. A hue and cry went out in the press, so we decided to open the next week's show repeating that scene, and then we went into the next show which had nothing to do with it."

Fortunately, it was uphill from there. The first major success of "Studio One" was a modern-dress version of *Julius Caesar*. In the show's second season, Miner stretched the boundaries of live drama to its limit with "The Battleship *Bismarck*" and "The Last Cruise." Miner not only had huge reproductions built of a battleship and two submarines, but he took realism in live TV to new levels by flooding the CBS studios with enough water to cause several actors to fall victim to seasickness (or perhaps it was Method acting).

After Miner departed for NBC, original scripts began arriving over the transom. The most distinctive belonged to Reginald Rose, an advertising copywriter, who found the gray-flanneled life too drab for his taste. The final straw for Rose was his three days of labor to find a suitable name for a new brassière, only to have the client reject his inspired suggestion, the "Upsa-Daisy."

No other writer so consistently used television to dissect then-current issues troubling American society, from conformism/individualism ("Twelve Angry Men"), racism ("Thunder of Sycamore Street,"), the McCarthy period ("An Almanac of Liberty"), juvenile delinquency ("Crime in the Street"), and mental health ("The Incredible World of Horace Ford"), the latter featuring an incredible performance by Art Carney.

CBS also specialized in half-hour mystery anthologies. "Suspense," "Danger," and "The Web" were referred to around the Grand Central studios as the

"Three Weird Sisters." The genre was also popular at NBC, which offered "Lights Out" and "The Clock."

ABC's anthologies were often excellent but short-lived. Their most successful was "The U.S. Steel Hour," presented in conjunction with the Theater Guild. However, it only lasted two years on the network before being snatched away by CBS.

NBC's accountants took the anthology series to a higher level in 1954 with "Producer's Showcase." What they were showcasing was color television. With RCA underwriting the budget, the ninety-minute adaptations were almost always spectacular, if not consistently successful. However, "Peter Pan," starring Mary Martin, "The Petrified Forest," with Bogart, Fonda, and Bacall, and "Darkness at Noon," with a three-tiered set and magical camera transitions, were instant classics. With "Producer's Showcase," "Hallmark Hall of Fame" and "Playhouse 90," CBS's outstanding ninety-minute anthology, television grew out of its adolescent stage. "Playhouse 90" 's "The Miracle Worker," "Requiem for a Heavyweight," "Judgment at Nuremberg," and "Days of Wine and Roses," among others, displayed television's limitless potential. The series just about owned the Emmy awards during its run—and deservedly so. In 1970, *Variety* polled editors and critics, asking them what they thought was television's best series between 1950 and 1970. "Playhouse 90" came out on top. "Everything we had learned the previous ten years came with that show," recalled Ethel Winant. "It was the best of 'Philco' and 'U.S. Steel,' the best writers and directors. It all came together and produced this magical moment. That was 'Playhouse 90.' "

The 1955–56 season featured some sixteen live anthology series, including a daily hour anthology, "Matinee Theater." Their success also paved the way for their downfall. After Philco's ad agency saw that "Marty" touched a nerve in almost every corner of America, it began to reassert control over the show and tried to pressure Coe to do more upbeat stories. The move backfired, and the series was off the air by October 1955.

Meanwhile, the Hollywood studios took notice of television's burgeoning talent and over the next few years siphoned off the best of what TV drama had to offer. Most of Coe's writers made the move, as did his top directors, Delbert Mann and Arthur Penn. The CBS stalwarts John Frankenheimer, George Roy Hill, Sidney Lumet, and Frank Schaffner, all pups raised under Worthington Miner's experienced hand, looked to the big screen for fame and fortune and found it. Of course, the likes of Woodward, Newman, and Lemmon are still enjoying magnificent movie careers.

The introduction of videotape in 1956 boded the end for live drama. Tape could capture a performance with no loss in picture quality, while offering the director the opportunity to reshoot until satisfied. Tape also allowed a show to be rerun until infinity. Rerun money was all profit. That more than anything convinced the networks to ring down the curtain on live TV.

While tape took care of live broadcasting, the anthologies themselves were dusted off by old-fashioned six-shooters, in the hands of western actors, who left the kitchen range for the home on the range and preferred bussing their horses to coping with neurotic women. Long-struggling ABC found its magic potion in "Davy Crockett" and "Cheyenne." The two shows sparked a western craze that peaked five years later when, according to TV historian J. Fred Mc-Donald, there were twenty-eight prime-time westerns, a quarter of the schedule. In March 1959, eight of the top ten shows were oaters.

"ABC introduced their horse-ass operas," said Fred Coe, "their Disneyland public relations shows; and they lowered television. . . . They didn't care about anything but the ratings. NBC and CBS had enough pride to do something worthwhile. ABC entered at the cheapest level of competition."

When ABC's ratings began to climb, their philosophy of win at all costs was met and matched by NBC and CBS. The Golden Age was over, its glory preserved only in scratchy kinescopes and the memories of those who recall a brief period when creative people were given the freedom to create a body of work the likes of which may never be matched again.

ROD STEIGER: When I came out of the Navy after World War II, I didn't know what I was gonna be, but if you had an IQ of a decimal point you got into the civil service, so I got a job in the Office of Dependents and Beneficiaries in Newark, making checks for veterans.

When I was there, the guys on my floor noticed that all the pretty girls were busy on Thursday nights. The office had a theater group, and all pretty girls signed up. When we heard that we descended on the group like a bunch of vultures. The woman who managed it was very pleased because they had no men in the group. In my neighborhood, they thought something was sexually wrong with you if you wanted to be an actor. I figured acting was better than sweeping floors and filing checks, so I went to the New School in New York on the GI Bill, and I became fanatic about it. Whatever anger I had, I could vent through acting, and I was very angry. In my neighborhood, people used to laugh at my family's name because of alcoholism. Something in me said, "I'll do something so good they won't laugh at the name."

NANCY MARCHAND: I came to New York with three friends from college in 1949. We found a dream apartment for thirteen dollars a month in back of a tenement on Forty-fifth Street between Ninth and Tenth. It was two rooms with hot water but no heat.

NORMA CONNOLLY: For those of us in New York in the forties and fifties, it will never again be what we had. It was a glorious time. We won World

War II, we were young, and had total freedom. We were all going to be Broadway stars and own the world.

RICHARD KILEY: I lived in a Brooklyn rooming house where everybody was poor. My little room was a dollar a day. I also ate on a dollar a day, and ate quite well. There were three or four actors and a few neophyte writers in the same place. If you got hungry, you could always go down and say, "Have you got a sandwich or something?" It was a real New Yorky experience. We had a lot of fun. If somebody got a job, they would automatically start the spaghetti and the cheap wine, and everybody from all the rooms would come down.

NORMA CONNOLLY: If you were rich you went to Sardi's, poor you went to Downey's, but if we went to Sardi's, Vincent Sardi knew we were all broke and he would give us a break.

BETHEL LESLIE: Actors also hung out at the Astor Drugstore on Forty-fourth and Broadway to comb their hair or apply lipstick or whatever. Half the time that's where you found your next job. Somebody would say, "They're reading for this at such-and-such, but I'm not right for it." It was that kind of community.

RICHARD KILEY: It was a nice camaraderie. Of course once they thought they had a foot in the door they shared nothing.

NORMA CONNOLLY: There were so many wonderful people. Eva Marie Saint was enchanting. Maureen Stapleton was wonderful, and Lee Grant, who was totally blacklisted, had the guts of a tiger. They were all young and basically decent people except Jimmy Dean. Jimmy was an asshole. He was also a trade kid. He would trade sexual favors to move up the ladder.

ANNE HOWARD BAILEY: Jimmy Dean was in a show I wrote. He carried all of his money in his wallet and was filthy dirty. He always wore this absolutely filthy coat. You could smell him down the hall. Nobody wanted to get near him.

NORMA CONNOLLY: He was a boring, tacky little boy. Norma Crane always used to give Oscar parties. At one of them, Jimmy tried all night to get attention. He was banging on the pots and pans, and he was wearing a T-shirt, and he would say, "If I drop my pants, you will all faint." This went on until Marlon came in dressed in a suit. He walked over to Jimmy, pointed to the T-shirt, and said, "That was last year, Jimmy."

ROD STEIGER: The first time I ever heard of television I heard of it disparagingly. It was considered lower than doing a movie. Our aim was to be in the theater, and movies were pollution. You were a whore if you went to films.

ETHEL WINANT: Television paid hardly anything, and it wasn't considered very prestigious, so film actors wanted nothing to do with it. That opened the way for all these kids who were hanging around while trying to break into the theater, people like George Grizzard, Paul Newman and Joanne Woodward, Jack Klugman, Rod Steiger, and Jason Robards.

I moved to Manhattan in the fall of '45 to work for an agency called Liebling-Wood. Audrey Wood represented Tennessee Williams, Truman Capote, Gore Vidal, Carson McCullers. She taught me how to read a script and analyze it. I did Tennessee's notes when he was working on *Streetcar*. I worked with Gadge Kazan on *Death of a Salesman*. It was pretty heady stuff for a kid from Marysville, California.

One day my friend Louise Albritton said she was doing a drama on television, and she wanted me to watch it. I had to go to Cavanaugh's Bar on Twenty-third Street and convince them to watch that as opposed to whatever sport was on. When I spoke to her afterwards, she said, "It's a lot of fun. You should find out about it."

I wrote to Tony Miner and Fred Coe. Fred never answered, but Tony answered instantly, saying yes, I could come watch a rehearsal of "Studio One" at Liederkranz Hall. It was exciting. There was so much more energy than in the theater. When I went to the studio I was dazzled by the technical stuff. I also liked the fact that everything was done so fast, and when it was over you just went on to the next show without looking back. I was dying to work in it.

GEORGE GRIZZARD: For actors, CBS started a stable like Hollywood. They signed Charlton Heston, Mary Sinclair, and Maria Riva, who became television stars. CBS would also have open casting calls and a thousand people would show up. When your turn came, you would walk across the stage and meet Bobby Fryer, the head of casting, and if you had a picture or a résumé you handed it to him.

TONY RANDALL: Shows were done out of the ad agencies and the talent agencies, so you went to William Morris and MCA and up and down Madison Avenue. I was always pounding the pavement. I know every free toilet in New York. I knew which buildings to cut through to save walking in the rain. I did it religiously. I had no pride, and I was never out of work. Every week I got something, even if it was just one fifteen-minute radio show that would pay the rent.

GEORGE GRIZZARD: In 1951, I got on my first television show. I was the barroom piano player on "Crime Photographer." I had no lines, and I was only on during the credits. My friends watching at home would say, "Oh, I think that was George's leg."

NANCY MARCHAND: I got started when I met a lady who was a friend of a lady who lived at the Dakota where Tony Miner lived. They were going to do "Little Women" on "Studio One." This lady said to Tony, "I know who can play Jo."

I went to a studio and read a scene. When I got home there was a message that I got the part. What excitement! It was a two-parter. The first night was Christmas Eve, and the Oyster Bar invited us down to have dinner. We went in costume. They opened this big window that looked out on the station, and with the crowd staring at us, we sat in hoopskirts eating roast goose.

JOHN NEWLAND: Any of the live shows you can name I did ten of. Back then, there were a handful of stars, Felicia Montealegre, Maria Riva, Margaret Hayes, John Baragrey, Richard Kiley later, and me. There was also Eileen Heckart and Vaughn Taylor, who could play anything.

TAD MOSEL: Vaughn played more parts than any actor in the history of the world. He was really the first television actor. He used to come out of one studio, change clothes, and go into another studio to go on the air again an hour later. They used him because he was reliable, which was terribly important.

DELBERT MANN: That was precisely why several actors became members of our stock company on "Philco." To get the timing right, there was a lot of cutting of lines between dress rehearsal and air, and we needed actors who could handle that kind of pressure. E. G. Marshall and Rod and Eva and Grace Kelly could handle it. Others who couldn't you didn't use again.

ROD STEIGER: Live television was the closest thing to repertory that an American actor could be in. In a month, I'd play a New Yorker, an English lieutenant, and an Irish rebel.

GEORGE GRIZZARD: I lived off [producer] David Susskind. On "Justice," Bill Prince would get me out of jail at least once a month.

TAD MOSEL: "Philco" was a character actor's holiday because so many of our plays were about character people, not beautiful people, and they never worked so hard in their lives.

NANCY MARCHAND: I'm very large and I'm not pretty and I have a kind of authority about me. It was good for me in those days, because I never played a part I didn't find interesting.

I did a show for Kraft about Elizabeth and Essex, the Earl of Leicester. I had to age from seventeen to seventy in an hour, so Dick Smith made these vinyl pieces to put on my face to age me during the commercials. It was like an assembly line. As I went along the line, somebody would take off a bodice, and they would be putting new clothes on me, and he would be slapping on these cosmetic pieces.

It worked perfectly in dress rehearsal, but when they had to start over again, they couldn't get the pieces off. They tried cleaning fluid and other stuff to get them off.

DICK SMITH: I really put her through hell because I didn't have foam latex for making facial appliances. I had this vinyl material, and to glue them on I found a medical adhesive. The problem was I hadn't had time to figure out how to get it off.

NANCY MARCHAND: It took them two-and-a-half hours. They also shaved my head and shaved my eyebrows. They never grew back.

DELBERT MANN: Of the live shows, "Philco" and "Studio One" were considered to be the class acts. When "Robert Montgomery" went on the air, it joined that group. "Kraft" was not in that group, with the exception of a few shows. "The Alcoa Hour" and "Pulitzer Prize Playhouse" did quality shows but they didn't last long. "Playhouse 90" came later. Hallmark was the class of the class, but they were not on a weekly basis.

NORMAN FELTON: One morning in December 1949, I arrived in New York from Chicago. I put my things in a locker and went straight to Robert Montgomery's office to talk about a job. I told him I wasn't so sure I could work with him looking over my shoulder. He said, "I'm the same way. On my last film I wouldn't let my producer on the set, so I understand."

It turned out that far from looking over my shoulder, Montgomery was in Paris or Washington all the time, so I really had to do the producing, come up with ideas, and write scripts and direct them.

PERRY LAFFERTY: There was nobody leading the Montgomery show. That's why it was probably the greatest training ground in New York. The other shows all had bright, wonderful, talented people controlling the productions. On Montgomery, we were on our own as long as you didn't go over budget or go crazy.

WERNER MICHEL: I supervised "Studio One." Tony Miner was a tasteful producer and Paley was personally behind it. If you wanted money for that show you could get it. That was Paley at his best. When he wanted quality, he fought for quality.

MARTIN MANULIS: He was also a heavy competitor. He wanted to be Number One, so he engaged people he thought would make CBS Number One.

TAD MOSEL: The dramatic shows started off with public domain material. When they ran out of that, they developed original work. That's when the excitement began because the young people came in. The established writers wanted nothing to do with it.

DELBERT MANN: These young playwrights wrote intimate stories that were later derided as "kitchen drama," but it was that kind of drama that gave us our best plays and seemed to make the strongest emotional connection with the audience.

TAD MOSEL: The reason why they were called "kitchen plays" was because the studios were old radio studios, so there wasn't room for a lot of sets. You really had to limit yourself to one or two. The room in the house where most of the action took place was the kitchen. You could bring your actors in and out. Exteriors were next to impossible in live television. They just were never believable, so you avoided them.

PHILIP BARRY: We did a live western on "The Elgin Hour" out of ABC. We had a terrible time. We had a street painted on the floor, and one of the horses peed on the street and all the paint ran. Another horse stepped on a camera cable and wouldn't take his foot off. The camera was trying to get from one set to the other and we lost it. Between dress and air, two horses shucked their halters and ran into Central Park.

DELBERT MANN: I grew up in Nashville. Fred Coe and I acted together at the very good local community theater. I followed Fred to Yale and to South Carolina. Then, he brought me up to New York.

Until then I had never seen a television show. I had never even seen a TV set, but I went to New York in the spring of '49 as a floor manager. I spent literally eighteen, nineteen hours a day haunting the studio and observing directors and control-room procedure to get some kind of information about cameras and camera technique.

ARTHUR PENN: Fred brought me to New York after I did a season as stage manager on "The Colgate Comedy Hour." He just called and said, "Hey, Pappy, I'm doing a show called 'First Person.' Do you want to come east and direct this?"

Phshew! I was gone like that. "First Person" was a summer replacement for "The Life of Riley." I got to rehearsal, and there was Joseph Anthony, Mildred Dunnock, and Kim Hunter. I thought I was going to die. I was absolutely terrified. Here were a community of actors who took my breath away.

For the first two or three shows I was extremely timid. It wasn't until "Tears of My Sister" with Kim Stanley, where I dared be bold only because she invited it. She would ask, "Is that all right, Arthur?" After that I gained more and more confidence, and by the fourth or fifth show I began to feel that I was directing, and soon after that I joined "Philco."

PERRY LAFFERTY: Preparation was the difference between life and death. I would sit for at least a week with a lens protractor and the ground plan, and I would figure out the camera moves and which lenses to use. That way I went into the studio with a plan. If you were organized technically you could concentrate on what was important to the people at home—the performances.

ROD STEIGER: With the best directors there's very little conversation unless there's something wrong. I had great respect for Arthur Penn, Vinnie Donehue, Sidney Lumet, anybody who left you alone. Sidney and I were like a team on "You Are There." I played Rasputin, Rudolph Hess, Dutch Schultz, Romeo. I'll never forget that one. First of all I'm doing the balcony scene to a boy, 'cause that's the way they did it then. Then I'm backing up to say, "but soft the light through the window shines," and a needle that was left in my costume goes right in my ass. The camera came in close, and I did that speech while pulling a needle out of my ass.

REGINALD ROSE: Sidney Lumet was wonderful. He does homework like no other director, and he is the warmest guy. Everybody was "my love," and "you gorgeous wonderful thing," and rehearsals were filled with kissing and hugging and wild exclamations of joy. Actors have never been more loved than when they were loved by Sidney Lumet.

RICHARD KILEY: That's his method because then if he tells you to explode, you'll do anything for him.

ROD STEIGER: He knew how to talk to an actor. You don't just say, "Get angrier. Get faster." You help them find a reason to get faster. The director is like the father of a family. He has to know his actors and what will turn them on. You talk to one person about painting. You say, "This man's the kind of guy who would shit on a van Gogh." The actor gets furious. That's called motivation.

PHILIP BARRY: Sidney didn't like talking to the actors on the loudspeaker, so he would tear down the spiral staircase to the stage, talk to the actor, and tear back up the staircase. O. Tamburri, our TD [technical director], once said to me, "If Sidney does that a little faster, he's gonna screw himself into the ceiling."

MARTIN MANULIS: Bob Stevens was the producer-director of "Suspense" until I was asked to replace him. He was gifted but not efficient. He wouldn't have the script ready for rehearsals. He didn't have a clue about timing a show. The axe finally fell when he put on a thirty-minute show that only lasted twenty minutes.

WILLARD LEVITAS: I designed "Suspense," but I never got any credit on the show because Stevens would almost always be *long*. You never knew if you were going to get off with the ending. His AD [assistant director] was Bob Mulligan. Bob would say, "You know, you're three minutes over."

Stevens would tear out pages from the script to pick up the time. How the actors did it I have no idea.

LEE POLK: Timing was one of the director's primary jobs because you had no leeway. He would have to know whether the actors should speed up the last few scenes or slow them down. If we were running fast, the actor would do some business before saying some lines, "Just a second, I have to check this out," and he might be looking around the set for something. In the meantime, they would slow his speech down."

ALVIN SAPINSLEY: I wrote a show that began with a rainstorm, and when they dropped the water from overhead, they blew out one of the cameras. Bob became hysterical. He shouted, "Cancel the show. Cancel it." He left the control room, and the assistant director had to direct the show.

WILLARD LEVITAS: Every time you would say, "Bob Stevens," the eyes would roll. He was brought up on charges by AFTRA for hitting an actor. If somebody screwed up during a show, he would run out during the commercial, grab 'em around the throat, and say, "You do it again, and I'll kill you."

RICHARD KILEY: Here's my favorite Bob Stevens story. "Suspense" was shot in a tiny studio. Bob had a script that took place in a Southern mansion. One scene had a character like Scarlett O'Hara coming down this winding staircase.

Martin Manulis said, "Are you crazy? The ceiling is hardly big enough. The lights are barely above the actors' heads."

Bob said, "No, I've worked with a guy who makes miniature sets. I've got it all figured out."

Marty agreed to commission this guy to build an elaborate model with a chandelier and a winding staircase. He also built a set of ornate doors to match the ornate doors of the model. When the Scarlett character appears at the top of the stairs, the camera is on the model and it goes up the stairs to the doors. Then there is a dissolve to the real stairs, and out comes this gorgeous woman. It was a wonderful effect, and, when it worked in rehearsal, there were cheers in the studio.

Terrific. It's going to be a legendary moment in television. They get on the air, and they start the shot on the model. Now, they had a new stagehand that day. He wasn't familiar with the show. At that moment, he is walking behind the model, and he sees this little flash of light in this little space. He walks over and peers into this little space, and on the air you saw this enormous fucking eye looking through the doors, and a cry of anguish came out of the room. All of Bob's work was ruined.

＊　＊　＊

REGINALD ROSE: In 1949, I was writing copy for a small advertising agency. I had been writing my own material since I was sixteen, but I never could sell anything. Then I got a television set. I watched all this stuff, and I said, "God, I can do that," me who had been doing this for fourteen years and never sold a thing.

I wrote this half-hour television play called "The Bus to Nowhere." It had to do with aliens who were on Earth to bring back some humans to their planet to study them and find out why they made war. It was now 1951, and I had a kid and my wife was pregnant, and we didn't have the money to pay the obstetrician. I knew Philip Minoff, who was the television critic of *Cue*. I asked him if he would read it. He did and called Sidney Lumet who agreed to read it. With great fear, I brought it over to Sidney, who was then I believe, twelve years old. The next day the producer, Charlie Russell, called; they bought it. I was thirty years old, and I finally sold something. I didn't even ask how much. It didn't matter. I went home a hero.

WALTER BERNSTEIN: In the beginning, these shows paid $250. I got up to $400 on "Danger." For an hour show I would get $650, maybe toward the end it went up to a thousand.

REGINALD ROSE: Whatever they paid, I said yes. By then I had two kids and was afraid to quit that agency. It was hard to come home and work at night and on weekends, but I did it. I wrote thirteen television plays while I was still working at the agency.

TAD MOSEL: I kept my job selling airline tickets until I had to quit because they were going into rehearsal for one of my shows. The producer said, "Are you going to sell tickets for Northwest Airlines or be a television writer?"

I thought if I could make a living writing for television that would give me the time to write the great American play. That's very patronizing and very young, but even when I was having my greatest success on TV, I still thought of it as a stopgap. It was a long time before I realized that television was a separate form of its own with its own virtues and liabilities.

The wonderful thing about live television drama was if you had a little bit of talent you couldn't help but get discovered because there was such a greedy need for talented writers and actors. The trouble was hanging on. Many people wrote one play and were never heard from again.

REGINALD ROSE: Because they were so desperate for scripts, television was a continuous learning process. I can think of no other place where that could have been done.

TAD MOSEL: At first, they didn't want anything I wrote. As a change of pace I sat down and wrote a play that I simply wanted to do. At that time, there

were two subjects that were absolutely forbidden on TV, adultery and suicide, and
the play I wrote dealt with both. Fred Coe bought it. He just said, "I'll do it."

J. P. MILLER: My coming into television was one of the great miracles
of our time. I was living in an apartment in Queens with two kids. There were
no rugs, no furniture. The kids slept on army cots in the little bedroom.

I was selling air-conditioning refrigeration and writing theater plays which
nobody would read. I'd see television in bars and say, "I'd rather starve than
write that crap." I *was* starving, but I was arrogant. I was much too good for TV.

In 1953, a friend of mine who was a TV repairman brought me a television.
It had the controls, but not the case. I put it in a cardboard box, which I painted
maroon, put it on the table, and started watching it. One night I tuned in
"Philco Playhouse" and I saw a play by Horton. I thought, "Boy, that's terrific."
I tuned in again and saw a play by Tad and then something by Paddy. By then,
I said, "Jesus, these people are trying to do something good. If I could write for
them, I would condescend to write for television." [Laughs.] Arrogance spoiled
by fucking youth.

I then watched a lot of Philco shows and made a bunch of notes about what
I needed to write to appeal to Fred: I had to concentrate on human relationships. I had to search for the rock-bottom truth of every character's motivations,
not fancy anything up. I had to make every line of dialogue true to that character and that situation without getting showy or melodramatic. I had to solve
the stories by natural progression of events, not with a gun, an axe, or a punch
in the jaw.

I wrote down these rules. Then I wrote a play called "Hide and Seek" about
an old blind woman in the South and her grandson who was an orphan. Not
having an agent, I took it up to Fred Coe's office and handed it to an assistant.
A week later I get this call, "J. P. Miller, I read your play. Who's your agent?"

"I don't have an agent."

"How did I get the play?"

"I brought it up there."

"Well, we don't accept unsolicited manuscripts, but now that I've read it, I
want to buy it. Can you come in and talk to me?"

I go to see the grand guru Fred Coe. It scared the living hell out of me, because he was *the* producer in television. He gets up with round Coke-bottle
glasses and his short haircut, little babyface, sticks his hand out. It felt like a
warm muffin. [Laughs.] He says [in a Southern accent], "Pappy, I love that play.
We're gonna do it. What do you think of Arthur Penn?"

"I think he's great."

"We're gonna ask Arthur to direct it. What do you think of Mildred
Dunnock?"

"I think she's a great actress."

"We're gonna ask Mildred Dunnock to be in it."

"God, am I dreaming? Yesterday I was walking on Third Avenue trying to sell air-conditioning and refrigeration."

"No, Pappy. We're gonna do this. You got any more of these plays?"

"Sure."

I told him an idea I had for a play called "Old Passel Foot." He said, "That's a good story. Go home and write it."

I went back and wrote it. In the meantime, they did "Hide and Seek." It got the best reviews I ever got. It was my first play. I should have quit right then. [Laughs.]

ROBERT MARKELL: When I had designed a show, I used to go on top of the light grid and watch the action below. It was like a ballet, to see the cameras and mikes and the actors all moving together, and that was what live television was, everybody working together.

LEE POLK: It was a little more frantic than balletic. You had cameras running into each other, people pulling cables, people getting out of the way, people running beneath the cameras so they could get to the other side of something.

BOB MARKELL: That was one of the keys to live television: figuring out how to get an actor from here to there for the next scene, and getting the cameras from here to there. This caused huge headaches for directors. Also, you couldn't have the cameras jump the cables, and with this mass of cable on the floor, the director had to make sure they didn't get tangled up.

LEE POLK: In thirty seconds an actor had to climb over cables, duck under cameras and mike booms, and run around the scenery. That's why an actor sometimes suddenly sounded like he was out of breath, because he was.

TONY RANDALL: At the end of a scene, if there were two of us talking, they would come in on a closeup of you and you would have to pretend you were talking to me, but I would be running over to the other set and changing my shirt. How would I know when the camera was off me so I could run? The stage manager would crawl on his hands and knees and hit your ankle. That meant run. It was hilarious and so fraught with the possibilities of mistakes.

ERNIE KINOY: We were doing "The Big Story," and somebody had been killed. The corpse was lying on the sofa. Behind it were two people who had just discovered it. The next scene had to start in the same locale the following day, so you had to somehow get the corpse out of there. The plan was for the camera to push in, and you could lose the corpse out the bottom of the shot. He had his eyes closed, so he had to wait for the stage manager to tap him on the ankle before he'd crawl away under the camera.

One of the actors behind the couch had a tray with a can of orange juice on it. He was so nervous you could see his hand shaking. The can fell off the tray, hit the back of the couch, rolled off to the side, hit the corpse on the ankle, and he got up and walked away.

NORMA CONNOLLY: Most of the time you would be running, and costume ladies would be running with you, and you would be tossing off clothes and throwing them on.

NORMAN FELTON: The second show we did on "Montgomery" was "Kitty Foyle." There were some scenes in which Jane Wyatt was supposed to be a little girl. These scenes came with such rapidity, and the girl would have to change costumes. Then I had an idea, and it worked. I was able to do one scene where the girl was speaking in a living room, and then dissolve to her in another scene in the middle of winter. After the show, Fred Coe called. He said, "Okay, Norman, what's the story?"

I said, "Twins."

DICK SMITH: I had to do makeups during those changes. For one show about a prize fighter, the guy had to get beaten up, so I dressed up as one of the trainers, and in between rounds, I would get in the ring, pretend to be mopping the guy off, but what I was really doing was making him up bruised.

TAD MOSEL: I once played a terrible trick. I wrote a play for the French actress Michelle Morgan, who was the most beautiful actress in the world, and while I was welcomed on other shows, on this one I was told that Miss Morgan did not want the author to be there. That annoyed me.

In the middle of rehearsal they called me and said that they had the most beautiful French actress alive but she had no chance to wear an evening gown. "Would you please write a scene for Miss Morgan where she could wear an evening gown?"

Well, I thought that was really rotten to ask a writer to write a scene just for that. There was a scene where she had been walking her dog in some old clothes, so I wrote "dissolve to Miss Morgan coming down the stairs in an evening gown." She didn't even have ten seconds to make the change. I was invited for that when it went on the air, and it really was funny to watch them try to do it. She was walking into a cocktail party, so they hired a pianist. The camera panned him and the guests, while behind the scenes they were tearing the clothes off this poor lady and pouring her into the gown. Writer's revenge. [Laughs.]

DICK SMITH: When you're talking about two minutes that's a lot of time. I learned, especially when I did my most triumphant change with Claire Bloom for Queen Victoria.

In the show, she starts off as the young queen and ends when she's eighty. The first change was during a commercial. We had three minutes and twenty seconds. First, she had to run from one end of the stage down to her next set where we were waiting.

I had an assistant with a stopwatch and a cue card that listed the tasks we had to do. He would call off each task. When he cued "Wardrobe," the wardrobe ladies had twenty seconds to rip off the panels that were stuck on her dress to make the costume change. "Okay, hair." The hairstylist moved Claire's bun from the top of her head down to the nape of her neck.

Then Claire ran over to the bench at her writing desk, and I and Bob O'Bradovich came in on either side of her. We had like cigarette-girl trays with all our makeup materials. There was another assistant standing by, and on cue from our emcee, he squirted some adhesive inside this foam latex appliance, which would give her fat cheeks and a double chin, handed it to me, and Bob and I plopped it on her face and squeezed down the edges. Then the assistant put adhesive in a rubber nose and gingerly handed it to me—if he had squeezed it, he would have ruined it—and we plopped that down on her face.

Then we patted on special makeup to cover the edges. We also went around her forehead covering up eyebrows and eye makeup. All this time, the man with the stopwatch read off the seconds, so we literally worked up to three minutes and fifteen seconds.

That was just to make her fat and forty. Within an act there was a scene change where she goes to sixty. For that we had a minute-forty. The costume change consisted of a black shawl with a dowager's hump sewn into it. That was thrown over her shoulder. There wasn't time to remove the wig. It was glued on, so she took another wig and got the damn thing on over—over!—the brown wig. Now Claire also needed eye bags and those heavy eyelids Victoria had, also a piece to cover her lower lip and chin. I put all that on. Then I took like a rubber stamp of forehead wrinkles and literally stamped wrinkles on her forehead. [Laughs.]

The play ended with a brief scene when she was eighty. To change her again was impossible. In reading the script, I saw that she is sitting talking to herself as her servants wheel her out in her chair onto this balcony, and she waves to the cheering multitudes.

I said, "Why don't we take a double, make her up ahead of time to look like the old queen and do it with Claire's voice-over?" They agreed, and it would have worked beautifully, except when they pushed her out to the balcony, her skirt got caught in the wheels of the chair. Now, the clock is running out. The director is screaming. Finally the guys shoved the goddamned chair out there for the closeup and the fadeout, but the hour was up, and they had to cut the credits off before the makeup credit appeared.

DELBERT MANN: Under those fantastically pressured circumstances there was a kind of electricity in the performances that I have not seen in any other medium. Even the worst shows had an electricity that was palpable.

ROD STEIGER: When it was live, television was the most difficult medium to work in. You had one shot. The pressure was hideous. You had to be a masochist to do it. The worst time was thirty seconds before you go on. At that time, if somebody showed you an open door you'd run home to your mother. Part of me is saying, "I won't remember, I won't remember. I won't remember." The other part is "Whatamidoinghere?whatamidoinghere? whatamIdoinghere? Oh, God, my friends are gonna see me."

I remember somebody saying, "You get so intense. You get so worried when you're working."

If *you* make a mistake your office knows about it. If *I* make a mistake, my office knows about it; my block knows about it; my state knows about; my country knows about it, and the world eventually knows about it. That will make you a little nervous.

DELBERT MANN: On "Darkness at Noon," Lee J. Cobb had a heart attack *during the show.* He didn't know it until the next day.

O. TAMBURRI: For a cameraman, five minutes before a live show is worry time. Certain shots are almost impossible to make, but you did it right once during rehearsal so you know you can do it. Then, when you do it right on the air, the control room lets you know how great you are. It's a nice feeling.

BOB MARKELL: Even when things went wrong, you didn't worry about losing your job, and there were some real disasters. We did a "You Are There" on the Alamo. Somebody said to me, "How do you get cannon balls going through walls on live television?"

They came up with these big rattraps and balsa-wood blocks, and on a signal you triggered the trap, and the trap hits a block and it shoots out. It worked beautifully in dress rehearsal. Comes the airtime, you heard *snap, snap, snap,* and none of the blocks were coming out. On the monitor, you saw the stagehands pushing the blocks out with their bare hands. Darren McGavin was playing Jim Bowie. He said, "I don't know if they're Mexicans, guys, but get 'em!" I think I left town for a day after that one.

On another show, Franchot Tone is going to strangle this woman in his attic. He says, "Nobody can help you." He opens a door, and there's a stagehand sound asleep. He slams the door and says, "He's not gonna help ya, either."

WILLARD LEVITAS: When I designed my first show for CBS, everything I learned in school went out the window. Everything had to fit on the trucks and in the elevator, so it was all five feet nine inches wide and made of canvas just like you would find in a theater, and every time somebody would close a door you would see the wall shimmer.

BOB MARKELL: I designed an art gallery scene for a "Studio One" I did with Frank Schaffner. When I went home and saw it on the air, I noticed that he had restaged the scene, and people were leaning against the wall. I called the control room right away. The assistant director picked up the phone, and I could hear Schaffner saying in the background, "I know who that is. Tell him that's what you have to do when the fucking walls are falling down."

DELBERT MANN: With your sets, you were always fighting time and space and money. In "Marty," Paddy had conceived this big ballroom scene, but the only space we had available was a truncated triangle between the butcher shop set and the bar set. I only had room for one sound boom and one camera, so out of necessity we staged the dance scene so they turned and turned and turned. It worked so marvelously I did the same thing with the film.

BOB MARKELL: When I did a show with Phil Silvers on Broadway, I brought in some amusing scenery, and he gave me some of the best advice of all. He said, "I'm funny. Scenery isn't."

*   *   *

REGINALD ROSE: After I sold a couple of scripts, I got a call from Donald Davis, who asked me to adapt a book for "Studio One." The book was a western, but the interesting thing is why they called me. When I wrote "The Bus to Nowhere," I said to myself, "Where the hell can I put this bus so that nobody will see that it has been stopped by an invisible barrier? I know, the Mojave Desert."

After I adapted the western, I asked Donald Davis why he called me. He said, "Because you know all about the West."

I knew nothing about the West. I had never been in the West. I didn't even like westerns. I just couldn't think of a place to put the bus. That's why they picked me, and that's how television was.

ERNIE KINOY: These days you go in with something to sell and three years later something happens. Back then, if you were clever, you went to lunch with Florence [Britton, the story editor of "Studio One"] and waited until she had her third martini. At that point you could sell her the menu.

MARTIN MANULIS: Claudette Colbert made her television debut on the opening show of "Best of Broadway," which was a major series of hit plays done in color. She was a major Hollywood star, and I felt I had to get her for "The Royal Family." In trying to convince her, I said, "I hope you'll decide to do this because Miss [Helen] Hayes wants terribly to have you do it. I don't think she'll do it with anyone else," which was a gross exaggeration, as Miss Hayes had already signed. That sat very well with Claudette, and she agreed.

Claudette did not leave her reputation as the best-dressed woman at the stage door. During rehearsals, she was constantly at Hattie Carnegie's for fittings. Helen wasn't very polite about it. One day she exploded in front of everybody.

She said, "When the lady gets here, if she has time for rehearsal in between fittings of her dresses, perhaps we can proceed." She then left the stage. Finally, Claudette came in. Things were very cool. Luckily, I was the only one who heard Claudette ask, "How can she be so difficult with me? After all, she wanted me. She didn't want anybody else for the part."

Then we did "The Man Who Came to Dinner." We had Monty Woolley who created the part on Broadway, and Merle Oberon and Joan Bennett as the two women. Joan was in Europe when we engaged her to play the secretary while Merle was to play the beautiful bitchy actress. Well, things got screwed up. When we came to the first rehearsal, Joan realized she was signed for the stagy actress and Merle for the secretary, the All-American girl. Merle was very happy because she wouldn't have played the other part, but Joan was miserable. She said, "I can't play this bitch. If you want a bitch, get my sister Constance."

Monty Woolley had been originally so perfect in the play, but this was twenty years later. I didn't know until we got to the studio that in the intervening years he had become incontinent. While he was sitting in his prop wheelchair, Joan came up to me in the control room. She said, "I'm not setting foot on that stage again until you do something about the old boy. All those cables are getting wet. We'll all be electrocuted."

I said, "I'll do what I can, but Merle isn't complaining."

"Well, have you seen those boots Lady Korda has on her feet?"

*   *   *

NORMAN FELTON: I shared a small office with Harry Salzman, the executive producer on "Montgomery." We had desks face-to-face. When he wasn't negotiating, he was arguing with his wife and calling her all sorts of unprintable names, but he certainly helped get things I needed for the shows.

The producers were greedy. The budget was supposed to be twenty thousand dollars, but Montgomery took five thousand off the top as producer and five thousand for acting and reading the TelePrompTer, and Gibbs took five thousand for producer. That was fifteen thousand out of the twenty. Salzman had to make deals to help the budget. When we did "Our Town," he made a deal with Coca-Cola. They paid for the drugstore set. Of course Coca-Cola was well displayed.

We did a show called "Evening Star," about an aging actress. The first act had a western scene on a Hollywood soundstage. In the last act, they are doing a show about Elizabethan times. We needed a lot of people, and they never had money for extras. I had an idea. We ordered forty dressmaker's dummies, forty western outfits, and forty Elizabethan costumes. I used about six live extras in that show, and I mixed them with the dummies. When the cameras moved past these groups you didn't know which were live and which weren't. Do you know that Gibbs said to me later, "Why did you even need the six?"

PERRY LAFFERTY: Because "Montgomery" paid so little, good scripts were hard to get. One of the few reliable writers we had was a guy named Irving Gaynor Neiman.

IRVING GAYNOR NEIMAN: I was pretty fast. I could turn a script in in a week, and the scripts could be tricky. They gave me "Ten Little Indians" to do. It had ten murders and we had forty-six minutes to find out who these people were before they were killed off.

I got my assignments from Gibbs, who was my agent at the time and kind of a crook, which was not unusual in the business. He took commissions on his own shows. That was not nice.

ALVIN SAPINSLEY: Gibbs always took ten percent, and he never hired anybody who wasn't a client. A lot of the scripts were awful. Some of the ones I wrote were awful.

PERRY LAFFERTY: The scripts would often come in in such pathetic shape. One night I rewrote seventy pages, starting at five-thirty in the evening until I finished at six in the morning.

IRVING GAYNOR NEIMAN: Everybody likes to think it was his contribution that saved "this awful script." These dreams of glory. There were more decent scripts than they remember. There were a lot of egos on the line between the actors, the directors, and the producers.

Actors couldn't resist making changes. One time, this director had let them get their head, and once actors sense that, they can hardly read a line without, "Oh, dear, can't I say it this way. This is terrible." The great lady of the theater, Judith Anderson, read a line in which she is playing a great actress. She said, "Oh, my God, who wrote this?"

And I had the greatest moment in my professional life. I said, "Shakespeare."

NORMAN FELTON: The difference between "Montgomery" and the other shows was the quality of the scripts, but if I do say so I was a very good director, and I got good performances.

IRVING GAYNOR NEIMAN: I think we were the first to portray a suicide on television with O'Hara's "Appointment in Samarra." I did the adaptation of the book, which was taught in a lot of English courses, and lo and behold the network let us do it.

STOCKTON HELFFRICH: I remember that one. At NBC, we had inherited some of the attitudes of the motion-picture code. One aspect of that was that you never show suicide as an appropriate conclusion to a life. Still, we believed that "Appointment in Samarra" was a fine piece of literature, so it was passed with our fingers crossed. People commit suicide whether it is something you encourage or not.

TAD MOSEL: In my case, Florence Britton turned down "The Haven" because it dealt with adultery and suicide, but Fred Coe bought it. Still, we needed approval from continuity acceptance [the censor's office]. Three days later, the word came down. It was fine except for one sentence which made reference to an old Chevy. They thought it was a gratuitous plug for Chevrolet. Could it be changed to "old crate"? So much for the rules about adultery and suicide. That was one of the greatest lessons I ever learned: if you wrote it well you could get it on.

ALVIN SAPINSLEY: I adapted *The Great Gatsby* for "Montgomery." To say at the end, "You're better than the whole damn bunch put together," we had to make a compromise. You couldn't say "damn" on television, but it would have ruined the play if he couldn't have said it. So in an earlier scene I had somebody say, "What the hell is going on here?" Then, when we had the big conference we gave them the "hell" if we could keep the "damn." I think that was the first "damn."

REGINALD ROSE: The writer's natural enemy is the censor, and you have to battle it. I used to sit in meetings and say, "Look, I'll take out the second 'son of a bitch' if you give me one 'fuck you.' "

Once on "Studio One," a guy from the ad agency was complaining to Felix Jackson about something he wanted out, and it couldn't come out. Felix was arguing like hell. Finally, he got so frustrated, he said to him, "Listen, you must understand this. You're a sensitive man."

And the guy said, "I am not sensitive!"

Felix just said to hell with him. He didn't take it out.

Most television writers can never be powerful enough to demand that what they write be done. There was a time in television when you could. They really wanted Paddy's plays, so he could do what he wanted to do. I touched sensitive issues more than most writers, because that was what I was interested in doing and most of what I wanted to do got done.

Issues that bother me are issues concerning people who want to impose their beliefs on others. That was the theme of "Thunder on Sycamore Street" and "Tragedy in a Temporary Town." In a way, almost everything I wrote in the fifties was about McCarthy. I was surprised I got away with the stuff I did. Television was so sensitive to criticism, and the criticism almost always came from the right. The network people were really petrified for their jobs. Yet, they were also afraid of being that way, so sometimes things got through.

*   *   *

NORMAN FELTON: One year at a Christmas party, I was off in a corner with a fellow who was doing a Ph.D. at Columbia. He said, "Do you know there was a novel about a prizefighter by George Bernard Shaw called *Cashel*

Byron's Profession that was never copyrighted, a pretty bad novel." I found the book and it was bad, but we could do it without paying a fee. We called it "The Prizefighter and the Lady." I got Alvin Sapinsley, one of our better writers, to write the script.

ALVIN SAPINSLEY: I wrote a brand-new Bernard Shaw. It wasn't intimidating because it wasn't a very good novel. I improved on it tremendously, and I think Shaw would have agreed.

NORMAN FELTON: The reviews were excellent. *Variety* said, in effect, "It's a pleasure in television to hear the sparkling dialogue of Shaw." The funny thing was every word was Alvin's.

DOMINICK DUNNE: On the Montgomery show, Bob would come to one rehearsal. Then he would read his narration over the air, and even though he was using one of the earliest TelePrompTers, he would usually blow it.

NORMAN FELTON: Generally, Bob would speak at the end of a show, thanking the actors. He would also introduce the show.

PERRY LAFFERTY: Sometimes, he would act in a play, and then he would be involved.

NORMAN FELTON: We had a hard time finding material he would do. He was supposed to do four shows a season, but it got so he only did one. Gibbs would say, "Norman, he's got to do another show. Can't we find something for him to do?"

He did one called "No Visible Means." After the second act began, I noticed that his fly was open and that a bit of shirt was sticking out of it. I had the cameraman push in on a closeup above his waist. Then one of the actors whispered to me, "If I go sit next to him, maybe I can reach down and zip him up."

I said, "Don't you dare, and nobody tell him," so we finished the scene, and he went to the next act where we had a costume change, and nobody ever knew if he knew. Had the others said something, he would never have come out for the next act.

After five years, I told Montgomery that I felt the need to branch out. He wouldn't talk to me during the last two shows. On the last show, I told him where to stand to read his last bit. He said, "I know where I'm going."

"If you don't stand there, we may have some difficulty."

"I know where I'm going."

Well, he went to the spot he wanted to go to, but there was a piece of furniture in the way. He had to walk behind this desk. From there he couldn't see the TelePrompTer without his glasses. That was the last time we worked together.

Still, it's easy to forget the good things he did. He was a good actor. When he performed he was certainly excellent. Because of the power of his name, he did cut through a lot of problems.

PERRY LAFFERTY: Near the end, we were doing a big color show out in Brooklyn. When it was over there were a lot of good-byes to the crew, except Bob. He got into his limo and was off into the night. He was true to form until the end. I never saw him again.

J. P. MILLER: I've worked with some great producers, but Fred Coe understood writers better than any of them. He could always find the essence of a problem. He never preached. He understood that to get five gallons of milk out of a five-gallon cow, you've got to talk nice to 'im. You gotta massage him in the right place. You gotta know how to squeeze his psyche to make it happen. Today, they're not producers, they're entrepreneurs, who think to make a cow give milk you've got to beat her.

ROD STEIGER: Fred was wonderful. He had a terrible temper, but he got things done. Was it Machiavelli who said, "I never heard of a leader that was a nice guy"?

He was the best mind that ever hit television for anything. He got you Chayefsky, Tad Mosel, J. P. Miller, Kim Stanley, Steven Hill. He had an eye for talent, an ear for talent, and a great compassion for talent. They were scared to death when he said, "I think Steiger should do 'Marty,' " but he insisted. I owe the bare foundation of my career to Fred Coe.

J. P. MILLER: He assumed you were in agreement on one thing: that you wanted to have the best goddamned show ever done on television. It was not, "Well, that's good enough." Then, to prove it, you got the director you agreed on who best understood the material. You got the best possible actors. If it wasn't the greatest thing ever done it wasn't because you didn't try.

TAD MOSEL: I was still working at the airline when I met Fred. He said he liked to have first refusal on scripts because it gave writers a sense of security, which it did. He said, "Now for the first year, how many plays would you want to write?" Can you imagine being asked that question? I said six, which I thought was a moderate amount. He said, "Okay, we'll make it six."

He said he would produce whatever I wrote. Now when you hear that, you either try to get away with murder, which means your life will be very short, or by God, you do your very best, and really with a man like that you did your best.

DELBERT MANN: Before Paddy Chayefsky met Fred for the first time, Fred had been told about this writer who had a story about a Jewish cantor losing his faith and regaining it. However, having heard about the terrible-tempered Mr. Coe, the WASP from Mississippi, Paddy came in and instead told him about this Methodist minister who had lost his faith. He went on and on, until Fred finally said, "Pappy, that's not the story you want to tell me. What's the story you really want to tell?"

"Oh, he's Jewish."

TAD MOSEL: I went to him with my idea for the play "The Lawn Party." I said, "Fred, I want to do a play about a woman who wants to give a party."

He said, "What kind of party?"

"Well, when I was growing up in Steubenville, Ohio, they called them 'lawn fêtes,' and people had them out on their lawns with Japanese lanterns. They made punch, and maybe there would be some games. It was just an evening party for the neighborhood."

"Why does she want to give this party?"

"Because she has an ugly life, and the party is beauty and excitement."

"Okay, go ahead." That was it. I never talked about it again until I turned it in, and he never called.

HORTON FOOTE: Fred liked you to tell him an idea, which appalled me, so I would write my plays and *then* tell him my idea. I just think you spend so much time pitching, there's nothing left after the pitch is done. When I told him about "Bountiful," I said, "It's the story of an old lady who wants to get home."

He said, "That's fine, write it."

I never told him it was already finished. I just gave it to him three days later. He thought that was so funny. After that I never did have to tell him anything, although I did read "John Turner Davis" to him while he was taking a shower because he was in a hurry. I'll never forget what he said, "You son of a bitch, you're gonna break another million American hearts."

Fred was a Southerner, and he understood my work in a deep, visceral way. Another producer could have crushed me in two minutes. You say, "Forget it, this is nonsense," and I would have gone home and never would have done it again. Fred had a devotion to writers. We were consulted about casting, and we went to all the rehearsals. He didn't move without consulting with us.

We had a press agent named Johnny Friedkin. It was his idea to publicize the writers. He said, "You know, Fred, you can't afford stars. Publicize the playwrights," so we became a household word, which wasn't too bad, you know, and the writers really *were* honored.

REGINALD ROSE: I loved it. In all the publicity it was "another Paddy Chayefsky play," not another "Philco" starring whoever. I actually heard people in the subway saying, "Hey, I heard there's a Reginald Rose play on tonight." Holy cow! A few years before I was barely making a living in an ad agency.

TAD MOSEL: It could have spoiled us, but I don't think it did. We were all different but we were all good friends. If there was any professional jealousy, I never knew it. We all wanted everyone else to be successful. When I saw a Paddy play, my only thought was, "Oh, I wish I could be as good as that."

REGINALD ROSE: Paddy and I both lived on West Eighty-sixth Street. I guess I admired his work the most. I went over to Paddy's when he won the Oscar for *Marty* just to look at it, and he let me hold it and everything.

DELBERT MANN: It was obvious from the beginning that there was something special about Paddy. The intimate style, the focus on an emotional problem or relationships, so strongly focused and yet on such a modest scale, was quite clear in Paddy's work from the beginning. I directed his second play, "Reluctant Citizen," which was about an uncle of his, an old man who had come over from Russia. This man wants desperately to become a U.S. citizen, but he's too fearful of government and authority until a teacher in a settlement house encourages him to take this monumental step forward and apply for citizenship.

J. P. MILLER: TV does microscopic examinations of human relationships, better than the movies, and different from theater. You can't take an extreme closeup in theater. Kim Stanley can't just sit there and let a tear pop into the corner of each eye and make a statement. She can on TV.

RICHARD KILEY: On TV, you could play an emotion as you would normally play it. Let's say it's a love scene. On the stage, you are saying [very loudly], "Jane, I adore you." This is a built-in problem with the stage. On television you are able to play as I'm talking to you. That's a wonderful luxury.

The trouble with most actors when they started television is they didn't realize how economical they could be and they overacted. If the camera is twenty feet away from you, you can play close to stage energy, but as the camera gets closer, you must reduce everything in terms of its complexity. People say, "Forget about the camera, let the director worry about it." That's bullshit. You have to be aware of the camera.

ROD STEIGER: Anyone who tells you that on television an actor doesn't have an audience is full of crap. Sometimes you had sixty people around you. That's a little theater audience. Don't you think the actor checks the reactions of the crew? Sure you do. If you make the grip put down his newspaper to watch the scene, you know you're doing good. If I was with an automatic camera, and there was nobody in the studio but me, the camera, and a cat in the corner, I'd be worried about how the cat liked it.

TAD MOSEL: I would sit in the control room as far back against the wall as I could and not say a word or make a move because it was such a tense time.

That was truly the most thrilling part of live television, sitting in that control room, because you had been through ten days of rehearsals when you really never knew what you were going to see, because actors are totally unpredictable. You don't know when you are going to lose a camera, when a set is going to fall in, lights are going to go off, or actors are going to drop dead. The fear was essential to the pleasure, but there was also a tremendous amount of pride that this was happening.

DELBERT MANN: As the second hand came up to the hour, the tension was just unbelievable. Then there's the release when the show finally ends. If you've gotten off on time without any major boo-boos, and you feel you've done a good job, it's exhilarating.

PERRY LAFFERTY: You had to be young. If somebody would ask me today, "What was the most interesting part of your career?" and I've been in television forty-five years, I would only have to think a second—"It was when I was directing live television." That was the most exciting, fabulous time.

Still, I had times where it was four-fifteen on a day when we went on at nine-thirty, and I didn't know how I was going to get it together. Despite all your planning, it was not working, and the panic is coming up in your chest. You've got to do it. Then, when you come off the air you would absolutely collapse. You get into the taxicab to go home, and you ache.

ARTHUR PENN: If you were vulnerable to the pressure, it was pretty bad. Kingman Moore ended up hemorrhaging in the control room. He had to be carried out during a show. Guys turned to drink. There were a lot of heart attacks, crazy kinds of behavior. What saved me was a deep attraction to the actors and the actors' process, so that the whole thing of "We're on the air!" never caught up to me. Plus, I already had two years on "Colgate" where we were always winging it, so I wasn't all that anxious.

NORMAN FELTON: On a "U.S. Steel Hour," the cast was nervous and needed something to break the tension, so about thirty seconds before air, I said on the talk-back, "You know, folks, things can go wrong. It's very difficult, and if you forget a line or you make a mistake, just remember I'll never use you on any show again."

There was a moment's pause and then everybody laughed like hell. I swear not a mistake was made on that show.

ROD STEIGER: I did Dutch Schultz on "You Are There," and three actors in a row in consecutive scenes went up on me. Now if you only learn your lines you're dead on live television. If you know the situation you can always say something that fits in. When the third actor came in and his eyes glazed, I knew I had to cover for him. "I know what you're gonna tell me. You think I'm taking over your territory. I'll never take over your territory," and I grabbed him by the shirt and threw him off the set.

Anyway, after all that, I let *my* concentration slip. I'm thinking, "Thank God, you've got two more lines and this is over. Two more lines and you can hide from your friends." Then all of a sudden I heard this voice say, "Isn't that right, Dutch?"

I didn't know where I was. I had a deck of cards in my hands. I never played cards in my life, but I started to shuffle them, and Sidney Lumet later said he never saw anybody shuffle cards like that in his life. I played with them until I remembered my lines and got shot and was the happiest corpse that ever lived.

PERRY LAFFERTY: Ralph Locke and Eva Marie Saint were doing a "Philco." In the play, they were talking to each other on an airplane. All of a sudden, Locke couldn't remember anything. There was this long, terrible pause. The dialogue was such she couldn't say anything. Finally, he said, "Well, this is where I get off," and he got up and walked off the set.

EILEEN HECKART: I was on a "Kraft" when an actor went up on his lines. Stanley Quinn just turned off all the sound in the studio and gave him the line. In effect he turned off all the sets all over America, and everybody was up jiggling their set trying to get the sound back.

PERRY LAFFERTY: Because he was a friend of Montgomery's, James Cagney made his one and only live television appearance on the show. It was a lovely script called "Soldier from the War Returning" about a sergeant who had been on the graves detail.

Cagney was very nervous. In the climactic scene with him and Audra Lindley, he has a monologue that's a page and a half, and halfway through it, suddenly I see that he's lost it. He doesn't know what the next word is. We have a problem, because it's a philosophical dissertation. She can't say anything. The stage manager can't whisper because the mike is right there.

The silence was maybe ten seconds, but it felt like ten years. I cut to him, cut to her, cut to the two-shot. I kept cutting back and forth until he found it again and finished it. The next day, Jack Gould wrote in *The New York Times* about the splendor of Mr. Cagney as an actor understanding the value of a pause, "like Beethoven in his Fifth Symphony, dot, dot, dot . . . dom."

NORMAN FELTON: I had some very unusual experiences. I directed a courtroom drama for "U.S. Steel" called "Survival" that was set in 1850. It was the story of a ship that sank, and in this lifeboat were so many people it too was going to sink. A crew member made the male crew members go overboard in order to save the lives of women and children. He was later tried for manslaughter. The two principals were the man on trial and his sister, who attended the trial.

About five minutes into the show, I noticed something on the sister's chest.

The set designer told me later he was wondering, "Why did Norman put that pearl necklace on her?" It wasn't a pearl necklace. She was vomiting from food poisoning she had gotten during lunch.

The saving grace was she didn't have a line in the show, just reaction shots. I'm watching the monitor, and the technical director is about to punch up the camera that is on her, and she's going, *"arrrrup."* I stopped him, and I took his script and threw it over his shoulder. I said, "We're gonna play this without a script." The rest of the show, I'd watch her and cut away when her head went down. When it came up I would cut to her. At the first commercial, I told everybody to hold their places, and I asked the girls on each side of her to help her and clean her up as best they could.

At the very end, she had to get up and be devastated because her brother was convicted, so they get her up and I had a camera coming towards her down the aisle, and the technical director says, "Jesus, she looks so terrible. Do you want me to cut away?"

I said, "No, push in!" It was cruel, man, but I thought, "I've got to do it. I'm a director," and she did look terrible, but just for a different reason.

*   *   *

DELBERT MANN: My routine on "Philco" was to direct a show every third Sunday. Fred made only one last-minute switcheroo and another script fell into my lap, and it was the most fortuitous there ever was. It happened after I read this one script on a Monday morning. It was such a disaster that Fred switched to a show that Paddy was still writing—"Marty"—which was originally scheduled for Gordon Duff or Vinnie Donehue.

"Marty" came into being because Paddy had some time during rehearsal of a show, and he got to wandering around the rehearsal hall, which was the ballroom of the Abbey Hotel. At night the ballroom was a lonelyhearts club, and there was a sign on the wall that said, GIRLS: DANCE WITH THE MAN WHO ASKS YOU. REMEMBER, MEN HAVE FEELINGS, TOO. At the break, Paddy said to me, "I want to write a story about a gal who comes to a place like this."

At the next break he said, "No, I've been thinking about it. I want to write about a man who comes to a place like this and meets a girl." He thought about it a little bit more and he said to Fred, "I want to write about a middle-aged guy who goes to a lonelyhearts' dance." Fred told him to write it.

We went into rehearsal with only two acts written. Even so, I knew "Marty" was a piece of extraordinary writing. We cast Rod when we had only one act. I don't think we ever had a strong second choice. He said yes on the basis of one act. Nancy Marchand was only in the second act. As soon as we got that in hand, we sent it to her.

ROD STEIGER: "Marty" changed my whole life. "Marty" changed television. Everybody started to do slice-of-life after that. I didn't realize what it was gonna do, but I knew it was a wonderful part to play, even though halfway through rehearsal, there still wasn't a last act.

DELBERT MANN: All we knew was that they were going to get together at the end, but we didn't know how. Paddy didn't tell anybody until he brought it in. We stopped rehearsal, sat down at the table, and read it together for the first time.

WILLIAM NICHOLS: I cast the show. I remember Fred made Paddy change the ending, which was a shame. The original ending was he was sitting there with his friends jeering him about this dreadful girl he picked up. There is this shot of him alone, in which he sits and muses to himself, "Oh, Jeez, I guess she was sort of a dog," and goes back and plays with the boys. That was much more true to life, but he and Fred had a terrible fight over it. Fred said, "You can't have a sad ending like this, not for television." He said, "It ain't pro-life," so Paddy changed it.

ROD STEIGER: To show you the immediacy of television, the next morning I got out of my little room and went to my coffee shop. A garbage truck is going by. The guy who drives the truck says to me just like the play, "What are we goin' to do tonight, Marty?"

I said, "I don't know, what do you wanna do tonight?"

Then I got to the store and a woman said, "What are you gonna do tonight, Marty?"

I said, "I don't know, what are you gonna do tonight?"

In the coffee shop, I get my corn muffin and coffee and the guy says, "What are you gonna do tonight, Marty?" Then I knew something special had happened. This play touched the core of loneliness in the average man and swept across the country.

DELBERT MANN: That show brought more phone calls and letters than any show we ever did. They were universally, "My God, that's the story of my life. How could you have played it so truly?" People were crying on the phone.

TAD MOSEL: On the fourth floor of NBC, there was a page's desk in the foyer, and you knew how successful a play was by how soon the phone rang at the page's desk when you went off the air. If you had to wait five minutes, you knew you were in trouble, trouble, trouble. If they couldn't even get the commercial in before the phone was ringing you were jubilant. You were a success.

REGINALD ROSE: After "Thunder on Sycamore Street," there were calls like, "You 'Studio One' commies. If you don't like this place, why don't you get out."

TAD MOSEL: When it was over, we would all go to Hurley's Bar, and everybody would wait for the reviews in the newspapers.

REGINALD ROSE: You could do a "Studio One" and then rush down to Eighty-sixth and Broadway to the newsstand at twelve-thirty at night and get the *Times* with the review in it.

TAD MOSEL: The day after the show, it seemed everybody in the United States of America was talking about it. When I went to the corner to buy cigarettes, the man who sold me the cigarettes would say, "I saw your show last night," and he would give me his review. While he was giving it, someone would else would say, "Oh, did you write that? Well, I'll tell you what I think about it." You could barely get home again.

When a play was finished, it was a little death in a way. It was difficult to cope with, but that was the nature of the beast. That's why it was wonderful to overlap everything. I never finished a play without already working on something new. I've always felt that was the saving grace for any writer. Before you get to the end of a project be sure to always start something else. Otherwise, when it ends you just feel so terribly empty.

*   *   *

BETHEL LESLIE: Everybody talks about the disasters, but there were also the wonderful things that happened that don't happen on film, like all of a sudden you look at an actor and you realize he's lit up, and he's lighting up everyone else. Things like that would happen and it would be breathtaking.

ROD STEIGER: I've always been, to put it in childish terms, "a shining knight in search of the Holy Grail." And the Holy Grail for me was the hope that I make a moment that will live after the time of my actual life. I think I've gotten close to it. When the pawnbroker puts the spindle through his hand, that's like a heavy poem. The curse of being an actor is that as you achieve a moment that may be remembered it dies 'cause you're moving on. That's why movies were great because scenes are preserved—like the taxi scene in *Waterfront*, which I am so bored with now.

HORTON FOOTE: It was my wife who had seen Kim Stanley off-Broadway and said to me, "Just trust me. Cast this girl in 'The Chase.'" I was very bold. I said to José Ferrer, "I have the best actress in New York." My wife was never wrong about that.

TAD MOSEL: Kim was one of the greatest actresses I've ever worked with. She just knocked your socks off. She played a fourteen-year-old girl in "The Waiting Place" even though she was thirty at the time, and she was absolutely ageless. She was a genius. You had to go through some difficult times with her, but the difficulty was always artistic, never temperamental.

RICHARD KILEY: Kim played my ex-wife in a play called "The Glass Wall." Her character had had a nervous breakdown seven years before and was totally out of it until a drug miraculously brings her back. But in that time, I remarried, and while Kim's character wants to get back together, it just can't happen.

On the day she is released I bring her to a motel, and I say, "Whatever you need, call. We're going to get you back on your feet," and I kiss her on the forehead. She had some lines saying, "I'll call you," which we had rehearsed.

We get on the air, and when I go to give her this avuncular kiss she turns around, and the tears are streaming down her cheeks. She doesn't say her line. She just looks at me, and her eyes go to the bed and she comes back to me. Now, we're live. This silence is attenuating. I look at her, and I start to fill up. We threw all the lines out and just stood there, and I just touched her face. I never did the little kiss. It grew into the most incredible kind of powerful unscripted moment, quite deliberately by her, but honest to God, I don't think she planned it. Kim was that kind of actress.

DELBERT MANN: The Method was the most significant theatrical movement the American theater has ever seen. It took us away from the declamatory, old-fashioned style of acting, which did not lend itself to the intimacy of the camera as the Method did.

HORTON FOOTE: In those days there was this great Method–anti-Method business. I liked Method actors and I was surprised to learn that Fred liked them too.

ROD STEIGER: My generation of actors, I believe, starting with Montgomery Clift, changed the acting of the world. All of a sudden actors around the world begin to identify more personally to what is happening in a play rather than conjecture about what is happening to the character.

I tried to make it like it was happening to me. I think the thing that worked with me in "Marty" was the loneliness I had in my childhood, when I had no Christmas trees.

PERRY LAFFERTY: The hardest thing for a director was the mixture of styles. I had Luther Adler on one show. He was Method to his toes. He asked me, "You mind if I ask you a few questions?" I said, "Of course not. That's what I'm here for." I should have said, "Shut up and deal." We were blocking a kitchen scene, and I said, "Luther, when you are finished here, take the cup and put it on the sink and then say your line."

There was this long pause, and he said, "I don't think I drink out of a cup."

"Okay, what would you drink out of?"

"A glass."

The week was a nightmare. He never learned a word. He asked about everything, and he drove the other actors crazy. They said, "We never get a cue. We don't know what's going to happen next." Of course, what happened was, on the air Luther was brilliant and the others were all just slightly off because they never heard the words being fed to them properly before.

TAD MOSEL: In "The Haven," the man who played the leading role with Eileen Heckart couldn't see reason to cry. Delbert gave him all these images and nothing worked. Eileen, who was no-nonsense, was pacing up and down. Finally, she said to him, "Look, honey, just pick up your cues and spit out the lines, and the scene will play like hell." Then he cried, because she was being mean to him.

Eileen was responsible for my play, "The Out-of-Towners." I wrote it for her because after we did so many plays together she said, "Honey, can't you get me out of the kitchen? I'm so sick of making the cocoa for Mama and the eggs for Dad."

I said to myself, "Where can I put her so she can't get near a kitchen?" and I thought of a hotel lobby.

REGINALD ROSE: I went on jury duty in early 1954. I got on a manslaughter case the first day. Until that moment, I had never been in a courtroom, and I was enormously impressed. The case was about a Bowery bum who inflicted wounds which then caused somebody to die. There were several counts, from manslaughter in the first degree down to assault. Everybody had him guilty, but on what count? There were people in the jury room who actually said, "Let's just drag this out. They'll have to buy us dinner."

There was a terrific fight in the jury room. The side I was on battled for assault because the guy he injured didn't take care of his injuries. It seemed to us his responsibility was to go to a doctor, but he didn't. He went to his bed and stayed there. His wounds became infected, and he died three days later. We prevailed, and the judge said we were absolutely right.

Within a week, I had an idea for a play about a jury with evidence that needed to be more thoroughly examined and the idea of one man holding out against the others and beginning to convince them. I wrote "Twelve Angry Men" in four days, and that first draft with very, very minor changes was what was done.

HORTON FOOTE: After a while it was time to leave "Philco." I had served my time, and I wanted to move on. I never had the great identification with television that Paddy did. Still, television allowed me to get certain material out that I probably would never have written, because in those days nobody did one-act plays.

I also sensed that television was going in a different way. Lillian Gish told me, "You all are making a terrible mistake by not doing anything to protect yourselves. Like they took the movies away from Mr. Griffith, they will take TV away from you."

ARTHUR PENN: In the beginning, the dramatic shows were not of any great interest to the advertising agencies. Philco had a benign agency until the end of 1953 when they discovered people were indeed watching, and, lo and behold, we felt their hot breath. It started with, "Oh, God, is she going to say that?" or "Can you get her not to have such a dirty nose?" Then it went to "Can we see the scripts before rehearsals begin?" The pressure got worse and worse, and eventually Fred had to capitulate. He kept it from the talent. When we would have a drink after the show, he would just say, "Those son of a bitches," but it began to permeate the atmosphere.

HORTON FOOTE: They began to attack the show, calling us the "neurotic playhouse." I was one of the first persons they attacked because they thought I was "introverted," that I didn't care about the world at large.

DELBERT MANN: They wanted more conventional drama. "Let's get some different kinds of stories in there." That ultimately led to Fred leaving the "Playhouse" and to my leaving.

※   ※   ※

MARTIN MANULIS: "Climax" was a major program for CBS. On its first show, there was a shooting in the first scene. The victim fell dead on the ground. The other actors continued playing the scene. Suddenly, to everyone's horror, the corpse, not aware that the camera was on him, rose, dusted himself off, and walked off the set.

The next morning all hell broke loose at CBS. The producer, director, even the story editor were all fired. I was asked to leave "The Best of Broadway" to go to the Coast post-haste to take over the show. While I was out there, I heard about "Playhouse 90." The show was born in 1955 when William Paley asked the program department for new ideas. Frank Stanton suggested a ninety-minute dramatic show. CBS wanted a quality leader, but they also wanted to use their new studios, Television City, properly and with distinction.

At first, the show was known as "Program X." It was to be a weekly ninety-minute live drama with thirty-nine shows a year. No one had done it before. I was chosen to be the producer, probably because I was already doing a weekly hour.

There were always three shows in various stages—one casting, one rehearsing, and one about to go on the air. It was a madhouse. Script meetings were usually on the weekends. We would try to work at the pool and pretend we were real live humans.

We planned a fifty-fifty mix of originals and adaptations. The writers were outstanding. We had Rod Serling, J. P. Miller, Tad Mosel, A. E. Hotchner, Horton Foote, Reginald Rose, and a few others. We also had top directors:

Franklin Schaffner, George Roy Hill, Delbert Mann, John Frankenheimer, Daniel Petrie, Robert Mulligan, Arthur Hiller, Ralph Nelson, and Arthur Penn. They came enthusiastically, because they realized the creative opportunity the program provided.

ARTHUR PENN: I went out there for the money. At "Philco," we really earned nothing. I was married and had a child. We were pretty broke. I had a couple of shirts where the collars were almost gone, and I didn't have enough money to replace them, so when Marty offered some forty grand, I grabbed it—shamelessly.

Our mission on "Playhouse 90" was to come in as the New York boys and take the Hollywood community and "Marty" them. Hollywood's way of dealing with New York was, "If we can't beat 'em, join 'em." They began to siphon us off.

MARTIN MANULIS: We recognized the true value of the writer. In addition to the ten-thousand-dollar script fee, we instituted audio credit for the writer as well as for the director and the producer. That was a first, and the network resisted it until I complained that everyone mispronounced my name. Also the writers were brought to Hollywood—all expenses paid—to attend rehearsals. When changes were needed, they did them, usually with grace. Usually.

ETHEL WINANT: People had never seen a show like this with the top writers and top directors and layer upon layer of stars. The idea was to do shows that would get people to say, "I didn't know he could do that." Or "Wow, that was exciting."

MARTIN MANULIS: "Requiem for a Heavyweight" was supposed to be the opening, but a CBS executive named Al Scalpone hated the script. He said, "You'll do this downbeat story and you'll kill the series." Well, we were allowed to do it if we didn't open with it, so we did it the second week and it won five Emmies.

ETHEL WINANT: There was a lot of stunt casting on "Playhouse 90." The idea was to cast people who were promotable, like Ed Wynn in "Requiem for a Heavyweight." The problem was everybody wanted to fire Ed because he couldn't remember his lines. Even his son Keenan, who was also in the play, was in a panic. I hired Ned Glass to play the bartender in the show. He was secretly understudying Ed, who was also in a panic because he couldn't remember his lines.

MARTIN MANULIS: If this had not been live, he would have been wonderful, but the strain of doing live TV was just impossible. Everybody wanted Ed replaced, including Ralph Nelson, the director, but I got stubborn. I knew he was in no way his public persona, a clown, and I believed he could play this well, so I took a flyer. I went to a run-through and did a real grandstand play. I gave high praise to everyone, especially to Ed, and left the studio.

Everybody thought I meant everything I said, and they were aghast. Well, he made it and got a lot of good press. They respected his courage. Here was a man of his age doing a totally different thing than he had ever done before. He was even nominated for an Emmy.

ETHEL WINANT: "Playhouse 90" was fun because we got to work with lots of stars, which I could never do in New York because I never had fifty cents. Sometimes a director would say, "I don't want stars. I want wonderful actors," but the truth is most people become stars because they're good and because people like to see them. The trick is to cast them correctly.

ARTHUR PENN: For one show, Martin said to me, "What about Tab Hunter?" This was to play a murderer.

"Are you crazy?"

"Listen, that guy . . ."

So Tab and I met and talked about it, and I was impressed. Tab responded to my New York style. I gave him a kind of license that he had never had. Until then, he had been sort of a manufactured creature, a name. As a result of something that he tapped into for that role, he was absolutely terrifying. Years later he said it was the best acting experience of his career.

MARTIN MANULIS: We got actors to do the show for a pittance compared to their movie salaries, but we also offered them parts that they normally might not get.

ETHEL WINANT: There was that famous problem with Paul Muni on "Playhouse 90."

MARTIN MANULIS: It was a coup to get Paul to make his debut with us. I figured that a man who had spent his life in the theater would have no problem with live TV, but when we began rehearsing in the studio, it confused him because studios are very noisy. I felt sorry for him, but my blood was running cold because he couldn't remember anything. His wife kept saying to me, "Muni is an old firehouse. When the bell rings he'll run."

Well, he wasn't running. It was the first and only time in my seven years at CBS that I had to call New York and say to Hubbell Robinson, "You will have to inform whomever that there may not be a show tonight."

It was George Roy Hill who made it work. He not only directed the show, but he also talked the lines into an earphone we gave Paul. At the beginning of the show, Muni put his hand in his pocket, and he realized that there were wires visibly dangling from his jacket. A minute or so later, he put his hand to his ear the way a deaf person does and leaned forward a little when someone else was talking to show that he was playing a man who had poor hearing. To think of that at that time was remarkable. This was a master actor out there at his finest.

We only had time to rehearse the first hour of the play. The last thirty minutes had big soliloquies by Muni in tight closeups. The cameras were so close together they made heavy static. In the control room, George suddenly said, "He can't hear me." Now we were up the creek, but fortunately Muni didn't have to throw many cues, and he took off on his own and he was superb.

DICK SMITH: In 1959, I did "Moon and Sixpence" with Laurence Olivier. That was something for me. He was my god and at that point one of the kindest, most considerate people I've worked with. When I worked with him on "The Power and the Glory," he asked me if I could make his lips bigger. I made rubber lips for the first time, and he loved them. Talking about it one day, he said, "My lips are so thin. My eyes are too deepset."

There I was standing by this man who was so handsome. I said, "Don't tell me you don't like your face. My God!"

He said, "Oh, I mean professionally it's a disadvantage," which was not entirely true. Then I said, "If you had your choice professionally, whose face would you like to have?"

"Gary Cooper. His expressions are very subtle, but you know when he smiles his face lights up so much."

I think that underneath that admiration was the desire to be the manly, strong, silent type, because with his experiences as a young man he wondered, "Am I a man?" Having gone through it myself, I sympathized.

MARTIN MANULIS: We had a bang-up success with "Playhouse 90" in its first year, and we began to feel there was almost nothing we couldn't achieve live. To open the second season, we wanted to do something challenging. Barnaby Conrad, who was a bullfighting aficionado, brought in the idea for "Manolete." We thought Jack Palance would be ideal for Manolete. It never occurred to us what a hoot we would get for building a production around a fake bull's head on the end of a stick, bobbing up and down.

ETHEL WINANT: "Manolete" was the worst show we ever did.

MARTIN MANULIS: We should have known better but we didn't. It was a combination of the fake bull, and everything else that went wrong. Jack, who had a body of steel, wore a pair of tights that were hanging down as if he had a load in his pants. Instead of this magnificent figure, there were his droopy drawers. As his love interest, we had the top model of the time, Suzi Parker, who was a great beauty, but really couldn't act.

ETHEL WINANT: It was another case of stunt casting. Suzi was the number-one model in America. She had signed this huge motion-picture contract. She was on the cover of every magazine in America. She was terrible in rehearsal, but we didn't fire her. It was a hopeless part. It didn't matter who you put in it.

ARTHUR PENN: When Bill Gibson was writing "Two for the Seesaw," he said to me, "Jesus, I need some money."

I said, "What do you got that we could do on television?"

"Well, I once wrote a modern-dance narrative based on Annie Sullivan and Helen Keller."

He told me about it, and we sketched it out. After he finished it, I took it to NBC. They said no. I couldn't believe it. It just jumped off the pages. CBS also turned it down. When I joined "Playhouse 90," I told Marty about the script. He read it and bought it.

MARTIN MANULIS: "The Miracle Worker" was the only time ever that we did nothing to the script after it was delivered except cut out the last scene. My wife, Katharine Bard, played Mrs. Keller. That scene was important to her, but it was so anticlimactic. You couldn't top that "wah-wah" scene.

After being "Playhouse 90" 's sole producer for two years, I decided to leave. I had offers from almost every movie studio, and I wanted to do that.

J. P. MILLER: Fred Coe was the producer of "Playhouse 90" when I wrote "Days of Wine and Roses." It began with a guy who decided he didn't want to be a writer anymore—me. I had such a terrible experience in California, I said, "If this is being a writer, I'm going back to New York to tell my wife I'm gonna buy a boat and be a fisherman."

So now I'm walkin' down the street in New York City, and I bump into Fred Coe. Fred says, "Hey, Pappy, I've been lookin' all over for you."

"Look, Fred, I'm giving up this goddamn writing game."

"Look, Pappy, I'm gonna do three 'Playhouse 90's, and I want you to do one of 'em. If you change your mind, call me up and tell me what story you want to do. We got a deal, one show only, the rights are all yours, but I want a powerful story."

I go home, have a fight with my wife, can't sleep. "Shit, maybe I'll go get drunk." I make myself a martini one o'clock in the morning, go back to bed, still can't sleep. I start thinking about my Uncle Fred, an alcoholic who lived with us during the Depression. Suddenly, a story pops out.

At one-thirty, I call Fred. I knew he was up drinking. "Listen, I got an idea. Two nice young people fall in love, and they like to drink, and the bottle becomes more important to each one of them than they are to each other. I don't know where it goes from there, but that's the story."

"Jesus, Pappy, that sounds great. Why don't you write it?"

That's the way it started. I didn't know anything except that equation. I tried to visualize a title that would be poetic and have to do with love and booze, and I thought of Ernest Dazen who wrote a lot of love poems.

I had a draft in about three months. Fred loved it, but he started getting heat about it before we even went into rehearsal. They wanted him to make a lot of changes. The show was undersubscribed when it went on the air. They had a lot of public announcements to fill it up. They said, "Fred Coe has screwed us up. He's costing us millions." Well, the goddamned show was one of the highest-rated shows. It got all these Emmy nominations, and Fred, who was the goat, became the hero.

I made my acting debut in it. I shush a drunk in an AA meeting. It made Actor's Equity very angry that I was doing the part. They said, "You're cutting an actor out of a job." I said, "I'm giving about fifty actors jobs. Go fuck yourself."

The only problem we had during rehearsals was when John Frankenheimer and Piper Laurie became, shall we say, close. They would come in in the morning having rewritten some of her scenes so that she was getting drunker and drunker—actors love to play drunks. This made Cliff Robertson rather hostile, because he didn't know what was going on. He was playing love scenes with an actress who was playing love scenes with the director.

Anyway, I turned down all the changes in the script and I called Fred in. I said, "Fred, they're turning this into a drunk play. Take a look at it." They did a run-through for him, and when they got through, John said, "Fred, did you ever see more real drunk scenes in your life?"

Fred said, and this is a quote I'll never forget, "You're right, John. You got the wine. Now see if you can get the roses," and he walked out. That's what I call a producer.

✳   ✳   ✳

JACK RAYEL: I was in charge of new programs and program development for NBC when a woman named Millie Alberg wrote a letter to NBC, saying she was representing the actor Maurice Evans. He wanted to put on a production of what he called "The GI Hamlet" on television. I had seen it, and I thought, "God, that's wonderful. Nobody's ever done anything like this." I proposed it to the man who represented Foote, Cone and Belding in New York, the agency that handled Hallmark. That was the beginning of the "Hallmark Hall of Fame."

I had to go to the vice president of sales, George Fry, in order to get his signature to approve the sale at a bargain basement rate, fifty thousand dollars for two hours, time and talent. He looked at me when he was about to sign it and said, "Are you sure you want to be responsible for this?"

"Yes, George, I do. Let's go with it."

Of course, it was a great success.

JANE AURTHUR: I worked for Ethel Frank, who was the story editor on Hallmark. She worked under Al McCleery, who was a madman. His dream was to make enough money in television so he could contribute to some political party and become Secretary of the Army. He had to be called "Colonel." He wanted us to address everybody at NBC by their military title. Of course there was "The General." You had to know what everybody was. I would call the secretary and jokingly say, "Is Commander so-and-so in?"

Sarah Churchill was our hostess on "Hallmark" and a very stiff actress, but Mr. Hall, who owned Hallmark, was a great admirer of Winston Churchill, so Sarah got the job. She also had to star in one out of four shows. It was not easy to find material for her.

One of my jobs was to come up with story ideas for the show. We would have to summarize them for Mr. Hall in one page. I would write, "We nominate *Pride and Prejudice* for the 'Hallmark Hall of Fame' because . . ." Imagine summarizing that in a page.

DELBERT MANN: "Producer's Showcase" was another star-oriented show. It was part of Pat Weaver's whole premise—taking the audience to an extraordinary event—but the shows were really devised, as much as anything else, to sell RCA color television.

They were a little unhappy with the first shows I did for them. One was "Yellowjack," all done in the tropics of Cuba with olive-drab Army uniforms about yellow fever, and "Darkness at Noon," which was dark and gloomy and not terribly colorful, and then the "Petrified Forest," with Bogart, Fonda, and Bacall, but which was set in desert colors.

ARTHUR PENN: When I was blocking "State of the Union" with Margaret Sullavan, I suddenly got a call from General Sarnoff, "I want more color in her clothes," so we had to go out and get a new dress for Maggie.

TAD MOSEL: I adapted "The Petrified Forest" with the Bogarts and Henry Fonda. The problem was in the play Bogart doesn't even appear for a solid hour. You could not go on television with the biggest star in the world and delay his entrance. If you didn't believe Bogart was the biggest star in the world, he would tell you so. He would say, "What I mean by a star is you could go to the loneliest crossroad in the world and say the name and they know who you mean. There are very few of us."

I had to manufacture a scene for the very beginning, so you saw him for about a minute. Also, in the original production, he had almost no lines. He just sat at a window with a gun in his lap. I had to make up whole passages for him. One problem I had with that was his difficulty pronouncing "s's." In the play, Bogart makes a reference to the American Legion and their "pansy" uniforms. Well, I couldn't use "pansy" on television, so I changed the word to "sissy," and he said it, but like no word you ever heard in your life. Finally, I quietly changed "sissy" to "fancy," and nothing was ever said about it.

He died the following year. There was no reason why with his stature he should do live television in a secondary role to Henry Fonda. I think he knew he was dying and wanted to get Lauren Bacall back into the midst of things. After she married him she had disappeared. If you wanted to get back into the swim in 1955, you went on television, and it led to a new career for her.

* * *

HORTON FOOTE: I adapted Faulkner's story "The Old Man" for "Playhouse 90." The script called for a flood, but I figured let them figure it out. That's not my problem. It didn't faze Frankenheimer. We were going to do it live, but just before we were to begin, John said to me, "We'll drown the actors. It will be terrible. We've got to put it on tape." That in a sense was the death of live television because the show was a big success. They repeated it about four times. After that people started thinking of tape. I've always felt bad about it, but I guess it was inevitable.

ETHEL WINANT: That was the first show that was ever shot out of sequence and then edited like a movie on tape.

NORMAN FELTON: I started a one-hour series called "Pursuit." They wanted to tape it live on Sunday and air it two days later. We set the cameras like we did for a live show. The idea was we would start and go straight on for an hour. At the end of the first act, Keenan Wynn suddenly stops in his tracks and says, "Shit, I blew it." Of course everything stopped. At that moment I knew that live television as I had known it was finished. As long as the actor knew it wasn't really live, you couldn't fool 'em.

TAD MOSEL: I think tape helped the performers a great deal. It made the production more flexible, and it gave them time to change their clothes, which was the biggest problem in live television.

In live television, we learned to write pure Aristotelian plays with unity of time, place, and action because we had to. Take clothes, for example: if there wasn't a legitimate way to keep your actor off to change from a fur coat to a bathing suit you didn't do it. That meant you had to telescope time, and the same actor had to wear the same suit all the way through, so the play could not cover ten years. It was best to cover one or two days and focus on a single dramatic event.

We could not afford many actors or many sets. In order to alleviate the set problem, the directors kept moving into the actors' faces, so that you had plays taking place within twenty-four hours with two or three characters.

ROD STEIGER: I was happy to go to tape, but tape made it possible for a lot of actors who weren't ready to survive because they could always do it over. I think it lowered the level of professionalism.

TAD MOSEL: After tape came in, we became old-hat. We represented something that was dead and gone as far as television was concerned. The movies were different. *Marty* revolutionized movies. That kind of smaller-scale movie had never been done before, and it was so successful a different kind of movie evolved, one that television writers could write.

Movies were looked down on until then. Famous writers got drunk and went to work in the movies. It didn't become an art form until after television. Those movies that we look back on and say, "Oh, those wonderful movies in the thirties" were not considered so wonderful in the fifties.

J. P. MILLER: The writer was important on live television because it had to be right when it went on the air. With tape, they could say, "I hate this fucking script. Let's get Joe Blow in here to fix up the ending." In the case of "Days of Wine and Roses," Joe Blow would have come in and you would never have heard of "Days of Wine and Roses" because they would have both been sober, and it would end in a big clinch and be just like every other piece of shit that has ever been done.

REGINALD ROSE: By the end of the fifties, I had written five movies and a lot of television. By then, the television audience was larger than the movie audience, but television only gave you fifty-two minutes to say something and movies gave you a hundred. I wanted to write bigger stories than television would allow me to write. What kept my career in television was the decision to do my play, "The Defender," as a series. Here was a chance to blaze trails and to get at all kinds of issues.

BETHEL LESLIE: When I went out to Hollywood, the first thing they did was fit me with falsies that went out to here. The whole atmosphere was different. In New York, there was always a sense that what was important was the work and the performance. Out there, the hair and the lighting was most important.

NORMAN FELTON: Hollywood was making half-hour shows—cops and robbers and westerns—and they got bigger ratings than "Playhouse 90." On live television, shows were selected in terms of the material. They were directed and produced by people who were out of touch with the growing audience. They should have kept in mind that we could do shows with substance but which the average person could enjoy.

ARTHUR PENN: It was always an adventure to work with those great writers. If Clurman had the fervent years in theater, these were the fervent years in television. I don't think the people involved ever felt as great about them-selves again as they did then.

O. TAMBURRI: We all worked hard. Three cameramen would have a beer at Hurley's. At midnight, Larry Elikann is there saying, "You should have been on this angle on that shot," and he's lying on the floor looking up. "You did it wrong."

IRVING GAYNOR NEIMAN: Television writing was a skill I had, a craft I learned. It was a nice way to make a living. I was a hack, but a good hack. It was a hack business, ninety-five percent of it, and either you do good hack work or bad hack work. I dreamed that someday I would write for the stage, but I never did.

A lot of my stuff was plain forgettable, but I don't want to denigrate it too much. I wrote it as well as I could, given the limitations of time and space and everything else, but if any of them was art, I doubt it. The Golden Age which was so fondly remembered was not so golden. It was a Golden Age because some rather interesting things were done, but a lot of pretentious nonsense was done, too. The impression now is that "Studio One" and "Philco" and "Good-year" did all gems. I did a few of each, but I'm not sure mine were gems. "Ap-pointment in Samarra" was a good show. And in one or two others you managed to get through the hassle or to be assigned a decent property if it was an adaptation. If you were assigned a piece of junk, you did a piece of junk. It was always a commercial medium even in the Golden Age.

TAD MOSEL: A Golden Age is not a zenith; it is a flowering and a period of good will because of the flowering. If television wasn't flowering in the fif-ties, I don't know what it was doing. The flowering ended when television be-gan to get rich. When you had to write your play with only two sets and four characters, you learned a discipline in writing which you lost when they said, "You want an army? Okay, we'll give you an army." It's my theory that the min-ute that happens the only freedom for a writer and director that is worthwhile is the freedom to choose your own jail cell. We liked the confinement.

O. TAMBURRI: Those were fun days, but even now when I am retired, I dream about the work, and it's not always good. It's sometimes hectic. Some-times it's a reminder of the problems that we had rather than the successes. Sometimes I wake up in the morning fighting a show that is not going right, and it just hasn't gone away. I hope it does. If I don't let up on those dreams, I'm going to have to visit somebody.

CELLULOID HEROES

A full hour dramatic show may cost the sponsor some $30,000 per week for the production. And, when the show is over, what does he have for his money?—Nothing!

Script rights revert to the author and union regulations prevent a reshowing of the kinescope—$30,000 gone with the wind.

Film . . . has that all-important re-run value which is the quality I feel counts most in TV.

One might guess those were the words of a Hollywood mogul or a typical agency hack. Er, no. They are excised from an article in *TV News* by Fred Coe, the guru of live television. Since there is no evidence that his children were being held hostage at the time, we must assume he was serious about what he said.

Actually, there was sound economic reasoning behind his comments. Reruns made filmed programs more profitable in the long run. Film also allowed a writer and director much more leeway in the breadth of their storytelling and in its presentation. Still, film, particularly in television's early years, seemed something like a four-star meal with Spam as the entree. Perhaps it was just the century-old conflict between East Coast theater and West Coast commerce, but if New York had its "Philco" and "Goodyear" playhouses, it also gave the world Howdy Doody, and what was more commercial than that?

On the other hand, Hollywood, more than New York, tended to regard its output as "product." "They aren't making shows, they are making widgets," said Ethel Winant, and Winant, who cast everything from "Studio One" to "The Mary Tyler Moore Show," knows from whence she speaks. "They make shows they hope will have a commercial shelf life of twenty years."

The first made-for-TV widgets rolled off the line in 1947. "Public Prosecutor," produced by Jerry Fairbanks, was an odd hybrid of mystery and game show. Each episode was seventeen minutes long, which made them perfect schedule filler. Fairbanks syndicated his films, meaning they were rented directly to local stations or advertisers, bypassing the networks. Syndication soon became big business. Because stations had large schedules to fill, syndicators, with either libraries of old feature films or first-run productions of their own, did well from the start. By 1955, the syndication business was grossing some $150 million a year.

Fairbanks was truly a pioneer. His other early offerings included "Jackson and Jill," the first filmed sitcom, and he was the distributor of "Crusader Rabbit," the first cartoon made for TV. However, Fairbanks's most lasting contribution to television was not in his product but in his process. He was the first to shoot with several cameras simultaneously in order to speed up production. Ralph Edwards used the same technique on "Truth or Consequences," and then the producers of "I Love Lucy" found that Fairbanks's technique made it possible to film comedy before a live audience (although Desi later claimed credit for the idea). It has been used for most sitcoms ever since.

Frederic Ziv, the George Washington of syndicators, going back to his days in radio, weighed in with his first film shorts in 1947. That year also marked the television debut of the first hour film on TV, the "Hopalong Cassidy Show." That series, however, was not specifically made for TV. They were Hoppy's old features edited to fit a one-hour slot.

Soon, filmed shows dotted local schedules. Most of them were westerns, produced for a double sawbuck out of the minor Hollywood studios. By and large, they were the same show, with interchangeable heroes chasing interchangeable villains. Nearly all of them were shot on location. Most of them had a good-looking star, who probably rode better than he acted, and most importantly did not command a fat paycheck. Nearly all of them had a sidekick for comic relief, but romance (aka "mushy stuff") was limited to the star and his horse, and never got beyond the petting stage.

In the early fifties, some of the locales switched from the Old West to India or Africa ("The Straw Hut Circuit"), which usually meant a move to a more verdant corner of the Western ranch. Such series also zoomed into outer space with shows like "Flash Gordon," filmed in Berlin (which explained why, wrote Hal Erickson in his history of syndicated television, "the principal mode of transportation in the twenty-first century seemed to be the Volkswagen"). Critics laughed at the show's papier-mâché sets, but "Flash Gordon" and the other quickie serials like the pseudo-African adventure "Ramar of the Jungle" were rerun for years.

"Who gives a damn about production values on TV?" asked Richard Carlson, the star of Ziv's "I Led Three Lives." "Nobody. The major film studios who went into TV have learned that production values will not sustain any show. What the people want is a story and people they don't resent in their living rooms."

Nobody gave it to 'em like Ziv. "Highway Patrol" had fewer production values than a bar-mitzvah movie, but it did have a bankable star in Oscar-winner Broderick Crawford, whose "Ten-Four!" made it one of the biggest syndicated hits of all time, and with "Code Three" and "Whirlybirds," et cetera, it spawned more progeny than Joseph Smith.

Film displaced live programming steadily through the 1950s. According to *Broadcasting Yearbook*, eighty-two percent of network programming was live in 1952. By 1961, the figure had dropped to twenty-seven percent. Most of the early filmed shows were of the action/adventure variety and were placed on the Saturday morning schedule. However, some, like the first twenty-six "Superman" episodes, were violent enough to be considered adult fare and were aired locally in adult prime time. As for the Man of Steel, a second producer completed the series in tamer fashion, felt to be more suitable for kids. Not all the syndicated series were done cheaply. "Superman" employed an expert crew, and "Foreign Intrigue," shot on location in Paris and Stockholm, garnered three Emmy nominations.

None of the early film shows were produced by the major studios, which eyed television with the same mixture of irritation and fear that the dinosaurs may have felt for the first furry creatures they squished under their toes. Paramount even refused to broadcast its movies on its own stations. The first minor studio to adopt an "if you can't beat 'em, join 'em" attitude was Hal Roach, but even that was from a distance. The Roach Studios were leased to producers of several early film comedies, including "My Little Margie," "The Stu Erwin Show," and "The Life of Riley."

Columbia was the first major studio to break ranks. In 1951, it set up a subsidiary, Screen Gems, specifically to make TV shows. Two of its earliest efforts were "The Adventures of Rin Tin Tin" and "Captain Midnight." Disney was not considered a major, but its decision to move into television had an enormous impact. The cheese in the mousetrap, so to speak, was $500,000 that Leonard Goldenson of ABC dangled in front of Disney. That money would be used to finish Disneyland. In exchange, Goldenson would get many hours of badly needed programming. Disney took the bait and signed a seven-year commitment. It was a good deal all around, unless you happened to be a raccoon, because after December 1954, when Davy Crockett made his debut, every kid in America was after your butt.

Quickly, the big-budget Disney shows pushed the westerns into a different arena. Beginning in September 1955, with the nearly simultaneous premieres of "Gunsmoke," "The Life and Legend of Wyatt Earp," and "Cheyenne," westerns became adult programming, with more realistic plots, shaded characters, and major-league acting. Warner Bros. even brought satire into the genre with "Maverick" in 1957.

Before he took the TV plunge, Jack Warner's antipathy toward the small screen had been legendary. His wife wasn't permitted to watch it, and TVs were banned from all Warner Brothers sets. Still, he may have had no choice when Goldenson approached him hat-in-hand in 1954. Perhaps more than the other majors, Warner's was severely affected by the slump in the movie business that began after World War II and peaked in the early fifties. Television's popularity only partly contributed to the decline, but it was the primary reason for Warner's recovery. By 1958, the studio, with "77 Sunset Strip," "Sugarfoot," "Maverick," "Hawaiian Eye," et al., was programming ten hours a week of ABC's prime-time schedule, and both the studio and the network were enjoying their salad days.

The rumor was they were all the same program. In some ways they were. When the writers struck Warner in 1959, script editors took the old scripts, transposed the names of the characters and, voilà, a "77 Sunset Strip" suddenly became a "Hawaiian Eye." The joke was in the credits, which listed the writers as "W. Hermanos," Spanish for Warner Brothers. Funny, except the joke was on the viewers.

TOMMY CARR: I made my first picture for Lubin in 1909 when I was two and a half. I had something to do with one picture or another every year after that until I retired.

I was too small to be an actor, so I went behind the camera. I became a dialogue clerk at Republic. Republic was a minor studio, but it was a famous minor studio. They specialized in serials and westerns. When TV came in, Republic had a western space on their lot, and they would rent out space. You could do your show cheaper there than you could in other places, and when I directed at Republic, I made westerns in eight or nine days. Once I made six of 'em in twenty-eight days.

HARRY GERSTAD: I worked on so many westerns as an assistant editor at Republic that I was bowlegged. I also worked at a film laboratory and at Technicolor, so I knew fine grains and duplications, dissolves, and I knew trickwork backwards and forward. All of that came in handy later when I did "Superman."

※　※　※

STANLEY RUBIN: Louis Lantz and I were a writing team at Columbia Pictures. In the fall of 1947, our contract was not picked up. While trying to find a way to make a living, we realized there were no filmed weekly series on network TV. We thought, "Why don't we be the first?"

We never considered doing a live show. I had a firm notion about residual values; that when the films reverted to us, we could sell them again and again.

People said, "Well, film doesn't have that *je ne sais quoi,* the pizzazz of a live show."

I said, "Bullshit, when you've got it on film you've got it forever."

We had no idea if TV shows would be fifteen minutes, twenty minutes, or half an hour. To make the financing easier, we decided it would be a fifteen-minute show. That first script ran long, thank goodness, because we realized the episodes would have to be a half hour. We called it, with a little hyperbole, "Dramatizations of the World's Greatest Short Stories." The truth was we used public domain short stories because we couldn't afford to buy any. The first one we did was de Maupassant's "The Necklace." Each script was introduced by a proprietor in a bookshop. We really needed him as a narrator to cover sections in the story we couldn't possibly afford to dramatize.

The series was sold to Lucky Strike who called it "Your Show Time." We spread the word amongst all our writing friends to come up with stories for teleplays. We also put stories by Pushkin and Chekhov on the list, but Lucky Strike said no Russian stories, so we had to take them off.

We shot two films a week at the Hal Roach Studios. We would start one on a Monday morning, finish it Wednesday at noon, then start the next one Wednesday after lunch and finish it Friday night at eight or nine or ten o'clock. After we had done five or six shows our accountant discovered that we were going $3,500 in the hole each show. Disaster lay at the end of the road unless we got some financing. I went to several banks. They asked, "What do you have for collateral?" I said, "These films will be worth something after Lucky Strike is finished with them."

I was proposing they would be valuable as reruns, but they never heard of such a thing, and they wouldn't give me a nickel. Then my partners wanted out because we were losing too much money, so we did twenty-six and that was the end. When we rereleased them through Ziv, our balance after expenses was over $200,000.

I think the show made people aware of the value of doing series on film. Also, we won the first Emmy, "Best Film Made in Hollywood for Television," on January 25, 1949.

FREDERIC ZIV: I am considered the father of syndication. I began syndicating radio programs in 1935 as an independent producer.

BUD RIFKIN: I was working for the CBS station in Youngstown, WKBM, in 1938 when I met Fred. He had a series called "Johnny Lawrence, The Freshest Thing in Town." He would sell that to Smith's Bakery in Cleveland or Jones's in Pittsburgh. He offered me a job working for him, making presentations to bakeries in Ohio, Pennsylvania, and New England. Then in '47 Fred suggested I move to New York because we were going to get into television one way or another.

FREDERIC ZIV: We did our first television program, "Yesterday's Newsreel," in 1947. It consisted of old newsreel footage, but we had no difficulty in finding a market for it. Most stations were desperate for programming.

BUD RIFKIN: People would watch you and me dancing in those days. We couldn't produce enough to fill the airwaves. The network went black after ten o'clock. We had "Yesterday's Newsreel" on from ten to ten-fifteen in New York. That's how hungry they were for film.

FREDERIC ZIV: In '48 we did "Sports Album." In 1949, we did our first full scale production, "The Cisco Kid." We shot it in color. There were no color sets yet, but I knew that color would come and we should be prepared.

BUD RIFKIN: Soon we were repackaging old films for the networks. You could sell them anything, especially since none of the major studios were doing anything in television.

RUDOLPH FLOTHOW, JR.: My father, Rudolph Flothow, Sr., co-produced virtually all of the B pictures for Columbia. He did hard-hitting dramas that were shot in twenty-one days, things like "Boston Blackie," "Red Rider," and the Ellery Queen pictures. When the film industry died in '47, my father met a guy named Edward Small, who created a thing called Television Productions of America. They wanted to do for syndication just what he had done before, hard-hitting, low-cost shows, a lot of male-driven action.

My father said, "Why don't we do something about Africa," which always fascinated him. When they needed a name for the show, a writer who had worked for my father at Columbia said, "Why not call it a palindrome? That would be catchy," and he came up with the name Ramar, "Ramar of the Jungle."

RICHARD BARE: Roach got into TV to keep the studio busy. I did the first hour-long TV show on film at Roach. It was called "Hurricane at Pilgrim Hill." We made the show in four days.

ERIC FREIWALD: My partner Robert Schaefer and I met in a writing school in Hollywood after the war, and we decided to team up. We wrote a western story for "The Durango Kid," which was a Columbia Pictures series starring Charlie Starrett.

ROBERT SCHAEFER: My uncle, Armand Schaefer, was a producer at Republic Studios, so I knew something about westerns. I also had horses as a kid. Eric didn't know which end of a horse ate. I sent this story to my uncle. He sent it to a producer at Columbia, and they bought it for a hundred dollars. I was twenty-three. Eric was twenty-one.

Then my uncle and Gene Autry formed Flying A Productions to make television pictures. As far as I know, Gene was the first personality to make television films. My uncle said we could take a shot at writing one of the Gene Autry films. We wrote a story in three or four days and it was accepted.

ERIC FREIWALD: Flying A produced "Gene Autry," "Range Rider," "Annie Oakley," "Buffalo Bill, Jr.," and "Adventures of Champion." We worked for all of them.

DICK JONES: I grew up in a little town in Texas. At the age of four, I was the youngest rider and trick roper in the world. Hoot Gibson brought me out to Hollywood. I played in almost every western there was because they didn't have to hire midgets or girls to double me.

When I got out of the service I worked on some of the "Lone Ranger"'s. They ran by their shirttails. Their whole system was in a station wagon. The front had a camera platform. On the tailgate was a guy with the sound equipment. They would do two shows at once. We would chase one way up a dirt road at Arvison's Ranch. When you'd get to the end, you'd turn around and get on a spotted horse that had been painted with white paint, change hats, and go shootin' the other way for the second film.

Once, I was the Apache Kid, and I wore a black hat. For the next show, I put on a tan hat and I was this girl's brother. I didn't even change my clothes. The producers of "The Lone Ranger" pioneered the industry, and Autry just copied him.

PAT BUTTRAM: Gene would shoot two pictures simultaneously. A heavy in one would be the sheriff in another. He would just change his badge while we set up. Gene would always be chewing gum, because Wrigley was our sponsor, and the sheriff would always take out a stick of gum. Of course, the bad guys never chewed gum.

TOMMY CARR: I directed the first "Wild Bill Hickok"'s. We'd make them in three days using every bit of light we could at a cost of fifteen-thousand dollars each. To keep costs down, you would go through the script and figure out how much everything was going to cost you. A stunt man would get twenty-five dollars if he is shot out of a saddle and hits the ground. Each extra costs a certain amount, and if he opens his mouth he gets that much more. So instead of having twenty-five people on a set you try to have fifteen, but you still have to shoot it so it looks like you have twenty-five. You used furniture and plants or automobiles in your establishing shot, anything to fill space and make it look like more people.

You always use stock shots. On "Rawhide," we used stock shots for the cattle. Fifty head of cattle would cost you close to a thousand dollars, so before we started the season, I would get maybe seven hundred head of cattle and shoot nothing but cattle scenes, big drives, and riding the cast right out in front, covering every situation that might come up during the season.

We did have problems with the steers. They were all steers, no cows in there, but they were mounting each other all the time. I'd be standing right by the camera operator. As he panned across he would say, "Humper . . . humper . . . humper . . ." My God, if you have five hundred or a thousand of them there was a lot of that going around.

DOUGLAS HEYES: I wrote a whole lot of movies for a quickie outfit called Clover Productions. Their production manager was a guy named Bert Leonard. One day he walked into my office and said, "Listen, I ran into a guy at a party who has a dog called Rin Tin Tin. His ancestor, the early Rin Tin Tin, was the biggest star in silent pictures." He asked me if I wanted to team up with him and do a series about this dog.

He said, "There's a fort out at Corriganville John Ford built for 'Fort Apache.' Maybe we can use that set."

"Yeah, why don't we put the dog in the cavalry?"

We quickly sold the concept to Shredded Wheat, and I wrote a script. When that was done, I said to Bert, "We ought to meet this dog if he's going to be the star of the series."

We went out to Santa Ana to see the dog's owner, Lee Duncan. He bought out this untrained old dog who was like the fourth or fifth descendant of the original Rin Tin Tin. I said, "He's a nice-looking dog. What can he do?"

"He'll be fine once the series starts."

"Can he do something now, like chase a bone?" Then I said, "Run, Rinny," and Rinny sat down. I pulled Bert aside, and I said, "Bert, we're in trouble. This dog can't act."

There was a famous movie dog called Flame. Frank Barnes was now training Flame, Jr., and that was the one that did all the acting in "Rin Tin Tin."

TOMMY CARR: On "Roy Rogers," we had six or seven Triggers. The real good-looking one was only used for closeups. You had one for stunts, one for tricks, and one that could ride like the wind. Gene Autry had more than one Champion, too.

DOUGLAS HEYES: When we would rehearse, Frank would say, "Just tell me where you want the dog to do something." I would say, "Here he's supposed to bark and go to the window."

"Okay." When it came to that time, Frank would say, "J. R., bark and go to the window," and he would do it. The dog understood everything. "Pick up the hat and drop it on the floor." He was amazing. An actor couldn't have done those scenes as fast. He did them in one take, and he never had to get in the mood to do his part.

We used the old one, too. He was brave, but he didn't know any tricks, so he ran with the horses. When you see the dog running with the cavalry, that's the original Rin Tin Tin. When you see Rin Tin Tin running for help, it's Flame. Then there was a third dog, the fighting dog. The kid, Rusty, would say, "Yo, Rinty," and the dog would attack the heavy. If you look carefully you'll see that halfway through the leap he turns into a smaller, darker dog.

JENNINGS COBB: A friend of mine was the story editor on "Rin Tin Tin." He asked me to write a script for him as a favor. I considered that beneath me, but I set aside my work and wrote it. I didn't want my name on it. Just think about writing for a dog.

Then I found out they played the show on Friday evening and repeated the show Saturday morning, meaning you got a hundred-percent residual the next day. It was more money than I had ever been paid anywhere else, so I started with "Rin Tin Tin."

The best actor on that show was Rand Brooks. He was in *Gone with the Wind*. He gave Lana Turner and Elizabeth Taylor their first screen kisses. I did so many shows about him, the producer took me aside and said, "Listen, this is 'Rin Tin Tin,' not the Rand Brooks Show." The dog was the star and don't forget it.

DICK JONES: "The Range Rider" came about because Flying A wanted to do a series around Jock Mahoney, who was one of the best stuntmen in the business. I was the sidekick for comic relief. I never got the girl. Little kids thought that was cute. I was twenty-five at the time, the oldest teenager in the business. They called me Dick West instead of Dick Jones because Autry didn't want me to own any rights.

LESLIE MARTINSON: After I left MGM, I joined Roy Rogers's show as supervisor. At MGM, we did three and four setups a day. On my first day with Roy, we shot like eighty-seven. We did two teleplays a week, at least twenty-three minutes of film a day. The cameras were turning sometimes at seven-ten. Still, it was a happy company. As hard as Dale and Roy worked, not even once was I morally disappointed with then. I never met two people like that in my life. They had both burned a trail in their day before they became religious. They didn't call Roy "Buck" for nothing.

DOUGLAS HEYES: A lot of shows were shot at Corriganville. A western actor named Ray Corrigan owned this movie ranch. Howard Hughes built a Corsican village there for "Vendetta." It had a section of trees called "Sherwood Forest," because "Robin Hood" was shot there.

It also had this rugged terrain going into the hills. We were always on a very tight schedule with "Rin Tin Tin," because there were two things we were always losing, the light and the kid. They'd say, "We're losing the kid," because he could only work a certain amount of time. We had a double, so if necessary I would shoot the kid in closeups, bring in the double, and shoot over his shoulder for the longer shots.

At the same time, we were always moving the camera a little uphill to catch the sun. There was one hill, the top of it was called Panic Peak, and we invariably ended the day at Panic Peak. That's the last place the sun would touch.

RUDY FLOTHOW: They shot "Ramar of the Jungle" at Lucky Baldwin's estate, about fifteen miles from downtown L.A. Baldwin was an eccentric millionaire, who created a kind of swampy dreamland with palmettos and thick foliage. Nobody on "Ramar" worried about botanic accuracy. They just wanted a lot of green. They would always throw up these two collapsible straw huts. You never saw any exterior longshots, because they didn't want you to see the parked Chevrolet just outside the frame.

LES MARTINSON: On "Roy Rogers," everything was done at the Arvison Ranch. If you really watch the shows, you'll see the same four shacks there that had no interiors, just windows.

We started early in the morning. Sometimes, it was still too dark to get a camera reading, so we took Nellie Belle and Roy's jeep and we'd turn all those lights on, move in, and get all those head closeups.

DOUGLAS HEYES: If it rained you shot. We were shooting "Bengal Lancers" and a sandstorm came up. I couldn't see the actors or anything. I called the head of production at Columbia, and I said, "I can't see anything. We gotta pull the plug."

He said, "Shoot anyway." He wouldn't pull the plug for any reason on a television show. We could shoot in the rain because unless it's backlighted, rain doesn't really show up on camera. On those early shows, if you see the shoulders of the actors starting to get darker and darker, that's because it was raining.

DICK JONES: The only way there was a retake was if you screwed up so bad they couldn't print it.

LES MARTINSON: It was the first take, then turn the camera twenty-five degrees to the side for the next scene. By the time you turned ninety degrees, you'd made three shots in presumably three different areas and in different parts of the script, working your way up toward Panic Peak until it got too dark.

DENVER PYLE: I've done chases where I ride by in the stagecoach and they're tryin' to get the last shot of the day in. The cameraman says, "You got a cigar?"

"Yeah."

"Well, just as you go by the camera, light the cigar," and he hands me a wad of matches the size of a half dollar and says, "Just light that and hold it up so I can see your face."

I was a character man. I played everything, a lot of heavies, lots of gamblers, whatever came down the pike. I just wanted to be working.

RUDY FLOTHOW: My father used a regular stable of heavies. He was very fond of these guys with mean faces who were actually very sweet.

DENVER PYLE: I did "Ramar of the Jungle." We were looking for ivory. I was egging on these guys in Ubangi or something. I kept saying, "Flowthowrudy Flothowrudy," until he caught on to it.

RUDY FLOTHOW: The "Africans" were a bunch of black football players, mostly linemen from UCLA and USC, who would work as extras for eight dollars a day. They wore leopardskins over the shoulder and leopardskin tights. They would run around saying, "Ug, ug." It was the kind of thing that Malcolm X became very incensed about.

On the set when the guys were relaxing, it was not the black guys sit over here and the normal people sit over here. The one reason there appeared to be complete integration was that a lot of people on the set were gamblers, and they loved talking to the football players, trying to get a line on who was going to win a game.

IRON EYES CODY: My mother was a Cree Indian. My father was a Cherokee, born in Fort Gibson, Oklahoma. He was a vet. These cowboys came to Oklahoma to make a picture, and my father took care of their horses. The people then brought him to Hollywood to be a technical adviser and actor.

My father brought me here to teach a little boy sign language for a C. B. DeMille film called *Squaw Man*. I've been in the movies ever since. I did a lot of westerns on television, but I never played a killer. Will Sampson was an Indian. He and I started a club, and we told all these Indians who were actors, "Don't do a bad Indian unless it's a true story."

I turned down a lot of scripts. Sometimes, we would cut things out—stabbing 'em in the back or getting called "Goddamned Indian." Some of the "Rin Tin Tin"s shouldn't have been made for children with all that fighting and killing, but it was popular.

JENNINGS COBB: Indians were the bad guys, and I empathize with Iron Eyes on that. When I did a show about Geronimo, I shaded him. He's being put upon, but hell yes, the Indians were the bad guys. That was the mold from the beginning, and nobody said a word about it. They were too interested in the money.

IRON EYES CODY: You've got eighty thousand Indians in Los Angeles. They were told, "Do this or we'll put somebody else in there." Many of them needed the money so they did it. Or they used Mexicans or Italians to play Indians. The white men and the women and even the children got billing, but none of the Indians got billing, and they got the Indians cheaper. For a "Rin Tin Tin," they got fifty dollars a day. If they were white they got seventy-five dollars.

* * *

TED ROGERS: I supervised the "Lone Ranger" for Dancer, Fitzgerald. In the early days, no matter what anybody says, the voice of the Lone Ranger on television was the radio Ranger, Brace Beemer. He also made personal appearances as the television Lone Ranger even though he was never in any television shows. The producer, George Trendle, interused those guys any way he wanted to. It was ingenious to put a mask on these guys, so all he ever had to pay somebody for these appearances was scale. If the guy wanted another ten dollars a month, Trendle would say bye-bye and get another guy.

DICK JONES: The very first day Jock Mahoney and I worked together on "Range Rider," we made a pact. Every stunt we did ourselves, so that when a little kid asked us, "Did you do that?" we could look him in the eye and say yes and not tell them a lie.

TOMMY CARR: The stars love to say that. Red Barry said it all the time, but he didn't, no more than we would let him do. It wasn't worth the gamble. Roy could do all those riding stunts, but we would never use him for the fighting stunts, because you can't take a chance of hurting him. If he gets hurt, you're dead.

LES MARTINSON: We always had a bulldog and three fights in every show. A bulldog is where Roy catches up to a racing heavy, leaps out of his saddle, and brings a man down. I've worked in many westerns, and I have never seen a man ride like Roy Rogers. Still, I wouldn't risk Roy in a bulldog.

TOMMY CARR: In the chase scenes you're using doubles, so mostly they had to learn to get on and off the horses. We knew the ones who were good, and the ones who weren't. With Autry, it would take three or four shots to get him on. Rogers, first time. There was a horseman. Autry, he couldn't stay on a horse.

ROBERT SCHAEFER: He was drinking a lot in those days.

TOMMY CARR: He was a lousy actor and a rotten singer, and he certainly wasn't any cowboy.

DICK JONES: Hoppy was scared stiff of horses. He hated kids, too. I worked in a film with him when I was eight or nine, and I could hear him cussing me.

TOMMY CARR: You'd be surprised how close you can get and still get away with a double. You could get any two guys roughly the same size, put the right wardrobe on them, cut it right, and that's all you have to do.

DICK JONES: The fights were choreographed about five minutes before we did them. The guys we worked with were professionals. When you worked with someone for a long time, you got to know all his moves, so you could do it blind. The sound was dubbed later. A punch was two rocks crashing together.

DOUGLAS HEYES: Rinty had fights with a bear, an eagle, and a mountain lion. The eagle was on an invisible wire, and Rinty was too, so they could get close but not touch. When we jerked the end of the wire, maybe they would flip, so that from a certain angle it looked like they were really mixing it up.

For the bear, we first got a guy in a bear suit. I didn't direct that one, but I was sitting in the dailies, and I said, "Jesus, Bert, this bear doesn't even act like a bear. He's walking like a gorilla."

And Bert says, "That's funny because this is the first time this guy has ever played a bear. He always plays gorillas."

JENNINGS COBB: Everything was done with intercutting. I remember a fight with a real bear. They tranquilized it so much that it couldn't even lift a paw. All it wanted to do was sleep. A couple of people had to hold him up, so they could get a closeup of his paw in Rinty's face.

TOMMY CARR: When you work with animals you have to think like one. Most of the time they want food. You don't beat them because you never get it that way. I had an elephant trainer who put a hook into the elephant's ears. This elephant was actually crying it was beaten so badly. You could see the tears falling down his face. I told him, "You hit that animal one more time I'm gonna take that thing from you and beat you with it." Oh, it was awful. It was just a poor dumb animal.

RUDY FLOTHOW: For "Ramar," when they wanted really tough stuff that the SPCA would not permit, like the python-fighting-the-water-buffalo crap, they got that from Mexico. The Mexicans would say, "You want the girl screwing the snake or the elephant on top of the three boys? Whatever you want, we'll do it," probably for a buck a foot. You couldn't shoot it in the U.S. but you could show it.

The professor and the doctor would be walking down the path looking for the wicked witch doctor and suddenly the doctor would say to the professor, "Wait a minute," and he would look off to the left, and with a cut you would see a water buffalo being strangled by a python. That would fill up a lot of time and give the film a little zip, especially since there was no sex queen. There was very little sex in those series.

If you got hold of a whole set of "Ramar" and timed them, you would find an amazing pattern. Somebody came in and said, "Mogamba is in trouble" at the same point in each show. Someone was taking the sacred jewel or the tribe's favorite idol. Then they would go into the jungle to look for him.

ROBERT SCHAEFER: It's the old KISS theory. "Keep it simple, stupid." You couldn't give Gene a lot of long lines anyway because he couldn't memorize them.

PAT BUTTRAM: In the shows, I was always Pat Buttram and he was Gene Autry because we were doin' two at once, and he couldn't remember what name I had in what picture.

DICK JONES: "The Lone Ranger" and "The Range Rider" had the same writers, so the plots would be the same, just different people. Each story went: who are the bad guys, where did they go, let's go get them, and let's get the horses and ride off in the sunset. They say there are only eight western plots anyway.

ROBERT SCHAEFER: I always heard thirteen. It's in between there some place, but it's very simple: man against man, man against nature, man against woman, man against the devil.

TOMMY CARR: Somebody robs a bank and gets away in a car. Change the bank to a store and it's a different plot. Change the heavy from a man to a woman, but it's all the same.

ROBERT SCHAEFER: Eventually, "Maverick" and "Colt .45" got us out of the oaters. Then, Bob Golden, the producer of "Lassie," asked us to do a couple of those for him, and we ended up doing 188 of them.

JENNINGS COBB: "Lassie" was a wimpy show. "Rin Tin Tin" writers looked down their noses at Lassie. Rin Tin Tin was a ballsy dog who took on Indians. Lassie was pretty effeminate. Eventually, they dumped the kid, and the dog was turned over to the Forest Service, and they asked me to write one. I approached it pretty seriously, but when I turned in my script, Bob called me. He said, "Jennings, I'll pay you for this, but I can't shoot it. It may be a great 'Playhouse 90,' but it's a lousy 'Lassie.' "

So I got a script from Bob and Eric. Now, on "Rin Tin Tin" you wrote, "With a savage snarl Rinty leaps up and over camera." But on "Lassie" they used an adverb with every sentence you put Lassie in. "Lassie barks happily." "Lassie barks nostalgically." The dog barks, right? The dog cannot bark happily or angrily, perhaps some shading but not nostalgically. On "Rin Tin Tin," they would have called you in and said, "You want Rinty to bark how?"

On my script, if Lassie barked, Lassie barked, but I added the adverbs to please them. I also saw they liked to get to the dog instantly, so I got to Lassie on page one instead of page four. They called me an hour after I turned it in. "I don't know what the heck you did, but this is a great script."

*　　*　　*

DICK FEINER: In 1953, there were two major syndicators that sold films to the TV stations, Ziv and Motion Pictures for Television, which was my uncle Matty Fox and his partners.

DALTON DANON: I was a territorial salesman in the West Coast office of Motion Pictures for Television. I was still a junior, so I had all the wonderful markets like Butte and Billings and Twin Falls and Eugene and Eureka.

At that time, the studios were still not acknowledging the existence of television, so our films came from the smaller studios like Monogram and PRC. We had some A films, like *Stagecoach* and *Foreign Correspondent*, but mostly they were serials like "Flash Gordon" and "Buck Rogers" and B's and C's. Still, they became very valuable to station managers, because with our films, they could program an hour at $32.50 instead of the $2,500 it would cost them to do a live show. My favorite sales pitch was, "You can't stand in front of the camera and wave for less than we could sell you programming."

We were not only salesmen but also program consultants. A lot of the old movies ran for sixty-five or seventy minutes. We showed them how a host could fill time by introducing the films. He could wear a western outfit, if they played westerns.

One of my great pitches was in Billings, Montana. They had a cliff there called Sacrifice Cliff, where the Indians used to throw maidens over. Their host was called Sacrifice Cliff. He was also the station's program director.

DICK FEINER: We taught them how to stay on the air, how to build time segments, how to use film, how to promote, how to advertise.

Our company got the Alexander Korda films from England. They were popular, but plenty of stations in the South didn't want them because they didn't speak "English." We also couldn't sell the Zane Grey series in the South because they wouldn't play the Sammy Davis, Jr., one. That was true all over the South. They even cut the black kids out of "Li'l Rascals."

DALTON DANON: When a station bought the package, they had access to our entire library for a certain number of program hours. We had a service department and film bookers. A booker would develop a strong relationship with a broadcaster, and he would suggest what to book. Most everybody wanted "Flash Gordon" or "Buck Rogers."

JOE GREEN: I did syndication for NBC. We "bicycled" films around. We would put the shipping instructions on the inside of the box. "Immediately

N

after your use send to WJRB in Indianapolis." Maybe they did it eighty percent of the time. Plenty of Saturdays I got a call at home from some guy in Indianapolis. His "Dangerous Assignment" hadn't come in. Usually, the guy at the previous station forgot to send it.

DALTON DANON: Ziv also created his own programming like "Highway Patrol." They were Number One there. "Duffy's Tavern" was the first full production we did. Then came "Janet Deane, Registered Nurse" and "Flash Gordon," which was shot in Germany, and "Sherlock Holmes."

FREDERIC ZIV: No one else created the kind of sales and promotional helps that we did. Let's say a bakery in Indianapolis bought one of our programs. He would receive posters, window displays, store displays, newspaper ads, and newspaper stories to feed to the editors. We also sent a man to conduct a meeting of his sales organization.

DICK FEINER: Ziv had a sales organization you wouldn't believe. They just blanketed a town. When they'd get an offer from a station, the salesman guy would go across the street to the other station. That guy would beat it, and they'd give him the show. People just hated them, but they had the product.

BUD RIFKIN: We built the best sales organization in the country. We had covered the country with offices in Atlanta, Dallas, Los Angeles, Chicago, New York, and so on. Every salesperson would be taught how to sell each of our shows. He had marvelous brochures and flip charts. When they were selling "The Cisco Kid," they sometimes wore Cisco Kid hats. If he was sent to a city, he couldn't leave that city until the show was sold.

DALTON DANON: We carried sixteen-millimeter projectors and film of the shows with us on sales trips. We would set it up in the bakery or in the back of the hardware store, so the owner of the business could see it for himself.

BUD RIFKIN: We sold the "Cisco Kid" in virtually every television market in the country. "Highway Patrol" and "Sea Hunt" were also very successful. Our concept in creating shows was to find attractive people doing interesting things.

FREDERIC ZIV: Instead of being called the "Father of Syndication," I could have been called the "Father of the Chase" because I recognized the value of the chase. We did the chase on horseback with "Cisco Kid," on the highway in "Highway Patrol," and underwater in "Sea Hunt." The idea was to attract the largest possible audience. The advertisers wanted ratings, and we wanted shows that would produce them.

We had some difficulty with Broderick Crawford. He would drink and be on his hands and knees. Because of that, we did not permit him to drive a car anywhere. Imagine the chief of "Highway Patrol" getting caught driving drunk. We had a man who doubled as Brod Crawford. He was also his chauffeur. He spent most of his life seeing to it that Brod did not get into trouble.

DALTON DANON: The series we made were done on low budgets with funny sets, but back then television audiences weren't jaded like they are today. It was visual radio, and it was exciting.

DICK FEINER: TelePrompTer became popular because Jack Webb was shooting "Dragnet" and dollars were so sparse they couldn't afford to reshoot a scene. Irving Kahn, who was the head of promotion for Twentieth Century Fox, had Underwood build the first TelePrompTer. It was nothing but a big typewriter with big type on a roll of paper.

The actor now had to read the dialogue, and he had to look to the side to do it. Webb had a cameraman move in for a closeup. People said, "All you're doing is shooting a picture of a guy's face." Well, it looked like the two guys were talking to each other, but what they were doing was reading their dialogue.

Sarnoff saw that Webb didn't have enough money to make it. In those days, banks would not finance television. They didn't think they'd ever be paid, but Sarnoff guaranteed them an order for thirty-nine and thirteen repeats. That convinced the Bank of America to make the loan. Other banks followed suit.

"Superman" was financed by getting Leo Burnett [an advertising agency] to pay for the series for the advertisers. They created the Kellogg's strip, five different half-hours a week sponsored by Kellogg's. "Wild Bill Hickok" was one of them, and "Superman" was another.

TOMMY CARR: I knew Bob Maxwell, who was connected with National Comics, and when they decided to make the TV "Superman," Bob asked me to do it.

Of the people we tested for the role, George Reeves had the best face and was the best actor. George was great. He had to say so much of that awful dialogue and make you believe it.

HARRY GERSTAD: Maxwell asked me to join the project, but I was at RKO, doing some of their better pictures. I did line up a lot of expensive technical talent for him because he told me he wanted to make a first-class series.

THOL SIMONSON: They brought me in to do wire work. They had an accident with George on the first day of shooting.

TOMMY CARR: They were trying to have him fly. They had him hanging on wires, and they dropped him fifteen feet.

THOL SIMONSON: He was not a complainer, but he refused to do any more. After that first day, seven of us were brought in. George looked all of us over, and I had just finished working with him on "So Proudly We Hail," so he said, "I know this joker. He's not too bad," so they picked me to develop something that he would go along with.

The Howard Anderson Company was a big special effects outfit. In talking with them, we developed this arm that would come through a blue backing. It had a pan on it that George would lie on. You wouldn't see the arm because you would paint it out and then superimpose whatever you want for a background. All you saw was George.

That pan would tilt, swivel, and turn, go high and low. The camera was on a big hydraulic dolly. It took twenty men pulling on the arm, while the cameraman would tell them, "A little right, a little left, a little up, a little down." He did all the flying in one day for five years of the show, with the exception of when we went to color and had to reestablish some of the shots.

TOMMY CARR: When he jumped out the window, there was a springboard beneath the sill. He would hit that and dive out, then land on a pile of mattresses. I put the springboard there because I was a little tired of him going out the side of the picture. If you're going into the sky, you're going up, not sideways. I tried it out one time. I didn't know they had it set for a guy who was 185 pounds. I hit it with my 125 pounds, didn't tuck, and came down on my neck.

HARRY GERSTAD: I came in when they brought in Whitney Ellsworth to replace Maxwell. The first twenty-six shows all had to be re-edited because most of them were either too long or too short.

To re-edit, you lengthen out scenes or extend your flying shots. There are a few things that you do when making a film which sound ridiculous but are important because they give you leeway. For instance, anyone who leaves a room goes all the way out the door. Anyone who comes into the room comes through the door. You can always pick him up on the other side. This gives you your six feet or your nine feet. Each three feet is one second.

You know why we never had a newsroom? You had to have people in it. They cost money, so they all had little tiny offices. If somebody walks down the hall and enters a door, that's the last you see of them.

The heavies are always two at the most. The only time you saw a group of people was the opening when they're looking up. I shot all those stock shots around Los Angeles. The entrance to the *Daily Planet* is the Carnation Building on Wilshire Boulevard. We had a library of stock shots. When he's coming down the hall, you shoot him with the hat on, and then you shoot him carrying the hat, and that covers you either way.

We shot two shows a week. We would start a picture on Monday in the office. Then, the next day you worked George in the underwear. If you finished with him in the underwear on Wednesday, that afternoon you started the next picture with him in the underwear so you wouldn't have to change the uniform. You tried not to work him all day in the underwear because it was too damn uncomfortable with all that rubber underneath it.

THOL SIMONSON: The original muscles were not too good, but then we made up a rubber mold instead of padding. The new muscles were hotter than the hubs of heck. The stages were not air-conditioned, and those lights were hot, so the sweat would roll off him. We got blocks of ice with a wind machine behind it, and we aimed that at him when we could.

HARRY GERSTAD: It took about an hour to sew the goddamn thing on. Our tailor was always running around with needles and pins to tuck it up.

THOL SIMONSON: Every year we reshot the opening where he is standing on the globe. I caught hell one year because after everything was wrapped, someone noticed that right at his crotch there was a star.

HARRY GERSTAD: Getting bullets to bounce off him was easy. We shot BBs at him.

THOL SIMONSON: The rifles and revolvers were of soft lead, so he could bend them. Most of the walls were of plaster and water, aereated foam. It was called Pyracel. You could poke your finger through it, but sometimes the wall would stand for a week, and as it dried it got harder. He would hit it a little too easily and only get halfway through. Then he would bounce through again real quick. Still, we never shot it twice. Believe me, this is strictly from hunger. What you see is what you get.

* * *

PETER LEVATHES: Once, I took a steambath with Daryl Zanuck. Outside the steambath was a television set they had to see sports. He said, "Peter, you worry about that postage stamp. We have Cinemascope, for God's sakes."

People like Zanuck thought that just wasn't the way to show a film. You go to a theater, it's dark and there's one hundred percent compulsory attention. In television, you are in a room. There are lights and commercials, you go to the toilet, you get a sandwich. They didn't think it would work. On the other hand, they were scared to death of television. They thought it would take up people's idle time, which was utilized to go to the movies.

After the war, I made a deal with Eisenhower to do a television documentary of his book, *Crusade in Europe*. When word got around, I got summoned to Skouras's office. He was there with Nicholas Schenck, the president of Metro. Skouras said, "Mr. Schenck, tell Pete what you just said."

He said, "I think you should be fired. You're gonna destroy the theater business by putting shows on television." Schenck left, and Skouras said, "I don't think you should be fired. We'll make this." He supported me, but not enthusiastically.

Even Eisenhower said, "Why do you want to do this?"

I said jokingly, "Maybe one day you'll be president."

He said to his daughter, "Amy, did you hear that?" like "What a silly thing this man is saying."

Skouras softened up a bit on television when Churchill asked to see some episodes. Skouras took them to England himself. He said, "If Churchill wants to see these, maybe there is something to television."

WILLIAM T. ORR: To Warner's, television was the enemy. A movie set could not be dressed with a television. It was not to be mentioned in dialogue. Jack, who was my father-in-law, didn't even like his wife to watch it. He would say, "Anna, go out and see the movies where they belong to be seen."

DOUGLAS HEYES: My first job as a screenwriter was at Warner Brothers in 1951. I was there for seven or eight months when Warner's began to feel the pinch from television so strongly there was talk of shutting down the studio. There were thirty-four writers in the writers' building the week I finished my assignment. The next week every project had been cancelled. Every producer had been fired, and every writer was fired except one.

BILL ORR: They weren't going to close down, but we did stop production to take stock of what was going on. Our grosses had dropped frighteningly due to television. One year we made $18 million. The next year we lost $18 million. Then Benny Kalmanson, Jack's executive vice president on the East Coast, convinced Jack to go into television. Benny had about four words to his vocabulary—fuck, shit, cocksucker, and son of a bitch—but Jack had a great faith in him.

Benny Kalmanson brought Leonard Goldenson to California to meet with Jack, and Jack gave in. A decision was made to make three series from "Casablanca," "King's Row," and "Cheyenne," which was not a very good western but it turned out to be the only hit of the three.

I think the promos for Warner films were the cherry that got J. L. to say yes. We were supposed to have ten minutes at the end of each show for what were essentially trailers for our films. After a while they found when the promos went on, people were going to the bathroom or tuning to something else, so the promos were reduced to eight minutes, then four, then two, and then they were out.

Leonard went after Warner's in part because he was only getting shows from producers when they couldn't sell to NBC or CBS. And he knew we had the facilities to make quality shows. When we did a cattle drive with Clint Walker, he would be sitting on a horse in the back lot with maybe one or two cows, but we knew how to integrate it with stock so it looked like he was leading the biggest cattle drive in history.

Still, at first we didn't know beans about doing a television show or who could do them for us. Then our public relations guy said there was someone in New York named Gary Stevens who knew all about television, and Stevens was made our head of television just like that. It turned out that his job had been to take actors over to some morning show.

RICHARD BARE: I did five or six B pictures for Warner's, so when Jack Warner decided to go into television, he said the only one who knew how to shoot fast and cheap is Bare. Bill offered me $500 to produce "Cheyenne." I told him I could make $750 by being the director. "All right. Who the hell can we get to produce this thing?"

I picked up his phone and called Roy Huggins, who had been my story editor on "Joe Palooka" over at Columbia. I said, "Roy, didn't you tell me you were leaving Columbia?"

"Actually, I'm cleaning out my desk."

I told him to come over right away. The next morning he was the producer.

Stevens, though, was really a screw-up. He called in several reporters and made a big announcement. He said television was going to be the savior of Warner's. If not, the studio would be turned into a parking lot, and he, for one, didn't want to see Jack Warner in a white coat parking cars.

BILL ORR: Jack was in Europe when he read this. He called and screamed, "Get that son of a bitch off the lot by noon!"

Then he says, "Who we gonna get for it."

His assistant says, "Bill can do it. He's the only one who knows anything about it."

Just like that I was in charge. I just thought we were just going to be television on film, that we could bring a bigger expanse of activity to the TV screen than they could do live. Bob Lewine really got us going. He told us stuff we never thought of, about using a "snapper" out front of the show to get the viewer's attention; how to end on a high note before the commercial so everybody would be fascinated with what was coming next.

RICHARD BARE: "Cheyenne" was not a hard show to do. There were no difficult actors. Warner Brothers wouldn't pay any money to anybody that had any clout, so you had people who were young and eager.

BILL ORR: We auditioned a few guys for the lead, and they were terrible. Then an agent told me, "There's a guy under contract to Paramount who's done a couple of spear carriers. I don't think they're going to pick him up."

"Fine, send him over."

RICHARD BARE: Norman Walker was then working as a bouncer.

BILL ORR: We chatted a bit. He was taciturn and soft-spoken. We tested him along with four or five other guys, including Lee Marvin. I took the test to the boss who at that moment was interested in television. He said, "He's a good-looking big old guy, isn't he? What's his name?"

"Norman Walker."

"We're gonna have to change his name."

The guy who did our trailers said, "Say, we had a picture with Gary Cooper and Ingrid Bergman. His name was Clint Maroon. Let's call him Clint."

Walker had nothing to say about it. We could have called him Orville Schiskavov, and he would have said yes.

TOMMY CARR: Clint Walker wasn't a good actor. Very few of 'em were. Basically, they were what we called "shit-kickers." On "Friendly Persuasion," Gary Cooper said to me, "Oh, c'mon, Tommy, I'm not an actor, I'm a shit-kicker." We called 'em that because like Cooper he would be talkin' to a girl, and he would be lookin' down and kickin' at the dirt, "Oh, I don't know, ma'am."

BILL ORR: We started off hoping to make good TV, but quickly we realized we just had to get them out, and so there we were in our cubbyhole off the lot, putting up with things I never would have countenanced before. The scripts were abominable. Finally, I fired the story editor, went to a local bookstore, and bought an anthology of western short stories, and used those.

That first year I was always up all night with scripts. The producer would be at my house on weekends trying to get a script into shootable condition for Monday. We didn't have any big-writer budget. We were getting $75,000 a show. Out of that we hired producers, director, writers, actors. One of the actors we hired for a bit part in the first "Cheyenne" was Jim Garner. Dick Bare found him in a bar on Sunset Strip.

RICHARD BARE: The bar was called The Rendezvous. I was in there one night, and a friend came in with a fellow named Jim Bumgarner and introduced me. I said, "Jim, are you an actor?"

He said he had just come off the road company of some show. I didn't pay too much attention to it. The next day Bill Orr told all the producers and directors, "Jack Warner wants new faces."

I said, "I ran into a new face last night."

"Go get him."

I called the bartender. "Who was the fellow that Bob Lowry introduced me to last night?"

"Oh, Jim Bumgarner."

He said he comes every night. I left a message for him to call me, which he did about three days later. We were going on location to film the first "Cheyenne." We had one small part left open. When he came in, I read him with Bill. Bill motioned me out to the hall. He said, "Maybe we can get somebody better."

"Bill, it's late. We're leaving at six tomorrow morning. I think I can get a performance out of him."

The next day, Jack Warner was watching the dailies when Garner's scene came up. He said, "Who's that?"

"Jim Bumgarner."

Warner, in his inimitable style, said, "Take the bum out and give him a seven-year contract."

That was a year before we made "Maverick." In the meantime, he played smaller parts in two or three "Cheyenne"'s. Then Bill and Roy concocted "Maverick," and they put Garner in there. I always said I created "Maverick" because I brought Garner and Huggins in there.

BILL ORR: Roy Huggins had told me that Universal made a successful picture with Ty Power about a riverboat gambler. He said, "Why don't we do a series about that?"

"We don't have a riverboat or a lake. We'd have to build them. We have a lot of western sets. Make him a western gambler."

Roy always said he wanted to do stories about an antihero. "Cheyenne" wasn't right for that. I said, "Clint can't be anything but the hero. He can't be tricky and duck out the back door." When we got Garner, I said, "Here's the guy that can do that."

MARION HARGROVE: My book, *See Here, Private Hargrove* was probably the number-one best-seller of World War II. I came out here in 1948 to do a screenplay for my second book. Then in 1955, I was called in to write "The Girl He Left Behind." While I was out there, the story editor kept suggesting I try television. They were doing a lot of westerns across the street. I said, "There are two things I can't do. I can't do television, and I can't do westerns."

Then Huggins called and asked me to work on this series, "Maverick." We sat down and worked out a story. I liked "Maverick" because the guy was basically a coward. As Huggins said, "Like everybody else, if a guy came in and pulled a gun, Maverick's hands went up immediately and he was ready to talk terms."

RICHARD BARE: The attitude of a leading man being almost a coward, almost a cheat, the antithesis of Cheyenne, who would never drink or smoke, and God knows what Maverick would do. That's why they called him Maverick.

ARNOLD LAVEN: One day my partner, Jules Levy, said, "I've got an idea for a television show. It's called 'The Rifleman.' "

"What's the idea?"

"Well, that's as far as I've gotten."

In the meantime, Jules met an unknown writer named Sam Peckinpah. Sam knew we had a title called "The Rifleman," and he said, "I've got a screenplay in the trunk that might fit the title." It was about a loner who comes into a town to win some money in a turkey shoot. Some people recognize him as a magnificent shot and start to take bets. Then the bad guys tell him if he wins the shooting match they'll kill him, so he loses because his life isn't worth it.

It was a marvelous script, but you can't have a western hero that turns tail at the end. Then one day, I was leaving my house and I kissed my eight-year-old son good-bye, and it hit me that I had the solution to Sam's teleplay: add a boy to the scene. If the man had a young son whose life was threatened, nobody could deprecate him for not risking his son's life.

We devised a situation where, after throwing the match and being booed out of town, he shoots up the bad guys and decides to settle down and bring up his boy in the West. Now we were in business. We sold it within ten days of completing the film.

In its early years especially, it was a show with kind of a moral point of view that came out of my own feelings about raising my son. The show was within the top five within the second or third week.

BILL ORR: "77 Sunset Strip" was originally a movie called *Girl on the Run*. We made it for $245,000. The detective was played by Efrem Zimbalist, Jr. Eddy Byrnes was a heavy. Every time Eddy Byrnes came on, we had some music to anticipate his entrance. At the preview, the audience got all "Here he comes." He played a raunchy, no-good son of a bitch who was combing his hair all of the time, but the audience loved him.

The manager of that theater said, "Jesus, that kid is getting such a big reception. You gotta look into him."

So when we wrote the first one, we put him in as Kookie, and we reformed the character. I knew this parking-lot attendant at one of the restaurants who was a real hustler. He made out he knew everybody and did a little procuring, so I said we should base Eddy's character on him.

DOUGLAS HEYES: I was at Warner's then. In the dailies, every time Eddy came on the screen they would refer to him as "that kooky kid." That's how he got that name.

BILL ORR: The combing of the hair came about because my assistant Hugh Benson and I were talking, and I said, "We can't get a good story every week. We've got to make our people worth watching," so we tried to get some shtick for him, and Hugh said, "You know my son is such a pain in the ass. He gets a comb out of his back pocket, and he and his friends are always combing their hair. Why don't we have Kookie do that?"

RICHARD BARE: We never released the picture theatrically. Instead, ABC put it on the first night of the new series. We changed the title to "77 Sunset Strip." At the end, Efrem came out and said, "Ladies and gentlemen, this show is gonna be on every week. I have a nice young man who is gonna be my partner, Roger Smith," and he came out. Then he said, "Hey, Kookie is not a bad guy, come out here. We're gonna keep him in the show."

BILL ORR: "77" was the first one of those shows. I liked "Hawaiian Eye." The other two, "Bourbon Street" and "Surfside Six" were obvious copies. "Hawaiian Eye" is a perfect example of people getting what they want. One Easter Sunday, Ollie Treyz called from ABC. He says, "We need another show like '77 Sunset Strip.' We've got so many advertisers wanting to get in on it, we can't handle 'em. How about a detective story in Bermuda?"

"That's no good. There are mostly blacks over there. Let's go to Hawaii where there's a polyglot of people." And that's how "Hawaiian Eye" came about. Just that quick conversation.

We also did "Bourbon Street Beat." People said, "It's the same damn thing," but we couldn't get away from it. Ollie kept saying, "Get me another one."

He would grab onto anything. Once, I just mentioned in passing that I was thinking about doing a series about the Alaskan Gold Rush called "The Alaskans." We were in Pebble Beach for the golf tournament. He says, "We're gonna go to New York and tell Lucky Strikes about, what did you call that story?"

" 'The Alaskans.' "

"That's right. We'll go back and we'll tell 'em."

We go to New York, and he's ad-libbing about how we're going to do this and that. I'm "blah-blah-blah-blah." Then I had to go and make a show out of it.

"Colt .45" was a show we couldn't get rid of. It always kept getting renewed. Don't ask me why. That show was our testing ground for talent. We used cutters who wanted to be directors, writers who wanted to be writers, actors who wanted to be actors.

We came up with "Surfside Six" after the first season of "Bourbon Street" when the network said, "It's too dour a location with weeping willows and all that stuff. We think the show would be better someplace else." It didn't take any time at all to come up with Miami Beach. "Bourbon Street" just went off the air. We got a different cast, and we had "Surfside Six."

All we did was send a crew over to the location for second-unit stuff. We cast a lot of girls to water ski and guys to drive motor boats, and then we shot the hotel and our principals in bathing suits and in clothes walking through the hotel, so we had a body of stock. We also did location shots for rear projection. Everything else was done at the studio.

RICHARD BARE: At one time, Warner's had ten hour-long shows on the air simultaneously. A lot of dialogue would be loused up because there would be gunshots going off on another set, so you were always dubbing in the studio afterward.

ANNE HOWARD BAILEY: They were just grinding out those crappy shows. I never watched that stuff. Never in my life have I ever looked at anything like that. In New York, we really tried to come up with quality scripts. In Hollywood, you quickly understood that all they were concerned about was mass appeal, to feed America's limitless desire for cheap, quick entertainment. Nobody ever wanted anything out of the ordinary. I tried to sell controversial stuff, but they never wanted anything that had to do with a racial problem, for example.

The producer I worked with at Warner's was named Jerry Davis. You would pitch a story to him while he was swaying around on an exercise machine. It was like a Hollywood farce. You'd never make eye contact. Then he was always taking calls from his bookie. He would be on the phone asking, "What are the odds," and he'd be saying to you, "Go on, go on, I'm listening."

Those guys were so weird. They were worried about girls, their haircuts, their exercise, and mostly their bookies. Jerry Davis never paid attention to what he was getting. They had dreadful actors. Troy Donahue couldn't remember how to say hello. It would take ten takes for him to learn to say two lines because he couldn't remember them. None of those people ever learned their lines. It was just madness.

BILL ORR: We wanted attractive people with good personalities. They didn't have to be good actors. That wasn't what was selling our shows.

TOMMY CARR: To me, Clint Eastwood is very fortunate, because he was never an actor. That taciturn *Fistful of Dollars* bit isn't acting. He was the same back then. Clint was lazy. He always cost you a morning. On "Rawhide," I never ever started a day with Clint Eastwood in the first scene, because you knew he was gonna be late, at least a half hour or an hour. No, I didn't care for Eastwood.

On the other hand, Steve McQueen wasn't lazy. He just thought he learned the business. I had him and Robert Culp and in the same show. I don't know why I didn't go crazy. They were two alike, but Culp was much smarter than McQueen. Culp would get impatient, but he would come up to you with the script and say, "Look, wouldn't this be better if we do this?" It had nothing to do with him. He was just smart.

They were both Method actors. These guys would say, "I have to go off in the corner to feel this before I do it." Oh, God. I walked on the set one time at Universal, and this guy said to me, "Go in there and look." I walked onto a soundstage, and I hear this awful, "Nyaaaaaaaaaaaaaah." It was this guy standing on his head, screamin' like hell. He's getting in the mood for the next scene. It was Dennis Hopper. They wanted me to do a picture with him. I said no way. I wouldn't touch the son of a bitch.

DOUGLAS HEYES: It was fun when we were doing all that stuff at Warner Brothers, but all those shows were interchangeable. A couple of my "Maverick"'s turned up on "77 Sunset Strip." All they did was take it out of the West and put it on Sunset Strip.

MARION HARGROVE: When I am connected with an ongoing series usually at some point I steal "Ten Little Indians." I did it with "Maverick" on a show called "Black Friar."

Roy Huggins and I used to get together on Saturday afternoons to start an episode. One day I said, "Roy, what the hell are we gonna do at this time? We've stolen everything but *Macbeth* and *The Admirable Crichton*."

He said, "I don't like the heavy in *Macbeth*. Steal *The Admirable Crichton*." I did, and it was my favorite "Maverick."

　　　　　　　　　*　　*　　*

BILL ORR: ABC was the last network to go to color. When they did, I told Jack and Benny Kalmanson that we should shoot in color, but print them in black and white. That way we would have the color when we get to syndication.

"It'll cost more to paint the sets."

I said, "So what?" but he killed it. In the long run it cost us millions. Today, all those shows would be on if they were in color. The only thing on is "F Troop." The first year of that was black and white and the second year was color, and then Benny had it taken off because we were three thousand dollars over budget.

LES MARTINSON: Bill Orr was the hero of that six or seven years. He was a twenty-hour-a-day man, a great storyteller and a marvelous editor. But Bill was well aware that when you make these pictures for x amount of dollars, and you satisfy the public, the office is not going to say, "We'll give you an extra thirty thousand dollars to bring up the quality of these shows to meet the opposition," and that's what happened to the empire. It just crumbled. We couldn't meet the competition.

JENNINGS COBB: I cannot write formula stuff. I cannot sit down and say, "What crap am I gonna write this time?" As the years went on it got worse. Then I found myself spilling my guts in a long poem about the suffering I was going through after being dumped by a woman. I gave it to my agent and he sold it. It was called "For You," and it was in print for seventeen years. I quit the business the day after it was published. I retired to Oregon to write my novel. I'm still writing it.

An odd thing happened. I started missing the business. Not the writing. I thought I hated it, but you can't devote that much time to something and just turn around and walk out the door. You miss even talking about the business. I still do.

MARION HARGROVE: I wrote the last "Maverick" script ever for TV. It was never aired. It had to do with Maverick's working to acquire the local franchise for a new invention, the telephone.

The producer called and said they wanted to insert a few story points. I went in, and they handed me two or three pages of a story outline that had sixty-two separate plot developments, this for a script that was forty-eight minutes. It was that Saturday morning cartoon influence that ruined comedy on television. I worked on it. I averaged between half a page and minus half a page a day. After about three weeks the producer called and said the show had been canceled. He told me to finish it up and they would pay me.

Then it occurred to me. When my other shows had gone off I was never able to wrap up the characters, so I figured, what the hell, I'll have fun and do it. The next day I did six pages. I was writing it the way I wanted to write it and nobody would ever read it.

At the end, Garner is in jail. The people were coming through making their initial payment on the telephones, and he's putting the twenties in one pile and the tens in the other. Louis Delgado comes rushing in, "Jimbo, Jimbo, Jimbo."

Garner looks up at him and says, "It's Bret, Bret Maverick."

"No, Jimbo, not anymore. We've been canceled."

Jimbo looks at him, looks at the money, and goes back to counting the money. "Fuck 'em, Louis," he says, "we can buy and sell the bastards." That was the last line of the last "Maverick" script ever written.

BILL ORR: What happened to westerns was like everything else, oversaturation. A lot of those shows went off about the same year because they weren't producing as they had been. Still, Leonard Goldenson had a tremendous impact on TV by bringing big-time film-making to it. His suggestion that the big studios get into it saved ABC, and it kept us going, so we were all saving each other.

It also changed TV by putting the New York shows out of business. Was that for the better? We probably didn't make as good theatrical efforts as they did in New York, but let's put it this way, the audience got bigger and bigger, so I guess it was for the better.

You start off with a concept, and you have some taste, you hope, and you try to find the best things you can find within the budget that you've been allowed. I'm proud of my work. First off, there was a lot of it. Second, it made a lot of money. That's what's important in the business. You can't make pictures just because they're good pictures in television because you've got that rating thing. You've got to be commercial and you've got to keep doing it week after week, so you aim for a quality. Hopefully you'll get some peaks. Hopefully, you'll never go below it, but you know that when you have to be on every week, something is going to get made that isn't worth a damn.

There were some shows I didn't like, but the network liked them and wanted them on the air. Jack Warner always said, "If they're looking for messages, have them go to Western Union."

LAUGH TRACKS

The fellow tapping out these words will surrender this space as quickly as possible, as there are a wealth of comic geniuses waiting a few pages hence to reminisce about their work. Their subjects need little introduction, but permit just a few notes as a guide through the chapter.

The "Texaco Star Theater" began as a radio show in 1948 with Milton Berle as the host. When Texaco decided to try television that spring, they auditioned a string of emcees through the summer, before settling on Berle in September. The Texaco program was an extension of Berle's hugely successful nightclub act. It was brash, rowdy, rude, and hilarious, just like its star. The show was television's first big-budget comedy and a smash hit. It generated a swarm of news stories about water levels dropping in cities during commercials and stores and theaters shutting their doors when the show was on.

Berle's greatest contribution to the medium was selling it to the public when the industry desperately needed a boost in circulation to survive. In that sense, his importance cannot be overestimated, but Berle was the proverbial big fish in the little pond. His Nielsen rating for the 1950–51 season was an extraordinary 61.6, but that is a misleading figure because the Nielsens indicate the percentage—not the number—of TV sets tuned to a show. Television was still playing to a relatively limited market when Berle was at his peak. As more stations joined the network, his numbers dropped drastically. Berle signed a "lifetime" contract with NBC in 1951, but Texaco dropped its sponsorship in 1953. The new "Buick Berle Show" show was revamped by head writer Goodman Ace and director Greg Garrison. It presented a less abrasive model Berle in a sitcom/variety format. The change worked for a while, but Berle's day had passed, and the show faded away after the 1956 season. Berle next did a program for Kraft and then the former king of television hosted "Jackpot Bowling" for a season before the network mercifully bought out the rest of his contract. "It's better to burn out than it is to rust," wrote Neil Young. Berle did both.

"Your Show of Shows" sprang to life as the "Admiral Broadway Revue" in the fall of 1949. It starred Sid Caesar, Imogene Coca, and Mary McCarty, who was hired as the show's original comedienne because the ad agency didn't think Coca could do comedy.

In February 1950, Admiral dropped the show because it was too successful. The company was selling so many television sets, it needed to reinvest in capital improvement instead of television programming. The show then became the first test of NBC programming chief Pat Weaver's "magazine plan." The idea was that instead of a single sponsor owning and controlling a show, the network would own it and sell advertising minutes to individual sponsors, in much the same way a magazine sells space to advertisers. The arrangement had the added benefit of putting the editorial control solely in the hands of the producer rather than some salesman, whose primary interest was not the show's content but its bottom line.

The next year, for "Your Show of Shows," producer Max Liebman dropped McCarty and paired Caesar and Coca. He also added Carl Reiner and Howard Morris to the cast, along with some of Broadway's freshest musical talent. The show soon set the standard against which all TV comedies have since been measured. How could it miss? In Caesar, Liebman had a comedian with a bottomless well of voices and characters and more hostile aggression than a New York City cab driver. Together with Coca's own blend of steel and whimsy they made an unforgettable team.

Of course, the terrific scripts were what made it all work, and stories about the writing sessions for "Your Show of Shows" have become legendary. Most of the tales involve Mel Brooks, and some of them are even true. Caesar really did dangle Brooks from the office window by his ankles, and Brooks would come in late, shouting, "Lindy has landed!"

With a half-dozen writers competing for space on a ninety-minute show, there was a lot of tension in the office. The scripts didn't roll off a typewriter as much as they were shot out of a pressure cooker, but the writers weren't competing to get one-liners into a monologue. There were no monologues on "Show of Shows." These were solidly built sketches that satirized everything from foreign films to television news interviews.

One of the show's staples was a series of sketches featuring Doris and Charlie Hickenlooper. Unlike the Kramdens, when these two said they hated each other, they meant it.

> *Doris: I'm tired of being taken for granted! What happened to the glamour that used to surround us? Where is the excitement of yesterday? Where did our romance disappear?*
>
> *Charlie: How do I know where you put things? I can't even find my shirts.*

Or:

Doris: You never treated me like this before we were married.
Charlie: That's the biggest lie of all! What a lie! I always treated you rotten.

There seemed to be no limits to the writers' imaginations. In one famous sketch, Caesar and Coca portrayed two lions at a zoo, casually commenting on the food.

Coca: Did you eat that meal last night?
Caesar: Don't remind me. Where did they get the idea lions only like to eat raw meat? I'm dying for a green salad or some creamed cauliflower.
Coca: Sounds good. And a nice caramel custard . . .

Then:

Coca: Who's our favorite keeper? Do you like the young keeper or the old keeper?
Caesar: I like the fat keeper. He has such nice blue eyes. A delicious looking man.
Coca: Looks like quite a dish.

While Caesar, Coca, and company were wowing 'em in New York, CBS was putting its top comedic talent to work on the West Coast. The first to take to the air was "The Perfect Fool," Ed Wynn, followed by Alan Young, Edgar Bergen and Charlie McCarthy, George Burns and Gracie Allen, and then Jack Benny. The Burns and Allen format was one of the first to break through television's "fourth wall." The cameras would occasionally pull back to reveal the sets as sets, and Burns would regularly address the television audience. Gracie, of course, was Gracie, delicious as a Hershey's Kiss.

Appliance Man: You'll really like this range, Mrs. Burns. For instance, you put in a roast, you set the oven control, then you go out all day. When you come home at night the roast is done.
Gracie: Haven't you got one where I don't have to go out?

Though all four shows did well, particularly Benny's, CBS's runaway hit was "I Love Lucy." America's favorite redhead (although Red Godfrey might have disputed that) made her television debut on "The Ed Wynn Show." The experience was an enjoyable one, and it convinced her she could take her hit radio show, "My Favorite Husband," to television, starring her real-life favorite husband (at the time), Desi Arnaz.

Desi turned out to be the big surprise for everyone involved in the show. He was an excellent straight man, a sensitive producer, and a sharp businessman. It was his decision to purchase the old RKO studios and convert them to Desilu Studios, which became one of the most successful television studios in Hollywood.

"I Love Lucy" peaked in the 1952–53 series with the story line that followed Lucy's "condition" (the writers still couldn't use the "P" word). CBS and the sponsor had been unhappy with the news that Lucy was in a family way and suggested that the situation be hidden from the TV audience. In a letter to the head of Philip Morris, Alfred Lyons, Desi said he had no such intentions and threatened to break off the sponsorship agreement if Philip Morris stood in his way. Lyons then wrote to his agency, "Don't fuck with the Cuban." The agency still insisted that the first episode about the impending arrival be prescreened by a priest, a rabbi, and a minister (this is not the beginning of a joke). After the screening, the three were asked if there was anything inappropriate in the material, and they responded in unison, "What's objectionable about having a baby?"

Forty-four million Americans watched the broadcast depicting Little Ricky's birth on January 19, 1953. Its 71.7 Nielsen rating was one of the highest in history. The next week, Dwight Eisenhower was sworn into office. A relatively paltry twenty-nine million people watched the ceremony, proving that they liked Ike, but they loved Lucy.

While "Lucy" ruled the ratings for CBS, NBC was still placing its faith in its New York variety shows. After the 1954 season, "Your Show of Shows" split in two like an amoeba, with Coca and Caesar each getting their own shows. "The Colgate Comedy Hour" was NBC's answer to Ed Sullivan. Both "Colgate" and the "All-Star Revue" had rotating celebrity hosts. Lonesome George Gobel was the only host of his sitcom/variety show, which was the smash hit of the 1954 season. The jokes on the Gobel show were so widely anticipated each week that the scripts had to be locked in a vault to keep the columnists from printing them before the show went on the air. "Here's a woman whose fans are legion," he said introducing a singer on one show, "French-Foreign and American."

Gobel's signature phrase, "I'll be a dirty bird," soon became part of the national lexicon, and his closing words of wisdom were quoted by columnists around the country. "This is Lonesome George reminding you that the camera adds ten pounds, so don't eat cameras."

The latter part of this chapter shifts the focus to sitcoms, which moved the variety shows off the schedule. One of the first was the gentle "Mama," about a Norwegian immigrant family who settled in San Francisco around the turn of the century. The show was based on the book, *Mama's Bank Account*, which was subsequently turned into the Broadway play and movie entitled *I Remember Mama*. "Mama" was sponsored by Chase and Sanborn Coffee and always featured at least one member of the Hansen family enjoying a cup of java at the end of the show. In the title role was the stage actress Peggy Wood. The teenaged Lars was played by noted tennis enthusiast Dick Van Patten, while Robin Morgan played little Dagmar. Ms. Morgan later left acting and became the editor of *Ms.* magazine.

The last two sitcoms to come out of New York were "Mr. Peepers," starring Wally Cox, which was done live and was produced by Fred Coe. "The Phil Silvers Show," originally called "You'll Never Get Rich," was filmed. Nat Hiken's brilliantly iconoclastic comedy about a conniving Army sergeant was probably too early for its time and never got the audience it deserved. This was, after all, the period of nice, fatherly men in the Robert Young–Hugh Beaumont–Carl Betz mode. When Ernie Bilko pleaded, "Come home to Papa," he was talking to his dice.

HARRY CRANE: I grew up in Brownsville. There was no affluence, no swimming pools. If you wanted to cool off in the summer, you went up to the roof and sat under the line of wet wash. Nowadays, kids go to Europe. The only people that went to Europe in my neighborhood were the ones who got deported.

I was naturally funny in school. The first time I got a big laugh was in assembly class. The dean of our high school was like Danny DeVito's height. He was talking about his beginnings, saying, "There's not much difference between me and you."

I said, "No, only about three feet."

HOWARD MORRIS: We lived in a cold-water flat off Moshulu Parkway in the toilet section of the Bronx. I went to DeWitt Clinton High, which must have had 12,000 boys, but no girls. I was the smallest kid in the school and apparently the prettiest, because when a play was done that had a woman in it I got the part. [Laughs.] Once, I played a ballerina. Afterward, my mother came to our dressing room with tears streaming down her face. I said, "Ma, didn't you like the play?

She said [crying], "Oh, I loved the play."

"Why are you crying?"

"You're so beautiful."

IMOGENE COCA: My mother once worked for Houdini. My father was a conductor for Keith Albee. When I was nine, my mother insisted I take dancing lessons. These ladies put on what they called a carnival, and my mother said to me, "You'll sing." I was so scared, I went kind of crazy. I was like Jerry Lewis and Martha Raye. The audience saw somebody losing their mind onstage, and they loved it, so my father got Keith Albee to book me into a couple of theaters. That's how I got my start.

HARRY CRANE: A friend of mine got me a job writing for Eddie Cantor. I used to write in an empty apartment in Brooklyn. My desk was a Sunkist Orange box, but I loved it. The first joke I wrote for Cantor: A guy comes into a store to complain about a suit Eddie sold him. The guy says, "This suit fell apart after a week. You said it would last a lifetime."

He said, "The way you looked that day, I thought it would."

EVERETT GREENBAUM: I would be the only person in the movie audience laughing at Robert Benchley. I loathed the Three Stooges while all my friends loved the poking their fingers in their eyes. I still loathe Ralph Kramden, where he is gonna hit his wife.

I wrote and performed a radio show in Buffalo called "Greenbaum's Gallery." We did very offbeat stuff. Instead of playing Top Ten records we played things like T. S. Eliot reciting one of his poems. We also had a series where we told stories of cowardly dogs, who ran away when the house was on fire.

PAUL HENNING: In 1942, my agent got me a job as a writer on the George Burns–Gracie Allen show. I wrote to mother that I was writing for George Burns. She wrote back, "Who writes for Gracie? She's the one with the funny lines."

AARON RUBEN: I worked for Burns and Allen. Then I went to work with Nat Hiken, my wife's first cousin, on "The Fred Allen Show."

PAUL HENNING: Fred came to see Ruth and I at the Algonquin once. The owner of the hotel had sent up a basket of fruit and flowers and placed them on the television. As Fred and his wife Portland came in, he looked at the basket and said, "That's the best thing I've seen on television yet."

AARON RUBEN: It killed him that Milton Berle was the king of television, while he couldn't make it on TV. I think it was because Fred had this acerbic wit that was evident in his face. He had these enormous bags under his eyes, and what looked like a perpetual scowl.

COLEMAN JACOBY: Fred loathed artificial comedy, and he considered Berle an artificial comic, because Berle would just stand there and do other people's jokes. He was not very good at physical humor. Once, as a publicity stunt somebody proposed erecting a statue of Berle in Herald Square. Fred said, "That will be the first time that people shit on a statue."

JAY BURTON: I started writing for Milton in 1948. I had just gotten fired by Bob Hope. The ad agency couldn't fire Hope so they changed writers. I called Milton. He asked me to write a monologue on spec. I did and stayed with him for eight years.

AARON RUBEN: Milton really started the business. Tuesday night, theaters and restaurants were empty. Everybody was home watching Berle.

JAY BURTON: You'd see signs in the store windows, WENT HOME TO SEE UNCLE MILTIE.

MEL DIAMOND: It was the novelty of it. TV was still in diapers, and everything Milton did was new and hilarious. A lot of people were discovering vaudeville and burlesque for the first time, on "The Texaco Star Theatre," and they loved it.

Berle remembered practically every funny thing he ever saw on the stage, and his sidekick Hal Collins remembered whatever Milton forgot. Between the two of them, there wasn't a routine they couldn't dredge up on a moment's notice. Shit, who needed writers when you had perfect recall, but in those days almost all comedians stole from each other. Early on in Johnny Carson's career on the "Tonight" show, I asked Jack Benny what he thought of Carson's copying so many of Jack's mannerisms, and he said, "So what? We all took something from somebody." Berle just took more than most.

Believe it or not, "The Texaco Star Theatre" never ran a "crawl" at the end of the show, listing the names of the writing staff, so there we were, writing the hottest fucking show in TV history and we never got any credit. What was Milton's rationale? He said, "The audience wants to think I'm making all this shit up myself." Other than that, he was a sweet son of a bitch and a joy to work for.

JAY BURTON: Milton was a big sport, but when it came to wages it was all the same. They always thought they gave you too much. After a few weeks, everybody quit. Milton's sister was in charge of wardrobe. She quit, too. She was the leader.

He was also a perfectionist. One time he had a bunch of nine-year-old kids dancing. They didn't get it right, and he kept saying, "C'mon, kids, this is high-school stuff."

STEWART MACGREGORY: In rehearsal, he wore a Turkish towel and a whistle around his neck, and he ran everything.

JAY BURTON: Milton used the whistle to stop rehearsal like thirty, forty times a day. Everybody hated him for it, so they had a pool, and they would bet on how many times he would stop the rehearsal. Once, eighty-seven won. Milton stood up and said, "I had eighty-five."

DICK SMITH: I didn't work on that show if I could help it. The entire crew hated Berle, so much so that one of the greatest and most memorable nights was the night he had on Lauritz Melchior, the opera singer. Melchior was to sing an operatic thing, and then with Berle he would do a parody of *Barber of Seville*. In the skit, Melchior plays a barber, and he is supposed to take a bucket full of suds and a large paintbrush, lather Berle, then shave him with a huge prop wooden razor.

Well, while Melchior was singing his aria in rehearsal, Berle started telling him he wasn't in time with the orchestra. Melchior, in high German dudgeon, went on the air boiling over. He began slapping Berle's face with the brush.

Then after he raked him severely with the wooden razor, he picked up the bucket and not only poured it on his head but pushed it onto Berle's face, cutting his nose. They had to ring down the curtain while backstage the stagehands were applauding Melchior.

AARON RUBEN: I didn't like the fact that a comic could be cruel to a stagehand, but there's nothing edgier than a comic who is about to go on or a comic who has just come off and died. A lot of times they're scared to death their material won't work. I remember Milton saying to me, "It's not lappy enough. You gotta put it in their laps or they won't understand it."

MEL DIAMOND: You'd give Milton a monologue, and he'd test the jokes on anybody, a cab driver, the elevator guy, the guy shining his shoes. If they laughed, the joke was in. If not, you came up with a new joke.

JAY BURTON: I used to give him six pages and hold out three pages. As you got closer to the show and you gave him more jokes, the more he liked them. "Oh, these are new. Okay!"

MEL DIAMOND: Milton always had about seven or eight writers. One of them was left over from his old vaudeville days. He'd show up at meetings and go to sleep, but he was a sweet guy, and he picked up a check every week because Milton liked him.

When I joined the show, I kept hearing about the size of Milton's penis. I figured it was a rumor started by Milton himself, but everybody kept saying, "Has he shown it to you yet?"

So you couldn't wait for him to invite you into the toilet so that you could take a piss with him and he could show you his dick. The rumor wasn't exaggerated, and it was one of the biggest joys of his life. Jay Burton said Milton would rather get complimented on the size of his dick than get five great jokes.

GREG GARRISON: After a few years, the Texaco show died because you can't do the same crap over and over and over again. Goody Ace was brought in to revamp the show, and Milton hired me to direct. We reworked the show from scratch, and he didn't fight with me because by then he was dead.

JOE CATES: Greg was a very physical and strong guy. If a star gave him a tough time, he would look at him and say, "You really want to yell at me?"

He would physically intimidate them. That wasn't my style. I'm a *kitzeler*. I like to smile, but to be fair to Greg, I've had stars run over me. Greg never had a star run over him. Greg would grab him by the shirtfront and not worry about the consequences.

GREG GARRISON: Milton is a coward, so he was physically afraid of me, which is okay. I took the whistle away from Milton the day I started.

AARON RUBEN: The Texaco show had been just a loose conglomeration of bits and pieces. Goody gave it a format with running characters, who were akin to the characters on the Benny show every week.

GREG GARRISON: Milton kept saying, "You've taken me out of my show," which was true. I had taken part of him out of it, and I made it more interesting. He fought it the whole two years I stayed with him. Goody kept saying, "Can't you give Greg a break and be more cooperative?" Actually, it was Goody we were trying to help. He worked his tail off.

Once his show was over, he ended up hosting bowling shows. Did you ever know a comic who knows when to get off? He always wants to do another joke, another stretch, or another series.

MEL DIAMOND: On the show, Milton loved to do Jewish schtick. He would use words like *hamentashen* [a kind of cake] that you wouldn't understand if you weren't Jewish. We were once discussing that in Lindy's, and I said, "Milton, you're one of the best comedians I ever saw, but it sure helps to be Jewish. If only the goyim knew what they were missing."

I punched up a very sensitive button. Milton's manager, Irving Gray, jumped in and said I didn't know what the fuck I was talking about. As far as they were concerned, Milton was just as big in the boondocks as Bob Hope was, and Irving had all the demographic statistics to back it up. I never broached the subject again, but I'll tell you this, when television moved out of the Northeast, Milton was never a smash in places like Peoria or Galveston, and Bob Hope was.

AARON RUBEN: Nobody stays king forever, but it's not easy being dethroned. When Fred Allen was Number One on radio, in typical Allen style he said, "Well, there's only one place to go from here." He was prepared for it. Milton didn't take it well when Bilko took off opposite him.

To this day Milton thinks he's the king of television. Leo Rosten told me Milton was playing one of these senior citizen homes. He was walking down the aisle to this little stage. He stops and asks a little old lady in the front row, "Do you know who I am?"

"No, but maybe the front desk can help you."

It's an indication, "Do you know who I am? I'm Uncle Miltie." I once had him over to dinner when my oldest son was about four. Milton approached him, but my kid started to run away from him. Milton chased him around the dining-room table. He says, "Come here, you little bastard. It's your Uncle Miltie."

＊　＊　＊

SOL RADAM: It was one of our agents at William Morris, Harry Kalcheim, who saw Berle and said he should be on television. Harry had an unbelievable eye for talent. One day, he said, "There's a guy up in Tamiment named Max Liebman, who is doing a weekly revue that would be wonderful on television."

We went up to see it, and it was wonderful. I was assigned to CBS and I got a hold of Charlie Underhill, who was their head of programming. I took him up to see it, and he said, "They can never do this every week, but thanks for bringing me."

So the next week we brought Pat Weaver. Max was a little guy, and either he or George Jessel had the worst hairpiece in the business. Pat, all six foot six of him, looked down at him and said, "Can you do this every week?"

Liebman said yes. Back we went next week, and it was a brand-new show, and it also was wonderful. Pat then said, "Could you go on the air in October?" That's how "Show of Shows" began.

HOWARD MORRIS: One afternoon I was walking around Broadway, and I bumped into the stage manager of "Call Me Mister." He said, "Howie, are you working?"

"No. I'm just going home." It was like three o'clock in the afternoon. We were on Fifty-second Street. He said, " 'The Admiral Broadway Revue' television show is looking for a guy Sid Caesar . . ."

"Who?"

"Sid Caesar. They need a guy Sid can lift by the lapels."

I weighed about 107 pounds then. "Go up there and ask for Max Liebman. He's the producer and tell him I sent you."

I had a choice. I was either going to do that or get the bus and go home. There come those moments in life. I thought, What the fuck? and I went to see Max.

When I got there, they didn't have any signs on the doors, but I heard some singing. I opened a door, and there were four guys singing and carrying a woman who turned out to be Imogene Coca. I asked them, "Where's Max Liebman?"

"Try the girls' locker room."

I went and knocked on the door, and there was this little man in a funny toupee. He introduced me to Mel Tolkin, Lucille Kallen, Sid Caesar, who was this hulk standing in the corner, and a Frenchman, Monsieur Bourée, who didn't speak English. Sid lifted me up and said [in a growly voice], "Oh, yeah, him get."

I didn't speak French, so I pantomimed a lot with the Frenchman. The next day I'm in the john. The Frenchman is at the urinal next to me, and he says, "Hi, Howie, how're they hangin'?" It was Mel Brooks.

LUCILLE KALLEN: I started writing in high school. There was a good-looking blond girl there who had fancy clothes and was very popular, which made me angry, so I wrote this twenty-five-page novel, in which the beautiful, well-dressed, popular girl gets impaled on the spikes of a wrought-iron fence, and the boy who thought he liked her realized he liked the other girl who was really much brighter.

I met Max in 1948 when he was recruiting people for Tamiment. He took me, my friend Marsha, and Mel Tolkin. Every week that summer, Mel and I turned out a two-hour original revue, music, lyrics, and sketches.

When we put it on television as "Admiral Broadway Revue," the big difference was that a star emerged—Sid, but Max still orchestrated everything. Max was a genius for picking talent, and he put together something that nobody had ever seen before or since. He made the basic decisions as to which ideas were worth even exploring.

IMOGENE COCA: Max was that show. First of all, he knew a lot about revues, which are hard to do. He engaged all the writers, the director, orchestra conductor, and choreographer. All of them were first-rate. The numbers made everything a little classier. They were just beautiful. Jimmy [Starbuck, the choreographer] was brilliant, and we had Bob Fosse and his wife, and Marge and Gower Champion, Denileva, and I even did a number with Lily Pons.

LUCILLE KALLEN: The show was born out of a theatrical tradition, not a radio tradition, so it had more scope. Even the comedy was different. What we were doing was not so much comedy as satire. We weren't doing gags.

JOE STEIN: Sid was like a postgraduate course in comedy. I worked with Gleason, Phil Silvers, and Jerry Lewis. They all had their areas, but Sid had no limits, except one thing, he couldn't stand up and tell jokes. The most difficult thing for him was to go in front of the audience and say, "Ladies and gentlemen, welcome to 'Your Show of Shows.' " He had a lot of difficulty talking as himself.

HOWARD MORRIS: He was a fucking ge-ne-ius, from whom I learned so much, a *goldena boychik*. Anything else, forget. The hostility inside him, which gave him such trouble, was translated into work. He was so fucking me; Jewish sarcasm and humor based on hostile reality.

LUCILLE KALLEN: Sid was a genius, but as far as I was concerned what made Sid what he became was Coca. Sid alone is like having a match without anything to strike it on. She was the perfect foil for him. She was diminutive, and he was large. She was stiletto sharp, and he was a roar and kind of bumbling.

Imogene took a real delight in other people. They existed for her as people.

For Sid, they existed in terms of himself and what they contributed. Imogene and I were two females lost in a sea of male interests, male behavior. That consolidated our relationship.

IMOGENE COCA: In the beginning, the writers were not writing for me. Instead, I relied on material from my revues. Then one day, I asked Max if I could do a sketch called "Better Go Now." I thought he would use my husband, but Max said, "Good idea. Do it with Sid."

Sid and I always rehearsed in different rooms. I barely saw him, and I never saw his work onstage. I thought, "How am I going to tell a fellow actor what the motivation is for this?"

Sid came in and looked at me peculiarly, and I looked at him, and I said, "This is a pantomime I did in the show." I told him the story. I said, "These people are going to see a movie. It's about the cliché things that people do."

He did it as if he had done it all his life. From then on Sid and I worked together.

LUCILLE KALLEN: On the "Admiral" show, we were in the old Mellon studios. Tolkin and I wrote in the boys' dressing room with their dirty jockstraps hanging all around us. With "Show of Shows," we had better offices, but it was still a pigpen. There were cigar stubs and remains of lunches, greasy paper from the sandwiches all over the place, splatters of stuff that Sid had thrown against the wall when he got mad.

GREG GARRISON: When I got there, the writing staff consisted of a guy who said very little named Mel Tolkin, Lucille Kallen, and a young borscht-belt pain in the ass who did not contribute much named Mel Brooks. The two people who get the least amount of credit did all the work. That was Lucille and Mel Tolkin.

LUCILLE KALLEN: Brooks was the third member of the team. At first, he was hanging around giving Sid jokes. I didn't know who he was for a long time, and he thought I was the secretary. At a certain point he was allowed into the writers' room, and we came to accept him. Then he said to Sid, "I want my name on there," and so his name appeared on the crawl.

Brooks was insecure enough that he had this overpowering need to dominate, to impress. He would come in five hours later than anybody else. The door would burst open. He would slide across the floor and yell, "Safe!"

HOWARD MORRIS: We put him on the show once. We wanted him to do this cat sound he does because he has this space between his teeth. He came over to the corner where the mike was, and I have never seen anyone paler in my life. He was petrified. I said, "You son of a bitch, just do the fucking cat sound." He did it.

LUCILLE KALLEN He would come up with forty lines every day, two would be brilliant; the rest would be forgettable.

JOE STEIN: He didn't behave like a writer. He behaved like a nut.

HOWARD MORRIS: One evening, I was walking around Greenwich Village when suddenly somebody came up from behind, pushed me up a dark alley, took my jacket, tied my hands behind my back, and then tied me to a riser. It was Mel. He said, "This is a stickup. Don't fuck with me. I get crazy. I want your wallet, your keys, your wedding ring, and your money."

He took all those things and left. I'm tied in this dark alley for about a half an hour. Finally he comes back and says [reluctantly], "Oh, all right, here's your stuff. I'll untie you now. Don't ever say anything about this. You know I get crazy."

For years I never said a word about it. Then, one day in the middle of May, Mel and I decide to rent a boat in Central Park. We get in, and I'm like a soubrette, laying there, my hand dangling in the water. He's rowing. Suddenly, I hear *splash, splash*. The oars go in the water. The boat starts to rock, and I turn around and say, "What's goin' on?"

"Remember the time in Greenwich Village I held you up?"

"Yeah."

"This is the real robbery. Put your wallet on the seat. Take off your pants. Get in the water."

Well, you know the word "meshuggenner." I took off my pants. I tied my shoes around my neck. I was petrified. You never knew what he was going to do. I got in the water and I waded ashore.

JOE STEIN: When they got back, Howie said, "Okay, give me back my money," and Mel said, "No, I held you up fair and square."

LUCILLE KALLEN: Tony Webster also wrote the show. He had a way-out sense of humor, too. He once pulled one of the funniest things I ever saw. We were at his apartment and the phone rang. Tony answered. There was a long pause, and then he said, "Roll 'em," and he hung up.

We said, "What was that?"

"I don't know. Some guy's got a bunch of long-distance trucks ready to go, and he said 'What should I do?' and I said 'Roll 'em.' "

Interviews with Carl and Sid made it seem like the show was ad-libbed. It wasn't. We wrote that show. There has also been a lot of mention of Woody Allen, Larry Gelbart, and Neil and Danny Simon, all of whom I respect, but Larry was never on "Show of Shows." Woody Allen came to Max for a job and didn't get it, and Doc and Danny as far as I can recall came on when I went to have a baby. I don't remember them being there after that. The basic staff was Tolkin, Kallen, Brooks, Webster, and then Joe Stein.

JOE STEIN: The very first day I was there was very peculiar. I was sitting around chatting with the guys when suddenly I heard a lot of vomiting. I said, "What's going on?"

They said, "Oh, Sid just came in." He usually came in and threw up his breakfast. Then he'd wander in and say, "Well, what are we gonna do for next week?" It was all very casual. There was a lot of cigar smoke and a lot of talk about psychiatry. Every one of them was seeing a shrink. Early on, we were having lunch, and they were talking about their psychiatrists, and I kept eating, and they said, "Who's your psychiatrist?"

"I don't have one." They looked at me like I was crazy.

The way we worked was we threw some ideas around the room. There was lot of screaming going on. Very often I thought I was saying a line that was funny, but I'd never get heard. You had to fight for your lines.

LUCILLE KALLEN: I couldn't override those big voices, and yet I had very definite ideas about what should and shouldn't be done, so I would stand on the sofa and wave this red scarf to attract attention.

JOE STEIN: There wasn't any real acrimony, but sometimes there were a lot of put-downs.

HOWARD MORRIS: We were tough. You had to protect your groin at all times.

JOE STEIN: Sid's instinct was infallible and he was immovable about his opinion. We would write a sketch, and he would go [delays a second], "Naah."

"Why? We think it's funny. What's wrong with it?"

"I don't like it."

"But it's funny, Sid. Read it again."

[Delay.] "Naah."

It was dead. You can't argue with "Naaah."

HOWARD MORRIS: At one point we said, "We've done it all. What if we just have four people come out and sit and do nothing." That engendered the four English people. All kinds of terrible things would be happening like the roof would leak and there would be a flood all around us and we would just be sitting there on the couch stone-faced. It was hilarious.

IMOGENE COCA: One Monday, Max said to the group, "Have you written anything?" which caused the usual laughter, and Lucille said, "I have," in this quiet voice, and everybody was startled, as if she had announced her death. Max said, "Can you read it?"

It was a satire on "A Place in the Sun." We had never done a satire on movies. Max said, "It's beautifully written, but . . ." and this was the only time I ever heard Max say anything like this, "I'm not sure the audience would under-stand it."

Lucille said, "Oh, well, it had such a good part for Coca."

And Sid said, "Then why don't we do it?" It was the first movie satire we ever did. We must have done two hundred after that.

JOE STEIN: One of the great ones was a takeoff on "From Here to Eternity." They played the scene of two lovers on the beach. In all the years I worked for him, I never saw Sid break up and go out of character, he had such control, so seeing them trying to keep it together when the stagehands were dumping all that water on them made it doubly hilarious.

IMOGENE COCA: Max did not approve of our breaking up on camera, and neither did we. When we did the movie satires, I was always playing the thing straight, but in that scene I inhaled just as they threw all that water on us, and I thought, "Oh, my God, I'm going to drown in front of all these people."

That struck me as being the funniest thing and that *was* terrible, because I was biting my lip and pinching myself to try and keep from laughing, and Sid turned to me and said, "Pretty rotten night, isn't it?" [Laughs.] I needed that like a hole in the head. Oh, God, it was awful.

LUCILLE KALLEN: When he had a few drinks, a few hundred drinks, Sid would get maudlin and sentimental about us, and other times I think he would have been very happy to have drowned us. No actor, no performer likes to feel dependent for his stardom and his whole persona on other people, so Sid would throw the script that we had slaved over on the floor. He was saying in effect, "I don't need you. I'm a big star."

When he threw the script on the floor I wanted to kill him. It was so disre-spectful of our time and effort. I've heard about a prisoner who drew pictures in his cell, and the guards broke in and tore them up. It was worse than a beat-ing, to take somebody's creation and destroy it.

HOWARD MORRIS: Sometimes Sid would sit there in his chair mim-ing an anti-aircraft gun shooting down jokes. "*Poooooch,* next." And don't ever get caught sitting in his chair. He'd grab you by the gills. I saw him rip phones out of walls and pick up couches to throw them out of windows.

There were two very large guys, Sid and Carl. It was like a Jewish family. I was "The Kid." You are either the oldest and the strongest or the youngest and the most pitiable. I was the youngest and most pitiable, but I was making the same impact they were, only they didn't know that. I didn't know it either. When in doubt, rip Howie's clothes off. Or have him climb over Sid. Rip, climb. I didn't mind. It got laughs. The most interesting morning was Sunday when I would look at my body and find the various bruises and great clumps of hair missing.

IMOGENE COCA: I would peek out the curtain before the show. There was nothing to suggest television. There were five cameras, but you weren't aware of them, and there was no applause sign and no TelePrompTers. "Show of Shows" was really like a New York show. You went into a beautiful theater and played to a theater-wise audience.

I didn't have any idea of the impact we were making until one evening I was taking my two aunts out to dinner, then to the Palace Theater to see Judy Garland. As we were walking down Broadway, one aunt said to me, "Do people always stare at you?"

I said, "What?"

"Everybody is staring at you."

I thought, "That's odd."

We get into the theater. The usher takes us to our seats, and the whole audience, I swear, descended. I was so embarrassed. I didn't know what to do. It was totally unexpected.

Toward the end of the last season, my agent said to me, "There are a lot of rumors going around that the show is going to close." A couple of days later, I was in the rehearsal hall, and Max's press person, Dave Tebet, came in. I thought, "What's wrong with Dave? He's so white." He said, "Coca, you have to come with me."

"Dave, I'm rehearsing a number."

"You've got to come with me," and so I followed him into this room. It was like a Marx Brothers movie. I had never seen so many people in a room that small in my life. All the cameras were clicking and people are yelling, "How do you feel about the show going off the air?"

Like an idiot I broke into tears. I could have killed myself for doing that, but that's how I found out. I have no idea why Max didn't tell me before.

HOWARD MORRIS: Sid wanted his own show. He staged that news conference unbeknownst to us. That's when they announced that each of them would have their own shows.

IMOGENE COCA: I wanted my own show like a hole in the head. I never did find out why the show went off.

MIKE DANN: Everybody had a point of view on why it went off, and they were all probably right. It's like backing into a buzz saw and asking which tooth cut your ass. The ratings were down substantially, and it was very costly. Four years is a long time for a major variety show like that, but there wasn't one reason. I think Max wanted to do something else. Maybe Sid wanted to split off. Sid and Max were a marriage made in heaven. They were never quite as successful without each other.

LUCILLE KALLEN: We were all given our choice, whether to go with Sid or Imogene. I went with Coca because I felt a little bit put upon by the predominance of male points of view. The men thought of Coca as inferior, too. They had three categories of females—mother, whore, and if she had any brains, lesbian. Mother and wife were the same. Those were good women. Anybody who was sexy had to be a tart. Anybody with brains had to be not female.

Coca's show didn't work. The combination of Sid and Coca was a miracle. You couldn't duplicate it, and Coca wouldn't buy anything less than that.

HOWARD MORRIS: Carl and I went with Sid. She is lovely, but Imogene is not the creator Sid is, and Sid's show was as good as any Broadway show, but he was getting crazier and crazier. The writing sessions were even wilder because we did not have Max to control us. Now, this was a Jewish family really screaming at each other all day long.

GREG GARRISON: Sid needed the editing of Max. Once Sid left Max it was anything he wanted. No one had the guts enough to say no.

CHARLIE ANDREWS: I got a job writing for the show for a season. Aaron Ruben, Phil Sharp, and Mel Tolkin were the staff. They used to call me the tamed Gentile.

Sid had an office in the penthouse of a building on Fifty-seventh Street. His desk was built on a platform, so when you sat down, you were looking up at him. His valet would bring in a tray of celery and salami, and Sid would eat and never offer you a thing.

When Sid would come to the office to hear a sketch read to him, he would be wearing a suit with padded shoulders that made him look like he was wearing armor, and the creases on his pants were razor sharp. He would sit in front of Aaron's desk and arrange himself. He would pull his trousers up, to preserve the crease, very slowly, and he'd run his fingers down and then cross his legs. Then he would say, "All right, let's hear the gold."

Aaron would start reading, and Sid, who would be smoking a big cigar, would rarely laugh. The tip-off that he liked something came when Aaron would finish reading and Sid would wet a finger and flick an imaginary piece of dust off his shoe. With that, everybody breathed a sigh of relief, because you knew he was gonna get up and leave the room. If he didn't flick that dust off his shoe, then you knew you had a lot of work to do.

HOWARD MORRIS: Thursday nights was usually the night Sid wanted to throw the show out and write a whole new show for Saturday. The truth is he just didn't want to go home. He wanted to drink with the boys.

One Thursday night he said, "We're in trouble, guys. We've got to write a whole new show." Everybody ran to the phones "blah-blah-blah, two or three or four hours, blah-blah-blah, son of a bitch."

Then about a dozen of us went out to dinner with Sid. He had just been put on some kind of pills. The dosage had not yet been worked out, and he had just taken them. We sat down at this big table and ordered. He ordered brook trout. When it came, he was saying, "Well, I think in the sketch you and Pat . . ." and his head went right down into the trout. He was laying there, and we didn't know what the hell to do, so we just kept eating, and we went around the table with different ideas about how we would kill him. Forty minutes later the head came up and he finished the sentence with his face all covered with trout.

JOE STEIN: I once saw him drink a whole bottle of gin before the show, and he was wonderful on the show, but he was an alcoholic.

HOWARD MORRIS: After a few years, NBC said, "Listen, don't do a show every week. Do one show a month," but Sid wouldn't have it. He said, "No, that destroys the fulcrum of what I have here to offer. My audience would not stand for me not being on every week." He was full of shit.

They said, "Oh, is that how you feel? Okay, good-bye. We'll call ya," and he kept waiting for them to call.

* * *

SEAMAN JACOBS: The first time I met Ed Wynn was at his apartment on Park Avenue. He said to me, "You can't be much of a writer. You're wearing a necktie."

In 1948, I wrote a radio show with Ed and Keenan that didn't sell. When he was going into television, I thought I wasn't qualified to be head writer so I recommended Hal Kanter.

HAL KANTER: "The Ed Wynn Show" was the first national show to emanate from California. We did it live, and it was seen by the rest of the country on kinescope. The only other person CBS had employed out here at the time was Ralph Levy. They brought him out to direct the show.

RALPH LEVY: Ed almost died when he met me. He called Paley and said, "Why did you send this child out here?" After a while, he trusted me completely, but sometimes in rehearsal he would start to giggle, and he'd say, "Oh, Ralph, I have the funniest story I must tell you."

He would take me away from where people could hear, and while he was laughing his head off he was really telling me what the hell I did wrong, but he would never embarrass me in front of the cast and crew.

SEAMAN JACOBS: One time a director asked him, "Ed, when you do that line are you going to move left like you just did?"

Ed said, "I don't know. Why can't you treat me like a baseball? When they do a baseball game nobody knows where the ball is going."

RALPH LEVY: George Burns and Jack Benny all thought Ed was the greatest of them all. Jack's wife Mary wouldn't go see an Ed Wynn show with Jack because Jack's laughter was so embarrassing.

Ed was funny about his material. Hal would write something, and if it was successful, Ed would say, "Of course, I did that years ago." All those comedians were like that, except Jack. After one show Ed got a call. Soon, there were tears in his eyes. Somebody said, "Who was that?"

"That was Fanny Brice. Imagine, Fanny Brice, the first comedienne of the American theater, called to say that I brought the theater back to television."

Hal said, "Why don't we get Fanny on the show?"

Ed said, "Why, what can she do?"

HAL KANTER: He said, "What the fuck can she do."

Ed was a courtly gentleman of the old school until their backs were turned. Gertrude Niesen was on the first show. He was so courtly toward her. Then she got a laugh during rehearsal, and he said to her, "Please, my dear, don't do that."

Afterwards in his dressing room, he said, "If that broad tries to fuck me up on the stage that way, tell her I'm going to fart all over her." He was furious.

RALPH LEVY: He had his problems, but as my mother used to say, "he was delicious." The show lasted only a year. I think the audience was getting too sophisticated for his silly puns. The next thing we did out there was a pilot for an Edgar Bergen show. The funniest thing about that show was we couldn't use half the rushes because the men on the mike booms were so carried away with Charlie McCarthy they turned the mike heads toward him, so every time the dummy "spoke" we had no sound.

The person who had the second show on the coast was Alan Young. His show was one of the funniest shows ever on television. It won the Emmy, and it won the Peabody, but I guess it didn't sell enough gasoline, and it didn't last.

I was on vacation in New Mexico when I got a call from Harry Ackerman asking me meet with George Burns who wanted to go into television. George was also worried about working with someone my age. He was always suspicious of anyone who didn't come up the way he did. He loves the fact that all of his Pee Wee Quartet group were electrocuted or something.

Fortunately, he calmed down when he realized this would be a visual version of his radio show. There were only a few sight gags, mostly with Gracie, who was so graceful with props.

PAUL HENNING: Gracie was more anxious about it. She loved her life in radio where you read from a script. She was afraid to have to memorize a half-hour show on live television.

A group of us went to Palm Springs to talk about how to do the show. The idea of having George participate in the show and talk to the audience came from *Our Town*. Fred Allen later told me, "You know, I could never get the right format for television. That would have done it."

RALPH LEVY: After a while, Jack asked me to do his show. George and I got along fine, but I was looking for a new challenge. George's show was pretty much set in a pattern, while Jack's show was different every week.

HAL GOLDMAN: I was writing for Jimmy Durante when an agent put me with another writer, Al Gordon. The theory was that teams do better. It was true, and soon we were hired by Jack Benny.

HARRY CRANE: The main reason for a collaborator is for meetings with producers who will never turn out to be icons. These people make suggestions on what you had written. That's why you need a partner because when you walk out the door you can turn to somebody and say, "Are they fuckin' crazy or am I crazy?"

RALPH LEVY: Jack's adjustment to TV was a little better than George's. George was nervous about memorizing the monologues even though he made them appear natural.

He became a bit more relaxed because of my mother. After the first shows, she said, "Ralph, the spotlight is catching the saliva on the end of his cigar. People won't like that."

I told George, and he whipped off to Dunhill and bought a cigar holder and that became his major prop, twisting the holder on the cigar. After that, if I didn't like something, he would say, "Now, let's get this straight. You don't like it or your mother doesn't like it?"

GREG GARRISON: George and Jack both took a liking to me. They used to call me "The Kid." George started to invite me to his house for dinner on Thursday nights, and Jack would be there.

The cook would make pot roast and potato pancakes. They used to drink a little schnapps, and we would sit there. I didn't know why I was there until one day I realized, "You're the audience." All they did was talk about the old days and with me there, they could tell their stories because they couldn't tell them to each other. One night, Jack says, "Tell Greg what the cigar is for."

George says, "Well, all right, watch me carefully. I'm gonna tell a joke, and after the joke I'm gonna take a little pause and then I'm gonna give you the punch line. Watch me."

[Imitates Burns's voice.] "Why does a fireman wear red suspenders? [Garrison takes an imaginary cigar and sucks on it, then takes it from his mouth and looks at it.] To hold up his pants. Did you see what I did?"

"No, I didn't. Show me again."

"All right. Why does a fireman wear red suspenders? [He takes the imaginary cigar, sucks on it, removes it from his mouth, looks at it.] "To hold up his pants. . . . Did you see what I did?"

"No."

"All right, watch me. I'm gonna do the setup for the joke: Why does the fireman wear red suspenders? Then I'm gonna take the cigar and put it in my mouth. Now, I'm gonna take the cigar out of my mouth and hold it over here. While I hold it there, the audience is gonna look at it, and while the audience is looking at it, I lick my lips. You see, I stutter, and you can't tell a punch line on a dry mouth."

PAUL HENNING: Writing for radio was stealing money compared to television. In radio, all you had to do was write dialogue. The listener did the rest with his imagination. With television, you had to have action to suit the words. Fortunately, Ralph was a very, very talented director.

RALPH LEVY: The equipment was a problem. It distracted the live audiences. It also bothered Jack, so I kept the cameras in the back with the lights off. I just wanted him to talk to the audience and not worry about the camera.

GREG GARRISON: Sid didn't want the cameras to be mobile. He felt—correctly—that if you move a camera while he is performing, the audience peripherally will watch the camera, not him. Milton used to say, "Don't anybody move onstage when I'm doing something. If I hear another voice, I'll kill you."

HAL GOLDMAN: Even without the distractions, television is a rough medium anyway for comedy. You were dealing with a minimum amount of rehearsal. If we had been on Broadway the bugs would have been ironed out over weeks and weeks of rehearsal.

PAUL HENNING: Gracie was nervous about it, but she was a flawless performer as well as a wonderful woman. She never tried to be funny. She was just a consummate actress.

RALPH LEVY: Lynn Fontanne said she was the greatest comedienne on America's stage. She was a natural in the sense that she came across so beautifully, but it was very, very tough, because she was a perfectionist, and there was no sense to her lines, which made them very difficult to memorize.

One of my favorite jokes was when Gracie was buying a Christmas tree, and the salesman told her how great cedar was. He said, "In fact, it's so good my wife has cedar drawers."

And Gracie said, "I'd love to hear her sit down some time."

PAUL HENNING: I wrote one bit for Gracie where George says, "Where's the morning paper, Gracie?"

"Oh, I wrapped the garbage in it."

"I wanted to see that."

"Oh, George, it was just a bunch of eggshells and rinds."

AARON RUBEN: They were very careful about her character. I remember George getting upset because somebody brought him some material that made Gracie out to be really nutty, but she was nutty as a fox. George could smell the difference a mile away. Gracie, too. If she wasn't sure about something, it was out.

PAUL HENNING: Harvey Helm came up with most of Gracie's lines. He was a very funny, imaginative writer, but he had a drinking problem. When we were in New York, George arranged with a doctor to take Harvey to Bellevue for treatment. They went to the hospital together, but Harvey got out of the cab first and went in and introduced himself as the doctor. He said, "Now, this fellow coming in will claim that he is the doctor, but he's really Harvey Helm." Of course, when the doctor came in and introduced himself, there was a big mess.

AARON RUBEN: Writing for Jack was like having a civil-service job. He had the same guys for twenty years. That was the mark of a good show, and he was just a lovely man.

HAL GOLDMAN: I don't think people really believed he was that cheap, although this may be a true story: he once gave a waitress a big tip. She thanked him and said, "I could have sworn you were Jack Benny." He overtipped all the time, and he was always helping people without telling anybody else.

RALPH LEVY: We used to kid him that he would go broke tipping. He did it because he was worried people would think that he was really like that, but I don't think he was bothered by the character he played. He didn't want to tamper with success.

Gracie's was a similar situation. My sister came out to visit me the first year. She was sitting with Gracie, and they got to talking about Jack. Barbara wondered if he was really stingy, and Gracie said, "Do you think I'm really stupid?"

HAL GOLDMAN: Jack was physically self-conscious. He was not relaxed onstage. He always needed to have a piece of chalk or a piece of paper to keep his hands busy.

RALPH LEVY: That's why he used the violin and developed all those motions with his hands.

HAL GOLDMAN: But like they say when someone can't walk and chew gum at the same time, Jack couldn't talk and, for example, dial a phone at the same time. I never saw anybody like that. He had to finish dialing then say his lines.

Also, when he forgot his lines he would go "Ah, ah, ah," and talk slowly. Because of that and his whole style of waiting and looking out at the audience, his scripts were ten pages shorter than other shows.

Our writing sessions were not like those for "Show of Shows." We'd get in by nine and usually leave by three. There were never any crises. Never once did Jack throw out a script. Most comedians don't care if they send you home at three in the morning, but Jack knew that writing wasn't easy, and he didn't want us killing ourselves. He didn't think it was necessary. He liked most of the shows. He knew some were weaker than others, but as long as their average was up to his standard he was happy.

We spent a lot of time with him meticulously rewording punch lines or building up jokes to get them exactly right. That's where his big contribution was. He would say, "The audience doesn't know who wrote this. I don't care if I'm wrong or right. The important thing is that we get the right line in here."

That was great because writers often think, "Gee, I better not say I don't think this is that funny because it came from the comedian." It's the case with everyone I've ever written for except Jack. You can't imagine how much better that makes it, because so many things are done out of politics rather than the professionalism of the creative people.

RALPH LEVY: Jack understood timing better than anybody. Timing is allowing the audience to get a joke a fraction of a second before you get it or react. If you react before they get it you either step on the laugh or you insult their intelligence.

HAL GOLDMAN: He realized the value of people expecting things and then seeing them happen instead of surprising them all the time. His delivery and his jokes were based on that. They all knew when he would say, "Well," or "Now cut that out," and they always laughed at it.

Jack was tops on radio, but not on TV. Still, it was a very successful show for CBS until Jim Aubrey, who was looking for better demographics, let it go to NBC. CBS then came on with "Gomer Pyle" and just killed us. Jack was crushed. He said, "I wouldn't mind if Lucy was beating us, but Gomer Pyle?"

RALPH LEVY: The audience reaction was so important to his humor. That's why I never enjoyed Jack as much when the show went from live to film. I don't think Jack enjoyed it as much either, but I think his business people talked him into it because of the residual values.

PAUL HENNING: "Burns and Allen" was filmed. Then the film was shown to an audience, and we'd record their reaction. Sometimes, they laughed so loud we had to lower it.

RALPH LEVY: The laugh machine was invented by a guy named Charlie Douglas. The machine was necessary. If you filmed a show without an audience, it just lies there, but the machine has always been a crutch. It's very seductive, and you have to resist overdoing it. Even if you film a show before a live audience, they still "sweeten" the laughter with the machine.

The machine is like a typewriter. You press one button for a titter and one for a guffaw, and you play it like an organ.

RAY EARLENBORN: I worked for Charlie. He was very proud of it. It made him a lot of money, but some of us are sad, because now the whole thing is fake. I started with him when he was an audio-man at KNX radio, and he was doing stuff for Lucille Ball. That's when he built his first machine. We had been using sixteen-inch transcriptions with a continuous laugh and a continuous applause, that you could fade in and out. He built the machine to get a variety of laughs that would be more to the point of the jokes.

The first one was like a big drum with a loop on it. Now, it has foot pedals for continuous laughter and continuous applause, and then I have "gozintas" and "gosoutas" on the push buttons going into a laugh and coming out of it and going into applause and coming out of it.

Most of the laughs in the later machine were originally recorded from the Skelton show. He's easy to get good clean laughs from because he does a lot of pantomime, and you don't have music or dialogue to come in and goof it up. I also used Marcel Marceau because he's a pantomime artist.

The way to lay in laughs is to look at a show and do it as you feel it. There are big laughs, small laughs, medium laughs. "Ooooooh"-type laughs, "Ah-haa"-type laughs. Today, they all use drop-your-pants laughs. There's no dynamics. You blink your eyelash and it's a big scream. That's for the advertising agency because they don't know what's funny, and they're afraid the clients won't think they've got a funny show. A laugh track is a form of insurance for them.

Milton Berle carried his own audience with him wherever he went. His mother, I think, cast it, and his mother was one of the laughers. They used cackling women and screams from every pants-dropping show. He would listen to the laughs and say, "That woman screaming, put that in."

MEL DIAMOND: That machine was the answer to every prayer he ever had. He didn't need the fuckin' audience anymore, which he didn't like anyway because he couldn't depend on 'em. To me the machine is as fraudulent as the phony quiz shows, but the comedians saw it as the answer to their worst fears.

✳   ✳   ✳

JACK CARTER: At first, I didn't know about plugs. Every week on DuMont, I had a joke about some girdle. Finally, I said, "What is this?"

"Those are plugs. We get cases of liquor and typewriters."

"Where am I in this?"

"You're supposed to get. Don't you know about it?"

I didn't know.

OSCAR KATZ: Cy Howard [a TV writer] had a garage full of appliances from all the plugs. He set his brother up in the appliance business with them. You'd read a script, and you'd find three plugs in one sentence. If somebody said their relatives came over on the *Mayflower*, they'd talk about Mayflower Moving, Mayflower Clothing. Then there were hidden plugs. Chicken and cranberry sauce was a plug because the cranberry guys were trying to promote using cranberries with chicken. If you said something nice about truck drivers that was a plug.

EVERETT GREENBAUM: A guy would come around and say, "Well, this week we have a special on bananas." And if you did a joke about bananas you got a gift.

JAY BURTON: I knew two writers who got so much liquor they threw a party for two hundred people.

JACK CARTER: There were a million jokes. "Some guy stole my wife's Diner's Club Card. I went to the police. He was spending less money than she does."

Hope did more than anybody. "I was walking down the street, and I got hit by a Mixmaster." Youngman would just mention five names. He wouldn't even do a joke. "Good evening, Abe's Linen Suits. Pepsi-Cola and Diner's Club were walking down the street, and they run into a bottle of Jeris Tonic Shampoo."

HAL GOLDMAN: We had Jack and Rochester take inventory in the icebox, and they rattled off like ten different things. They were all plugs. Another time Rochester mentioned some kind of an electric blanket. Jack said, "We don't have a so-and-so electric blanket," and Rochester said, "We do now."

EVERETT GREENBAUM: The Jerry Lewis writers would get the list and put all the things into one paragraph. They ruined it for everybody, because after that it became illegal.

MOREY AMSTERDAM: "Who Said That?" didn't allow any plugs, but a guy asked me to do one for Adam's Hats. I said, "How the hell am I gonna get a plug in on a show like this?"

"You'll think of something."

Sure enough, one question had to do with what was written on King Tut's tomb. I knew it, and I added, "Incidentally, that same expedition later went on to another part of Egypt where they found what was the original Garden of Eden. They even found Eve's fig leaf, and now they're lookin' for Adam's hats."

AL GORDON: The censor didn't bother us on plugs or anything. Benny censored himself. He wouldn't do anything that would hurt people or anything that was political or dirty. "The Dean Martin Show" was different. The censor would come into our room and say, "You gotta take out this tit joke."

"Listen, we couldn't use it, but they could [on another show]?"

"Okay, keep the tit joke, but take this out." They allowed Dean to do dirty jokes because he was a success, but if another show wasn't a success they wouldn't let you say hello.

JACK CARTER: The censors flagged you on everything. When you did Sullivan, you couldn't say belly button. You couldn't say navel. You had to say aperture. Sullivan once said to me [in Ed Sullivan's voice], "That's an aperture in the human body."

I said, "It's an asshole, but I'm not saying it."

"You can't say that on my show. I don't want any belly buttons or navels."

*   *   *

MIKE DANN: When Pat Weaver created NBC's programming department, the acquisition of Martin and Lewis was the first function of the department. We had lost Jack Benny and other stars to CBS, and NBC now had to sign talent to replace them. That was a big thing to convince General Sarnoff. "Sign talent ourselves? We're just a delivery system."

PAT WEAVER: Gleason wanted $250,000 to do an hour show for us. Sarnoff said, "That's more than I make."

"You can't do the falls, General." He wouldn't do it.

MIKE DANN: "The All-Star Revue" was the department's first programming effort.

CHARLIE ISAACS: It was originally called the "Four Star Revue." It had rotating comics. I wrote Jimmy Durante's segment. It became the "All-Star Revue." Then it was folded into "The Colgate Comedy Hour." They were all big-budget variety shows.

MEL DIAMOND: You know the Big Bang Theory? The variety shows were the big bang for television. They caught the attention of the public faster than anything else.

MIKE DANN: At NBC, all major new ventures were in color because RCA was fighting not only CBS but also to get the public to buy their color sets. RCA underwrote these expensive shows because there was no point in buying color sets unless there were color shows. They even gave us color sets and paid us to have color parties in our homes with important people and opinion makers who would be invited over on Saturday nights to watch "Show of Shows" in color.

ARTHUR PENN: I got assigned to "The Colgate Comedy Hour" while I was still in New York. Unlike "Show of Shows," on "Colgate," the producers were subservient to the comics, who were Martin and Lewis, Eddie Cantor, Bob Hope, Jimmy Durante, Abbott and Costello, Danny Thomas, and others. For them it was like summer stock. They would come in and do everything their own way, and there was nobody in charge of the total show. As a result, perhaps with the exception of Martin and Lewis, we never had the best of these people.

Martin and Lewis were the most out of control, but they were also using the medium as contemporaries of television in a way the others were not. For example, usually everybody was terribly concerned that you not show the other cameras. Jerry would come tearing out of the frame and make the cameras follow him and photograph each other.

CHARLIE ISAACS: Durante used the cameras, too. I thought he did more innovative things than any of the others. We never threw a pie or squirted seltzer.

At first, Jimmy was uncomfortable with the show. When I first talked to him about it, he said, "I don't know. You gotta memorize all that stuff." He really was fearful. What changed his mind was the money. He had been making about as much as he could in the clubs. On TV he was making a fortune, and he could still play the Copa, but now for much more money.

MEL DIAMOND: Bob Hope had to adjust to television. He was a very diligent comedian, but he never learned his lines. When he did dialogue with his guests, he was always looking over their shoulders at the goddamned cue cards. Put them away and the show is over.

Gleason's memory was as close to photographic as I have ever experienced. He could read a sketch once and know it cold. And what he didn't know he could improvise and still be hilarious. Hope, as they say, couldn't ad-lib a belch after a hearty meal. He lived for the monologue, the one-to-one contact with an audience, and he was probably the best monologist of the time.

ARTHUR PENN: He was a perfectionist when it came to his monologue. He would come offstage swearing at himself for having blown in the most imperceptible way the [snaps his fingers] of a line.

MEL DIAMOND: Hope was wise enough to know that he was strictly the creation of writers. He was a great laugher, which was rare. Gleason would glare at you and give you a sense of fucking fear. Hope appreciated writers, but whether that reflected any special encomium for the writer I doubt it. I can say a lot of nice things about him, but spreading any real bread around was never one of his great assets.

Writers generally were fired very quickly. It was no great dishonor to be fired. "Red Buttons," they had a shuttle from L.A. to New York every week, bringing in a fresh load of writing meat. The minute there was flack from the sponsor they fired the writers. It never occurred to them that it might be a director, or the producer.

That's why most writers never wanted to be on a show when it started because as sure as the sun comes up in the morning those guys in the trenches doing the creating will be fired, so never go in with the first platoon. Let some other guy be killed. Then the new writers can come in and walk on those bodies.

CHARLIE ISAACS: Skelton really had a hate for writers. He thought of them as slaves. He fired his head writer almost every other year. When he fired [Bob] Schiller and [Bob] Weiskopf, they told the *Times* they were fired "for being Number One." He fired me.

With Durante, there was always this crappy publicity. "What will he do when he runs out of material?" I quit the show three times saying, "You say these things to the press when we are writing a goddamned show every week." He mumbled a half-apology. We were a big hit, and every damn word on that show was ours.

EVERETT GREENBAUM: Gleason was a shit. Once I was sitting in the Fox commissary. It was near a stage, and we heard a big argument. A door opened and Gleason screamed to somebody inside. "Go to hell. I'm not having anything more to do with this."

And then Lucy came to the door and said, "You fat fuck."

His culture didn't interest me, the boozing and the broads. I loved Carney. I thought everything he did was wonderful.

MEL DIAMOND: Most of us came from radio. We thought TV was radio with pictures, so we wrote just the way we had done all along.

EVERETT GREENBAUM: They would follow what we called "the rules." They were radio rules. When you watch a show written under the old rules, you say, "Oh, now they're getting into a routine." Or you say, "That's a rule of three." A rule-of-three joke was, "Police are on the alert for an escapee from Federal prison. The man is six feet tall; he is wearing a gray suit; and he is driving a blue Chevrolet coupe that he cleverly carved out of soap." Two set-ups, then the punch line.

In sitcoms, the rules said you were supposed to lead up to the block comedy scene. A typical block comedy scene was when Lucy was wrapping chocolate in the factory. Also, you had to have a climax at the end of the first act to make you tune back. That was a rule. Another rule was you had to have a sidekick. We had Tony Randall on "Mr. Peepers" and Don Knotts on "Andy Griffith."

"The George Gobel Show" worked so well because we were willing to break those rules. That was Hal Kanter's genius. Hal is probably the greatest joke maker in town. I remember when I said to him that Colonel Sanders had died. He said, "I know. I saw chickens tap-dancing in the street."

One of his jokes on the Gobel show was very controversial. It was Decoration Day weekend. Gobel came out and said, "As of Saturday night there have been three hundred traffic deaths from driving. You people just aren't trying."

HAL KANTER: Jack Douglas wrote a line for George, "There's an old saying that money can't buy you happiness. Money *can* buy you happiness, so pick up a fifth on your way home."

That caused a tremendous outcry from Baptists all over the country. We hit the front pages with that.

EVERETT GREENBAUM: Then there was one about a cookie going door to door selling Girl Scouts. When we introduced pretty, perky Peggy King, I wrote the line, "We could have gotten a French singer or a Spanish singer or a British singer, but we got an American singer, because it's so easy to get parts." I still hear that joke in different forms.

BUD YORKIN: That show was as funny as any show of the fifties. George had wonderful timing, and everybody kind of related to him as Peck's Bad Boy, always getting into trouble with his wife.

HAL KANTER: I learned early on from my association with Groucho Marx that one of the basics of humor was taking a cliché and standing it on its head. Whenever we could get away with it, we did—even with the credits: "Directed by Bud Yorkin, Carnegie Tech, '38. Produced by Ed Sobol, Columbia, '09. Staged by Harvard 23, Yale 46." Every week it was something different. We would always throw strange things into the credits, like that something was by the Brontë sisters.

EVERETT GREENBAUM: The Gobel show worked because of Hal. The executives were afraid of him because the ratings were so high, so he became very powerful. That's what happens if you have a hit under your control: the advertisers don't bother you.

But when Hal asked for a piece of the show, Gobel wouldn't give him one—

tenth of one percent on it. He was the most disloyal comedian in the world, so Hal left, and all of George's relatives came out of the woodwork to write the show, and it went downhill.

HAL KANTER: George did not fight for me. He just wanted everything to be nice and smooth and happy. I'm sure he was told that other people could do the show. He found out too late that it was not so.

EVERETT GREENBAUM: I wrote a joke where the grandmother put her false teeth in a glass of water at night, and the agency said, "Put the teeth in a glass of condensed milk"—because that was the sponsor. I said, "That's crazy, it kills the joke," and they fired me. George didn't fight for me either. Later, when he was a neighbor of mine he used to invite me up for a drink, and I would say, "George, I don't drink and you fired me."

❉   ❉   ❉

ARTHUR PENN: Dean Martin had one of the funniest, fastest minds I have ever seen. Jerry was a *tummler,* but just plain standing around being funny, Dean had him every which way.

BUD YORKIN: Dean would come up with these great lines in rehearsal. Then Jerry would do them on the air as if they were ad-libbed and get an ovation. It was down and dirty for a while.

HARRY CRANE: They hired me to do their pilot for Colgate. On the show is Leonard Barr, Dean's uncle from Steubenville, Ohio. He started Dean in the business. He was going to do a dance routine with his partner. The show was eight minutes over. An hour before showtime, Pat Weaver says they have to cut Barr and Estes. Dean says, "Oh, you can't touch that. He's got everybody from Steubenville watching. It'll break his heart."

"We've got to cut him."

"If you cut that, I don't do the show." He stuck to it.

JOE CATES: I never heard of another star doing anything like this, but when Dean made all that money he went to Greg Garrison, who produced his show, and said, "You've got a piece of it," and he gave it to him. He is a mean man and a distant man, but he recognized that Greg made it for him.

GREG GARRISON: We have been together twenty-seven years. There has never been a piece of paper which has existed between us. He always makes me laugh. I've never enjoyed working with anyone more, and with the exception of George Burns, no man was ever a better straight man than Dean.

ARTHUR PENN: Dean would always drop back and one under Jerry, recognizing that that was the strength of their act. The only discomfort that was ever in evidence was when I would go into the dressing room, and I would see him drinking.

Now Abbott and Costello, they really hated each other. Lou's contempt for Bud Abbott was really palpable. He thought he was dumb. In a way he was like a horse with blinders. He knew the stuff he had to do, but if there was any variation on it he would not get it, and Lou would be, "Ugh, Jeez, Lou, listen!"

CHARLIE ISAACS: There was something fantastic about these old performers. I had a great respect for them. I worked with Jolson on "Kraft Music Hall." People would ask me, "Wasn't Jolson a son of a bitch?" Well, I had some battles with him, but I would see him waiting in the wings, this little old man in a cashmere turtleneck, looking about five foot four, and then he would get his cue and suddenly he was six feet four and he would strut out there. I've gotten so damn mad at Berle. Nevertheless when I saw him out on the stage and the people were screaming, you had to admire him.

ARTHUR PENN: Eddie Cantor's segments were always meticulously rehearsed, but Dean and Jerry could get pretty crazy. My headphones were connected to the control room, and when the two of them were on, you would hear all kinds of things. "God, where are they going? Watch it, three, Jesus Christ, pan over! Get 'em over there, Penn, get 'em back onstage!" Well, you couldn't get him back onstage. He knew what he was doing. I was doing what I could to control the circumstances, but usually I was laughing.

BUD YORKIN: Jerry liked to tear up things. Once when we were short, he grabbed a fire hose and turned it on. He blew out two cameras and tore up the curtain, which was about fifty-five years old. [Sarcastically] Jack Gould thought it was genius.

✳   ✳   ✳

CHARLIE ISAACS: Jimmy Durante had some strange friends. In Chicago, he took me to a restaurant called Fritzl's. Downstairs was a large den with paneled walls, and there are ten guys around a table playing cards. He introduced me, and one of them was Jake Fiaschetti, the guy who inherited the Capone gang. After we left, Jimmy said to me, "Weren't they fine gentlemen?"

Jimmy said that when he grew up on the East Side, these neighborhood guys would go away for a while. Then they would come back in limousines, dressed in expensive suits and loaded with money. That meant they had made good, so they became role models in a strange way.

Eddie Jackson told me that very early in Chicago they were having a rough time getting decent bookings. A guy who had seen their act, heard them talking about it. He said, "Where can I get a hold of ya?"

They told him, and he said, "Wait till you hear from me." Two days later they were booked in a hell of a club. The guy's name was Al Brown, later known as Al Capone.

ROD ERICKSON: Guys at William Morris and MCA were told when they were assigned a nightclub with an act, "You're going with the Mob, whatever they offer don't take it or you'll be beholden to 'em. Don't even let them buy you a drink. Keep it a business relationship and nothing personal." If you're talking about Sinatra and Dean Martin, you're talking about the Mob.

CHARLIE ISAACS: Jerry and Dean are appearing at the Chez Paree in Chicago. Dean doesn't show up for rehearsal. Finally, he walks in with this little man who looks like a short George Raft. That was Johnny Ambrosio. The producer looks at Dean and says, "Dammit, Dean, you're late."

Johnny steps in front of Dean and says, "He ain't late. He was with me."

We rehearse a while, and then Johnny says, "You come with me." We get in two cabs and go to Halstead Street, which was a tough area. Sheldon Leonard and Dean and myself and Johnny are in one cab. Johnny starts pointing out spots, "Right there is where the Bertinelli family got it." On another corner he says, "This is where the Carotti mob was hanging from lampposts when it was all over." On another corner he says, "They still got blood on the sidewalk here. They killed someone every night for a week." He was taking us on this tour of all the great Mob hits.

Finally, Sheldon says, "We ought to get back to rehearsal."

Johnny then says to Sheldon, "You know, the hoods really like you. They think you take off real good on 'em."

Sheldon swelled up like he just got an Academy Award.

ARTHUR PENN: Jerry and Dean had these kind of henchmen around. Dean had this guy named Killer Gray, who made us a little nervous. "Hey, Killer," Dean would say, and Killer would go off to get something. We found out later that *killer* was Yiddish for hernia. He had a "killer." When that came out it was hilarious.

CHARLIE ISAACS: The gangsters loved show people. They went out of their way to do favors for them, figuring someday they'll pick up. Once, Jimmy had a show that needed a lot of rehearsal, but he disappeared for two days because they asked him to play some benefit, and he had to do it.

ROD ERICKSON: Keefe Brasselle and Jim Aubrey [performer and former head of CBS programming, respectively] were good friends in a funny way. Keefe's godfather was Joe Profaci, the head of the Brooklyn Mob. Keefe fascinated Jim. Somebody once said, "Jim was born a gentleman, and he's working very hard to become a gangster."

I don't know what the nature of their relationship was, but there was a lot of talk about it. One night, Jim invited my wife and me and some of the guys who were heads of sales to the opening of Keefe's Hollywood Night Club in Edison, New Jersey. The real reason why the hoods opened the place was to have a floating crap game for the workers in the area.

At one table was everybody who counted in decision making at CBS, except Bill Paley or Stanton. At the other table were all the guys who were picked up by the FBI at the Mob's big Appalachin conference and had just gotten released from jail. In the back of the room were the families at one table and their mistresses at the other. It was fascinating. Keefe said to me, "I want you to meet my godfather, Joe Profaci," who looked like your grandfather who didn't make it and is now holding up a sign at the railroad crossing. He spoke broken English, but there was something in the eyes. Maybe he thought I was a cop, because he said to me, "I'm glad to meet you," and started patting me down for a weapon.

Keefe performed with the DeMarco Sisters and, at some point, pointed to Bill Hyland of CBS and said, "If you don't pick up my contract, I'm gonna sic Uncle Joe on you."

Two days later, the hoods blew up the place. Profaci was moving in on somebody's territory.

GREG GARRISON: Jim Aubrey signed me to do a series with Judy Garland. After we made the deal, he calls me and says he would consider it a personal favor if I also do a summer replacement series starring Keefe Brasselle.

I knew he was a part-time hood. This is the guy he wants me to do a summer show for, but why not. He just gave me one hell of a deal, so we do five shows. Everything is going very well. Then Keefe begins to read his notices. He goes to a restaurant. He gets a good table. Everybody recognizes him. He's Charlie Studley.

One night at a quarter to seven I go up to his dressing room to go over some notes with him and he's not there. Someone says he's in the bar across the street.

"Are you crazy? We're gonna hold an audience up." I go crazy when you hold an audience up. I believe like my comics taught me. "Don't move a camera, and don't fuck with an audience."

I go inside the bar, and I say, "Hey, Keefe, let's go."

He stands up and says, "I'll tell you when I'm ready to go. I'm the star of this fucking show."

Big fuckin' announcement. [Sighs.] I grab him by the fuckin' scruff of his neck. I yank him out of the fuckin' chair. I pop him on the back of his head. I throw him out of the goddamned bar. I roll him across the street, throw him into the goddamned theater, and I say, "I want you on the stage in fifteen minutes, and I'll break every goddamned bone in your body if you're not."

Unbelievably, he does a hell of a performance that night. During the show, I turn around and Rocky Graziano is standing next to me. I say, "Rock, how the fuck are you?"

He says, "What the fuck did you do to that wop?"

"I kicked the shit out of him for not being here."

He sighs and then he says, "He's got a thing goin' for ya. They're gonna knock you off tonight."

"What?"

"I'm tryin' to square it. Come with me to my fuckin' hotel. You're goin' to stay with me. He's a fuckin' crazy idiot."

I go to Rocky's place. He got three calls. Each time he said, "No, he's with me and he's my friend and I don't give a fuck, you square it." And he squared it. The next day I was fired, and it took a year to buy off my Judy Garland contract. Six months later Aubrey was canned for some business he had with Keefe, and Keefe was in jail for shooting somebody. Charming people you run into.

MEL DIAMOND: I met Greg on "The Kate Smith Show." Kate's voice was like spun gold, and on camera she embodied all the sweetest virtues of American life, decency, kindness, and good taste. Meanwhile, behind the scenes her show was more like an orgy. I remember "Boom Boom," our resident schtupper, not to mention this heir to an oleo margarine fortune, who ran an expensive call girl operation on the side. As it happened, his girls began appearing on the show as models, so when Kate was downstairs on the air singing "God Bless America," some of us were in the dressing rooms upstairs getting laid. That's why when I think of "The Golden Age" of television, I'm not remembering the "Philco Playhouse."

CHARLIE ISAACS: Comedians are a horny breed. Hope was the worst. It's quite common knowledge, but the press has been good to him. Hope had what they called a beard, a guy that pretends the girl is his date. His beard was a guy named Barney Dean. I remember when I did the Walgreen show there was a gorgeous girl sitting in the audience during rehearsal. I started to talk to her, and Barney sits down on my right and whispers, "Leave her alone. Bob's girl."

MEL DIAMOND: Hope kept a lot of young chicks around. They used to say he could get into his car, and it would automatically take him where he had a chick stashed.

CHARLIE ISAACS: The press protected him in part because they said he was doing such a wonderful job entertaining troops. First of all, most of his flying was done at government expense, and he put together shows that paid him hundreds of thousands of dollars.

MEL DIAMOND: Milton was quite a cocksman. One time he's in the lobby of the Essex House and he spots this gorgeous girl using the house phone. He's trying to figure out some way to hit on her, so he saunters over, picks up the phone next to her, and asks the operator to ring his room. After a beat, he says loud enough for the chick to hear, "Hello, Mother? This is your son, Milton Berle."

CHARLIE ISAACS: When I was producing and writing "The Gisele MacKenzie Show," which Jack Benny owned, I went to Vegas to see Jack. Backstage, he said to me, "Come here."

We went to his dressing room. He looks both ways in the hall and closes the door. He says, "This girl is just fantastic. She can sing. She can play the piano and violin. She's attractive." Then he says so plaintively in that Benny delivery, "Some people say I'm fucking her. I'm not fucking anybody."

✳   ✳   ✳

MIKE DANN: The variety shows eventually died because we ran through the stars of radio and weren't developing new stars. Bob Newhart couldn't do song and dance, and Johnny Winters, he was a strange guy who made Jackie Gleason look straight. Variety shows were also huge and difficult to do, and the pressure of doing them in color was enormous, so they went off the air.

MEL DIAMOND: I once tried to peddle a talk show for kids called "Teenage America," but there was no interest. They said, "Who gives a shit about kids? They don't have any buying power." Elvis proved they were wrong. Now, they saw the zillions being shelled out for concerts and records and realized he had uncovered the motherlode. It was true then, and it's even truer now: kids own the fucking business.

Before then there were some sitcoms, but those of us who were writing stand-up material never paid any real attention to them. If anything, we joked about them, but now as the kids shifted their loyalties away from their parents and away from the old-style comedians, if you wanted to keep eating you had to learn to write some inane fucking sitcom, no more funny monologues, no more funny sketches, no more pretty dancers to hit on. It was a tough transition, and I broke my ass trying to write that drivel, but go complain. It got me a house in Encino and supported my family for years, but the fucking pressure also contributed to my divorce.

MAX WILK: I wrote one of the first sitcoms, "Mama." I had already been writing television for four or five years when I got to "Mama." It was one of the few times that nobody ever wanted anything from me but my best. The day after my name appeared at the end of "Mama" for the first time, I was walking down Main Street in Ridgefield, Connecticut, and people were coming up to me and saying, "You wrote 'Mama.' What a wonderful show." Never had anybody ever said that to me before.

I learned to write on that show. I learned to get plots out of the characters. We were not just doing stories. We were doing character stories. It's a big difference. We never did jokes. Our humor was subtle and gentle. "Mama" had no middle commercials. That gave you twenty-four minutes to develop characters from beginning to end without an interruption. The network wanted a middle commercial, but General Foods said, "No, we like this show the way it is."

Also, it was done live. With a live show, your actors bring a validity to it they don't bring to film. You had to be absolutely right with that show. You couldn't fake anything.

DAVID SWIFT: "Mr. Peepers" was also done live out of New York. It came about after Philco bought an original of mine called "The Copper," about an inept little policeman. For the lead, Bill Nichols saw Wally Cox doing his act at the Village Vanguard and cast him. It was the first time he ever acted. Fred wanted a series created for him. I dreamed it up on a plane to Chicago. Bill then found Marion Lorne and Tony Randall.

TONY RANDALL: The show was originally a thirteen-week summer replacement, but when they announced the run was over, there were so many protests they decided to put it back on the air. I was so busy directing that I asked them to release me from the show, but they wouldn't, so I did it reluctantly, and it was the turning point in my life. "Mr. Peepers" made me a name.

EVERETT GREENBAUM: When I first went to New York, I brought a pile of acetates of my radio show with me and left them at Talent Associates, which packaged "Peepers." They heard them and offered me a two-week trial to see if I could write with Jim Fritzell. That two weeks lasted thirty years. We wrote more than anybody else. We wrote 560 half-hours that were on the air. Three hundred of them were in the top ten. We did 120 "Mr. Peepers," five years of "The Real McCoys," eight years of "Andy Griffith," three years of "M★A★S★H." Hal Kanter once said of us "They've had their fingers in more pilots than an Air Force proctologist."

When we wrote "Peepers," the character of Mr. Peepers was so free of hostility that you usually wound up writing Mr. Weskit, who was Tony, and then involving Mr. Peepers in the story. Mr. Weskit could make a fool of himself and be obnoxious, but Mr. Peepers was perfect.

TONY RANDALL: Wally was so muscular we never could take a shot of him with his shirt off, because it would ruin the image of this meek little character. He was built like a gorilla.

EVERETT GREENBAUM: He also had an amazing mind. He knew five or six different languages, and he knew everything about biology. He really was "Mr. Peepers," except Mr. Peepers didn't have a sex life. I'd say to Wally, "What did you do last night?"

"Well, I came back from not getting laid about ten."

With "Mr. Peepers," Fred Coe encouraged us to get away from the Hollywood customs and make it more literary like *The New Yorker*. Jim would whirl in his grave if he heard that, because he was a small-town San Francisco Swede, who hated anything chi-chi. His talent was on a much higher level than his taste. He watched quiz shows all day long and read the sports pages.

TONY RANDALL: I would always pick up the phone when it rang. Jim Fritzell knew that, and he would always say on the phone, "How's your cock?" And I would go helpless with laughter. He knew he could get me with that line, so he wrote a whole show about it. He had Wally buy a car, and five times on the show, I had to say to Wally, "How's your car?" knowing that I couldn't say those words. This was before millions of people [shrieks of laughter].

EVERETT GREENBAUM: After a while, we began to repeat ourselves. The show where he got married broke all the records, but it was a mistake because it destroyed the character more or less, but we did it to get it renewed for the third year. That year was a disaster. Jim was drinking. We were offered a wonderful deal but Jim and I were so sick of each other by then, we turned it down.

Three years for a little show like that is not bad. It doesn't have to stay on forever. In England, they don't go twenty years with a show. "Fawlty Towers" was something like twelve shows. That's the way you should do it.

MAX WILK: General Foods was very happy with "Mama." They didn't have a huge audience, but what they got in terms of the quality of the audience and class made it very worthwhile. Then the last year they shot it on film, and the life went out of it.

That's the story with television. After the film boys got hold of television, you got "Highway Patrol" and "Harbor Patrol" and this patrol and that patrol. The symbol of what happened to television when it went out to California was the flashing blue light on the top of the cruiser. Television was now product, homogenized down to the lowest common denominator. Gresham's Law still applies to television: bad money drives out good. Bad television drives out good television.

EVERETT GREENBAUM: I didn't like many shows from that period, but I loved Bilko ["The Phil Silvers Show"]. That's the show that holds up best. It was a wonderful character and supporting cast.

AARON RUBEN: Nat Hiken created Bilko. Nat was the best. When he was working for Fred Allen, there was a guy named Doc Rockwell, who would come in with off-the-wall ideas. Once, he came in with a notion that the city is getting so overpopulated, you can't just keep building skyscrapers up, up, up. "You have to start building down," so we wrote this stuff and gave it to Nat, and he put in an incredible joke. Why didn't it occur to us? Because we didn't have Nat's mind. He said, "Groundscrapers, you see, you're building the buildings into the ground, and then if somebody dies, you just throw him out the window."

COLEMAN JACOBY: He had an original way of defining a character and getting humor out of it. He did a sketch with Bert Lahr and Nancy Walker where Bert is insanely jealous over his homely wife. He sees her as a beauty. He shouts out the window to the neighbors, "Eat your heart out."

AARON RUBEN: I became the director on the Bilko show because Nat produced it, directed it, and rewrote everybody's scripts, and he burned himself out after two years. When I took over, Nat said to me about Phil Silvers, "He's the best." He was an incredible performer, but he was a terrible insomniac, and he gambled all the time. That ruined his life. He would come in around seven A.M. for makeup, purple bags under his eyes. He'd plop down in the chair. I felt so sorry for him. His head would be slumping down. Then, "Okay, Phil we're ready for you," and the guy who a moment ago looked like he was near death, the face, the eyes, and the teeth would light up as if he had just been plugged in. When they said, "Okay, cut," he would just flop down again.

Phil resented that Doberman got more mail than he did, that this freak would suddenly become a star. We were in this studio on Twenty-eighth Street in the middle of the garment center. When we'd break for lunch there were guys standing on the curb, rocking on their heels, and they'd see Phil, and they'd say, "Hello, Bilko, how's Doberman?"

That's all he had to hear, "Fuck you."

Nat saw himself as a hotshot gambler like Bilko. He was a Walter Mitty type. First thing he did in the morning was put on his glasses so he could see where his cigarettes were. He smoked all day long. He ate all the wrong things, and he never went to a doctor. He was all alone watching a basketball game in his house when he had a heart attack and died. Guys who have to do everything themselves literally just burn themselves out. That's what happened to Nat.

COLEMAN JACOBY: Nat's point of view pervaded on Bilko, which was very realistic and very satirical of human nature. It was about a con man working his score. It was not a family show, like all those other shows at the time. That was one reason why it never accumulated the ratings it was worthy of.

EVERETT GREENBAUM: Most of those family shows sickened me. "My Little Margie" was stupid, "Father Knows Best" and "Danny Thomas," with that sermon at the end. These shows represented American life in a dishonest way. No one had any bodily functions. You usually didn't know what the father did for a living. No one ever used bad words. It was an America that was really created by Louis B. Mayer with the Andy Hardy pictures, only it was done better by them than it was on television.

ROBERT YOUNG: I had been under contract to MGM for fifteen years when they took on an assignment from General Foods to do a radio show. The idea was some of the MGM stars would do one-act plays. I hosted the show and found I liked doing radio, and it was an easy way to pick up a few extra dollars. After the show ended, I said to a friend of mine, a producer named Eugene Rodney, "I'd like to have my own show." I had wanted to get away from Metro anyway. I was tired of being the king of the B pictures.

Rodney and I kicked a few things around, and then one day I said, "Gene, I'd like to do a family show. I'd like to be the father, but not a boob. I don't want to do William Bendix in 'Life of Riley.' " Out of that came "Father Knows Best" which was on radio for a few years. When we had the chance to take it to TV, I thought it was a step down, a sign that you couldn't work anywhere else, but Gene convinced me otherwise.

* * *

EVERETT GREENBAUM: Irving and Norman Pincus had a children's television show, "Mr. I. Magination" in New York. Then they came out here, and Irving sat on Walter Brennan's doorstep for a couple of months and got him to do "The Real McCoys."

What a bastard Brennan was. We were there five years, and he thought my name was Phil, and he thought I was gentile. He was always confiding in me. He'd say [in Brennan's voice], "You know, Phil, a nigger smells bad because they got poison in their pores and you can't get it out." He also told me, "Phil, I can tell a Jew by their back. Their back ain't round like ours. It's straight down."

Everybody knew how I felt about him. Everybody felt the same way. In one show, a Japanese servant girl walks on Grandpa McCoy's back to straighten out his back trouble. Well, I was late for a story meeting, and they decided to punish me, so Irving says, "You've got to do a whole new script. Walter won't appear in a scene with an Oriental woman walking on his back."

"Well, we'll take that scene out."

Then Jim said, "Walter will not appear on the screen with an Oriental woman."

So I said, "I'm gonna kill him," and I started running toward the set. They were yelling, "It's a joke! It's a joke!" And they were chasing me through the streets of the studio. Even after they told me I still wanted to kill him.

CHARLIE ISAACS: I worked with Walter and I didn't find him to be that way at all. He was conservative, yes, but I found him to be one of the kindest, most generous men I ever met in show business.

MADELYN DAVIS: Bill Frawley, who played Fred on "Lucy," was a crusty old guy. I didn't really see the tension between him and Vivian Vance, although they weren't crazy about each other. Vivian and Lucy got along great.

RALPH LEVY: I knew Vivian very well, and some of Vivian's stories about Lucy were pretty horrific. Lucy insisted Vivian look like the slob she did.

Vivian also told me about one show when Lucy was pregnant. There was a quick costume change. Lucy had her dressers right by the exit on the stage, so as soon as she came off she just stood there and her dressers did everything. Vivian had to run about fifty yards to her dressing room, and she got back just before the cue, huffing and puffing. Lucy said, "Where have you been?"

Vivian looked down at her overextended stomach and said, "I'd tell you to go fuck yourself if I didn't see that someone beat you to it."

EVERETT GREENBAUM: I took a course in acting from Lucy. I didn't like her. Oooh, she was tough. I remember one day, two young people in the course did a scene from Chekhov, and she said, "What's that?"

"It's Chekhov."

"I don't allow no Chekhov here."

RALPH LEVY: Somebody said once when they asked her if Lucy was tough. She said, "Tough? she's got muscles in her shit."

But she had to be tough.

MADELYN DAVIS: If she got mad, she would be the first person to be sorry, because she had a temper. She was impatient, and she wanted it right. She didn't have any tolerance for people who weren't doing their jobs.

Desi had a terrible temper, too, but he never got mad at us. I think he realized that if he yelled at us too much we might leave. I respected Desi's talents and so did Bob. He was very undervalued. He was intuitive. He knew what worked. He was good with audiences, and he kept everything together. We could always do what we wanted. He never said, "That's too expensive," or "That's a dumb idea."

We were spoiled by those two. You could write anything, and Lucy would do it enthusiastically, and when you work with Lucille Ball what you write comes out a lot funnier than you ever hoped.

We put her in clay. We starched her, and she never said, "Oh, I don't know if I'll look good." The one exception was when we had her working with an elephant. She had to talk into the trunk. This time, she took a look and she almost got teary. She said, "I don't know."

We went into the office and redid the whole last scene. Then Vivian called. "It's okay, she's gonna do it."

"How come?"

"Well, I said, 'Lucy, if you don't want to do that funny bit with the elephant, I'll do it.' "

Sometimes she would have doubts about a routine, so we put in the scripts, "We tried this." We did try them out first. You find funnier things that way. Also, we had to make sure it would work. We would be lying on the floor handcuffed together, saying, "If anybody walks in, they're gonna think we're absolutely crazy."

Lucy was marvelously coordinated. Some of these things were very difficult. Not only could she do them, but she would find all the funny stuff. She loved to rehearse, because the more she rehearsed the more fun she could have with it.

We never discussed story lines with Lucy, but we did with Desi. He liked talking to writers better than business. Desi was also the fastest person to pick up lines that you could imagine, even though he didn't always understand them. He'd say, "If you guys think it's funny, it's okay with me." We ended up using his difficulty with English in our scripts.

AARON RUBEN: I produced "The Andy Griffith Show," and there was definitely some of Andy in Andy Griffith, and while I wouldn't say that Don Knotts was a schnook, there was a little bit of that ungainly quality in him.

ROBERT YOUNG: I wasn't Jim Anderson, but it was hard for the public to accept that, and it got to be a pain in the ass. People would ask me about social conduct and raising a family and I'd say, "Why are you asking me?"

"Because of 'Father Knows Best.' "

"That is a film of a script written by writers. Life isn't written by writers."

JANE WYATT: A couple of years before "Father Knows Best," I played opposite Cary Grant and Gary Cooper. I was getting every part there was. Then suddenly it stopped. I couldn't figure it out until a friend told me I was blacklisted.

I had gone to Washington with the group that protested the Hollywood [anti-communist] hearings. I also was seen wearing a Russian costume at a meeting during the war to push for a second front, which President Roosevelt was pushing for too. I had to go to New York for a couple of years where it didn't seem to make a difference. I did lots of live television in those two years.

When they were putting together the television version of "Father Knows Best" they asked me if I would do it. I said, "No, I've done live TV. I don't want to do a serial." I never read a script of the show. I never listened to it on the air. I just knew I didn't want to do it.

Finally, they convinced me to read the script, and it was enchanting, but before I could do it, Screen Gems insisted I appear on Radio Free Europe and read some kind of narration to the Russians. That got me cleared.

Still, I hated doing the pilot. It seemed so antediluvian to me. It was done at

Columbia where we shot *Lost Horizon*. They still had those great big awful arcs, and they had to lay down tracks for the dolly. You could only walk a straight line, and that goddamned stage squeaked so.

Mostly, I missed the electricity of live television. The night we finished the pilot, I wrote my agent, saying I wouldn't sign a contract unless I got a royalty. That was the only word I knew because there were no residuals. The result was I got a very good deal on the reruns, but then I also got stuck with the show.

PAUL PETERSEN: Donna [Reed] hadn't worked much after *From Here to Eternity*. For her, TV not only had financial benefits but it also resurrected her celebrity. Carl Betz [who played her husband] had misgivings. Here was a guy who had shared the Carnegie Award with Edward Ludlam. Now he was second banana on Mother Knows Best.

BARBARA BILLINGSLEY: Hugh Beaumont wasn't happy in the beginning either [as Ward on "Leave It to Beaver"], but he appreciated the show as it went along. We always laughed at what Ward was supposed to do for a living. We never knew. That was deliberate. It was like Ozzie Nelson. He was always home. It was always Saturday in that house.

I liked the idea of doing a series. I had two small boys, and the series meant security for me. I would go to bed at night thinking about what I would like to do, and it was a show just like "Beaver." I said to myself, My God, I'm doing the show of my dreams.

PAUL PETERSEN: Donna and Carl were so wonderful to work with. It led to some confusion on my part as to who my real parents were—and to my parents' breakup. My mother says today, "How could I compete with Donna Reed?" I spent more time with Donna than I did with my parents. I went to work at seven in the morning and got home at six and was out being famous in the afternoon. Why should I listen to my parents?

BILLY GRAY: I never confused Jim and Jane with my real parents. Young was always cordial, but there wasn't anything parental to the relationship. We were professional actors and this was a job. You showed up and knew your lines and you hit your marks. I liked that part of it, being respected as a contributing member of the group.

BARBARA BILLINGSLEY: Jerry [Mathers] and Tony [Dow] had their mothers with them at all times. While we ended up feeling almost like a family, there was no question who their parents were.

We all got along beautifully. I believe that if you are loved, and there's some discipline and you feel secure, you are going to be all right. The kids on our show were. Some of those other kids had problems. Lauren Chapin probably had it the worst.

JANE WYATT: Lauren had a very rough home life. Once, her mother came on the set wearing a mink, and I said, "Oh, what a lovely mink cape."

"Isn't it sweet? Lauren gave it to me for Christmas."

BILLY GRAY: Her mother would be juiced out of her melon and would create a scene. Eventually, she was barred from the set.

EVERETT GREENBAUM: It was generally very nice on the Griffith set, and Ronnie was such a terrific person, mainly due to his parents, who were marvelous.

AARON RUBEN: They were the most un–show business parents you ever saw. They dealt with him like a pro, and as soon his bit was over, "Can I go back to school now?" and he would go racing to that little room. He was quite a kid.

EVERETT GREENBAUM: Now Aunt Bea was different. I just hated her guts. She made it a point, every time we were together socially, of saying, "There's only one thing wrong with the show. The writing is terrible."

She was nuts, and people got fed up with her. Some fans in a Southern town invited her to come and visit. She got along fine for a while. They even helped her buy a house. At the end of six months, no one would talk to her.

PAUL PETERSEN: School was a lot of fun on our set. The teacher, Lillian Barkley, was excellent.

BILLY GRAY: She was a nice lady, but it was a total sham. The "school" was just eight-by-eight canvas with one-by-three slats holding the thing up. You heard everything that was going on on the set. There was no blackboard, nothing, just a card table and a couple of chairs. You do a shot and come out and go to school for a half hour until they relight the set. It was just back and forth and back and forth. You can't learn fifteen minutes at a time.

There wasn't really any course of study. All that was required was that you spend the time, which I think was three hours a day. Lillian gave me the answers to the test I took to graduate from high school. She just said, "Don't get 'em all right." I wasn't going to learn anyway. I didn't want to, and she knew it was a lost cause.

JANE WYATT: Billy was the first hippie. He was always in trouble. He got a million traffic tickets until they took his license away, so he got a bicycle. Then he kept going through red lights, and they took his bicycle license away. Then he was thumbing his way and getting on a bus. He came in late one morning, looking like a thundercloud. I said, "What happened?"

"Oh, I got a ticket."

"They took away your driver's license. They took away your bicycle license. How could you get a ticket?"

"I got a ticket for jaywalking."

ROBERT YOUNG: Gene and I decided that "Father Knows Best" would be shot like a motion picture. It would not be what was standard TV filming at the time, a two-shot over the shoulder, a closeup, and that's it. We wanted to give it some care and to indicate we cared. That made it harder to shoot one of these things in six days, but we did it.

BILLY GRAY: The kind of work Rodney and Young did was so different from regular television. They didn't cut any corners at all, except in what they were paying me, but there was carte blanche for the director. He could have as many takes as he wanted to until he felt he got it right.

JANE WYATT: The show was Gene Rodney's whole life. He was very strict about the scripts. You couldn't change one jot or one tittle. An "and," "if," or a "but" would take a call to the front office, and Mr. Rodney would come down and discuss it with you. On live TV, scripts were being changed all the way through, but in Gene's office there were piles of scripts that had been finished and polished. That's why those scripts still hold up. They worked so hard over them.

BILLY GRAY: I always felt the lines were shitty. We had to say stuff, like, "Golly, gee." I tried to get things more current, to use the vernacular of the day. "Crazy" was happening then. "Crazy, man." They said that would offend people.

BOB CARROLL: We were busy writing all the time.

MADELYN DAVIS: We did thirty-eight shows a year. I don't know how, except we worked on weekends and dated each other.

On the weekends, we used to go to the studio and climb over the wall because it wasn't open. We preferred working there because there were no interruptions.

You know those numbers you take when you go to the butcher? We brought some in and we had them backward, so we would start with thirty-eight and we had a big ceremony each week when we would take one off until we got down to the last one.

BILLY GRAY: It's work when you have to get up real early in the morning, but it's fun when you get it right the first time. Still, I couldn't wait to get off work and go smoke grass. That was great fun. Nobody else on the set smoked grass. Nobody in my high school knew what grass was. I had to go to Mexico to get it.

JANE WYATT: I was unhappy doing the show. I was away from the world. You got up at six in the morning and got into your car, said a sleepy hello to the gate man, ran out to the same makeup man you had all the time, got to the set with the same cast, the same director, same everything. That night you went home, ran the lines, and went back the next day.

In New York, we rehearsed on First Avenue and Fifth Street. Whether you took the bus or the taxi, there were different people, people in babushkas, people in fur coats, people who said hello, crazy taxicab drivers. There was a whole other world, and in California we were cut out of that world. It was stultifying.

BARBARA BILLINGSLEY: I didn't mind it. I still get a thrill when I drive into a studio. You think you don't want to work until you get on that lot. Then you can't wait to start.

I had a wonderful life during "Beaver." I had a new husband that I adored. He worked long hours, too. When we saw each other it was wonderful. Sure I was seeing the same people, but I loved seeing the same people. I never wanted to do more.

JANE WYATT: Whenever we had a hiatus, I always wanted to get myself another job. I'd go to New York and do live television. I was going to do a show out here, "Matinee Theater," in which the woman turned out to be a murderess, but I had to get permission from Rodney, and he would not let me play a murderess.

BILLY GRAY: I lost the part of James Dean's sidekick in *Rebel Without a Cause* because Rodney wouldn't shoot around me. Who knows what that would have done for my career.

JANE WYATT: The first year, Billy had no beef. They did all these scripts from the radio show where the best scenes turned out to be between Bud and Dad, and Mom had nothing to do.

I was so frustrated the first year. I went absolutely mad. I read all of the Old Testament in my dressing room. I took Spanish lessons. They kept saying, "Wait until the second year," and the second year was much better. Still, I got frustrated at times. I was never shown reading a book. On the other hand, what kind of show would we have had if Mom was off having a career. I think for the time it was okay.

RALPH LEVY: One of the ideas behind "I Love Lucy" was that she was always trying to get into Desi's act. George Burns used to say to me that with Lucy's great talent anybody would love to have her in their act, so the show was just not believable.

MADELYN DAVIS: This was in the fifties. I would have trouble with that character today, but then I didn't think about it. We wanted to do the norm, all that husband-and-wife stuff. "You never take me anywhere," and "I need a new dress for the party."

Lucy's character developed a little bit over the years, but we were not gonna change her or any of them. We dealt with timeless subjects, which is why it has lasted.

BARBARA BILLINGSLEY: I didn't mind playing June. I was playing the ideal mother. I don't sound as though I had any brains, but it seemed to be a normal family to me. It didn't seem unusual that the woman would be serving breakfast and be there when the kids came home from school.

Sure, there were a lot of working women, but nothing like today. My mother worked, and I was brought up in a one-parent home. Of course that shocks everybody, but I think there was a lot of me in June. My children were surprise guests when I was on a television talk show, and they were asking them about me, and they said, "She's just like June Cleaver."

Being in a dress all the time was the producers' idea. They always wanted us to be the ideal, which meant I had to be dressed, no curlers. They had me wear pearls, which became a symbol, but that started because I have a hollow in my neck, and in those days our film wasn't as good, so the cameramen asked me to wear the pearls because the hollow created a shadow.

ROBERT YOUNG: The Andersons came out of my conversations with Gene about what we thought would be representative of a middle-class American family, if there was such a thing. There probably isn't, but that was what we were looking for.

BILLY GRAY: They got the kind of quality they wanted, but it told people things that they shouldn't hear. On one show, Elinor wants to take a course in civil engineering, but the instructor tells her that a woman's place is in the home. At first, she wants to prove to him that she could be a civil engineer, but the upshot is, in order to suck up to the guy and win him over, she appears in this very feminine, coquettish dress that she has pooh-poohed earlier. She does the feminine wiles things and everybody applauds. It just sucked.

There was another one where the message was just 180 degrees wrong. Lauren plays baseball with her friends, and there is a party and no one has invited her. Mother and Dad say, "Well, you shouldn't dress the way you do. You can't beat 'em up the way you do." Anyway, she comes down the stairs, and she falls and gets all this attention. It turns out it is just a gimmick to be a little girl, and she is applauded for it. Everybody says, "All right, now you're starting to figure out how it works." I mean talk about manipulation, this was big time.

In another show, the parents have a quarrel. I look Father right in the face and ask him if he and Mom were fighting, and he says no. Talk about a bad lesson. It's a scary notion that a family can't fight, that people don't get angry with each other.

JANE WYATT: We had a couple of quarrels. Other families that weren't Anglo-Saxon had much more temperament. We had little undercurrents of things going on all the time between Mom and Dad, not in front of the children of course, but Dad would come around and soothe my ruffled feathers.

ROBERT YOUNG: People did perceive it as real life. I know that. I don't know if people compared themselves unfavorably to us, but maybe it helped with the realization that a family can exist without killing each other.

BILLY GRAY: Whether or not Rodney and Young intended "Father Knows Best" as an example to live by, it has been taken that way. Over the years, people have said to me that they've gained a great deal of sustenance from it somehow. I never understood what they were talking about, but it's had an effect, and I'll be damned if I'm happy about it.

ROBERT YOUNG: The role of Jim as I played it seemed to influence the writers to write more strength into the father role. Originally, the show was supposed to be called "Father Knows Best?" When Scrappy Lambert, our representative, went back to New York, he called and said, "I think we got a deal, but there is a condition. The question mark has to come off."

We said, "Good Lord, that's supposed to be a joke. Who the hell are you talking to? Are they idiots?"

It was supposed to be a jab at Father, who always assumes he is the head of the household, but everybody else knows that Mother is. We thought "Mother Knows Best" would be too obvious, so we called it "Father Knows Best?" but the sponsor, Kent cigarettes, didn't like it. Actually, the deal rested on the question mark coming off.

BILLY GRAY: It doesn't surprise me that a murderous outfit like Kent would want to maintain a father-knows-best gestapo gestalt. Perfect. Later, Scott Paper was our sponsor, but we couldn't show toilet paper on the air, because that would suggest that people had assholes. If they did, they would have to admit that people take shits. The saddest part about it is television is probably the most important invention since movable type.

The incident with the question mark perfectly illustrates the fact that they don't want people questioning authority. Objectively speaking, that is a more important lesson for a child than "Shut up and do what I tell you."

They also didn't want you questioning their commercials. They just want you to buy what they're selling, so they don't want you questioning anything. It's all perfectly logical if the bottom line is your entire consideration.

Remember also that this was the 1950s when the Un-American Activities Committee went berserk and *Brown* versus *the Board of Education* was decided. If you are producing a show that pretends to be a lesson to live by, you drop the ball if you don't at least address some of the problems that are happening in so-

ciety. The fact that there were no blacks anywhere on the show wasn't an accident. We had a Mexican gardener, Frank. He was a caricature. There weren't
any black people on the set, even. Maybe we had a black utility man, who kept
the water cooler filled up.

It was as if we were in a vacuum or some kind of enchanted forest. It wasn't
taking into account the reality of the world. It was just an advertiser's vision of
what the world should be.

JANE WYATT: Integration didn't happen in Springfield [the fictional
setting for the show]. My dentist was born in Minnesota. He said, "There was
one black man, but he just collected the trash, and he lived on the outskirts of
the town. And I'd never seen a Jew in my life." There were places like that. We
were supposed to be in a small town.

MEL DIAMOND: Television was playing a game, and we had to adjust.
We had to make up lines we would never say in real life. We knew what life was
about, but you couldn't say it on television. I'm not just talking about bad
words, I'm talking about mature concepts about how people relate to each
other. I wrote "Bachelor Father," which was truly a show of its time. Bentley Gregg dated all the time, but he wasn't screwing anybody. That was the
big lie.

As a writer, if you had experience and balls, you got neutered very fast.
Harry Crane had his own take on what we did for a living. He used to sing a
little parody of "Love and Marriage," which he called "Lies and Bullshit" and
which was mainly what we did to satisfy the insipid requirements of the advertising agencies, not to mention the imbeciles running the standards and practices departments at the networks.

PAUL PETERSEN: I think, especially today, in the absence of a strong
nuclear family, family shows provide emotional instruction, in a way saying,
"Look, this is a way things can be done correctly."

BILLY GRAY: That goes along with a feeling that I've had for a long
time that this wasn't just accidental that children are brainwashed by society.
Somebody makes a decision what to leave out of a textbook, what lies to spread
to get a docile work force. It ought to be our moral responsibility to make sure
that each child gets a proper education, and if we don't, this is what we get, a
fuckin' cesspool where people are afraid to leave their houses.

MEL DIAMOND: I never came out here to be a rebel. Guys were making a lot of bread, writing all the sitcom crap, and I took the check and gave
them what they wanted.

*   *   *

BARBARA BILLINGSLEY: In the beginning, Jerry didn't need any directing. They just had to tell him where to go. Tony needed a lot. He was not a natural like Jerry, who was unbelievable. He couldn't read a line badly, and he couldn't read, but once he grew up and became self-conscious it all left. If an actor cannot concentrate and is not relaxed, the juices aren't there. When that happened to Jerry, Joe Connelly said, "We have to stop the show. What are you gonna do with a big clunker kid like that?" I was looking forward to the show ending, but soon after it was over, I reminded myself of *Our Town*, and I would have done anything to go back one day and do it all over.

MADELYN DAVIS: "Lucy" was a great combination of our loving to write for her and her appreciating what we wrote. People say, "I want to thank my writers," but they remain nameless. She would give our names. It was the best of circumstances, to be on a show where people valued your scripts, valued your opinion.

ROBERT YOUNG: I was tickled to death about the end of the show. The pressures of TV were quite a strain. Motion pictures were a piece of cake compared to TV.

JANE WYATT: When the show was finished, I was offered one television show after another, but I vowed I would never do it again. They always turned out to be "Mother Knows Best" with a working mother bringing up three children herself.

PAUL PETERSEN: Jeff Stone didn't do me any good when I left the show. This was 1966. A different work environment had begun in Hollywood. It was sex, drugs, rock 'n' roll. It was antiwar. If you stood for anything "American," you were the personification of evil. That hurt because Jeff wasn't me and I wasn't him, and yet the two were inextricably linked, but as years have gone by, I have kind of turned out to be Jeff Stone, a very conservative Republican fellow. I make no apologies for it. I think I'm in the majority, but it's still an unpopular thing to be in Hollywood.

HARRY CRANE: Show business is just like baseball. They're always bringing up young kids. I know theater. I was weaned on E. B. White and Thurber. I can direct. But these kids today at the networks, when I go to a pitch session, before I tell the kid the story I put him on my lap. Larry Gelbart said that's nothing. "Last week I pitched a story to a fetus."

AARON RUBEN: Sheldon Leonard invited me to join a group of old writers for lunch, and it was very pleasant. I came home and my wife said to me, "What do you talk about?"

"Dead writers, dead comics." But you know what's amazing, we're the only ones who can talk about them. Nobody else would know what we're talking about. Ed Wynn. If somebody today doesn't know who Sid Caesar is, who would know Ed Wynn?

I was never a club type of person, but I started to look forward to it. You're talking about a period that's over and done with and about the type of people that you don't see anymore. I'm talking about the giants that we all worked for, Sid Caesar, Phil Silvers, Milton Berle, George Burns, Danny Thomas, Bert Lahr. These were the giants of the century. Who is there today that can be likened to any of them?

AND NOW THE NEWS

Go figure: Edward R. Murrow, whose stance on "See It Now" against Senator Joseph McCarthy is sometimes credited with saving the country, was also responsible for "Person to Person," which legitimized the kind of cheesy entertainment journalism that today seems as dangerous to our system as Tailgunner Joe ever was.

Probably the person least bothered by such irony was Murrow himself. He realized that "Person to Person," which featured him in stilted conversation with the likes of Yogi Berra and Zsa Zsa Gabor, gave him a much wider audience than he ever got on "See It Now." With the higher ratings came more acceptance from the American people. That, of course, was an enormous benefit when it came time to take on McCarthy.

Such is the nature of television where the most banal pictures often carry the same weight as the most important journalistic stories, and where image is more important than reality. It is an issue that troubled historian Daniel J. Boorstin, and led him to write his influential book on media, *The Image*. The book appeared in 1961, not long after the Kennedy-Nixon debates, where the presidency of the United States was in effect decided on the fact that one candidate's skin was more transparent under the lights than the other's (as if answering questions about complicated affairs in two and a half minutes was any indication of presidential ability either). Perhaps Boorstin had that in mind when he wrote, "We are deceived and obstructed by the very machines we make to enlarge our vision."

Pictures have always fascinated people, but televise them and they captivate. Television has created two whole generations of pie-eyed Americans. David Sarnoff predicted it would happen in 1939 when RCA was about to inaugurate its program service. He said:

With the advent of television, the combined emotional results of both seeing and hearing an event or a performance at the instant of its occurrence become new forces

to be reckoned with, and they will be much greater forces than those aroused by au-
dition only. The emotional appeal of pictures to the mass of people is everywhere
apparent. We have only to regard the success of motion pictures, tabloid newspapers,
and modern picture magazines to be convinced of this.

Beginning with CBS in 1941, those who assembled the first TV news programs thought less about the larger issues of television than about the simple
mechanics of putting together a newscast. Producers labored over basic questions about how news was to be gathered and presented, while coping with
daily crises brought on by the infant technology. They did seek through their
limited means to take advantage of television's two-dimensional capabilities.
Maps, stills, and newsreel footage were the best they could do, since the setup
time for live remote equipment curtailed their ability to capture unscheduled
news events and bank robbers did not generally cooperate by phoning in their
expected arrival times.

There wasn't much they could do anyway with the fifteen-minute nightly
newscasts, an indication of the priority network executives assigned to news.
Only ABC, whose president, Robert E. Kintner, was a former newspaperman,
carried a longer show. "All-Star News" was an hour newscast that ran nightly
in prime time and featured not only straight news reporting but also interviews
and discussion. The show, however, was a financial disaster and was replaced
within a year by a fifteen-minute broadcast anchored by John Daly. ABC did
not go to a half-hour show until 1967, four years after NBC and CBS extended
their news programs.

NBC, CBS, and DuMont all had news telecasts after the war. DuMont's
"Walter Compton News," broadcast between New York and Washington, was
the first network news show. CBS, which employed the first regular TV news
anchor, Richard Hubbell, in 1941, did experiment with a variety of different
formats after the war before settling on Douglas Edwards as its anchor in 1948.
NBC's first postwar newscasts were newsreels, spliced together for television by
Paul Alley out of a dingy office on Manhattan's West Side. Alley not only did
the editing but also narrated the show and made the assignments until his operation was finally replaced in 1949 by the "Camel News Caravan," starring
John Cameron Swayze.

NBC's most important news show of the early 1950s wasn't even done under
the auspices of the news department. "Today," which premiered in November
1951, was conceived of by Pat Weaver as a wake-up show called "Rise and
Shine" that would combine news and entertainment. It was a bold move by
Weaver. Most observers doubted that Americans would be interested in watching
a news show at seven A.M. They were right, so the producers teamed host Dave
Garroway with a baby chimp named J. Fred Muggs, and the ratings shot past even
Weaver's expectations. NBC executives could boast all they wanted about "To-

day" offering the latest news, the finest experts, the best pictures, and the most advanced technology, but ultimately it was the antics of an ape that made the program the most successful in the history of television. That said volumes about what Americans were looking for when they turned on their television sets, and Murrow, for one, took heed when he agreed to do "Person to Person."

If "Person to Person" gave Murrow his fame and fortune (he co-owned the show), "See It Now" gave him greatness, even beyond the reputation he earned on London's rooftops during World War II. With the debut of "See It Now" in 1951, television graduated from observer to creator of news. "This is an old team trying to learn a new trade," said Murrow on the first broadcast. That neither he nor his producer, Fred Friendly, knew quite which end of the camera to look into worked to their benefit. They employed the finest newsreel cameramen, who were used to conserving film, and instead instructed them to keep shooting until they got what they needed. The two radio veterans ended the practice of dubbing in audio tracks and instead went for actual sound. They also sent their reporters to the front lines, whether it was in Korea or Washington, without concern for the political or commercial consequences. Murrow and Friendly saw "See It Now" as television's equivalent of Teddy Roosevelt's charge up San Juan Hill. Its two "Christmas in Korea" shows, focusing less on battle footage than on the lives of individual soldiers, brought home the horrors of war in a way never before seen. The cameras revealed not fighting machines, but men and boys, scared, lonely, bored, and above all, human. Jack Gould of *The New York Times* wrote, " 'Christmas in Korea' was a visual poem, one of the finest programs ever seen on television."

But "See It Now" will always be remembered for the Sunday night in 1954 when Murrow put his career on the line against Joseph McCarthy. Friendly and Murrow were well aware of the risks. CBS had thrown in the towel four years before when it required that its employees sign loyalty oaths and blacklisted certain artists it considered to be security risks because of their political beliefs, and while William Paley guaranteed them his support, CBS now refused to pay to advertise the broadcast. Who knew how long Paley's guarantee would last. Yet Murrow was unrelenting in his conclusion:

> . . . We will not be driven by fear into an age of unreason if we dig deep in our history and our doctrine, and remember that we are not descended from fearful men, or from men who feared to write, to speak, to associate, and to defend causes which were for the moment unpopular. . . . We cannot defend freedom abroad by deserting it at home. The actions of the junior senator from Wisconsin have caused alarm and dismay amongst our allies abroad and given considerable comfort to our enemies, and whose fault is that? Not really his, he didn't create the situation of fear, he merely exploited it and rather successfully. Cassius was right, "The fault, dear Brutus, is not in our stars but in ourselves. . . ."

It was the first time television was ever used as a political mallet. The attack was hailed in many quarters, although there was some dissent, surprisingly, from liberal commentators. Gilbert Seldes and Jack Gould of *The New York Times* sided with Murrow, but they expressed concern about turning television loose to silence a political voice. "In the long run, it is more important to use our communications system properly than to destroy McCarthy," wrote Seldes. Gould went even further:

> It is difficult to see how Mr. Murrow could have done other than he did without abandoning his and television's journalistic integrity . . . but what was frightening about Mr. Murrow's broadcast . . . was . . . what if the camera and microphone should fall into the hands of a reckless and demagogic commentator?

McCarthy took another bashing from the television cameras that spring, but this time he was hoist by his own petard. The Army–McCarthy hearings were televised live by ABC and DuMont. On June 9, after McCarthy attacked the patriotism of a lawyer, Fred Fisher, the Army's counsel Joseph Welch brought a burst of applause from the hearing room, and no doubt around the country, when he asked the now-historic question, "Have you no sense of decency, sir, at long last? Have you no sense of decency?"

McCarthy had little decency and even less understanding of television. The man who used the cameras so skillfully to engineer his rise to power forgot that the lens that made him could just as easily break him, and it did. If "See It Now" caused many Americans to examine their consciences, the Army–McCarthy hearings made it clear that this was a man who didn't play fair. Emboldened by the shift of popular opinion, the Senate censured him in December. Three years later he was dead.

But Murrow didn't emerge from the McCarthy program unscathed either. After the broadcast, "See It Now," which had operated as an independent unit within the company, was deemed too dangerous to remain that way. When Murrow was granted rare interviews with Yugoslav President Tito and China's premier Chou En Lai, CBS demanded that their words be counteracted by panel discussions on the dangers of communism. After a "See It Now" report on farm foreclosures, CBS took another slap at Murrow when it gave the Secretary of Agriculture, Ezra Taft Benson, a half hour of free time to rail against Democratic agricultural policies.

Murrow ran out of cheeks in 1958 after CBS offered up its cameras to a crackpot Southern congressman named John Pillon following a program on statehood for Alaska and Hawaii. Pillon contended that Hawaiian statehood would guarantee congressional seats to the Communist Party because of the alleged influence on the islands of Harry Bridges, the West Coast head of the National Maritime Union. That was too much for Murrow, who resigned from "See It Now," and the show, which had garnered three Peabodys, four Emmys, and every other major television award, was canceled.

Its death did not, however, signal an end to documentary film-making on television. Quite the opposite. From the beginning, "See It Now" was a boon for TV documentarians. Reuven Frank remembers "See It Now" 's debut causing NBC executives to wonder, ". . . why we weren't doing things like that. A new question was heard in the corridor of 30 Rockefeller Plaza: 'Who is, where is, our answer to Murrow?' "

There were no more Murrows to go around, but both networks produced excellent documentary programs. NBC's "Victory at Sea," the story of U.S. Naval operations during World War II, was a mammoth effort presided over by Henry "Pete" Salomon, a former student of the historian Samuel Eliot Morrison. Salomon and his staff took two years to edit some sixty million feet of film into twenty-six half-hour programs, which aired over the 1951–52 seasons.

Another early NBC effort was "Battle Report," a quasi-government-sponsored examination of the Cold War in Europe. The twin newsmen, Charlie and Eugene Jones, who had been the first TV cameramen to go to Korea, were then virtually the only American television crew on the Continent at the time. Only twenty-five years old, they interviewed nearly every major head of state and snared some of the biggest scoops of the year for the program.

NBC's "Wide, Wide World" was less a documentary than a live news magazine show. It was hosted by Dave Garroway, although the real stars were NBC's technical crews, which beamed home live pictures of everything from a rocket being launched to skiing in Switzerland.

CBS's documentary unit thrived under the leadership of Irving Gitlin. In 1956, Albert Wasserman produced and directed "Out of Darkness," one of the most stunning films ever aired on TV. Using a hidden camera, the documentary followed a catatonic woman through intensive therapy. The movie came to a climactic end when the woman spoke her first words in many months.

The documentary series "CBS Reports" was born out of twin public relations disasters that befell the network, the demise of "See It Now" and the quiz scandals brought on in part by CBS's "The $64,000 Question." No matter the network's motive, the new series, produced by Fred Friendly, aired a number of honored documentaries. "Biography of a Bookie Joint" was a landmark investigative report about a bookmaking establishment in Boston that operated with police protection out of a key shop on Commonwealth Avenue. Over several months, CBS cameras from a window across the street watched thousands of people enter and depart from the store. To clinch the report, producer Jay McMullen, using a camera hidden inside his lunch box, entered the store and placed bets himself. To its credit, the documentary looked beyond such dramatic footage to trace the business to a network of organized crime operating nationwide.

The most celebrated documentary in the series, and of all TV documentaries, was David Lowe's "Harvest of Shame." Aired on the day after Thanksgiving, 1960, this searing look at the plight of a group of migrant farmworkers—narrated by Murrow in one of his last appearances for CBS—was television's most impassioned hour. As powerful as it was, the film had little effect on legislation, the growers' lobby being too strong, and for once demonstrated television's limitations. Since the original broadcast of "Harvest of Shame," CBS has produced two follow-up documentaries. Both clearly show that despite public awareness of the problem, the workers' situation is generally unchanged.

The week "Harvest of Shame" was broadcast, NBC brought out the first documentary in its new series, "NBC White Paper." After ten years of trying to find another Murrow, NBC apparently decided the best way to beat CBS was to hire its rival's top documentary talent, so in 1960, Irv Gitlin and Albert Wasserman arrived at 30 Rock to assemble a top-flight documentary unit. As for Murrow, he left CBS in 1961, but not before firing a warning shot at the medium in a speech before the Radio and Television News Directors. His words still resonate with truth today:

> . . . I do not advocate that we turn television into a twenty-seven-inch wailing wall where longhairs constantly moan about the state of our culture and our defense. But I would just like to see it reflect occasionally the hard, unyielding realities of the world in which we live. . . . This instrument can teach, it can illuminate: yes, and it can even inspire. But it can do so only to the extent that humans are determined to use it to those ends. Otherwise, it is merely wires and lights in a box.

Murrow moved on to briefly head the United States Information Agency, under President John F. Kennedy. There, he stunned his former colleagues when, under pressure from the government, he attempted to prevent the BBC from broadcasting "Harvest of Shame." It was an unfortunate end to a brilliant career.

HARRY AROUH: I'll never forget the first time I heard the radio. I was a little boy in New Brunswick, New Jersey. One afternoon, my father came home from the store in the truck. We all ran toward him, because we weren't accustomed to seeing him during the day. He said, "I have a surprise for you."

He opened up the back of the truck and pulled out a wooden box. We wrestled it up the stairs to our apartment. When we opened it up, there was this glistening piece of furniture on four spindly legs. He said we now had a radio. I didn't know what that was. He plugged it into the wall. At first we didn't get anything but lots of weird noises. Finally, he got someone speaking. I was flabbergasted. I asked him where is this person doing this talking.

"He's in New York."

"Are we the only ones who can hear what he's saying?"

"No, anybody who has a radio can hear him."

I wanted to be the person whose voice is heard everywhere. I listened to the news all day long. I thought H. V. Kaltenborn and Lowell Thomas were wonderful. Then I learned that they were also writing that stuff. My teachers had always told me to be a writer. My heart told me to be a broadcaster. Here was a field where I could do both.

HENRY CASSIRER: I was working for the BBC when I met Ed Murrow. He gave me an introduction to Davidson Taylor at CBS. He hired me to work for their shortwave listening station, translating foreign languages into English.

CBS had a big problem in that the news services didn't want radio to use their stories, so CBS had to set up its own news sources. That was when Paul White put together the great network of newsmen and commentators, headed up by Murrow. I got my whole education at CBS from White and the others.

HARRY AROUH: There was William Shirer, Elmer Davis, and H. R. Baukhage. I loved those voices, but nothing had ever equaled what Murrow was doing. There was no such thing as covering a story live from overseas with the bombs bursting in the background. His style was impeccable, his words stark and simple. He told the story without emotion. Everyone talks about Walter Cronkite being the most believable man. In those days it was Murrow and only Murrow whom you could believe.

HENRY CASSIRER: In the glamorous culture of America, Ed Murrow was the great man, but to me it was Paul White. He had the vision as to what was needed to make CBS News the top news organization. He created the roundup at eight o'clock in the morning, when you got the correspondents worldwide live on radio. Nobody else could match that. It was the equivalent of what we have today with satellite programming.

When I picked up the German invasion of Russia on the shortwave, the *Times* on its front page announced it "as picked up by CBS." This was a great achievement for CBS because people realized the top news comes from CBS and not CBS picking up the top news. Also, it wasn't NBC.

ROBERT SKEDGELL: I was working as a copyboy in the spring of '41 when Paul asked me, "Would you like to go down to Grand Central and write for television?"

"Sure, what is it?" He didn't know much about it, but he explained they were starting this experimental station, and I guess they wanted a young kid they didn't have to pay very much. Starting in July, we did two fifteen-minute shows a day, one at two-thirty, one at seven-thirty, and I would write the copy.

The newsroom was a tiny area separated from the rest of the office by a wooden stairway. All we had was two desks, a couple of filing cabinets, and a United Press Radio machine. I would show Gilbert Seldes my copy. One time I showed him what I wrote, "President Roosevelt claimed . . . ," and he said, "Mr. Skedgell, presidents don't claim, they state."

The set consisted of three huge maps on swivels. Dick Hubbell had a desk in front of the main map bay. He would perch himself on the edge of the desk with a pointer in one hand and his copy in the other. Sometimes, they would put stills on an easel and bring the camera in. We had no film and we couldn't switch anywhere.

On December 7, I was in my apartment listening to the symphony when I heard John Daly break in. I got dressed and ran up Park Avenue. We got on the air around three-thirty and stayed on until one-thirty Monday morning broadcasting news and interviewing guests. It was the first live instant special.

The next day we had Roosevelt's "day that will live in infamy" speech fed into the studio. We didn't have any visual, so Rudy Bretz put an American flag up with a large fan behind it so it would wave in the breeze. That was our visual.

HENRY CASSIRER: I first heard of CBS-TV through Ned Calmer, who was doing a news show for them in 1944. There was no TV news department. We only put on one fifteen-minute show a week. Nobody took it seriously, but I knew my own job at shortwave was going to stop after the war, and I was looking for something. I was hired to help with the news and work on graphics.

RUDY BRETZ: Occasionally we put maps on the floor, and a guy would walk across it and point with a stick. You can do a lot on the floor, which is part of the camera's view anyway. If it's just blank it's wasted. Very rarely do they use it now.

Back then the news shows were actually more complicated than today's news productions. We had still pictures on easels, film segments, a large studio map, and live commentary. There could be some real foul-ups. One show was just terrible. Instead of changing just one card on the easel, the stagehand pulled the whole stack of them off while the camera was on the air, leaving nothing but the easel. The next story was a film piece, and they cut to that, but a splice broke on the film. By then, the stagehand got the cards back, but he put them in the wrong order. The announcer was just reading his copy. The next story was about a funeral in New York, but the announcer was reading about demonstrations in Germany.

Then, the director tried to just go to a shot of the newscaster reading his copy, forgetting about any more pictures and film. But at the point the announcer was supposed to walk over to a map. The director had set up the cameras to shoot in on him sitting there, so when the announcer got up he walked right off the picture.

Generally, all this elaborate stuff kept the face of the announcer pretty much out of there. We wanted to avoid having the newscaster's face on TV. We figured that the commentator was secondary to the news itself.

HENRY CASSIRER: One question we had to solve was, is TV a replica of radio? Of the newsreel? The newsreel did the spectacular, the fire and the fashion shows. That wasn't real news, but it was something people looked for. The anchor's role was a part of this. We had a notion that television news was visual; radio news was personal. We didn't realize until later that people are the most telegenic material in television.

PAUL ALLEY: I came to television from newsreels. One day I read in the paper that NBC had acquired the Army Signal Corps films. I called up John Royal and said, "What are ya gonna do with 'em?"

They didn't know, so I just walked in and created the job. We put on a news show called "The War as It Happens." The show ran whenever we got film. I wrote the copy, directed the editing, did the narration, and picked the background music. I was called "Alley, The One-Man Newsroom." Eventually, we had film crews in Washington and on the Coast and in Texas.

GERALD GREEN: They were still on staff when I joined a few years later. These were newsreel guys who were always covering things like an elephant on water skis and the fattest man in the world going to the bathroom. There was Bill Burch in Chicago and Harry Walsh in Miami, who covered the bathing beauties and was great on crotch shots.

EUGENE "GENE" JONES: People tend to denigrate them as just Lew Lehr and the dancing bear on the surfboard, but actually the caliber of these cameramen with their ponderous equipment was excellent. That's why Fred Friendly hired Hearst cameramen for "See It Now."

My Dad was a foreign correspondent and later the editor of various distinguished newspapers. He died when my twin brother Charlie and I were kids. By the time Charlie and I were seventeen, in the 1940s, we were covering FDR's White House as photojournalists for Washington papers, but we didn't intend to be cameramen for long. We always intended to be foreign correspondents like our father. During the war, we enlisted in the Marines as combat photographers.

In 1947, we saw our first television set. There was a bar/restaurant adjacent to the *Times-Herald* called the Showboat. The owners had a television on the bar. At six o'clock, there was a regular news program. This was news that talked as well as moved, and we were mesmerized. We were convinced this was the future. Newsreel footage sometimes wouldn't get into the theaters for five days. Here, film could be shot and seen the same day.

On our days off from the paper, we began to shoot out-of-town stories for the local NBC station. We would go on a train or bus or sometimes chartered a plane to take us to some disaster, like a flood or a plane crash. Sometimes, it would take us eight hours getting to these stories and another eight hours getting back.

We often came back hungry and covered with dirt, having slept in anything from trucks to freight cars. Bob McCormick of NBC paid us seventy-five dollars a story, which in no way covered our expenses, but we practically would have given him the footage just for the thrill of getting it on the air.

BOB DOYLE: I was newswriter at the NBC station in Washington when David Brinkley was the bureau chief for about three months, the worst bureau chief that anybody ever had. I'd ask him what I should do, and he'd say, "I don't know. Go to Fourteenth and New York and interview the cop."

"What about?"

"I don't know."

He gave up that job very soon.

MARTIN HOADE: When I came out of the Army in 1945, Paul Alley was then doing his three fifteen-minute shows a week out at Ninth Avenue and Forty-fifth Street, which was like Siberia. Anyone who wanted to move up wanted nothing to do with that place, mostly because of Paul, but I got assigned there.

ARTHUR LODGE: Paul was a miserable son of a bitch. He used to show nude pictures of his wife.

MARTIN HOADE: We had three cameramen. If there was a fire in town, you'd say to Joe Vadala or Harry Turgander or Santino Sozio, "There's a fire at Fourteenth Street and Ninth Avenue, chase out." We didn't even have our own cars, we'd have to take taxis.

GERALD GREEN: Sozio was a little fat Italian with a white mustache. He looked like Toscanini. Actually, he knew Toscanini. He used to talk of seeing him coming off the ships, and when the cameramen bothered him too much, Toscanini would yell out, *"Non mi rompere i coglioni."* Don't break my balls.

MARTIN HOADE: Those old guys were extraordinary. I remember we got one guy to cover the American Legion parade. He takes out a satchel with his camera. He has it resting on his chest with the eyepiece, and he's cranking, and I said, "Oy, gevalt." I found a public phone, and I said, "Paul, this guy's cranking this thing. I need twenty-four frames a second."

Paul said not to worry about it, and when I developed the film, that hand crank was as steady at twenty-four frames a second as if it were run by a motor.

There was great animus directed against us from the newsreel people. I covered the HUAC hearings. Inside the hearing room, the tripods were set up in such a way that there was no room for mine, so I complained to the chairman,

J. Parnell Thomas. He said, "Well, those newsreel cameramen have been here for years."

I said, "They're gonna shoot this today, and it will be in the theaters in two days. If I shoot this it will be on the air tonight, and the stories are longer." All of the sudden there was space for another tripod in the room.

CHESTER BURGER: I went to work for CBS television after the war. The two guys running the news operation were Leo Hurwitz and Henry Cassirer. They hired me as a "visualizer," to add visuals to stories that they didn't know how to report with pictures, like complex economic stories. How do you present them visually?

Henry was a scholarly, thoughtful man. He wanted to use the media to develop a real understanding of complicated issues, and he encouraged me to dig out unusual thoughtful stories and figure out ways of showing them.

We had one film crew, Larry Racies and a technician. After a while, Henry and Leo began sending me out with them just to facilitate the story. I would interview people. We didn't have sound, so I would write the script when I got back, quoting what the person said. In a sense, I was the first television reporter.

HENRY CASSIRER: Once we realized we had to use an announcer on camera, we had trouble finding someone who was suitable. There was a notion that a journalist was a hard-driving white man. The anchor person would have to be sensitive to others, he would have to be able to interview, have a certain warmth, and be able to relate to the audience. He would have to have enough knowledge to be able to deal with a range of subjects.

CHESTER BURGER: Should it be a man of authority? Should it be a working journalist? None of the CBS radio news stars wanted to have anything to do with television. We tried a sportswriter named Stan Smith a few times, but he didn't go over. We tried an older man with a beard, thinking he would be a symbol of authority.

HENRY CASSIRER: The person we were looking for couldn't be the boss; he had to work with the team. Teamwork was really the key on television as opposed to radio, where a man could do a whole broadcast by himself. Radio people weren't used to that.

CHESTER BURGER: Doug Edwards was from radio, but he was so unpretentious and so pleasant that he went over very well right away. He didn't regard television as slumming as the others from radio did.

HENRY CASSIRER: He wasn't a brilliant man; we didn't want a brilliant man. We wanted a man who was likable and steady, who could fit into a team and not impose himself. That was Edwards.

BOB DOYLE: At NBC in Washington, we used Bob McCormick for a while. He was one of the best newsmen I ever knew, but he got fatter and fatter, and they didn't like that. We also tried Richard Harkness and Morgan Beatty, who were two of the most popular radio newsmen of the day. Harkness was scared to death of the camera. Beatty had that magnificent voice and presence, but he was too much of an idiot to work in television. Eventually, Brinkley got it.

CHESTER BURGER: After a while, I began pressing the engineering department to develop more portability with the sound equipment. Then a camera called the Auricon came in. It was the first sixteen-millimeter sound camera. When Truman was president, he often came to New York and stayed at the Waldorf. Every day he would go for a walk up Park Avenue. With our new portability, we were able to mount the camera on the roof of a station wagon, and film him walking down the street talking to people. The first night we had it on the air, it was a sensation in the industry. It was a real technical landmark.

BOB DOYLE: Because I knew Truman so well, I was the one who had to walk into the Oval Office and tell him he had to leave so we could set up for a speech. The others would say, "You tell him. You're his fair-haired boy."

It took all day to set up. I once blew out all the power in the White House with Eisenhower and Dulles. Here's the difference between Truman and Eisenhower. After I blew all the power, I went up to Ike's press secretary Jim Hagerty, and I said, "I don't think we're going to get on. You better tell the president."

"You tell him."

So I went up to where he was sitting next to Dulles, and I said, "Mr. President, there's a chance we might not get on."

He stared at me for ten seconds and said, "Get on."

Truman would have said, "What's the trouble? Can I help you? Where's the electrician?"

GENE JONES: Truman used to refer to Charlie and me as "my twins." There was no b.s. with him at all. He was marvelous with the camera crews. We were members of his "One More Club," because we would always be saying, "One more, Mr. President." He had laminated membership cards printed up for us.

✳   ✳   ✳

BOB BENDICK: The '48 political year was a turning point in the history of communications, especially in terms of the political conventions. I got a great deal of satisfaction from being in charge of the three conventions that year for CBS. We competed with radio, with newsreels, and we came out ahead.

At CBS, the sponsors had no control at all. You had such a strong news organization. All our decisions were made within the normal CBS television group, or the correspondents.

ANDREW HEISKELL: I was then the publisher of *Life*. For me, the conventions had been very exciting on radio. I thought, "Wouldn't it be fun to be associated with that on television?" Using television was like consorting with the enemy. Television *was* a threat, but if a medium has a big future and you don't use it, you're hanging yourself instead of letting somebody hang you. So I made a deal with NBC for maybe $100,000. Then a couple of days before the convention, one of the NBC people said, "What do you want to do?"

That literally meant, "What *do* you want to do?" I had total control, even though it was the last thing I wanted, but bit by bit, I found myself saying to the technicians, "Maybe we can do this. Maybe we can do that."

DAVID LEVY: They were called the Life/NBC conventions not NBC/Life. We were on morning, noon, and night. I was there with Young & Rubicam, *Life*'s ad agency. Together, we created all the programs that went on and shared the decision making.

NOEL JORDAN: If Time/Life had not been involved, we would have done the same things, but we would not have done them half as well. They had all the contacts. They could get hold of Vandenberg's headquarters or Dewey's people. Still, NBC News by no means relinquished control of the news. Everything was done with the approval of NBC News. Frank McCall and Ad Schneider from NBC were there all the time.

Heiskell says their people said to the "technicians": "Why don't we do this?" Well, you can't do all that stuff in ten minutes, or ten hours. Starting that March, I went down with three engineers and we plotted all this stuff out, long before *Time* was in the picture. We were very concerned that the conventions might be dull, so to keep it moving we set up power lines into all the headquarters and other key locations in Philadelphia.

ANDREW HEISKELL: I remember saying, "You mean we've got a camera in Washington and we can use it?"

"Why not?"

So we had Truman getting onto the train, Truman getting out at Baltimore, and then arriving at the station in Philadelphia. That was incredibly dramatic then.

BOB BENDICK: It was tough convincing the radio people to come on television, because radio was more important than TV.

LARRY LESUEUR: Also, doing television was hell. We had to carry these heavy packs, and there was no air-conditioning, so you melted under the lights. They were always powdering your face and putting eyebrows on you, although that was okay after a while because some pretty girl did the makeup.

MARTIN HOADE: I had an argument with Governor Dewey, because even though he had a heavy beard, he resisted makeup. He said, "Well, has Senator Taft consented to using makeup?"

You were some kind of a fairy if you used makeup, and if Taft wasn't going to use it he wasn't going to either.

ANDREW HEISKELL: Whenever I got bored I switched to something else. Nobody ever said, "Hey, you can't cut off the main speaker." All the big mucky-mucks from NBC would just come by and leave, like, "Look at the animals performing," and we were the animals.

HENRY CASSIRER: All the CBS bosses were down there, but all they were interested in was "The Ed Sullivan Show," which started during the convention. For them that was the future.

CBS News got a sponsor after the convention, Oldsmobile, and things changed. Ed Chester, who was the head of CBS, told us, "Don't criticize the military. General Motors produces materiel for the armed forces." That shocked us, but we became more careful about our stories. Also, Larry Lowman criticized me for pitching the news too high. He said, "You've got to pitch it to a fourteen-year-old boy in Texas."

I didn't do it, but I couldn't argue with him. It was the audience rating breathing on our neck.

Then, on the night of the election, Ed Chester took me around the shoulder, and he said, "Henry, sorry to say this on a night that you did such a good job, but we have decided to put Larry Haas in your place."

I was told that Chester wanted to give his buddy my job, but it was also that I was a man of the left, and they didn't trust me. They also let me go because I refused to tailor the news to a fourteen-year-old boy.

BOB BENDICK: Henry and Leo were heavy-minded fellows, and their news was heavy-handed, while we wanted to get more visuals into stories. Around that time, Don Hewitt was hired. Don was a kid with a lot of razzmatazz. He understood visuals. Actually, he was something of a madman, but he had an innate sense of entertainment, and he made the news more dramatic and commercial.

DON HEWITT: When I first walked into the studio at Grand Central, I felt like Judy Garland in the Emerald City. There were cameras, booms, and lights. "Holy shit, this is like Hollywood."

The director was Fred Rickey. The show was only on three nights a week then. I remember Fred saying to me, "You couldn't do this five nights a week. You'll kill yourself."

Fred smoked like crazy. On my first broadcast, I was sitting next to him when in his excitement he dropped a lighted cigarette in my pocket. I'm trying to follow the script and I'm pounding my coat, trying to put out the fire in my suit, while he's yelling, "Follow the script!"

"My suit's on fire!"

"The hell with your suit. Follow the script!"

I said, "Fuck this place. These guys are crazy." But as time went on, I got a reputation of being crazier than they were. CBS was full of academic elitists. I brought in the Hildy Johnson "Kill 'im, kill 'im, kill 'im." I realized that out there were cops, firemen, and homemakers. I've always had a genuine affection for Kiwanis and Rotarians, "the people." I like "the people." We were trying to reach the mass audience. This was BROADcasting. You reach the lowest common denominator. The trick is to do that without losing your soul.

BOB BENDICK: Don can talk about going tabloid, but he was not his own boss in terms of what went into the news. There was an overview that kept it within the Murrow tradition.

MARTIN HOADE: After the convention, it was decided that NBC could do on television what we do on radio—a daily hard news report that wasn't just tits-and-ass like the newsreels.

ARTHUR LODGE: Still, to cover the world with cameras would be very expensive. Camel wanted to do a show five nights a week. The Esty Agency got NBC and CBS competing with each other over the account. NBC already had Paul Alley's "Camel Newsreel Theatre," which gave us a leg up, so they stayed with us, and we started the "Camel News Caravan."

REUVEN FRANK: One of the first things they did was fire Paul Alley. He originally went on the air because nobody cared who went on. He was most famous mostly for his expense accounts. When he ran the news, it was small time. Now, those days were over.

MARTIN HOADE: Now, we needed an announcer. We had John McVane, who had a show out of the United Nations, but if Christ was coming down the Jersey Turnpike, John would lead with a story out of East Gambia. Bill Brooks, who was vice president for news, said, "It's either him or Swayze."

So Swayze came aboard. I'll tell you how hand-to-mouth we were. The guy worked out of like an electric closet. In there he had his toupee. He'd spend more time in there on his toupee than he did with the crew. He did everything you asked him to do, but he was not a congenial man. What none of us had really cottoned on to was that his face and his connection to the people would be important as what he was reading.

REUVEN FRANK: Swayze was known for his photographic memory. There were always two gaps to fill in the broadcast, and for those, he memorized the leads of major stories we weren't covering. We called that "hop-scotching the world for headlines."

ARTHUR LODGE: He liked to portray himself as a brain by giving that two-minute spiel from memory, but he spent all his time memorizing those goddamned two minutes. He had no interest in anything else. He wouldn't even see the film before the show. He was more concerned about whether his toupee was on straight. How can you be involved with the first news program and not give a shit about what goes out over the air?

CHESTER BURGER: He was a gladhander. "Everything is great in the world" kind of thing. That wouldn't go today, because expectations of what the anchorperson should be have changed. Then, nobody knew what would go over best. I thought the anchor was a guest in someone's home, which means you don't yell. You talk intimately. The newsmen—as well as the politicians—who learned that, were the most successful.

GERALD GREEN: Before I joined NBC, I was working for the INS, the "Unintentional News Service." It was a terrible, pinch-penny, ass-dragging organization. We stole everything from the *Times*. One of the rewrite men, James Powers, sent me to Art Lodge. They were both from Minnesota, and they even looked alike, tall, skinny, wonderful guys. Art hired me right away.

REUVEN FRANK: Jerry invited me up and introduced me to Lodge. He hired me right away. Later, I asked him why he hired me. He said Jerry had told him I must be good because I could type faster than he could.

GERALD GREEN: Arthur Holch had come out of NBC radio. He was our main newswriter.

ARTHUR HOLCH: I was a twenty-five-year-old kid, and it was exciting just to be there. If you could drink two martinis at lunch and come back and put the show together and feel fine, it must have been exciting.

REUVEN FRANK: The guy in charge was Frank McCall. He was smart, but he had no feeling for television. He admitted openly that all he had to do was hang on until he got a pension. Ad Schneider was McCall's number-one guy. He was often at these lunches we had once a week at Garrah's. These people used to drink something called a "Torpedo." I had one once and couldn't work the rest of the day, but they carried on the tradition of the drinking newspaperman.

BOB DOYLE: There was constant drinking. In New York, it was at either Hurley's on West Forty-ninth Street or Healey's on West Fifty-fifth Street. The Murrow group were all pretty heavy drinkers, too. Ed was. Hurley's even had a phone with a direct line to the studio.

ARTHUR HOLCH: Generally, after a couple of martinis, you would go back and look at the wires and decide what stories we could do that day.

REUVEN FRANK: Maybe NBC didn't have the Murrow gang, but we did have correspondents everywhere they did and we were better at switching and getting direct reports.

GERALD GREEN: We had a better show, but we didn't have a better news program. There was very little news anyway in a fifteen-minute newscast, but they at least tried to cover the news with their talking heads. The whole dispute in TV news back then was talking heads bad, head cracking, as we used to call it, good. People getting beat up on the street was great. We used to sit in that screening room with Lodge and Reuven Frank, "Look, they're beating somebody up. Get a minute of it!" But Murrow or Collingwood in London talking about an important vote in Parliament that day was no good.

NBC felt you should be like *Life.* They led with great film because it was great film. It was a more interesting show to watch, and it steadily outdrew CBS, but in telling the news it just didn't get the job done.

REUVEN FRANK: The big difference at CBS was that Paley got his rocks off with the news. His ego was appealed to by being seen around town with Ed Murrow. Sarnoff did not have a smaller ego than Paley, but it got expressed with the NBC Symphony and Toscanini. News was supported. Sarnoff fought off sponsors who tried to interfere, but the kind of cachet the news got at CBS was always denied at NBC until Robert Kintner came along.

ARTHUR LODGE: It was a terrible thing to get film on the air. Let's say an airplane crashed in Dallas, Texas, early in the day. If the cameraman got pictures, depending on the network situation, it might be originated out there or sent here. We had to figure out airline schedules. Then, we had motorcycle couriers at the airports to get the film from the stewardess or the pilot.

You got the lab to turn down all other business and stand by with the machines all threaded up and ready to go. They'd slap the film on there and edit it quickly. The film editor sometimes would tear the film with his teeth.

We would then write the script, put it in the can, and start a mad dash down Park Avenue in a red jeepster. We'd get to the RCA Building, and they'd be holding an elevator. "Here it comes through!" It was like gangbusters every night of the week. Sometimes we wouldn't make it.

ARTHUR HOLCH: We had a feature bank just in case. One story was called the "Blue Baby." It never went off the list. The line was, "We're gonna have to run the 'Blue Baby' tonight."

REUVEN FRANK: When it came to deciding what got on, Camel had certain taboos. You could not use a NO SMOKING sign. You could not show a picture of a camel. To them a camel is not a stinking animal, it's a cigarette. You could not use anybody smoking a cigar. I got the rule changed for Churchill. He was probably the most famous living human being, and every time you took a picture of him he had a cigar. Camel said okay, but that was it. I couldn't use Groucho Marx.

ARTHUR HOLCH: You could not mention cancer, any cancer. If a person died of cancer, it was "of a long illness."

ARTHUR LODGE: The show always ended with a triangular ashtray with a cigarette burning.

REUVEN FRANK: The ashtray said "Camel." Sometimes there was a carton in the background.

GERALD GREEN: Camel had a special Christmas box. There was a typical agency guy whose job it was to set up this can of cigarettes with a sufficient number poking out. He would poke the cigarettes and study it, and then poke a few more. He was there one day setting up the commercial when he says to Reuven, "I'm not gonna be here next week. I got a promotion."

"Oh, yeah, what are you gonna be doing?"

"Same as here, producing shows."

$*$ $*$ $*$

GERALD GREEN: We were slaves to film in those days. Some of the feature film from overseas was really old. In Damascus an Islamic fundamentalist group got the shit beat out of them by the cops, and there was great film of guys being hit on the head. That film had no relevance to anything, yet there was a compulsion on the part of NBC to get it on the air, so you'd concoct a lead. You'd find something in the AP budget that said, "Israel rejects Syrian claim to border villages," and you'd say, "Israel today firmly rejected any Syrian protests about . . . ," et cetera, "as a consequence of which there was rioting," and up would come these guys getting banged on the head. We were still a newsreel operation to a great extent.

ARTHUR LODGE: The Joneses thought differently than most of the old-time newsreel cameramen. They figured that covering the war meant getting up to the front line and shooting the troops coming at you. They sent back some spectacular footage. One sequence they shot was dive-bombing, which they shot from over the pilot's shoulder.

GENE JONES: Three or four days after the Korean War erupted, we called McCormick at his home and asked him to set up a meeting with Schneider and McCall. They were aware I had just been nominated for a Pulitzer Prize at *The Washington Post* and Charlie, at the *Times Herald*, had won many White House News Association awards. They also knew of our citations as marines at Iwo Jima five years earlier and reviewed all those freelance stories we sent to the network. What really appealed to them was our determination to focus on combat in Korea using the absolute minimum of film, editing in the camera so that each story we sent back would be a complete entity, virtually ready for telecast. Charlie told them we both would probably be wounded. McCormick just grinned and said, "No need to ice the cake, laddie. We've decided to hire you— and besides, no one else wants to go." They said they could pay us each a hundred dollars a week, no expense money and no insurance for death or injury. Before we left, Ad Schneider equipped us with spring-wound recorders so we could also make radio spots for NBC. He told us, "Go out there and cover the war as you see fit, but we'll fire you immediately if the coverage isn't what we want." At age twenty-four, it was a dream assignment for us. We grabbed it.

In Korea, we never had any instructions from NBC. We just went where we knew we had to go. Occasionally, messages from NBC got through to us. They would be weeks old and smudged from being passed hand to hand, but they were filled with appreciative words, and we treasured them.

We decided to be right at the point of impact on the front line, to put our cameras on their faces, their trigger fingers, their tensed bodies, rather than taking the typical panorama shots. It's no different shooting combat than filming anything else, other than one basic factor: the considerable probability that you are going to get wounded or killed. It is impossible to film for a protracted period closeup and not get wounded.

Generally during combat, because the cameraman wants to save his life and has a still camera, he pops up, takes a picture, and drops down. We went with movie cameras, where you've got to rise up out of your hole for a take of generally five to eight seconds while somebody is taking shots at you. We did it with teeth clenched and hearts in our throat every goddamned minute expecting lead to lance into us, and, of course, it did eventually, and it hurts like hell. There's no sense of bravado. You're grinding your molars and a small cold voice is saying, "You've got enough. Drop down and go back."

We never knew from one moment to the next if we would be pounced upon by an enemy force. There was a bounty on Americans in those early days, and there was a sense of terror in the air. We were in the midst of what was a continuous retreat for the first five or six weeks of the war. There were no front lines. We had to run into the hills and sometimes hide for two or three days until we saw what we thought was an American vehicle, then frantically run down through the brush, waving at these people, who were often lost and bewildered themselves.

We lived most of the time like animals. We were covered with slime from crawling through rice paddies, exhausted from hiking over mountains carrying everything we had on our backs. We were hungry all the time. Sometimes, we rooted turnips and cabbage out of the fields and wolfed them down on the move. What little sleep we had was in foxholes within grenade range of the enemy or in roadside ditches.

It seemed that we were perpetually under fire. You would be talking to a man beside you and suddenly his face would be drilled by bullets.

Getting the film back to New York wasn't a problem. The Air Force had Piper Cubs as observation planes landing on dirt roads just in back of the front. You would throw a package of film into the plane, and it was immediately flown to the rear. Then it would be hand-carried to a plane that would take it back to Tokyo where the bureau chief quickly sent it on to San Francisco and then New York. The film would be aired about three or four days after it was shot.

We sent in an average of three hundred to five hundred feet every five days, which was maybe about ten minutes of viewing. We were desperate for film. We brought in twenty thousand feet of film, and received a few thousand more during our five-month stay. NBC sent additional film, but it never got through.

Charlie and I were the only journalists who requested to be with the first assault wave of Marines at Inchon. Only one of us was permitted to go, and I won the coin toss. I scrambled out of the Amtrac with shells screaming over me like flaming meteors. I ran inland, ducking and weaving, and as I turned to shoot some Marines behind me, a mortar burst nearby. The shrapnel sliced into my side and my stomach. Somehow I crawled toward the sea, dragging the camera along with me. It took me about a half hour before a frogman spotted me and dragged me into a boat, which took me to the hospital ship.

The next day, Lemuel Shepherd, commander of the Pacific Marines, and Carl Mydans, the *Life* photographer, saw me and assured me they would get word to Charlie, who had already been told I was dead. Carl also made sure the film was sent back to New York, although he couldn't resist adding a note saying, "This film found on the body of Gene Jones."

Two days later, I awoke to find Charlie asleep beneath my bunk. His nursing saved my life. We returned to the United States that fall. Soon he left to cover the attack on Seoul, where he was wounded, but later we parachuted thirty-eight miles into North Korea on a POW rescue mission. Then NBC said they wanted us in Europe, and we left Korea.

※   ※   ※

GERALD GREEN: In November '51, Frank McCall asked me to go on the "Today" show, which was being formed and needed someone with a strong news background. In the beginning, "Today" was run by disk jockeys. Garroway and Jack Lescoulie were disk jockeys. Mort Werner, the producer, and Joe Thompson, the associate producer, were disk jockeys. All they would talk about was, "What kind of music do you play in the morning?"

Meanwhile, Weaver didn't like the news department, and the news department hated the "Today" show with a venom. They were convinced it was gonna fail, and with reason. Pat wanted philosophers on. "Let's get Reinhold Neibuhr"—at eight in the morning. The news people would look at each other, and the disk jockeys would say, "What kind of music do you play?"

PAT WEAVER: I had so much trouble getting "Today" organized because I was mixing up news and entertainment. We wanted to cover all the stuff they couldn't get on the Camel newscast, but the news people were holding back all the good stories for Swayze to go hopscotching around the world.

I also had to find a host. Because we had so much to do, I had in mind a guy named Rush Hughes, who got his name because he talked fast. Then when I saw the range of stuff we were going to do, I decided that a guy who was totally relaxed would be a better choice. That's when we came up with Garroway.

RICHARD PINKHAM: I couldn't sleep the night of the first show, so I went over to the studio. Dave was loose and easy. He said, "You need the doctor." He brings out this bottle. God knows what was in it, but I drained some of it and felt much better.

GERALD GREEN: Originally, the set had big headlines behind the desk, "TODAY"'s BOOK, "TODAY"'s THEATER, "TODAY"'s MAGAZINE, "TODAY"'s HEADLINE. Eisenhower's Secretary of Agriculture was Ezra Taft Benson. One day he backed down on his farm policy, so the headline Jim Fleming put up was BENSON HEDGES.

Abe Schecter was actually the first producer. He was real news and a wild, profane, tough, little guy about five feet tall. His feet barely touched the ground when he sat in his chair. Garroway loved sports cars. One day, we decided to have a parade of them by the window on Forty-ninth Street. Abe said, "Sports cars? What the hell are we showing sports cars for?"

Somebody said, "Abe, they're Dave's hobby."

And Schecter said, "Well, fuckin's mine, but I ain't putting that on the air."

CHARLIE ANDREWS: The control room was in the basement. There was a ramp that went up to the studio. I would sit alongside Schecter in the control room, and he would scream, "No, not that shot, that's too long!" Then he would run up the ramp toward the studio. There was a monitor at the end of the ramp. By the time he got there, the shot had changed, so he would come back and sit down. We used to call that the "Schecter Ramp Dance."

LEN SAFIR: I was hired about a month after it started to do the remote work. One of my jobs was to call up every morning to make sure everything was all set up. One morning, we had Cleveland Amory scheduled as a guest. I called up and spoke to an engineer. "Is everything all set up for Cleveland Amory?"

I heard this silence, then, "Whatjasay?"

"Is everything set up for Cleveland Amory?"

"Yessiree."

I hung up the phone. The next morning, I'm sitting next to the director when they fire up the cameras, and suddenly we're in this huge room. I said, "Where are they?"

We called the engineering department. "We're in the Cleveland armory."

GERALD GREEN: Technical things didn't work. The announcers wouldn't say their cues so the control room couldn't roll the film on time. I never could get Garroway or Fleming to read a roll cue. They would ad-lib and then say, "Where's the film?"

I would say, "Read your fucking roll cue, and you'll get the film on time."

Nothing drove me crazier than that [his voice rising]. When I was managing editor, I would watch the show at home, sometimes with my daughter, who was a year and a half, sitting in her little rocking chair. Fleming would say, "Meanwhile, in New Delhi another demonstration took place to protest Nehru's . . ." and I could see he was not reading the roll cue. And then he'd say, "There's supposed to be some film here, and I don't know where it is." I'd be sitting there shouting, "Run it. Run the goddamned film." One evening, I'm in the kitchen, and I hear my daughter yelling in the den. I go down there, and she's watching Felix the Cat, yelling, "Run it. Run the goddamn film." She thought that was what you did when you watched television.

One day about six months in, this ruddy Irish guy with a patch over one eye walks in, and he says "Hi, I'm Joe Culligan. I'm sales manager of the show."

He was a Bronx Irishman. I'm Jewish from Brownsville. We got along right away. I said, "I hear the show's going under."

"No way."

"Well, the word around the news department is that they're throwing us off the air. John Crosby says we can't last."

"Don't pay any attention to that. The show just has to be sold. It's a great show. I'm gonna go out and sell a couple of big ones. Don't worry, I'll take care of it."

MATTHEW JOSEPH "JOE" CULLIGAN: The show was losing $1.5 million a year. I was told to either to make it succeed or liquidate it.

GERALD GREEN: Joe was the unsung hero of the "Today" show. Forget about the geniuses, and the great program people, Joe Culligan sold that show when no one else could, and he's never gotten enough credit.

JOE CULLIGAN: I was so impressed by Garroway as an engaging personality, I picked potential advertisers and challenged them. I said to the fellow at Fram Filters, "I'll pay for the telegrams to fifty of your distributors. Ask them if they know Dave Garroway from the 'Today' show."

Out of the fifty telegrams, he got thirty-five responses, saying, "I watch the show. Dave Garroway is a hell of a guy."

We signed them up, and I leaked that story to the press. That brought others in. Also, we did funny things with the commercials. We had Saran Wrap, and Dave wrapped a piece of Saran Wrap over the camera lens to show how clear it was. We dumped four tons of snow on Forty-ninth Street, and Dave sat on it for an air-conditioning commercial.

GERALD GREEN: I always had a theory that half our audience watched the show because of our commercials. Then of course, the chimp came along. Many people say that was the key.

LEN SAFIR: I thought we needed some comedy. I remembered a *New Yorker* cartoon—a gorilla is leaving a desk, and a guy sitting down says, "And now with the human side of the news." I thought, Get a monkey dressed as a newspaperman. Sit him in front of a typewriter, and every once in a while we would cut to him banging away.

I called a pet shop. They said they would look around. I told the other guys, too. Then one day Charlie Spear comes rushing into the office. "There's one out by the elevator!"

I ran out, and there are two guys holding Muggs, who was in a diaper. He was about the cutest-looking thing you've ever seen. The next morning we put Muggs on. All we did was sit him next to Garroway. It was an immediate sensation. The chimp was irresistible. He ran all over the studio, while Jack Heyman followed him with his camera. He would pound on the window and wave hello to all of the people.

RICHARD PINKHAM: Len Safir, bless his soul, made like a hundred million dollars profit for NBC. He said, "If we put him on every day, the kids will see this little monkey, and their parents will realize there's wonderful news on," and that's why the ratings went up. Until then, I thought they would cancel the whole damn thing and I would be back in the newspaper business.

GERALD GREEN: I never had anything against the monkey. He bit a couple of people, but he liked me. He bit people who usually deserved to get bit, like Martha Raye.

You were okay with Muggs if you talked softly to him and petted him. Paul Cunningham, who put the newscast together overnight, was always "Hairbreath Harry." At seven o'clock, Fleming would be waiting for his newscast, and Paul would come in with his shirttails flying, scripts under his arm, and paper falling. In the morning, the chimp would be sitting in the corner. Anybody who came in, Muggs would want to say hello and shake hands. Paul would usually stop and say, "Oh, hi, Muggs, how are ya?"

One morning, he came in and the chimp held out his hand, and Paul said, "Oh, fuck off." He went to his desk and started typing. In two minutes, someone cracked him across the back and Paul literally fell off his chair. It was Muggs. He was pissed that Paul hadn't greeted him.

LEN SAFIR: He began to get nasty as he got a little older. He would snap at Garroway, who would be smiling while his hand was bleeding. It didn't improve, and Mort told me to find ways to get him out of the studio. Once, I called Marlin Perkins of the Chicago Zoo, and he agreed to throw Muggs a birthday party.

RICHARD PINKHAM: We had two or three Cadillacs and a lot of newsmen to escort him to the airport. Then Perkins called me. He said, "Incidentally, has anyone ever found out if he has worms? He can't come out here if he does."

"My God, we've got all these people here, what can I do?"

"Put the monkey facedown on your desk and then approach his rear end." At that point I thought, "I have a B.A. in English from Yale. What the hell am I doing?" I didn't bother, and nobody got infected.

*   *   *

HARRY AROUH: In 1953, I was working for a station in Houston. The news director was a crusty Irishman named Pat Flaherty. He had this idea that the audience shouldn't think that we were so unfamiliar with our stories that we had to read our copy, so we had to memorize everything. It was the most agonizing experience, sitting in front of a camera, trying to keep names and details straight. One guy got so frustrated with the pressure, he pulled his typewriter, which was bolted to his desk, and threw it across the room and said, "I quit." He left and never came back.

There was one broadcast in which my worst fears came to pass. It was a story about the county commissioner, who had nine children. I launched into the story, and suddenly I couldn't remember the guy's name. I said, "And the county commissioner, Commissioner . . . ," hoping that it would come into my mind, but it didn't. Finally, I said lamely, "Well, you know, the guy who's got nine kids."

Finally he decided that if Edward R. Murrow could use a script, we could too. After a while, it became wise to let the audience see the script because they realized if they didn't, the audience would think these people were just spouting this stuff without reference to notes, and maybe there were inaccuracies. Even after TelePrompTers came in, you still referred to the script as if you were reading from it. We didn't want the audience to know there was a TelePrompTer. We were supposed to be smart and articulate.

DON HEWITT: People laughed at me, but I suggested that Edwards learn Braille. Everybody thinks that's silly, but it's a hell of an idea.

GENE JONES: When NBC sent Charlie and me to Europe in 1951, our Auricon sound camera took a roll of film that ran three minutes. It was appalling that during every single interview we did with a chief of state, we would have to hold up a hand and say, "We have to reload." They were often not amused. Tito was quite angry.

I guess we were among the inventors of cinema verité, because sometimes one of us hung the Auricon on his chest while the other hung the sound box around his neck. You also had to carry the batteries. The person doing the sound had to hold the microphone, ask the questions, and sometimes even hold the light.

Our cameras were run by an automobile battery. The batteries NBC had sent us were inadequate. All our clothes had holes in them in the lap area from the batteries we took out of Citroën cars. The cameras had no tachometers to tell us if they were running at the right speed. When we did the first sound–film coverage of the Pope, Charlie was lying virtually underneath him on the Vatican balcony. We sent the film in and got a cable back saying, REGRET TO ADVISE YOU KEYSTONE KOP ACTION MICKEY MOUSE SOUND. FILM TOTALLY UNUSABLE. CHECK BATTERY.

There were always incidents during our interviews. While we were doing [British Prime Minister Clement] Attlee, Charlie dropped a bulb on his head. We interviewed King Paul of Greece at what was called the summer palace. It was so old, as soon as we plugged in, all the power in the house blew. Without a moment's hesitation, Paul said he knew what to do. One of the staff drove an enormous old Cadillac right up against the wall of the house. He attached our clamps to the car battery. While we did the interview, somebody sat in the car with his foot on the throttle to power the lights.

DON HEWITT: The big changes were one, TelePrompTer; two, color; three, not film to tape, but optical sound to magnetic sound. Magnetic sound was unbelievable. It's your ear more than your eye that keeps you in front of the television set. What you see is the icing on the cake. The cake is what you hear.

BOB BENDICK: I remember when the biggest thing we could do was punch up Philadelphia. Tony Miner said, "One day we'll push a button and get Tokyo, another button and get Jerusalem," and we all said, "Nonsense, it's not possible." That's the most astounding change to me.

DON HEWITT: Sometimes we made up the graphics as we went along. We created a model of Sputnik from a cloth golf ball and a coat hanger. Today, a computer does it. We did it with chewing gum, spit, and Scotch tape. During the Korean War, I built a clay map and went to a toy store, bought toy soldiers and tanks and jeeps, and we re-created the war every night.

You couldn't super names. Then at the '52 convention I was in a diner, and I'm thinking, Jesus, how can I put the names up there? You've got to get them photostated so they come out white on black. And that takes time. By the time you get the thing made the shot is gone. As I'm sitting there, I look up, and just as the waitress asks, "What will you have?" I said, "That board."

"What board?"

"That board that says HAMBURGERS, 35 CENTS."

I bought that and all the little white-on-black letters for twenty bucks. I took it to the studio, and I said, "This is where we put the names up in a hurry. If you can put up S O U P 25¢, you can put up ROCKEFELLER." And those were the first supers.

✳   ✳   ✳

DONALD HYATT: I was in NBC's training program in 1949 when somebody told me to go see a guy named Salomon who was doing a project called "Victory at Sea."

"Pete" Salomon was a brilliant student at Harvard. He shone in Samuel Eliot Morrison's classes. During the war, Roosevelt asked Morrison to do a history of naval operations. Morrison asked Salomon to be his assistant. Together, they went anywhere there was action. Peter later got the idea that Morrison's history would make a good television series. He went to his former college roommate, Bob Sarnoff, who took it to the General. For two years, they hemmed and hawed about whether this was something the network could do. Finally, they said okay.

Peter saw himself as a dramatist, and "Victory" was put together with more poetry than plot. That's where it broke new ground. Because of Peter's vision, the ratings were huge. It opened the doors for other documentaries because the network, which tried to bury it at first, saw not only public acceptance, but that they could make profits and be good guys too.

ALBERT WASSERMAN: I grew up in the day of the great film documentaries of the 'Thirties. They were concerned with social ideas. They used people as symbols rather than as individuals. Comes along television with the small tube, and the logic had to be different, because the image quality was not nearly as good, and it was more intimate. Now, you told your ideas through individual stories and then enlarged that thematically to make it more universal.

When Murrow did his half-hour interview with Robert Oppenheimer, practically the whole thing was a tight closeup. By most standards, that would have been terribly static, but I was mesmerized. His reactions were so powerful on that tube. You couldn't do that in a theater.

TV was a great boon to documentary filmmakers, mainly because we got paid to make films rather than spending most of our time looking for work.

FRED FRIENDLY: In 1951, Alcoa wanted to sponsor a weekly program that Murrow and I would do. Ed told them, "Fred doesn't know anything about television and neither do I. Fred's even color-blind," but they kept saying, "You've got to do it. We just lost a big antitrust case, and if you do this, we'll never tell you what program to do. We'll leave you alone."

Finally, I said, "We'll try it for thirteen weeks."

PALMER WILLIAMS: Alcoa wanted to sponsor a show with class to clean up its image. Because of that, "See It Now" became a law unto itself. No one from Madison Avenue ever saw the program before it went on the air, neither did anyone from CBS. On the second broadcast, Ed read his contract with Alcoa over the air. He said, "The contract says we will turn out this television program and Alcoa will turn out aluminum. They have given us a free hand to do whatever we see fit."

JOSEPH WERSHBA: I worked on "Hear It Now," and I was hired for "See It Now," even though I knew nothing about film. Murrow was also very uncomfortable with TV. He thought it was much too theatrical. There was too much equipment that got in the way of doing a story.

FRED FRIENDLY: To this day, radio at its best is far superior to television, but Alcoa kept their word, and "See It Now" went on to be the most important program that CBS ever aired, the most important that Ed, and therefore I, had anything to do with. People suddenly saw, "This is what television can do."

JOSEPH WERSHBA: We never used the word "show" on "See It Now." We used the word "broadcast" or "the story." Murrow had used the words "good show" as a reference to World War II if a British airman came back alive from the Battle of Britain. Ed didn't want the term "good show" applied to something as trivial as a television broadcast. We were not in show business.

PALMER WILLIAMS: We drew our camera crews from the Hearst newsreel. We had Joe Wershba and Eddie Scott as reporters. Fred also hired Gene Milford, a film editor who won an Oscar for "On the Waterfront." Then Bill Thompson showed up as the second editor followed by Mili Lerner.

MILI LERNER BONSIGNORI: I had never heard of Murrow when Gene told me he needed an assistant for a "pilot." I thought that meant there was going to be a flyer. That's how much I knew about TV. I said, "How long is the job?"

He said six weeks. I stayed there the rest of my life. My first day, there was

Palmer, who knows film, and Fred, this big guy who's as nervous as a cat. Every time something goes wrong he turns to Palmer and tries to kill him. The whole floor was full of film. There was an assistant in the corner with tears rolling down her face. She says, "Thank God you're here. I am leaving. These people are crazy."

Everybody was saying to me, "Hi, dearie. Hi, sweetie."

I said, "No, dearie, no, sweetie. I'm sitting outside. You clean up the room, and then I'll come in and you can dearie, sweetie." And they did, and we made the pilot, which was a story about following a pint of blood from a donor to a patient.

JOSEPH WERSHBA: Fred was the impresario. He made it possible for Murrow to be as effective as he was.

PALMER WILLIAMS: The relationship between Ed and Fred was interesting. Fred was the junior partner and very respectful of Ed, and Ed, most of the time, was respectful of Fred's energy and talent.

JOSEPH WERSHBA: Fred was the most difficult man I ever worked for. He would get irascible if things didn't go his way. One day, he didn't like the way Bill Thompson edited some film, and he kicked a cot through a speaker.

MILI LERNER BONSIGNORI: Fred was a maniac. He's a big man. I'm little. I came in as an assistant, but they promised to move me up to editor. After a month, I said to Fred, "Time is up. I'm an editor now. Give me a story to cut."

"No way, you're only a woman. What do you know about this?"

I said, "Good-bye, Fred. I quit." I put on my coat, and I was ready to go. He chased me around the room and grabbed me by the neck. He said, "You're driving me crazy."

I said, "You're killing me."

Then he says, "Okay, cut the Trieste story."

But you could always call him for help. Sometimes, I'd call him at four o'clock in the morning. I'd say, "Fred. I'm having trouble. It won't come together."

He'd say, "How about if we do it this way?"

"I'll try it."

No matter what time, he was ready for you. If I called him when he was in with Paley, he would come out to talk to me.

PALMER WILLIAMS: Fred was constantly pushing to do different things. When I joined, Friendly had already dispatched a crew to Korea with a sound man. I had looked at millions of feet of military footage. Nobody ever had a sound man. Sound was always dubbed in. But here was a radio man coming into film. His whole thing was pushing toward the natural sound. It was revolutionary to have this additional sensory use of it.

I still remember Ed climbing out of a plane looking haggard and worn, saying, "The things we do for Fred Friendly." After that, any time we were pushed to the limit, "the things we do for Fred Friendly."

MILI LERNER BONSIGNORI: I can go right back to being a young woman again, entering the cutting room at 550 Fifth Avenue in back of a long office. We all worked in the same room with the clatter from the Moviolas that was so horrendous. The working hours were very hard. The first year we went on on Sunday, so we worked from Tuesday through Friday. Saturday we would come in at ten o'clock and we wouldn't go home until twelve thirty on Sunday. Our social life was really almost nil. I lost more boyfriends, but we felt we were changing the world. That's what Murrow inspired in us.

JOSEPH WERSHBA: We never had a ten-minute orientation on how films were made—fortunately—because much of our stuff was people talking, and we were not afraid of that. We might have felt otherwise if we had known more. Since we didn't know about filmmaking we depended on the cameramen. He was like my editor in the field. "What is your thinking," was his favorite phrase. His other favorite phrase was, "Well, if that's the way you want it, but I'm reporting this to the union."

MILI LERNER BONSIGNORI: When you cut a film, each scene has to talk to you. It says, "I'm what you want." Another one says, "But I'm what you want." Then you say, "Let me take a good look and feel you out," and then I just choose.

When the reporters or cameramen scream at you, you have to tell them, "You cannot fall in love with a shot." That's why they don't make good editors. Cameramen break their necks to get the shot. "Oh, boy, this will make the whole story." The editor looks at it and says, "It's a gorgeous shot, but it doesn't support the story. Also, if I put that in, the rest of the story falls apart because it's not as gorgeous. You upset the balance." Our job is make an audience pay attention and not turn the knob.

REUVEN FRANK: At NBC, there was always talk about our answer to Murrow, which got louder and sillier. We ended up with Joe Harsch and "Background," which was not an answer because it got no support. You can't just *say*, "We've got to do something like that," you've got to *do* something like that. CBS had a major commitment. They put in money and hired people.

GENE JONES: Charlie and I wanted to do documentaries, and I used to talk to Bill McAndrew all the time about this. He would say, "God, won't you ever leave me alone." With few exceptions, there was no nurturing of anybody.

They hired some marvelous talents, but they didn't have the eccentric, some-times despotic, near-genius individuals who would risk all or cared deeply for things.

In early 1952, Charlie and I and my wife, Natalie, who was the first woman foreign correspondent at NBC, ended up going to Europe to feed material to the "Camel News Caravan," the "Today" show, and a show on the Cold War called "Battle Report Washington." We created our own assignments, which were essentially mini-documentaries that took us all over Europe, Asia, the Middle East, Africa, and eventually Russia. Europe was then a very tense, com-plicated, dangerous place, but most people had no idea of what was going on in Eastern Europe. When we sneaked our cameras into East Berlin, we felt we were showing Americans something that was so alien to them, the way the *Vopos* [secret police] were, and the terror on the faces of the people.

Our goal was to reveal this horror in every way we could. We reported on how the Nazis were being restored to various high positions in West Germany. We saw intense racial hatred in the Yugoslavian countryside. We shot what we called the communist riots, especially in the communist section of Paris. We also filmed the poverty, because we assumed that at the heart of it was not the communists but the outrage that the systems were failing the people in the af-termath of World War II.

We made our own assignments. Many times it was extremely melancholy, es-pecially in the former ghettoes of Warsaw or Berlin. I was very conscious that we were often working with local cameramen who a few years before would have burned my wife alive because she was Jewish.

We asked tough, complex questions about important issues. These were the first interviews of this kind on television. When we asked John McCloy why Nazis were being put back into power in Germany, he rose like a rocket out of his chair and pointed to the door and said, "The interview is over."

Konrad Adenauer [West Germany's Prime Minister] hemmed and hawed when we asked him if he would commit troops to NATO. We talked to Attlee about the terrible postwar poverty that we saw. Chocolate was rationed, meat rationed, and fish was not abundant, while we saw immense chocolate stores in the ruins of Berlin.

We were covering the NATO conference in Lisbon when NBC sent word there was fighting at the Suez Canal. The Egyptian fundamentalists had orga-nized a guerrilla army and were determined to kick out King Farouk and the British. We covered the street-fighting in Ismalia, where Egyptians had killed a number of British and made the mistake of holing up in a police station, which tanks then leveled. At that point, the terrorists started burning Cairo. One group dragged many British women and children from the British Turf Club into the street, wrapped chains around them, poured gasoline over them, and burned them alive. The bodies were still smoldering when we got there. We met up with the fundamentalists, young guys brandishing rifles and shouting gleefully at what they had done, and they told us everything.

At that point, the Egyptian police grabbed us and threw us in jail for three days. My wife, Natalie, was extremely concerned, being a Jew, but we were released with our film hidden in a box of her Kotex. As soon as we got to Paris, we shipped it to NBC.

*   *   *

OTIS FREEMAN: In 1951, I was working for WPIX in New York. Somebody got the idea to cover Senator Kefauver's hearings on organized crime. We didn't know it would turn out as big as it did. At first, WPIX was there by itself. We went down to the courthouse and set up our equipment in a bathroom, which was the only place available. At one point I walked into a place where the government people were holding the witnesses. I opened the door, and nearly everybody inside went for their guns.

Then Frank Costello complained about the lights, so we had to turn most of them off. Then he didn't want to be shown on television. Lenny Leff was told to take the camera off his face, so he just panned down to his hands. Of course, if Kefauver asked a tough question, Costello's hands would clench up. We had no idea that that would become a famous shot. We were just trying to get the best pictures and best program we could.

JOSEPH WERSHBA: Those hearings demonstrated the power of TV. Most of us at CBS enjoyed Costello's discomfiture, except Alex Kendrick. He said, "Just a minute. This guy's got rights. They're being violated right there on television. He's being forced to take the Fifth Amendment in order to make him look like a criminal. If they can do it to him, they can do it to anybody."

I think Murrow felt the same way. After the hearings, we went out for a drink, and Murrow raised his glass and said, "Let's have a king's ransom, one for Uncle Frank." He was very, very tough on this rule of law, meaning accusations must be made through the legal process. That's what this country's all about, but there was no getting away from the power of television.

BOB DOYLE: I was the pool director for the '52 conventions. The shots were better in '52 than they were in '48. The cameras were better. The audience was now between fifty and eighty million. All the stations took it unless they were smart and put on movies.

The Democrats tried to make it more interesting for television, but you can't shut up a politician, except when Bess Truman kicked Harry. He objected to something and she gave him a boot in the ankle. I had that on the air. Bess was a tough cookie.

DON HEWITT: Television took over America inch by inch. At the 1952 conventions Eisenhower and Stevenson were nominated, and so was Walter Cronkite. I thought "Holy shit, Cronkite is almost as big a name as these two guys."

BOB DOYLE: I was talking to Jake Arvey of the Illinois delegation, who was a political pro. Nothing happened in Illinois without his say-so. He asked me how many people were watching. I told him fifty to eighty million. He said, "We can't fight on the floor anymore." And there never was again. They had secret caucuses in '52. Hewitt tried to poke a lens through the wall, but I called a meeting of the three network vice presidents and we put a stop to it.

DON HEWITT: I did things I would fire people for. Television gets caught up in it own *meshugas.* I know. I started a lot of it. At the Democratic convention in 1948, India Edwards held up a steak and a bottle of milk as a symbol of inflation. I went down, stole it, and brought it back up to Murrow, and he did a whole piece on it. I figured, if you steal stuff and give it to Ed it cleanses the process. Ed thought it was great. He said, "Hot damn."

GERALD GREEN: Stan Rotkewicz was a big Polish guy from Jersey. He was business manager at NBC News. At the convention it was very tough to get on the floor with credentials. The Republicans had issued badges with a color-coded ribbon. White was best. With that you could get on the platform. There weren't enough white ribbons because CBS had stolen them, so Rotkewicz took a bottle of bleach and bleached the blue-and-red ribbons. They came out off-white, but he had thirty guys walking around with cream-colored ribbons. He said, "I made so many of them, the real white ribbons weren't getting on the floor. The guards were saying, 'That don't look like a real ribbon. Get outa here.'"

DAVID LEVY: I was head of the television/radio campaign for Citizens for Eisenhower. The Taft people didn't want an Eisenhower rally when he was nominated, so they tried to clear the hall of his supporters. I had about six or seven credentials. I gave 'em to one of my advisors and said, "Get six people in." As soon as six came in, we passed the credentials out again and again. The networks let us stash these people around the hall as extra cameramen, makeup people. We even put them in closets. We brought in maybe 150 people, and they put on a big parade for Eisenhower's nomination.

DON HEWITT: I invented the word "anchorman" in 1952. Sig Mickelson and I were talking about how we were going to have a relay team of Cronkite, Doug Edwards, John Daly, and Quincy Howe, and Cronkite would be like the anchorman.

I believed that you lived or died on how popular the anchorman was because the conventions were a bellwether of who was winning the news battle. Nobody thought much about nightly newscasts. Now, I wonder what we were competing about. Who gave a shit? I was competing for my own satisfaction in sinking the enemy. I really thought of them as the enemy and this was war.

BOB DOYLE: [NBC President Bob] Kintner said, "This is not a convention to elect a president, it's a war between the networks," and it was.

DON HEWITT: We went to the conventions in '48 when television was radio's little brother and suddenly it was, "Holy shit, we can do what radio does." We never got over the fact that we had this big, wonderful moment, and the conventions became the be-all and end-all. They're still a big deal. In the newsroom, when they posted the list of who was going, people would burst into tears if their names weren't there.

For years, I've asked, "Why are we doing this?" There's no news anymore. At least in the beginning you could see a credentials fight or a platform fight. You want to see a fight at a convention now? Let NBC's sign be two inches bigger than CBS's.

REUVEN FRANK: I think real news came out of the conventions, at least until '68. In 1960, for example, our people were convinced that Johnson would get the nomination. The nominations became a foregone conclusion when the primary system took over. Since then, two great issues of American life were acted on out on the convention floor, Vietnam and civil rights.

* * *

TED ROGERS: I was on the set of "The Stu Erwin Show" when Rose Woods [Richard Nixon's secretary] called in 1952. She said, "The boss wants to talk to you."

I had worked for Nixon on his television campaign in 1950. I was with Dancer, Fitzgerald, and a man from the Los Angeles Republican Finance Committee invited me to talk to them about using television for the campaign. I told them that they should get into it; television was the wave of the future. That night, Nixon himself called me at home. He said, "I was in the back row, and I agree with what you said a thousand percent."

I went to work for him, even though I had no interest in politics. I saw it as a way to get my foot in the door for things that otherwise would never have been open to me. Now, he was calling again.

In 1952, TV for the first time was the main focus of the advertising. It was also the first time that a candidate was really packaged.

The Kudner Agency wanted to show Ike, the educator, because he was president of Columbia. Christ, Ike couldn't give a damn about Columbia. That was just a way point. I suggested we emphasize Ike's folksiness, his ability to communicate with the average human being. We ended up doing these informal chats with voters. They were controlled, yes, with big outlines in large type if he needed them, but at least he was comfortable.

The Checkers story began in September, when the story about Nixon's "slush fund" broke in the press. We were doing the kickoff of a whistle-stop tour when a guy in the crowd yelled, "Hey, Nixon, tell 'em about the sixteen thousand dollars."

Right there we canceled the tour and sat in a hotel in Portland for three days waiting for the General to either throw Nixon off the ticket or keep him on. I wanted Nixon to go on TV. I kept saying, "Take it to the people."

Finally on Sunday night, Nixon was in his hotel room on the bed with his shoes off, his back up against the headboard, talking to Eisenhower on the phone. "General, I never thought I'd ever say this to you, sir, but there comes a time in everyone's life when you have to shit or get off the pot."

That did it. We were given the go-ahead to plead our case on TV. We bought time on all three networks for Tuesday night. I called a friend of mine, John Claar, an excellent director and a liberal Democrat. I said, "Forget that. I've got a job for you, if you want it. Find a crew. Get a studio and a library set."

He said okay. The only studio available was NBC's at the El Capitan Theater. There was no rehearsal. Nixon made notes on four pages of legal paper. He brought those to the studio. We waited for financial material from Price Water-house [the accounting firm] regarding his personal finances, but they couldn't get them to us in time, so he had to fill with anecdotal comments and explanations of his own. That's why he used the story about his dog Checkers, which was ad-libbed. The "Republican cloth coat" line was one he used all the time. It was one of those "winners" that every politician uses on the stump until hell freezes over.

He got so emotionally involved in what he was saying, he ran over, on live TV on all three networks. I had to pick the end of a phrase where I just felt a pause. I had already whispered to the cameraman to iris to black when I hit his hip, and that's what we did. People thought the end was planned. Bullshit. It was a desperate move to get him off the air without a disaster.

After the telecast, Nixon walked right into the camera. The cameraman grabbed him and said, "Steady, sir." He thought it was a failure. He thought all his broadcasts were failures, but it worked. Eisenhower had no choice. TV forced his hand. Maybe everything he said on the broadcast wasn't true, but people identified with him as a guy in trouble just standing there and talking. It confirmed TV's incredible power.

* * *

FRED FRIENDLY: People used to say to Ed, "Why don't you do something about McCarthy?" And Ed would say, "We're not a civil-liberties bureau. When we get the right story we'll do it."

JOSEPH WERSHBA: Fred was a partisan, like the old days of the newspaper *PM*. We're against people who are kicking other people around who aren't strong enough to kick back and defend themselves. They went as far as they could without being a civil-liberties union, but they were.

FRED FRIENDLY: I was going to lunch one day when Ed and I passed in the lobby. He gave me a slip of paper from the *Detroit Free Press* and said, "Fritzl, maybe this is your McCarthy story." It was about an Air Force lieutenant named Milo Radulovich who was asked to resign because someone said his father was a communist. We sent Joe out to Michigan to interview him.

JOSEPH WERSHBA: Within two minutes I knew I had a great story. Radulovich not only knew this was wrong but he also had ideas about what the hell America is supposed to stand for.

FRED FRIENDLY: I asked Joe, "Is Radulovich verbal?"

And Joe said, "He's more verbal than you are."

JOSEPH WERSHBA: The only problem was how to balance it. The Air Force wouldn't talk. I looked around town, and I found this guy who was the head of the local American Legion. I figured he would say, "Oh, that son of a bitch. His family is guilty, and he's as guilty as they are."

This guy says, "They do this to him, they're gonna do it to you and me and anybody else. We're gonna have to cut this thing off now before it gets too big." That was a big shock. The police officer, the marshal, and a gas station man were all of a piece.

When I brought the story in, Fred said, "You're fired. I'm fired. Ed's fired, and we've got the greatest story that's ever been on television."

After the Radulovich show, McCarthy's hatchet man, Don Surine, said to me, "What if I tell you that Murrow was on the Soviet payroll?" He shows me a story from the *Pittsburgh Sun-Telegraph,* 1934. It's an attack on George Counts, who was a great liberal, saying he was part of this conspiracy to send our students to Russia and bring their students here. Murrow was listed as the group's secretary. I said, "Don, this was a student exchange program."

"But it was handled by VOKS, the Russian agency for cultural relations. He was going over there on their money, so he was on their payroll."

I asked him if I could show it to Murrow, and he magnanimously said okay. I took it to Murrow. He looked at it, and said, "So that's what they've got."

The next day I'm at the water fountain, and he says, "The question is, when do I go against these guys?"

That was the moment that he started to consider when. We broadcast the McCarthy show four months later.

PALMER WILLIAMS: We began by digging out McCarthy's speeches from various film libraries and stockpiling the stuff.

MILI LERNER BONSIGNORI: We kept collecting, and I couldn't understand why we weren't using it.

JOSEPH WERSHBA: Meanwhile, I was covering McCarthy at every opportunity. Once before a meeting of the Sons of the American Revolution he put his arm around me and says, "How's Ed?"

I said, "Be good, Joe, we've got a camera in there." He was good, better than good. He was very warm toward people, but he was a first-class bully, a very talented opportunist and almost invulnerable in that the whole thing was kind of a joke to him.

BOB DOYLE: McCarthy knew that he had to say whatever he was going to say by six o'clock to get it on the news. Then just before six, he would say something outrageous like, "George Catlett Marshall is a communist," and it would get on the air.

JOSEPH WERSHBA: We were used by McCarthy, but that's the nature of reporting and television especially. It was a terrible dilemma. I'm sure every responsible news office in the country was worrying, "How the hell do you handle this kind of stuff when you know the son of a bitch is lying?"

You have to say what the guy is saying, but we couldn't catch up with his lies fast enough before another one came out, so we were giving him this buildup. The more you wrote about him, even attacked him, the more powerful he became. This is what demagoguery is all about. The hope is eventually you catch up with the truth, but meanwhile the devastation that takes place lasts a long time. And this is why it took something like the Murrow-McCarthy broadcast to cut the guy down to size.

PALMER WILLIAMS: When they finally got to a point where Ed and Fred decided we had enough material, Murrow saw fit to tell Paley he was going to do it. It was that big.

JOSEPH WERSHBA: Paley said, "I'm with you today. I'll be with you tonight, and I'll be with you tomorrow."

PALMER WILLIAMS: Then Fred came down to talk to us. He said, "We have to be sure that we don't have an Achilles' heel in our midst as a way for a McCarthy to get back at us by getting at somebody. If there's something we should know, speak up."

Well, I had been divorced in 1947, and my first wife was a card-carrying communist. I told this to CBS's lawyers, and they said I had to resign. I called Fred and told him. He turned up in twenty minutes and said, "Don't worry, we'll get through this." Then Ed called and said, "We're not accepting your resignation."

JOSEPH WERSHBA: When we were looking at the film, people were still worrying about whether or not we should go ahead with it. Ed said, "The terror is right here in this room. No one man can terrorize a whole nation unless we are all his accomplices."

I asked him what he would say at the end of the broadcast. He said, "If we had a country where nobody ever joined an organization, read a controversial book, or had friends who were different and was accused of this and ruined by it we would be just the kind of people that McCarthy wants."

"Mr. Murrow," I said, "it's been an honor to have known you."

"Wait a minute," Fred said, "what do you mean, it's been?" That broke the tension.

FRED FRIENDLY: The Saturday after the show, I ran into Frank Stanton on the elevator. He asked me to come by his office. I went upstairs. He had a notebook of poll results, which showed that the American people were more for McCarthy than for Murrow.

I said, "Isn't that more reason to do the program, that more people believed McCarthy? Maybe we changed some minds?"

"Well, the affiliates think they might lose their licenses because of it."

JOSEPH WERSHBA: Since then people have asked, "What the hell did Murrow do? He just rode in on the crest." Well, Murrow took McCarthy on at the high point of McCarthyism. McCarthy's fatal flaw was that he didn't understand the power of television. If he did, he would never have allowed that Murrow broadcast to stay out there unanswered for so long.

PALMER WILLIAMS: Three weeks later we were advised that McCarthy would answer us the next week. We knew he was filming it at the Fox studio. Later, the production manager told me of the trials and tribulations they had propping McCarthy up and getting him to look like something because he went on a complete debauchery when he came to New York. It took a lot of coffee to get him to speak easily, and they had to put on the heaviest pancake makeup that anybody ever saw on a man. He looked like a waxen figure, and his normal roar was virtually inaudible.

Anyway, before the broadcast he said he could get me a copy of the audio track for a hundred bucks. I got the money and picked up the track. Our stenotypist took it down, and it was sent over to Murrow so he could respond to it. Just before it aired, the McCarthy people showed us the film, and they were disappointed we weren't bristling. They didn't know we had already heard it.

After the broadcast, we marched out of our studio to where the press was waiting. There stacked up neatly on a table was a complete mimeographed reply to everything. Someone asked, "Mr. Murrow, I understand you saw the program at the same time we did, that you had never seen it before. How did this mimeographed answer come to be?"

Murrow looked at him sagely and said, "Does Macy's tell Gimbels?" They never found out.

JOSEPH WERSHBA: The McCarthy show was Murrow's high point of influence. From there on, it was down because he had become controversial. Once you take a stand you lose the viewers who don't agree with you. He also began to lose influence with Paley.

FRED FRIENDLY: Once, we were having a fight with Paley. Ed said, "We've got to keep on doing this program. Don't you want a program like this on the air?"

And Mr. Paley said, "Yes, but I don't want a pain in my belly every time you fellas do a program."

Murrow said, "That goes with the job."

That was the beginning of the end.

JOSEPH WERSHBA: People complained that we were like a rogue outfit who could do anything we wanted to. They were really worried about the illusion that one man could stand apart from the company and have his own viewpoint expressed. They worried that a loose cannon could cause sponsor withdrawals and cut away from CBS profits.

Ed helped give CBS a conscience and a soul in the thirties. Murrow saved the company and helped save the country with that McCarthy broadcast. Now, there was no place for him. The documentaries that followed, while they were all first-rate, were essentially traditional investigations, not controversial in the same way McCarthy was.

FRED FRIENDLY: We were in the control room when they ran the first "$64,000 Question." Ed said to me, "Any bets on how long we'll keep this time period now?" He was right, and we were soon off altogether. They knew they could sell the time for more money than they were getting from Alcoa.

Later, I became president of CBS News. I thought I'd have all the power Ed had. Ed didn't think so. He said, "Don't take it. They'll cut off your balls." He was right. I left after they put on reruns of "I Love Lucy" instead of Gulf of Tonkin hearings, and I thought I would be there until the year 2000.

✳   ✳   ✳

GENE JONES: In 1953, I worked briefly in Saigon and wanted to do a long documentary, knowing it was the most important story in the world. In 1954, I begged NBC to let me go back to Indochina, and they agreed. Throughout South Vietnam, people told us that their own communists were preferable to the French or Americans or any outsiders. In Hanoi, I interviewed the French High Commissioner while he sat in a lounge chair at the sporting club. There was actually a sign there saying, NO DOGS AND NATIVES ALLOWED.

After that, I kept bugging Dave Taylor about doing hour-length documentaries, but he said they were starting up something called "Wide, Wide World," and he wanted me to become a producer-director and help figure out how to do it. The show was sort of a live-feature documentary. With each show we tried to be more and more daring in terms of live television.

GERALD GREEN: I hate to say this, but it became brainless muscle-flexing on the part of RCA. It was mostly pretty pictures and action of some kind. We traveled a lot. A lot of things at NBC News were done so producers could travel. They would sit around looking at lists of hotels and airlines, "Where can we go now?"

"I'd like to go to New Orleans."

"Okay, let's go to New Orleans." They would invent trips just to go somewhere. Barry Wood started that.

GENE JONES: Wood was an entertainment guy. Nobody could ever figure out why he was put in charge. Sometimes my brother and I would do things on more serious subjects, such as poverty, and Wood would say, "How long is this piece of shit?"

Much of the stuff was legitimately history-making. The first missile launching on live network television was done specifically for "Wide, Wide World." It was a scheduled test launch, but we convinced them to change the date so we could cover it live. Charlie had nineteen cameras at White Sands. I even cued the missile.

We also went to Juarez to interview the chief of the border patrol. He was standing on the border, saying how their new impregnable system would prevent any Mexicans from getting across. As he was speaking, about a hundred Mexicans ran across the border behind his back. Several of them were giving him the finger as they crossed. It was the funniest goddamned thing ever.

The show was reasonably journalistic, but some dreck got onto it. The classic example was the Malcolm Campbell caper. Campbell was a famous speedboat racer. A guy came to the office and said he represented Campbell. He offered us exclusive rights for his next world championship run. Wood paid him $25,000 and I made arrangements to fly Campbell's boat, the *Bluebird,* over with Campbell and take him to Lake Meade, Nevada.

Three weeks later, the day comes, I'm on site with a crew plus ten cameras, no Campbell, no agent. We wait another day. I called our London bureau chief Romney Wheeler. When I mentioned the agent's name I heard raucous laughter. "Gene, you've been conned. This guy has pulled that stunt all over the world."

He gave me Campbell's phone number in Scotland. Campbell was intensely sympathetic. He agreed to come over and do the run for free if we paid his expenses. Barry decided to get one of his old cronies, the famous old-time announcer, Ted Husing, to narrate this dramatic event. The day comes. I'm in the control room. We cut to Lake Meade. I say, "Cue Husing."

There isn't a sound except Garroway's breathing. I shout, "Cue that son of a bitch." The AD calmly says, "I can't, Gene."

"Why?"

"He's laying in front of me dead drunk. He's been drinking all night because he's so terrified about going on live." Dave did the introduction, and then I said, "Cue the *Bluebird*."

Nothing happened. "Cue that goddamned boat!"

The AD very calmly said, "I can't, Gene."

"Why not?"

"It just sunk as it crossed the start line."

We immediately switched away. NBC announced the boat had had an accident, and in typical "Wide, Wide World" bravado, on the next show we showed them winching the *Bluebird* out of Lake Meade.

* * *

DON HEWITT: In 1956, I made the dumb suggestion of teaming Murrow and Cronkite at the conventions. It was a disaster. They were two strong egos who didn't like each other and couldn't work together. Meanwhile, NBC paired Huntley and Brinkley, who complemented each other. They each brought different strengths, while Murrow and Cronkite brought the same strength.

REUVEN FRANK: Huntley was working on the Coast when he was hired by NBC in part as an answer to Murrow. I knew him only because some woman called him a communist, and he sued her and won. That was kind of famous because nobody did that.

Brinkley was just this kid who replaced McCormick. People in New York didn't get to know him until they saw a talk piece he did about how to go to a Washington cocktail party, saying you take your drink and walk from the front of the room toward the back door, stopping only to pour your drink into a plant. It was vintage Brinkley.

I wanted Brinkley to anchor the convention. The director of news wanted Huntley. When Davidson Taylor suggested pairing two people, then we knew we had the answer—Huntley and Brinkley. As it turned out, everybody inside liked them, but they didn't make much of a flash outside until '60.

DON HEWITT: In 1960, I thought I got run over by a steamroller. I turned around to see Huntley and Brinkley. I said, "Who the fuck are these guys?"

REUVEN FRANK: I put them on the convention, but I thought putting them together on the nightly news was a dumb idea.

BEN PARK: Pat brought me into New York as head of public affairs. The first thing he wanted me to do was fire Swayze. There was CBS with their heavyweight journalists and that really provoked Pat. Swayze was a real thorn in his side, so I just took him to lunch and said he was fired.

I was a terrific admirer of Brinkley's, and I thought he should do the newscast, but I got a lot of resistance from Bill McAndrew, who thought Huntley should do it. Everybody was lining up, and I suggested using them both as a compromise.

REUVEN FRANK: Huntley made Brinkley possible. Brinkley alone could never make it, because he doesn't have the authority that the audience wants. Huntley did. He had that great leonine head and that Murrow-like voice. Sure, that image of probity or authority is a lie, but people want to believe it.

I wrote the "Good night, Chet. Good night, David," because it was the shortest closing I could think of. They hated it. They said it made them sound effeminate. I said, "Every program has to end, and this is the shortest ending I can think of. If you can think of a shorter one, I'll take it," but they never did.

In early '56, Huntley and I started a program called "Outlook." We started covering the civil rights movement very heavily on the show. That's where we found Frank McGee. He was the local guy in Montgomery. We covered the story on the news, too, and were very bitterly resented throughout the South, where we were known as the Nigger Broadcasting Company.

HARRY AROUH: After I quit my station in Houston, I went to Little Rock and was the news director of the radio and TV station. I had a couple of reporters and a cameraman, who barely knew how to load his camera. He wasn't trained in news. He was just a local guy who needed a job.

I was there when the biggest story in the world hit the wire: the Central High School civil rights thing [the battle over the integration of the school in 1957]. I handled it the way I handled any other story, right down the middle. I had enough experience to know that you don't take an editorial stance on any story on the air.

That doesn't mean I wasn't angry at what I was seeing. I had never run into anything like that before. It was universal hatred that you could cut in the air. All the rednecks were doing things in full view they normally would have been ashamed to do. You couldn't say what was on your mind for fear that you could be attacked. It was like being in Germany when the Nazis were first taking over.

I couldn't take a position anyway. I would have hurt the station. They couldn't afford to come out on one side or the other for fear that the advertisers might withdraw. The *Arkansas Gazette* almost went broke as a result of its editorial stance in favor of desegregated schools.

REUVEN FRANK: When "Huntley-Brinkley" started, a whole bunch of Southern affiliates wouldn't carry it. A station in North Carolina followed the broadcast with their local editorial fellow who told the "real truth." His name was Jesse Helms.

HARRY AROUH: I wanted to do special coverage, but I needed more people and equipment. The network sent down armies of people. For the first time, I saw what producers did, what the camera crews did; how reporters wrote their scripts and developed stories. It helped us become more sophisticated.

I wanted to be like them, to operate without shackles. A year later the network called. They wanted to do a follow-up on Central High. I told them I could do it. I went out with my inept cameraman, did the story, and sent it to New York. Soon after that, I received a telephone call asking me if I wanted to go to New York for them. I said, "Yeah."

*   *   *

GERALD GREEN: Over time, "Today" improved, and we got over the hump. We supplied a need. Nobody else was doing morning news on a nationwide basis. People tuned in to learn what was happening, not only in news, but in movies and books.

You can go through the list of shows that failed opposite "Today." They kept setting people up, and we kept knocking them down, Cronkite, Collingwood, Jack Paar, Faye Emerson, Will Rogers, Jr., on and on.

The "Today" show introduced the hourly newscast, which was like a radio newscast so you really got the news. We had guest experts, people who really knew what they were talking about, like Hanson Baldwin, the *Times*'s military expert, and Abe Raskin of the *Times,* the finest labor writer.

When Stalin died, I brought [former Russian premier Alexander] Kerensky in. He was very old and was living in New York. He said to me [in a thick Russian accent], "I don't vant to get up that early, much too early."

"I'll send a car for you with a pretty girl."

"All right. I'll go."

I sent Mary Kelly. "If he gives you a bad time, buy him a case of vodka," and she did. I asked her, "What did he say?"

"Make it a case of Scotch."

He was great. He was our Russian expert. We threw out the whole show when Stalin died. It was marvelous television. I ordered an enormous blowup of the Kremlin. Fleming stood in front of it with Kaltenborn, who said, "Yes, Fleming, you and I have stood many times in front of the Kremlin." We should have been throwing snow at them.

We also had byline reporters. Except for "See It Now," where Bob Pierrepont and others would stand in front of the camera and say, "I'm standing on the thirty-ninth parallel in Korea," if you look at the "Camel News Caravan," there are no byline reporters. We started it with Joe Michaels covering the Wanamaker's store fire downtown and Mary Kelly reporting from the MGM lot in Hollywood.

LEN SAFIR: I did the lighter feature stories. We had a hole-in-one tournament on the "Today" show. We set up the cameras on a golf course and watched these golfers trying to get a hole in one. It was fascinating.

BOB BENDICK: We would put a twenty-dollar bill in an old glove and place it on the sidewalk in front of the window. Then we would focus the camera on it to see what would happen. Some people would look at the glove. Some would kick it. Some would pick it up and not look at it very thoroughly. The intensity of the suspense, because it was real and live, was great fun.

GERALD GREEN: The street was great. Truman walked by once when Tom Nord was out there with a microphone. Truman was with Georgie Jessel, the biggest schmuck that ever lived, and Tom said to Truman, who was no longer in office, "Mr. President, wouldn't you like to come in? Mr. Garroway would love to talk with you."

"Well, I think I might. George, what do you think?"

Jessel says, "You can't, because I'm on another network."

We did skits. I always thought sports interviews were so dull, so when we had Sal Maglie on, I had Lescoulie dress up in a New York Giants uniform, and we had Maglie in a suit and tie interview him.

Ernest Gross was the first American ambassador to the UN. He was so dignified, I always thought he was Sir Ernest Gross. One morning I picked him up, and in the car he said to me, "Oh, I've never seen the program." Stupidly, I let it slip out that there was a chimpanzee on the show. I thought he was gonna jump out of that car. [In upper-crust tones] "A chimpanzee? You are putting me on a program with a chimpanzee."

BOB BENDICK: Muggs got to be kind of tough after a few years. He and Garroway weren't getting along so well. Every so often off-camera Garroway would take a whack at him.

CLAY CASSELL: He bit Mary Kelly one day. Boy, was she pissed off. "That damn chimp. I'll kill that son of a bitch."

BOB BENDICK: He would jump up into the lights and tear everything to pieces. Any chimpanzee when he gets older is an enormous beast. After a while, we couldn't trust him any longer. We had the poster girl for the March of Dimes sitting on the edge of this desk. We brought Muggs over to this sweet little girl on crutches, and he knocked her right off the table.

Finally we got rid of him. We tried to get another one, but we could never find the right one. None of them had his intelligence or personality. He was a great actor.

LEN SAFIR: I left the show at the peak of my career. I was burned out. I wasn't getting enough sleep, and I was drinking too much. There was a lot of that. We were so exhilarated from the work we couldn't go to sleep, so we went to Toots Shor's and drank. I stopped after I left. I haven't had a drink in thirty years.

GERALD GREEN: In *Network,* Paddy Chayefsky used a story about Lenny Safir. One morning we send a mobile unit out on the George Washington Bridge just to see the traffic coming in from New Jersey. Lenny is the location producer and he oversleeps. When he gets up, he runs down to Second Avenue in his bedroom slippers and pajamas with a topcoat thrown over them. He flags down a cab, and gets in. The driver says, "Where to, buddy?"

Lenny, who was gaunt with sunken cheeks, says, "The George Washington Bridge."

LEN SAFIR: He asked, "What for?"

"I'm gonna do a television show up there."

This guy thought he had a suicidal nut on his hands. He said, "Why don't we sit down and have a cup of coffee and talk about the whole thing. Life can be better."

"Look, I'm really in a rush. I've got to get there. Here's twenty bucks if you can get me there."

"Twenty bucks?"

"Yeah."

"You want to go to Bellevue?"

"No."

Everything I said compounded it, but for twenty bucks he was willing to go. After I finally got there, I told Jack Lescoulie the story. He repeated it so often, Chayefsky heard it and used it.

GENE JONES: I was the last surviving body after they folded "Wide, Wide World." I wanted to go overseas, but Kintner told me, "It's the 'Today' show or you're fired."

I was there about twenty months. It was exhausting but a damn good experience producing "Today" on a daily basis because it was much more of a news program than it is today. I arrived in the studio at three-forty-five each morning, and I left at seven-thirty at night. NBC sent me home in a car. I would get into my pajamas, and jump in bed.

Sometimes, the night news editor would call Natalie and say, "Wake up Gene. There was a plane crash," or "a railroad accident. Should we order a mobile unit out to cover it?"

Natalie would say, "Sure, I'll wake him up." She would put down the phone, think about it, and then she would say, "No, don't do it," or "Okay, do it."

Garroway had his eccentricities, but he was okay. He wanted ultimate control to insure maximum quality. That created sparks between him and the producers, including myself.

BOB BENDICK: Garroway was one of the best interviewers who has ever come along. It was tragic what happened to him. The hours were very difficult. He had to be up at three in the morning, and he'd go out at night. The Doctor sustained him and brightened him up, but it also killed him eventually.

LYNWOOD KING: The Doctor was liquid codeine. Around two minutes to seven, out would come the little bottle, and he would take a slug of it. Then the sweep second hand would hit seven and he would smile and sparkle and be Dave Garroway until nine o'clock when he would go back to depressed Dave Garroway.

BOB BENDICK: Once, I was very tired. He said, "Take some of this." Boy, they practically had to scrape me off the roof.

Garroway was complex and insecure to start with, and the Doctor propped him up. As the years went by, he took more and more of it, and it began to befuddle him. He became unreasonable. He thought of himself as the final authority on everything.

GENE JONES: Once when he was negotiating his contract, a minute or two before airtime he lay down in front of the desk and started picking his nose and flinging the boogaboos in the air. The stagehands said, "Well, it's contract time."

He insisted that we do a feature on his bomb shelter to encourage other people to build them. There was a steel door with a big bank-vault-type closer. Over the doorway was a double-barrel shotgun on pegs. I said, "What's that for, David?"

"So if necessary I can kill anybody that tries to come in."

On the opposite wall was a bicycle on pegs. I asked him what that was for. He said, "After the bomb drops, I'm going to open the door, get on my bike, and pedal away."

LYNWOOD KING: By then he was convinced his phone was being bugged. I'm not so sure it wasn't, knowing how corporations work, but David was paranoid about the communists, too.

GENE JONES: He said ghosts were menacing him. He said machines had human antagonisms toward him. Sometimes he would grab the microphone in a rage and twist the wire back and forth, muttering, "I'll kill you. I'm strangling you."

We had these one-minute "pad" spots, which were about little objects that were placed off to the side. If an interview fell out or a switch to a city didn't work, Garroway could pick up an object and say, "Did I ever tell you about this?"

He had a man who would come in and scoop up these items in a big bag. Some were quite valuable. Dave's house was filled with them. Some of the writers would put on the script, "This must not go to Garroway's home. It must be returned."

BOB BENDICK: We were in Rome when he began giving one of the writers a horrible time. The guy had worked all night making the changes he wanted, which was true all the time. Finally, I chased everyone away, and he and I had a confrontation. I didn't know it, but the mike and the camera were on—I think purposely—while I laced into him something fierce. After that I was fired. He continued to take the staff to task, and he was fired shortly after that.

LYNWOOD KING: I left when Garroway left. At that point, the show was transferred to the news department. They tried a bunch of different hosts, Edwin Newman and Sander Vanocur, and finally they decided on John Chancellor. Garroway was as good as any of the news people. Over the years, none of the people who made the show a hit were news.

* * *

MIKE WALLACE: I was still doing commercials and game shows when my son Peter died in a climbing accident in Greece. I was so busted up about it, I thought, "I'll do something for Peter. You've been making compromises in the name of having kids to support," so I decided to go straight. It was a wonderful decision to have to make because it was what I wanted to do.

In 1956, I was anchoring the seven and the eleven o'clock news on DuMont with my partner Ted Yates. He came with up with the notion for an interview program at eleven called "Nightbeat" to replace the news. The idea was to do something that had never been done on television before, an interview show in which we would ask tough questions. It was astonishing. It became a success overnight. The cab drivers, the cop on the beat, and the people you went out to dinner with, were all talking about it, and my hard-news reputation was made.

REUVEN FRANK: NBC's news department really came together with Kintner's arrival in 1956. The first important thing he did was say, "News reports to me." All of a sudden we could get a news bulletin on. Before, by the time we got permission from the various layers of management it was no longer a bulletin.

His vision was very simple. He wanted the average person hearing something was going on to switch to NBC, and I think he achieved it for a few years.

JAY MCMULLEN: The news was a showcase for the public, so CBS could, in effect say, "Hey, we care about what's going on in the world and informing the public about what's going on." The truth of the matter has to do with the terrible mess the networks got into with the quiz scandals and the pressure that was applied by the FCC which was, in turn, getting pressure from the Eisenhower administration to force the networks to start doing more public service programming.

There were also people beating the drums for more public service broadcasting. I was then making radio documentaries for CBS News under Irv Gitlin, who was a great leader.

ALBERT WASSERMAN: Irv was a large man, full of energy and enthusiasm. He was Fred Friendly without the temper. Also, Irv left you alone. Fred couldn't do that.

JAY MCMULLEN: Irv encouraged people to go out on their own and come up with ideas. In 1957, I was in close touch with Bobby Kennedy, who was then chief counsel for the Senate Investigations Committee. He was conducting hearings on the Teamsters and giving Jimmy Hoffa a lot of bad publicity. I suggested that CBS do a documentary on Hoffa. He said CBS wouldn't go for it because the Teamsters could shut down the network, but Irv told me to go ahead. He teamed me up with Al Wasserman, one of the great innovators in TV documentaries.

AL WASSERMAN: Hoffa was then perceived as the devil incarnate. He was very suspicious of us.

JAY MCMULLEN: My argument with him was, "Things can't get much worse for you in the press, so how about us doing a broadcast which is not just an attack on the Teamsters, but also an explanation of the Teamsters, how it started, their problems, and what's good and what's bad about what they're doing."

Eventually, he agreed, but when I handed him the release to sign, he said, "If I sign this you can knock the shit out me. You can kick me all over the place and make me look sick."

I looked him in the eye and said, "We could, but we're not going to go out of our way to do that. We're interested in the truth."

He said, "If you hadn't said that I wouldn't have signed this fucking thing."

There was a big meeting after the documentary was finished. Every bigshot at CBS was there except Paley. The lawyers said we shouldn't air it because the Teamsters could shut down CBS. Stanton felt very strongly that we should put it on the air and we aired it.

ALBERT WASSERMAN: What came out was not a simple black-and-white story. Hoffa was a complex, enormously capable man and was not personally corrupt. That doesn't mean he didn't like the power, but his motivation wasn't money. I thought because we did not present Hoffa as an unalloyed villain we were going to get roasted by the press, and I also thought, because the documentary was very critical of him, that Hoffa wasn't going to like it. To my great surprise, the critics thought it was a devastating portrait, and Hoffa said, "Well, you gave me a fair shake."

JOHN SCHULTZ: Jay told me that when the film was over Hoffa said to him, "Mr. McMullen, you don't like me, do you?"

He said, "Well, Mr. Hoffa, I don't believe anyone, no matter who I interview, about sixty-five percent of the time."

Jay is tenacious and not show-biz. He was like a police investigator. In "A Real Case of Murder," he got a real aggressive ambulance-chasing attorney to reverse himself.

I had a job editing commercials when I heard there was an opening at "CBS Reports." People stayed home at night to watch "CBS Reports." I really wanted to work on that show, despite the stories about Fred's temper, and I was hired.

JAY McMULLEN: I was one of the first people hired when they started "CBS Reports." "CBS Reports" worked very informally. You proposed ideas and you discussed them with Fred. I never had an idea imposed on me. Fred believed you did better work on something you were interested in personally than on something that did not interest you.

JOHN SCHULTZ: Fred wanted new editors to work with new producers, and David Lowe was brought in to produce a film. He had also directed "Captain Video" and several game shows. He had done several documentaries and had a law degree, so he knew how to question people. He cared a great deal about the plight of the migrant workers and wanted to do a film about them. That became "Harvest of Shame."

"Harvest of Shame" took about eight months on and off. It took David a while to find the people who knew where the bodies were, so to speak, and to get the right crew leaders to talk. He was a very elegant man and absolutely guileless. There was no aggression in his questioning. That was one reason why it worked. There was a grower who said, "Oh, they're happy people."

David said later, "I hate to do that to him. He was such a sweet guy, but these growers exploit the workers."

There are also things you can do as an editor. Fred was always going, "You gotta keep it moving!" But this woman says on film, "I know what you're thinking, my children don't like milk. They like milk, but you know, all I can afford is one quart every two weeks." [Silence.] Then I cut. I gave it that extra beat. I always liked to do that and I could get away with it if they didn't sell an extra twenty-second commercial.

I developed an ending for "Harvest of Shame" using a sound recording of a little girl singing, "Oh, Jesus loves me." It was such a plaintive beautiful non-professional voice. I put it together with some pictures of migrant workers and showed it to some people. A couple of them cried. Fred didn't know what he thought about it. David loved it. Murrow just sat there and said, "It's very moving. We don't want it. We don't want people to go, 'Oh, tsk-tsk, isn't that awful.' " He wanted to get on camera and say, "These people cannot speak for themselves. Only an aroused, enlightened public opinion can do it."

It was this conflict between art and information, but in this case, everybody realized he hit it right. I certainly did. "Harvest of Shame" didn't win an Emmy or a Peabody. DuPont was giving awards then, but nothing for us, and now it's the most famous documentary in television history. It did generate more letters than any other program ever aired on CBS up to that point. Some were even written in crayon, "May the glory of Jesus Christ be upon you."

It brought about some changes in the laws. They required registration of crew leaders, and it pricked the conscience of people. I don't know if television can mammothly change things, but maybe you can get people to think, on let's say civil rights, "Hey, maybe I'm a little wrong." That's about the best we can do.

ALBERT WASSERMAN: "Out of Darkness" was a film I made with the idea of helping remove some of the stigma from mental illness. The film followed a mute catatonic woman through three months of therapy. At the end, she said her first words. When the show was aired, that same week they also ran a production of *Richard III*, which was quite acclaimed, and the reviewer said that, in its own way, "Out of Darkness" was as shattering an emotional experience as *Richard III*. More importantly, the show had a very significant impact. The National Association of Mental Health reported a major increase in membership—something like a third, as a result of that film.

A TV documentary can have an immediate effect if your target is very specific. For example, we did a film that discredited the city manager of Newburgh, New York, who was campaigning against welfare. But if you are doing a documentary on larger issues, these problems are generally so fundamental that they don't change as a result of an hour on television.

JOHN SCHULTZ: "Biography of a Bookie Joint" was sort of the first television investigative report, especially with hidden cameras. It brought down the chief of police of Boston. I think it was the first time that politicians in an entrenched political system realized they were vulnerable to television.

JAY MCMULLEN: Bobby Kennedy sparked the idea of "Bookie Joint." He was then attorney general and was very much annoyed with the pronouncements of J. Edgar Hoover that the power of organized crime operating nationally was a myth.

Kennedy suggested I look into illegal gambling, which he said gets to the heart of organized crime. A few months later I showed him some snapshots of a bookie joint with police walking in and out. He kept asking me, "Where is this place?" I told him, and he smacked his forehead and said, "Boston! Home!"

We rented an apartment across the street and began filming activities outside the store. The documentary resulted in a total of 180 grand-jury indictments. The control of the police department was removed from the mayor's office to the governor's office. Quite a few people went to jail. We were being told at that time that there wasn't any such thing as organized crime, and we proved that was wrong.

There was enormous pressure put on CBS up in Boston after the documentary. Cardinal Cushing did not like the broadcast. To this day, "Biography of a Bookie Joint" cannot be shown anywhere. Why? I suspect the Cardinal made a deal with Paley: "You don't show that film anymore and we'll get off your back."

JOHN SCHULTZ: Toward the air date of "Harvest of Shame," the Citrus Growers of America threatened to either sue CBS or pull their advertising. Fred came thundering in, "Don't we have anything on citrus growers?"

I said no, and he was disappointed. He wanted to put something in. Philip Morris sponsored the documentary. They were told beforehand about the nature of the story, and they said it wasn't a problem. After it aired, there was a movement to boycott them. They sent a representative down there, saying, "We had no part in the film. We think it was a lying, deceitful program, so please buy our cigarettes."

ALBERT WASSERMAN: I went to NBC to get the "NBC White Paper" off the ground. Kintner was very gung-ho about it. He wanted a series that would be comparable to "CBS Reports." They wanted some new blood to do it, and they wanted new blood from CBS.

We had carte blanche the first few years. The White Papers got an enormous amount of attention and were compared very favorably with "CBS Reports." The first one was the "U-2 Affair." We also did "Sit-In," which was an examination of the sit-in movement in Nashville. Both of them won major awards.

Still, I found the climate at NBC different from CBS, which was a small company, and broadcasting was their business. NBC was part of a large conglomerate, much more corporate, with many more bureaucrats and much more incompetence in the hierarchy.

I also realized that television basically looks at programs as a commodity. It's a great, insatiable maw that has to filled, and the people who do best are the people who are able to turn out product, and that wasn't what I wanted to do, so I left.

JAY MCMULLEN: There was a lot of disillusionment after a while. Television opened up entirely new possibilities in terms of photography and journalism, and it was very exciting. That opening, as far as journalism was concerned, was encouraged and enlarged by some people who had made their careers in radio—specifically Ed Murrow. Here was a man who had brought us World War II and who had certain standards and ethics about what journalism was really all about. He set the pattern, and we followed him.

But along the way, those standards began to be shaped differently. Suddenly, there was more competition for the audience. The networks talked openly to the news departments about what kind of ratings we were getting, and talk like that always leads to "How do we improve our ratings?" The search began, not to abandon all the rules of journalism, but to tap into different ways of doing things, what might draw the attention of the audience.

Then, I hate to say this, but it's true that some semi-news programs, like Murrow's "Person-to-Person," were doing Marilyn Monroe and other Hollywood stars. Yes, it's news in a sense, but in another sense it was purely and simply entertainment. Now, a lot of the programs that are in the field of news and public affairs are really entertainment. "Person to Person" started it all. When I retired, "CBS Reports" was still running, but we were doing maybe a quarter of what we had been doing before. It started as a weekly show. We weren't even doing one a month anymore. It all came down to ratings.

*   *   *

LEW GOMAVITZ: Adlai Stevenson was a fan of "Kukla, Fran & Ollie." He also did Burr's legal work. Newt Minow was Adlai's lawyer. When Adlai was running for president Newt asked me to counsel him. I became his television coordinator. Adlai was great in small groups where there was no pressure, but he couldn't speak on television. He'd freeze and forget his lines.

Newt wanted me to get Adlai to relax, but Adlai was afraid to ad–lib. I just couldn't get him to loosen up.

TED ROGERS: Stevenson didn't listen to his people. Eisenhower did. That was the difference. He also didn't have the kind of leadership qualities that could be visually transmitted as well as Eisenhower's.

Nixon was a child of television. It didn't scare him. He was a very effective presenter, but there were problems. He perspired profusely, so we always had to lower the thermostats in the studios. People would come in and think they were in a goddamned refrigerator.

Still, I always had confidence in him on TV. In '56, we sent him into the lion's den at Cornell with eighteen brilliant leftist students, no holds barred. He did fine, but he literally went for my throat afterward. The press corps had to pull him away. He was out of control, shrieking and screaming that I had exposed him in an unfriendly arena, that I had handpicked these "little commie bastards." He kept saying, "Goddamnit, why didn't you control it?"

The next day Jack Gould called it the best telecast he had ever done, and James Reston said it was the best telecast of the '56 campaign. Nixon apologized to me all over the place.

MOREY AMSTERDAM: I still feel that JFK's becoming president was due in part to me. I was up in Hyannisport, and I went to play a round of golf, but there was nobody around at the course. Finally, I see these two guys come up. One of them is a politician named Chuck Roach. The other is Pierre Salinger. I said, "C'mon, guys, let's play golf."

"Wait a minute, Jack will be here any minute."

Just as I said, "Jack who?" up he comes. He says, "Morey, what are ya doin' here? I just saw you get killed in a movie last night."

We were friends from then on. At one point, he asked me if I had seen him on television. I said yes, and then he asked me what I thought. I said, "Whatya mean what do I think, you got a brother-in-law [Peter Lawford] who's an actor. You're friends with Sinatra."

"They say it's great, but I think it stinks. I just don't like the way I'm comin' over."

"Well, if you really want to know, I think they're being too pedantic with you. What do you care if the women think you're cute, if they vote for you?"

He says, "Listen, I'm doing a press conference tomorrow morning. I want you over there to help me."

The next morning he sends a car for me. I watch as the reporters ask him questions. Every time he would look at me I would shake my head. Finally, he says, "Wait a second." He comes over to me and he says, "What the hell are you doin'?"

I said, "Jack, you're buggin' them. Every time somebody asks a question it takes you ten minutes to come up with an answer."

"That's my New England background. I've got to think about what I'm going to say."

I said, "Well, while you're thinkin' about it, somebody else is gonna be president."

"What do you suggest?"

"Well, yesterday you said you got a kick out of watching me go into the audience and people yell at me for a joke. People always call out something I've never heard of in my life, but the second they ask a question I start talking, and as I'm talking the wheels are grinding and the right thing comes out. You've got to do the same thing. Let's say someone asks you about civil rights and up to that moment you've never heard of civil rights, you can still start saying things like 'It's the number-one thing on my agenda' or 'I've got men working on it.' "

He finally got the idea. In his debate with Nixon he was marvelous. Two days after the debate, I got this letter in pencil on his stationery: "Dear Morey, How do you like your pupil? Love, Jack."

TED ROGERS: Kennedy would just make his point and shut up rather than go on and on. It was a brand-new Kennedy. I don't think Nixon realized the magnitude of the first debate when he got to Chicago. He had been out in the boonies and had no idea of the national and international media buildup. The staff kept it from him. I never told him because I was never permitted to talk to him. Meanwhile, the Kennedy staff was right at Ground Zero in Chicago, days before the debate, and they knew what was happening.

DON HEWITT: He knew what was going on. I met with him five days before the debate to go over everything. I never saw Nixon until that night. They just didn't think it was that important.

TED ROGERS: He didn't understand because the people around him didn't understand doodly-shit about television or about electronic media. They thought I was a pain in the ass because I was always trying to get television into their plans.

Kennedy was well prepared for the debate. Bill Wilson, his campaign coordinator, showed me the list of fourteen things that JFK had memorized, that no matter what the question was in the first debate, JFK was to turn the question around and cover these fourteen subjects because the Harris polls had said they were most on the public's mind. Somebody would say, "What do you think about such-and-such and North Korea." Kennedy would say, "That's well and good but think about how it impacts on the people in Detroit and the automobile," and off he'd go. They didn't give a damn what the question was. In the first debate he covered the whole fourteen.

That never even occurred to Nixon, who was a purist as a debater. The first debate with Kennedy was a beauty contest and he lost. People who heard the Nixon-Kennedy debates on radio thought that Nixon won hands down.

That night Nixon was certainly at the lowest point of his presentation facilities in his political career. He had had a staph infection in his leg, and that night I saw him bang his knee and grab it in pain when he was getting out of his car. I also didn't realize how much weight he had lost until four o'clock the night of the debate.

There was no way I could compensate for his loss of some twenty pounds and all the various aftereffects of his illness and the fact that they overworked him like he was a perfectly well candidate, which he wasn't. If I would have had any power I would have canceled the debate, but I didn't. I couldn't even get him a smaller shirt. He wasn't listening to me anyway. He was totally preoccupied.

DON HEWITT: I'm standing there with Kennedy and Nixon, and I said, "You guys want makeup?" Kennedy had been campaigning in an open convertible in California. He looked great. He didn't need any. Nixon looked like death warmed over. We offered to put some makeup on him, but he said no because he didn't want people to say he used makeup and Kennedy didn't.

TED ROGERS: We put some kind of Pan-Cake on him in 1950. He didn't object then. Even then we used to tell him if he was on television more than thirty minutes we could see his beard growing.

DON HEWITT: When the first debate was over, I said, "My God, we don't have to wait for election night." I said, "I just produced a television show that elected a president of the United States." That was a travesty.

FADE TO BLACK

June 26, 1950, was the red-letter day—literally—for anti-communists in the television field. On that day, the blacklister's bible, *Red Channels*, was published. After that, no self-respecting red-hunter could be without a copy. Consider this endorsement from Ed Sullivan, in his *New York Daily News* column.

> . . . *the entire industry is becoming increasingly aware of the necessity to plug all commie propaganda loopholes. Network and station heads, with a tremendous financial stake, want no part of commies or pinkos. Sponsors, sensitive in the extreme to blacklisting, want no part of commies or their sympathizers. Advertising agencies . . . want no controversy of any kind. For that reason,* Red Channels' *listing of performers who innocently, or maliciously, are affiliated with commie-front organizations will be a reference book for any programs.*

Red Channels was a 213-page paperback that listed 151 names, 130 organizations, and 17 publications, and the citations that supposedly justified the listings. The names were compiled from organization lists, petition signatures, and the like. What could qualify a person or group for inclusion in the book? One could have been a member of the Communist Party, of course, but there were actually very few members in the book. The more likely scenario was that someone signed a petition in support of Jackie Robinson's entry into baseball, protested civil rights abuses, or backed the presidential candidacy of former vice president Henry Wallace. Such was the nature of subversive behavior as judged in 1950.

It would be a mistake, however, to lay all the responsibility at the feet of *Red Channels*'s editors. The blacklisting game had many eager participants. A scorecard of players would include all four major networks, the country's leading advertising agencies, civic organizations, labor unions, senators and congressmen, professional witnesses, along with a few independent "security consultants" and a supermarket owner in Syracuse, New York.

The television industry's efforts to keep track of potentially subversive elements nearly predates the industry itself. In a 1990 letter to *The New York Times*, Gertrude Berg's daughter Harriet wrote that her mother, who played the beloved Molly Goldberg in radio and TV, appeared in a 1944 CBS memo, naming those who publicly supported the reelection of President Franklin D. Roosevelt. Following the president's death in April 1945, and the end of World War II, anti-communist fervor mushroomed, with the entertainment field first targeted in 1947 by the House Committee on Un-American Activities (known as HUAC).

That year also saw an early attempt to return fire. A Greenwich, Connecticut, woman named Hester McCullough pressured local authorities to cancel a performance by the dancer Paul Draper and mouth organist Larry Adler because of their alleged pro-communist sympathies. The two retaliated by filing a libel suit against her. The case resulted in a hung jury, however, and the two rarely performed together again.

Still, the television industry remained relatively immune to attack until three former FBI agents formed a company called the American Business Consultants and began publishing *Counterattack*, a weekly newsletter that set out to expose and defeat not only communism but those involved with "helping communism." According to the "Report on Blacklisting" by the Fund for the Republic, among those charged with being in league with the communists were both houses of Congress, the television networks, the ACLU, and the YMCA.

Following the HUAC hearings on Hollywood, *Counterattack*'s editors turned their attention toward radio and television, listing names of those whose politics wandered to the left of center and insisting that they be barred from the field. Their influence was boosted by their alignment with other right-wing groups, particularly veterans' organizations whose members could often be counted on for bulk phone calls or picket duty.

Even more influential was a fervently anti-communist Syracuse grocer named Laurence A. Johnson. How could a man who owned four supermarkets in a small Northern city reduce the head of General Foods to something resembling his own quivering dessert dish? Easily. This was an industry not known for its courage in the best of times, and when Johnson kicked he knew just where to aim. He paid regular visits to the offices of the major advertising agencies who hired "controversial" performers notifying them that he intended to post a notice on his shelves that the sponsor of a certain television program hired "subversives." The sign might say, YOU CAN BUY THE PRODUCT MADE BY THAT FIRM OR A COMPETING PRODUCT MADE BY A COMPANY THAT DOES NOT HIRE COMMUNISTS.

All he had to do was threaten. In not a single instance was Johnson shown the door. Quite the opposite. "It is indeed heartening to know you are continuing your crusade," wrote the vice president of Kraft Foods in a typical response to Johnson, the man threatening to cut off their livelihood. Ironically, Johnson had the least sway over those who knew him best. When the veterans in his American Legion post demanded that phonograph records by the folk group The Weavers be banned from radio, television, record stores, and jukeboxes in Syracuse, they were simply ignored and the protest ended. "I don't know what's the matter with those people in New York City," said one Syracuse station executive. "Maybe they're so big they have to be stupid."

The right-wing line was bought—literally—by most industry figures in New York. For a fee, *Counterattack* would supply advertising agencies with a list of names from its own files. Similar services were provided by other publications and independent "security consultants" such as Vincent Hartnett, who was the uncredited author of *Red Channels*.

At times, the McCarthy period seemed to create more jobs than the WPA. Aside from "security consultants," there were also the professional witnesses, men and women who made themselves available to testify against those who they claimed served the communist causes. Louis Budenz, Whittaker Chambers, Isaac Don Levine, and Elizabeth Bentley were star government witnesses, confessing not only their own past sins but those of their neighbors. The oddest of the lot was Harvey Matusow, a self-proclaimed ex-communist, who later recanted his testimony, claiming he had been a "false witness." The government then charged him with perjury, not for his original testimony but for his retraction. A trial ensued and Matusow was convicted for what was, in essence, telling the truth.

Hartnett was not only a witness, but also judge, jury, and executioner. This was a man for whom hubris was no sin. He once published a magazine article under a pseudonym in which he praised his own work blacklisting and clearing actors. He found no shortage of clients and actively solicited business not only from advertisers and their agencies (charging five dollars for every name they gave him to look up in his own files) but also from the people he exposed, indicating that Hartnett studied not only the workings of the left, but also the shakedown techniques of the Mob.

Hartnett offered to protect actors from people like himself for fees upward of two hundred dollars, the figure he cited in a letter to actress Kim Hunter. Hartnett would write a letter, informing an actor of his left-wing history. The letter would go on to suggest that to prevent protests against the actor's employment, it would be wise to submit to either an analysis of his past or a clearance process, which Mr. Hartnett would be happy to arrange.

There were several ways an actor could be cleared. One, of course, was to name his friends before a congressional committee. Another was to submit to an interview with a leading right-wing newspaper columnist such as George Sokolsky or Ed Sullivan. If the subject pleaded his case effectively, the columnist would announce that the actor, who only moments before had been a threat to national security, was now safe enough to appear in a drama or situation comedy without infecting the American public with his heretofore dangerous political opinions.

Sokolsky was an interesting case. Upon being twitted by the press critic George Seldes, he advised, "Be a crook, Seldes; but don't be a little crook. I'm a big crook. I've made a lot of money. Be a big crook, Seldes."

This self-appointed guardian of American values was openly paid by the Japanese government, in return for generous notices in his columns. He once wrote, "In spite of the bellicose talk, the Japanese want no war with us." That appeared in his syndicated column on December 2, 1941.

Right-wing activists labeled their cause "Americanism." The idea that one must prove his innocence was a concept against which this country was formed. Yet that was precisely the position in which those named as communists found themselves. The tragedy was that those with final say over hiring consulted *Red Channels* rather than the Bill of Rights. Three months after *Red Channels* first appeared, the editors celebrated their first scalp in Jean Muir. The actress was scheduled to star in the TV version of "Henry Aldrich," when General Foods fired her the night before the show's premiere, citing her *Red Channels* listing.

By the year's end, scores of TV's most talented performers, directors, and writers found themselves waiting in vain for the phone to ring. Sometimes, as in the case of director William Sweets, a sponsor canceled a contract in the wake of public protests. Other times, as in the case of Muir, a listing in either *Red Channels*, *Counterattack*, or other publications, such as the American Legion's *Firing Line*, were sufficient to warrant firing.

Generally, a blacklisted artist, who refused to participate in the clearance process, had few places to turn for help. There were only pockets of resistance. David Susskind, a packager of shows, hired "tainted" performers when he could. Some blacklistees wrote under pseudonyms or used "fronts" to represent their work. However, there was no help forthcoming from network executives, who demanded casting lists from producers so names could be submitted to security consultants for clearance. By 1950, CBS, in part because it was known as the liberal network, was requiring a loyalty oath of all its employees and also operated a security office that would have been the envy of the FBI. ABC also had a security operation that worked hand in hand with HUAC. Only NBC was somewhat more resistant; more, not completely.

The unions were also of limited help. Actor's Equity, the American Federation of Radio and Television Artists, and the Radio Writer's Guild, were horribly split over the issue. At AFTRA, the atmosphere seemed especially poisonous. There, a pro-blacklisting organization headed by Hartnett called AWARE was opposed by a group of moderates and progressives who called themselves "The Middle of the Road" ticket, headed by Charles Collingwood and John Henry Faulk. With AWARE, Hartnett took his own arguments even further, declaring that those who opposed blacklisting should be blacklisted because they were, in effect, helping the communist conspiracy.

Faulk himself was blacklisted. In 1958, he filed the most widely publicized suit of the period against Hartnett and Johnson, emerging victorious in 1962 with a $1.3 million judgment in his favor. However, his career was never the same. The suit did, at least, put an end to Johnson's reign of terror. He was found dead in a Bronx motel room as the jury was deliberating. By then, many of the blacklisted artists were gradually finding themselves employable again. Still, the McCarthy period had cost them the best years of their lives. Considering the talent that had been shut out of the industry for years, it cost television a lot more.

HARVEY MATUSOW: A character named Cockypoo has ruled my whole life. He's been my fantasy character ever since I was five years old, growing up in the Bronx. Everybody in my club was supposed to come up with a nickname. I came up with Cockypoo. Somebody else liked the name, too, so we took a vote, and I lost. That traumatized me, because Cockypoo could do everything.

I was in the infantry during the war. When it ended, I would sit in cafés with these communists and listen to their stories about fighting the fascists. They would say, "We always felt the informer was immoral, but when Germany conquered our country, we removed that layer of immorality. Now, we had a patriotic reason for doing what we thought was repugnant, infiltrating and spying."

When I went to work for the McCarthy forces, just as those communists had infiltrated the fascists and helped destroy them, it was my fantasy that Cockypoo was infiltrating the McCarthyites and would wipe them out. This was my fantasy, not reality, but that is how I justified what I was doing. Anyone who does something despicable tries to make it palatable to himself. Cockypoo did that for me.

ABRAHAM LINCOLN "ABE" POLONSKY: I came from a family that believed in education. My grandfather was kind of a superintendent of schools in Russia. My father was a socialist and very literary even though he was a pharmacist. He read and spoke four or five languages. I grew up in the Bronx. We had a very good library in our house. We talked about literature, so when I announced at the age of seven that I was going to be a novelist, it was accepted.

I went to City College, which was an exciting place in the late twenties and early thirties. My circle consisted of Leonard Boudin, Paul Goodman, and William Christopher Barrett. They turned out to be a distinguished radical group, very much influenced by the Depression.

After graduation, I went to law school, and then wrote and practiced law. One of the partners in our firm was related to Gertrude Berg, who had decided to do a radio show about a court case. Naturally she came to us for help, and who did they pick to work with her? Who was the most unimportant person?

Me. Eventually I began writing for her beginning at $250 a week, which was an incredible sum.

I joined the OSS during the war. They investigated me first and found out I was a member of the communist left. I told them. I told everybody. Still, they thought my background would be useful to them in Europe.

At the same time, I was hired by Paramount to become a screenwriter. I thought it would be a good thing to sign with Paramount because under the law when you got back from overseas, they had to give you your job back, but when Bill Dozier, the head of the writers, heard I was leaving, he went into a goddamned fury. I later saw a note he left in my file, saying, "Fire the son of a bitch when he gets back."

I wasn't fired. I did a picture with Marlene Dietrich called *Golden Earrings*. I did *Body and Soul* with John Garfield. Then I directed and wrote until I was blacklisted. I was blacklisted because I was a member of the Communist Party. That qualified me for the OSS, but it made me too dangerous to work at Paramount.

WALTER BERNSTEIN: I fought for this country. I wasn't disloyal. You didn't have to risk your life in the war to make it a shame to be blacklisted, but it was. Who were they to say I was disloyal or to say what loyalty consists of?

ABE POLONSKY: I went to New York because there was no use hanging around Los Angeles, which is a company town, while in New York they don't give a shit who you are or what you do as long as you don't bother them.

It was tough in the beginning, but I lived through plenty of excitement during the war, so this was tame stuff. I rented an apartment from a painter named Gwathmey on Central Park. I got a job doing this and that, writing screenplays, fixing them up. That's when I got together with Walter and Arnie Manoff and started to do television.

HARVEY MATUSOW: I joined the Communist Party in 1947. I was an officer in the Tompkins Square Club on the Lower East Side. Nobody ever talked about overthrowing the government at those meetings. That was rubbish. These were people like myself who wanted to change the world. Eventually, I left the party because I felt it was as much bullshit as everything else. That's when I started testifying against them.

ROD ERICKSON: In 1950, Young and Rubicam put "The Aldrich Family" on television. We had Jean Muir playing a mother until some busybody broad in Westport, Connecticut, said she was a communist. I was at the rehearsal on Saturday night. I came back on Sunday and nobody was there. I didn't know what the hell happened and I was executive producer of the show. It turned out she was fired by General Foods's top man, Charlie Mortimer.

They had no cause for the accusations except for *Red Channels*, which was worthless, but firing her started the feeding frenzy. Suddenly, they were playing court, and everybody was a commie and there weren't any rational people anymore.

IRA SKUTCH: One day in February 1950, a lawyer came to our agency, which handled the Philco account. He said, "I used to be an FBI agent, but several of us thought we could carry on the fight better from outside the FBI than within, so we've left."

I said, "What fight?"

"The fight against communism." Then he said, "We've been criticized for printing the names of communists and companies who have employed them without giving them any warning, so we're now giving warning and you had a communist on your show last week."

"Who was that?"

"Jean Muir."

"Jean Muir? She played Abraham Lincoln's mother. I don't see what's communistic about that."

"That's not the point. The point is that all the money that you pay her she gives to the Communist Party."

"Is she a card-carrying communist?"

"As far as we know, she's not, but they're the worst kind."

I asked him for substantiation, and he pulled out a two-page mimeographed list. It said she appeared at a rally for Russian War Relief during the war. She went to a dinner honoring somebody. He also had an unsigned statement from someone, saying that he borrowed her car to drive three communists to a meeting and that they got into an accident.

Philco's reaction was exemplary. The president said, "We're not going to have these sons of bitches telling us how to run our company."

We never did have anything to do with them until the show was sold to Goodyear, which said they would not allow anybody in *Red Channels* to appear on the show. From then on, my boss had a copy of *Red Channels* in his desk. When Fred Coe would call him and give him the names of the actors, he would secretly take a look and give him a yes or a no.

HARVEY MATUSOW: I worked for *Counterattack*. Besides the newsletter, for five thousand dollars we also set up security systems for companies. If a company bought our services, they would send us lists of names, and we would check them out in our files and let them know if they were acceptable or not.

We had a humongous index file. If a name appeared in an ad in the *New York Post* we put it on a card. We also had all the Congressional testimony cross-indexed. We would go through the cards, and we would find out that so-and-so signed a petition in 1941 and we would tell the client.

IRA SKUTCH: There was also a payoff. The guys who came to see us said if we subscribed to their service, they'd clear everybody we called, so this whole business of clearing people was a blackmail scheme.

HARVEY MATUSOW: Lennon & Mitchell paid me $150 for a list of actors that we had indexed. It didn't take a lot of convincing. They were eager to have it because now they could just look at the file and—"Boom, we don't want him."

They bought it because they were afraid of us, and also because they believed in what we were doing, which was to get communists and left-wing sympathizers out of the industry.

TOM BOLAN: I was Roy Cohn's law partner, and I defended Vincent Hartnett and Laurence Johnson when they were sued by John Henry Faulk. Hartnett believed that it was proper and almost mandatory to oppose the appearance on television of anyone who was in the Communist Party or significantly connected with it. He felt it was proper to approach sponsors and say, "Why are you sponsoring someone who is a member of the Communist Party or connected with it in a significant way?"

He saw it in the same light as the Nazi Party, an organization that deprived you of your liberty and would execute you at the drop of a hat. Someone who was just a left-winger or a liberal, that was not his goal, nor was it in the case of any of the organizations involved.

PAUL DRAPER: Neither Larry Adler nor I were ever members of the Communist Party, nor were we ever accused of it when we were blacklisted. Being left-wing or being in favor of certain communist front groups was sufficient.

HARVEY MATUSOW: The net was very wide, but they said it was narrow. If you signed a civil-rights petition or if you questioned whether the Rosenbergs were guilty, you were a suspect. We went after anybody who publicly got up and was in the way of what we were doing, like the American Civil Liberties Union.

DANIEL PETRIE: There was a real terror in that time. One night we got a phone call in the middle of the night after we had gone to bed. The person said, "I just want to warn you to have your wife be careful about what she says about the blacklist at cocktail parties."

Click. I never found out who it was.

KIM HUNTER: What got me on the list was my participation in a peace conference of the arts and sciences at the Waldorf in 1949. I thought it was an absolutely marvelous idea, getting people together from all over the world in the arts and sciences to talk. I was in good company. There were four hundred sponsors besides me, including Albert Einstein and Eleanor Roosevelt. Still, it was immediately labeled pro-communist by HUAC.

I also signed a bunch of petitions in favor of civil rights, and [in mock horror] I worked in a Lillian Hellman play, *The Children's Hour*! I was also a member of Actor's Studio, which they decided was as red as a firecracker, even though politics were never discussed at the Actor's Studio.

DAN PETRIE: Really, it was an honor if you could get into the Actor's Studio, but all the Actor's Studio people were blacklisted. I once went into a men's room with Vinton Hayworth, who was president of AFTRA. At adjacent urinals I asked him about Lenka Peterson, who was in Actor's Studio and was having a hard time getting work. I said, "She's from Omaha, Nebraska. I know her family. They aren't leftists. She has simply been tarred with the brush of being in the Actor's Studio."

He started to froth at the mouth. [Loudly, in a slow, menacing tone] "DAN, MY LIFE STARTS AT LABOR DAY, MAKING FRUITCAKES FOR OUR BOYS IN KOREA. NOW, IF THERE'S ANYTHING WORSE THAN A COMMUNIST, IT'S AN ANTI-ANTI-COMMUNIST.

CHARLIE ISAACS: In the beginning, most of the television writers who came to New York worked for ridiculous salaries. Most of us were not Sam Gompers types. Nevertheless we decided to start a union. I was made president. Jess Oppenheimer was the vice president. Immediately we got into a terrible jurisdictional fight with the Screen Writers Guild.

Some clique over there decided they couldn't beat us because we had most of the TV writers, so they began smearing us, saying we had communists in our group. I was particularly angry because I was a combat veteran. To be called a communist after that was just terrible. Letters were sent around with the names of myself and Jess. Kids at school were told by their teachers if they see any of these names on television they should write postcards to the sponsors. I sure lost my virginity about writers. Just the word "writer" was holy to me at one time, but not after that.

KIM HUNTER: At AFTRA, if you supported the AWARE side at the union, you were a loyal American. If you were against them, you were disloyal, and you were blacklisted.

LEE GRANT: This was a whole new world for me. I didn't read newspapers. I was a self-involved Jewish princess actress. It started for me in '52. I had worked with J. Edgar Bromberg in a play. He had a bad heart, and the committee kept badgering him. Anyway, then he went to work in England, and he died of a heart attack. At his memorial, I said that HUAC had killed him. The next day I was told I was on the list. I almost fainted. I knew it could happen and now it did. I felt the blood drain out of me. I had crossed that line, and in those days we thought blacklisting was forever.

At the time I was a very hot actor. I had done *Detective Story* and won the Critics' Circle Award. I had been nominated for an Oscar, and I won the Cannes Film Festival Award for Best Actress. Now, I couldn't get any work in television or movies.

KIM HUNTER: They didn't tell you you were blacklisted. You just didn't get work. I had my Oscar, for god's sake, for *Streetcar,* and I couldn't get anything. I went to Bill Dozier, who was a vice president at CBS. I asked him, was I blacklisted or just being paranoid. He said, "No, it's true. We can't hire you."

My publicity agent was told to write to Vincent Hartnett, which he did, and he got a letter back saying that for two hundred dollars he would tell me what my problems were. I said, "No way, I know what I've signed."

LEE GRANT: I ran into Mike Wallace. He said, "Tell me you're not a communist and I'll fight for you."

I said, "That's the whole point. I may be a communist. I may not be, but that can't be the basis on which you decide to go to bat for me." There was nothing to say after that.

PAUL DRAPER: I *was* connected with left-wing organizations. When Larry and I filed our libel suit against Hester McCullough, we wanted to show that you could have those affiliations and beliefs and still not feel that you wanted to overthrow the country by force and violence. That was important.

I had known Ed Sullivan for quite some time. He volunteered to be a character witness for me. A lot of people did, but as the case came closer, all of them said they couldn't afford to. When Ed reneged on his offer, he said, "If you come on my show, we can knock this off in a minute."

I went on, but within an hour after the show, they said they got 150 calls from war veterans. We later discovered that most of them had been made from the same phone booth. Also a lot of letters came in. As a result, in his column, Ed apologized to CBS, the sponsor, Ford/Lincoln, the ad agency, Cardinal Spellman, his readers, the administration, the Army and the Navy, and anybody else he could think of.

After that, everybody who came on his show was screened. It was as if you were applying to the CIA. They would check everything in your history to make sure there was nothing that could link you to anything left-wing.

He told me it was a shame that it had happened and that the Roman Catholic Church could use young men like me. He said he could fix everything up if I joined the Church. I have never done any television since.

KIM HUNTER: The networks went out one by one. CBS first, ABC last. I said to my agent at William Morris, "What can you do to help?" And they said, "Oh, c'mon, we've got hundreds like you."

I left my agent. The hell with 'em.

HARVEY MATUSOW: It may have been Hartnett who wanted me to meet Johnson, who took a liking to me. He would take me on his visits to the agencies. We would be taken in very quickly to see the executives. They would treat him with the same kind of fear they would treat anybody who could cut their legs off. And Johnson could cut their legs off.

He would make his demands. We would say, "You can't use Jack Gilford." I'd be there from *Counterattack* backing him up. I'd make all kinds of wild charges. It was theater. If I saw them reacting I would do it more.

Johnson wasn't looking for money. He was looking to control the industry and tell them who they could or couldn't hire. He could do it, because we knew that Madison Avenue people are cowardly. That was the key. Whether Johnson could have affected their sales was not the issue, they believed he could.

The publicity was his power. It was a newspaper world then, not a television world. Winchell or Sokolsky could say in five hundred newspapers that your product hired communists, that would have affected your sales, and those columnists loved Johnson.

All those reactionary columnists were on the take, and Johnson probably paid them, too. Howard Rushmore, Victor Riesel, George Sokolsky, and J. B. Matthews, they all were on the take. Leonard Lyons also played the game. I know because I was close to a lot of them. I hung out with Winchell, riding around in his Cadillac all night. You never offered him money. He would have knocked you down, but if you said, "Walter, you need a new typewriter. Let me get you a new one," that wasn't money. That's how it worked. They got everything free, and they were always hustling for it.

I was also on the take. As Johnson's deputy, they would kiss my ass. Sam Levinson's agent gave me an envelope with two hundred dollars in it, "Go buy yourself a dinner." I would go back to *Counterattack* and say, "He's ready to cooperate. Let's take the heat off him." Levinson was in no position to name names. He was just a liberal Jew. We just didn't want him to say anything against the blacklist or *Counterattack*.

Johnson found out that Gilford was going to be on "The Colgate Comedy Hour," and Yogi Berra was also supposed to be on the show. Johnson was upset about that, so I got on the phone with a P.R. man from the Yankees, and I used a phony voice. I said, "How can you have Yogi Berra appearing on a show with communist sympathizers?"

I used to do puppets in those days. I had a hundred voices. I must have called twenty times in different voices, and they took him off the show. We laughed a lot about that at *Counterattack*.

TOM QUINLIN: At Revlon, they worried about every letter they received. When we were casting a commercial, Revlon would tell the agency, "Don't give us anyone who is in *Red Channels*." They didn't want their products boycotted.

It went to ridiculous extremes. We had a lipstick shade called Red Caviar, and people said we were procommunist. I remember our TV executive was on the phone with this woman. He was holding the phone about a foot away from his ear. Finally, he said, "Madame, do you shop at Macy's? What about their red star?"

ROD ERICKSON: When I bought "Robin Hood" for Johnson & Johnson [unrelated to Laurence Johnson], General Johnson asked to see me. He said, "Why are we sponsoring that commie show?"

"I beg your pardon, General. This is a classic story. What do you mean a communist show?"

"Doesn't he rob from the rich and give to the poor? Isn't that communism?"

SAMM SINCLAIR BAKER: Most of the top people in advertising had no conscience. The creative people were more liberal, but they had to keep it to themselves. The network people who gave in to it would say, "You know, personally I'm against this, but clients are extremely skittish."

FRANK STANTON: You had the federal government and Madison Avenue on your back. You had the press on your back. We could have gone out of business if we couldn't get any income.

It wasn't Mr. Johnson the quarrel was with, it was with General Foods, for example. Talk to them. Don't talk to me. We were the victims. We [set up a blacklist] to survive. When the chairman of the board of General Foods and the chairman of the biggest agency in the business says, "We're gonna wipe you out," that's pretty powerful talk.

If we would have said go ahead and do it, it might have been disastrous. We didn't know. He was the biggest advertiser we had. We set up a security system because we thought it [communists at CBS] was a serious problem. In retrospect that wasn't the case, but we had a person who devoted a lot of time to it. We didn't do it frivolously.

We examined the character of these people as to their loyalty to the country. The public established those standards. Liberality was perceived of as being disloyal. That's incomprehensible today, but not at that time.

What made a person disloyal? Behavior, as perceived by God, the courts, by the man in the street. I didn't believe they were disloyal, but I had no evidence to the contrary, and when I was confronted with the evidence that was brought to bear on us from the advertisers and from our affiliates, I had no choice.

I'm not proud of that period for my country, my industry, or my company, but we lived in those times and that's the way it was. We acted on what was the wisest course to pursue, economically, anyway. I don't know where the moral issue comes in if you don't exist.

Yes, we instituted a loyalty oath, but some pretty thoughtful people, Ed Murrow included, went along with it.

OSCAR KATZ: I didn't like it but I signed it. The only person who got fired for not signing the oath worked for me. She was a Republican. She was a clerk, lovely girl. She said, "I'm not going to tell anybody what my politics are."

Joe Ream, who was in charge of this, said, "Tell her to see me if she wants to." She spoke to him for about an hour. He fell in love with her and then he fired her.

ETHEL WINANT: I never signed. About every three months somebody would call and say, "We don't seem to have your loyalty oath." I'd say, "Really, I'm astonished." They would send another one. Several months would pass, and they would call again. John Housman even said to me, "Honey, sign it, and you can stop getting these phone calls," but I wouldn't.

BOB MARKELL: I was forced to sign it, and I still have very strange feelings about it. It was a very big trauma for me. I asked Marty Ritt and Yul Brynner what to do. Marty Ritt said sign it. Yul said, "Fuck 'em."

"Oh, yeah, what are you gonna do?"

"I got a play I'm gonna do. It's about the King of Siam."

BOB BENDICK: I was head of news and special events when all this broke. Tony Traber was involved in special events as an assistant. They saw him on the list and said, "We have to get rid of him. He's a communist."

I was shocked. He was no more anti-American than anybody. I talked to various people above me to help him, but nobody would listen. Management's line was, if you're in *Red Channels*, you're a communist. It was a terrible wrong, and I suppose I considered saying, "If he goes I go," but I was not that dedicated to valor. I had kids and everything else, so Tony was fired.

CHARLIE ANDREWS: There was a blacklisted writer named Lou Solomon. I was head writer on the summer replacement of "Caesar's Hour." Aaron Ruben and Phil Sharp asked me to hire Lou. I did. He wasn't a comedy writer, but he was such a sweet guy. It could have blown up in my face, but I didn't have that much to lose. Then I introduced him to Bob Bendick, who had come over to NBC, and Bob hired him for "Wide, Wide World." To hire him on a show as big as that was chancy for Bob, but he did it anyway.

FRANK STANTON: All the networks had a policy. NBC was doing the same thing we were doing.

PAT WEAVER: All that McCarthy stuff didn't really bother us at NBC because I said, "Fellas, here's the rule. Anybody who doesn't like our casting or what we're doing, we relieve them of their contract. They don't have to stay another second."

EZRA STONE: Bullshit. I produced and directed the Fred Allen Chesterfield series on NBC. Jack Gilford was hired as a guest on one episode. Pat Weaver came down personally to the rehearsal hall and took Fred and me aside and said, "We've got to let Gilford go. We can't clear him." Fred turned absolutely crimson. He was so incensed and humiliated, but there was no recourse.

DELBERT MANN: I'm a great admirer of Pat Weaver, but he's wrong. I can give you a list of names of people we could not use. Elliot Sullivan, Phil Loeb, Kim Hunter, Judy Holliday, Jean Muir. Tell me there was no blacklist.

DAN PETRIE: When I was doing "Treasury Men in Action" at NBC, I had scripts that were awful. I used Madeline Sherwood a lot until she got blacklisted because she could take that material and make it palatable, even exciting.

Then she came to me when I was doing "Justice." She said, "I want to go to Montreal for Christmas. My mother isn't feeling well, and I don't have a nickel. Can you hire me as an extra?"

I said, "Absolutely. I know we can sneak you in." I had a scene in a campus coffee shop, so we sat her in there with her back to the camera. You didn't see even her profile. After the dress, suddenly an agency guy walked over to me and said, "Isn't that Madeline Sherwood? Get her out of here."

"Why? Nobody knows her. It's a blond-haired girl."

"I know who it is."

"Because you walked onto the set and recognized her. Nobody else will, and she needs money."

He said, "Dan, get her out of there." I had to. I never met fanatics like that. They were extraordinary.

MADELINE GILFORD: It was frustrating because we couldn't prove that Jack was blacklisted. He just wasn't getting called, or they'd say, "We're going another way." That was a great euphemism. The union kept saying, "Get proof. You have none."

Well, I got the goods on them. After Jack was fired off a show sponsored by Kellogg's and Pet Milk, I called Laurence Johnson, pretending I was Pat Weaver's secretary. I said, "I took home some papers. One of them has your number on it, and it says 'urgent.' Is there something I can do? Did you call him?"

He said no, so I asked him, "Did you call anyone at NBC?"

"Oh, yeah, Pete Barnum."

"Oh, I see something about Jack Gilford."

"Yeah, I called Kellogg's and Pet Milk. We're not gonna carry those products if you're gonna have those people on your shows. You people down there in New York may think it's all right, but it isn't all right with us up here in the country. I told him you can't have those people on like George Kaufman and Sam Levinson," and he proceeded to name only Jews, so "you people down there in New York" was another euphemism.

I said, "Did Mr. Barnum take care of it?"

He said, "Oh yeah, he said he would take care of it."

I was jumping out of my skin. Jack confronted Pete Barnum and George Heller at AFTRA. They got him on Jerry Lester's show—but only on a local segment, so they got us after all, and they didn't use him again for eleven years.

ROBERT SAUDEK: I worked with Bob Kintner at ABC. He was a liberal, but he didn't make a big deal of it. Gypsy Rose Lee was hired at ABC when he was there. She had been named in *Red Channels,* so the word went out that she was unacceptable. No advertiser would touch her show. I went to see Kintner about it. We decided to stand firm and keep her on the network for the thirteen weeks, and we did without any advertising. In fact, Kintner and I got a Peabody Award for it. That was a big case at the time.

BOB LEWINE: I was head of programming at ABC. I couldn't fight them. Maybe Kintner could have in the beginning, but mostly my instructions were to check with our lawyer, Gerry Zorbaugh, on all casting decisions. I was a good servant. I wanted to stay in the business. Whatever they wanted, if it made sense I did it.

GERALDINE ZORBAUGH: The blacklisting was the most heart-rending thing I've ever done. I remember telling my minister, "I'm not sure I can take this any longer, but somebody has to do it." I could have said no, but I knew I could be fair, and I think I was. I don't think I made a mistake on anybody.

I worked with HUAC to get all the material I could get on the person's background. You checked where they worked and found out what their co-workers said about them. I also tried to find out which organizations they belonged to. If somebody had simply attended a party for an organization, that was okay, but if they marched three years in a row in a May Day parade, they'd be out.

When I talked to them, they had to say they were not now a member. If it came out that they had been in the past but were all right now, that was okay. When I went to college, our whole crowd were members, so what? There was one director I was very fond of. I said, "Look, we're alone in this room. Just tell me you are not now a member of the Party," and he wouldn't say it.

KIM HUNTER: Communism made no sense to me, but to have to say I'm not one? It wasn't against the law to be a communist.

I was up for a role at ABC and I never got it.

LETTER FROM VINCENT HARTNETT TO GERALDINE ZORBAUGH, OCTOBER 7, 1953. REPRODUCED AT THE JOHN HENRY FAULK TRIAL:

Dear Gerry,

I received from you the enclosed list of names for the purpose of evaluation. To keep my own records straight I note that on the list appeared the following names . . . and one of these is Kim Hunter. . . . In my opinion, finally, you would run a serious risk of adverse public opinion by featuring on your network Kim Hunter.

GERALDINE ZORBAUGH: I don't remember that letter. There must have been another reason why she didn't get the job. We had to run a business, and we were very careful to do it as efficiently as we could. A person had a right to belong to any organization, but that person didn't have to work for us. We didn't want Party members in the broadcast business. What they had done to the motion picture business was not going to be for us. One person moved in, and pretty soon you had a whole echelon of them. They undermined morale in the whole place.

ABE POLONSKY: No one ever ruined Hollywood except incompetent producers shooting pictures every year, and no one ever ruined television except producers making shitty things that people don't want to watch. Nobody politically ever could take control of Hollywood or of the television industry except those who own it.

The fear of people who are different has a long history in this country going back to the Abolitionists and before then to the Alien and Sedition Act. People always exploit that fear. This is part of the general disrepute the human race is held in by gorillas and chimpanzees. When you ask a gorilla or a chimpanzee what he thinks of human beings, he says, "You can't trust 'em."

I understand the position of people like Stanton because I heard it. It wasn't a question of principle. It was a question of fear and profit. For a capitalist to lose his profit is part of being a capitalist, but to lose his capital is a violation of the eleventh commandment: "Never jeopardize your capital." [Laughs.]

In the case of this woman, principle does come into play. "Everybody has a right to be a communist as long as they are very young and stupid, but if they get to be communists when they are older, then they shouldn't be on the air." Why shouldn't they be on the air? Because they're going to preach communism?

WALTER BERNSTEIN: At the beginning of the blacklist, but before I was blacklisted, I got a call from an agent, asking me if I would do an audition script. I said sure. When I gave it to him, he said I shouldn't put my name on it. When I asked him why, he said, "to be safe about it." That was the first inkling I had. He called a couple of days later and said the producer at the advertising agency wanted to see the writer. I said, "I can't go up there as this other guy. People know me."

He called me back and said, "I fixed the whole thing. I told them I'm taking the other writer off because he's uncooperative and I'm getting him another writer."

"Who?"

"You."

I had to go up there and listen to what an uncooperative shit this other writer was. When I did the changes, the guy said "Why didn't they get you in the first place? You're obviously a much better writer than this other guy."

The first year was tough. I slept on Marty Ritt's couch. He was blacklisted also. His wife was making thirty dollars a week selling space in the Yellow Pages. Marty supported himself by being a gambler. He was wonderful at it, and I did the cooking. We were young, and we had a lot of resilience. We were also very committed politically, which sustained us.

LEE GRANT: There was no blacklisting in the theater, so I got parts in various plays. I also taught and helped fight the "war." I liked being involved in something larger than myself, especially something moral where the rights and wrongs were so clear.

WALTER BERNSTEIN: When I look back on the period—and it would be different for those who couldn't work—the friendships and the support were very powerful and positive. I miss that. We were always there for each other. Polonsky, Manoff, and I always functioned as a group. We would meet for lunch at Steinberg's Dairy Restaurant on Broadway and Eighty-first Street.

ABE POLONSKY: We met there every day, except if Charlie Russell [a TV producer] was paying. Then we would eat at the finest restaurants in midtown. A lot of us blacklisted writers lived on the Upper West Side. Zero Mostel lived there, too. He was the king of the vegetarian restaurants. He would walk in and stop at everybody's table and taste everybody's food.

Isaac Bashevis Singer ate there too. One day he came in when a beautiful girl was having lunch with us. When she left, Singer came over and introduced himself to us. We talked for a while. Then he said, "This girl, who is she?"

"She's an actress."

I'll never forget this line. "Does she fuck?"

You know what we said? "We presume so, but not with us."

We had our favorite waiter. At first, he couldn't figure out what we did. He thought Arnie had a job early in the morning down in the food markets. That's the way Arnie looked, but one day after he listened to us talk, he said, "I know who you are."

"Who are we?"

[Accusingly] "Writers!"

LEE GRANT: Arnie, Abe, and Walter created the front system. Arnie was a gambler and a street fighter, and he and Walter and Abe had a great time licking the odds in such creative ways. Arnie was the tactician and the strategist.

ABE POLONSKY: Arnie says, "It's absurd to try and make a living each on our own. We ought to get together and take over a show. Walter just got blacklisted. He's got all the connections, so Walter will be the outside man. I'll be in charge of the production group. You (meaning me) can be the crazy designer," which is what they used to say in the garment industry.

Charlie Russell was a very brave man. He immediately employed Arnie and me, so we did the "Danger" series for him. He even raised the price so we made more money.

WALTER BERNSTEIN: Charlie was a real hero. He was totally non-political, and if it was found out he was hiring us, he would have been out. I did a play for Fred Coe called "Rich Girl," but when I was blacklisted, he wouldn't hire me. I told him I could get a front, but he still wouldn't do it. That surprised me.

In the beginning, we thought I would just put another name on my scripts. We used the name Paul Bauman. Then they became suspicious, so we had to get a front. In the meantime we dropped Bauman. If they asked about him, "He moved to Denver."

Then came that whole process of getting fronts. Leo Davis, who became a producer, was the first one I used. He was poor, and he was sending money to his old parents. Then he started getting a few more scripts, and it made his life impossible. Friends kept telling him, "You've living in a shithouse making this money." Then his parents wanted more money, so he couldn't do it anymore.

It was difficult to hold onto a front. Either they wanted money or they had ego problems. Howard Rodman was a sweet funny man, who fronted for me on a couple of scripts. It was a bad time in my life, and these were two comedies that weren't very good. Well, his name was on it, and he took me for a walk in the park and he told me I wasn't writing up to his standards.

The front who lasted the longest was Leslie Slote. He had no aspirations to be a television writer. He was working for a civil-service paper called *The Chief.* Since he was in the writing game, people accepted him, and he got a kick out of it. He liked the play acting, and he wouldn't take any money.

LESLIE SLOTE: I had known Walter since we were kids, but when he told me about the blacklist, I didn't have a television set, so I didn't know what the hell he was talking about. He asked me if I would let him use my name, and I said sure. He explained that every once in a while I would get money from CBS. I would deposit it in my checking account and then write a check for that amount to him. I didn't want any money for it, but some guys were charging.

WALTER BERNSTEIN: Somebody even tried to capitalize on our situation. A story editor at NBC offered us work. I didn't have a front at that time, so I said I couldn't do it. He came back and said, "The producer knows you're lying," because somebody had gone to NBC and said he was my front. That was the final grotesquery.

LESLIE SLOTE: At one point, I had to show up at the studio to watch a performance of "Danger," because everybody wanted to meet this wonderful writer. I just sat in a booth and watched this thing, and that was all. I wasn't nervous.

Another time Walter called to say, "The agency people want to meet you," so I put on my tweed jacket and got a pipe so I looked like a writer, and I showed up at the advertising agency. Russell was there. He later told Walter I was a big hit.

I didn't even know I did one series, "Colonel March." I must have done about twenty of those. Then one day Walter calls me and says, "You've got to go up to CBS's spook department," to see this former FBI guy. I went to the CBS building. I got off the elevator on the eighth floor, and there was no name on the door of his office. Inside was a secretary and not a paper to be seen anywhere. It was the cleanest office I have ever seen. He asked me a few very cursory questions, and thank you and good-bye.

After that Walter said I was blacklisted. That was the end of it. The last script that carried my name was "The Prince and the Pauper," for which I received a Christopher Award in 1958. Walter gave me the plaque, and I still have it.

WALTER BERNSTEIN: The TV show we did that I liked the best of all was "You Are There." The conceit was modern-day reporters are present at the fall of Troy or the Battle of Gettysburg. They interviewed the participants. Walter Cronkite narrated it, and we had three or four actual CBS correspondents. It was a wonderful show, and it was written by myself, Abe, and Arnie.

ABE POLONSKY: We were conducting guerrilla warfare with that show. Every forbidden subject in the United States was treated: free speech and John Milton, Galileo, the Alien and Sedition acts, all this stuff that no one would dare open his mouth about. Ed Murrow once said to Charlie, "I always watch your show. How do you get away with that stuff?"

WALTER BERNSTEIN: The only flack we got was one outraged letter from the wife of the president of Miller Beer. I don't recall if she called us communists, but she said we were cruel and unfair to Marie Antoinette.

ABE POLONSKY: Toward the end of the series, Bill Dozier becomes the producer, and he wants to take it to California. They said, "It's a New York show. It's very successful there." That's when he said, "but he's using blacklisted guys." He knew all along, because one day he said to Charlie, "Tell Polonsky this is a very good script." The son of a bitch.

They sent it out to California so they wouldn't have any fronts. It was the end of "You Are There" for us, and it was the end of "You Are There" for him too because they started putting crap on, and people stopped watching it. It was known as one of those dangerous shows, because history was dangerous in those days. History is always dangerous.

LEE GRANT: I was subpoenaed to testify in Washington. Leonard Boudin was my attorney. He explained that they would try to trick me. If you answer questions about "Danger," then you have to answer questions about your family and your friends. He said the best thing for me to do was take the Fifth Amendment from the beginning, and it wouldn't open me up from then on.

I felt like I was in the principal's office. I was a bad girl with eight grown men leaning over me. When I walked in there, one of the guys on the committee said, "What's a nice little girl like you doing in a place like this?"

I said, "What's a big grown man like you doing in a place like this?" I wasn't afraid. I had no temptation to break into movies or television. I knew I was not going to lose my Broadway job. What they wanted was for me to name Arnie, and I wasn't going to do that.

WALTER BERNSTEIN: The only way I could get un-blacklisted was by doing some kind of *mea culpa* thing. The FBI would come to the house or approach me in the subway station. It was always the same two guys, very polite. "Walter Bernstein? We're from the FBI, and we'd like to talk to you."

"Thank you, I have nothing to say," and they would leave. They were letting me know they knew where I was. That was scary. After a while they would call me on the phone, and we got friendly. He would say, "How are the kids?"

"Fine. How are your kids?"

KIM HUNTER: Hartnett suggested I write a letter, saying I was against battling AWARE. That's what got me off the blacklist. I said, "AWARE is going to exist or not exist, why should we get involved?" I worded it the best way I could to feel reasonably honest about doing it, but I didn't feel reasonably honest about it. That's why it is still so painful.

MADELINE GILFORD: It was awful what happened to Kim, but we were too busy feeling bad for those of us with children that we couldn't feed or take to the doctor. Those who cooperated were turncoats. Kim and Billy Redfield we were sorry for.

ETHEL WINANT: He stood up before the Guild and made a *mea culpa* speech and got a job offer before the meeting was over. It was a disgrace. It was a disgrace that we all let it happen, that we were all scared, that we didn't just refuse to make the shows.

ERNEST KINOY: Sam Moore was about as thoroughly blacklisted as anybody. It got to the point where if you had to bail out and inform on somebody, you figured, "Well, I'll name Sam. It can't hurt him anymore," so everybody named Sam. The strange thing was he was enormously well liked in the union and continued to be reelected to positions.

HENRY MORGAN: The worst part was a man named Jack Wren at BBD&O, a bald man in his thirties who had an office lined with reference books. He sent for me to talk about my blacklisting. I said to him, "You certainly know that I am not a communist."

He said, "I know, but if you want to clear yourself there are certain things I'd like you to do."

He said I would have to go to this party. I didn't know what the party was but I went. I remember somebody said to me, "The fact that you're here means you're an anti-communist."

I said, "I'm not like all the anti-communists. Some of them I find despicable."

"Like whom?"

"Like Whittaker Chambers."

He just turns me around and standing there was Chambers and he heard me, so I went home. They wanted me to be seen at a party with a guy like Whittaker Chambers, and I didn't want to be seen at a party with a guy like Whittaker Chambers.

Then I went on a show hosted by Conrad Nagel, in which I played a part. The point was if you appeared on Conrad Nagel's show you are pure. Then Wren says there's an AFTRA meeting to consider the case of Phil Loeb. "Here's the speech I want you to make." I say, "I can't read that." It was slander. I said, "I'll make a speech, but not this one."

I didn't know Phil. I felt then as I do today. If you're a communist or an Islamic Fundamentalist, I don't give a shit if you're a nice person. I always understood that that was what the country was about. At the meeting, I raised my hand and I guess this had been preset because they recognized me. I went up to the microphone, trembling. I said, "I'm a little nervous." Big laugh. I start to read my version of this, which was that Phil Loeb shouldn't bring his case to AFTRA. It was an actor's union for wages and time. I didn't bring my case and he shouldn't bring his. I didn't read the next few pages, which said how wrong it was in America to have communists working.

Wren called me after the meeting. He wanted me to write him a letter saying he cleared me, "to show the evenhandedness" of his office. I prefer to think I didn't write the letter, but I did.

MADELINE GILFORD: For these people, the blacklisting clearing racket was a money-making racket, just a scam.

ETHEL WINANT: The way the blacklist worked was you would call this number and give them a list of names you might want to use. Then they got back to you with either a yes or a no for each name. It was never done in writing. It was always done by telephone, and they charged money to do their research.

DANIEL PETRIE: They would charge five dollars to twenty-five dollars per name. The producers didn't like it because if you cleared twenty or thirty people you went into several hundred dollars in charges.

ETHEL WINANT: I would submit two hundred names for every show, and the agency would complain to my boss, but my bosses hated the blacklist as much as I did and were not sympathetic to the agency. Sometimes it would take a couple of days to get back, which hurt our negotiating position with an actor, so they created a rule that they had to get back to us within twenty-four hours. I would dial the number and say, "I want to clear Viveca Lindfors." Then I would say to my secretary, "What time is it?" She would say, "It's three-nineteen."

"Okay, tomorrow at three-eighteen dial Viveca Lindfors's agent. If they call at three-twenty-five to turn her down it's too late."

Certain names were submitted every week just in the hope there would be a clerical error because if they were cleared once they could be hired.

DANIEL PETRIE: "Treasury Men" had a white list of people who had been cleared. The first year I did the show we cleared lots of people, and that first year we used two hundred people. The next year we were given a list of eighty-seven people, from which we could cast. We couldn't cast anybody else outside of that list because it would cost to clear.

There was one guy, let's say his name was Lewis Vincent. He had previously been on the white list. This year he wasn't. I looked at the previous year's list. There was a guy named Vincent Lewis. His name was misprinted on the current list, and I couldn't use him.

ETHEL WINANT: When we were doing Armstrong Circle Theater, the man in charge was named Max Vanzoff, who was a little right of King George III, but I think he was an honest man. He really did believe we could be wiped out by these dangerous people. One day at a meeting he said, "Does anybody have any problems?"

I said, "I have a terrible problem. I can't cast the show because of the blacklist."

He said, "Oh, Mrs. Winant, you're a mother and a good American. You don't want to see your money going to communist Russia because you pay these communist actors."

I said, "First of all, it's not any of my business where their money goes, but it's your show. As much as I disapprove of it you have a right not to have an acknowledged communist on your show if it really offends you, but the blacklist is a fraud. Ninety-seven percent of the people who are blacklisted don't know where Russia is, have probably never voted, and certainly aren't sending their money anywhere except to Sardi's or to Daddy. The blacklist is political fear. It has nothing to do with overthrowing the government."

"You can't prove that."

"I can. I can tell you people who are blacklisted, and I can show you that they never belonged to the party."

He said, "I'm shocked. Can you tell me that there is no recourse, and that these people are being falsely accused?"

"That's absolutely true, and if they were members, half of them didn't know what they were joining."

He said, "I'll tell you what. If there's an actor that you think should not be blacklisted, call me and I'll look into it."

We cleared about ninety percent of the blacklisted actors. I would submit about four or five people for a part. If I got a no I would call him, "Richard Kiley is blacklisted."

He was blacklisted because he had once appeared in a play written by Robert Ardrey. About twenty-four hours after I called I got an okay on him, because Max asked them for the exact information.

BILL ROSS: Ezra Stone and I were Phil Loeb's adopted children. Philip was one of God's angry men. He was very involved in politics, but he ever joined anything except Equity.

EZRA STONE: Phil was multi-talented, as a director, as a musician, as an actor, and as a teacher. As an actor, he was very much admired by Brooks Atkinson and the top critics of the day. He and Sam Jaffe were the leaders of the rebel movement at Equity. They were responsible for the creation of rehearsal pay and for secret balloting. The entire existence of AFRA, now AFTRA, came as a result of their leadership.

BILL ROSS: He always fought with a sense of humor. At one meeting, someone got up and said, "Mr. Loeb, are you or are you not a member of the Artists Committee to Win the War?"

Phil said, "What, then to Lose the War?"

EZRA STONE: During rehearsal for "Parade," which he directed in 1935, we were seated in chairs facing the footlights, and Philip and his staff were at tables in front of us. Phil was pacing around. As he passed me I said, "Phil, your fly is open."

He said, "Ventilation! I am protesting the management's lack of air cooling," and he refused to button up.

LEE GRANT: Phil and Zero had this running gag where they would show up naked at each other's houses.

BILL ROSS: Once, Katie [Mostel] was serving roast beef for dinner, and Zero said, "Great. Did you tell Phil?" Because Phil loved roast beef. "Call him up and tell him to get right over here," so she called him and he said, "I'm not dressed."

"Look, it's just us, come as you are."

So Phil came over. When he got to their floor he undressed completely except for his tie, and then he rang the bell. Katie answered the door and never blinked an eye. He came in and sat there with Katie and Zero and the two boys. When he got ready to leave, Katie whispered to him, "Phil, your fly is open."

When Phil was first blacklisted, we treated it as if it were a joke. When they closed the Goldbergs down, it stopped being a joke. After holding out courageously for a while, Gertrude Berg said to Philip, "They won't do the program with you. I have to let you go, but I will get you a good settlement."

When he accepted that money, it was disastrous. He had to accept it. His son was in a sanitarium, and Ezra's father was paying the bills. He didn't want that to continue, but he felt he had sold out. He moved in with Zero and Katie. I think he needed the company.

But Phil got more and more depressed. Sam Jaffe was more aware of it than any of us. Phil was staying with a mutual friend, and Sam had to put bars on the windows and make sure there were no razors or poisons in the medicine cabinet.

EZRA STONE: I wasn't attuned to his depression until he invited me for brunch at the apartment of a friend of his. Phil was not his fun self. He was bemoaning that he was losing his eyesight, and how could he ever work again if anybody would hire him. He reminded me that I had to sign a will he had written in longhand in which I agreed to be executor of his estate and to look after his son Johnny, who was schizophrenic. When we were done, he walked me around the corner to my car. I got in, and he said good-bye. I insisted that I wait to see that he got back across the street safely, but he just waved me off, and that was the last time I saw him.

BILL ROSS: He was getting ready to go into rehearsal for a play, and I started calling around to find him, but the line was either busy or no answer.

EZRA STONE: Sam called me because Zero called him that Philip had left their apartment and had not returned. The next day they found his body. He had registered at the Taft Hotel as Fred Lang, which is a name he always said he would have liked to have because in German it meant "forever peace." He had committed suicide there by taking an overdose of barbitures. It turned out that that night, he had made a number of calls from his room, and one of them was to me, but my line was busy.

HENRY MORGAN: He killed himself not too long after I made my speech to the union. I've always felt a little bit responsible. That may have been the one time in my life in which I did something for which I don't truly forgive myself.

LEE GRANT: All those people who were in their forties, fifties, and sixties and had made names for themselves were crushed and never came back.

WALTER BERNSTEIN: When the blacklist began to break up, I had a couple of meetings with the guy at CBS who was responsible for the clearances. He said, "You have to give us a statement saying that you are not a communist and whether you were or not, what you've been involved in, and what you've thought about it." I wouldn't do that. I was blacklisted until 1958.

LEE GRANT: CBS wanted to hire me, but they couldn't because I was still on the list. HUAC refused to take me off. They said, "Not until she names her husband."

When I was separated from Arnie, I knew I had to earn money. My lawyer suggested I hire a lawyer with influence on the Hill. He recommended someone who was very close to Hubert Humphrey. The new lawyer spoke to them and came back to me and said, "Lee, you have to name your husband."

I said I wanted to work, but I still have to sleep at night. A couple of months later, the head of the committee called this lawyer to ask for a favor. He said, "I'll tell you what. I'll do the favor for you, and you let Lee off."

He said, "Okay." They sent it to the network and the studios, saying Lee Grant is no longer considered whatever. Immediately, Herb Brodkin called me and said, "When can you work." It ended with a whimper and not a bang.

My very first show was a "Nurses." I was starring in it, and one of the blacklisters was playing a small part. I remember this great feeling of being in power. When he showed up at the door of my dressing room, our eyes locked, and I looked at him, and I waited for him to say something. I was going to say, "I'm off the blacklist. What are you going to do now?"

He said, "They didn't give me a bed to sleep in. I have no bed. What am I going to do?"

I couldn't believe we were gonna miss the moment. He had made the jump past the confrontation into dependency. I found myself running around saying, "Why doesn't he have a cot to sleep in?" and while I was doing it I was thinking, "Oh, God, the irony of it." I never did say anything to him. There was no enemy.

It was the same thing I felt when I got the Oscar. I was standing up there, thinking, "Them. There is no more them. They're gone, and the fight is over." I felt so bereft. I hated those people when I was fighting them. I still do.

HARVEY MATUSOW: I was about to marry Arvilla Bentley, the financier of the McCarthy people. I was moving into a mansion in Washington. Then one day I was sitting on Fifth Avenue, looking up at the Theological Seminary, and I just read over and over again the inscription in stone on the building, "Do justice, love mercy, and walk humbly with thy God." I sat there all day, and it became a mantra for me. That became my breakthrough. I realized my Cockypoo fantasy had to be reality.

I decided I would write a book exposing them. I wrote it on Jack Anderson's typewriter, using stationery from the organizing committee of the J. Edgar Hoover Foundation. I don't know where they got that from.

Years later, I met Millard Lampell after he had won an Emmy. When he received his Emmy he thanked everybody for getting the award, "especially since I was blacklisted all these years."

He got a standing ovation. Then, he said, as he came down from the podium, the first person who patted him on the back and said, "Great, it's about time somebody said this," was the producer who'd blacklisted him.

That was so typical of the agency people and the business people. Those who were deeply involved in the blacklist never saw their own responsibilities.

REGINALD ROSE: We did a triumphant show on "The Defenders" called "The Blacklist." It happened because I had submitted an outline about a black DA, who was prosecuting a black criminal. They were very nervous about it. I had wanted to do a show about blacklisting, but I had never even brought it up. Television? Blacklisting on television, impossible, right?

They wanted to talk about this outline. I kept insisting I had to do this show and they kept resisting. Finally, I said, "I'll tell you what, let me do a show on blacklisting and I'll forget this show." There was a long astonished pause, and one of them said, "Well, if you do it in good taste."

And I said, "You got it," and walked out. That's how I got that show on. It was Ernie Kinoy who wrote it.

ERNEST KINOY: We invented a situation that paralleled the situation with Johnson. We didn't want to focus on a big star because he would make it somehow. We created an ordinary working actor, and when he's blacklisted he's finished. Then we picked the actor to play the lead, but CBS said, "You can't hire him." They were still blacklisting him!

ROBERT MARKELL: Then when CBS saw the script, they said, "It has to be about the movies. It can't be about television, because there's no blacklist in television."

* * *

ABE POLONSKY: It was a terrible struggle, and we were all angry, but there was also the *joie de vivre* of being young. The struggle was successful, and no matter what horrible things happened, they didn't destroy us. We were hurt by it. An artist's identity lies in his work and the public's recognition of the work. That had to be abandoned. In that sense we were of assistance to each other; we were our own audience for each other.

The blacklist lasted into the sixties, because it was a business enterprise. People made a living at finding communists. Very late in the sixties, I was still blacklisted. Marty Ritt tried to get a movie for me at Universal, and they turned me down. Then a TV producer wanted to do a series on the OSS. I said, "Why should I? I'm writing movies. I make much more money. Would you want me to use a pseudonym?"

He said, "No, I'll put your name on it."

"You have a deal."

Universal said, "Use someone else besides Polonsky."

"No, we're gonna use Polonsky. Go fuck yourself." That was the end of the blacklist.

After I became successful again, Bill Dozier did a movie that was bad. He called me up and asked if I would come and look at it. I said to myself, "God, revenge is sweet."

I went out and looked at it. It *was* bad. He said, "How can I fix it up?

I said, "Burn it," and I left.

SOAPY STUFF

Fill in the blanks:

> Soap Heroine, *who is* an age acceptable to the advertiser's target audience *and lives in* a location acceptable to the advertiser's target audience, *loves* Soap Hero, *who suffers from* a disease acceptable to the advertiser, *but* Evil Woman *who wants* Soap Hero *for herself convinces* Soap Heroine *that* Soap Hero *has committed* an acceptable sin to the advertiser *so that* Soap Heroine *drops* Soap Hero *and* commits a dastardly deed acceptable to the advertiser *and lands herself* in a bad place deemed acceptable by the advertiser.

That's about six months' worth of action in your favorite soap opera, or "daytime serial" as they are respectfully called in the halls of Procter & Gamble—and for a very good reason: since 1932, the serials have been the major force behind Procter & Gamble's $30 billion in global sales. By the late 1940s, the Cincinnati-based conglomerate was spending over $20 million a year on its radio serials and was about to increase that by moving to TV.

And why not, the soap operas were an advertiser's dream: an audience that believed everything it heard! The problems of Rosemary or Helen Trent were so real to the listeners that when a baby was born on a soap opera, the studio would be flooded with gifts. Weddings and anniversaries brought in sacks of cards. Such loyalty translated into big dollars for the networks. According to one estimate, soap operas currently account for a sixth of all network profits. That's a lot of suds, and whether the programs were any good or not was beside the point, according to Tony Converse, formerly the director of CBS's daytime programming. "Strictly from the network's point of view a good soap opera is one that has a high rating, and a bad one is one that doesn't."

What is a soap opera? The feeling here is that if it looks like a soap opera, sounds like a soap opera, and has characters who are even more miserable than you are, then it is a soap opera. The humorist James Thurber probably concocted the best definition: "A soap opera is a kind of sandwich, whose recipe is simple enough, although it took years to compound. Between thick slices of advertising, spread twelve minutes of dialogue, add predicament, villainy, and female suffering in equal measure, throw in a dash of nobility, sprinkle with tears, season with organ music, cover with a rich announcer sauce, and serve five times a week."

Soap operas go back to the earliest days of radio, although because the definition of a soap can be rather slippery, the first soap is a matter of some dispute. In his academic overview of the genre, "Speaking of Soap Operas," Robert C. Allen declares that WGN's "Painted Dreams," by the doyenne of soap opera writers, Irna Phillips, was the first in 1930. Others have cast their votes for "The Smith Family," which bowed in 1925, and "The Rise of the Goldbergs," which first aired in 1929.

By Thurber's definition, "Painted Dreams," the story of Mother Moynihan and her family's search for eternal love and happiness, probably qualifies as the first. It certainly was the first for Phillips, a former Dayton schoolteacher turned radio actor.

In 1932, P & G broadcast its first "washboard weeper," "The Puddle Family," for Oxydol. "The Puddle Family" evaporated quickly, but their next entry, "Ma Perkins," by Frank and Ann Hummert, lasted some twenty-eight years.

In 1932, Elaine Carrington, whose fanny would share the soapland throne with Irna Phillips, found herself taking refuge in the lobby of WGN during a rainstorm. Carrington was a fiction writer for women's magazines, and while she was drying off she realized she had some of her stories in her pocketbook. She took them upstairs in the hope of selling them to the station. They weren't interested in the articles, but they did offer her the opportunity to lather up a soap opera. She returned with "Red Adams," the story of a typical American teenager who just happened to fall in love with some of Hollywood's biggest stars and a bevy of other exotic women. What a lucky kid!

"Red Adams" was soon picked up by P & G, which renamed it "Pepper Young's Family," and it became a big hit for them. Carrington went on to have a lucrative career for P & G. Her next effort, "Rosemary, When a Girl Marries," was probably radio's most popular soap. She became one of the highest paid people in America, with a penthouse in New York and a mansion that she called "The House that Camay Built" in Bridgehampton, Long Island.

While Carrington and the Hummerts never made the transition to television, Phillips—whose characters were generally more three-dimensional than Carrington's or the Hummerts'—did well on the new medium. Her principal radio show, "The Guiding Light," moved easily to TV in 1952. Another Phillips creation, "As the World Turns," is still on the air some forty years later.

There is evidence that the first television soap opera nearly preceded the first radio soaper. In 1931, Don Lee's experimental station in Los Angeles, W6XAO, aired one called "Vine Street." Popular wisdom said soaps wouldn't work on television, primarily because the housewives didn't have time to sit and watch, whereas on radio they could go about their business and still enjoy the troubles of Pepper Young's long-suffering family. Irna Phillips was among the doubters. In a 1948 letter to P & G vice president, William Ramsey, she wrote, "I have had very little interest in television from a daytime standpoint, and unless a technique could be evolved whereby the auditory could be followed without the constant attention to the visual . . . I see no future for a number of years in televising the serial story."

The naysayers saw other problems with television. Radio actors could read their lines, but on television they would have to memorize five scripts a week. Also, the radio soaps expanded the listeners' imaginations, taking them to exotic locales all around the world. That would be impossible on live TV. TV was also much more expensive than radio.

Despite the doubts, in 1946, DuMont attempted the first network soap with "Faraway Hill." It ran for twelve weeks and was considered a success despite its limited distribution to only two stations in New York and Washington, D. C. DuMont's second effort was "A Woman to Remember" in 1948, which featured one clever gimmick. To get around the difficulty of having actors memorize their scripts every day, the story was set in a radio studio. It was a soap opera about a soap opera, which allowed the actors to read some of their lines from their scripts.

NBC's first TV serial turned out to be a real-life tragedy. In March 1951, it broadcast "Miss Susan" from its sister station, WPTZ in Philadelphia. The show starred Susan Peters, a minor movie star, who had been shot by her husband and paralyzed in a hunting accident. Peters played a wheelchair-bound criminal attorney, but the daily grind was too much for her. Forced to rely more and more on painkillers, she weakened over the course of the year and died that December.

"The First Hundred Years," starring Jimmy Lydon, Robert Armstrong, and Anne Sargent, was Procter & Gamble's first television soap. The story of a young married couple in New York City, it debuted in 1950 and lasted two years on the CBS network.

Two of TV's most successful soaps premiered in September 1951. "Love of Life" was the story of two sisters, one good, one bad, and "Search for Tomorrow," another Procter & Gamble production, was the tale of long-suffering Joanne Tate. Indeed, Mary Stuart spent thirty-five years searching for a better tomorrow in the role. When "The Guiding Light" moved to television in February 1952, P & G continued to produce the radio version and protected its high ratings by starting the radio broadcast at one-forty-five, while the same episode on television didn't begin until two-thirty.

In the long run it didn't help. Television doomed network radio, and the daytime serials were chief among the casualties. The last radio serials were canceled in 1960. The old numbers game that was responsible for their rise finished them off.

AGNES NIXON: When I was a child, I used to listen to "The Guiding Light" on the radio. One of its characters was a minister named Dr. Ruthledge. Every now and then, he would recite an Edward Markham quatrain, which was the theme of the show:

> *There is a destiny that makes us brothers*
> *None goes his way alone*
> *What we send into the life of others*
> *Comes back into our own.*

That philosophy moved me even as a child, and I loved that program. If I had been told then that someday I would be writing "Guiding Light" on television, I would have been just stupefied.

ROD ERICKSON: I was with Procter & Gamble when the most significant programs for them were their daytime serials. I always called them soaps before I went to Procter. Either Bill Ramsey or Gil Ralston said to me, "We call them daytime serials here." The word "soaps" was derogatory.

Bill invented the daytime serial at WLW in Cincinnati for the sole purpose of selling to women, and Procter knew more about selling to women than anyone else. First of all, you gave them a story about someone who was worse off than they were. Also, in all these stories the women were dominant figures.

My job was to read every episode of ten different serials. I developed a lot of respect for the writers. The scripts were well constructed and their characters so well defined. Procter kept a "bible" on each show. The bible told very specific things, where they lived, who were their neighbors, what they ate, when they went to the john. This way, if the writers changed, there was no way the listener could be smarter than the writer.

The daytime serials gave solace to women who were alone doing drab work. We tried quiz shows and comedies, but they didn't work. The characters on the serials were their friends. You knew much more about them than any friend you had. We paid Virginia Miles, who played Ma Perkins, seven hundred dollars more a week not to put her name on it. Everybody wrote to Ma Perkins, and we didn't want her identified as an actor.

Procter was a very smart, efficient advertiser. They ran their serials the same way. Everything was researched. You could jump the plot ahead only one and a half times a week, because the ratings indicated that that was the number of times the average viewer tuned in. The plots moved very slowly. Elaine Carrington once wrote a breakfast where they sat down to eat and didn't finish until nine months later.

There was sex, but married sex, no adultery, and not many divorces. The characters were very Midwestern to reflect our customers. I don't remember any black characters. Had they found out that blacks were ten percent of their customers, they would have had ten percent of their characters black.

AGNES NIXON: I was an only child of divorced parents in an Irish-Catholic enclave in Tennessee. We Catholics were less than one percent of the population, and because of that and because I lived with my mother, grandmother, and three maiden aunts, and had few playmates before starting parochial school, my imagination became my boon companion.

I played a game of paper dolls where I would make up stories about them and have them walk through everything I was pretending. Those stories sometimes went on for months and were akin to the long-term story projections I write today.

I was in all the high-school productions, and I was sure I would be a famous movie star someday, but at Northwestern I saw quite a few classmates who were better at acting than I was, and I decided I liked the writing medium better. I also realized that in writing, one can play all the parts.

JOHN HESS: I wasn't going to write soap operas. I was going to be a playwright, but I got a job in radio, writing everything from drama to commercials. Then, in 1950, a friend introduced me to Elaine Carrington, who was some character. She was blowsy, immensely self-confident, essentially a very vulgar woman who thought she was not. She hired me as a writer for a few weeks.

ROD ERICKSON: I dealt with Elaine a lot. I thought she was a real lady, although she looked like George Washington. She would sit in her apartment on Fifty-fourth Street or in her gazebo in Bridgehampton and dictate to her secretary and play all the parts of the show.

DICK DUNNE: Elaine and Irna were great rivals and were always accusing each other of stealing material. When Elaine died someone said, "Now I know Irna will never die because Elaine did it first."

JOHN HESS: Elaine didn't write much herself, and when she hired me, I found the characters were so shallow and one-dimensional, it was not difficult at all. All her shows were plot, not characters, the opposite of the way they would be on television. To tell you how ridiculous it was, my goal was to write a script faster than it could be performed. I made it once.

AGNES NIXON: A few days after I graduated from Northwestern University, I got an interview with Irna who, I thought, had no peer. Her subjects were different from Elaine's and the others'. Her subjects were more controversial, and she covered them in depth. She had three-dimensional characters.

DICK DUNNE: Irna wrote about tangled emotions while other writers wrote melodramatically. In her way she was the Freudian daytime serial writer. Her whole life was soap opera. She had two adopted children, and she would drive them crazy because she was always writing about people looking for their roots, and she would use them for plot lines.

Most people were intimidated by her, but she amused me. She was lonely and about as neurotic a person as I've ever known. She would phone in after every single show to speak to the director and mostly rip the show to shreds. Then when she really got lonely she'd create a storm so that everybody from P & G would bring her to dinner and have meetings in her apartment.

Her apartment was really an insight into Irna. It was beautifully furnished, but every chair had a plastic cover, and there wasn't a magazine or a book or anything personal to be seen. It was as if she had moved into a hotel room.

ROD ERICKSON: Irna was certifiable. Bill Ramsey took care of her. He'd get her drunk, neck with her, whatever she wanted, in contrast to strict Procter policy, "Don't fuck the talent."

AGNES NIXON: I went to her apartment and gave her the script I had written for Northwestern Playshop. Her secretary was there, and to my horror, the three of us sat down at a card table, and Irna read my script aloud. I was so nervous I wanted to hide in the dumbwaiter, but when Irna put the script down, she asked me if I would like to write dialogue for "Woman in White," five scripts a week for one hundred dollars a week.

ROD ERICKSON: The thinkers who made policy never doubted the serials would move into television. The only question was how and when. There was a big concern when I moved to Young & Rubicam that we would not get the same number of homes viewing in daytime. It's one thing to listen to radio when you're working, another thing to sit down and watch television.

It took about ten years to make it really viable. By then there were multiple sets in the home. Also, the appearance of dishwashers, washing machines, and dryers gave the housewife time to sit down and watch.

JOHN HESS: In 1951, a friend told me that a friend of his, Roy Winsor, was coming into town. Roy was the head of radio for the Biow advertising agency and was being sent to New York to take over as the vice president in charge of television. We invited him for dinner, and over a lot of drinks we got into a big argument about the fate of soap opera on television. I knew nothing about it. I had two weeks of work with Elaine Carrington. He had produced and written a whole bunch of things.

The next day I felt bad, so I wrote Roy a long letter which was a burlesque of our conversation in the form of a soap opera. I said our new television soap opera ought to be set in such and such a place, and the lead should be named Vanessa, because V is for virtue and A is for ardor and so on. I got a note back from him saying, "Take the jokes out of it and I'll sell it."

I also suggested it be called "Love of Life" because it sounded good. He said, "It's a perfect title. It has Love. It has Life, and it even has 'of.' "

It lasted thirty years. He put on two soaps at the same time with Biow money, that and "Search for Tomorrow," which starred Mary Stuart. These were the first two that made it on TV and like those that followed were a way for aspiring actors to make a living until the big break came along, so you had a lot of good actors as well as writers, producers, and directors.

LARRY HAINES: Charlie Irving, the producer-director of "Search," asked me if I would be interested in a short run on the show. When the character started catching on they offered me a contract. I said, "How long do you think this role will run?"

And Charlie said, "Probably the rest of your life."

He wasn't kidding. I was on for thirty-five years.

MARY STUART: I met Roy Winsor through my boyfriend. I knew he was going to put on soaps, so I auditioned over dinner. I had read one article in the *Times* about American housewives, so I was an expert. He thought I was the cutest thing there ever was.

I didn't even audition.

Everybody said, "How can you do a soap?" I just thought having a job was wonderful. I never figured that it would last thirty-five years, that I would spend my entire life on that show.

LARRY HAINES: You had a great deal of talented people in soaps. My first television soap was "The First Hundred Years." Robert Armstrong and Jimmy Lydon were on that show.

JIMMY LYDON: When Jean Holloway made a deal with CBS to do "The First Hundred Years," they wanted some people with stage experience. Bob and I both knew Jean, and she hired us.

When we got to New York, nobody knew if we could handle a daily show. It was a first for everyone, and Procter & Gamble and Benton & Bowles let us alone until we established that a cast of six people could learn twenty-six pages of tripe every day. I don't know how we did it, but we did. I do know that I threw up at least twice a week about five minutes before airtime.

LARRY HAINES: I didn't find it that difficult because most of it was "Let's have a cup coffee and talk." That's what we did. We sat down for a cup of coffee and for nine minutes threw the dialogue back and forth. At first, the scripts were written like radio shows. "Oh, Mary, look who just came through the door, John." Meanwhile, you already saw who it was. That changed once they learned that people did sit down and watch.

MARY STUART: On "Search," we never rehearsed the whole show, so there was always some scene we were faking when we got on the air. I talked to God a lot in those days, "Please, please, just get me through this."

JIMMY LYDON: We were among the first to use a TelePrompTer, which really only helped the radio actors. They would be fine with the script in their hands and the blocking and everything else, but then before the show you could see the glazed eyes, and the terror. Then Bob or I would say, "Listen, don't worry. Just look over my shoulder and take everything off the TelePrompTer."

LARRY AUERBACH: I directed "Love of Life." At first, we didn't use TelePrompTers on "Love of Life." The actors would help each other out, except once when Jared Reed, who was an old man and a renowned left-winger, was brought in. The guy who played opposite him was very conservative, and when Jared couldn't remember his lines the guy would just let him stammer.

JIMMY LYDON: Bob Armstrong was always letter-perfect. On one show we had about seven pages of dialogue, and about a page and a half into it Bob went up. I thought, "Well, the mighty have fallen." I ad-libbed a little bit and threw him a cue. Bob just looked up from his coffee with a grin on his face. I figured, "Well, he's really gone. I'll give him another chance," so I ad-libbed a little more and threw another cue in his lap. Now Bob is really grinning. Suddenly it struck me, he wasn't up. I was! He knew what was happening and he was enjoying it. He wouldn't save me because I had the temerity to think that he was up.

LARRY AUERBACH: We did a restaurant scene with the napkins on the tables formed in nice little peaks, but one was in my shot and I didn't like it. I went to take it away after dress, and the actress said, "Don't do that. My lines are on there."

MARY STUART: I wrote my lines any place that my eye would normally fall. The stagehands used to say, "If Mary has a heavy day, don't anybody bend over." I was at the sink a lot, so I would write in the sink with a little grease pencil.

LARRY HAINES: One day, she wrote a couple of words inside a coffee cup, forgetting that on air we were going to pour coffee in it, which we did.

JIMMY LYDON: Everything that could happen happened, not just with the dialogue. We photographed everybody in the crew at one time or another, sets fell down, wardrobe changes didn't work because we didn't have the time. At least once a week one of our four cameras would explode.

MARY STUART: It was difficult to act when you have no set or just doorframes hung in thin air with a black cyclorama behind it.

LARRY AUERBACH: "Love of Life" was sponsored by American Home Products, which had about five hundred brand names, including Preparation H and Franco-American spaghetti. Our budget was tight. We could only have twenty-five cast appearances every week, which included principals, extras, and everyone else. We did everything in front of black velour. We hung pictures in the air and used wainscoting to keep you from seeing the floor behind the set.

DICK DUNNE: The sets drove me crazy because we would be doing these sketchy things, and then the commercials would come on with these gorgeous sets, which was the reverse of what it ought to be.

MARY STUART: Our whole budget was under nine thousand dollars a week, including our salaries. At the end of thirteen weeks, there was money left over, and Charles ran over to tell them. They said, "Don't ever admit that you didn't use all the money." He went right out and spent money, and for the first time we had sets, but they were just gray walls.

JIMMY LYDON: We had complete sets. We also did forward projection and all sorts of tricks. We did the interior of railroad cars by waving a stick in front of a lamp as if it were a telephone pole going by the window, or they would wave trees in front of the lamps as if they were going by. We taught the technicians that stuff, because we were well versed in the phony art of motion pictures.

However, as motion picture people, we were used to technical crews that were the best in the world, but this was IATSE, which was stage crews. These people own the world as far as the unions go. Our electrician was drunk every day of the week, and he got to snoring right in the middle of the show, and distracting us. This happened so often that we complained to the union. After the third complaint, we were visited by two goons, who said, "Listen, that's your head electrician. Keep your mouth shut or we'll take every electrician off the show," and he stayed drunk for the entire run of the show.

MARY STUART: You would open a closet door, and always there would be a stagehand in there.

JIMMY LYDON: Everything about it was so god-awful we wanted to get back to Hollywood, where the money was better, where it wasn't anywhere near as difficult and was a little bit satisfying once in a while. No matter what you say about actors who do it for the money, and most of us do, we are professionals and we do care about what we do, and it hurts when you don't have much of a chance to do anything decent.

We went to see Walter Craig at the agency to quit once a month at the beginning. He would say, "Now, you fellas know you can't do that. Read your contract and go on back and behave yourselves."

It became a running gag. He would say, "You want a drink?"

"No, we don't want a drink. We have to learn twenty-six pages of drivel for tomorrow."

The scripts just got worse. After two months they said, "We know what sells soap," and so a quiet family situation suddenly became even more driveling, with gangsters and murderers.

DICK DUNNE: American Home Products didn't really care what you put on the air as long as it stayed within the budget and the ratings stayed up.

JOHN HESS: There were restrictions. Pregnancy was something you had to be very careful about. Extramarital affairs, which are now the staple of television, were iffy.

DICK DUNNE: We didn't have any adulteresses, but we did have an unmarried affair going on. There was another thing I did. John created a bartender who was a friend of one of the leading women, and I said, "Do you know, that could be a black actor?"

John said, "Yeah, it could."

That was the first black actor with a continuing role in a daytime serial. I had about six fellas come in and read. It was embarrassing because I knew that every single one of them had starred on Broadway, and yet daytime was very slow to use them.

We did have to change the script for him. When he was a white man he called the woman by her first name, but when he was black, she was "Miss Whoever." We didn't want to indicate that they were too friendly. Back in the fifties you had to be careful about that sort of thing.

JOHN HESS: A directive came down from Program Practices with a list of phrases that couldn't be used. With most of them I couldn't figure out why not. One of them was "Hold on to your hats, boys," which turned out to be the tag line of a very old dirty joke. You couldn't name body parts or use the word "breast."

LARRY AUERBACH: None of the scripts were *Moby-Dick*. Some were good; some bad. The toughest job in the business is writing soap operas.

When you are doing some 260 shows a year, no repeats, no hiatus, you are bound to get some bad ones.

JIMMY LYDON: Jean Holloway would go to the hairdresser, and while she was sitting under the dryer she would write twenty-six pages.

JOHN HESS: The basic notion of writing a soap opera is all so-and-so has to say is such-and-such and the story is over, but they don't ever say it because then you would have nothing to write about it. "Why doesn't Beany go to his father and tell him he took the book?"

Well, because then you've shot about a month's worth of scripts. The great secret was how to attenuate and retain interest. How did I? You approach the same set of circumstances from different directions. If you have a couple talking about divorcing one day, the next day, you have another couple talking about the first couple's divorce.

I tried very hard not to write down, for my own sake as much as for anybody else's. You do that by writing characters that are interesting, not writing dialogue with holes, and also by having some variation of character. Soap opera on radio had no variation of character whatsoever. On "Love of Life," my good and evil sisters were not purely good and evil. Our villain Steve Gethers had all kinds of nuances. That gave me an opportunity to have people argue about whether or not he was a good guy.

I could write dialogue quickly and well. I would try to get far enough ahead so I could take time off to write a play. Once I got ahead thirty-five weeks by writing two, or sometimes three, a day, which was a little more than three hours of work. Then there were times when I was only one day ahead, and I was phoning pages in. It was extremely informal in that regard. I also had great leeway in what I could do. We were Number One, which didn't hurt.

DICK DUNNE: We used to say that, if you had a slump in the ratings a murder trial always put you on top.

MARY STUART: After Agnes did the first thirteen weeks, Irving Vendig wrote the show from Florida. We weren't carried there, so he never saw it. This is how much he cared. He said, "Charlie if you cut out two pages, save it so I can use it again."

*   *   *

JOHN HESS: The amazing thing was the world at large was addicted to this. Mary Stuart could not walk down the street without being accosted fifty times a block. We would get sad letters from people, identifying so closely with this stuff, believing so intensely this rather shallow fiction. I knew there was literature that could affect people that profoundly, but this wasn't literature.

MARY STUART: We were an instantaneous, huge hit. I read the letters. We really touched people's lives. They saw themselves in a different environment than they would have otherwise. We were not elegant, but we were eloquent. Everybody on our show was thoughtful. We spoke wonderful English, and we had wonderful actors, who were inviting. People could imagine themselves in that room with those people.

LARRY HAINES: Soap fans feel very close to you. I've had people pull up a chair and sit with us in restaurants. Most of them didn't even know my real name, but they knew Stu Bergman.

MARY STUART: I got hugged and kissed a lot. I liked that. Mostly, they talked about themselves as though they were talking to a friend, although once, a lady hooked her umbrella over my arm. She said, "You never even wrote me a thank-you note."

"I beg your pardon."

"There was a party at my house."

"Ma'am, I think you are mistaken."

"[Sternly] You were in my house. It was a Tupperware party in Teaneck, New Jersey."

LARRY HAINES: It was in my contract that if I were offered a play or film they would write me out for the time I needed. P & G was very gracious about that. I did shows on Broadway, film. I did *The Odd Couple* with Jack Lemmon and Walter Matthau. I did a play with Henry Fonda. During one matinee, I made my entrance long after his initial appearance. He had been warmly received, but when I walked out and got an even bigger hand, he kiddingly said, "Who the fuck are you?"

AGNES NIXON: In 1955, Irna and I collaborated on the first half-hour soap opera, "As the World Turns." When she told them she wanted to do it, they said, "It'll never sustain," so she spent her own money to make a kinescope. As soon as P & G saw it, they said, "Wow, this is going to be hot stuff," and they immediately told one of their advertising agencies to get another one ready to premiere the same day. That's how "Edge of Night" happened to go on the same day in 1956.

Toward the end of her life, Irna was telling P & G that the hour soap opera was the future of the genre, and again they said, "No way." She died before she was proved correct.

JOHN HESS: I got burned out. I was determined to break into nighttime. I did, but it was goddamned hard. I don't know many writers who made the jump. I quit in 1957, and I never watched a soap again.

AGNES NIXON: Procter & Gamble did not want to do any public service. Then in the early sixties, I suddenly felt there was something we could do that was more than just entertain. My obstetrician mentioned to me the Pap-smear test and that uterine cancer was one hundred percent curable if caught in time. I mentioned to P & G that I'd like to have Bert have uterine cancer, and they went into orbit.

CBS said, "What? This is entertainment time. We have a public service time," and of course public service time is early on Sunday morning when people are either in church or asleep in bed, so I wrote an eight-month projection, showing how I would incorporate this story. They said, "Well, you may do it, but you may not say cancer, and you may not say uterus, and you may not say hysterectomy." By now my Irish was up and I was mad. I wrote the scenes the way I wanted to, and finally they agreed, but it was rough going.

JIMMY LYDON: We were hoping the show would be dropped. After a year and a half, it was, and we cheered. It was that ugly.

The show ended on a Friday, the first of July. My wife had my car packed, and Saturday morning at six o'clock we drove over the George Washington Bridge on our way to California, and I didn't look back.

MARY STUART: I wanted to work in nighttime, but I didn't know how to go about it. Then I had children and was no longer mobile, and I didn't have the ambition to work on nighttime.

Still, I never stopped caring about my work. If you are going to take up people's time it matters. What they get out of it is that they feel. Many people have very little human contact in their lives. We give that to them. The stories on "Studio One" were more interesting, but you didn't know the people as well. I don't feel I sold my soul. I think I had a wonderful career.

LARRY AUERBACH: In the early days I wanted to do the hour dramas at night, but I was never willing to leave and make myself available, and I did have this soap-opera smell about me. There was an elitism toward directors who worked on soaps, but I liked the idea of a check coming in every week, and I liked working. I liked going into the studio. I still like going into the studio. I hope there's a studio up there when the time comes.

KIDS' STUFF

There were doubts about whether or not the soaps would make it on TV, but there was no such concern when it came to children's programming. Ever since Philo Farnsworth experimented with bits of Disney's "Steamboat Willie" in the 1920s, local and network broadcasters have included children's programming on their schedules.

Most broadcasters claim they program for children out of duty. Forget it. Broadcasters like kids' shows because advertisers like them. Let Buffalo Bob Smith tell his young fans that Wonder bread builds a body twelve ways and the next day nearly half the kids in America are tugging on their mothers' sleeves when they walk by the packaged loaves of white bread in their local supermarket.

Most of the children's-show hosts were hucksters in the guise of father figures. There was the friendly hunter (Buffalo Bob) or a friendly museum watchman (Captain Kangaroo). That combination of warmth and authority, an animated version of the typical Norman Rockwell patriarch that was also brought to life in sitcoms by Hugh Beaumont and Robert Young, was a powerhouse sales tool. If Dad says Wonder bread is good for you, then it must be true. Actually, there was no better model for exploiting the kids' market than Howdy Doody. After the show found its audience, Smith and his manager Martin Stone set up the Kagran Corporation to mine the gold in their young viewers' pockets. "We were real hucksters. You might say we were real whores," Smith told Gary Grossman, for Grossman's terrific history of children's shows, *Saturday Morning TV*. Grossman writes that by the end of 1957 sales of Howdy Doody–licensed merchandise totaled some $25 million.

That was just fine with Cy Schneider, who spent more than forty years in the business end of children's television, beginning with Mattel toys in 1953. In his book, *Children's Television*, he wrote:

> . . . *commercial television, even for children, is just another business. It is a business that makes its money by helping sell products.* . . .

The television business works on three simple principles: keep the audience up, the costs down, and the regulators out. The reformers forget that television's first mission is not to inform, educate, or enlighten. It isn't even to entertain. Its first mission is to entice viewers to watch the commercials. If commercial television cannot move goods, it cannot be in business. Just because commercial television devotes many of its hours to the special audience of children doesn't change the fundamental point one iota.

The concept of children as consumers has been greeted with horror by others. Even Bob Keeshan, who, primarily in his role as Captain Kangaroo, made his living from kids, has expressed his dismay. "Advertisers and their agencies have a responsibility to the public and especially to young audiences who are immature and uninformed consumers. Exploitation of such an audience in search of profits is unconscionable."

On the other hand, Keeshan has sold his share of Kellogg's Frosted Flakes to youngsters, which may account for why sugary cereals don't alarm him today. "That's not an issue with me. There are more important issues than that." One imagines that dentists everywhere would be thrilled to hear that.

In his book *About Television*, Martin Mayer takes a more absolutist point of view. "Pushing goods to children is an abomination, and allowing the most popular shows to float along on the surface, buoyed by the ratings, clearly abdicates adult obligations to children."

Still, no discussion of children's programming should ignore the fact that a lot of the shows were fun. This writer couldn't get enough of "Andy's Gang" ("Pluck your magic twanger, Froggy") and still believes that Chuck McCann is one of the great comedy geniuses of all time. While television is not a good baby-sitter and cannot take the place of a book, the oft-heard arguments that television hinders the imagination are absurd. The science-fiction fantasy shows, "Tom Corbett, Space Cadet," "Flash Gordon," or "Captain Video and His Video Rangers" sparked hours of inventive play when the shows were over, especially the latter with its rayguns made from automobile tailpipes and ashtrays. No one could have enjoyed that show *without* a half-decent imagination.

Even before NBC went commercial in 1941, its experimental New York station offered a regular children's feature, "Paul Wing's Spelling Bee." Probably the first Saturday morning kids' show was "Children's Matinee," which was aired on the now-commercial WNBT in 1941 from three-thirty to four-thirty in the afternoon. Each show had three twenty-minute segments with either Captain Tim Healy, Marion Bishop's Marionettes, story-telling, or pet features.

DuMont, which seemed to pioneer everything in programming, broadcast the first postwar kids' show as we know them today, "The Small Fry Club." From six to six-thirty, Monday to Friday, Big Brother Bob Emery played some piano and showed films or drawings his viewers sent in. He invited kids to join his club. Within two years over 150,000 small fries had signed up.

In 1947, NBC's Warren Wade, who had survived at the network for ten years despite near-complete incompetence, finally did something right. He gathered together the talent for a Saturday afternoon children's show called "Puppet Playhouse." The first broadcast featured the marionettes of Frank Paris and radio personality Bob Smith, nicknamed "Buffalo" after his hometown, not the nickel. He was originally brought to New York in 1946 as NBC's early morning entry against Arthur Godfrey. Smith also hosted a Saturday morning kids' show as Big Brother Bob Smith. It was on that show that he used a Mortimer Snerdish voice he called "Elmer" to greet his listeners with the immortal words, "Howdy doody, boys and girls."

"Puppet Playhouse" premiered on December 27, 1947, and Smith and Co. were such a hit that Wade's original plan to have rotating hosts was scrapped. Within a few weeks "Elmer" was reborn as a puppet named "Howdy Doody." The show went to six days a week, and purveyors of everything from Howdy Doody lariats to Howdy Doody bowties moved in for the kill.

Both "Howdy Doody" and "The Small Fry Club" were hits with the critics. *Newsweek* was especially positive in a 1948 overview of the small screen.

> As every parent knows, the chief child-bait on radio is little more than comic-book entertainment—a grotesque mixture of Jack Armstrong, Superman, and Buck Rogers. Yet somehow, possibly because blood curdlers are as yet too expensive for video, television has developed real children's programs of a type more akin to Tom Sawyer than Orphan Annie.

The *Newsweek* piece cited "DuMont Kindergarten" (a forerunner of "Romper Room" and "Ding Dong School"), hosted by twenty-five-year-old Pat Meikle, who drew on an easel and told stories directly into the camera. The idea was not only to entertain kids, but to keep them in front of the set long enough to give their mothers a chance to take care of other business without interruption. Thus, the notion of TV as a baby-sitter was born. Even *Architectural Digest* liked the idea. "A television set is better than hashish in calming active children in the late afternoon."

The one show that DuMont will always be remembered for is "Captain Video." DuMont signed Broadway actor Richard Coogan to play the role of Captain Video, and fifteen-year-old Don Hastings to be his youthful sidekick, "The Ranger." The original idea was that the pair would simply introduce some old westerns DuMont had bought, but kids found the live pair to be so much more fun than their celluloid counterparts that the network decided to build a show around them. DuMont was still obligated to show the old westerns, so after the Captain and the Ranger had spent ten or fifteen minutes hunting down the evil Dr. Pauli in the twenty-second century, they would turn to their magic screen to see how their other Rangers were doing—and, lo and behold, there was someone who looked suspiciously like John Wayne, leading a posse. Once the chase scene was over, the action returned to the twenty-second century for the rest of the half hour. Nobody cared that the old westerns had no relation to the rest of the show. And despite a prop budget that averaged around twenty-five dollars a week, and some of the worst dialogue since Tarzan, "Captain Video" was an enormous success.

Paul Tripp was an exception to the exploitative father figures. His show, "Mr. I. Magination," was never a commercial success, which was its saving grace. "Mr. I. Magination" was CBS's first postwar children's show. It was created and written by Tripp, who also played the title role of the friendly train engineer in a pair of candy-striped overalls with no fly. (Mr. I. Magination drove a train but he didn't go to the bathroom.) The show used rear projection to take children on trips from Imagination Town through "I Wish I Were Town," where Tripp, his wife Ruth Enders, and a different child actor each week reenacted historical events.

The first made-for-TV cartoons were created in 1949 by Alex Anderson, whose uncle, Paul Terry, had founded Terrytoons. Anderson teamed up with a Harvard Business School graduate named Jay Ward to make "Crusader Rabbit," a series of five-minute films whose somewhat sophisticated slant made them a cult favorite among adults as well as kids.

Five-minute theatrical cartoons required hundreds of drawings and took months to make at costs upwards of $50,000 each, impossible for TV, which also needed new material every week and could never recoup that kind of money. The only way cartoons like "Crusader Rabbit" could be done for TV was to cut down on the number of drawings in each cartoon and limit the action. The first studio to attempt "limited animation" was UPA, with its "Gerald McBoing-Boing" series, which was actually done for theatrical release. Anderson and Ward employed the same techniques on the "Crusader Rabbit" series. In 1959, Ward and another animator, Bill Scott, took two characters of Anderson's, Rocket J. Squirrel and Bullwinkle Moose, and fashioned an unforgettable series around them.

Their primary competition came from two old MGM hands, William Hanna and Joseph Barbera. Hanna and Barbera had been turning out "Tom and Jerry" cartoons for MGM since 1938 when the animation studio was shut down in 1957, due to TV's inroads against the movies. The two then decided to try their hand at the small screen and were almost immediately successful with "Ruff and Reddy," a dog and cat variation on Tom and Jerry.

From there, the two created Huckleberry Hound, Quick Draw McGraw, and Yogi Bear, all of whom got their own shows and had long, profitable runs on the networks. Cartoons became a huge business on television. For producers like Hanna and Barbera, the best thing about it was the stars never demanded to renegotiate their contracts, although the bear was said to have demanded a piece of the pie.

*   *   *

ROGER MUIR: After I got to NBC, I used to say to Warren Wade, "We've got to do something for the kids." This went on for six months. Finally, he said, "Your wish has come true. We're going to start a kids' show." Warren's idea was to do three alternating shows each Saturday afternoon under the title "Puppet Playhouse." I would do the first one with a puppeteer named Frank Paris. The second week would be Paul Winchell and Jerry Mahoney, and the third week would be Ed Herlihy and another puppet act.

When I asked Warren who would host my show, he said, "Well, there's a guy named Bob Smith who's been doing a kids' radio show. Go see what he does. If he's any good, we'll consider him."

It was kind of a quiz show called "The Triple B Ranch." Bob would greet the kids in the radio audience in a real Mortimer Snerd, dumb-sounding voice he called Elmer. He'd say, "Well, howdy doody, boys and girls." After a while the kids would come into the studio and say, "Where's Howdy Doody?"

The show was good, and I told Warren we should use him. Then, I sat down with Bob and his writer Eddie Kean to get a show together. We decided to use Elmer but call him Howdy Doody.

EDDIE KEAN: Bob said, "That's all well and good, but what do I do for a puppet?"

I suggested that until we got a puppet we say that Howdy is too shy to show himself on camera. He's gonna hide in a drawer. So on the first "Puppet Playhouse," nobody saw him. He just talked to Bob whenever Bob opened the drawer.

ROGER MUIR: We also had Frank Paris do a little puppet show called "The Adventures of Toby Tyler."

RHODA MANN: Frank was an amazingly talented puppeteer, who Bob Smith couldn't stand because he was a little light on his feet. I was his leading lady. I did male, female, and children's voices while operating the puppets.

MARTIN STONE: There was a hell of a snowstorm the day of the first show, and as a result the kids were inside, so it got an audience by default.

ROGER MUIR: We got a rave review in *Variety*. NBC told me right away, "You've got to go on again next week," and the next week, and the other two never got on in that time slot.

EDDIE KEAN: I wrote "It's Howdy Doody Time" for maybe the second show. The music is a French theme, "Ta Ra Ra Boom Der E." Marty Stone suggested that tune because it was his camp song when he was a kid.

ROGER MUIR: We still needed to figure out what Howdy Doody should look like. We wanted a cowboy puppet that was Mortimer Snerdish with chaps and a plaid shirt. Paris made what we asked for, but it was ugly. It didn't look anything like the familiar Howdy.

RHODA MANN: There was an argument over who owned the character, so Frank took the puppets, including Howdy, went over to WPIX, and did "Pixie Playhouse." I went with him. Meanwhile, they got a new Howdy puppet and asked me to work him, so I came back and stayed with the show for five years.

SCOTT BRINKER: Meanwhile, they took another marionette, wrapped his head up, and said Howdy was having a face-lift. In the meantime, they had Velma Dawson make a new Howdy Doody, which looked much better. Unfortunately, he was also heavy and out of balance.

I designed and made furniture. I make my first marionette for that show in 1947. One day, my kids were watching "Howdy Doody." I watched for a while. Then I got an idea for a premium. I went down to my cellar, and I made a little gadget. It was the head of a marionette with a little string. You'd pull on it and the mouth would open and close.

I called up NBC and got Bob Smith. I didn't sell him the idea, but he said to me, "Do you make marionettes?"

I said, "Sure." I'd never made a marionette in my life. They had a drawing of how they wanted Mr. Bluster to look. I went to the library to find out how you make a marionette and I made Mr. Bluster. They liked it and asked me to make a better Howdy, which I did. Then I took the old Howdy, redid the face, and he became The Inspector. I also made the Flub-a-Dub and the Princess.

I also made literally hundreds of props, the Flapdoodle, the Air-o-doodle, Marbledoodle. My accountant made a list of all of them and how much they cost for tax purposes, and I got audited. Imagine explaining to the examiner what all these things were.

EDDIE KEAN: The character of Howdy Doody was a sissy. He was me as a child. I always preferred to study than to play baseball. I never hit anybody. No one ever hit me. He was the dullest character on the show, no offense to Bob, but he was because I made him so. Jack Benny was bland. Phil Harris was the one who drank. Dennis Day made idiotic remarks. Everything was happening around him.

ROGER MUIR: Clarabell was not on the first shows. Bob Keeshan was there, but he just wore street clothes and handed out prizes. Bob Smith was wearing a lion tamer's outfit because the show had sort of a circus motif. After a few weeks, Warren said to me, "Why the hell is that guy in street clothes coming into the circus? If he's gonna come on, put him in a circus costume."

We got a clown costume for him, and Dick Smith put together Clarabell's makeup. Keeshan was not an actor, so we stole the honking horn from Harpo Marx. We wanted him to be a menace without being violent, so we came up with the seltzer bottle.

EDDIE KEAN: Keeshan's success was enormous and inexplicable. He was totally unemotional and just the most untalented person I ever met.

ROGER MUIR: Bob Smith is a talented musician. Everybody in the cast played a musical instrument. We had to find the simplest instrument for Keeshan to learn, and we came up with the marimba. Then we had to hire a music teacher to teach him to play the thing. The idea was he would play something like "Around the Mulberry Bush," and when he gets to the last note he would play it wrong. But every time he got to where the gag was, he'd hit the *right* note. I can't tell you how much time we wasted trying to get him to hit the wrong note. We finally just gave up.

DAYTON ALLEN: I met Keeshan in a men's room. I recognized him by his smile. I was doing "Oky Doky Ranch" on DuMont. He said, "You do a lot of voices. You'd be great for us."

"Oky Doky Ranch" was some piece of crap, but that's where I learned to work with a puppet. That thing must have weighed about a hundred pounds. I think it was made by King Kong, but I was okay with it because I was very powerful. My breath alone could have lifted it.

RHODA MANN: I thought Dayton was the funniest man I ever met, but he was so undisciplined.

DOMINICK DUNNE: My first job in TV was stage-managing "Howdy Doody." Dayton was so funny, but the cheapest humor. Nothing was too low for him. The rehearsals were the dirtiest, the dirtiest!

DAYTON ALLEN: People came from all over NBC to watch the rehearsals, because they could get wild. You had to be sometimes. Otherwise you went bananas with all that baby shit.

RHODA MANN: It's gotten exaggerated over the years. What was the worst thing? Maybe the Flubadub humping Mr. Bluster.

SCOTT BRINKER: Bob would get so hysterical he couldn't go on. Dayton would feel Howdy's crotch and go, "Oh, boy," but he didn't have anything there, so once I made a set of genitals for Howdy. When he put his hand in there again, he almost fainted.

RHODA MANN: He groped anybody and anything. During the movie I would take my mike off and walk around on the bridge. One time I didn't bother, and they forgot to turn it off in the control room. I was bending over, watching the movie when Dayton came up behind me and did a major grope. I screamed, "Goddammit, Dayton, take your goddamned hands off me." It went coast to coast!

HOWARD DAVIS: I came on the show to direct in '52 after Bob Rippen was moved up to associate producer. Dayton would proposition the Peanut Gallery mothers, sometimes successfully. Judy Tyler would come to rehearse her lines with the puppets, and Dayton would have Bluster say things like, "I hear you're available, toots."

DOMINICK DUNNE: She played Princess SummerFall WinterSpring. I loved her.

ROGER MUIR: We got her to appeal to the little girls. Well, she appealed to the little girls and the big daddies, too.

DOMINICK DUNNE: She fucked, sucked, couldn't get enough, and the foulest mouth, but just gorgeous.

BOB RIPPEN: There were a lot of stories about the road trips and Judy and lots and lots of guys. Once in a nightclub in Kansas City she ended up drunk and standing on a table and said something that would have been very, very bad for a kids' show. We pulled strings to keep it out of the paper.

HOWARD DAVIS: I don't like it when Judy is made to seem like a borderline whore. She wasn't. She had round heels, but she was such a delight. Had she lived, she would have been a major star. You could see it in *Jailhouse Rock* with Elvis. She was a professional, and she was tough. When Bob grabbed her ass she was early feminist enough to say something about it. She was a very independent spirit. The makeup people and the wardrobe people and the stagehands really loved her. They were her friends.

ROGER MUIR: We also hired Bill Lecornec as a puppeteer, and so we could get more mileage out of him he also became Chief Thunderthud and umpteen other characters.

EDDIE KEAN: He had a little mustache that he would not shave off. He was the only Indian in history with a mustache.

BOB RIPPEN: We were once out in Hollywood, and in those days you could buy liquor in the newspaper stands of hotel lobbies. Bill was with me in full regalia as Chief Thunderthud when he asked for a bottle of Scotch. The clerk looked at him and said, "I'm sorry, sir, but we can't sell liquor to Indians."

ROGER MUIR: The studio was very small. We could handle maybe fifty kids in the Peanut Gallery. I had a two or three year backup. We got letters from mothers who were pregnant, so the kids could come on in two or three years.

EDDIE KEAN: The problem with the Peanut Gallery was kids sit home and think everything is neat and tidy. Then they come in and see this wild set, and they are really shook up when they see Clarabell talking to the director, and that Howdy isn't real.

BOB RIPPEN: When they saw Bob talking for him, you could see that puzzled look on their faces.

EDDIE KEAN: The secret to the show's success was that the kids were always in on the jokes. It was never played on them, and when Bob talked into the camera it was like he was talking to each one of the children at home. That and the Clarabell slapstick made it work. The show was a mixed blessing for me. It was exciting and wonderful, but it was also extremely tedious and difficult. When the show was on five days a week, I'd wake up in the morning around seven-thirty, make myself coffee, go to the desk, and spend the day at the type-writer alternating between cigarettes and coffee. I didn't even get dressed or take a shower until I was through. It's a miracle I didn't die of cancer at an early age. I did my damndest to get finished by four or four-thirty, so I could see the show at the studio, just for a break in the action. I was very alone while everybody else was having fun.

SCOTT BRINKER: Eddie used to call us with the script for the next day's show at eleven o'clock at night. Eddie would say, "There's something called a Flapdoodle in the script," and he would tell me what it was supposed to do, and I'd build it overnight. For two years, I got two hours of sleep a night. It was tough, but I loved my work and I worked hard. Thank goodness I had a wife who worked with me.

The props were fun. It was a very clever show that never got its just deserts. The Flapdoodle was a mailbox made with a model of a goose. The Marbledoo-dle was a thing you stood on, like a pedal. You pushed it up and down. That worked a bagpipes, which in turn started the marbles down a series of runways. The Air-o-Doodle was a conveyance for the puppets. It was several things in one, a car, an airplane, a boat. Bluster went to the moon on that. Then there was the Clarabus. That was actually a battery-operated car that he could ride.

EDDIE KEAN: When Marty said we needed an animal, we went nuts trying to figure out what animal to have. We only had enough money for one puppet, so I suggested we use parts from several animals. That's how the Flubadub came about.

SCOTT BRINKER: I built him from a pig's tail and a seal's feet and a dog's body and a giraffe's neck.

EDDIE KEAN: I found the name by doing what I always did when I was stuck for script ideas—I looked in the dictionary or encyclopedia. In the dic-tionary, the definition of a flapdoodle was a flubdub.

I had a rule, and this was something imbued in me by my parents. Howdy was a cowboy, but there were no guns, no knives, no lassoes, no lariats. Everything wasn't always sweet. Everybody was fighting everybody, but there was no violence.

ROGER MUIR: The critics used to blast us because it was such a noisy show, but behind everything was a positive attitude. The songs, "You don't cross the street with your feet, you cross it with your eyes." "Be kind to animals." They weren't educational in a "Sesame Street" sense, but "Howdy" was a good show for kids. We won the Peabody Award and lots of others.

EDDIE KEAN: For seven years, I never took a rest. When I went on vacation, I took a typewriter and mailed my scripts to New York. I wrote every word for seven years, and after that I had had enough. After I left, it went on tape, and the writers who succeeded me got residuals.

Before I left, there was a meeting with some NBC brass about what to do to counter the oncoming Disney show. Our thought was to have cartoons, which Howdy never had, but was Disney's forte. The answer from NBC was no, and we couldn't succeed against Disney without cartoons.

On the show, I had Princess SummerFall WinterSpring say, "Cowaboopa." I just made it up. It sounded like Indian to me. The "cowa" stuck with me. Then, when the chief got angry, we had him say, "Cowabunga," instead of "damn you" or "darn you."

A few years ago, I walked into a Burger King and saw a huge poster billboarding a promotion using the Ninja Turtles, and on the Michelangelo turtle was the word *Cowabunga*. I nearly fell over, because I had never heard of the Ninja Turtles. I was totally unaware that surfers in California were using the word the same way parachuters did when they shouted "Geronimo" when jumping out of a plane. The word has since turned up in the New Oxford Dictionary, which is in every university in the world. It is defined as "a cry of exhilaration."

You know, I shot down a couple of Japanese suicide planes during the war, but when I talk to people about what I've done, the only thing that means a damn thing is that I invented the word "cowabunga."

* * *

LARRY MENKIN: One day Jim Caddigan, the program director at DuMont, said to me, "Listen, everybody's going to science fiction. Did you see that thing out of Chicago called 'Captain Marvel?' Why don't we do a science fiction Captain something?" Someone said, "Video." I don't know who. I came up with a structure—Sherlock Holmes and Dr. Moriarty.

CHARLES POLACHEK: I was the first director of Captain Video. The show was a science fiction soap opera for kids. Dick Coogan played the lead, and his young ranger was Don Hastings.

We went in the first day with no preparation. I said, "Where is the prop department?" They had no prop department at DuMont. I said, "The script calls for a telescope that sees around corners called the 'opticon scillometer,' and a special raygun."

Larry White and I went into Wanamaker's toy department and tried to find something that we could gussie up to look like a raygun. This old-maid saleslady said, "We don't carry guns." Next to the toy department was auto accessories, so I said to Larry, "Let's see what we can find over there." The opticon scillometer was made from a combination of a spark plug, a muffler, a rear-view mirror and an ashtray. I made it with my own two hands. We created a lot of props out of automobile parts.

DON HASTINGS: The atomic rifle had one of those stickum ashtrays on it for the sight. It was held together by a part from an automobile muffler.

Our scenery budget was fifteen dollars a week. The X-9, our first rocket, was just a painted set.

LARRY MENKIN: Instead of having them take off in their spaceship, we had them lying down, and we'd shake the camera. Also, when they were going through clouds, we took a great big tank of water, poured cream in it and shot through that.

DON HASTINGS: Our mountain hideaway was literally a four-by-four card on an easel. Sometimes it fell off while we were shooting it.

Coogan was a very funny man. We would do whole run-throughs with him as Clark Gable and me as Peter Lorre. The stagehands were always having fun with it. One time Coogan had to pick up some suitcases. He said to a stagehand, "C'mon, put something in these." Well, they put so many stage weights in there he couldn't lift it.

STAN EPSTEIN: Captain Video would bust through a wall and then fall on his ass, and you would see them turn their backs to the camera, their shoulders shaking.

My favorite guy for ad-libbing was a guy named Eddie Holmes, who played a space bum named Tucker. Whenever we were a minute short, I loved it because we would give Eddie the okay, and he would tell a story about his brother who raises kumquats on some planet.

CHARLES POLACHEK: Sometimes we couldn't hire enough actors because we didn't have the money, so we would double as much as we could by putting beards on people. When we ran out of doubles, we used the stagehands' shadows to fill out the cast.

STAN EPSTEIN: Liz Mears, the casting director, kept a lot of actors alive by putting them on the show.

DON HASTINGS: Stephen Elliott was a regular. He later became Dr. Pauli.

RICHARD COOGAN: Every night at his home was Halloween. The kids knew where Dr. Pauli lived and were always egging his house.

DON HASTINGS: Ernest Borgnine played one of the villains. Jack Klugman was on it.

LARRY WHITE: Once, I called Ernest Borgnine up, and he said, "I'm givin' up the whole thing. I'm starvin' to death. My father-in-law has a hardware store out in Far Rockaway."

I begged him, literally, "Look, twenty-five dollars a day, you get six days' work. You can start in the hardware store next week."

After one show that week, the phone rang in the control room, and this elegant voice says, "May I speak to the actor Mr. Borgnine." It was Louis de Rochemont. From that appearance Ernie got "Whistle at Eton Falls," and the rest is history.

RICHARD COOGAN: While I was playing Captain Video, I was also doing a Broadway show with John Garfield, a big star. He says to me, "Dick, you've got to do me a favor. My kids were watching you on TV, and I said, 'Hey, I know that guy,' and they looked at me incredulously, 'What do you mean, Dad. You don't know Captain Video.' "

"Yeah, that's Dick Coogan. I'm workin' with him."

So I had to give him a picture autographed *To my friend, John Garfield*.

DON HASTINGS: Benton & Bowles would fly us everywhere. We opened supermarkets, fruit shows, the Allegheny County Fair. I made more doing an appearance than I did on the show. I loved it. We did a lot of parades, a lot of saluting.

RICHARD COOGAN: For the Thanksgiving Day Parade, I made up a song. We had a microphone on the float, and we sang the song. It carried from block to block, so by the time we got halfway through the parade everybody was singing along with us.

> *Captain Video rangers and all his gallant crew*
> *When there is trouble we know what to do*
> *We're loyal to our country, faithful to our God*
> *We put down the bad man wherever he has trod*
> *We are brave. We are strong. We are dum ta dum*

At the end, and you go, "Yaaaaay!" That was a barrel of fun.

OLGA DRUCE: My reputation was as an educational broadcaster. I was hired originally by the "Superman" people to clean it up, because it was too racist, too violent, and parents were objecting. I was the one who wrote "fights a never-ending battle for truth, justice, and the American way." I'm not proud of that. [Laughs.]

"Captain Video" horrified me at first, because it was hardly in English. Also, they had no sense of drama, and, as someone with a background in child psychology, it wasn't the kind of show I wanted children to see.

I didn't know beans about science fiction, but I said I wanted the best writers. I didn't want the show laughed at. Women are different from men in regard to these things. It becomes like your child, and you want it taken seriously.

I met Arthur C. Clarke. He used to laugh his guts out about Captain Video, but he introduced us to the best writers. We also put some of the first science-fiction special effects on the air. When Arthur and Kubrick were making *2001*, they called me for the names of the people who were making our spaceships.

We introduced themes of international conflict, the dangers of space. There were superior races, but the basic theme was the hero who fought for world peace and world unity, freedom of religion, freedom of the individual.

Still, in the middle of all these high thoughts were these western films. I sat at every conference at Benton & Bowles and said, "For God's sake, get those films out of my hair," and they finally did.

"Captain Video" built a very respectable following among intellectuals. One time Adlai Stevenson was supposed to make a big speech. He said, "Seven o'clock on a weekday? No sir, not opposite 'Captain Video.'"

DON HASTINGS: The show ended right around my birthday in 1955. I was sad. We just had such a good time, and it wasn't just the acting company, it was the crew, the production people. Those were good days for me. There was a real *esprit de corps* at DuMont. It was a great place.

*   *   *

ALEX ANDERSON: My uncle, Paul Terry, created Terrytoons, which were distributed by Twentieth Century Fox. My uncle was sort of the Daddy Warbucks of the family. He didn't have any sons, and he was grooming me to follow in his footsteps. He had me work in every department, but what I really loved was the writing and the drawing.

Around that time, Disney made a movie called *The Reluctant Dragon* which had a segment that showed Bob Benchley visiting a cartoon studio. The story people tell him the story by showing a series of storyboard stills that are up on the wall, but they also added a few sound effects and reactions. I said to my uncle, "Couldn't we set up a television department and do a similar thing, comic strips on television?"

He said, "Alex, if we had anything to do with television, Fox would drop us like that. If it's something you want to do, Godspeed, but you'll have to do it on your own, and for God's sake, don't tell anybody whose nephew you are."

I had an old fraternity brother named Jay Ward, who had gone to Harvard Business School. I told him my idea about doing a comic strip on television, so we went into partnership together. We set up shop in a little studio apartment over my garage in Berkeley. We had a team of eight people. We worked for peanuts—and not even salted peanuts—but it was like the Wright Brothers. Money wasn't what it was about. It was about the thrill of doing something new, and they were glorious days just in the comradeship we enjoyed.

When I was back at Terrytoons, I talked to someone there about doing a takeoff on Don Quixote with a donkey I'd call "Donkey Otee." He said, "Donkeys don't really have the personality. Use a rabbit. They're always so timid."

There was a little kid in the movies named Butch Jacobs. He was a freckle-faced kid with eyes that were sort of too wide apart. In fooling around, I drew Crusader Rabbit with his looks. Once I had the rabbit, I thought, If you are going to have a Don Quixote, you need your Sancho Panza. I thought if I had an aggressive rabbit, the counterpart should be a tiger who was kind of a patsy. The name Ragland T. Tiger came from Tiger Rag. It was rather a stretch, but we were dumb and sophomoric, and we thought it was funny. The "T" may have come from Jay. His name was Jay T. Ward, and he liked to put a "T" in the middle of all names.

ART SCOTT: To make their cartoons, they used several basic shortcuts. For example, if a character runs toward you or away from you that took a lot of drawing because the character had to change size. If he moved from left to right or right to left, there was no change of size.

You could also have "a cycle of action," where he would just be running in front of some background. That way you could get a lot of mileage out of just a few drawings. Also, when you had a character crash into something, everything would fall down on him for a funny effect. For TV cartoons, they would have him run offstage and you'd hear the crash. Then the camera would shake. Then you would cut to the result, which would be the guy sitting in a heap of rubbish. That took very few drawings. It was like radio, where you would imagine the action.

ALEX ANDERSON: You would also do limited lip action when the characters spoke. It was more like talking heads. That's how we could do it for $350 a cartoon.

ART SCOTT: The character would be held still, and they would put some mouth drawings over him, opening and closing his mouth.

ALEX ANDERSON: Somebody said I was the father of limited animation. That's like saying, "You're the guy who invented polio." We just couldn't do anything more.

LUCILLE BLISS: I was the voice of Anastasia in the original "Cinderella." I also did "Tom and Jerry"'s and "Droopy" cartoons. One day, my mother called to tell me, "They're auditioning for a dog or a rabbit. They asked for you."

I auditioned in Alex's garage in Berkeley, and I got the job. Because they didn't have much money we worked in the recording studio from nine at night to four in the morning.

Jay was very particular. If there was a little thing, we had to do it over. It was tough, because people were tired. They would be sleeping on the sofa when they weren't on. Jay always did it with a smile, so when he came in smiling, we said, "Oh-oh, we gotta do it over."

ALEX ANDERSON: Eight of us did four five-minute episodes a week. I was working seventy-five hours a week. I wrote the episodes and did storyboards. Back at Terrytoons, turning out two five-minute cartoons a month took a staff of 120 people. Fortunately, our competition was wrestling. It was a window of opportunity that never would have later existed.

LUCILLE BLISS: They paid us five dollars an episode, and we would get paid by the week. It was always, "Who needs the money most this week?" The guys were saying, "I have children to raise. I can't pay the rent. I need that money!" Me, I was just going to school, so I usually was the low kid on the totem pole.

Jay went to New York to sell the show. He was afraid to fly, so he would take the train with his St. Bernard. Now, a St. Bernard can't go in the baggage car, so we would say, "Oh, the dog is going to New York again. There goes somebody's salary."

ALEX ANDERSON: "Crusader Rabbit" had tongue-in-cheek parody, but not quite the height that Bullwinkle and Rocky reached. Our fan mail for "Crusader Rabbit" came almost entirely from college kids.

Jay wouldn't let me watch it because I got so upset with all the glitches. I got an ulcer out of it, but it was so exciting. Those first days of television if you were involved in it was like a new world. I didn't think of it as anything but the best time of my life.

*　*　*

ROGER MUIR: I kept in touch with Bob Keeshan after he left "Howdy Doody." He had an awful time getting work. One day he told me his father-in-law, who was an undertaker, offered him a job. He didn't know whether to take it or not. I told him he should take it. At least he would be able to feed the family. Then, I got a call from Jack Miller, a producer in Chicago. He was looking for someone to play a clown-host for a lunchtime cartoon show. I put Bobby and Jack together. They went from there to do "Tinker's Workshop."

BOB COLLEARY: I was working at ABC as a cue-card man on the "Hopalong Cassidy" show when Bob was doing "Tinker's Workshop." Even then he was ahead of his time in terms of television's effect on children. On "Tinker," they had those "Farmer Grey" cartoons which were violent and had racial overtones. If he saw something he didn't like he would yell in to the director, "Cut. Take it out. Put me back on." Then he would come back on and say, "I don't think you really want to watch that."

DAVE CONNELL: After "Tinker" was on ABC locally for about six weeks, CBS saw that it was out-drawing its early morning "Jack Paar Show" in the New York market, so they thought, "Aha, that's what we'll do, a children's television show." They had four people prepare pilots. Keeshan and Miller developed the kangaroo idea, the premise being a children's museum with Keeshan being the caretaker. He had big pockets with stuff inside. That was the Kangaroo part of it. Their pilot was the one CBS accepted.

The show went on the air in October 1955. I started in January, having come from the University of Michigan, with a masters in television. I was ready to become the next John Frankenheimer. Instead, I got a job on this kiddie show. For six weeks I was a clerk. My first job was to forge Keeshan's name on postcards when fans sent in letters. He found me doing it and put an end to it. Then I just hung around for a while until a production assistant job opened up and I took it.

We were live six days a week. The show was sloppy. The directing was bad. Everything was bad, but it didn't matter. It worked. It worked because of the magnetism of Keeshan, Lumpy, and Gus. Lumpy [Hugh Brannum, Mr. Green Jeans], who I adored, was the perfect second banana, and Gus [Cosmo Allegretti, Mr. Moose, Dancing Bear] added a spice that was just fabulous. Bob would often screw up the technical crew by being in the wrong place at the wrong time, but there was a magic he had in looking at that lens and communicating to kids that was very, very special. Bob himself did not understand why he worked. His pat answer was "If I ever stop to think about it, I won't be able to do it."

BOB COLLEARY: The rules came from him. He didn't want any slapstick or extensive noise. If you were going to do comedy it had to be relatively soft, never too inside or too adult. We had to educate the guests as to what they could and could not say. People weren't as sensitive in those days to young people, so they might use street talk or get too glib.

The show was in jeopardy so often and he was frequently fighting the sponsors. Only the kids and the parents appreciated the show. It was not a business success. We had one champion at CBS, Lou Cowan. Then he was bumped upstairs. Jim Aubrey, his successor, was not a friend of ours.

OSCAR KATZ: "Captain Kangaroo" was a financial drain. We were always threatening cancellation, but every time it got up to cancellation, somehow the mothers of America knew about it, and they were constantly threatening to tear down the CBS building, so we kept reluctantly renewing it. I finally came up with a plan to change the financing, which made it more tolerable to us.

DAVE CONNELL: The real pressure to keep the show on the air didn't come from the letters, but from the local stations, because they were getting audiences at that hour which they had not gotten during all those abortive attempts to compete with "Today." During one meeting with the affiliates when they announced the cancellation, WCAU, among others, said, "If you cancel 'Kangaroo,' you can have our affiliation back." That's when they realized they were stuck with it.

Bob also took on the issue of commercials and our control of the commercials. It didn't matter if CBS Program Practices approved a commercial, we had to approve it.

BOB KEESHAN: I can remember hearing Dick Tracy or Little Orphan Annie on the radio saying, "Now, get your mother and tell them to bring a pencil and paper, we want to talk to her." That carried over to television, but I didn't want to do those kinds of commercials. It wasn't until "Captain" was a success that I was in a strong-enough position to enforce it.

DAVE CONNELL: Short of saying, "You can't say, 'Force Mommy to buy this,' or 'We're not gonna sell guns,'" the rules were subtle and had to be worked out in negotiations. It was only a big deal when a company got approval from CBS Program Practices for the commercial and made sure the contract said the commercial only had to be approved by Program Practices. That happened with a product called "Johnny 7," which was a stock, to which a kid could attach seven different things, an automatic rifle, a shotgun, a machine gun, a bayonet.

When we turned it down, the company went to CBS and said, "Here is our contract. You can't turn this down." CBS called us in, and they told Keeshan, "You've got to run these things."

When Keeshan refused, CBS said, "Well, we may have to cancel the show for violating the contract."

To his eternal credit, Keeshan said, "We're not going to run them, and there's nothing more to discuss, but if the show is canceled—and you have the right to do that—I will probably get a call from Jack Gould, and I will, as Captain Kangaroo says, 'Tell the truth as to why the show is canceled.' " In forty-eight hours it went away. That was a gutsy move on Bob's part, because there were still elements at CBS who wanted to dump the show, and this would have given them an excuse.

BOB KEESHAN: I helped change a lot of continuity policies, certainly in the way they regarded young audiences, and they allowed me to do pretty much what I thought should be done after that.

※　※　※

ALEX ANDERSON: When we created "Crusader Rabbit," another idea we had was that a bunch of animals in the North Woods owned a television station. We saw a chance to parody shows like wrestling. I had worked with Mighty Mouse at Terrytoons, but I never understood how he managed to gyrate through the air. Squirrels, at least flying squirrels, can fly, and I thought why not go closer to reality and have a squirrel that can fly.

I was also looking for other animals in the Canadian region. I tried reindeer, but reindeer aren't funny. I always felt there was something unique about a moose. I went to work sketching this character, but it wasn't quite what I wanted. Then, one night I had a dream and the personality came to me. In the dream I had gone to this poker party, and this moose joined us and he embarrassed the hell out of me because he kept doing these card tricks. "Pick a card, any card." I woke up and said, "You're working too hard," but that dream formed the basis of Bullwinkle for me, goofy but show-biz, a kind of performing moose.

Down the street in Berkeley on College Avenue was a Ford dealer, Bullwinkel Motors, owned by Clarence Bullwinkel. Bullwinkel was a wonderful name. I changed it to "le" on the absurd idea that I was free from litigation.

CHRIS HAYWARD: I started writing in my twenties. I always had a funny turn of mind, and I always thought in visual terms. I worked on "Time for Beany," which was fresh and witty and sassy. I also worked on some things for Hanna-Barbera when they were still at MGM. They were sensational, extraordinarily visual, great humor, but they went into limited animation and it became totally commerce.

WILLIAM HANNA: We had no choice. Joe Barbera and I assumed we would be making "Tom and Jerry" for the rest of our lives, but we were wrong, so when MGM closed down their cartoon studio, we formed Hanna-Barbera with the intention of trying television.

We had to do it more cheaply, so we used lots of dialogue, which eliminated a tremendous amount of the animation, and also we used fewer drawings per foot. This way where we made a six-minute "Tom & Jerry" at MGM for thirty to forty thousand dollars, we made a four-minute "Ruff & Ready" for TV and sold it for five thousand dollars and made a profit on it. From the time it went into production until the time we saw it on the screen was five or six weeks. A typical "Tom & Jerry" cartoon was in production for five or six months.

ALEX ANDERSON: I never liked cartoons that were so namby-pamby. We wanted to put more bite into it, like UPA's "Gerald McBoing-Boing," which appealed also to adults. Jay put Rocky and Bullwinkle together with that in mind. He hired Bill Scott. Bill brought in Boris and Natasha from the Addams Family.

We wanted good voices that would give it that right note of satire. At the first session, Bill was auditioning people to do Bullwinkle, and he was explaining how it should be done when Jay said, "Hey, you can do it. To hell with these other guys." Jay wasn't a writer or an actor, but he had a great ear.

CHRIS HAYWARD: I wrote some story lines for "Yogi Bear," which I didn't find very witty. Everything seemed to rhyme and was reduced to "Let's steal the pie off the windowsill." Then Jay showed me the first episode of "Rocky." I was stunned, because the soundtrack was so clever you didn't mind the fact that the animation was limited.

You could laugh listening to it. You couldn't do that with the other limited-animation shows, and it was just so fast. They told the story with driving dialogue and marvelous puns that Bill Scott wrote. Hanna-Barbera wrote and produced their cartoons for kids, whereas Jay produced them for himself, and that was the difference. I think that is what gave them a timeless quality.

ALEX ANDERSON: Jay had to do an awful lot of fighting to get them to allow him to put "adult humor" into it. You have problems when your sponsor is a cereal and thinks it should be for kids. They kept saying, "You're pleasing yourselves, not the public." NBC also felt it was too sophisticated for kids.

CHRIS HAYWARD: They wanted the show to be like Hanna and Barbera, and Jay refused, but the kids did understand the humor. The voices were hilarious. Kids are so much sharper than what the producers of kids' shows give them credit for.

The people who worked for Jay were great visual thinkers and gifted, funny people, and they were willing to work for nothing. Jay was a dear, sweet man, just cheap. He did have a great studio with popcorn machines and milkshake machines for us, but he paid slave wages. I got $135 a week.

His way of showing you gratitude for work that was done was taking you to the races or to lunch. He was like an uncle. If you asked him for a raise he would look at you and chuckle. That's why after a while a few of us just said, "We've got to get into a different line of work," and Allan Burns and I created "The Munsters" and I did "Barney Miller" where the big bucks were.

WILLIAM HANNA: With the success of "Ruff & Reddy" we went to a half-hour format. That's when we came up with Huckleberry Hound and the others. Huckleberry was created in the typical way. In this case, Dawes Butler came in and said [in a slow western twang], "I wonder what ya could do if ya had kind of a talkin' thang like that."

One of us said, "Well, that sounds like an old hound dog."

ALEX ANDERSON: I invented Dudley Do-Right. I had seen *Rosemarie* with Nelson Eddy and Jeanette McDonald. It was so absurd for a mountie to sing, "Give me some men, oh, some stout-hearted men," it was funny. I was also inspired by a book by Milt Gross called *He Done Her Wrong*. It was the story of a villain and a dumb hero. Maybe it was also an outgrowth of Robert W. Service's poems. Plagiarism is only when you steal from one person. I was stealing from everybody.

CHRIS HAYWARD: Bill Scott said, "Do you have any idea how he sounds?" I said, "Yeah, we're thinking about Johnny Weismuller," because Weismuller had no bottom to his voice. That was the voice we gave to Dudley. Bill did it.

WILLIAM HANNA: We were asked to consider doing a nighttime show. We thought "The Honeymooners" was the funniest show on the air. Joe and I thought that was the route to go in cartoon form. First, we considered doing a family of pilgrims or gypsies as contemporary people. Then Dan Gordon made this very rough sketch of characters in skins, and we knew that was it. We called the family the Flagstones to begin with, but somebody else had the name, so we had to change it.

CY SCHNEIDER: In 1959, ABC came to my agency with a library of old theatrical cartoons done out of the Harvey Comics characters, Casper the Friendly Ghost, Hughey. It was a tired old library, but we thought there was enough to construct a show.

Because Mattel sponsored the show, we created two characters, Matty Mattel and his sister Sister Belle. We used them for the wraparound to get television exposure for merchandising purposes. We called the show "Matty's Funday Funnies."

The show caught on, and Mattel used Matty Mattel and Sister Belle as dolls and various other products. They also had the merchandising rights to the other figures, including Casper, who became very big. That kind of blending of the cartoons and the commercials didn't become an issue until later when we made it an issue because we went too far.

ABC offered us "Beany and Cecil" as a cartoon show. We thought the pilot was wonderful, but we wanted to add some things that we could merchandise. Beany always had a beany, and we wanted to make that into a product. We had come off Davy Crockett and Mickey Mouse hats. We talked Bob Clampett into putting a propeller on top of the beany, and we sold something like two and a half million of them.

EDDIE KEAN: On "Howdy Doody," we didn't incorporate the licensed products in the scripts, we just used them as prizes. In 1948, I wanted to have something to go along with the election, and it occurred to me to have Howdy run for president. It kind of made the show. Kids really lit into it. The signal thing was the offering of the buttons.

ROGER MUIR: I went to Warren Wade and said, "We've got this Howdy-for-president theme. I can get five thousand buttons, and we could tell the kids if they are for Howdy Doody they could send in a request and we'll send them a button." He said all right. On a Saturday we did the first plug, and Monday morning I got a call from Warren. He said, "I think both of us are going to get fired. We've got to go see John Royal."

It turned out that sixty-six bags of mail were in the mailroom, which was ten times the normal volume of mail. We plugged it three more times and ended up with over 250,000 requests. That was the first indication of how popular the show really was. Right away, they took the response to major sponsors and said, "Look at the power of this thing." Colgate came in first, then Kellogg's.

EDDIE KEAN: Soon, every damn company in the country was calling us for licenses. If the product was decent Marty did not turn them down. One of the reasons I finally left the show was because the fights were so unpleasant over the marketing. They used Bob as a spokesman so the kids wouldn't know a commercial was starting and get up and go to the bathroom. I think it was taking advantage of kids.

ROGER MUIR: We didn't worry about Bob selling products as Buffalo Bob. All of the products were blue-chip products. In 1949, Wonder bread was considered a good product.

HOWARD DAVIS: Wonder bread builds strong bodies eight ways. Later on it was ten. We were terribly venal.

CY SCHNEIDER: Before Minow's speech there was no talk of responsible programming. If we thought of social benefit, it was "Let's not do any harm." In the commercial mainstream, anything pro-social, uplifting, or creative was simply not on our mind.

In my own personal terms, there is a special responsibility toward kids, but in terms of television, there isn't. Television is not there to instruct kids. Kids don't want to be instructed. They go to school for that. They expect to be entertained by television, but that isn't television's responsibility either. Television's real responsibility is to corral an audience to watch commercials, because without the commercials it doesn't exist, except public television.

BOB KEESHAN: That's nonsense. Of course, television is a mass medium, but whether they like it or not they are part of the nurturing system. There are people who spent time in advertising and merchandising who recognize they have a responsibility to special audiences, and they act accordingly.

CY SCHNEIDER: Minow's wasteland speech really scared the hell out of the networks. He threatened to shut them down unless they offered quality shows for children. ABC came up with "Exploring." Then there was "1, 2, 3, Go" and "Discovery." These shows stunk of the classroom. We sponsored them, but they didn't get any ratings.

I invented the word "edu-tainment" in an article I wrote for *Broadcasting*. I said we should combine elements of popular programming with education. We did it with a show called "The Funny Company" about a kids' club. It got an excellent critical response, and Mattel got a lot of benefit out of it because we developed a lot of characters which they made into products, so everybody came out ahead.

DAVE CONNELL: It is an interesting question, how far do we go? Is the purpose of an hour of television to learn how to deal with a bully on the block, or these days when your neighbor pulls an automatic weapon out of his belt. I'm not sure television is the right vehicle for that.

We tried to go with what we called the "medical model." We may not do good, but we don't want to do any harm. At "Sesame Street," I was deluged by people who wanted us to solve all the social ills of the world, but TV can't do everything. It really can't do a hell of a lot, actually, and frequently people expect it to do more than it can or ought to try. It isn't a parent.

GAMES PEOPLE PLAY

Answer: They played "Jeopardy!" on this show twenty-three years before "Jeopardy!" premiered on television.

Question: What was "The CBS Television Quiz"?

Only they didn't call it "Jeopardy!," they called it "Answers in the Questions." Here's one from the May 5, 1942, broadcast that was worth five points:

"Answer: Because there were no more worlds to conquer."

You will have to wait for the correct question.

"The CBS Television Quiz" was commercial television's first game show. It required both mental and physical dexterity with tough questions like, "What is the difference between shoat and stoat?" and difficult stunts for the contestants, like balancing a pan of marbles on their heads.

What they didn't do was play for money. Neither did the contestants on NBC's first game show, "Play the Game," which was nothing more than charades played in a living room set. "Play the Game," having moved over to DuMont (and later ABC) after the war, joined five other game shows on the air that first postwar television season. One of them was DuMont's "Cash & Carry," hosted by Dennis James, in which viewers at home were invited to call in to guess what was under a barrel. There were so few TV sets in New York City at the time, that Harry Dubin, who watched from his Upper East Side apartment, won nearly every week.

That same year, Mark Goodson and Bill Todman sold their first game show, "Winner Take All," to CBS radio. The show moved to television in 1948, the first radio game show to make the switch. It joined more than a dozen new game shows on the four networks that season. Since 1946, nearly five hundred game shows have appeared on network television, and it only seems like Bill Cullen hosted half of them. (Actually, he did twenty-three.)

Goodson-Todman's first made-for-television effort was "What's My Line?" which debuted on February 7, 1950, and didn't leave the air for seventeen years.

The show established a pattern for Goodson-Todman shows, which later included "I've Got a Secret," "To Tell the Truth," "The Price Is Right," "Concentration," and "Match Game," among others. They were all simple, straightforward games with an emphasis on personalities.

The Goodson-Todman producers paid as much attention to the mix of panelists as they did to refining the games themselves, and it showed. The longstanding "What's My Line?" unit of Arlene Francis, Dorothy Kilgallen, Bennett Cerf, and until he died, Fred Allen, was a perfect blend of disparate elements; Francis's warmth and intelligence and Kilgallen's icy determination (she really did want to win), the breezy Cerf, and the more caustic Allen. Stirring the pot was the veteran CBS newsman John Charles Daly, with his South African accent and the linguistic dexterity to handle what was really a difficult game for an emcee.

While money was given away on Goodson-Todman shows, it was never the dominant factor; the game was. Even on "The Price Is Right," which was about money, the genial Bill Cullen skillfully kept the focus on the personalities.

That wasn't the case with "The $64,000 Question," which made its debut in 1955 and within a month had turned television on its ear. The idea of giving away $64,000 was unheard of at the time, and while the producers did their best to play up the personalities of the contestants, the amount of money involved overwhelmed the show—and the good sense of the industry.

The show was produced by Entertainment Productions, Inc. EPI's principal partner was Lou Cowan, who on the heels of the show's success, was made vice president in charge of creative programming for CBS. Creative he was. Before "Question," Cowan had produced several game shows, which employed "controls," an industry euphemism for rigging.

"The $64,000 Question" was just a summer replacement show, but within three weeks it shot past "I Love Lucy" and Ed Sullivan to become the number one program in America with an astonishing 84.8 share in the Trendex ratings. Erik Barnouw writes that when Captain Richard S. McCutcheon of the U.S. Marines became the first to win $64,000, a convention of wholesale druggists in Sulphur Springs, West Virginia, was halted with the announcement, "The Marine has answered the question!"

It didn't take long to fire up the competition. That fall, NBC answered back with "The Big Surprise," another Cowan show, this one with questions valued as high as $100,000. Cowan struck again in 1956 with "The $64,000 Challenge," a kind of graduate school for "Question" champions. It was followed by "High Finance," "Twenty-One," "Treasure Hunt," and "Break the $250,000 Bank" (no subtlety there), all big money prime-time shows.

Quiz-show champions became national heroes. Their winning totals were listed in the newspapers like baseball box scores. There was Teddy Nadler, a cab driver from St. Louis, who took home $224,000; Robert Strom, the young genius who won $160,000, Elfrida Van Nordroff, the all-time winner on

"Twenty-One" with $220,500. Charles Van Doren won a relatively paltry $129,000 on "Twenty-One," but the twenty-nine-year-old college professor and literary blue blood became the biggest hero of all, accumulating besides his winnings, a *Time* magazine cover and a job with the "Today" show.

The possibility that gobs of money could be won or lost was the reason why most viewers tuned in to the quizzes, but what kept them glued to the most popular shows was clever direction and the behind-the-scenes manipulation intended to maximize the tension and the ratings. The producers worked the dodge to excess. The format for "The $64,000 Question" was designed by Joseph Cates, who originated such brilliant gimmicks as the isolation booth and using bank guards to protect the sanctity of the questions.

On "Question," the producers sought contestants whose area of expertise seemed out of character: Mert Powers, the Southern grandmother on baseball, psychologist Joyce Brothers on boxing, Redmond O'Hanlon, a New York City policeman, on Shakespeare.

Once a contestant was selected, the manipulation began with an extensive interview to determine the contestant's "matrix of knowledge" within, for example, the category of history. If the contestant was a ratings draw, and his area of expertise was determined to be American history, he would be asked questions within that field so that he would win and continue on the show. If he was a ratings drain, he might be asked questions on European history, in the hope that he would fail, making way for a new and potentially more popular contestant. A similar technique was used on "Tic Tac Dough," "Dotto," and "Twenty-One," as well as "The $64,000 Challenge," which differed from its parent show in that it involved two contestants playing each other.

Other methods were also used to fix the contests. Sometimes on "Question" answers were given in advance to insure victory for a contestant whose pleasing personality had pushed up the ratings—or the defeat of an unpopular opponent.

"Twenty-One," which was created by Jack Barry and Dan Enright (as was "Tic Tac Dough"), involved much more tinkering. The show premiered in September, 1956, and was loosely based on the card game "21." Two opponents would play against each other, selecting questions with point values that rose with the difficulty of the question. The first to achieve twenty-one points was the champion.

There were problems from the start. Questions on "Twenty-One" demanded general knowledge rather than the specific expertise required on "Question." As a result, the material on "Twenty-One" was simply too difficult for even the brightest contestants. Fortunately for Enright there was a simple solution. He just made sure that when necessary the contestants were given the answers in advance. They were not only instructed when to give correct or incorrect responses, but they were also told which point values to request, insuring that a series of tie games would heighten the tension before a handpicked victor emerged.

One of the more enduring images of the fifties is of Charles Van Doren, sweating and grimacing in the isolation booth on "Twenty-One," looking like a man who had just eaten a bad hot dog. What he really was doing was acting out the role of a man struggling to retrieve information from the deepest recesses of his brain. Along with his money, he should have gotten an Emmy for following so effectively a script laid out for him.

Although he didn't work directly with Van Doren, the man pulling all the strings was Dan Enright, a man so crafty he would have given Tricky Dick Nixon fits. Contestants were shown how to build tension by pausing dramatically before answering questions, instructed on the proper way to scrunch their brows and purse their lips to indicate doubt; and taught to exhale deeply if they gave the correct answer, indicating great relief.

Nobody did this better than Van Doren, but the seeds of his downfall were sown with his accession. The man he vanquished, Herbert Stempel, was an Army veteran, enrolled at City College on the GI Bill. Stempel took exception to the notion that Van Doren was chosen to win their match by virtue of his pedigree. After he was "defeated" by Van Doren, Stempel sought revenge by approaching several newspaper reporters with his insider's account of how the show was rigged. Only the *New York Journal-American* seemed interested in the story. The paper even went to NBC to get a reaction from them before deciding to drop the story out of fear of running afoul of the libel laws.

Network executives are a nervous lot to begin with. The call from the *Journal-American* probably drove blood pressures at 30 Rock up past the Dow Jones Industrials. There was a lot at stake. "Twenty-One" was so successful that the network had entered into negotiations to buy it outright from Enright and Barry. The rigging remained an open secret for another year. Then, on August 15, 1958, Edward Hilgemeier, Jr., walked into the office of Assistant New York City District Attorney Joseph Stone with a story about the backstage goings on at "Dotto."

Unlike Stempel, Hilgemeier had proof in the form of a page he had torn from the notebook of contestant Marie Winn. Hilgemeier, who had made a career out of being a quiz-show contestant, had seen her writing in the notebook during a meeting with "Dotto"'s producers before the show. He suspected it wasn't somebody's recipe for oatmeal cookies she was jotting down, but rather the answers to the questions she was about to be asked on the air. That turned out to be true. Winn left the notebook in her dressing room, so while she was on stage, Hilgemeier tore out the telltale page and took it with him to the *New York Post*.

The reporter, Jack O'Grady, was willing to write the story, but needing a hook for it, he convinced Hilgemeier to take his complaint to the DA. That kicked off a year-long denouement which saw all the big-money quiz shows taken off the air, a grand-jury investigation and finally Van Doren's November 2, 1959, *mea culpa* before a congressional committee and his subsequent indictment on perjury charges. The grand jury, unlike the TV audience, didn't buy his act.

GIL FATES: At CBS before the war, we sweated like mad to do fifteen hours a week of programming. One night, a bunch of us were sitting around, and we decided to do a quiz show. "The CBS Television Quiz" was an hour show once a week. I was the emcee and Frannie Buss was the scorekeeper. She was the first Vanna White. The contestants were mostly friends of Tony's and Gil's. Bennett Cerf and Dick and Dorothy Rodgers were regulars.

They would answer questions and attempt stunts. The "Jeopardy!"-type questions were tough. We also did "What's the difference between?" For example, you had to explain the difference between antimony and alimony. The stunts were hard too. For one, the contestants sat in a chair, and between their knees was a bowl of peanuts. They held a milk bottle on their heads, and against the clock they had to see how many peanuts they could spoon up into the bottle. At the end of the show, the winner got a warm handshake.

GERALDINE ZORBAUGH: Before the war, we used to play charades with our friends. On the way home one night, my husband Harvey said, "This game would be good on television." I said, "You're always having these ideas, but you never do anything about them," so he went into NBC and met with Tom Hutchinson. He said to bring in the group. We went in and played it for him, and they put us on the air the next week. At home, somebody would just say, "Let's play the game," so it was called "Play the Game." Harvey was the emcee, because as a college professor he was used to that kind of thing.

Television was closed down during the war. We came back on ABC because I was working there. We also had a sponsor, Alexander's, because his wife was taking her Ph.D. under my husband. Now, we had people suddenly telling us where to sit and to look in a certain direction. We also had guests, like Hazel Scott. But I was on ABC's legal staff, and the general counsel said, "You can either be a lawyer or be talent. You can't be both," so I left the show. I wasn't very good anyway.

GIL FATES: CBS was then experimenting with several game shows. On one of them you would get a person on the phone and show a picture of something on the air and ask them if they recognize it. Sometimes we'd get a picture of an apartment house on Park Avenue and call people in that building, and they wouldn't recognize it.

BOB STEWART: I was a staff producer at WRCA in New York, now WNBC. I practically begged the station manager to let me put on this game show I created called "The Auctioneer." I got the idea from an auction I used to watch on Fiftieth Street during my lunch hour. The auctioneer would put up a clock or some silver. His aim was get at least one buck over the retail price. The people in the crowd scored, in effect, if they could get it for less than what they could buy it for in the retail stores. That one line between the two became the idea for "The Auctioneer," which later became "The Price Is Right."

FRANKLIN HELLER: Bob Bach created "What's My Line?" He got the idea on a subway. He was looking across the aisle at a guy and he thought to himself, I wonder what he does for a living? He told the idea to Goodson, who liked it. In return, he gave Bob a lifetime job booking the guests. The price for that was to never say it was his idea, and he never did take credit for the show.

BOB STEWART: Mark Goodson claimed credit for the earth. He also claimed "The Price Is Right" was his show.

FRANKLIN HELLER: He liked people to think that he made up these shows. "I've Got a Secret" was made up by Allan Sherman and Howard Merrill. What he did do was hire creative people like Bob Stewart. Goodson was very bright and driven, but not amiable. I didn't share his enthusiasm for money, but he was loyal to a fault. I never had any respect for Todman. He was a drunk.

BOB STEWART: Todman was the money and a little alcohol or maybe a lot of alcohol. He'd be sauced by ten-thirty in the morning. Mark was a superb editor, but he could not begin with a blank piece of paper and give you a show. You could bring him your idea, and he would say, "You've got a problem here," and then you had to go and fix it.

GIL FATES: The first "What's My Line?" was a disaster. The cast and the set were terrible, so they brought in Frank Heller.

BOB STEWART: Frank invented something that seems very simple today, but somebody had to be the one to invent it—that was where to put the panel, the players, how you make the entrances.

FRANK HELLER: If I have any claim to fame, that's it. Even today, everything is a variation on my design. Those first shows *were* awful. The microphones got into the shots. The camera was never on the person speaking. I made models of the panel desk and Daly's desk and a new kind of blackboard. Then I moved them around until I found an arrangement that the camera couldn't louse up.

Then I found the panelists were saying funny things, but the studio audience wasn't laughing. They were distracted by the cameras, the mikes, and everything. The cameramen knew this, and they wore Hawaiian shorts and were showing off for the audience, so I made them wear black alpaca coats. Then I got seven-and-a-half-inch lenses, which meant they didn't have to move for their shots. It worked. My second program was a big success.

IRA SKUTCH: Next came "I've Got a Secret." They put the contestant in a witness box like at a trial. The emcee was the judge, and the panel were the lawyers. They even walked around. It was a mess, so they flip-flopped Frank's design. On "What's My Line?" the panel was on stage right and John Daly on stage left. They just reversed it, and it worked.

BOB STEWART: I got to Goodson-Todman in a roundabout way. In August '56, I was out of work, and I bumped into Monty Hall on the street. He said, "I know the attorney who represents Goodson and Todman. You got any ideas?"

"Sure."

So we saw Mark, and I presented him an idea called "Three of a Kind," which became "To Tell the Truth." The idea grew out of something we worked on but never aired at WRCA called "Cross Examination." On that show, we permitted a contestant to invent any identity he wanted, and we had a panel behaving like police interrogators. They asked questions, and the contestant lost if they caught him in a contradiction.

I said to Mark, "I have three people who pretend to be the same person and a panel of professionals cross-examines them to try and guess who the real person is."

He said, "Impossible. How are amateurs going to stand up under cross-examination by professional panelists?"

"You get the panelists. I'll bring in the amateurs."

I brought in three people. One of them had been in the infantry in World War II and was now managing a grocery store. Mark brought some of his producers and they questioned these people for fifteen minutes. Then they had to vote separately. I said, "Before you vote, if anybody is positive about who the real person is, raise your hand." Nobody did. The show went on that December.

GIL FATES: People think anyone can do a game show. It is true you're not doing Shakespeare every week, and once you get the format down, it's not that hard, but the creation and refining takes a lot of sweat.

IRA SKUTCH: All shows start out with an idea by an individual. For example, Frank Wayne came in one day and said, "Write down something about an elephant." The idea was you would try to match what the others wrote down. That was an idea, not a show, but from that idea came "Match Game" and several other shows.

BOB STEWART: Mark used to have these regular meetings to come up with game ideas even though nobody ever created an idea with twenty people in a room.

IRA SKUTCH: They never came out with an original concept at the meetings, but we did push other concepts along.

FRANK HELLER: Mark liked the meetings, because then he could say, "I brought that to perfection." Believe me, "Password" was as good as it would be before Mark ever saw it. They did inspire one thing—"Heller's Law of Television: Never permit the other fellow to finish a sentence since he might know what he is talking about and thus prove that you do not." The corollary is, "If you miss your chance to interrupt, change the subject."

BOB STEWART: Before one of those meetings, Mark told me they were working on an idea about merchandise and what it cost and that's when I told him about "The Auctioneer." We tried it out in his office by having people bid on the lamps, the furnishings, and everything in there.

FRANK HELLER: One day, Bob came into my office and closed the door, and he said, "I've got an idea and want to tell you." That was "Password." We worked on it. I helped bring it along to where it was viable game. Then he brought it to Mark.

BOB STEWART: The original idea for "Password" didn't work. That was, you had two opponents facing each other. When one looks at the other, behind his head he sees a word. Each one gives the other a one-word clue to see who gets it first. The problem is, what's to stop one from giving the other deliberately bad clues. We kicked it around until we came up with the idea of having two teams of partners, and now each of the teams was trying to communicate instead of competing.

When I presented the show to Mark, he said, "If you can only give one-word clues, it won't work because what are you going to do if somebody says 'mother-in-law.' Who is gonna know if it is one word or two?"

Gil Fates said, "Why don't you get a judge?"

I said, "What a wonderful idea. We'll get the best etymologist in the world."

I go to the *World Book Encyclopedia* and find out their etymologist was a guy named Reason A. Goodwin, a wonderful name. We would plug the *World Book*, and he would be the judge. It was fabulous. Goodson agrees to do it. We sell the show in fifteen minutes, and we're now in the first or second week of taping. Sure enough, someone says something with a hyphen in it, which would be unacceptable. Everybody now looks anxiously at Reason A. Goodwin. Is he gonna accept it? Reason A. Goodwin very calmly opens up a dictionary, looks up the word. We were hysterical. We could have had a girl do that twice as fast.

IRA SKUTCH: Some shows fell in very quickly. Others took all kinds of torturous work.

BOB STEWART: On "Password," we had to decide whether or not to show the word on the screen. Finally, we decided that we had to because for the people at home much of the humor came from their knowing it while the panelists didn't. The show also had Jack Clark whispering, "The password is." He did that for my mother. She was a Jewish immigrant who couldn't read English. I knew that she would watch the show and that she and some of my other relatives couldn't read.

IRA SKUTCH: Once you had a form to work with, then you would set up run-throughs with people in the office, telephone operators, whoever was around. That way you quickly found stuff that didn't work. You'd make adjustments and try it again.

FRANK HELLER: For "Beat the Clock," Bob Howard and Frank Wayne created the stunts, things like roll a ball down a slide so it goes in a hole; any obtuse thing they could manufacture out of oatmeal boxes. During the day, we hired actors to try out the stunts. If they were too easy or too hard we adjusted them or just didn't use them.

Jimmy Dean was one of the actors, but we had to fire him. He was so well coordinated we couldn't tell from him what the average person could do.

BOB STEWART: After a show was sold, you made a pilot to see whether the machinery on the stage was working. "The Price Is Right" pilot was the ultimate disaster. Bill Cullen, who was on the turntable and had a bad leg, had the microphone around his neck, and when the turntable started to move the mike began strangling him. He wasn't nimble enough to jump up. I remember screaming to the stagehands, "Hold it!" They stopped and jerked the turntable, and he fell against the desk.

Then the totaller, which was supposed to punch up the numbers, broke down. It was such a disaster that NBC wanted to buy us out. Bill Todman, who loved a buck when he could smell it, suggested we take their money and then put it on CBS. I said, "No way. They bought the goddamn show. Force them to give us the thirteen weeks."

NBC reluctantly let us go on the air, but they put us opposite the most successful daytime show of the generation, "Arthur Godfrey," figuring, "Okay, thirteen weeks and good-bye." Within thirteen weeks we were beating Godfrey. It was unbelievable. We had no idea what we were getting into. My staff was two people. Ultimately we had a warehouse filled with merchandise.

We invented the "Showcase" on that show. It was a weekly contest where we showed seven items, one of them handmade so you couldn't check the price. We invited people to send in postcards, guessing the retail prices.

On Tuesday or Wednesday morning after the first "Showcase," the postman comes in with maybe fifty cards. The girls quickly go through them. Thursday, he comes in with a bag of postcards, and the girls work to eleven o'clock. On Friday, he comes in with about six sacks of postcards, and we knew we were out of business. We hired a guy named Bobby O'Donnell, who had a company called Radioland Service. He had literally hundreds of housewives in Queens going through the postcards.

In the show's heyday, we averaged forty million postcards a month. Plus the stores were threatening to close us down because people checking the prices were tying up their telephone lines.

IRA SKUTCH: The best shows were the simplest shows.

FRANK HELLER: "What's My Line?" is the quintessential show, and it couldn't be more simple. "What does that guy do for a living?" That's all it is. "The Price Is Right" is, "How much does that cost?" "Jeopardy!" has the fundamental question, "Who is buried in Grant's Tomb?"

BOB STEWART: You have to do something that causes the viewer to sit on the edge of his chair and shout the answer or the clue out, even if he's alone. If he doesn't say it out loud, you haven't gotten him. A panel show is different. In most panel shows you are in on the secret, so there is nothing to shout about. There, the key was having a panel that you could identify with and enjoy.

"What's My Line" was the only panel show where we didn't let you in on the secret. You were involved with the questions being asked and listening to the answers. Then you could judge for yourself what was true and what wasn't.

IRA SKUTCH: It was a difficult show for the emcee, John Daly, because he had to interpret many of the questions so people could answer them. That called for great language skills.

BOB STEWART: There are instances when an emcee can make or break a show. Garry Moore's personality went a long way toward making "I've Got a Secret" work. The same show with Bud Collyer, who was not as warm, and didn't have the same kind of friendship with the celebrities, might not have worked out as well.

IRA SKUTCH: An emcee is a much underrated job. I think Bill Cullen was the best of all of them. He was very, very quick-witted, and he was able to play the role of himself. That sounds ridiculous, but that's where actors fail. You hire an actor to be an emcee, and he plays the role of an emcee. The phoniness of it comes through.

BOB STEWART: Here's another reason. It's not too tough to host a show with celebrities, who make it funny and clever, but for a guy to take the average person on the street and get great humor out of just normal conversation is about as tough a thing as there is, and Bill was the best at that.

IRA SKUTCH: Bill was also excellent at being what Goodson called "an onstage producer." When a question didn't work or the scenery fell down, an emcee had to know how to handle it. Bill was also the best at that. On the other hand there was someone like Lee Bowman.

GIL FATES: Lee Bowman might have been the worst.

IRA SKUTCH: Goodson hired Lee to host "What's Going On?" They thought he was urbane and polished because that was the character he played in the movies. The first or second week of the show, they ended up three minutes short. Goodson gives Bowman a stretch signal. Bowman looks at him and says, "Well, that's all the time we have for the day. Good-bye."

Bob Noah once worked with an emcee he said was the densest person he ever worked with. Everything had to be written down and gone over and over again. One day, this guy asked Bob, "At the end of the show today, I'd like to say happy birthday to my father. Is that all right?"

Bob said it was fine, but after the show was over, the guy said to Bob, "Goddammit, you said I could say happy birthday to my father."

Bob said, "Yes, why didn't you do it?"

"It wasn't on the cue card."

FRANK HELLER: John Daly was embarrassed by "What's My Line?" but he made his peace with it. He also made $10,000 a week. That gave him comfort.

IRA SKUTCH: It's true that a lot of the emcees were alike. It's sort of self-perpetuating, because the people who were good at it kept working, and there were only a limited number of shows on the air, so the tendency was to use the same people.

It was just assumed that emcees were male. We always felt that if we could find a woman it would be a tremendous promotion, but we couldn't. A lot of the announcers came out of radio, and there were never any female radio announcers. We did use Sarah Purcell as a co-emcee on "The Better Sex," and she was very good, and Betty White was excellent when she hosted "Password" for a while, so was Arlene when she substituted on "Price Is Right."

IRA SKUTCH: The panel shows made big stars out of people. Bennett Cerf was a publisher nobody knew. Henry Morgan was just a radio personality and Dorothy Kilgallen was a name in a newspaper. They all became major personalities.

Putting a panel together was like casting a play. We would try people out and make changes if it didn't work. You tried to get contrasting people who still were compatible.

FRANK HELLER: The caliber of the panel on "What's My Line?" was a step above the others. Bennett Cerf was literary, and Dorothy Kilgallen was a famous journalist. Arlene was an actress and a darling person.

I protected the women. I made sure they were properly lit. On the camera that took the ladies' pictures, I put a silk stocking over the lens. It degraded the picture, but they were my friends, and it softened their appearances.

The first four panelists were Dorothy, Governor Harold Hoffman of New Jersey, Dr. Richard Hoffman, a psychiatrist, and Louis Untermeyer. Governor Hoffman was a politician and Dr. Hoffman was a pedant. Besides, having two people named Hoffman was dumb. We replaced them with Arlene and Bennett. Then Untermeyer got mixed up with McCarthy, and he was dropped. It was deliberate that everybody hated Dorothy. That was the point. If they were all sweet and lovely it would have been boring, so one of them had to be a pain in the ass.

HENRY MORGAN: I was the heavy and the funny guy on "Secret." I was an amusing Dorothy Kilgallen. [Laughs.] Isn't that an oxymoron? I had a great joke one night: I was wearing a striped seersucker suit, and she said, "It looks like you are wearing mattress ticking."

I said, "Dorothy, you know a lot more about mattresses than I do."

FRANK HELLER: "Secret" was a much more relaxed show. It didn't matter whether anybody got it right or not. There was no Dorothy Kilgallen on the show. On "Secret," Henry Morgan couldn't have cared less.

HENRY MORGAN: I enjoyed "Secret." Most shows were work; this was even less than work. The show went on at seven-thirty. I used to arrive promptly at seven-twenty-five, and I was out of the studio before the credits. I was being paid $1,650 a week. Is that fun?

BOB STEWART: It was fun to work at Goodson-Todman. I was a top producer. I made great money, but it frustrated me that I couldn't determine my own fate. Mark always had the final say. I had this idea where you name a series of things and I've got to tell you what you are talking about. Somebody would say, "a photograph, a license, a social security card," and I'd say, "things in a wallet." Mark didn't like the idea, and it frustrated me that I couldn't get it out there. It later became the endgame for "The $25,000 Pyramid."

I walked out on an awful lot of money. I never got a nickel from any of my shows. Goodson just couldn't understand why I would want to leave. People always think you are doing it for money. Over lunch at the Four Seasons the first thing he said was, "Okay, let's negotiate. What can we give you?"

I told him I just wanted to try it myself. He said, "Bob, I've made you my prince."

I said, "Mark, I want to be a king."

* * *

ALBERT FREEDMAN: Traditionally, all panel and quiz shows, from the time of radio, had a form of control. Entertainment was the key. Without entertainment you had no show. Everybody knew what was going on—the agencies, the sponsors, the networks. A producer knew what he had to do to make a show successful, or he would no longer be producing. It doesn't make it right, but that's the way it was.

JOSEPH CATES: In the thirties, "Quiz Kids" and "Information Please" always used a system of feeding questions within your area of knowledge. It wasn't an accident that they asked John Kieran questions on nature and Oscar Levant questions on baseball. Those shows set the patterns, and when we came on we followed them.

ALBERT FREEDMAN: Was it wrong? Of course, but there are various types of wrongs. Much more destructive than those quiz shows is the violence on television, whose influence has cost this country untold grief over the last forty years.

When television was just starting, I worked with my brother who was a writer on "You Bet Your Life." I left Groucho and came to New York in the early fifties. Here, I produced a kids' show called "Make a Wish." Then I was with "Life Begins at Eighty" and "Juvenile Jury." All the shows I worked on were controlled. With Groucho, we knew from interviewing the contestants what was funny and what was not. The repartee was scripted. Also, the show was filmed for an hour and then cut to twenty-three minutes, so you could edit out all the dull stuff.

On "Juvenile Jury" we knew the funny things the kids would say from interviews we did with them beforehand. Sometimes we fed them answers. Sometimes, we didn't have to. They were very bright.

JOE CATES: I did "Stop the Music" in '54 and '55. The show was controlled. The people who came on were music tested.

PERRY LAFFERTY: Harry Salter did "Stop the Music," also "Name That Tune." Harry wasn't crooked. He was out in the open about it. He was a crazy man. On "Name That Tune" we had a thing where, if you kept a contestant on five weeks, he would get up to $25,000. Well, the audience would go nuts because he had a hot couple going, and Harry didn't want them to lose, so the band is playing and he's going [in a loud whisper], "Blue Skies. Blue Skies," three feet from the mike boom.

I said, "Harry, we're gonna get arrested."

He did it because he loved his show, and he was doing everything he could to make it work.

ALBERT FREEDMAN: A friend of mine produced "Name That Tune." He gave the answers to John Glenn, who won a lot of money.

OSCAR KATZ: In their minds they weren't cheating. A friend of mine was head writer on "Name That Tune." He said it was easy to knock off people they didn't want to win. They had "A" tunes where the title was in the second line, not in the first first line, and you would give the first line and that was wrong. They had tunes in pairs that sounded alike, and you would give both "A" and "B" and they would knock you off because it would be "B."

One time they had this obnoxious kid on the show, and they couldn't knock him off. The put the other kid's chair closer to the bell. That didn't work. You know what they finally did? The idea was if you knew the song you would run down the stage and ring the bell. Now, this is in front of the audience, they weren't hiding anything. They raised the bell! He couldn't reach it. That's how they knocked the little son of a bitch off.

BOB STEWART: With "The $64,000 Question," the story was the money, not the game. Before, the biggest money game that existed was "The $64 Question." The difference was amazing.

JOE CATES: Mark Goodson didn't like the show. He said, "It's a big mistake. You're substituting money for the entertainment value of a show like 'What's My Line?'"

FRANK HELLER: Actually, CBS and the sponsor wanted "What's My Line?" to raise the ante to a thousand dollars. Goodson wanted to do it, but John and I absolutely refused to let them. We said, "If you do that, we will both quit and we will expose it to the press." We knew the other shows were crooked.

JOE CATES: In June of '55, I was going to California to produce and direct Lawrence Welk. When I told Lou Cowan, he said, "Joe, you can't go. I have this summer replacement I want you to do for me—'The $64,000 Question.'"

Lou gave me a half-page outline, that's all. Now, I had been attending Lee Strasberg's classes in direction. How do you apply decomposition to a quiz show? I broke down every single action involved in a quiz show. Start with the set. All quiz shows had a boxed set, like the interior of a living room. I said to the designer, Eddie Gilbert, "Give me a space stage."

He designed a set with latticework. You could look through and see the cyclorama and lights. When a contestant enters he is generally brought on from the side. "No, I want a center entrance, and I want him coming down the stairs." I did that because a center-door entrance is the most dramatic, like coming down the stairs in the old Ziegfeld Follies.

Where does the emcee get his question? Usually, there is a card with the questions in his pocket, or sometimes a girl brings him a card. That's okay on a normal quiz show. What do you do for $64,000? "Shit, you'll get 'em out of a computer." It was bullshit, of course. We used a sorter. There is no such thing as a computer that separates. There were thirty buttons, one for each category, but what happened was from behind, a stagehand lit up the one you chose with a little bulb, but it always sorted out the same way. It was fake but very theatrical.

At $4,000, we needed something even bigger. Where do you keep the questions? "You get them out of a safe." Steve made a deal with Manufacturer's Hanover for a plug. They would send a banker named Ben Fite, and he would get the questions out of a bank safe. You know how stupid that was? We used to give it to the banker the day before to put it in the safe, right? And then he would bring them with him, but Ben didn't look imposing, so I put two bank guards there. It was hokey. I was a young guy without much taste. What are they going to do, pull guns to protect the questions? But it looked good. At $8,000, 16, 32, and 64, I wanted to make it even more dramatic. What could it be? We were working in a radio studio where there was an announcer's booth, so *boom!* We used the announcer's booth. To justify it we said, "Well, there's so much money involved, he could have an associate in the audience with a book, and he could yell out the answers."

There was more. It was Lou's brilliant conceit that the money is so consequential, the decision so big, that you should have a week to think about whether you will quit and take the money or go ahead. The real reason why we did that was because we couldn't afford to give away so much money every week, but by giving the contestants a week's grace in five weeks of big money, one guy will lose and one guy will quit, so the total budget was held to $11,000 a week for prizes.

STEVE CARLIN: The show wasn't about the money. It was celebrating the working class. Our contestants were guys who had an extraordinary knowledge of a particular subject. We had a garbage collector on Grand Opera, and just so nobody would figure we were fooling, we followed him on his route with a camera.

JOE CATES: We were looking for the classic dichotomy. We didn't want a history teacher on history, we wanted the law of opposites, an immigrant on history, a Southern woman on baseball.

I also understood, which the sponsor, Charlie Revson, never did, that for the winners to have credibility, there had to be losers. Charlie's idea was everybody should either win or quit and take their money. He didn't want to offend anybody.

STEVE CARLIN: Charlie Revson was the kind of man who walked into a room and gave the impression that everyone was farting, and he was the only total gentleman.

JOE CATES: He was an obsessive-compulsive guy. That's why he was successful. We had regular meetings with him, and he wanted to discuss each contestant, the performance the previous week, the contestants for next week.

JUDGE JOSEPH STONE: He was a horrible human being. All you had to do was meet him. When we were investigating the quiz shows, Martin Revson, who was really second fiddle in Revlon, told me that he and his brother were continually at each other's throats. One Friday they had a terrible row. Martin stormed out of his office. When he returned Monday, his office was gone. Everything on the walls, his furniture. Gone.

JOE CATES: Before we started one meeting, one of his assistants gets up and walks into a corner and stands there. Charles says, "Let's start the meeting," and starts talking. I said, "Excuse me, is this *Alice in Wonderland*? There is a man standing there with his face in the corner."

Charles says, "Get on with the meeting." Martin is shooting me glances. I said, "No, I don't understand this. You want me to stand in the other corner?"

Charles reluctantly says to the guy, "Okay, come sit down."

I said to the guy afterwards, "You have more brains than anybody else in the room. How can you take that shit?"

He looked me right in the eye, and he said, "You should have minded your own fucking business. I'll tell you how I take that shit. Before I came here, I was making $10,000 a year. They started me here at $40,000. If he wants me to stand in the corner I'll stand in the fucking corner."

STEVE CARLIN: They threatened and threatened us at those damn meetings, but we produced the show as we damn pleased. It was as simple as that. If he wanted us to knock off Joyce Brothers, I didn't know it while it was going on. If it worked out that way, does that mean that the orders were carried out?

JOSEPH STONE: Oh, bullshit. In both "The $64,000 Question" and "The $64,000 Challenge," the Revsons ordered what should be done.

JOE CATES: He'd say, "I fuckin' hate [that contestant]." Charlie wanted Joyce knocked off, so I gave her tough questions. She had one of those mnemonic memories. She memorized the little *Ring* book and she won.

GILBERT CATES: When we did "Dotto," the sponsor would say, "Oh, that's a wonderful contestant, we're lucky to have her." That was a signal to the producer that we had to keep that person on. Or he would say, "What a shame that person is on the show."

It was clear even though I never heard anybody say, "Get that person on," or "Get that person off."

JOE CATES: When I was on, we never gave anyone any questions or answers, but this is what we did do. If a guy knew opera, like Gino Pratto, who knew Italian opera, we just didn't ask him anything on French opera, German opera, or American opera.

JOSEPH STONE: Maybe Carlin or Cates never gave anybody any questions and answers, but Mert Koplin, who ran that program after a while, did, and Richard McCutcheon, who was one of the champions, admitted it.

REV. CHARLES "STONEY" JACKSON: In '55, I was tryin' to wriggle out of debt, so I wrote to "The $64,000 Question" and got no response. I had asked for categories on boxing and football. I was a football player and a referee. I also spent eight years on the ham-and-eggs circuit in boxing. Then I found out they wanted categories that were far away from your normal interests, so I conned them a little. I sent them a telegram and said add to my choice of categories "great love stories." I'm sure my ex-wife got a big laugh out of that.

I got a call and went up for interviews. Mert Koplin gave me a hundred questions in the "great love stories" category. They kept track of the answers I gave them, and they knew in what areas I was strong and the ones where I was weak.

On the show, I got up to $16,000. Then, I said to one of the girls in the office, "I don't seem to be gettin' the attention from Koplin that I had been getting before."

She said, "That's a signal that you better take your $16,000 and move on." So I quit at $16,000 so I could go on "The $64,000 Challenge." You had to go to $16,000 to get on the "Challenge."

JOE CATES: If we agreed with Charlie that maybe a contestant's personality didn't come across, maybe less attention was paid to him in the routining; or they would put him on earlier, not in the big spot, or we would ask him a harder question, or simplify someone else's question.

That was part of the reason why I left the company. The biggest problem was at the $32,000 level, because a contestant would say, "Wait, I've got $32,000. If I lose, they're gonna give me a $4,000 car. I've lost $28,000. If I win, what do I keep out of the second $32,000 after taxes? Eight, ten, twelve. I'm gambling to lose twenty-eight against twelve. That's not a good deal."

I had asked everyone not to have any contact with the contestant while he was making his decision, but it was clear to me that Mert and Steve were trying to affect the contestant's decision. They might say, "Look, we never leap in the difficulty of questions. The $16,000 questions were well within your area of knowledge. What's the big difference to go to the next step?"

For me, the true excitement came from not knowing if the contestant would continue or not. That doesn't mean I was perfect. Inevitably you are tempted. There is an ebullient, attractive person against a dour personality, so you would tend to give the attractive contestant a question he might know.

Mert and Steve also suggested the pre-show warmup, which I did not permit. The week I left they started it. An hour before the show, they would say to the contestant, "Let me ask you twenty questions to get your brain going," and they would ask the component parts of the questions that would be used in the show.

I didn't permit it, not out of ethical concerns. It was purely a pragmatic question. If you rig four contestants a week, at the end of fifty weeks that's two hundred contestants. They have wives and husbands and friends, so four or five hundred people know. Inevitably, a reporter for *Time-Life* is going to find out what you're doing.

STONEY JACKSON: On "The $64,000 Challenge," you played against an opponent. My opponent was a Miss Doll Goostree, who was also from Tennessee. We had the $2,000 question and we both answered it.

Then we got to the $4,000 level. At that time, they had a star system, and they were starring Teddy Nadler and Joyce Brothers. I think they were also afraid of my mouth or my typewriter or both, so they didn't want me to lose, but they didn't want me to interfere with the stars either, so the producer, Shirley Bernstein, asked me to come into her office for a screening. I said, "Why? I'm a champion defending my title. I don't need a screening."

Well, she wanted to talk to me. She said, "Do you know who, other than Christopher Marlowe, wrote a song about Hero and Leander?" Before I could say "No," she said it was Thomas Hood. The boy I brought along with me, who was later mayor of Tullahoma, said "Well, I guess you're supposed to remember Thomas Hood."

On the show, they gave that question to Miss Goostree. She blurted out Shakespeare, which of course was wrong. When I answered it, I was strongly tempted to say, "I know the answer because Shirley Bernstein gave it to me," but I didn't because I had visions of my bullet-riddled body in an alley somewhere, but that would have made me eternally famous, wouldn't it?

When I got home, I called Miss Goostree, and she said that that same week that Shirley Bernstein had told her to study up on Shakespeare because that was what the questions were going to be about. That's why she blurted out Shakespeare, so they shafted her and kept her from winning and they shafted me by making me the winner at that level. Once I won the match, I couldn't go further. I did send Miss Goostree $400, which was the same that the Internal Revenue Service got.

SHIRLEY BERNSTEIN: After Steve and Mert would meet with Charlie, they would look either happy or depressed. They would say, "Shirley, so-and-so has to lose. Charlie is off the wall."

I would say, "I'll do what I can do, but I can't promise."

I could control it up to a point by writing questions to their strengths or weaknesses. I was right about eighty percent of the time, but there was hell to pay when I was wrong. Steve would say, "Charlie is not happy with you."

What could I do? I was right most of the time. With Jackson, it's possible I was being sat on very hard by Charlie, and I may have given him that answer among twenty other questions.

JOE CATES: I kept telling Steve to stand up to Charlie, but he wouldn't. I said, "If you have the number-one hit and you don't stand up to him, what will you do the rest of your life?"

All clients put on pressure, but it was Carlin who was responsible. In the same way, Dan Enright was responsible for "Twenty-One" even though NBC later bought the show.

ALBERT FREEDMAN: Before I joined "Twenty-One," I worked on "The Big Surprise" which was produced by the Cowan organization. A few times I was told to feed answers. One of the kids knew the stock market. Yeah, with my help, and you know the great investigator, Mike Wallace, was the emcee of the show. I was also the producer of "Tic Tac Dough," which was quite successful on daytime television. That was controlled a little bit.

ELISE BARRON: My sister and I began performing when I was seven and she was five. One day, when I was sixteen, we took the test for "Tic Tac Dough." Afterward, Dan Enright said, "Wow, you guys did wonderfully on your tests." I wasn't a great tester, so I thought they were mostly interested in the entertainment value of two sisters. I turned out to be right.

It was decided I would play against a gentleman who was then the champion. The producer, Howard Felsher, said, "We hope you'll tie him a few times and create a little interest, and at some point maybe you'll even defeat him. Then maybe we can bring your sister on, and the two of you can sing together and then compete against each other."

They had me sign a statement. When I asked them to explain it to me, Felsher said, "We don't want you to tell anybody what's happening here backstage, not your girlfriends, your boyfriend, not even your mom."

I asked why not. He said, "You know the competition between shows. They don't want anyone else to know how they do their shows, and we don't want them to know how we do ours."

I was then shown into a room with many filing cabinets. He said, "Obviously, we can't show you the questions, but this is where they are chosen from. We like to give people a chance to browse, to trigger their memories about things, so they will feel more comfortable about answering the questions."

There was a tall man going through the drawers. They told me he was the man I would be playing against. They gave me a drawer to take into another room. I was concerned that I would never have time to scan all the files in that room, but they obviously knew which ones I had studied.

I went on the show, and lo and behold, up came some of the questions I had seen. I managed to tie with this gentleman, who was an academic. That first day's game felt open and fun, but the second day was different. I was told beforehand to go for specific subjects, which did not happen the first day, but I mixed up the categories and instead of tying like I was supposed to, I won right off the bat.

They took a station break, and there was this flurry of activity. Felsher came out and put his arm around me, and he said angrily, "Do you realize what you have done?" It was like I was being scolded. Out came a woman I had never seen before, and questions came that I did not know and she did, so she beat me, and I was out of there.

* * *

ALBERT FREEDMAN: When Barry and Enright started "Twenty-One," the show was straight, but it was so dull the sponsor wanted to take it off the air. They had to control it.

JOE CATES: When I investigated "Twenty-One" for NBC, I came to the conclusion that it was Enright's decision to rig it. It was just an untenable format, and he had to rig it.

SHIRLEY BERNSTEIN: I found that out later when Granada Television hired me to produce "Twenty-One" in England while it was the hottest show in America.

There was one basic difference between "Twenty-One" and "The Challenge." "Twenty-One" required enormous general knowledge, whereas for my show you had to know about one subject. Many people know enormous amounts about Shakespeare, or about Wall Street, but you can't find anyone who knows everything about everything.

I started screening people. They are very insular over there. They know everything about Shakespeare or about English history, but they've never heard of Connecticut or French literature or American history. I thought, "How am I going to do this?"

Plus, in the dry runs they didn't play right. The game is based on Blackjack. In America, they say, "I'll take a six" or an "eight." In England, they'll say, "I'll have a two, please." "I'll have a one," and then they'd fail.

They were so boring. I used up about ten contestants in a half hour. After two or three runs, it dawned on me that something was fishy, so I called Dan Enright. I said, "Listen, Dan, how do you control the show?"

He flew into such a temper. "Control, what are you talking about? I don't know what the hell you're doing over there."

It was such a suspicious temper, but I said to the head of Granada, "There is no way you can do this show unless you cheat." He said they couldn't, at which point I had to go home anyway because I got a job on "Playhouse 90."

ALBERT FREEDMAN: After a while, Enright wanted me to take over "Twenty-One." I wanted to stay with "Tic Tac Dough," but he basically insisted, "You either do it or you're out." I had to start looking for contestants. Stempel was already on the show, although I never met him.

HERBERT STEMPEL: I was born in the Bronx. My father died when I was seven. There were not many books in the house. My parents were not very educated. I spent a good part of my time at the library, devouring facts. I have a retentive memory. I don't remember everything, but things stay in my mind a long time.

I never thought of applying to a quiz show until 1956, when I happened to turn on "Twenty-One." I didn't think it was fixed. I just thought, "This is not difficult at all." I sat down and wrote them a letter, saying I had thousands of odd facts at my command, and I'd like to try out for your fine show, if not "Twenty-One," maybe "Tic Tac Dough."

A few weeks later, they called me in and gave me the hardest test I ever took in my life. There were 363 questions, and I got 250 right. It was the highest score ever on this test.

ALBERT FREEDMAN: The test was broken down into categories so I knew the areas that the contestant was good in and bad in. I would then play to that. I only gave certain contestants the answers.

HERBERT STEMPEL: I didn't hear a thing for about a week or two. Then one evening when my wife was out with her friends, I got a call from Dan Enright, saying he would like to see me. I told him I was baby-sitting, but he could come to my home.

He walked in carrying an attaché case. He sat down on the sofa, opened up the case, and pulled out a bunch of cards and started asking me questions. I answered most of them. The ones I didn't know he filled me in on. After he finished he leaned back and said, "How would you like to make $25,000?"

"Who wouldn't?"

I immediately understood what was happening. He said something to the effect of, "Play ball with me and you will."

I said, "Fine, what do I have to do?"

I didn't think it was wrong. I knew it wasn't honest, but how many people would actually say, "Here's the door."

ALBERT FREEDMAN: The people we had on the show all had a tremendous amount of knowledge and intelligence. They were lawyers, professors, writers. None of them ever turned me down, including Van Doren, because no one thought that they were doing anything that would hurt anybody. In fact, they were grateful to be on the show, even those who lost. The money they won helped many of them to further their status in life.

HERBERT STEMPEL: I was a struggling guy with a bunch of wealthy in-laws who treated me with no respect. Here, I could get some money for myself, become independent of them, and raise my self-esteem, so we made an unspoken agreement that I would go along. Then he said, "Let me look at your wardrobe."

I showed him my closet, and he took out an old, ill-fitting suit that once belonged to my late father-in-law and a frayed shirt and a terrible-looking tie. Then he said, "You're gonna be on the program tomorrow. I want you to go and get a haircut." He wanted me to get one of these old whitewall Marine haircuts.

That night I told my wife, "Toby, I'm going on this program tomorrow, and I'm letting you know now that it's fixed. I don't know where it's gonna lead, but I'm gonna go along with it and see where it takes us." She didn't have any qualms either.

I would have preferred to have played honestly, but you either played his way or not at all. I deluded myself into thinking it was just entertainment. I knew it wasn't kosher, but $25,000 was an absolutely mind-boggling amount of money. I never had more than fifty dollars in my pocket at one time.

Enright also ran a kickback operation. One day he said to me, "You know, Herb, we have to guarantee our investments," and he showed me a letter that said if I won between $80,000 and $100,000 I agreed to take $80,000. On sums between $60,000 and $80,000 I agreed to take $60,000. It was a sliding scale. Pharmaceuticals Inc. was giving him $10,000 a week for prize money, which he wanted to stretch out. That was the reason for all the ties on the show, because if he could dispense only $5,000 a week, he pocketed the other $5,000.

Before the first show, we went through the question. Some of them were identical to the questions he had asked me the night before. Then he started to coach me on the gestures, the lip biting. He said, "I want you to answer question number one in the following manner, answer the fifth part first, then the second, and don't answer right away. Count five or six." This was the hardest part of the whole business, the stage directions, because it was all choreographed, every single thing.

He said, "After you answer, breathe heavily. Keep your watch near the microphone so the audience can hear it to build up the tension. And after you answer the last part of the question and you hear the answer is correct, light up and beam." He told me never to mop my brow but to pat it because I had makeup on. Of course, they turned off the air-conditioning in the booth so you would sweat. It was hot in there.

I could not use my own voice. He gave me this fake high voice [imitates himself on the show], "I'll take ten points, Mr. Barry." I was the only contestant who ever had to humble himself and call him "Mr. Barry" and had to shake hands with this little wimpy handshake. Enright taught me how to do that. He wanted to create an image of a nerd, of a Univac, as they used to call computers back in those days. I was supposed to be a total encyclopedia, a guy who does nothing but pop out answers, has no personality. You know, every account describes me as a short stocky man. Look at me. [Stands.] I am five eleven.

I was never nervous. I knew my opponent had to be rigged, too, because they arranged so many tie games. I just followed the instructions. After the first show I thought, "Gee, this is easy."

Towards the end, I got disgusted at having to wear that suit every week, so the last week I wore my nice single-breasted suit and a nice shirt and tie. He said, "Look, you're not paying attention to your lessons." I didn't care. I also let my hair grow out, and he was very, very angry. That's the kind of fanatic he was about this. He was a meticulous planner, but he didn't understand the human element and that's what cost him.

Then in the fifth week of the show I saw Van Doren backstage. I didn't know who he was, but then I heard his name and I knew it was the beginning of the end.

ALBERT FREEDMAN: I had nothing to do with Stempel. I did hear through Enright that Matty Rosenhouse from Geritol had called Enright and said, "The ratings stink. Stempel has to go."

By a fluke I had met Van Doren through some friends. He didn't know anything about quiz shows. I told him I was about to take over "Twenty-One," and I asked him if he would like to take the test. He said he wasn't interested. We then had lunch, during which he mentioned he liked to travel, but his salary at Columbia was low. On that basis, I convinced him to take the test.

When I was told he got the highest score of any of our contestants, I was more determined than ever to get him on the show, and we talked about the money and how he would bring honor to the teaching profession. He didn't need a lot of convincing. I then explained the show had to be controlled, that we were providing entertainment. He wasn't surprised. He understood what it was all about. Before the show, we went over the questions. I made sure to ask him questions that were within his range of knowledge. The most important thing I told him was the points he should request for each question. That created the tie games.

No one knew this except me, because no one ever had anything to do with Van Doren except me. Not Barry, not Enright, not anyone. It was just between Charles and me.

HERBERT STEMPEL: I knew I was dead because they weren't going to put on the scion of a very famous family unless he was going to win. I found out for sure the next week. Enright told me in his office that I had reached a certain plateau. He said he had been nice to me by putting me on the program. I had won a certain amount of money. Now it was time to go.

In the beginning I was supposedly a poor guy going to school on the GI Bill, who had a lot of knowledge, but didn't have a pot to piss in. Of course, anybody who noticed that I lived in Forest Hills knew that there was something not kosher there. Now against Van Doren, I was suddenly the villain and he was the good guy. Enright would say, "Everybody's daughter would want to marry Charles Van Doren." Well, why wouldn't they want to marry Herb Stempel?

Enright's real name was Errenreich as Barry's was Barish. Enright was a typical self-loathing Jew. These people cater up to the *goyim*. He actually became a born-again Christian before he died.

I felt like shit when he told me I had to take a dive. I said I wanted to play Van Doren honestly. I was getting pressure at school. It had turned into a cultural thing, a Jewish boy from City College vs. a WASP from Columbia. The campuses were abuzz about it. He said, "No, you made a promise. You've got to go."

On "Twenty-One," they had you lose on an easy question because that flattered the audience. Herb Stempel had to lose on his favorite movie, which he had seen three times, *Marty*.

When it came time to lose, they asked me which film was the Academy Award winner of 1954, I thought, Fuck, what happens if I say *Marty*? Then I thought, Maybe he won't give me all the money, so I decided to say *On the Waterfront*, and I lost.

ALBERT FREEDMAN: I had no idea how long Van Doren would be on. I just needed an appealing personality to start off, but it turned out he had extraordinary charisma, tailor-made for TV. It was the first time on television that an intellectual became a hero in America. Until then it was only athletes and Hollywood people. Nothing like this ever happened on any of my other shows. Then he appeared on the cover of *Time*, and I realized the extraordinary power of television.

Van Doren didn't know what the hell hit him either. I didn't know what to say to him. It had gone too far, and it was out of control, but it was too late to do anything. Once you have a tiger by the tail you just don't let go.

After a while the pressure and publicity became too much for him, and he wanted to get off the show, so we had him lose. At that point, I could have quit, but I had two kids and had just bought a house. I decided to stay. That's where we start lying to ourselves. "Well, I'm providing entertainment."

HERBERT STEMPEL: One day I went to the office, and I said to Enright, "I want to play a charity match with Van Doren." He said, "Charlie won't do it, but Vivian Nearing [Van Doren's opponent at the time] will." I immediately understood that Van Doren was about to take a dive. I got a few thousand dollars together and took it to a bookie, and I doubled my money.

Losing to Van Doren didn't bother me as much as the fact that Enright had promised me a $250 a week job as a research assistant. When I asked him about that, he said, "I don't know what you're talking about."

He had also promised to put me on another of their programs, "Hi Low," but instead they put on Van Doren's brother, who won $78,000. It was also a totally fixed show, so he double crossed me on two occasions. Enright was so cocksure of himself. He just used people and discarded them. He used me, abused me, and got rid of me, so I did him in. With all his calculations, he never figured that somebody might be so angry with him, he would pull down the temple of Samson.

*   *   *

[*Marie Winn, the author of the highly regarded book on television* The Plug-In Drug, *was the "Dotto" contestant whose appearance sparked the scandals. The following is taken from a letter to the author. She refused to elaborate or answer any more questions.*]

MARIE WINN: The producers of "Dotto" called me in for a "warm-up" session before the first show. They'd throw a sample question at me, and I'd give them the answer as if I were playing "Dotto." If I didn't know an answer, they would casually throw it in—something of this sort. But I began to suspect, after the first show, that in fact the warm-up session included real questions that had appeared on the show. Still, I had been pretty excited. They had tossed out a lot of questions, and it wasn't at all clear that I wasn't imagining it all. But I wanted to know. So on the day of my second appearance I spent the half hour after the warm-up and before the actual show writing down in my school notebook what I remembered of the warm-up session questions. By the time it was clear, after that second appearance, that the seemingly innocent warm-up session was actually feeding me answers (an infuriating realization, as I recall, because I believed I would have won on my own—such is the nature of being eighteen years old!), it was too late. Another contestant who had seen me writing in my notebook—I didn't think I had anything to hide—tore out the page. . . . That second appearance was also my last. . . .

RICHARD PINKHAM: "Dotto" was the number-one daytime show. Then they put it on at night and it died. I got hold of a public relations guy. I said, "We've got to get some publicity for the show. Get me on the front page of the newspapers." About a month later, he put on my desk a copy of the *New York Post*, and there in thirty-two-point [type] was DOTTO RIGGED.

FRANK COOPER: I packaged "Dotto." It didn't take very long before CBS and Colgate decided to take the show off. That resulted in many of the shows going off because many of the shows were being produced the same way, and the networks knew it.

There was no villainy. You couldn't put a person on and have him staring at the camera and not have the answer. That was dullsville. When the first "Dotto" show went on the air, the first contestant was dull, and in the control room a representative of the network and a representative of the sponsor started to yell, "Give him the answer."

ALBERT FREEDMAN: When NBC bought "Twenty-One," it was very happy to rake in the profits. Lou Cowan was made president of CBS television because his company made CBS a lot of money. That's the name of the game, money, and if you make a lot of money by doing something wrong, you are a hero, as long as you don't get caught. NBC never asked me about the operation of "Twenty-One" during the quiz investigation. The network, the sponsors, the ad agencies, all said they knew nothing, which was a lie.

JOE CATES: There never was a meeting in the whole year that I did the show that did not include in a prominent capacity the network vice president, the ad-agency vice president, and the client vice president, but when they all turned, in this capitalist system of ours, and I'm a capitalist, they all protected each other, and the government went after all the lesser individuals. That's why the scandals were a fake.

JOSEPH STONE: In 1959, I was head of the complaint bureau of the New York City District Attorney's office. The bureau was almost like an emergency room in a hospital. If anyone wanted to make a complaint, they would come to the bureau and see one of the young lawyers on duty.

The office was open for business on Saturdays. One Saturday Edward Hilgemeier came in. One of my assistants interviewed him and thought that he might be one of these crazy guys who came in all the time. He couldn't make out what crime had been committed or why we should get involved since our only function was to investigate and prosecute crime.

He asked me to come in and listen. Hilgemeier said he had been on "Dotto," and he felt a crime had been committed, but he didn't tell us the story. I didn't know what the hell he was talking about. I never watched these programs.

Anyway, we just told Hilgemeier we'd think about it and let him know. Unbeknownst to us, what had really happened was Yeffe Slatin, who was Winn's opponent, and Hilgemeier, had gone to a lawyer after Hilgemeier tore out this page from Winn's notebook, and the lawyer got in touch with the producer. He said, "Look, my client has been wronged, blah-blah-blah." They settled with Slatin for $4,000, but this was where he made a big boo-boo. He only offered Hilgemeier $1,000. Hilgemeier said no. They raised it to $2,500. He turned that down. If they had offered him more, none of this would have come out.

Hilgemeier went to the *Post*, and told a reporter the story. The reporter needed a hook for the story. The hook was sending Hilgemeier to us. The story appeared Monday. It said the show was being canceled. Hogan saw the story.

That's when we began to take notice, but then we couldn't find Hilgemeier. The reporter wouldn't give me his address. That's when Stempel came in.

HERBERT STEMPEL: After the "Dotto" story broke, I called them up and said, "My name is Herb Stempel. I was on 'Twenty-One.' I have knowledge about what went on in the program." At last, I was going to get my revenge.

JOSEPH STONE: We began to bring in people connected with the shows. With a few exceptions, they all lied, the producers, the contestants. They were being controlled like puppets by lawyers. Had they told the truth, I would have researched the law, found out there wasn't any crime, and that would have been the end of it. By their lying, this thing kept expanding.

If I had a contestant in and I didn't think he was telling the truth, I would give him the lecture. I explained that we weren't interested in making any kind of a criminal case against him and that the only way he could get into trouble was if he perjured himself, and then only if we could prove it.

A lot of them were scared of what their friends and relatives would think if the truth came out. They had been heroes at one time, so this would be devastating to them. I assured them that we could not take away their money, but they didn't believe it. I pleaded with them to tell the truth.

HERBERT STEMPEL: Right after I came forward Enright tried to smear me as a crazy man. I was the bad guy who was accusing this fair-haired boy of being a cheat. Van Doren was also insisting it was scrupulously honest. That was insulting my intelligence, and that's one thing you don't do to Herbie Stempel.

JOSEPH STONE: Stempel was no angel. We didn't know what to believe at first. He was a gambler. He had pissed away his money by handing it over to a racketeer, who was going to invest it in a racing stable. After the racketeer disappeared, Stempel concocted a scheme with a friend of his to get $50,000 from Enright or they would expose the show. Enright put him off. Then he secretly tape-recorded a subsequent meeting with Stempel, in which Stempel admitted the scheme and apologized for it.

When Stempel appeared before the grand jury, he had to sign a waiver of immunity because the grand jury was interested in pursuing an extortion case against him, but in the end they couldn't because Enright never testified.

While I was questioning Stempel, I got a call from a lawyer who represented Hilgemeier, so Hilgemeier finally told me what happened on "Dotto."

When Stempel originally told the story I thought he was full of shit, but after I heard Hilgemeier again, we began to investigate Stempel's story. It turned out he had told people what was going to happen in advance of his appearance on the show. He told his barber, his doctor, the guy who sat next to him in school, his pharmacist. He told everybody. Once we talked to them, we realized Stempel was telling the truth.

What really clinched it for Hogan and me was Harold Craig, who also appeared on "Twenty-One." Craig, just being who he was, made him much more believable. My assistant called him up in Hebron, New York, to ask him to come in, but he said he couldn't come down because he had no one to mind his cows. I said, "Tell him to hire someone, and we'll pay for someone to mind the cows."

He came back and said, "Mr. Craig said that if he could come down on Saturday his brother could do it, so we wouldn't have to pay any money to mind them." I said fine. He came down.

My assistants saw him first, and he denied getting answers. I asked them to leave the room, and I talked to him softly. All of a sudden, he put his arms on the desk, put his head in his arms, and started to weep. He kept saying that he couldn't lie. Maybe five minutes elapsed before he raised his head. I suggested he go into the men's room and I would wait for him to return. When he came back he told the whole story. That's when I really became convinced that Stempel was telling the truth.

Now [District Attorney] Frank Hogan was a great patron of Columbia University. He was very friendly with Mark Van Doren, Charlie's father. This case broke Hogan's heart. He knew Charlie Van Doren, and he kept saying that Stempel was a nut.

After I got through with Craig, I went upstairs and told Hogan all about Craig. It was really heart-rending. His face became red. He didn't say a thing. He just walked over to the window and stood there in silence. Finally, he shook his head and said, "I can't believe it." That was all he said. He was just overwhelmed because he now saw that there was something phony-baloney about this. Needless to say he never told me to stop the investigation.

ALBERT FREEDMAN: Suddenly, the newspapers were playing up the story like it was World War III. There were headlines every day. It was terrifying, especially for young, naive, middle-class boys, being charged in the newspapers with lying and cheating. The whole world came crashing down at my feet.

BOB LEWINE: When the scandal broke, Kintner and Sarnoff asked me about Stempel's charges. I said I knew nothing about it. Kintner bet fifty dollars that his complaint was phony. I called Enright in. I said, "Dan, NBC is accusing you of fixing the show."

Dan literally cried. I said, "I don't mean to offend you but that's what they're saying."

"I'm surprised NBC would not show me any more courtesy." He continued to deny it. When the news later broke that he had confessed in Washington, I was shocked. He had put on such a great show for me in my office.

JOSEPH STONE: Enright could bullshit you to death, and it was clear that NBC weren't anxious to find out the truth. They just accepted what he told them. This was a big moneymaker. They weren't interested in destroying it.

FRANK COOPER: CBS and Colgate tried to escape their responsibility. They put the onus on me to pick up the tab for the cancellation of "Dotto," which would have amounted to close to a million dollars. I said, "Okay, what you'll do is break me, but I'm going to call the press and tell 'em what I know about the operation about these kind of games." They picked up the tab.

JOSEPH STONE: The way to get at what really happened was to have subpoena power, and the only way to get subpoena power was to convene a grand jury. I wasn't after the contestants. I've always felt sorry about them, but most of them did lie, including Van Doren.

ELISE BARRON: I was working at Schirmer's when I heard about the scandal on the radio. Then I got consecutive calls at Schirmer's from the DA's office and from Felsher. The person from the DA's office said I would probably be contacted by the producers of the show who would try to convince me to testify that I did not get any answers.

Felsher's office did call. They wanted me to come see them. The DA told me to make the appointment, which I did. Then a plumber's truck arrived at our home in Westchester, and guys got out in their plumbers' uniforms and their plumbers' kits and came into the house and set up a tap on our phone. When Felsher called again, I feigned some excuse about not being able to come in. Felsher told me to tell the truth to the grand jury, that I didn't get answers. I said, "But I did get answers."

Then he told me to *ssh,* that the lines may be tapped. One of the plumbers then gave me the sign that they had gotten what they needed. Then I went down to the DA's office to see Joseph Stone.

ALBERT FREEDMAN: I knew nothing about grand juries. I asked the lawyer if we did anything illegal, and he said no. I learned about our legal system the hard way. Meanwhile, Enright hired eighteen different lawyers. One of them had access to Cardinal Spellman. This lawyer said he could get the Cardinal to convince Hogan to ease off the investigation. It didn't work, but he took his fee in advance and kept the money.

JOSEPH STONE: Enright was really a button pusher. He spent about a quarter of a million dollars, hiring every lawyer in sight who he thought could get to me. He hired at least four lawyers who had once been in the DA's office. He hired one who was a friend of the judge. He hired friends of mine.

The only one I ever ordered out of my office was Myron Greene, who had once worked for Hogan. He intimated that somebody was paying me off. He also intimated that if Hogan wasn't running for Senate this investigation wouldn't be happening. Meanwhile, he should have been disbarred for misadvising his clients.

ALBERT FREEDMAN: Greene was my lawyer. He also represented Enright. He never told me to do what Enright and the others did, that is, take the Fifth Amendment. He knew I would not admit to working with some contestants and that I could be indicted for perjury, but he didn't say anything.

Before I testified, Van Doren invited me to lunch. He told me he was afraid that if I told the truth before the grand jury, he didn't know what it would do to his father. I assured him that I would protect him.

The grand jury wanted me to rat on NBC, about the sponsor, about Dan Enright, and I wouldn't. I felt it was not my business to play ball with an investigation which I felt was phony. I wanted to protect my contestants, and I was indicted for testifying that they didn't get answers. Then I was taken in handcuffs to the police station. The two detectives with me apologized. They said, "Well, kid, this is for publicity," and they took the handcuffs right off after the press left.

JOSEPH STONE: We had Freedman come again after he was indicted. The grand jury was frustrated because we weren't getting the truth from anyone. The bait was that we would consider dismissing the charges if he told us the truth.

ALBERT FREEDMAN: I was told in no uncertain terms that if I did not go back and tell the truth, not only would I go to prison, but Van Doren and the others would get into deep trouble. I was assured my testimony would be kept confidential, and the contestants would be protected. There was little choice, so I agreed to talk about Van Doren and the others.

Little did I know that a scoundrel named Richard Goodwin would get access to the grand-jury minutes and illegally use this confidential material to frighten Van Doren into testifying down in Washington, thereby causing himself immense grief.

JOSEPH STONE: This thing with Van Doren was a horrible experience for me, and what made it even more horrible was this jerk Goodwin double-crossed me. He was working for the counsel to this Special Subcommittee on Legislative Oversight. They came to New York and made a motion for the grand-jury minutes and got them. They promised to use them only for reference and perhaps to cross-examine witnesses. If the witness lied before the committee they could confront him only with *his* grand-jury testimony.

But Goodwin was a wily opportunist. According to what Van Doren told me, Goodwin interviewed him a number of times, and he read him Freedman's grand-jury testimony, which we supposed to be secret, where Freedman named him, so Van Doren now knew that the authorities had evidence that he lied. That's how Goodwin illegally pressured Van Doren to confess to the congressional committee.

ALBERT FREEDMAN: He made Van Doren think I would double-cross him by testifying against him in Washington, despite the fact that he had the assurance of my lawyer that I would not.

When the hearings began, I was living and working in Mexico because I was blacklisted and Mexico was the only place I could work. When the committee contacted me, I knew their investigation would turn into a circus, which it did. I didn't want to testify, but the committee said if I didn't, they would see to it that the contestants I was protecting would be ruined by the hearings.

I was very reluctant to leave. I had a wife and three little children, but I said to them, "If the function of this congressional hearing is to understand how quiz shows are produced, I will testify, but I will not answer any questions dealing with specific contestants who had not already testified." They agreed, and I did not mention Van Doren.

JOSEPH STONE: What happened next with Van Doren was very complicated. Stempel testified before the committee and told his story. In the meantime, Van Doren was summoned to the office of some of the NBC executives, and they asked him whether he had told the truth to the grand jury and whether Freedman had given him the questions and answers. He denied it.

They pressured Van Doren to send a telegram, volunteering to testify that he did not get the answers. To this day, that doesn't make any sense to me. All he had to say to NBC was, "Gentlemen, I'm sorry. I have already testified before the grand jury and that's it." The committee had already voted not to call him. They were scared stiff he would stick to his story and say, "Come now, you are talking to a Van Doren. This is insulting to me and my family."

Instead, he sends them this telegram, which in effect dared them to call his bluff, and they took him up on it. They knew he was lying. Remember, Goodwin had Freedman's grand-jury testimony. Did Van Doren think they wouldn't come after him? I couldn't believe he did that.

If Van Doren hadn't been such a schmuck and sent that telegram he would never have been subpoenaed. The worst thing that could have happened was NBC got rid of him. He would have made a terrific settlement with them because in his contract there was nothing that said he had to be morally correct.

He would not have been indicted for perjury because you needed two people to testify in a perjury case. Only after he confessed in Washington, did the grand jury have enough to indict him. I'm not saying that morally he shouldn't have confessed, but from a legal point of view, if Van Doren had a really tough lawyer, he would have just told him to forget about it.

After he drafted the telegram, Van Doren was summoned to a meeting with Kintner and Sarnoff. On the advice of his attorney, Van Doren declined to answer questions. At that point he was suspended from the network pending a resolution of the allegations. The following morning Van Doren dropped out of sight for a week.

BOB BENDICK: At that time, we had him on the "Today" show regularly as an essayist. His essays were just enchanting, and he enjoyed the recognition he was getting from "Today."

JEANNE BENDICK: When he supposedly disappeared, he and his wife were actually at our house. Bob kept answering the phone, saying he didn't know where he was, and they were here.

BOB BENDICK: At the house, he still didn't admit it to me, even though it was pretty clear that he had.

JEANNE BENDICK: He did say, and this was really sad, "The thing that I really wanted to do most in my life is teach, and who is going to let me teach their kids now?"

JOSEPH STONE: After he emerged, but before he testified before the committee, Van Doren's attorney brought him into the office and he apologized to Hogan for lying to me and the grand jury. Van Doren then apologized to me and finally told the truth. Then he went down to Washington to testify.

STONEY JACKSON: The day I testified, Van Doren came on in the morning with an entourage of attorneys and whatever. You would have thought it was a presidential appearance. This was after they had to catch him. I came on accompanied by a ballpoint pen and a notepad. I didn't know until after the hearings that I was entitled to have an attorney with me.

HERBERT STEMPEL: The obsequiousness of the Harris Committee was unbelievable, except for [Representative] Darounian, who said to Van Doren, "A man of your intelligence shouldn't be patted on the back for telling the truth."

JOE CATES: After I testified, I was blacklisted from the three networks. They just said, "We better stay away from him." It was terrible. Better to be a communist because you can recant being a communist. You couldn't recant being a quiz fixer.

JOSEPH STONE: For Enright, the cover-up was to protect Jack Barry's name. Barry ["Twenty-One" 's host] always claimed he didn't know, but he had to know what was happening. The number of tie games was unbelievable. Van Doren and Van Nordroff played something like fifty-five ties. A mathematician told me that according to the law of averages that was virtually impossible.

IRA SKUTCH: I can't believe he didn't know what was going on. A few years later, Mark Goodson made a deal with Barry to do a show that involved interviewing people on the street. Howard Felsher and I also worked on it. Barry made some tapes, and we made some tapes. His tapes were much funnier than ours, and we couldn't figure out why. It turned out he was giving them funny answers. Mark said to him, "You know you can't do that."

Jack said, "What difference does it make? It's only a pilot." He never learned his lesson.

ERIK BARNOUW: In the wake of the scandals, the quiz shows disappeared from the air and took a number of years off before they started to come back. When they did, they were a little bit more carefully policed for disasters of that kind.

IRA SKUTCH: The rules were you had to disclose whatever you were doing. That worked both ways. One is you will say, "Well, if I have to disclose I am cheating, I'm not going to cheat." On the other hand, as long as you disclose it, you can cheat.

ERIK BARNOUW: The networks had been wanting for some time to get control over their own schedule. Because the sponsors still owned the time and created their own programs to put on the network, there was no audience flow to the schedule. There would be something that appealed to women and then something that appealed to children, and they would sort of cancel each other off. The networks used the scandals as an excuse to take over their own programming so they could create an orderly schedule. This intersected with proposals for the "magazine concept," which Pat Weaver had introduced long before, and ABC had used to move forward. Now, it became the order of the day.

JOSEPH STONE: After Van Doren appeared in Washington, we reconvened another grand jury. The grand jury wasn't sympathetic to him. He and several others who had lied to the grand jury were indicted, and their lives were shattered, but Enright got away with it and so did the network executives who put these shows on.

JOE CATES: It is important to ask yourself, "Who made the money?" What about the guys who went from 25 million to 150 million in gross? What about CBS, which was doing 60 million in billing in an evening? What about the big money made by EPI and Charles Revson? What happened to them? Nothing.

JOSEPH STONE: The law was such that operating fraudulent programs was not against the law. It was only after the investigation that the federal law was passed. What does it say about those who got away? It says that justice wasn't done. In the end, the scandals all came down to one thing: money; money for the networks, money for the sponsors.

GILBERT CATES: The packager or the producer wanted a high-rated show. He wanted to do what he felt would accomplish it. It was also the advertising agency, which wanted to deliver that high-rated show to the sponsor. These two similarly guided entities were like a little atomic chamber driving one another.

ALBERT FREEDMAN: In the fifties we did not know the inherent power of television. When I found out, it was too bloody late. Believe me, I regretted the hell out of it, but was I evil? Was I a villain? I'm a very decent person, and I didn't hurt anybody. As a matter of fact, the people on my shows used that money to change their lives. The last thing I wanted to do was hurt Van Doren and the others, and that's what got me into trouble.

STONEY JACKSON: If they had advised the public that it was an entertainment then it would have been all right, but they led the public to believe that it was an honest endeavor. The folks that I talked to said, "Why don't you just take the money and run. Why bother with all this stuff? Whom are you cheating?"

That is an indication of where we are morally in this country. Those quiz shows showed a growing not immorality but amorality. The whole American public was betrayed.

ALBERT FREEDMAN: Believe me, the decadence in America started long before the quiz scandals. What the scandals showed me was the extraordinary power of this visual medium. It thrusts a person right into the living room, so he becomes part of the family. It creates celebrities and even elects presidents.

The power of television started branching into everything in the fifties. Yet why did the press make such an extraordinary thing about these shows while the role played by television in the violence that this country is going through goes unnoticed. By the time a kid is twenty-one, he can see thousands of different types of murder and mayhem. On television every form of violence is okay in this country, but nudity and sexuality is forbidden.

Wal-Marts refuse to sell a video of cars and pretty girls in bathing suits. Yet they sell thousands of copies of *The Texas Chainsaw Massacre*. What can I say? Welcome to America.

EXECUTIVE SUITES

Had he been president of NBC instead of the United States, Calvin Coolidge's major contribution to *Bartlett's Familiar Quotations* might have been slightly altered to read, "The business of television is business," and he would have been right. It has been that way ever since Bulova paid nine dollars in time charges for the first commercial back in 1941. The system really goes back to the fall of 1922 when AT&T, which already owned several stations, made a startling announcement that its flagship station, WEAF in New York, would operate in effect like a phone booth. AT&T would provide no programming. Instead, customers could come in, and for a fee based on the amount of time they wanted to purchase, air any message of their choosing. AT&T was proposing commercial broadcasting.

Many responsible people were scandalized by the idea that the airwaves could be used for commercial gain. A bill was introduced in Congress to ban advertising on radio. Herbert Hoover, then head of the Federal Radio Commission, declared, "The reader of a newspaper has an option whether he will read or not, but if a speech by the president is to be used as the meat in a sandwich of two patent medicine advertisements, there will be no radio left."

Nevertheless, AT&T went ahead. WEAF's first commercial program was a sales pitch by a Mr. Blackwell for an apartment complex in Queens, New York. The ten-minute pitch cost the company fifty dollars and drew a moderate response. What really blew the lid off the kettle was a ten-minute talk a few months later, delivered by the glamorous Marion Davies. Her lecture, "How I Make Up for the Movies," was done for Mineralava soap. She closed by inviting listeners to write in for a free autographed picture. Over 100,000 requests poured into the station. Commercial radio was here to stay. Soon, the music of the Ipana Troubadours and the A&P Gypsies dominated the airwaves in shows produced and directed by the advertising agencies, not the networks.

The Lucky Strike Orchestra was the brainchild of George Washington Hi the legendary president of the American Tobacco Company, and a seminal figure in the history of commercial broadcasting. The flamboyant Hill drove a Cadillac festooned with enlargements of the Lucky Strike package, chain-smoked Luckies despite a wracking cough, and insisted that all his employees smoke them, too.

Hill, along with Procter & Gamble, was one of the first big-time advertisers to use radio. He knew instinctively how to program for a mass market. He believed the upbeat music played by the Lucky Strike Orchestra could help America dance its way out of the Depression. Hill also broke through the early restrictions on low-class advertising with his classic line for Cremo cigars, "There's no spit in Cremo!" on the CBS network. Hill was a proponent of loud, obnoxious, repetitive advertising. His "Lucky Strike has gone to war!" ads, aired during the early stages of World War II, were one of the great success stories in advertising history. Hill depended mostly on his own instinct for his ad campaigns, but with the help of pioneering public relations man Edward Bernays, a nephew of Sigmund Freud, he was also an early proponent of employing psychoanalytic theory to develop commercial and marketing strategies.

When the Federal Communications Commission approved commercial broadcasting for television in 1941, network executives figured the best way to hook big advertisers was to offer them the same deal they got in radio. After the war, viewers could choose from familiar sounding programs, "The Kraft Music Hall," "The Borden Show," "The Kelvinator Kitchen," or the "Gillette Cavalcade of Sports." There were exceptions. William Paley, tired of CBS radio losing its stars to NBC, decided the best way CBS could get a competitive edge was to control at least some of its own programming. By owning its own shows, the network could tie the shows and their stars into long-term contracts. He set up a program department, headed by Hubbell Robinson and Harry Ommerle. Robinson hired three of the most gifted writers in the business, Cy Howard, Harry Ackerman, and Goodman Ace, to create programs for CBS radio. Their efforts had their impact on CBS television, too. For example, it was Ackerman who found Lucille Ball performing at the Stork Club and signed her with CBS.

For the most part, however, the old radio system ruled TV through the mid-fifties, which also meant a continuation of program practices so successful in radio: programming was aimed toward the lowest common denominator; sponsors combed through scripts to delete what they considered to be offending words or characterizations; controversy, either in dealing with serious social issues or simply in using black actors, was frowned upon. The latter policy was conducted particularly with an eye toward appeasing Southern stations.

Sponsors paid particular attention to anything they thought would boost the competition. This often went to ridiculous extremes. Westinghouse at first refused to allow "Studio One" to broadcast an adaptation of Kipling's "The Light That Failed," believing that the show would reflect badly on their bulbs. As Worthington Miner pointed out in his memoirs, Westinghouse became so wound up over the light–bulb issue that it completely overlooked its sponsorship of a homosexual love story!

Chevrolet wouldn't allow a pioneer on one of its shows to "ford" a river, and Ford wouldn't allow a shot of the New York skyline on a program it sponsored because the Chrysler building was shown. Chrysler wouldn't allow Abraham Lincoln's name to be mentioned on a CBS show about the Civil War, while Mars Candy Company objected to a script in which a little girl was given a dollar to buy ice cream and cookies.

On the "Camel News Caravan," in an interview with "Lucky" Luciano, only the mobster's first name, Charles, could be used, so viewers would not confuse it with an ad for Lucky Strikes. The word "lucky" seemed to pose a particular problem for American Tobacco's competitors. Scriptwriters regularly combed through thesauri to dredge up synonyms like "fortunate" or "providential" whenever the forbidden "L word" popped up. How bad could it get? This bad: even the word "American" was proscribed on one show.

Advertisers often pushed to get their products into scripts. Westinghouse, the sponsors of "The Adventures of Ozzie and Harriet," preferred kitchen scenes, the better to show off the Nelsons' sparkling Westinghouse appliances. How Ozzie earned the money to pay for them nobody ever knew. Ozzie was always at home wearing a tie.

Such overzealous behavior was rooted in the enormous profits generated by television exposure. The Hazel Bishop cosmetics company was a $50,000 annual business in 1950. After two years of television advertising, the company's annual sales topped $4.5 million. As sole sponsor of "The $64,000 Question," Revlon made sure the viewer remembered who was paying for their entertainment. George Feld was an advertising manager for the company. He laughed as he recalled the show's opening:

> The opening billboard said, "Revlon, New York, Paris. If it's the finest of its kind in cosmetics, it's by Revlon." Then the announcer said, "Revlon presents the 1,2,4,8,16,32,64, Revlon presents 'The $64,000 Question.' "
>
> During that time the camera was first on the Revlon logo, and then the camera pulled back to show an artist's palette, and in place of the chunks of color was the "1,2,4,8,16,32,64," and of course the big Revlon logo. Then it dissolved to "Revlon's $64,000 Question," and the letters were like light bulbs.
>
> Then the announcer said, "And now here's the host of Revlon's '$64,000 Question,' Hal March."
>
> He would dissolve to Hal March. He would be standing in front of the isolation booth, which had a huge Revlon illuminated on top of it, and on either side of the isolation booth were giant mockup lipsticks that said Revlon. Hal would do his introduction. Then he introduced the first contestant. We would cut to the gangway which had a Revlon sign on it, and the lady would walk towards Hall, and we would superimpose "Revlon presents," and the contestant's name.

It worked. A new shade of lipstick would be introduced by actress Barbara Britton on the show. The next day all its distributors would be sold out. According to records released during the quiz scandals, net sales went from $3.3 million the year before the show was broadcast in 1954 to $11 million in 1958. "The television quiz shows transformed the cosmetics business from a sleepy department store little nothing to . . . a worldwide global mammoth industry," said Evan William Mandel, Revlon's advertising manager.

Television affected the toy industry the same way. Before television, most toys were sold during Christmas season. The industry was small. In 1955, Mattel was one of the larger toy companies with annual sales of four million dollars. That Christmas it brought out a toy called a "Burp Gun," which it advertised on a new Disney show, "The Mickey Mouse Club," three times on Wednesdays during the weeks before Thanksgiving. Within a month, orders for over a million Burp Guns deluged the company.

"We came back after Thanksgiving weekend, and there was one entry door to the factory, and we could not get in the door," said Cy Schneider, who handled Mattel's advertising campaign. "Mail sacks were piled up in front of the door. The mail was from wholesalers and representatives. It was all orders." Schneider added that one of the orders came from General Eisenhower for his son David. "We ran out of guns and we had to put one together by hand for him." Mattel's sales more than doubled that year. Within a few years sales topped $35 million.

Companies that owned their own television shows generally had strict rules regarding how their products would be portrayed in their scripts. Camel cigarettes prepared mimeographed instructions for writers on its series "Man Against Crime." A heavy could not smoke; any smoking had to be smoked gracefully, not nervously; coughing was strictly prohibited; fire could not be portrayed (because that might indicate the dangers of a cigarette); and, ever mindful of the necessity of maintaining a relationship with the medical profession, doctors had to be portrayed in a positive light.

There were also rules regarding what sponsors saw as potentially offensive material. General Mills's written regulations were apparently designed so not one single American would be offended by any of its programs:

> There will be no material that may give offense either directly or by inference to any organized minority group, lodge or other organization, institutions, residents of any state or section of this country, or a commercial organization of any sort. This shall be taken to include political organizations, fraternal organizations, college and school groups, labor groups, industrial, business and professional organizations, religious orders, civil clubs, memorial and patriotic societies, philanthropic and reform societies . . . athletic organizations, women's groups, etc., which are in good standing.

By far the single most notorious instance of censorship was one which resulted in great embarrassment for CBS and nearly destroyed one of the best productions of the Golden Age. In 1958, "Playhouse 90" broadcast "Judgment at Nuremberg," a play by Abby Mann and directed by George Roy Hill. The show was sponsored by the American Gas Association. The AGA demanded, and got, all mentions of the word "gas" in connection with the Holocaust blipped from the show.

Producers were only able to air a show on a subject as troubling as the Holocaust because most Americans agreed that Nazis were bad. On the topic of integration and civil rights, there was no such unanimity, so when Rod Serling wrote a script, "Doomsday at Noon," about the Emmett Till case (in which a black teenager in Mississippi was lynched for whistling at a white woman) for "The U.S. Steel Hour," company officials went into apoplexy. After the racist Southern White Citizen Councils threatened a boycott, the company pressured Serling to sanitize the script. When it finally aired, the opening scene depicted a white church spire to indicate that the play was set in New England rather than the South, and the details of the incident were altered to remove every last hint of the Till case from the story.

Years later, Serling bitterly recalled the experience in an interview with Mike Wallace. "The black [character] was changed to suggest an unnamed foreigner. The locale was removed from the South to New England—I'm convinced they would have gone to Alaska or the North Pole and used Eskimos except that the costume problem was of sufficient severity not to attempt it." He added, "I went down fighting, thinking in a strange, oblique, philosophical way, 'better say something than nothing.' "

It didn't work. U.S. Steel had succeeded in reducing three hundred years of shameful treatment of blacks to a neighborhood dispute. With small exceptions like "Amos 'n' Andy" and "Beulah," which featured blacks in demeaning roles, television would remain white into the sixties, when the situation slowly began to improve with the appearance of Ossie Davis as a prosecutor in "The Defenders," and a black woman as one of Jackie Gleason's June Taylor dancers. Still, General Motors threatened to withdraw sponsorship from such a mega-success as "Bonanza" when its producers introduced a black character. It wasn't liberalism that finally opened the doors; it was sheer practicality on the part of the sponsors as they discovered black purchasing power and decided that potential profits outweighed possible losses from anti-black boycotts.

The lessening of sponsor interference was only one of the reasons why Pat Weaver introduced his "magazine" concept at NBC. Weaver, who had worked for George Washington Hill at American Tobacco and produced Fred Allen's radio show for Young & Rubicam, was hired by NBC as vice president in charge of television in 1949. The lanky, six-foot-four-inch Californian was a true anomaly in the television industry. He actually thought about the future of television, and television viewers in Weaver's eyes were not merely purchasers of potato chips and dishwashing soap, but citizens whose position in society might actually be elevated by television.

He wrote long, convoluted memos, which upon translation by his staff, were found to contain some striking thinking on the future of television. "Let us dare to think, and let us think with daring," he charged his staff in one of his few straightforward sentences. Weaver's interests were wide-ranging. He could discuss Arthur C. Clarke and Norbert Weiner and Sid Caesar and Jackie Gleason in the same breath. He also wrote about satellites and cable television years before anybody else did.

Weaver brought creative young people into the business and inspired them to think up new programming ideas. In turn, they were devoted to him. In Weaver, NBC had the most innovative network executive the industry has ever seen. His magazine plan brought television programming out of the dark ages and gave the network new scheduling flexibility, since it could place its own shows where it wanted. That opened up the possibility of controlling its audience. For example, by placing a blockbuster hit early in the evening, a network could guarantee high ratings for the shows that followed. A network could also block-program (air similar types of programs in a string) to control audience flow, and counterprogram (strategically place one show opposite another) against the other networks.

Actually, the plan was probably a harder sell within NBC than it was to the ad agencies who liked the magazine plan because it meant they were no longer responsible for a show's failure. By the early fifties, a prime-time network show had in any case gotten too expensive for a single sponsor to produce and support. According to TV historian Martin Mayer, between 1949 and 1959 the cost of producing and transmitting a television show jumped 500 percent. Gone were the days when the entire "Ed Sullivan Show" could be purchased by a single sponsor for $8,650.

ABC soon adopted a similar plan to open up its daytime programming. Called "Operation Daybreak," and engineered largely by Young & Rubicam, sponsors would buy minutes on many shows throughout the network's afternoon schedule, instead of putting all their dollars into one program. That way, the sponsor was guaranteed "total reach" of the audience, meaning at some point during the day nearly every viewer would see at least one of the sponsor's commercials.

With this transformation and the downgrading of the agencies' program departments, many creative people were lost. At Young & Rubicam, former vice president Rod Erickson recalls, half his staff left to try their hand in Hollywood. Some Y & R staff directors, like Tom McAvity, Grant Tinker, and David Levy, moved to NBC and enjoyed long TV careers.

Weaver's other unique idea was that television could elevate *and* entertain. While some network executives liked to talk about broadcasting quality programs, Weaver actually did it. Weaver creations include the "Today" and "Tonight" shows, "Wide, Wide World," "Your Show of Shows" (which combined comedy and highbrow music and dance), and the "Home" show, a women's service program with Arlene Francis and Hugh Downs. His "Producers' Showcase" provided some of the most memorable live drama and ballet ever done on TV. Weaver also took the concept of the special and turned it, in Weaverian fashion, into "the spectacular." While some spectaculars were clinkers (Betty Hutton in "Satins and Spurs"), many provided national television audiences with their first look at Broadway-level entertainment.

Weaver left NBC in 1956 after he was bumped upstairs into a toothless job by General Sarnoff, his place taken by the General's son Robert. Weaver was never again involved in television to the extent he had been. He was too independent for any of the three network heads, and his notions about their obligations to network audiences too radical for their taste.

The early 1950s brought two major changes to the TV industry. Following a titanic battle between RCA and CBS, color television (using the RCA system) emerged as a reality in 1953, the same year that ABC replaced DuMont as the third network. ABC was born in 1943 when RCA was ordered to divest itself of one of its two networks, the Red or the Blue. Since the Blue had the weaker schedule, it was sold for $8,000,000. The buyer was Edward Noble, the Life Savers king. Noble renamed the network ABC and tried to make a go of it. He gave up in 1953 when he sold a controlling interest in the company for $30 million to United Paramount Theaters, headed by Leonard Goldenson. UPT money enabled Goldenson to compete with CBS and NBC and also doomed DuMont, which finally collapsed in 1955.

Under the direction of ABC president Robert Kintner and his successor Oliver Treyz, ABC's programming had a huge effect on the industry—much of it negative. It was Kintner who hit upon the surefire recipe for a hit television show: sex and violence. Under his prodding, violent westerns and action/adventure series became the staples of the ABC schedule and were a spectacular success for the struggling network. Soon, the other two networks were mimicking the ABC formula.

The increasing amount of violence on the airwaves earned the attention of Congress in the wake of what was deemed to be a national epidemic of juvenile delinquency. The first hearings on mass media and violence were held in 1953. On a much larger scale, Senator Thomas Dodd of Connecticut, chairman of the Senate Subcommittee to Investigate Juvenile Delinquency, opened hearings in 1961 specifically to look into violence on television.

The congressmen heard testimony from several researchers who claimed studies of children linked exposure to violence on television and an increase in violent behavior. A Stanford University psychology professor, Dr. Alfred Bandura, reported, for example, that children played more aggressively after seeing a violent film than children who had not seen the film. Another study by Professor Richard H. Walters, of the University of Waterloo in Canada, showed that hospital attendants who had seen a violent movie became more aggressive in their handling of patients.

The Dodd hearings really exploded when the committee staff subpoenaed the internal memoranda of the three networks. The memos proved that the networks had ordered an increase in programs containing sex and violence for the express purpose of boosting ratings. The staff also gathered evidence that Kintner, who had moved to NBC in 1956, had lied about his intentions to the committee. However, as the committee staff contemplated taking legal action against Kintner, the hearings were suddenly terminated and their report suppressed.

The Dodd committee wasn't the only government body casting a jaundiced eye at television. In 1961, the Kennedy Administration, which owed its existence in part to the beneficence of the television camera, appointed a thirty-four-year-old Chicago lawyer, Newton Minow, as chairman of the FCC. Minow took his role as one of Camelot's white knights seriously. He laid out an activist agenda on such issues as children's programming, public television, and improving the viability of UHF broadcasting.

Despite the backing of the administration, it was an uphill battle not only against Congress, but within the FCC itself, which for more than a decade had been in hibernation as a regulatory agency. The FCC had been created in 1934 to protect the public interest. Its ability to do so rested in its power to issue broadcast licenses and revoke or refuse to renew them if a broadcaster did not fulfill his public responsibility. However, its seven-member boards had been filled mostly with political appointees distinguished only by their mediocrity.

Since Minow had only one vote on the commission, he could only go so far. He did make headway on UHF and was responsible for converting Channel Thirteen in New York to a public television station. However, he failed in his efforts to get a public TV station on VHF in Los Angeles, nor was he particularly successful in improving children's programming, although his activism did force the industry to clean up their practices for a little while. His attempt to apply stricter standards for broadcasters in terms of their public responsibility also fell short amid industry-wide and Congressional opposition.

Minow's greatest impact was in applying a label to commercial television that has stuck for more than thirty years. In a speech to the National Association of Broadcasters on May 9, 1961, he shocked broadcasters used to being gladhanded by previous FCC chairmen when he admonished them in what amounted to a State of the Union address on television in America. His words bear repeating:

> When television is good, nothing—not the theater, not the magazines or newspapers—nothing is better. But when television is bad, nothing is worse. I invite you to sit down in front of your television set when your station goes on the air and stay there without a book, magazine, or newspaper, profit-and-loss sheet or

rating book to distract you, and keep your eyes glued to that set, until the station signs off. I can assure you that you will observe a vast wasteland.

He could have made the speech yesterday.

ROBERT SAUDEK: In the late thirties, I had an office at NBC opposite the office of James Rowland Angel. He had been president of Yale and was now a consultant on education for NBC. He made speeches about how public-minded NBC was. He was an amusing man and was willing to put his feet up on the table and chat. Once, I said, "Dr. Angel, what do you do as consultant on education?"

He said, "Well, I'll tell you. When Trammell and Sarnoff are in the back room robbing the bank, I'm supposed to stand out in the street and say, 'They went that way.' "

ERIK BARNOUW: In 1931, I was hired at Erwin, Wasey & Co., after the agency had acquired a million-dollar account from Camel. The agency, which was developing a radio department, needed a director. I was hired because I had written the book and the lyrics for the *Princeton Triangle Show*. I never listened to radio.

The first program I saw them produce was Les Reis and Artie Dunn for Chiclets. They sat at the piano and sang in close harmony. I still remember their theme song [sings]:

*When you're feeling kinda blue
and you wonder what to do,
Cheeeew Chiclets and cheeeer up!
When you've lost your appetite
Here's the way to set it right,
Cheeew Chiclets and cheer up.*

It was very quaint [laughs], like vaudeville. During the next few years, I sometimes directed nine programs a week for Maxwell House, H & O Oats, Barbasol, and others. These programs were produced by the agency and aired on the networks. As the networks saw it, this was a perfectly natural thing to do.

This was the concept of the network as a phone booth—you buy time and do what you want with it. The networks weren't responsible for what went on, any more than the phone company was responsible for what was said over the telephone.

PAT WEAVER: Clients like American Tobacco and Procter & Gamble had total control of programming. The networks had no program departments.

EDWARD BERNAYS: For thirty years I worked with George Washington Hill at American Tobacco. He masterminded "The Lucky Strike Radio Hour," and he spent hours in the studio.

ERIC BARNOUW: He had this idea that we were gonna dance our way out of the Depression. Radio *did* have incredible power. People had enormous faith in the personalities like Evangeline Adams, the Queen of all Astrologers, for Four Hands Toothpaste. She got thousands of letters each week.

My first job in radio was to direct a program for Camels every night. The program—not just the commercials—was addressed to women to get them to smoke. The whole point of nearly every Camel campaign in the late 1920s and early 1930s was that very few women smoked, and if we got women to smoke we would double the market.

The networks did exercise some controls. Through the thirties there were no ad-libbed interviews on NBC. They were done beforehand, transcribed, and reviewed. Then people would read them on the air. Otherwise, somebody might offend somebody or say something that was dangerous from an ideological point of view. You were entering people's homes, so you behaved as such.

EDWARD BERNAYS: When William Paley took over CBS, he hired me to develop public acceptance of radio. I also worked with Sarnoff. We tried to tell both of them that they were working with a medium that could become *The New York Times* of the ear, and that to help insure the continuity of democracy they should not treat it simply as a means of making money based on appealing to the lowest common denominator.

ERIK BARNOUW: After a while, they did have programs like the "Chicago Round Table," "The American Home Forum," and "The Town Meeting of the Air," which were much more democratic than what we have now. They would have Norman Thomas and Earl Browder and a Democrat and a Republican debating an issue, but these shows were not sponsored, and they lasted only through the hegemony of radio. When television started, those shows expired.

The best shows were often the result of a corporation's desire to clean up its public image. I wrote for "Cavalcade of America," which DuPont produced to counter its image as the "merchants of death," after the revelation of its enormous profits made during World War I. Alcoa had the same intentions when it sponsored "See It Now" on television after they were accused of monopolizing the aluminum market.

Year after year, "Cavalcade" kept on winning prizes for having the best educational program. Their shows were written by people like Maxwell Anderson, Robert Sherwood, and Arthur Miller. But, while "Cavalcade" did shows on

American history, none of the programs dealt with war. You couldn't hear a shot fired on that program. We couldn't have stories on labor relations. I once suggested a program on the TVA, but I was told, "That's socialism." Every profile was a celebration, but they never did a black until after World War II. When they did, it was Booker T. Washington, who wanted blacks to be patient. Schools loved the series, but students got a very distorted picture of America.

TED SMITH: We were working on television in those days, but we didn't know what kind of programming television would have. Radio was home entertainment, so if anything the thinking was television would be home entertainment, too.

DONALD GLEN FINK: Television was going to be strictly entertainment. I don't think there were higher hopes for it. The networks realized early on that now with the visual medium you could do a much better job of selling things. There were smaller voices here and there of people who had hoped for a higher standard, but this was an expensive business. It took many dollars to put a station on the air. The guy who was pushing television hardest from a commercial point of view was Sarnoff.

ERIK BARNOUW: Sarnoff didn't think about the impact of television. He just thought the people would buy the sets. CBS hired Gilbert Seldes on the basis of an article he wrote on the future of television. He was about the only person thinking about that kind of thing. Nobody was in the upper echelons of NBC.

It always puzzled me that Sarnoff was so sure television would be even bigger than radio, and everybody believed him because he was so sure of it. I didn't go along with it. It was going to be much more expensive. You couldn't walk around the room enjoying it. You had to sit there and watch it, and it wouldn't be like a movie because it was smaller.

SAMM SINCLAIR BAKER: In 1938, I started in advertising at the Keyswater Agency. Since advertising was composed of very conservative people, they fought television, but I and some other people saw how radio had taken over from print media, so anybody with any sense at all knew that adding sight to sound would make for a tremendous sales tool.

JACK SIEGRIST: Pierce-Phelps was a major appliance supplier in the Philadelphia area. After the war, we brought in a number of wonderful things: vacuum cleaners, air-conditioners, washers, driers. Now, your mother didn't have to go out and hang up the clothes on a cold day to dry. It was a marvelous thing. I did more for women's lib, selling these drudgery-eliminating products than all the big-mouth broads giving speeches about how women were abused—which they were.

Then television came in. We had a television station in town called WCAU, but there was nothing on the air in the afternoon. We had to put something on in order to sell television, so we dreamed up "Homemaker's Matinee." My part was the last quarter of the show, which was a drama that was really a fifteen-minute commercial. It was the life of an appliance salesman. We would run a story through all the appliances during the week.

ROD ERICKSON: At Procter & Gamble, we knew television was coming; it was just a question of when. In 1946, Gil Ralston, Gail Smith, and I cornered Howard Morgens, who was then head of advertising. We told him we should begin preparing for television, but Procter never took risks. He wanted to wait for the cross period where you could afford to give up radio and take up television, which was not affordable yet. The costs per thousands was still way high.

Morgens said, "When it hits we'll be there. Let somebody else play around with it."

He was right, so I decided to leave the company and go to New York where eventually I joined Young & Rubicam, which was one of the first agencies to get involved with television.

NICK KEESELY: In '48, Lennen & Mitchell was looking for a guy to head up radio and television and I got the job. Television still wasn't anything. In advertising, it's only worth the circulation you get and the cost per thousand you get, and the circulation was still low. That year we put out a report showing that a fifteen-minute sitcom with a cast of four could be had by a client for less than six hundred dollars. "Howdy Doody" was two thousand dollars for a quarter hour.

Our intention was to educate clients like Colgate and Lorillard. We said, "You better get into it now 'cause the franchises are going to become more and more valuable."

We sold "The Amateur Hour" to Old Gold, and the impact was immediate. For $150 a week, I hired Dennis James to do the commercials with Julia Meade. That's when we created the dancing cigarette pack. Old Gold was a product that stood still for fifteen years, never increased. With that show, sales took off like you wouldn't believe. When that happened, we had no problem getting other clients into television, and from all the money we were making, I bought four more shows for Old Gold.

DAVID LEVY: At Y & R, we knew the big radio shows would be transferred to TV. We also knew that one day they would wind up on film. With film you could get much better production values, and you could do reruns. At first, Paley was embarrassed at the idea of reruns. He insisted on calling them "encore programs by public demand." There was some truth to that. A lot of people liked to see these shows more than once. I thought it made television a dollar-and-cents instruments rather than an artistic one. Reruns gradually replaced the summer shows and were also very profitable for the agencies, which always added their fifteen percent.

TED ROGERS: I was with Dancer, Fitzgerald, and Sample out on the Coast when many of the agencies out there were staffing up with people who knew something about movies or theater or TV.

We had just gotten approval for four shows to move to television almost at the same time, "My Little Margie," "The Stu Erwin Show," "The Lone Ranger," and "Beulah." Imagine if you were an agency in New York producing those four radio programs and in one summer they were all going to move to television. Who is going to do them? Where are they going to be done? How much do they cost? It was staggering what was thrown at us without any preparation.

LOU WEISS: At that time, the movie studios were letting their contract players go, and the only people who had anybody under contract were agents, so now when Texaco needed a big variety show, with the biggest comedy star around in variety, nobody knew how to put a show like that together. I started at William Morris in 1937. In 1948, we made the deal with Berle. We also got someone we represented to book the show, a producer and writers and the talent to put on the show. That's a package. We put a lot of those together. The whole concept of an agent changed in those years. An agent used to be a guy in a derby with a cigar. All of a sudden an agent's input and his knowledge of the business was needed.

We were good at the business because we had these great relationships with all the agencies. "You're looking for so forth? Who do you think might be good?" You tell them about different concepts we're working on. We always had a top group of people putting together ideas.

JOE CATES: When I was at MCA, my boss used to say that you are not to think of yourself as a salesman. Rather, think of the buyer as the guy sitting there rather remote, and you are bringing him knowledge of the business. You had to think of what his needs and his fears were. Your job was to allay his fears. You were his connections to major stars, writers, and producers. It was his job to see you and work with you. If he didn't, he wasn't doing his job, and we would go to his boss and his clients and tell them. It was a very aggressive approach.

ROD ERICKSON: Those MCA guys were raised that way. Old Jules Stein used to throw stink bombs in Chicago to get his bands in places and to get them to buy his glasses. When you heard Lew Wasserman talk for the first time, it was startling. "Am I hearing this accent right?" He began in the business by running a carnival. Some of that never wore off, but they were brilliant.

LOU WEISS: You had lunch with your clients. You drank with them. A lot of deals were made in bars. If you didn't drink, you were in big trouble, because they didn't speak to people who didn't drink. They wanted you to be as drunk as they were. That's how you got your foot in the door, because the guy liked you and he told you a lot. They learned from you, too. Deals were done in the agency, at the houses of the creative people, at the "21" Club, at restaurants. Agents don't make money sitting in their offices.

SOL RADAM: When I was at William Morris, I sold the "Pulitzer Prize Playhouse" to Schlitz at Columbia University. Eisenhower was the president of Columbia, and Dean Ackerman was head of the journalism school. We were at a stalemate, because Columbia [which administers the Pulitzers] didn't want to be associated with a beer. Then Dean Ackerman took Eisenhower for a walk one morning to a restaurant around Columbia. Two members of the board were having lunch and drinking beer. The General said, "Gentlemen, how are you? Enjoy your lunch." After that we had no problem.

ROD ERICKSON: MCA was notorious for having a dinner for a client, and then when he got back to the hotel there would be a girl in the room.

JOE CATES: I've heard the same stories, but I never did that. I imagine the agent better know that client damn well or that kind of thing could backfire.

It wasn't only agents who did funny things. I know several TV executives were paid off. One was a network's head of programming. Another was head of the TV department of a major advertising agency. David Susskind paid him off. Every week he gave him an envelope with five hundred dollars in it. The buyer would say, "Okay, I bought your show, what are you going to do for me?" It was that blatant.

ROD ERICKSON: A client and I went to see the summer replacement for "I Love Lucy" with Desi. The replacement was "The Whiting Girls." In those days, Desi owned the Luau at the Beverly Hills Hotel. At dinner there he said to me, "Let's go to the john."

He gets me in there, and he says, "I got two girls just in from Las Vegas for you and Jack. I haven't tried 'em, but I understand they're just great."

I had to think, What can I do that won't offend Desi but will help me get rid of this problem?

I said, "Desi, I'm embarrassed to tell you, but John and I are married to younger women, and we came out here for the rest."

Desi said, "Whoa, I understand. I'll take 'em both!"

You made regular pilgrimages to California in the fall to check out the shows you bought for the following season. Clients loved to go on those. The advertising director of General Foods, who could drink a quart of Canadian every single day, could hardly wait to get out there.

JOE CATES: Clients were all starfuckers. The easiest way to sell a show was if I could get Steve Allen or Hal March or somebody to have lunch with them. That made their day.

Every now and then someone would ask, "Do you think you could do a good show?"

My answer would be, "I guarantee I will not do a bad show. It may not succeed in the ratings, but you will never be taken to task because it's a terrible show," and that's what sold it.

NICK KEESELY: More accounts were lost through failures of shows than anything. That's why I lasted. I played it safe.

ROD ERICKSON: You tried not to take many gambles. Still, nobody can tell you definitely whether you got a good one or not. If I told you I was half right, I'd say I was a bleeding genius. I'd take ten percent. You're always guessing. I turned down "I Love Lucy" and "Danny Thomas."

I used to say to executives, "If you like it, don't buy it." What I was saying was, we were addressing a mass audience. The executives were upper educated and upper income. They had to divorce themselves personally when they were making a decision. I told them, "Your job is to reach the most people and set up the proper atmosphere to sell them something."

SAMM BAKER: The clients you dealt with didn't care about the quality of the program. They didn't care if they entertained. Sometimes they didn't even look at the programs. They just wanted to know, would we be able to deliver the numbers? Most advertising people considered the public to be a bunch of idiots. I remember one character: "Oh, they're a bunch of washerwomen. What do they know?"

NICK KEESELY: I avoided violent shows. I was a happy guy, and I liked happy things, so I always bought happy shows. "The Amateur Hour" was doing something for little people. Seeing Ted Mack give a little black boy a boost was great. I bought the Nelson family. If somebody asked, "What was the ideal wholesome American family?" I would have to say, Ozzie and Harriet.

PETER LEVATHES: General Foods only wanted shows that were not controversial. They didn't want to alienate any group.

ROD ERICKSON: Controversy divides your audience. Half the people will hold it against you. The other half will think you're wonderful but they won't buy your product, so what's the purpose? Procter bent over backwards to avoid controversy. They don't want one box of something not to be bought. That's why shows like "Father Knows Best" were ideal.

ANNE HOWARD BAILEY: At the agency where I worked you had people who would just not stick their necks out on the line. Ira, my immediate boss, was a lovely man, but he was terrified because he lived waaaay beyond his means. He had a wife and two daughters in Darien, Connecticut, and he was having affairs on the side.

He shopped at Brooks Brothers and it was always Sulka ties, and he had naturally developed his wine palate. He and his wife were always off to France or Italy. He was just hopelessly beyond his means and he was so afraid of losing it. I've never seen a man under such stress. His boss would walk into the office, and Ira would break into a sweat, and at the end of a meeting in the middle of winter, the whole back of his suit would be soaked from under his arms to his belt line. He wasn't alone. They all got themselves into this bind by one-upping each other.

CHARLIE ANDREWS: I made up a story. In "21," the client, the account executive, and two copywriters are having lunch. The headwaiter asks them, "Can I get you gentlemen a cocktail?"

The eyes all go to the client. He says, "Not me. I've got a desk full of papers. I'll need a clear head when I get back."

The account executive says, "Me, too, not at lunchtime."

And the copywriters, "Never, I've got a lot of work to do."

As the waiter takes a step away, the client says, "I guess I'll have one little martini. It's just one, and it's a little martini, not a regular martini."

The account executive says, "If you're going to have a little martini, I'll have one."

The copywriter: "I'll have one, too."

This is at one o'clock. At four-thirty, the account executive turns to the client and says, "You know your wife is a real cunt."

That happens all the time, all from one little martini. They're all stoned out of their skulls, and the next day the account executive can't figure why he lost the account.

STOCKTON HELFFRICH: Because this fear of offending people was so pervasive, all sorts of ludicrous things happened. The first thing that comes to mind is the show on the Holocaust that a gas company sponsored, and they didn't want the writers to mention the gas chambers. That kind of thing still happens.

ETHEL WINANT: "Judgment at Nuremberg" was such a humiliating thing for CBS. It became the joke of the industry.

NICK KEESELY: I told the American Gas Association, "What you need is a prestige show," so I sold them "Playhouse 90." We read the script for "Judgment at Nuremberg," and when we asked the client what about it, they said, "Well, they'll think it's our kind of gas, and ours is a different kind of gas. You don't need it in there," so we had them take it out.

ETHEL WINANT: The story of how it happened actually began a couple of weeks before, when we did this show called "Portrait of a Murderer." In the end, the killer was put in the gas chamber. They closed the doors and turned the handle and a commercial came up that said, "Nothing but gas does so many jobs so well." The next day, all hell broke loose. That's why they were so determined it should never happen again.

GEORGE ROY HILL: When the script for "Judgment at Nuremberg" came in I knew immediately that it was going to be trouble, so we prepared for it. Herb Brodkin, the producer, backed me completely when they told me to cut any references to gas out of the dialogue. I said, "If you want to cut it out you do it, but I'm not gonna do it."

ETHEL WINANT: All CBS had to do if they really wanted to serve the American Gas Company was say, "Look, why don't you change nights? You're an alternate sponsor. Bristol-Myers will go tonight, and you guys will go next week."

But everybody got crazy, and they began to do wonderful things. Hubbell Robinson was head of programming. Under him was Bill Dozier. Both of them saw that this would be big trouble and were suddenly unreachable for a week, leaving Guy Della Cioppa in charge. He was a stupid little man, who was known as "Paley's Pimp." He was a tower of Jell-O. He said to me, "Tell Herb Brodkin and George Roy Hill that if they don't take the word 'gas' out of the show, you will be fired."

I warned him that they would just laugh at me, but he insisted [in an angry voice], "Just go down there and tell them."

So I went down to the control room and told them. Everybody started laughing. "Guy Della Cioppa is gonna fire Ethel."

I went back and I said, "That didn't work out too well, Guy, but it got a laugh."

"I'm telling you. Heads will fall if this doesn't happen."

Nobody would take it out. They ended up sending a guy up to master control. After the show was fed out of the studio, master control was to bleep the word out before it was broadcast.

Just before the show went on the air, Guy called all the telephone operators and said no calls were to be allowed through to master control. If *he* called and pleaded to speak to master control they were not to let him because somebody might have put a gun to his head—he actually said that—and be forcing him to make the call. He also ordered me to watch the show in his office because he said I would break under the stress. After I heard the first word bleeped out, I would go down to the booth and beg them not to cut the word "gas" out of the show.

God sometimes helps you in moments of real horror. Just as the logo came up I said to Guy, "I hope the guy in master control understands he's not supposed to take the word 'gas' out of the commercial."

Guy went crazy. For an hour until that commercial he tried to get through to master control, and they wouldn't let him. Unfortunately, the guy in master control was smarter than that and he did not bleep the word 'gas' out of the commercial.

DAVID LEVY: There was advertising interference and network interference, but most of the network interference were mandates, while most of the advertising interference were suggestions. We made, at least in my experience, reasonable suggestions which the producer was free to accept or reject.

MARTIN MANULIS: As far as sponsors were concerned and therefore the network, there were certain subjects that were absolutely taboo. You couldn't do homosexuality or miscegenation. We did a show about the birth of a baby, and their restrictions were so heavy it was as if the baby came out of an ant hole.

ETHEL WINANT: There were no blacks on TV, except on "Amos 'n' Andy." There were no porters. It was a white conductor who put your bags on the train. It was so stupid and so terrible. It drove me crazy that I couldn't use them on television.

Sidney Poitier was put through the most degrading experience to do "A Man Is Ten Feet Tall." He was questioned about his politics and his sex life by a committee from the agency. He was willing to do it to make a point. The show won some awards, but the sponsors hated it so much, they wouldn't accept it.

NORMAN FELTON: It wasn't just the agencies. I wrote a show for Montgomery that had a scene in a laboratory where they were trying to find a cure for cancer. One of the doctors was black. Montgomery asked me, "Norman, does that guy have to be black?"

I said, "Yeah, of course he does."

"Does he have to be called Doctor?"

"That's right."

"Well, why?"

"Because I wrote it, Bob."

He said, "All right," and hung up.

REGINALD ROSE: I came up with "Thunder on Sycamore Street" after the Cicero race riots. I saw these photographs of mothers and little children with hatred on their faces outside the homes where blacks were moving in. I sent the outline in to Florence Britton, and she said, "Let's meet for lunch."

She just told me, "Everything in it is perfect except we can't do a Negro, and that's the end of it." The advertisers simply wouldn't allow it. This was 1954. Blacks were then still your maid or your local tap dancer.

She said, "We have got to find something else that this guy is," and I said a Jew or a Catholic, and she said no. Finally, ex-convict came up, and she said, "Yes, that's okay."

BOB LEWINE: At ABC we hired Sammy Davis, Jr., to do a pilot. It was based on Andy Hardy and had Sammy singing, dancing, and playing the drums. I remember Sammy saying, "We gonna have an all-black cast." I said fine. We showed it to Y & R, and they walked out in the middle of it, so we gave up.

JOE CATES: On a show celebrating the Fourth of July, Tom Moore, the former head of broadcasting at ABC, said, "What are you doing with the niggers? Cut the niggers out," but what's the point in singling out network executives. That was the situation in the country. We didn't make the value system. Those attitudes are formed in the home, in the school, and in the neighborhood, and I just think we reflected it.

It wasn't only blacks. I worked for fuckin' ad agencies, one of them where a guy used to brag to me, "Blacks, fuck, Joe, I don't have an Italian working for me yet." When he finally hired one, he said, "Hey, Joe, I hired my first Eye-talian."

You got out to Bloomfield Hills with a presentation and the guys are sitting around telling Jew jokes.

SAMM BAKER: Mennen, who was one of our clients, was a considerable anti-Semite. I would listen to cracks about a Jew who tried to get into the country club. For certain markets it would be better not to have a Jewish-looking actor, whatever that is. I felt lousy about it, but I was making a buck. I wasn't going to raise a row.

JOE CATES: It wasn't always the advertisers. It was also the affiliates, you know, the guy in Mobile, Alabama, who if you had that actor on he wouldn't carry your programming.

MARTIN MANULIS: If you *were* able to use black people, they couldn't touch a white actor.

EARTHA KITT: I did Salome on "Omnibus." During dress rehearsal, Mr. Paley came into the studio and saw this soliloquy where Salome says to the soldier, "Get me the head of John the Baptist," and she rams him down the stairs in anger because he refuses. When Mr. Paley saw this, there was a conference, and the result was the whole soliloquy was cut out because Mr. Paley said, "A white person can hit a black person, but a black person cannot hit a white person."

OSSIE DAVIS: All of us knew that TV was closed to us. We knew when we looked into the mirror in the morning and saw that there was black skin on our faces that it was gonna be tough that day. We took it for granted that we would be the last hired if hired at all and the first fired, and that we would wind up doing the same stereotypical crap that we did on Broadway. It was a source of great amusement to us too.

I signed petitions. I was part of a group organized by Dick Campbell to ask everybody in Harlem to turn off their television on a Saturday, which scared the bejesus out of the broadcasting community. That helped open things up.

There was an actor named P. J. Sidney. He used to walk around with a sign, accusing the broadcast industry of discriminating against black folks. As a response to P. J.'s accusations, CBS didn't give him a job, but they gave me one.

P. J. SIDNEY: I didn't give a shit about jobs for blacks. I was concerned about the image of black people in television. I picketed a few places, including David Susskind's offices in front of the *Newsweek* building. My sign read, PHONEY LIBERAL SUSSKIND. He came down and said, "You're killing me. Do you realize that I just bought five lifetime memberships in the NAACP?"

I said, "Sir, I am not for sale." So I continued my picketing.

I did my first television show in 1951 on DuMont when their casting director, Liz Mears, asked me if I wanted to do a show for her. I said since 1949 I had been trying to get into television with no success. Since then, I've been on hundreds of shows. I had a whole goddamned career of "Yassuh, can I git ya another drink, sir?" But I did what was available. I did not mix feelings with the fact that I needed money to live. You can't change things by refusing to do parts. All that does is make you poor, and everybody else who wanted to do things a certain way continued to do them the way they wanted to do it.

I felt about it the same way any whore felt about it. I needed money. Still, I was enraged at that image, but I went on to do over five hundred voice-overs, and I made a lot of money, and I live comfortably because I have worked the system the way the system works.

When it came to jobs, I was the only one who had proof of discrimination. I recorded a conversation with a Daniel Sutter at NBC, who admitted to me, "Yes, there is a law [against discrimination in casting], and there is a rule against it at NBC, but it is never followed."

ROD ERICKSON: Remember, you were in a mass medium. With blacks, you are still talking of the real interest and empathy of eight percent of your audience.

ERIK BARNOUW: Larry Menkin got very good reviews for a show on WOR called "Harlem Detective." The formula was the one "I Spy" used years later, a white detective and a black detective.

LARRY MENKIN: My partner Charlie Spear and I were poker players. One of the guys in our group was Ted Cott, who was about to go to NBC as program director. He had started tolerance spots on TV. In 1950 or 1951, Ted said that NBC had discovered that more and more blacks were buying television sets, "but we don't really have anything for them. Do you have any ideas?"

I suggested "Harlem Detective." "It's about anti-discrimination but it won't be a lecture." We got him a script a week later, but his boss turned it down. We sent it to the other networks and they all said, "Do you think we're gonna take this piece of shit to the Southern stations? Are you guys out of your fuckin' minds? They're gonna lynch us."

We couldn't give it away. Three years later, Ted has moved to WOR-TV where he is vice president and general manager, and he's bombing. Now, he remembers the script, and he thinks that even if it would be controversial, it would work, because people would buy spots in front of it and in back of it.

We cast the show and went into production. The biggest problem was the crew, which was hostile. The tension on the set was awful. The owner of the station was an arch-conservative, but the show was making money, and we began winning awards. I am sitting on top of the world, but suddenly we begin to be called communists and nigger lovers. At first the owner was on our side, but then about a year and a half after it started I was told "Harlem Detective" was out.

SAMM BAKER: Letters from viewers complaining about anything drove them nuts. A threatening letter from a church frightened them out of years of growth, so they didn't want to make waves. After a while when you're writing commercials and scripts, that becomes inbred. You just didn't use black babies in commercials to avoided offending white viewers.

JOE CATES: Self-censorship is the worst censorship, because after you've been doing it a long time, you may not be part of the times. The times might permit it, and you're still censoring.

On the first show I ever did, I put on a mixed group of dancers. It aired in Washington, D.C., and Virginia, and the station got about fifty complaints. When *Variety* called me I said, "Television is a wonderful medium. You've got a little knob. If you don't like what you see, you turn it off."

But you know, I didn't do it again for twenty years.

SHELDON LEONARD: I was doing a Van Dyke episode which was a flashback to where his child was born. He comes home with the baby, but he thinks the baby was switched with another at the hospital. It turns out the baby he thought was his belonged to a black couple. That man was played by Greg Morris. Neither the agency nor the network wanted us to do it, but then Procter & Gamble said, "If he wants to do it, let him do it."

So we put the show on the air, and, in a strange way, that experience was responsible for Bill Cosby. How? In "The Danny Thomas Show," we had a black actress who played a housekeeper. Sometimes Danny would put his arm around her shoulder or in one case kisses her on the cheek, and we'd get mail saying, "If I want to see a white man make love to a gorilla, I'll go to a freak show."

I kept that mail. When we aired the Van Dyke episode, we got mail of an entirely different nature, saying how refreshing it was to see a black man one up on the white man. How refreshing it is to see a dignified presentation, et cetera. I kept that also.

When I was getting ready to do "I Spy," the network had cast approval of my leading characters. They had already approved Bob Culp. Cosby had just visited the Van Dyke set. He was just what I was looking for. I wasn't looking for a black man. I was looking for an attractive, athletic man with a sense of humor.

I went to New York to persuade Robert Kintner to take a chance with Cosby. I brought the mail with me. After the usual amenities, I told him I saw a guy I wanted. He said, "Well, why didn't you sign him?"

"Because he's black."

"What difference does that make?"

I said, "Mr. Kintner, as of this moment it makes no difference whatever. I apologize for even thinking it did." Cosby got on the air, and after that the door opened.

ERIK BARNOUW: In radio, there were programs which were not explicitly white, but when television came along everything was explicitly white. I think that was one of the things that precipitated the Negro revolt. The only company I recall which didn't mind controversy was Xerox. They said, "We don't mind it because we're aiming for a more sophisticated audience."

PETER PETERSON: I was brought into Bell & Howell in 1958. One reason I was interested in Bell & Howell was that through Chuck Percy, the CEO, it had a tradition of being a company with a social conscience on hot subjects.

Eastman Kodak was then out-advertising us by huge margins. We looked into ideas that would differentiate us from Kodak and the other companies, but also be true to itself. I wanted to appeal to the upper end of the market, as we tended to put out a quality product.

One Saturday morning, I was watching cartoons with my son. When he went to the bathroom, I began clicking the set until I came to a show on NBC called "The Face of Red China." The show made the point that morale in China was rather high, and they were doing many things to increase their economic power. Here was a meaningful show on a country considered to be a threat to America that gave insights which were contrary to what one had been led to believe. I thought it was a tragedy that it was seen only by accident on a Saturday morning.

Around that time, there had been massive criticism of television in regard to violence and also the quiz scandals. I thought we could tie together a public need, a Bell & Howell need, and perhaps a network need to do something different that was genuinely a positive-sums gain, in which everybody benefited.

Nobody was doing public service documentaries in prime time. Those shows were at odd hours or on Sunday afternoons where only the cognoscenti would watch them. I thought we could do network prime-time documentaries, where the networks could have full freedom to do anything that they wished to do.

My plan was altruistic in that I thought we would get much better shows that way, but also, if there was a risk, we could say the truth that we had nothing to do with the content.

Chuck took to the idea. He knew Frank Stanton and suggested we take it to CBS, whose commitment to news went all the way to the top. CBS agreed to do it. We wanted to call it "Bell & Howell Closeup," but Frank said it was important that it be called "CBS Reports," because they were very concerned about their image and the way they had been positioned in Washington.

Very quickly, they got into two controversial subjects. One was civil rights, the other abortion and birth control, which upset the Catholic Church. But we also got acclaim from all over the country about how this company was courageous and had a conscience. We won the Peabody Award and others, and Bell & Howell's visibility grew a great deal.

My market-research background was important because I insisted that we not react emotionally to a few letters. With most corporations, it doesn't take more than a half-dozen landing on the CEO's desk for them to get very upset. Rather than relying on those letters, we did studies on what the company's image was in the aggregate. This way, when somebody walked into a store and said they would not buy a Bell & Howell product because they were a "nigger-loving company," I could say, "Well, we appreciate we're going to have that, but let's look at the company's overall interests." The data we had on our commercial success and the data we had on our company's reputation actually improved. Being involved in controversy did not hurt us at all.

DAVID LEVY: Cigarette companies were the most chauvinistic advertisers.

FRANKLIN HELLER: "To Tell the Truth" was sponsored by Marlboro. We had on two people pretending to be Israeli aviators. Before the show aired, we had a panel of actors, who would play a game with the liars to give them a chance to practice. In the course of the rehearsal, the agency man heard one of the actors ask, "What is the name of the Israeli parliament?"

Afterward, the agency man came up to me and said, "You're going to have to change that question."

I asked him why. He said, "This is a Marlboro show. Parliament is a competing cigarette."

IRA SKUTCH: On a Philco show, there was a line where somebody said, "That man has reached the zenith of his career."

We had to change it to "acme."

DAVID LEVY: It wasn't much to ask them to find a synonym if it was offensive to the client. He was paying the bill. Creative people were childish if they objected. They were always crying "censorship" with the slightest thing. Well, everybody is censored, whether you write a book, a play, or a movie.

NORMAN FELTON: On the "Montgomery" show, Lucky Strike had to approve all scripts. In one show, we had an ashtray in which a cigarette was to be placed. Just before air, an executive came up to me white as a sheet. "That's a penguin ashtray."

"Yeah."

"That's Kool cigarettes. You can't use that."

I had to send everybody I could to search the building for an ashtray with an animal on it that wasn't a penguin. About fifteen minutes before the show, they found one. They also wanted clean ashtrays. The last thing we did before every show went on the air was have someone make sure all the ashtrays were clean.

*   *   *

PAT WEAVER: When I moved to NBC in 1949, my world of tomorrow went beyond television. I wanted to build an inspiring, elevating, mass-communications business. We knew about satellites. Cable was already in existence, and Ampex was already working on the VCR.

RCA also agreed that I could run a program service. From now on, we were going to control the programming and sell advertising to support it. That way we could build what was impossible under the old system—a vehicle to convey information to people that they ought to know to enrich their lives by giving them things they might not want but that they ought to be exposed to. We would elevate taste and standards and make the common man into the uncommon man. That was worthy of our killing ourselves for.

MIKE DANN: I thought Pat was the most exciting man in the *world* when I met him. He changed the atmosphere around NBC completely. He brought in a coterie of people from the ad agencies who knew programming: Sam Fuller, Tom McAvity, Pete Barnum.

GIRAUD CHESTER: I worshipped Pat. You couldn't help but be excited at the vision this man had of the potential of television, to see him shake up the industry the way he did, with the "Today" show, the "Tonight" show, the spectaculars, "Wide, Wide World." He just was pure excitement.

ROD ERICKSON: He may have had a hundred ideas and one was good, but nobody minded because he had ideas. I just wondered how long he could exist with General Sarnoff, although he got along with another tyrant, George Washington Hill.

DICK PINKHAM: They were at each other's throats because Pat would never kowtow to anybody. He kept telling the General, "You don't understand broadcasting. You make the hardware. Let me do this for you." That didn't go over very well at all.

PAT WEAVER: He didn't like programming. He didn't understand it. When we had a chance to buy into Disney, he said, "I'm not gonna go in with Disney on Disneyland. That will put me in show business."

I said, "General, what business are we in?"

He said, "Communications."

MIKE DANN: Pat used to lecture us about what he wanted out of television like a coach talking to his football players. He would bring in scientists like Brewster Gitlin and Norbert Weiner to talk to us. He was truly interested in the creative mind. But Pat was not an intellectual snob, he was interested in the science of the world.

PAT WEAVER: Broadcast managements have always underestimated the public. They always say give the public what it wants by which they deign the crumbs. We didn't play down. We said, "Experiment with whatever you do. Try to push toward innovation; at the very least add enrichment to whatever you are doing."

We had a policy called "enlightenment through exposure." It meant that on "Your Show of Shows" we got the stars of Broadway and of the music world to perform. We wanted the best of everything, so on the spectaculars, we had Margot Fonteyn dance in *Sleeping Beauty*—thirty million viewers no drop in the Nielsens against "Godfrey" and "Lucy."

Operation Frontal Lobes was an idea I took from a Canadian scientist who said, "The only reason that we are different from chimpanzees is our frontal lobes have greatly expanded." The idea was to go to a company like General Foods, which had "Roy Rogers" and say, "Look, once a year, Roy will greet the children and say, 'Today, the show's gonna be different. We're going to see this country.' We could take them to Washington, see the Constitution or the White House. Milton Berle could do the same thing." Well, the clients really hated it. [Laughs.]

ROD ERICKSON: With "Jack Carter" and "Your Show of Shows," Pat created the first example of block programming on prime time.

PAT WEAVER: The basic concept was, we can give the people at home a marvelous Saturday night. We take them first out to a club where they would have vaudeville, then a movie followed by a stage thing. We would bring all that to you for nothing.

DICK PINKHAM: There were all kinds of interesting things which really never came around, unfortunately. One of those was the TV center in Radio City designed by Norman Bel Geddes for live television. I worked on it for about a year. The main studio was bigger than Rockefeller Center. It was seven floors, with an unencumbered arch 440 feet high. It would have been one of the greatest tourist attractions in New York.

PAT WEAVER: It would have had this marvelous dome at the top for our news programming.

DICK PINKHAM: It had space for seven live programs. We took it up to General Sarnoff. Norman was a marvelous salesman, and the General's eyes were snapping away, but he said, "It's a wonderful idea, but we're not going to build it."

We said, "What?"

He said, "We're not going to have live television. This is going to be a medium for film." Saying no made a big difference in all of television. I think he realized that the only way he could make television pay off was with the reissues of film and later tape. Pat believed in live television, but it wasn't economical.

PAT WEAVER: I knew tape was coming. I went down to Ampex when they were working on it. They called the room where they were developing it "the run-for-your-life room," because the spools had to be so big and the speed so fast that if the tape would break, the stuff would roll out and fill the whole room, and the guy who was running it had to run for his life.

MIKE DANN: Between 1951 and 1956 came a mammoth change in television. It was like a switch from the horse to a combustible engine as far as who was responsible for programming. An hour of television had become so costly for the show and for the commercials. That's when the networks came in and began to own their own shows and sell spots on the minute plan, while the agencies concentrated on the commercials.

For years, the major advertisers controlled radio. A small manufacturer couldn't get on the major networks. Even Johnson's Wax had to wait three years to get on the NBC television network in the early fifties. Now, under the minute plan, advertisers could buy a minute instead of having to buy a whole show. Suddenly, all sorts of advertisers could come into television and did.

PAT WEAVER: People thought the changeover was just an automatic thing that would have happened anyway, but everybody was against this when we started. Then "Show of Shows" immediately showed the smart guys how many good things there were about this change. Before, selling shows was always nerve-racking for the agencies because if it flopped you lost the account.

TED ROGERS: Now, agencies could say, "It's not our fault."

MIKE DANN: Howard Morgens, the head of P & G, said, "Let them be in show business. We'll buy guaranteed circulation. We don't want ownership." That wasn't true of Mr. Hall [Hallmark Hall of Fame], but other than him and one or two others nobody wanted to own a show, and they all accepted it.

JOE CATES: I didn't like it. Yes, Pat Weaver's people were excellent, but I think the democratic process works better with a hundred buyers rather than with three. As a producer, you could always find one advertiser to buy your show, so you were never stopped dead. There's a big downside to agency control, when guys like Nick Keesely control the show, but would I rather have a hundred Nick Keeselys than three? You bet your life I would.

Also, Texaco did the Met opera for years. Now, the networks charged for shows based on the ratings they delivered, so suddenly ratings were important. Now Texaco had to get ratings.

PAT WEAVER: I came in with the idea for an eighteen-hour program service, run by us, with a beginning show and a comedy show at the end and "Home" in the middle. The day would start with a "Rise and Shine Show" that had been so successful in radio. Seventy-five percent of the country listened to morning shows in radio. We worked for a long time on "Today," much longer than I expected to get it started.

DICK PINKHAM: NBC thought it was a dumb idea typical of Pat, but to him, the basic idea was that the television should no longer be a toy. This is something that can tell all of America what is happening. A lot of people thought, Who's gonna watch television at seven o'clock in the morning? Not many people did until we were saved by that goddamned monkey.

PAT WEAVER: I also wanted to build a show around women, beauty, children, and cooking, the kinds of things you find in a service book [magazine]. The idea was to be sure that our spectrum of programming had a total reach, meaning everyone would be looking at something. "Home" is the best example. Most of our viewers were women who did not watch television. It took us two or three years to get that one organized, but "Home" was a big success.

JACK RAYEL: I used to hear this show out of Chicago in which an announcer and a piano player exchanged some of the warmest, funniest comments, so I made a mental note of the announcer, Hugh Downs. When I was putting "Home" together, I had everybody in from Mike Wallace to Gene Rayburn. I was in Chicago and I asked the program director if Hugh Downs was still working. He said, "Yeah, he's somewhere around here right now."

Hugh came down, and I talked to him about "Home" but he said he had no desire to leave Chicago. I talked hard, and he finally agreed to audition. When Weaver saw it, he said, "I see you found your guy." I was delighted, and Hugh, when he saw the setup and realized what it meant financially, decided to give up Chicago. Years later I told Charlie Andrews this story. He smiled and said, "I'm happy that you liked them." He wrote those exchanges that made me so delighted with Hugh Downs.

I hired Arlene Francis, despite objections from above. They wanted Betty Furness. I liked Betty, but it seemed to me for this show and the material she would be handling, Arlene had a warmth in addition to the intelligence and all the rest that Betty had, and Arlene did it splendidly.

TED ROGERS: When I took over the show, the big objective was to sell color TV. The only product that Weaver had that was on when the stores were open was "Home" and in those days ninety percent of your television receivers were sold in department stores. We did nearly half our shows from department stores around the country with Arlene wearing a colorful outfit.

PAT WEAVER: We also started "Matinee Theater," a live daily anthology, to try and get people away from soaps.

GIRAUD CHESTER: I was the principal involved in "Matinee Theater." I still have the memo I wrote to Pat suggesting we do a version of "The Robert Montgomery Show" five days a week. He sent it back to me and said, "We'll do it in color."

Nothing has ever been on television comparable to "Matinee Theater." It was a massive logistical challenge. You had a live hour drama going into the studio on Monday, another one rehearsing for Tuesday, one rehearsing someplace else for Wednesday, Thursday, and Friday.

When the show debuted, Jack Gould wrote, "Housewives couldn't believe their eyes," but "Matinee Theater" didn't make it. One of the concepts behind it was that it would bring additional viewers to daytime. It didn't.

PAT WEAVER: "Wide, World World" was another way to show people what was going on in the world. The fundamental idea there was, on any given Sunday if you had all the money in the world and you had immediate transport to any place in the world, where would you go and what would you do? It was a marvelous idea, but the best series was "Producers' Showcase," which was an attempt to rebroadcast the great theatrical shows, premiere new movies, and create new shows for ourselves.

GIRAUD CHESTER: Eventually, Pat was pushed out by the General because he had become too important.

PAT WEAVER: I knew he was a publicity maniac, and that it would be bad for me to get publicity, but I had to get it to help sell these shows. He got mad about the profile of me in *The New Yorker*. He had asked again and again, but he had never gotten one. Then he really blew his stack when *Life* did a big takeout on me. I said, "Look, General, I know you want publicity. I don't give a shit about publicity. I only care about operations, but if I can help them by getting publicity, I'll do it."

Ray Schuster, Max Schuster's wife of Simon & Schuster, told me that before she was married she was at a spa in Europe where she was introduced to then Colonel Sarnoff. He chased her around the room a little and asked her to go to dinner with him, but she said no and went to her room. Soon, there was a knock on the door. A man stepped in and said, "I'm representing Colonel Sarnoff." He had with him a great big book, and he told her, "Just so you understand who is inviting you to dinner, he thought you might like to look at these press clippings." She couldn't believe that he took this book of press clippings with him, but she still wouldn't have dinner with him.

For me, the end came when I returned from a fishing trip and found out that while I was to be made chairman, the chief executive, Bobby Sarnoff, would be the important position. I said, "I'm not going to stay." Bobby pleaded and pleaded. He said he would take advice and counsel from me and wouldn't do anything without me, particularly that he wouldn't fire my people without consultation. Then I came back from a week's vacation and I learned that Fred Wile, who had been head of programs through our great years, and George Fry, who had been with RCA and NBC for forty years and had been my chief of sales, had both been fired.

I said, "Well, that's the General. That means he's turning it up another notch. Who knows what will be the next one to make me mad, so to hell with him." I just called him up and said, "General, we have contracts that prevent me from leaving and you from firing me, and I want to leave, now what happens?"

"Will it be peaceful?"

"That depends on you."

He said, "Okay, I'll have my lawyer call your lawyer."

* * *

ROD ERICKSON: In the fifties, the agencies began to focus on making commercials. Before that, there was no commercial department in the agencies. All that evolved.

EDWARD BERNAYS: George Washington Hill's whole life was devoted to selling Lucky Strikes. He had no other interests. In the thirty years or so that I worked for him, I never heard of anything he did outside of Lucky Strikes.

EVERARD MEADE: Everybody at American had to smoke Lucky Strikes. When Pat Weaver hired me, he offered me a cigarette. I said I didn't smoke, and he said, "You better learn."

EDWARD BERNAYS: Regardless of whether he was talking to a man or a woman, he always kept his hat on in the office. From a psychological point of view, he was a king, and this was his crown, and the people who visited him were simply his subjects.

He began in radio in 1928. Hill's approach to advertising was simple: spend more money than anybody else. Hill didn't do any research before going into radio. He always relied on his hunches, and he was generally correct.

ROD ERICKSON: Research was more of a crutch than anything. Mostly, it was a comfort for a brand manager in case he was wrong. He would say, "I don't care if they're accurate or not. Just give me some figures to help me make a decision."

IRA SKUTCH: At Philco, in order to show that the "Playhouse" was valuable, the agency subscribed to the Nielsen ratings. There was so little acceptance for ratings then, that Nielsen had to go around and sell it. They said when the Department of Agriculture checks a farmer's wheat they check a pint out of a carload, which is a sample of 140,000 to one. "Our sample is 80,000 to one, so it is much more scientific." How anybody can compare human beings to a cup of wheat I don't know, but that's what they did.

Still, my boss subscribed, and they would supply him with these numbers which he used to show Philco what a tremendous bargain the "Playhouse" was. Then they would take the same numbers and juggle them around and call Fred Coe to say, "Look, you've got to do better." The same numbers.

ROD ERICKSON: When I was executive vice president of the American Research Bureau, we hired mathematicians from all over the world. One night I sat dumbfounded listening to them arguing about how in a major market they had one diary from a teenager, and they were gonna extrapolate a rating of teenagers from that. Now that's literally not possible, but they justified it. They kept saying some bullshit about the coefficient correlation.

EDWARD BERNAYS: In the late 1920s and early thirties, every large advertising agency employed a psychologist because when you deal with people you have to know about how and why they function. Freud was my uncle, and I was undoubtedly influenced by him. When psychologists became as important as the copywriter, I asked my uncle about it, and he said, *"Echt amerikanische,"* typically American, meaning relating these ideas to business, which was regarded as outside the pale of a psychologist.

ROD ERICKSON: Procter put a marketing man with a research man and a manufacturing man. That way you had all three working together. If you do just R & D, you may get a wonderful product that nobody wants. Most of these guys were Harvard Business School. They didn't understand what moved people. That was a dimension I gave them. They would come up with a new product and ask me what I thought of their name for it. Sometimes these names were spit out of a computer. Once, one of them came out with a shampoo they wanted to call "Drek." They actually put it out and test-marketed it until a couple of us set them straight.

PAT WEAVER: Mr. Hill in effect said, "Advertising is simply selling. If you think of selling to each person that you are talking to, even though you are reaching millions, you'll do a good job."

EVERARD MEADE: The radio campaign "Lucky Strike has gone to war" was on for only six weeks, and only on radio, not in newspapers or magazines, but it has been in the language ever since. That again was the power of radio and Mr. Hill's intuition paying off in a gigantic way. To sell his new white package, he got an announcer to come on and just say, "Lucky Strike has gone to war. Yes, Lucky Strike Green has gone to war. Lucky Strike has gone to war," and then the music picked up, and that was it.

He had it thirty-nine times on one show, deliberately creating a gigantic irritation. There was no explanation. The announcers just went on as if they were idiots, but people would hear it and say, "What the hell is that?" Then they went to the store and bought Lucky Strikes, and they got the white pack.

PAT WEAVER: And with the white pack, we went from third to first place.

EVERARD MEADE: He had no problem irritating people with his ads. During those six weeks those ads were on the air, I said, "We're getting five thousand letters a week of complaints." He slapped the desk and said, "Not enough."

ROD ERICKSON: I remember when I worked for Hill we had to say Lucky Strikes three times in the introduction of a show's theme song. He said, "When people get up in the morning, instead of saying the rosary, I want them to say Lucky Strikes."

EDWARD BERNAYS: Hill's legacy was really the corporations' spending a lot of money on radio. Without his being conscious of it he made radio a very lucrative industry for the people who invested in RCA or in radio stations throughout the country, and of course he set the stage for advertising on television.

EVERARD MEADE: It's too bad he died before he ever got a shot at television. Heaven knows what he would have done.

SAMM BAKER: I hated commercials, but I did a lot of the worst of them. After the war, we started feeding commercials to a shopping program that DuMont had. People in the business were laughing at the show, and we were surprised because we figured there was no audience. Still, it was like a miracle. The woman or man would hold up a product and say some stupid stuff about it, and you could immediately see the impact on sales.

TOM QUINLIN: There has never been an advertising medium like television. Nothing. It's phenomenal.

E. LAWRENCE DECKINGER: We used to say that you could just put a commercial on a test pattern and get a recall.

EVAN WILLIAM MANDEL: When my wife and I got married, our first piece of furniture was a seven-inch television set. I was unemployed, so I glued myself to that set, studying every aspect of it. Eventually, I got a job for Block Drugs. I was put in charge of Polident and Poligrip, which were small, sleepy products. We put Polident on late-night TV, three spots a week. We showed an animated set of false teeth with the effervescent liquid bubbling through, changing tobacco stains to almost white. You couldn't do something like that on radio. Within a week, the sales went right through the roof.

ROD ERICKSON: Not all advertisers were consumer product companies. Some companies will do institutional advertising because the stock needs a boost. Sometimes they put on specials because they have excess profits and they want to invest in something. Usually there was a vanity involved on the part of the guy running the company. His friends were telling him about what great shows they had, and he didn't have any.

There are other reasons to advertise. Everybody knew about Jell-O, so what we were selling was usage, to remind people if they like Jell-O, use it for salads in the summertime, Jell-O puddings for desserts tonight.

On the other hand, Kaiser said to me personally, "We're going into television even though the only product I sell directly to the consumer is aluminum wrap. The entire gross we get from the aluminum wrap will not pay for the television show, but I am known as the guy who made ships that broke in two during the war. I'm the guy who made a lousy car. People think I'm wacky, and investors are worrying about investing in my company. Television will change the image of my company."

SAMM BAKER: The commercials that worked best were the demonstrations. We had a client—Kalistron, which was a vinyl sheeting with a unique feature that protected the color from fading and scratching. We invited people to scratch the plastic, and you couldn't see any difference in the color. It worked because it was simple.

ROD ERICKSON: We studied people's habits of listening to commercials, and every year it came out the same. When the commercial came on, two-thirds of them were either distracted or they go to the john or get up for a sandwich or a drink. The one-third who said they were paying attention, really weren't. They were talking or reading, playing cards. That means you have to use an attention getter.

If two-thirds are out of the room, not all are out at one time, so you don't put everything into one show. Also, you avoid putting your commercial into a large pod. A large pod means you're cutting about half your audience.

To keep people in front of the set, we tried to do an intro for the show and then put the commercial behind that. People are less likely to leave the room, because they don't know when the show will really start. We also used a second ending for the show and then put a commercial before that. If you follow a high-rated show, put your best commercials forward. You have no risk then. You get flow that way.

NICK KEESELY: Sometimes the ratings would be high and the sales were down. Lucy never did much for Philip Morris.

E. LAWRENCE DECKINGER: Sales actually went down because there was a lot of competition, and filter cigarettes were coming in. Still, Milton Biow begged them not to give up the show. He said, "If sales are going off with all that audience, just think what will happen if you don't have that audience." They didn't listen and sales went down precipitously.

LARRY BRUFF: I wish I could say that we could measure the impact of any show on sales, but I've spent a life wishing I could and being unable to prove it. For example, "Gunsmoke" became the number-one show in the country, but our salesmen would complain that it wasn't really selling people. But Godfrey did seem to produce overnight results.

CHARLIE ANDREWS: At his peak, Arthur had several shows on a week, and his ratings were incredible. He was the most powerful man in the industry, and he could take a sponsor to the top. It didn't always happen, but it did with Lipton and Chesterfield.

I was his producer for five years. I remember one day when these Madison Avenue types came in and tried to bribe him. They said, "Arthur, we have this spot, and we really want you to do a job with it. Give it a couple of minutes on the air.

"And by the way, isn't it your wife's birthday? We thought she might appreciate this." One of them brought out a little Tiffany box and gave it to Arthur. He opened it, and inside was a diamond ring—and not a little diamond.

Arthur didn't say anything. He just took it out and examined it, nodded his head, then opened up his desk drawer and just tossed it in.

BETTY FURNESS: I was successful at commercials because people believed me, but did I know that Westinghouse was a better refrigerator than any other? Hell, no—or cared. I was paid to sell a product, and it was a good product. I don't know how I would have reacted if I were asked to sell a bad product. I might not have done it—unless I needed the money.

HERB HORTON: Some of the stuff I did was awful. We said things you knew darned well weren't true. For forty-nine dollars you could get a suit and two pair of pants, and we were trying to get them to believe that bank presidents wore those things.

SAMM BAKER: Mennen's ads had a lot of atmosphere, of a mother holding a baby or cuddling a baby instead of showing the baby powder or the baby oil in use. The inference was that mothers who truly loved their babies used Mennen products, and the copy carried through with that too. I received a red-hot letter from a woman I respected highly. She had left the agency because she couldn't stand it. She said, "You didn't write that commercial. You have too much sensitivity." But I did. I felt queasy about it, but I said to her, "It's my job and it worked."

Hell, I wrote so many commercials that were nonsense, but they worked. Mennen's Baby Powder wasn't really better than anyone else's, but we wrote that it was. I even devised tests to show that it was better. They were accurate, but they were faked. If you got a fresh can of baby powder off the line, it's smoother than another brand that has sat around for a while. I wasn't proud of it, but I felt good when my commercials sold stuff.

JACK SIEGRIST: There is a kind of promise in the advertising business that you make. We will tell you about a new product that might help you, and while we might not tell you the whole truth, we will not lie to you. That is generally the way you *try* to work it, but lies and misdirection occur almost cyclically.

One time at Philco, I heard the engineers talking about a golden grid tuner. "What's a golden grid tuner?"

"Shit, everybody has it. It's to keep the contact points there from corrosion, so there's a little gold on it."

We were so poor for things to advertise that we jumped on that, "Philco, with the golden grid tuner." We didn't say that everybody else had it too. Where's the harm? I'm giving you a good set with a good tuner at a fair price.

HUGH DOWNS: My loyalty was with the person tuning in. It was expedient. If I lost my credibility, what use would I be to a client? I did commercials for a floor covering that was supposedly a high density vinyl, but people wrote to say they put it in their kitchens and the nailheads came through it. I distanced myself from the copy by saying, "The company assures me that they have made proper tests for this."

They said I couldn't do that, so I told them to get somebody else. They sued me, and I thought that was the end of my commercial career, but it had the opposite effect. On the Paar show, other people might do five of the six commercials. I asked the guy from the agency, "Why don't they do all of these?"

"Because if you don't do any of them the public will think you don't approve of the product."

JACK RAYEL: I did "The Hunting and Fishing Club," which was sponsored by Melocremo Cigars. Bud Collyer did the commercials wonderfully. He would take a cigar, puff on it, and say that this is one of the joys of the world. One night the agency guy said to him before the show, "Bud, I hope you'll have a little time after the show tonight. My friend and I would like to take you out to dinner. What do you usually do after the show?"

Collyer looked him right in the eye and said, "I throw up and go home," which was the way he felt about those goddamn cigars, but he looked as though he loved them.

DENNIS JAMES: In my case, everything was sincerity. I only had one thing to sell, and that was Dennis James. I did Old Gold commercials. I smoked, and I smoked Old Golds.

IRA SKUTCH: I did Old Gold commercials. Smoking Old Gold supposedly made you more glamorous, so the actor had to take a long puff and get the smoke out properly. They also wanted us to keep using younger people in the ads to get younger people to smoke. I objected to it, but there was nothing I could do.

NICK KEESELY: Dick Clark sold a lot of cigarettes for us on "Bandstand." I never smoked. That's why I'm healthy. I know I helped sell cigarettes, but I didn't know they were bad until Sloan Kettering began reporting on the dangers of cigarettes. As a result of the report, we launched filter cigarettes. We showed how the filters took out the gook. Yeah, they said some stuff still goes through, but they didn't prove that until the sixties and the seventies. By that time I was retired.

ROD ERICKSON: Everybody knew cigarettes were bad. That's why we called them "coffin nails."

LEE COOLEY: Of course. From my present perspective, yes, it was morally wrong to advertise them. Here was Arthur Godfrey for God's sake with lung cancer, and he was a Chesterfield guy.

LARRY BRUFF: I fired Godfrey on the air. He had lung cancer and started to publicly smoke a cigar. Now, we couldn't have him smoke another tobacco product when he was selling Chesterfield cigarettes. I walked into Stanton's office and said, "Look, he is violating his contract."

Frank said, "I'll call him as soon as he gets off the air."

"No, you won't. I'll call him right now in the studio. He has a line. That's it. No more Chesterfield commercials."

Before he worked for us, he smoked Camels, so who knows if it was the cigarette he was smoking now or the one he was smoking twenty years before. We never discussed his going public about lung cancer, but we didn't want him to smoke a goddamned cigar.

CHARLIE ANDREWS: That's not true. Arthur dropped Chesterfield before he got sick. He had read that cigarette smoking was harmful to your health, and he didn't want to do the commercials anymore, and he didn't.

E. LAWRENCE DECKINGER: Biow's ads used to say, "Philip Morris's superiority is recognized by eminent medical authorities. No other cigarette can make that statement!" They were able to prove that you would be less dead when you smoke Philip Morris. In any case, it was a medical story, and it propelled Philip Morris to a ten percent share.

Advertisers are like sheep. Camel surveyed doctors who supposedly said, the "T-Zone" is easier on your throat. They sent a carton of cigarettes a week to every doctor in America. Then they made a survey of what brand they smoked. What brand do you think they smoked? Camel came out ahead and they said so.

LARRY BRUFF: My boss believed that health claims sold cigarettes, so we came up with "no adverse affects to noses, throats, and sinuses from smoking Chesterfields." I thought it was negative advertising and unsubstantiated, but I don't believe cigarettes have an adverse effect on health.

EVERARD MEADE: It was embarrassing because Hill had emphysema. He would have these paroxysms of coughing, and then clear his throat and then light up a fresh cigarette. It was painful to watch. His eyes would water. He would take a handkerchief out, flick anything that had fallen on the desk, straighten himself out, pull out a cigarette, and start all over. He died of emphysema in 1947.

ROD ERICKSON: He was an ad for his own product.

EVERARD MEADE: The next two heads of American Tobacco also died of emphysema. When Hill died, I stopped smoking.

BETTY FURNESS: After the war, I needed to work. I took any job I could get, and the easiest things to get were commercials. "Studio One" was sponsored by Westinghouse, and I got the job of doing their commercials.

JUNE GRAHAM: Having done commercials for Westinghouse in St. Louis, Betty said to me, "Listen, they don't have a standby for me. If I got sick, they'd be up the creek. Check with them to see if they'll give you a contract." I did, and they did.

BETTY FURNESS: The poor woman stood by all those years. I never got sick. The only time she was on was if I was working for Westinghouse out of town. That was the famous commercial when the damn door wouldn't open. People think it happened to me, but that was June.

JUNE GRAHAM: That was February 14, 1954. The interesting thing was, the sound man, Artie Strand, used to play tricks during dress to see if I could cover up without dropping a line. I'd point to the egg keeper, and he'd put on chicken noises, or he would put on a sound of a woman screaming. That night we didn't have a dress rehearsal, so when the door didn't open, I just thought, "Okay, Artie, you're not gonna get away with this."

The problem was the refrigerator opened electronically, but just before the commercial, Geraldine Fitzgerald had accidentally kicked the plug out, so when I pressed the button, it didn't work. I said, "This is not April Fool's Day, somebody has kicked out the plug, but if the plug had been in . . ." and then I did the rest of the commercial.

Betty, with her usual sense of humor, called me and said, "Well, you've made your career," which I did. They sold seventeen percent more refrigerators the next day from everybody coming in and saying, "I want to see the refrigerator that doesn't work."

HERB HORTON: Some not-so-good things happened on live commercials. We did a thing with a swan for a cake mix. The swan was in a tank in a set that looked like a backyard. At rehearsal, the account executive decided that we should attract attention. He said, "Have the swan do something. He's a trained swan."

The trainer says, "Maybe I can get him to wiggle his wings." The swan did nothing, so the account executive says, "Christ, Horton, I thought you said you got yourself a trained swan. Make him do something."

He didn't know what he wanted him to do, just something, so I got hold of the head electrician. I said, "Hook up a wire to the tank, and give him a little smidge just to wake him up."

In rehearsal the swan goes "quaaack," and there is glee in the control room. Now, we wait for our cue to go live. The account exec goes, "Gee, that was great. Get him to do a little more."

I tell the electrician, "Give him a smidge more." I give him the cue. The electrician gives him a shot. The swan goes "quaaack" and drops dead as a doornail.

The account executive is dying. Nobody knew who executed the swan except the electrician and me. The trainer walks into the pool and picks him up, "Oscar, Oscar, please, wake up."

I just went to the product shot as soon as I could.

IRA SKUTCH: In an Admiral commercial with Henry Morgan, a girl opened the refrigerator door and something fell off. Henry picked it up and screamed, "Hey Admiral, come up here and tell me how to put this thing back on." They cancelled the show on him.

ROD ERICKSON: In part because of the accidents, commercials went to film as soon as it was technically feasible.

PERRY LAFFERTY: In 1952, a friend of mine, who was the agency man from Westinghouse, asked me if I wanted to do the commercials at the national political conventions. I said commercials were below my dignity. Then, like the Godfather, he made me an offer I couldn't refuse.

He wanted me because I had done shows in the Air Corps that required huge logistical planning, and the conventions were a logistical nightmare. They were done in the stockyards, which were just a big building. They built one control room for both the news anchor set and the commercial set. Flip cards with prices had to be supered over the picture. There were something like four hundred cue cards of prices. I really earned my money. You never knew when a commercial break was coming, so you were constantly on the alert like the fire department. You can't believe the problems in going to the bathroom, which was in the hall and always packed. If you went and got back in time, it was a real triumph.

Despite those fourteen-hour days, Betty had to look wonderful, so she kept changing her dresses. She became a huge icon partly because her clothes were always different.

BETTY FURNESS: Nobody remembers that Ronald Reagan did the commercials on NBC while I was on CBS. I looked better!

My primary function was to keep people from going to the bathroom so I could sell them a product.

I did ninety-six commercials during the convention. I was on the air more than anyone from either party. I became famous overnight. There was a cartoon on the front page of the *Indianapolis News.* A little boy and his father are watching the Republican convention, and the little boy says, "Who's ahead, Pop? Ike, Taft, or Betty Furness?" After twenty years I thought, "My God, they know me!" Telegrams came in suggesting me for vice president.

JUNE GRAHAM: Betty Furness did more for women in television than anybody else, by just being Betty Furness, by not giving anybody a chance to say, "Oh, you can't trust women." Betty was a consummate professional, the most consummate professional I have ever known, male or female, without a bone in her body that is interested in anything but getting the job done.

BETTY FURNESS: The reason that I have been a pro, and the reason I started out being a pro, was that I thought I might get fired. You don't act up, you don't misbehave, you don't complain because they can always get somebody else. Some people don't do their best or look their best, and I have never understood it because I always thought my best was barely good enough, so I better put it forward.

JUNE GRAHAM: A day in the life of the commercial spokeswoman in the Golden Era. Sundays, I got up at five to do the Hoffman Beverage com mercials on "The Children's Hour." Then I would go rehearse for the "Good-year Playhouse," leave "Goodyear" and run up at six P.M. to do Buitoni on "The Igor Cassini Show," changing my clothes in the back of a cab. Then I returned to do "Goodyear" at nine, then back in the cab to do the "Cassini" show at eleven. Afterwards, Giovanni Buitoni would take us out for a drink at the Stork Club. I was constantly moving. I once had to hire an ambulance to get from CBS to NBC.

Seven of us, Joyce Gordon, Vivian Ferrar, Betsy Palmer, Julia Meade, Kathi Norris, and myself, did ninety percent of all of the commercials. Betty, too, but she never did anything else but Westinghouse. We all helped each other because there was enough to go around. "Hello, Vivian, I went up for something. I don't think it's right for me. Why don't you call so-and-so?"

Our male counterparts always made more than we did because someone would say, "This is a man's commercial."

Why are cigarettes more for men than women? They always were. They had as many men doing cosmetics as they had women. Revlon was one of the few that allowed women to do commercials. How many female announcers did you have on soaps, shows aimed mostly at women? Not one. Why? Most people say that men are more authoritative.

I didn't think about it then. Only now that I'm a Monday-morning quarter-back can I say that the commercials stereotyped women as barefoot, pregnant, and in the kitchen.

BETTY FURNESS: I didn't define it. That's who they were. Women were homemakers. Very few of us saw a woman's role in another way. It was re-inforced in the dramas much more so than in my kitchen. The dramas didn't in-clude women who were unhappy. Neither did the sitcoms or the soap operas. It wasn't until Betty Friedan said, "We are not John's wife, we are who we are—women," that the light was turned on for me and other women. Until then, most women were scared to be different.

The commercials did perpetuate the stereotype, and sometimes I objected. They wanted me to wear an apron and I refused. I wasn't cooking, why the hell would I have an apron on? I said, "That's not who I am. I am the salesperson on these commercials."

By 1960 I was bored to death, so I quit. I had never paid any attention to the outside world until '52 when I saw the world of government. I became very excited by that world. It was real, unlike show business, so when I quit I decided I wanted to be a convention delegate, and I swore I would never do another commercial and I wouldn't act.

I tried to get a reporting job, but nobody would hire me. I did get an offer from CBS radio to do a show called "Dimensions of a Woman's World," a five-minute show three times a day that was really about a woman's world, not about recipes and diapers.

I never got to be a delegate at the convention, but I got to address the political convention in '68. That for me was the whole circle. I won, and goddamnit, I was thrilled.

✳   ✳   ✳

GERALDINE ZORBAUGH: In 1943, I was working for NBC when the government told RCA they could not own two networks, and the Blue network was sold to Edward Noble. I went to work for them. One day I said to my boss, "The Blue Network isn't a good name for the company. We should change it." I suggested we get a name that begins with A so we would be first alphabetically and then get CBS's call letters, which were WABC. He suggested to Noble that we change the name to the American Broadcasting Company.

Our offices were on the third floor of the RCA Building. Noble was content to stay, but Mr. Sarnoff wanted us out. I was listening in when Mr. Noble was talking to Mr. Sarnoff on the telephone about our not moving. They didn't need a phone. They could be heard screaming at each other across Manhattan. Finally, Mr. Sarnoff said, "That's it, out you go!"

DONALD LAUNER: They bought a riding academy on Sixty-sixth Street because it was very cheap, and also because the old riding ring inside was large enough to convert to a studio. When it opened, they were still cleaning out the horse stalls. We had problems with pigeons in the studio for quite a while. We did everything out of that one studio. We also had one control room and one film department. That was it.

BOB DOYLE: ABC was really a poor third cousin. Edward Noble was cheap. He lived in the Waldorf Towers. To make a call from his suite cost fifteen cents. He would go downstairs and put a nickel in the pay phone. He almost fired a girl for putting a special delivery stamp on a piece of airmail that he knew wouldn't be delivered until Monday anyway.

When ABC moved from Radio City to West Sixty-sixth, he made his executives take the subway. All of these guys in blue suits going down into the subway was one of the funniest sights I ever saw.

GERALDINE ZORBAUGH: Noble was not a broadcaster. He owned the Rexall Drug Chain, but he made most of his money with Life Savers. When he bought the network, the next day on everybody's desk was a carton of Life Savers.

ROBERT SAUDEK: This fellow I knew expected a bonus at Christmastime, but instead, Noble sent all the executives a book. You opened it up, and inside were ten rolls of Life Savers. That was the bonus. This guy got so mad when he opened it, he threw it through the picture window of his house, and he had to spend two hundred dollars to replace the window.

Noble was cheap, darn, yes. Joe McDonald, the general counsel of ABC, told him in 1946, "Mr. Noble, there are five licenses available, all Channel Seven in five of the six top markets. You can apply for them now and own them." Noble didn't want to do it because it would cost him twenty-five thousand dollars, but he finally relented just to get Joe off his back. A few years ago, the network was sold for four billion dollars.

DONALD LAUNER: We had to construct a huge amount of equipment on our own because we couldn't buy it. The men's room became our echo chamber. Our remote truck was an old wagon people used in the 1930s to deliver pies.

BOB DOYLE: After a while, things got even worse financially. They told us, "Nobody is going to get fired," and the next week they fired four hundred people. There was just no money, no nothing.

DONALD LAUNER: I'd get a paycheck on Friday but we couldn't cash it until Wednesday because there was no money in the bank.

BOB DOYLE: Our so-called big stuff, like "Paul Whiteman's Teen Club," came out of Philadelphia. I ran the auditions for his talent show. I remember thinking if I ever hear "Lady of Spain" on the accordion one more time, I'm gonna kill somebody.

DONALD LAUNER: At first, I was thrilled to be working with Whiteman. Then I was devastated when I saw that down behind the podium, where the camera couldn't see, was actually the director of the orchestra. Whiteman was just following him.

BOB DOYLE: He was an irascible son of a bitch. He fired me over something dumb. I told Kintner, "My God, Pops fired me."

He said, "Great, now he'll call you in a week and ask you to come back at double your money." He did. He fired me about four more times. He fired everybody.

He used to buy a case of Scotch and two cartons of milk, get drunk, and hole up in a hotel, and the only one who could get him out was his wife. She would bang on the door and make him open it. Then she would clean him up and get him on the air. The booze really got to him.

That was a great thing when a new station would open on the network, and ABC would send all its stars out there. We opened a station in Milwaukee. Pops was leading the orchestra, and he fell off the stage into the pit.

DONALD LAUNER: We had the station in New York. We also owned stations in Philadelphia, Chicago, Detroit, and San Francisco. Then we had affiliates wherever we could pick them up.

MALCOLM "BUD" LAING: I took over station clearance in 1951. Then I moved to affiliate relations. That was a challenge. Nobody would affiliate with us. I had to wheel and deal. In Pittsburgh, for instance, there was just one station. It was owned by DuMont. We owned WWJ in Detroit, so we made a deal with DuMont, you clear for me in Pittsburgh, I'll clear for you in Detroit.

BOB LEWINE: I got to ABC in 1953. It was tough on the station-relations people because we had so few shows to sell. We had the MCA murder series, which we bought to fill empty time. At the end of thirteen weeks, we took the same series, moved the shows around, gave them new titles, and put them on again.

We took anything. We had a show called "Take a Chance." A couple of brothers in Baltimore had a product called Lanolin, and on this show they gave away prizes, usually Lanolin. The show was really a half-hour commercial.

The owner of the Cleveland Browns, Art Modell, was on local ABC, selling pots and pans and cookie cutters. He would come on at midnight and do it himself. It was just a commercial for his stores. We did "You Asked for It." They'd manufacture stunts and claim that people wanted to see them. We knew it was fake, but we were happy to have the show. Most of our shows were so bad we used any persuasion at all to clear the shows.

BUD LAING: I did it by conning 'em. I would get friendly with 'em, intentionally lose at golf, drink with 'em. Some of those guys got bagged all the time, so before meeting them I would drink a lot of heavy cream to line my stomach.

BOB LEWINE: The guy who ran the Cincinnati station was a bastard. He would always try to make a deal. "I'll take it if you take one of my shows." He was apparently having an affair with a young lady named Dotty Mack, who would lip-sync to records. He said, "If you gave her a time period in the summer, I'll take Disney." That's how we got Disney on in Cincinnati.

BUD LAING: Station managers and owners in those days were decent guys. The guy in Cincinnati was generally the exception, although there were others. Some would ask for women when they came to New York. ABC would not provide them with women intentionally. I never did. I knew a guy at NBC who would supply 'em like no one's business.

Sometimes a client himself would try to clear a station by putting pressure on a station manager. Pabst Beer had the Wednesday-night fights. Binghamton was a one-station market, so we really needed that station for the fights. The local Pabst distributor said to me, "Whattya want me to do with this guy?"

I said, "Christ, don't go out and shoot him."

We got on there. [Laughs.] I think he might have said, "If you want to see your family you should pick up our fights."

BOB LEWINE: There were little triumphs. ABC did the first Miss America show with John Daly and Arlene Francis. We did the first muscular dystrophy telethon. I met Dean and Jerry in New York. NBC said, "You can't use them. They're exclusive to us," and Dean said, "Fuck you," and they did it.

One of my favorite stories is about the coronation of the queen of England. CBS and NBC allegedly spent a million dollars each to be the first to get it on the air. They had both arranged for these pilots to fly speed planes with the film back to the states. ABC paid ten thousand dollars for a feed from Ottawa which was going to get it from the RAF. Both of the planes had trouble. I got a call from Bud Barrie, who was head of programming for NBC. He said, "Our plane turned back. Can we take your feed?"

Kintner said it was okay, so I told Bud it would cost ten thousand dollars. He said fine. Then I said, "Bud, monitor your screen, because I have no idea when it is going to start. It could be in five minutes or five hours." They didn't watch, and we scooped them by six minutes.

Kintner was the one who kept the ship afloat at ABC. We had to use every resource we had. I never got home until eight at night. Kintner hated his entire family. He would drink and drink and drink, and finally he would say, "You want to have dinner with me?" It was not a happy time.

BUD LAING: He used to pee in his flower plants, even at NBC, but he was a brilliant guy. You would go to his office for a meeting of department heads. Kintner would ask everybody's opinion on a show. If everybody thought it was bad, and he thought it was good, it was carried by a vote of one.

GERALDINE ZORBAUGH: Something fell through for Saturday night, and at a meeting Bob Lewine said, "There's a bandleader on the coast named Lawrence Welk. I think I can get him."

Kintner said, "Get him," or else. He did, and it turned out to be one of the big winners.

BUD LAING: We cleared fifteen, twenty stations as a summer replacement for Dodge. That show took off. By September, we had over 120 stations.

BOB DOYLE: Kintner was as bright as they come, but he was also mean and a drunk. Still, I liked him. He'd send for you at one A.M.: "Come to '21,' " then hang up. He'd be on his eightieth drink of the day, but he'd remember everything that he told you.

It was Kintner with that great brain of his, drunk or sober, who made the two great deals that saved ABC television. One was the Mouseketeers, and two was the National Football League, which I directed for almost three years.

BOB LEWINE: I came out with Kintner and our attorney to make the deal. Walt Disney was shrewd enough to realize that ABC would give him money, which he needed desperately, to build Disneyland. In return he agreed to produce twenty hours of film for us. Out of that came "Davy Crockett," "Zorro," and "The Mickey Mouse Club." Those shows and the deal with Warner Brothers got us to crack the top ten.

BUD LAING: We were clearing Disney on CBS and NBC stations. Also, with new stations starting up we had more affiliates. The Warner Brothers shows were particularly good for us, so was "The Untouchables."

GERALDINE ZORBAUGH: After a few years, I started hearing that Mr. Noble was going to sell. Then his daughter died and he got very depressed. The business just didn't interest him anymore. One time when just the two of us were working together, he said, "Oh, I'm gonna be glad to get out of this."

Not long afterward, he sold it. He bought it for ten million dollars and sold it to Leonard Goldenson for thirty million dollars, so I guess he did all right. Three years later, Goldenson fired eight vice presidents in one day. When he fired me, he didn't even have the guts to tell me himself. Somebody else told me.

BOB LEWINE: Kintner was a heavy drinker, and Leonard Goldenson was a teetotaler. In October '56, Leonard got the votes he needed from his board, and then he said to Kintner, "You're through."

He brought in Oliver Treyz. I knew I couldn't work with him. Ollie was a slick salesman. He could sell you your own toothbrush. He'd promise a time period to some guy and then keep trying to sell it to someone else. If he made that sale, he would tell the first guy, "I never said that." "But, Ollie, you said" became a cliché in the business. It happened too often, so I left.

ROD ERICKSON: Ollie was crazy, but he was great for ABC. He really put them on the map. Ollie was probably closer than anyone to the real common denominator, the very common denominator.

*   *   *

MIKE DANN: Network ownership of the shows gave us the ability to control our schedules. For the first time we could have block programming and control audience flow. I became terribly interested in the techniques for scheduling. For example, I learned quickly that where a program was put was far more important than the program itself. "December Bride" was a terrible show, but it was a big hit because it followed "Lucy." An audience had to be developed for a program. The best way to introduce a show was to put it in a "hammock"—between two hits.

ROD ERICKSON: If you really are going to program scientifically, you really have to know people's living habits.

MIKE DANN: Generally, the audience in terms of numbers is constant in any given time period, except if man lands on the moon at three A.M., then the sets-in-use is higher. The only difference might be when it's daylight savings time in the East when nine to ten becomes the peak time period instead of eight P.M. Even with the remote control, there are no massive changes to other stations.

ROD ERICKSON: People are lazy. They would rather not get up and move.

MIKE DANN: Therefore, nothing is more valuable than to win at eight o'clock because eight-thirty will follow and nine o'clock is even better. Sometimes at ten o'clock at night, major audiences move from comedy to drama, but if you're successful at eight, the worst you do at ten is you're just as good as anybody else.

ROD ERICKSON: Every night's a good night, but there are differences of two or three points, which represent a lot of people. Friday, the man cashed his check and went out with the boys. That meant there were less males home watching TV Friday night, so you wouldn't waste a good show on Friday.

The men went to work Monday morning so they weren't catting around Sunday night. The family was home together, so Sunday night had the largest audience. That's where you put a good show.

MIKE DANN: Sunday night is two nights of the week because prime time is four hours, and it's peak viewing. Sunday night you fight like hell. He who wins Sunday night is king.

ROD ERICKSON: Saturday night the family went out. You could put a good show on, but you wouldn't want it there badly because people may be diverted. Monday, they're home. Nine o'clock Monday was probably the best chance to get the most people in all the time zones. Nothing was left to chance with "Lucy" being on Monday night.

MIKE DANN: We made mistakes in the beginning, when we had dramas and specials on too early in the evening, believing that we could control the audiences. We put "Producer's Showcase" on at eight, wonderful dramas like "Petrified Forest" with Bogart and Bacall and Fonda, but nobody gave a damn about it. You have to be a moron to put it on at that time. Sid Caesar at eight o'clock was terrible. You needed visual comedy for kids.

OSCAR KATZ: At CBS, my philosophy was if you spread the schedule out in a straight line Monday through Sunday and put the NBC schedule opposite ours, it's like two armies lined up opposite each other. You don't fight the strong salients. You look for the weak spots. I told CBS, "Don't compete against Berle. You're wasting your money. All shows have life spans. Wait for it to peak. Then go in."

MIKE DANN: The most formidable problem is programming against a hit. My worst record at CBS was the ten years of programming against "Bonanza." That was a disaster. I put everyone on from Garry Moore to Leslie Uggams. Nothing worked.

When the other network has a runaway hit, like "$64,000 Question," you don't know where to hide. You try to fix up your show, but it never works. No producer worth his salt will let his show go against it. That network's shows end up dominating the whole evening. You can't do anything until it starts to burn itself out. Until then, you just hope for enough of an audience to break even.

OSCAR KATZ: We had a show that was very serviceable for six years, but it was getting soft. Intuitively, we felt that the next season may be its last. So we thought, let's cancel it now because if it becomes a weak spot the other network can hop in with a big hit, and we can lose that time period for five years.

But you have opposition within the company. Sales says it's still saleable. Research says its studies indicate that the new show wouldn't get as high a rating as this show is getting. Sometimes you can get it out, and sometimes you can't.

MIKE DANN: Filling fifty-two half hours in prime time every week is a horrible responsibility. You can't go dark like a theater, so you say, "Wednesday night and Saturday night we'll throw away." You try to throw away the end of the week rather than the beginning. You never throw away Sunday night. We played percentages constantly. You wouldn't gamble unless you had to. Then you'd say, "Let's throw that in. It just might work."

BOB LEWINE: You never know till you put the show on whether it will make it. It's all instinct. As a network executive, if a third of your shows last two or three years, you're doing well.

MIKE DANN: I had two shows for seven o'clock Sunday, "Lassie," and a variety show with George Abbott. I saw the "Lassie" pilot, and I said, "What can the goddamned dog do the second night?" So I turned it down. "Lassie" ran for fifteen years. I must have programmed fifty shows against it. George Abbott went off after a few weeks.

BOB LEWINE: The first thing you must do is forget New York and L.A. and put on your hayseed glasses and program for Middle America. That's where your strength comes from. I was embarrassed by "Gilligan," but people in Jockstrap, Missouri, love those things. We forget that people eat dinner, sit down in a T-shirt with a glass of beer, take their shoes off, and watch wrestling. The minute you got fancy with the shows that didn't depict their lives in those small towns and cities you lost your audience.

MIKE DANN: If a theater doesn't have a good play, the house is dark. In television, you can't go dark, so most programming is mediocrity. Most programming I wouldn't look at, but I'm in the business of keeping commercial television popular and active. You don't willingly put trash on the air. You put on the best show you can that will appeal to the widest audience.

REGINALD ROSE: "The Defenders" was a quality show that dealt with serious issues. It made them nervous as hell, but whenever they were criticized for doing terrible shows they would say, "Yeah, but we do 'The Defenders.' We don't always do crap," and that was the only real reason they kept it on.

MIKE DANN: "The Defenders" was put in the schedule because we had a failing show. Mr. Paley turned to me in front of the existing management that was fighting it and said, "What have you got available?"

I said, " 'The Defenders,' Mr. Paley."

He said, "That seemed like a nice show."

"I thought so," and we scheduled it. It had been kept off the air because Jim Aubrey said, "We don't want that junk on the air. It's just pleading causes." He wanted trash. Every episode of "The Defenders" dealt with a social issue, abortion, picketing, racketeering, homosexual problems. It became a hallmark around the world. It was the most important show I ever put on the air.

"The Defenders" proved that you should never rule against the producer. Pat once said to me, "The function of bureaucrats is to pick the producer, then support the producer. Once in a while he'll be wrong and you will be right, but about ninety-nine times in a hundred he'll be right, because his life is on the line with it."

We are not there to lead, but things change. Television finally grew up because it consumed so much material, that you eventually put on things that were atypical. "The Smothers Brothers" took the first step. They gave me a lot of problems. I got calls from the White House, but they were our biggest hit. If they were weaker we would have canceled them.

ROD ERICKSON: When my wife and I first went around the world in 1960, that's when I realized the power of this medium to change the world. In the Philippines, there were houses on stilts to keep the rats out, and every one of them had an antenna. Karachi, the asshole of the world, they all have TV.

What do you think they're watching? American television. Even the Russians had it. You know what caused the Russian government to collapse? It was "Dallas." People are people. When they see guys bangin' beautiful broads, and snappy cars and money, and everybody's bowing at him, that's what changes people.

Everybody would have liked to elevate the audience, but it wasn't our job. Our job is to tell our clients how to move merchandise. It's not to educate the people. You can't force a lowest-common-denominator audience to listen to things that are not entertainment.

I saw the interviews with Frank Lloyd Wright and Sandburg that NBC did. Those were fine, but he was not gonna put those at Monday night at nine o'clock. He put them at Sunday in the afternoon, and that's where they belonged. Those kinds of shows will find their own audience. You can't force them on people. Of course, football came along and finished off much of the Sunday cultural ghetto. They couldn't compete with that.

DAVID LEVY: There was always lip service paid to elevating the audience. We did put on decent programs. We looked for what we called a "balanced schedule," to have shows that appealed to younger audiences and older audiences. Eventually, that gave way to the necessity of winning every time period. This was beginning in my time in the early sixties. Documentaries and special unsponsored reports began to disappear from network TV. The anthologies disappeared.

JOE CATES: In this country, you get the government you vote for. They chose to abdicate a meaningful supervision of the public air. It was once a presumption that the network that got this public air had an obligation to operate in the public interest, convenience, and necessity. That included an independent news department, special programming, a certain amount of children's programming. That's all gone because the business of America is business. The television business is a reflection of our society. It doesn't lead. It reflects.

MIKE DANN: The number of people who have contributed to the mediocrity of television is legion. Ollie Treyz helped build ABC by reaching down. It worked and it had a huge influence on television because it helped television grow.

DAVID LEVY: It was Kintner at ABC who invented sex and violence on TV. He needed a way to get visibility for ABC programs. Sex and violence was a way of attracting younger people, so there was a practical reason for it.

Kintner liked the idea that Clint Walker had his shirt off a lot. That equated sex to him. Before then, you didn't see male bodies on network TV.

CARL PERIAN: In the 1950s, I was a graduate student at the University of Maryland. I majored in criminal psychology. At that time, the so-called wartime babies were coming into their teens and raising hell all across America. Congress set up a committee to investigate. They called my professor and said, "Do you have a brilliant graduate student who can write, et cetera, et cetera?" and my professor said, "No, but I have Carl."

They were concerned about the mass media—particularly television—and its influence on children. In 1957, I set up hearings under Estes Kefauver. I had psychologists come down from Harvard and the usual flacks from the networks, who gave us the usual crap, "We're only reflecting society, we don't cause it."

They laughed and said they can show Elvis Presley dressed a certain way, and half the juvenile population of America would want to buy the stuff, but they wouldn't take any blame for the negative effects of television, namely crime and violence. One of my strongest supporters was the head of the Federal Bureau of Prisons, James Bennett. He said, "I can list a hundred inmates who directly learned the acts of crime off of television."

PAUL LASKIN: Carl organized another series of hearings as the chief investigator for the Senate Juvenile Delinquency Subcommittee. The chairman was Senator Thomas Dodd. These hearings were the most extensive investigation ever done into the relationship between juvenile delinquency and television.

DAVID LEVY: The networks were frightened to death of those hearings. Nobody knew what would come out of them.

PAUL LASKIN: Very little was known about the effects of televised violence, so there was a research component to the hearings, to see what had been done, what needed to be done. We also wanted to see what was actually on the air.

CARL PERIAN: Over eight weeks, our staff watched every prime-time show on the three networks and Metromedia.

PAUL LASKIN: We were surprised to find that the percentage of violent programming was quite high. We found also the number of children watching the violent shows, even at nine or ten at night, to be quite high.

CARL PERIAN: We were also concerned with how these shows got on. Clearly the networks bore the ultimate responsibility even though they were trying to pin the blame on the writers and the producers, but the producers and writers told us, "Hey, if we don't produce this crap we don't get on television."

We went out to California with subpoenas and came back with cases of files. That's when the famous memo came out about Jim Aubrey, the head of CBS, saying he wanted more "broads, bosoms, and fun" in "Route 66." The writer

Christopher Knopf said to me, "They told me, 'We don't care what you write about, but you have to have at least three fights,' " et cetera et cetera. They especially wanted the violence just before the commercial break, so people will continue to watch.

The Hollywood people didn't want to testify. They were threatened. A friend of mine was told to put violence in "Lassie," explosions, gunshots. This guy was a veteran, the kind of war hero who leaned forward in the foxholes. He wrote the committee that he was fed up with it, that he was ordered to do it, and he would be glad to come and testify.

I had breakfast with him the morning that he was going to testify. He repeated everything that he was going to say. Unfortunately, there were two or three minutes before Dodd got into the caucus room. While he was standing at the witness table, some CBS people came up to him and said, "Hey, you like your big house and your swimming pool? You like the school your children go to? You want to keep that?" They walked away, and he was destroyed. He couldn't remember anything. That's when Dodd said, "Go subpoena the goddamned files."

PAUL LASKIN: We singled out individual shows on each of the networks, and we had a separate hearing for each, basically to determine how violence got on. There was "Cheyenne" on ABC, "Whispering Smith" on NBC, and "Route 66" on CBS. We also looked into "Man and the Challenge" after an allegation by the producer, Ivan Tors, that somebody at NBC, either Kintner or Levy, had said that NBC would not give the program airtime unless he put sex and violence in the show. Through Levy we were able to get the facts.

DAVID LEVY: I liked the show, but Kintner said at a program meeting, "The show needs a female attraction. It needs sex and violence." Then he leaned over to Mal Bevel, who was taking the minutes, and he said, "Listen, Mal, that's not for the minutes."

After the meeting, I summoned two of my associates. I said, "You'll not believe what I just heard. Bob Kintner specifically ordered as a condition of acceptance of that show that it must contain sex and violence.

"But," I said, "we won't implement it." We didn't.

During the hearings, I was with Kintner when he tried to get an agency man named Joe Daly to say that I gave the order. He said, "Didn't you get those instructions from David?"

Joe said, "No, Bob, you were the one who told me to do it." Bob then cut the conversation off. The day I was removed I asked my secretary for the file on "Man and the Challenge." It was gone.

CARL PERIAN: It was clear from the hearings that Kintner started the policy, but Treyz honed it to a fine edge. He had an anthology show called "Bus

Stop." It wasn't doing well in the ratings, so he came up with a story about a psychopathic teenager who kills his father. It starred Fabian. Sure enough, after they advertised it a great deal, the ratings rose like threefold.

Before Treyz testified, the network executives told him, "Say you put on 3,800 shows a year. This one was a mistake, and you won't do it again," but he was an arrogant little bull. He told us, "It was a great show. I'd do it again."

He was fired three days later. Dodd said, "Well, we've got one scalp under our belt."

At one point, Dodd asked Treyz if he would allow his children to watch it, and Treyz said, "I wouldn't let my kids watch this crap."

ABC was just a bunch of schlockmeisters. We showed a film of a guy getting his hand crunched. You could hear it vividly in the caucus room, and I said to their program-practices editor, "Do you think that was a violent scene?"

"What scene?"

"The crunching of the man's hand."

"I didn't hear any crunch."

We made films for each hearing. ABC complained that we took them out of context, so I said to Laskin, "If they don't want us using excerpts, let's show their own trailers." The next week, I ran thirty minutes of trailers for "The Untouchables," and, honest to God, when it was over the room was shell-shocked. It was nothing but machine guns, bombings, and stabbings. We said, "All right, now what's your complaint about showing excerpts?"

One day, we had "The Shirley Temple Show" on. The NBC people said, "Boy, do we got them by the balls." They didn't even know their own show. Their vice president said, "Senator, you people are tracking the wrong thing, this is 'The Shirley Temple Show.' "

Even Dodd was waiting for them. This was an anthology show, and the episode in question was one of the most violent shows of the series. We even had a letter from Shirley Temple, objecting to the show. All she did was lend her name to it and do the introduction. When Dodd got through reading this to the NBC vice president the guy was practically under the table. It was the only time I ever saw Dodd laugh. This was before the fix was in.

PAUL LASKIN: The hearings really became hot when the memos surfaced, especially the one quoting Aubrey on "Route 66."

CARL PERIAN: That memo was devastating. I'll never forget even Walter Cronkite laughing at Aubrey's testimony that "broads, bosoms, and fun" meant healthy young ladies and their children.

Aubrey was really pissed because Stanton was the one ordering him to get high ratings, and it's the usual thing, just like they did with Oliver Treyz, they get him in the room and they say, "I don't want to know how you do, just do it."

PAUL LASKIN: Stanton came to see Dodd before he testified. He said he would be pleased to answer any questions about policy or philosophy, but that he had nothing to do with "Route 66."

CARL PERIAN: He said, "I don't want to have my skirts muddied with broads, bosoms, and fun." When Stanton came on, Dodd thought the guy would meet him halfway, so we showed the clips from this particularly savage "Route 66," and Dodd says to Stanton, "Do you approve of that type of television?"

Stanton said, "That was never shown on CBS."

Dodd said, "Those clips were subpoenaed from your company."

"That show never appeared on CBS."

Dodd asked me if I was sure. I said, "Senator, I've got twelve witnesses. It was on."

Stanton kept saying, "That show was never on CBS," and finally Dodd threw his hands up and said, "If that's the position you're going to take, there's no hope."

It was the only time *Variety* gave us a good headline. It said, THE WHITE KNIGHT HAS FINALLY BEEN TARNISHED. Stanton was either in denial, or he didn't know what the hell was going on.

PAUL LASKIN: Kintner did not want to appear, and NBC didn't want him to either. If it had come out that the president of the network had ordered more sex and violence, there would have been an outcry. The network would have dumped Kintner to save its own neck. There were also possible threats to NBC's station licenses for cynically espousing these policies.

CARL PERIAN: At first, David Levy didn't have anybody supporting him against Kintner. NBC said Levy was just a disgruntled employee, but we telephoned James Stabile, who was in the room when Levy claimed Kintner made the remark. Stabile remembered it all, so now we had someone else saying that Levy was telling the truth.

PAUL LASKIN: Before Robert Sarnoff appeared, his lawyer asked me if it would be proper for Sarnoff to make a courtesy call on Senator Dodd. I said there was nothing improper at all. He came in, and while he was in with Dodd, Dodd's secretary said the senator would like to see me. I came in, and Dodd suddenly started to scream at me. He didn't want these people harassed and one thing or another. I was so mad that when I left I wrote out my resignation, but Perian told me not to.

Levy appeared in open hearings in January. The whole idea was that we would question him about "Man and the Challenge," but the message went from Dodd to Perian to me at the last moment that Dodd did not want any of the facts relating to the Kintner-Levy dispute to come out. Dodd was closing the thing down.

DAVID LEVY: Walter Scott, the NBC president, called me up on Friday, June 30, 1961. He said, "David, you've brought an *esprit de corps* here, but it's been our thinking that perhaps now would be an opportune moment for a change in the program department."

We walked into Kintner's office. He wanted to assign me to the news department as an executive producer or I could go to India to do a project there. They were doing that only to be able to say to Dodd, "We've made a change in our program department in response to your attacks on sex and violence."

I elected to resign. I also insisted on a statement that my resignation had nothing to do with sex and violence and that David Levy as head of programming never espoused sex and violence on network TV. They wanted to say, "Nor did anyone else at NBC." I said, "I can't stop you from doing that, but I don't like it."

PAUL LASKIN: Most senators would never have taken on the networks, but Dodd was fearless. He savaged Frank Stanton. He savaged Aubrey. It wasn't fear of the networks that stopped him. For a while I thought General Sarnoff might have gotten to him through friends. It wasn't until later that I discovered Kintner's close relationship to Lyndon Johnson. Then I recalled the phone call from Frank Dooley. Dooley used to work for Dodd. Then he worked for Vice President Johnson. He called up Carl after Johnson's office had received a call from Kintner, who apparently told them, "After all I've done for you guys, why is this shitty committee after me?"

CARL PERIAN: Dooley told me they wanted this harassment of Kintner to stop. Of course, the report on the hearings was suppressed. Dodd rejected my first two drafts because they discussed the Levy-Kintner affair. We also included research that pointed to a causal relationship between violence on television and in general society. He didn't want any of that in there. He hired a Dr. Glick, a third-rate professor at American University, and told him to take the report and "take the crap out and sanitize it." They tried to get me to change the report. I said, "No, those were the hearings and those were the conclusions."

We also put in Laskin's recommendation for licensing the networks, and NBC went through the ceiling. It was also in our original report that Kintner was clearly lying. That was taken out. Dodd had his assistant personally deliver the report to Peter Kenney, who was NBC's "vice president in charge of Dodd." NBC read the report. You know what they said? "We would prefer to have no report at all, but if one has to be issued this one is acceptable to us." Can you imagine that?

PAUL LASKIN: We wrote to Abe Ribicoff, who was then Secretary of Health, Education and Welfare, and while it took many years to develop, ours was the first seed leading to the Surgeon General's report in 1972, which said there was a causal relationship between televised violence and increased aggression in young people.

CARL PERIAN: What did Dodd get out of it? We monitored Dodd's fund-raising, and we would find relatives of NBC people were paying him through the nose.

Jim Boyd was Dodd's assistant. His girlfriend was Dodd's secretary. Kenney of NBC used to take them out to expensive meals. It was at a urinal that Kenney offered Boyd eight thousand dollars for Dodd. Boyd asked Dodd, who said, "With what we've got on them, they should at least come up with fifteen."

Boyd went back and said, "Dodd wants fifteen."

Kenney said, "That's out of the question."

After the election, Kenney told Boyd, "I thought Dodd didn't want the eight grand if he could get fifteen."

Boyd said, "Yeah, that's the way I understood it."

"Well, one of his flacks called to say he'd take the eight."

Subsequently, in New York there's a fund-raiser for Dodd, and who's a thousand-dollar contributor but Mrs. Robert Kintner and crap like that. It went on and on.

The networks didn't stop. I went to work for Congressman Murphy from New York. He got on the violence kick, too, testifying and making statements. One afternoon, I have lunch with this flack from NBC. He says, "Can you please get Murphy to get off this violence kick? We're stopping it next season."

Then he says, "You see what I have in my hand?"

It was a mimeograph of a TV-news interview with Murphy. He said, "These are really important to a politician, and you can tell Murphy if he gets off his violence kick and the networks, he can have a lot more of these next year."

"You stupid bastard. You know what you've just done?"

"What?"

"You've offered me a bribe. I ought to have you arrested." I told Murphy. I said, "The guy that sent him was a friend of yours. What should I have told him?"

He said, "Tell him to go fuck himself."

The point is they are very mean, nasty people.

*   *   *

BERNARD SCHWARTZ: When the Subcommittee on Government Information was set up, I was hired as a counsel to conduct a study of the regulatory agencies. I didn't realize that the cards were stacked against me. The subcommittee chairman was under the thumb of Orrin Harris, the chairman of the parent committee. The staff was hired without any consultation and most of them were there to keep the investigation under control. The FCC was one of the first agencies that I looked into. Nobody ever told me what not to do, but there were intimations.

ERIK BARNOUW: The FCC has a terrible history of scandal. One member became a secret owner of stations in Albany and Worcester and Cincinnati. Eventually, the station in Albany lost its license when somebody found out.

BERNARD SCHWARTZ: We looked into the awarding of the television license for Channel Ten in Miami. That led to Richard Mack's resignation from the FCC and his suicide. We not only dug up records on it, but Mack also told our investigator everything about his relationship with Thurman Whiteside, who was operating for one of the petitioners. Whiteside gave him gifts while the FCC was in the process of awarding the license. Mack not only didn't try to hide it, he apparently didn't see anything wrong. He was a drunken bum. He was not competent. He didn't know what he was doing. How anybody like that could be an FCC commissioner is hard to understand.

The nature of the appointments to the FCC was crucial. With a handful of exceptions, the appointments weren't particularly good. It was the kind of position that nobody would take unless they wanted to use it as a springboard to private practice afterwards with clients from the industry.

JOEL ROSENBLOOM: I joined the litigation division of the FCC in the summer of 1957. It was not an activist commission then under the chairmanship of George McConnaughey and John Doerfer. Doerfer was discovered desporting himself on a yacht owned by George B. Storer, the owner of several television stations.

BERNARD SCHWARTZ: I think the Doerfer and Mack cases were the tip of the iceberg. With a lot of the TV licenses the tendency was if somebody had political connections, he got the license regardless of the merits. The FCC in effect gave away untold millions of dollars every time they awarded a license. It was really a case of the fox guarding the henhouse.

It was generally known that Orrin Harris owned a part of a TV station. Other people in Congress, including Lyndon Johnson, either through themselves or relatives, acquired interests in stations. There were leads to others, but I was fired because they wanted the investigation to die out.

HENRY GELLER: I joined the FCC in 1949. I left and returned twice, the last time when Newt Minow was appointed by President Kennedy.

JOEL ROSENBLOOM: It changed immediately with Newt's appointment, even though he was only one vote. It was the difference in expectations, concerning the broadcast industry.

HENRY GELLER: It was the same thing throughout the New Frontier. There was this feeling, "By God, let's try to accomplish a great deal in the public interest," which included encouraging public broadcasting and serving children.

JOEL ROSENBLOOM: The FCC rules required prospective licensees to present proposals as to how much public-service programming they would put on. When they would come up for license renewals their performance was matched against their proposals. That rule had been enforced with increasing laxity. Newt came in, and there was a particularly egregious example that had come up. He said, "How much worse can he do? He promised six-percent local programming and he did zero."

He garnered the votes for a hearing, which was stunning. Ultimately, the counsel for the station managed to persuade Newt and others that it was unfair to the station and we granted it a short-term license, but we issued a manifest to the industry saying from here on the commission is taking this stuff seriously. The station did improve its service to some degree. Still, it was a tiny station in Pascal, Washington. It was not exactly the kind of scalp that Newt was forever looking for.

HENRY GELLER: He proposed that the networks jointly work together to program for children. The idea was, if the children's programming didn't attract the same amount of advertising, they would all take the hit equally. The idea wouldn't work if one of them refused to go along, and that's what happened. ABC pulled out, and that was the end of it.

JOEL ROSENBLOOM: He helped push through the all-channel bill, which required that every television set manufactured in the U.S. needed to receive both VHF and UHF stations.

Another major thrust was public television. That was the one where we "stole" Channel Thirteen in New Jersey. The station had been owned by NTA Television, which was on the edge of bankruptcy. They had to sell. Here was an opportunity to get a VHF public television station in New York. The commission didn't have the power to dictate to whom anybody sells. Still, Newt said, "I've got to figure out a way to do this."

We instituted a proceeding which said it was a shame and a *shanda,* neither New York nor Los Angeles had public TV stations on VHF, and we're gonna consider any and all means. While we're considering this situation, sales in these markets will be carefully vetted. We wanted to give the impression that anybody but educators would have a hard time getting that station. We were muscling them, which was of borderline legality.

In addition he went to network people and said, "I will get you anti-trust immunity if you will make some donations to help finance a public acquisition of the station." It was to their benefit. If you were a commercial station in the market, would you rather have six competitors or five competitors? With six, there's that much less advertising inventory available.

Bobby Kennedy at Justice cooperated. In the meantime the Ford Foundation came through with some financing, and a deal was made with the owner. The governor of New Jersey was furious. Here was New Jersey's only VHF station. He took it to court and got a stay, but we got a rehearing and won.

HENRY GELLER: Newt showed his "vast wasteland" speech to a number of people before he made it before the NAB [National Association of Broadcasters]. I thought it was a very good speech, but I'm a First Amendment nut, and I said, "I would not refer as much as you do to quality of programming." The "vast wasteland" summed up the fact that it was not quality. I told him to take that part out, proving I shouldn't be a speechwriter.

JOEL ROSENBLOOM: None of his advisers liked "the vast wasteland" concept. We all said, "Take it out." I said, "It's too intellectual. Nobody will get it."

He talked to his wife and put it back in.

HENRY GELLER: The broadcasters applauded his speech at first. Even when he said, "Never before have so few owed so much to so many," they applauded. I was amazed, but they were so used to applauding chairmen, they didn't really understand at first what he was saying, but they understood by the end.

JOEL ROSENBLOOM: After the speech, he went to a reception. Every once in a while a guy would come up to him and say, "That was an irresponsible speech." He would go away and he would come back and say something equally hostile. After a while his host at the party said, "Don't pay any attention to him, Newt. He just repeats what other people tell him."

Newt only stayed another two years. There were a lot of good people during Newt's period. They were intelligent, and they cared, and they tried to accomplish something. But it was a question of how much anybody could accomplish in the face of an institution, which doesn't change easily. You can't go out there and just say, "Stop producing crap and start producing good things." That's not the way it works.

The government can't dictate to a network what is quality programming. The best anybody can do is to try to create conditions under which people who have some creativity have a decent shot at it. That's the most you can ever hope to accomplish.

THE WITNESSES

(in the chapter where they first appear)

SOMETHING IN THE AIR

ERIK BARNOUW *(1908–)* is the former script director for NBC and one of the founders of the Radio Writers Guild of America. His three-volume history of television and radio is the acknowledged standard on the subject. Now a professor emeritus at Columbia University, he divides his time between his homes in Vermont and New York City.

HAROLD BEVERAGE *(1893–1993)*, one of RCA's original employees, was twenty-seven when he invented the Beverage Wave Antenna, which dramatically improved radio reception and is still in use today.

ARCH BROLLY *(1900–1991)* worked with Philo Farnsworth in California and at Philco in Pennsylvania. He was later the first chief engineer at WBKB in Chicago, one of the country's first television stations.

BENJAMIN CLAPP *(1894–1991)* was one of John Logie Baird's first assistants and later was Baird's chief engineer. A true television pioneer, he received the first transatlantic television signals in 1927. During World War II, he worked on radar development and later became a successful businessman.

LEE COOLEY *(1909–)* is a former member of the Merchant Marines, journalist, and advertising executive who began his career in radio in 1937 at station KHJ in Los Angeles. He went on to become a successful television producer with "The Lanny Ross Show" and "The Perry Como Show," among others.

WILLIAM CRAWFORD EDDY *(1902–1989)* was a submarine commander who later worked for Philo Farnsworth and NBC before founding television station WBKB in Chicago.

WILLIAM C. EDDY, JR. *(1931–)*, is the son of William Crawford Eddy. He is the executive director of the product development group of Allied Signal Corp. in Detroit.

ELMA "PEM" FARNSWORTH *(1907–)* is the widow of Philo Farnsworth. She worked closely with her husband on the development of electronic television.

DONALD GLEN FINK *(1911–)* is a graduate of M.I.T. and a journalist who wrote *Principles of Television Engineering*, one of the most respected works on the subject. In 1940, he played a key role in setting the technological broadcast standards that are still in place today. He is retired and lives in Westchester, New York.

THOMAS T. GOLDSMITH *(1910–)* is the former chief of research for Allen B. DuMont Laboratories and is the namesake of TV station WTTG in Washington, D.C. He is retired and lives in Tacoma, Washington.

ARTHUR HUNGERFORD *(1911–)* worked for NBC on its pioneer broadcasts. After World War II, he became director of the Metropolitan Educational Television Association to help bring educational television to New York City. He later taught at Penn State University. He is retired and lives in State College, Pennsylvania.

HERBERT IRVING *(1899–)* started his radio career as a radio operator with the Merchant Marines, where he heard the historic first broadcast of the world's oldest radio station, KDKA. In 1924, he became an announcer-engineer with KDKA. He is retired and lives in Saxonburg, Pennsylvania.

IRMA KROMAN *(1905–)* was the program manager of Jenkins Television Corp. She later became an actress, working primarily for WGY, in Schenectedy, one of the nation's first television stations.

AGNES FARNSWORTH LINDSAY *(1908–)* is a sister of Philo Farnsworth. She lives in California.

EDITH ALEXANDERSON NORDLANDER *(1910–1992)*, a daughter of Ernst Alexanderson, was a schoolteacher. Her sister, Gertrude Alexanderson Young, also participated in the interview.

WILLIAM N. PARKER *(1907–)* had a long career in television, starting with the inventor U. A Sanabria, and then working for Philco and RCA.

LOYD SIGMON *(1909–)* was an assistant to the Boston inventor Hollis Baird and later became a college professor. Today his name is heard every day on radios in Southern California as the developer of the "Sig Alert," a system that measures traffic congestion.

THEODORE A. SMITH *(1905–1994)* was an engineer and vice president of RCA. He set up the company's first TV station in 1928, and played an especially prominent role getting television started after World War II.

W. GORDON SWAN *(1904–)* was one of radio's first announcers with WBZ in Boston. He later became WBZ television's first program director.

STUDS TERKEL *(1912–)* starred on the NBQ show "Studs' Place." After the show's cancellation, he left his TV career behind for a hugely successful career as a journalist and radio personality. He is the author of several oral histories, including *Hard Times*, *The Good War*, and *American Dreams: Lost and Found*.

THE RACE IS JOINED

LINCOLN FARNSWORTH *(1915–)* worked in his brother's lab, where he lost an eye in an accident. He later became a building contractor. He is retired and lives in Arizona.

LES FLORY *(1907–)* is the last surviving member of RCA's original electronic television research group. He is retired and lives in Princeton, New Jersey.

LOREN JONES *(1905–)* is an engineer who worked for Ernst Alexanderson at GE and Vladimir Zworykin at RCA. He is retired and lives in Chestnut Hill, Pennsylvania.

ROBERT SARNOFF *(1918–)* is the son of David Sarnoff and the former president of NBC. He lives in New York City.

TV COMES TO 30 ROCK

BETTY GOODWIN BAKER *(1908–)* was NBC television's first announcer. She lives in San Diego, California.

RAY FORREST *(1916–)* was NBC television's leading personality and announcer from 1939 to the start of World War II. He later produced and hosted "Children Television Theater," an Emmy-winning children's show. He is now retired and lives in New Jersey.

HILDEGARDE *(1906–)* was a longtime cabaret star. She lives in New York City and is still an active performer.

GIANT STEPS

LENORE JENSEN *(1913–1993)* was a radio actress who appeared in some of television's first commercials and hosted several early TV women's shows.

NOEL JORDAN *(1914–   )* started at NBC as a property man and later became a director. He is retired and lives in Colorado.

EDWARD PADULA *(1916–   )* was one of W2XBS's first directors. After he was fired because he was deemed not commercial enough, he went on to a successful career directing in Hollywood and on Broadway. He later conceived and directed the musical *Bye Bye Birdie*.

REINALD WERRENRATH *(1915–   )* was Bill Eddy's assistant at W2XBS. He later joined Eddy at WBKB in Chicago, then left that station to join NBC as a producer-director in 1948.

DUMONT (THE RISE)

BRUCE DUMONT *(1905–1992)* was the brother of Allen B. DuMont. For many years, he managed the DuMont plant.

DENNIS JAMES *(1917–   )* was DuMont's first on-air personality. He emceed many shows during TV's first four decades and still hosts the annual cerebral palsy telethon.

CBS OPENS ITS EYE

EDWARD ANHALT *(1914–   )* worked for CBS primarily as a cameraman until World War II. He did not return to television after the war. He became a Hollywood screenwriter and won Academy Awards for *Panic in the Streets* and *Becket*. He also adapted Irwin Shaw's World War II novel *The Young Lions* for the screen. He lives and works in Pacific Palisades, California.

CARL BEIER *(1920–   )* was hired as a general assistant at CBS. After World War II, he worked on television shows produced by the advertising agency Kenyon & Eckhardt.

BOB BENDICK *(1917–   )* was hired as a cameraman and became director of news and special events for CBS after the war. He was later the executive producer of the "Today" show and "Wide Wide World" on NBC. He is retired and lives in Connecticut.

RUDY BRETZ *(1914–   )* was the first person hired by Gilbert Seldes for the CBS television department. He later helped get WPIX in New York City off the ground. Mr. Bretz also collaborated with a colleague, Ed Stasheff, on one of the early bibles of television production, *The Television Program*. He has also taught television production and written several nonfiction books on the communications field. He lives in Malibu, California.

JOHN HOLLYWOOD *(1910–   )* went to work for CBS in 1936 as an assistant to Peter Goldmark. He stayed with Goldmark until his retirement and now lives in Red Bank, New Jersey.

JIM LEAMAN *(1911–   )* was a producer-director at CBS until 1941. After World War II, he became a producer-director for KFI in Los Angeles. He taught at the University of California until his retirement. He lives in Santa Barbara, California.

PETER MINER *(1930–   )* is a television director and the son of Worthington Miner.

MARIAN SELDES *(1928–   )* is an actress and the daughter of Gilbert Seldes, the first head of CBS television.

CAPTAIN BILL EDDY AND THE STORY OF WBKB

HUGH DOWNS *(1921–)* has been on television longer than any other TV personality. After his Chicago days, he moved to New York to co-host the "Home" show. He co-starred with Jack Paar on his late-night show and was also co-host of the "Today" show. He now co-hosts "20/20."

FELICE KERRIGAN ELIAS *(1923–1991)* was one of WBKB's original camerawomen. She later became the personal secretary to Faye Emerson.

LEW GOMAVITZ *(1912–)*, the director of "Kukla, Fran & Ollie," went on to direct many television shows, including "Sanford and Son" and "The Dinah Shore Show." He is now retired and lives in California.

WILLIAM PETER KUSACK *(1915–)* was one of WBKB's original staffers and later succeeded Arch Brolly as chief engineer. He is now retired and lives in the Chicago area.

STERLING "RED" QUINLAN *(1916–)* started in radio by writing a show called "The Open Road" for NBC. He later wrote many "Captain Midnight" scripts. He was general manager of WBKB and is also the author of a history of ABC entitled *Inside ABC* and several other books. He lives and works in the Chicago area.

DICK SHAPIRO *(1919–)* was one of the original staff engineers at WBKB. He is now retired and lives in the Chicago area.

MIKE WALLACE *(1918–)* is a television news reporter and mainstay on "60 Minutes." He began his television career in Chicago, where he was also heard regularly on radio as an actor and news broadcaster.

OVER HERE AND THERE

FRAN BUSS BUCH *(1917–)* began working for CBS television before World War II and went on to become the division's first woman director.

JACK BURRELL *(1905–)* was in charge of NBC television's remote crew before World War II. He later moved to the West Coast, where he continued his remote work.

OTIS FREEMAN *(1921–1993)* began his career in television as an engineer with the DuMont Television Network and then moved on to WPIX in New York until he retired.

HEINO RIPP *(1925–)* was a technical director for NBC for many years.

PAUL WYMER *(1914–)* was an engineer with RCA, where he was instrumental in the creation of the Image Orthicon tube and the later Image Isocon tube. He also worked on the development of color television.

NOW IT'S FOR REAL

MOREY AMSTERDAM *(1914–)* is a veteran radio and television entertainer. He was one of early television's biggest stars in the 1940s as host of "Cavalcade of Stars" on the DuMont network. He also hosted one of the earliest late-night shows, "Broadway Open House" on NBC.

BUDDY ARNOLD *(1918–)* was a writer on "Texaco Star Theater." He co-wrote the show's theme song with Woody Kling.

TED BERGMANN *(1920–)* is the former president of the DuMont Television Network. After DuMont's demise, he moved into the advertising industry and produced a number of TV shows.

JACK CARTER *(1923–)* is a veteran comedian and actor who hosted "Cavalcade of Stars" on DuMont and starred in his own show, "The Saturday Night Revue," on ABC.

JOSEPH CATES *(1924–)* is a veteran television producer and director.

HARRY COYLE *(1922–　)* began his career as a studio technician with DuMont and eventually became the preeminent sports director on television. He is now retired and lives in Iowa.

JERRY DANZIG *(1913–　)* was the program manager of CBS under Worthington Miner.

MADELYN PUGH DAVIS *(1921–　)* co-wrote "I Love Lucy" with her partner, Bob Carroll. The two later produced the sitcom "Alice."

MILTON DELUGG *(1921–　)* is a popular television bandleader who has appeared on many shows, including the original late-night show, "Broadway Open House."

AL DURANTE *(1913–　)* was an advertising executive in the publicity department of J. Walter Thompson.

GIL FATES *(1913–　)* was the producer and moderator of CBS's first game show, "The CBS Television Quiz." He also produced "What's My Line?," "Password," and "To Tell The Truth."

WALLY FERRIS *(1930–　)* was a cameraman with DuMont and later a writer. His novel *Across 110th Street* was made into a movie.

DON HASTINGS *(1934–　)* played the Ranger on "Captain Video" and for more than thirty years has appeared on "As the World Turns" as Dr. Bob Hughes.

FRANKLIN HELLER *(1912–　)* was a longtime director for CBS and later for Mark Goodson Productions, where his set designs for shows such as "What's My Line?" and "I've Got a Secret" set industry standards.

OSCAR KATZ *(1913–　)* began his career at CBS in the research department under Frank Stanton. He was later head of the network's daytime programming.

ALICE LESTER *(1918–　)* was married to the comedian Jerry Lester, the host of "Broadway Open House" and "Cavalcade of Stars."

PETER LEVATHES *(1911–　)* is a lawyer who began his career in the entertainment industry as an adviser to Spyros Skouras of Twentieth Century Fox. He became a vice president of Young & Rubicam and was later head of Twentieth Century Fox Television.

RALPH LEVY *(1919–　)* was the first CBS director on the West Coast. He directed the pilot of "I Love Lucy." He also directed "The Ed Wynn Show," "The Jack Benny Show," and "The Burns and Allen Show," among others.

STEWART MACGREGORY *(1917–　)* was an engineer and stagehand at NBC in New York.

HENRY MORGAN *(1915–1994)* was a longtime radio and television personality.

CHARLES POLACHEK *(1914–　)* was a staff director at CBS and then a director and producer at NBC. He was also the first director of "Captain Video" on the DuMont network.

AARON RUBEN *(1914–　)* wrote, directed, and produced many comedy shows, including "Caesar's Hour," "The Phil Silvers Show," "The Andy Griffith Show," and "Gomer Pyle, U.S.M.C."

IRA SKUTCH *(1921–　)* is a veteran television director. He primarily worked on commercials for Philco and game shows with Goodson & Todman.

DICK SMITH *(1922–　)* is regarded as the finest makeup man in the entertainment industry. He has created original makeups for many live dramas and films, including the *Planet of the Apes* films and *The Exorcist*.

MAX WILK *(1920–　)* began writing for television right after World War II. He wrote for "Mama" and "The Ford Television Theater." He is also the author of many books, including the fine television history *The Golden Age of Television*.

CHRIS WITTING *(1915–　)* is a former president of the DuMont Television Network. He left DuMont to become a vice president of Westinghouse Broadcasting. He now lives and works in Syracuse, New York.

SETS FOR SALE

E. LAWRENCE DECKINGER *(1917–   )* was head of research for the Milton Biow advertising agency, where he studied early television viewers. He teaches advertising at St. John's University.

HARRY DUBIN *(1910–   )* was one of the first Manhattanites to buy a television set. He was the owner of the popular Regent Food Shop on Manhattan's East Side for many years. Mr. Dubin is now retired and lives in New York. His son Ron also appears in this chapter.

BOB ELLIOTT *(1909–   )* is a retired television and electronic appliance dealer.

LEONARD FAUPEL *(1920–   )* is a former advertising director of P. Ballantine & Sons. He was also a senior vice president with the William Esty Company. He is retired and lives in New Jersey.

JERRY FISHMAN *(1921–   )* is a retired television and electronic appliance dealer.

MEL GOLDBERG was the head of research for the DuMont Television Network.

WILLARD LEVITAS *(1925–   )* was the set designer for many live CBS shows. He later produced shows for all three major networks, including "That Was the Week That Was," two Barbra Streisand specials, and "The Fabulous 50s." He is now retired and lives in New York City and Southampton.

JAMES MCMANUS *(1919–   )* owns the McManus Bar and Grill, a fixture on Seventh Avenue in Manhattan since 1920.

IRVING NEEDLE has been in the wholesale appliance business for more than fifty years. He is now with Panasonic in New Jersey.

JACK SIEGRIST *(1917–   )* has been a marketing executive with DuMont, Philco, and Motorola. He teaches marketing on the college level in New Jersey.

THE SPORTS SECTION

MEL ALLEN *(1913–   )* was the voice of the New York Yankees for many years and remains active in the broadcasting business as the narrator of "This Week in Baseball."

JACK BRICKHOUSE *(1916–   )* is a veteran TV and radio broadcaster and the longtime "Voice of the Cubs."

ALVIN "BUD" COLE *(1919–   )* was an engineer at NBC in New York before moving west to work with the legendary Klaus Landsberg at KTLA.

BOB DOYLE *(1922–   )* was a longtime television producer and director, beginning at WRC in Washington, D.C., after World War II. He was later an executive with *National Geographic*, and is now retired and living in Maryland.

JACK JACOBSON *(1922–   )* began his television career as a cameraman for WGN and eventually became general manager of the station.

WES KENNEY *(1926–   )* was a staff director at DuMont. After the network folded, he directed many shows on ABC, CBS, and NBC.

SAM LAINE *(1913–1992)* was a radio audio engineer when he met Dennis James and became his assistant during James's boxing and wrestling broadcasts.

HARRY MARKSON *(1906–   )* is the former head of Madison Square Garden's boxing department.

RUSS MASSRO *(1929–   )* was one of the best-known skaters in the Roller Derby when the sport was at its peak.

ROGER MUIR *(1918–   )* was a producer-director at NBC and the original producer-director of "Howdy Doody." He later became head of all children's programming at NBC, New York.

SAM MUNCHNICK *(1905–   )* was a wrestling promoter in St. Louis.

KEN NYDELL *(1915–   )* was the official announcer for "Roller Derby."

ED STASHEFF *(1909–   )* was a director with several television stations in New York in the mid-to late 1940s. He later taught television at the University of Michigan and is the co-author with Rudy Bretz of the seminal book on television production *The Television Program.*

LOU THESZ *(1916–   )* wrestled during the sport's more legitimate days and into the entertainment-oriented TV period. He is generally regarded as one of the finest wrestlers of all time.

TOM VILLANTE *(1928–   )* is a former advertising executive who was instrumental in bringing major-league baseball to network TV. He was later baseball commissioner Bowie Kuhn's chief adviser on television issues.

TV GOES NATIONWIDE

JOE BEHAR *(1926–   )* was the director of "Three to Get Ready," Ernie Kovacs's morning show at WPTZ in Philadelphia.

WILLIAM BODE *(1926–   )* directed "Action in the Afternoon," the legendary daily live western on WCAU in Philadelphia.

GREG GARRISON *(1924–   )* is a veteran television director whose credits include some of the finest comedy variety shows and specials ever aired, including "The Buick-Berle Show," "Your Show of Shows," and specials with Gene Kelly and Fred Astaire.

MARGE GREENE *(1929–   )* is a veteran television actress, comedienne, and writer. She worked with Ernie Kovacs in Philadelphia and later with Allen Funt on "Candid Camera." She also starred in a nightly ad-libbed drama, "Marge and Jeff," which appeared on the DuMont network.

JAMES HIRSCHFELD *(1929–   )* began his career as an assistant director with WCAU in Philadelphia. He subsequently produced and directed "Captain Kangaroo."

HERBERT HORTON *(1920–   )* began his television career with Philco before World War II. He later became a director for several advertising agencies.

CAL JONES *(1925–   )* was a director at WPTZ in Philadelphia. He later became an executive with the Westinghouse Broadcasting Co.

JACK KENNEDY was a cameraman and assistant director at WPTZ in Philadelphia. He later worked for the BBD&O advertising agency.

ROBERT "DOC" LIVINGSTON *(1913–   )* is a former television director who started his career with W6XAO Los Angeles in 1936.

HARRY LUBCKE *(1905–   )* is the father of television in Los Angeles. He set up Los Angeles's first television station, W6XAO, in 1931. He is also responsible for naming television's highest award, the Emmy.

TRIGVE LUND is a former cameraman and stage manager who worked with Ernie Kovacs in Philadelphia and New York.

MONTY MARGETTS *(1912–   )* began her career as a radio and stage actress and later created and hosted a Los Angeles cooking show, legendary for her inability to master the intricacies of boiling water.

ANDY MCKAY *(1913–   )* was Ernie Kovacs's stage manager and man Friday in Philadelphia and New York. He was responsible for many of Kovacs's most successful comedy bits.

HAROLD PANNEPACKER *(1922–   )* began his career as a cameraman with WPTZ in Philadelphia. He later became a time salesman for the station.

MAXIE SOLOMON *(1906–   )* was a time salesman for WFIL in Philadelphia.

JACK STECK *(1897–1993)* began in radio in 1926 and later helped start up WFIL in Philadelphia, where he was director and program director.

PRESTON STOVER *(1918–   )* was a cameraman with WPTZ in Philadelphia. He later became program manager at two other TV stations.

WILLIAM SWARTLEY *(1908–   )* was the general manager of WBZ in Boston, the first television station in New England, from the station's inception until his retirement.

SYLVESTER L. "PAT" WEAVER *(1908–)* worked for the Don Lee network before he joined Young & Rubicam and eventually became a vice president of the agency. He left Y & R in 1949 to become the head of NBC television, where he left an unmatched record for innovation.

KARL WEGER *(1924–)* was an engineer at WPTZ, where he invented several of the camera bits used by Ernie Kovacs.

JOHN ZACHERLE *(1918–)* is a television actor and radio deejay who appeared on "Action in the Afternoon" in Philadelphia. He later hosted "Chiller Theatre" and several other popular afternoon movie shows on television and is still a deejay in the New York area.

KTLA: PROMISE FULFILLED

STAN CHAMBERS *(1923–)* has been with KTLA almost since its inception, and today remains one of Los Angeles's most respected television newsmen.

JOE FEATHERSTON was a cameraman and technician at KTLA under Klaus Landsberg and still works at the station.

JOHNNY POLICH *(1915–)*, a former member of the New York Rangers 1940 championship hockey team, joined KTLA as a technician and remained there until his retirement.

EDDIE RESNICK *(1915–)* was the first cameraman hired by Klaus Landsberg at KTLA.

BUD STEFAN *(1921–1994)* was a popular performer at KTLA who also wrote and produced several shows before leaving the station to eventually head up the television and radio department of the advertising agency BBD&O.

BILL WELSH was a popular sports announcer and emcee at KTLA, then became the director of sports and special events at KTTV in Los Angeles.

THE CHICAGO SCHOOL

CHARLES ANDREWS *(1916–)* came to WNBQ after a stint with a Chicago advertising agency, where he created the radio show "Sky King." He left Chicago for New York in the mid-1950s. After spending a year as a writer on "Caesar's Hour," he became a television producer. Among his credits are "The Arthur Godfrey Show," "Candid Camera," and the Miss Universe pageants. He is retired and lives in New York.

BOB BANNER *(1921–)* earned his directing degree at WNBQ and later became a producer. He now heads Bob Banner Associates, an independent production company.

NORMAN FELTON *(1913–)* is native of England. After he he got WNBQ off the ground, he left Chicago to produce and direct "Robert Montgomery Presents" in New York. He also directed episodes of "Studio One." Later he became head of MGM television and was the creator of "Dr. Kildare" and "The Man From U.N.C.L.E."

WILLIAM HOBIN *(1923–)* was a director at WNBQ until he left the station to direct the classic television comedy "Your Show of Shows." He later directed numerous sitcoms and musical comedy specials. He is retired and lives in Arizona.

LYNWOOD KING *(1925–)* was hired at WNBQ as a stage manager. He later directed many network shows, including "Today" and "Mr. Wizard." He is retired and lives in New York.

TED MILLS *(1916–)*, the program manager of WNBQ, would leave the station to join NBC president Pat Weaver's staff in New York. He is retired and lives on Long Island.

BEN PARK *(1920–)* produced documentary programming for WNBQ as well as the popular soap opera "Hawkins Falls." In 1955 he joined Pat Weaver's staff in New York, where, as director of public affairs, he conceived the idea of putting Huntley and Brinkley together to anchor the news. He later worked as a producer for Westinghouse Broadcasting. He now lives in Toronto and New York City and is still active as a producer.

DANIEL PETRIE *(1920–)* began his television career in Omaha, Nebraska. After directing at WNBQ, he moved to New York, where he directed numerous live television dramas. His work as an active director in feature films includes *A Raisin in the Sun*, *Resurrection*, and *Fort Apache, the Bronx*. He won Emmys for two installments of "Eleanor and Franklin."

DUMONT (THE FALL)

LES AIRRES, JR. *(1924–)*, joined DuMont as a cameraman and technician. He directed the first major-league ball games aired by the network and was later general manager of the DuMont station WTTG in Washington, D.C.

HAL COOPER *(1923–)* was a staff director for DuMont and was producer and director of the popular children's show "Magic Cottage," which starred his wife, Pat Meikle. He has since been an active TV producer and director.

HAROLD CRANE *(1914–)* has written many comedy shows for Eddie Cantor, Dean Martin, Jerry Lewis, and others, including Jackie Gleason, for whom he created the comedy classic "The Honeymooners."

ART ELLIOT *(1924–)* worked in network sales for DuMont.

STAN EPSTEIN *(1925–)* was a staff director for the DuMont network.

PAT FAY was a staff director for DuMont. Among his shows was "The Growing Paynes," the network's first sitcom.

COLEMAN JACOBY *(1924–)* co-wrote with his partner, Arnie Rosen, "Cavalcade of Stars," starring Jackie Gleason. He also wrote many episodes of "The Phil Silvers Show."

LARRY MENKIN *(1911–)*, along with Charlie Speer, formed one of the most prolific of television's writing teams. The two created a number of shows on the DuMont network.

WERNER MICHEL *(1910–)* was a programming executive at CBS and at several advertising agencies. He is now a senior vice president at Kenyon & Eckhardt.

LEE POLK *(d. 1993)* began his directing career for the DuMont network and was active producing children's television shows at the time of his death.

JACK RAYEL *(1915–)* began his career as an announcer with the DuMont network. He went on to direct and produce before joining Pat Weaver's staff at NBC in New York, where he created "Hallmark Hall of Fame." He now lives in Upper Black Eddy, Pennsylvania.

ROY SHARP *(1919–)* was in network sales and affilliate relations for DuMont and later served as traffic manager until the network's demise.

CHUCK TRANUM *(1916–1994)* was one of DuMont's first announcers. He then became a popular on-air host and later a talent agent in New York City.

LARRY WHITE was a staff director for the Dumont network, where his work included "Captain Video."

THE GOLDEN AGE

JANE AURTHUR was an assistant stage manager on several of NBC's big-budget dramatic shows. She was also married to the highly respected TV and screen writer, the late Robert Alan Aurthur.

ANNE HOWARD BAILEY *(1924–)* is a writer with numerous television credits, including "Robert Montgomery Presents," "The U.S. Steel Hour," "Armstrong Circle Theater," and "Kraft Television Theatre," among others.

PHILIP BARRY *(1923–)* is a producer whose credits include "The Alcoa Hour" on live television and the TV films "First You Cry," "Kent State," "Strange Interlude," and "Friendly Fire." The latter won an Emmy for the best television movie of the year.

WALTER BERNSTEIN *(1919–)* wrote many plays for live television (often under a pseudonym because of the blacklist). His movie credits include *The Front*, which is based on his experience during the 1950s, *Fail Safe*, *The Money Trap*, *The Molly Maguires*, and *Semi-Tough*, among others.

NORMA CONNOLLY *(1927–)* is a veteran actress who performed in many shows on live television.

DOMINICK DUNNE *(1925–)* was stage manager for "Howdy Doody" before his current career as a journalist and novelist. He was also a film producer with credits that include *The Boys in the Band*, *Panic in Needle Park*, and *Play It As It Lays*.

HORTON FOOTE *(1916–)* has written numerous teleplays and movies, among them *The Trip to Bountiful*, *The Traveling Lady*, *1918*, *On Valentine's Day*, *Tender Mercies*, and the Oscar-winning *To Kill a Mockingbird*.

GEORGE GRIZZARD *(1928–)* has acted in numerous roles on Broadway, in television, and in the movies. In 1980, he won an Emmy for his role in "The Oldest Living Graduate."

EILEEN HECKART *(1919–)* has also acted in numerous roles on television and in the movies. In 1972, she won an Oscar for Best Supporting Actress for her performance in *Butterflies Are Free*.

STOCKTON HELFFRICH *(1911–)* was the NBC censor for many years. He joined the network in its script department in 1933, then moved into the department of continuity acceptance. He is retired and lives in Queens, New York.

RICHARD KILEY *(1922–)* has acted in many Broadway shows, including *Man of La Mancha*, for which he won a Tony. He has also acted in television, and won Emmy Awards for his performances in "A Year in the Life" and "The Thorn Birds."

ERNEST KINOY *(1925–)* wrote several live and filmed television shows, including "Roots" and a script called "Blacklist" for "The Defenders," which won an Emmy.

PERRY LAFFERTY *(1920–)* amassed a host of producing and directing credits for "The Twilight Zone," "The Danny Kaye Show," "The U.S. Steel Hour," and "Robert Montgomery Presents." He later became vice president in charge of television programs for CBS on the West Coast. He is now a novelist, living in the Los Angeles area.

BETHEL LESLIE *(1929–)* has enjoyed an excellent acting career in television and in movies. She appeared in *The Rabbit Trap*, *The Molly Maguires*, and *Captain Newman, M.D.*, among other films. She also starred in *Long Day's Journey Into Night* on Broadway.

DELBERT MANN *(1920–)* has directed many television shows and feature films. He won an Oscar for *Marty* in 1955.

MARTIN MANULIS *(1915–)*, the creator of "Playhouse 90," also produced numerous Broadway shows, including *The Philadelphia Story* and *Private Lies*, and produced the film version of "Days of Wine and Roses."

NANCY MARCHAND *(1928–)*, a popular character actress, won two Emmys for her role as Mrs. Pynchon in "Lou Grant."

ROBERT MARKELL *(1921–)* designed many shows for CBS before becoming a producer. Among his credits are "The Defenders" and "N.Y.P.D."

J. P. MILLER *(1919–)* has written many teleplays and screenplays. He won an Emmy for "The People Next Door." His other credits include "The Rabbit Trap," "Days of Wine and Roses," "Behold a Pale Horse" and "Helter Skelter."

TAD MOSEL *(1922–)* wrote many plays for the "Philco Television Playhouse" and "Goodyear Playhouse" shows. He is also the author of *Impromptu* and *All the Way Home*, which won a Pulitzer for playwriting in 1961.

IRVING GAYNOR NEIMAN *(1916–)* is an award-winning writer whose live television credits include "Appointment in Samarra" and "Child of Our Time."

JOHN NEWLAND *(1917–)*, one of television's earliest stars, is still an actor and producer with many shows to his credit.

WILLIAM NICHOLS was the head of casting at NBC during the Golden Age.

ARTHUR PENN *(1922–)* has directed numerous stage and television shows as well as feature films. He began his career as a stage manager on "The Colgate Comedy Hour." He then became a director of "Philco Television Playhouse" under Fred Coe and "Playhouse 90" under Martin Manulis. His Broadway credits include *The Miracle Worker,* for which he won a Tony, *Golden Boy,* and *Wait Until Dark.* Among his feature films are *Bonnie and Clyde, Alice's Restaurant, Little Big Man,* and *The Missouri Breaks.*

TONY RANDALL *(1920–)* is perhaps best known for his role as Felix Unger in television's "The Odd Couple." He also played Harvey Weskitt, the sidekick to Mr. Peepers. He now runs the National Theater.

REGINALD ROSE *(1920–)* was one of live television's most highly regarded playwrights. His "12 Angry Men" was subsequently made into a movie starring Henry Fonda. Among his other movie credits are *Crime in the Streets* and *Whose Life Is It Anyway?* He also created the classic television show "The Defenders."

ALVIN SAPINSLEY *(1921–)* wrote for live and film television, for forty years. His credits include shows for "Robert Montgomery Presents," "The Alcoa Hour," "Omnibus," "Goodyear Playhouse," "Playhouse 90," and "Studio One." He is retired and lives in the Los Angeles area.

ROD STEIGER *(1925–)* was one of the greatest actors of television's Golden Age. He later moved to feature films, where he starred in such classics as *On the Waterfront, The Pawnbroker, Al Capone, In the Heat of the Night* (for which he won an Oscar), and *The Harder They Fall.*

ORLAND TAMBURRI *(1921–),* known professionaly as O. Tamburri, was one of the most highly regarded technical directors in the days of live TV.

ETHEL WINANT *(1925–)* is a veteran casting director who began her career with "Studio One" and eventually moved up to be vice president in charge of casting at CBS.

CELLULOID HEROES

RICHARD BARE *(1913–)* was a producer-director who directed many of the early Warner Bros. TV shows.

PAT BUTTRAM *(1917–1993)* was a popular comedic actor who played Gene Autry's sidekick for many years and later appeared as Mr. Haney on "Green Acres."

TOM CARR *(1907–)* directed numerous quickie westerns for Monogram Pictures before moving into television, where his credits include many episodes of "Superman" and "Rawhide," among others.

JENNINGS COBB wrote many early TV westerns, including "The Gene Autry Show," "The Adventures of Champion," and "The Adventures of Rin Tin Tin."

IRON EYES CODY *(1916–)* appeared as a guest on many westerns and also had his own show on KTLA in Los Angeles, in which he explained Native American traditions to young viewers, but he achieved his most widespread fame as the Indian with a tear in his eye for the "Keep America Beautiful" advertising campaign.

DALTON DANON *(1924–)* was an early salesman of film libraries for Motion Pictures for Television, a leading film syndicator.

DICK FEINER *(1926–)* worked for Motion Pictures for Television. Joe Green and Larry Stern, who were also in TV syndication/sales, also participated in this interview.

RUDOLPH FLOTHOW, JR. *(1926–),* is the son of Rudolph Flothow, the producer of the syndicated TV series "Ramar of the Jungle."

ERIC FREIWALD *(1927–)* wrote many westerns for Gene Autry's Flying A Productions, including "The Gene Autry Show," "Annie Oakley," and "The Adventures of Champion." He and his partner, Robert Schaefer, later wrote for Warner Bros. and also wrote nearly two hundred episodes of "Lassie."

HARRY GERSTAD *(1909–)* won two Academy Awards as a film editor, for *Champion* and *High Noon,* and went on to direct many episodes of "Superman."

MARION HARGROVE *(1919–)* wrote the big World War II best-seller *See Here, Private Hargrove,* which was made into two movies. He later wrote many episodes of "Maverick" and other shows.

DOUGLAS HEYES *(1919–1993)* directed "The Adventures of Rin Tin Tin" before moving on to direct for Warner Bros. TV and later "The Twilight Zone."

DICK JONES *(1927–)* played the sidekick to Jock Mahoney in "The Range Rider." He also starred in his own show, "Buffalo Bill, Jr."

ARNOLD LAVEN *(1922–)* was the co-creator and producer of "The Rifleman" with his partners Arthur Gardner and Jules Levy. He has also directed fourteen feature films and co-produced twenty others.

LESLIE MARTINSON directed numerous television shows, including "The Roy Rogers Show" and many for Warner Bros. TV.

WILLIAM T. ORR *(1917–)* was the head of television for Warner Bros.

DENVER PYLE *(1920–)* is an actor who appeared in many early westerns.

BUD RIFKIN *(1913–)* was executive vice president in charge of sales for the Frederic Ziv Company.

TED ROGERS *(1920–)* got his start in television with the Dancer, Fitzgerald & Sample advertising agency. He was with NBC during the 1950s and also helped direct Richard Nixon's media campaigns from 1950 to 1960.

STANLEY RUBIN *(1917–)* produced the first filmed series for network television, "Your Show Time Story Theatre," and later went on to produce feature films, including, *White Hunter, Black Heart* with Clint Eastwood.

ROBERT SCHAEFER *(1926–)* co-wrote many early TV westerns with his partner, Eric Freiwald.

THOL SIMONSON *(1912–)* was a special-effects man in Hollywood who worked on many shows including "Superman" and several productions for Frederic Ziv.

FREDERIC ZIV *(1905–)* was the founder of the Frederic Ziv Company, the biggest syndicator of filmed television shows. His productions included "The Cisco Kid," "Highway Patrol," "Sea Hunt," and many others.

LAUGH TRACKS

BARBARA BILLINGSLEY *(1922–)* played June Cleaver on the popular sitcom "Leave It to Beaver." A cameo in the movie *Airplane!* (1980) helped revive her career, and she has since made frequent guest appearances on TV.

JAY BURTON *(d. 1993)* wrote for Milton Berle for many years. His other credits include the Dean Martin roasts, "The Kraft Music Hall," and "The Big Party."

BOB CARROLL *(1918–)* teamed with Madelyn Davis to write "I Love Lucy." The two also worked together as producers on "Alice" and other shows.

IMOGENE COCA *(1908–)* starred in the classic NBC variety show "Your Show of Shows." She later had her own variety show and also starred in a sitcom, "Grindl." As of this writing, she and Sid Caesar are still performing together around the country.

MICHAEL DANN *(1922–)* began his television career at NBC, where he worked under Pat Weaver. He was also head of programming for CBS and later helped develop the Nickelodeon network. He is now with ABC in New York.

MEL DIAMOND wrote many television shows, including "Jack Carter and Company," "Bachelor Father," "Jackie Gleason and His American Scene Magazine" and "The Kate Smith Show."

RAY EARLENBORN *(1915–)* operated Charlie Douglas's laugh-track machine for many years. He is now retired and lives in Arizona.

ROD ERICKSON *(1916–)* was a director for both NBC and CBS in New York. He then moved to Procter & Gamble, where he supervised some forty-five radio shows before leaving the company for Young & Rubicam, where he was vice president and manager of the television department. He was also vice president at Warner Bros., where he was in charge of worldwide television, and president of Filmways.

HAL GOLDMAN *(1919–)* wrote for many leading television comedians, but most notably for Jack Benny and George Burns.

AL GORDON *(1924–)*, teamed with Hal Goldman, worked for Jack Benny and later George Burns, among many other shows.

BILLY GRAY *(1938–)* played Bud on "Father Knows Best." He later had a successful career as a motorcycle racer.

EVERETT GREENBAUM *(1919–)* wrote a number of sitcoms with his partner, Jim Fritzell, including "Mr. Peepers," "The Real McCoys," "The Andy Griffith Show," and "M★A★S★H."

PAUL HENNING *(1911–)* wrote for George Burns and Gracie Allen for many years. He later created, produced, and wrote "The Beverly Hillbillies," "Petticoat Junction," and "Green Acres."

CHARLIE ISAACS *(1914–)* is a comedy writer with many credits, most notably for Jimmy Durante on "The All-Star Revue" and "The Kraft Music Hall" with Al Jolson and Oscar Levant.

SEAMAN JACOBS *(1912–)* is a veteran comedy writer with numerous credits, including many of the Bob Hope and George Burns specials.

LUCILLE KALLEN was, along with Mel Tolkin, the lead writer on the landmark NBC comedy variety show "Your Show of Shows." She has since enjoyed a second career as a writer of mystery novels.

HAL KANTER *(1919–)* directed and wrote "The George Gobel Show." He later produced the sitcom "Julia."

HOWARD MORRIS *(1919–)* starred on "Your Show of Shows" and "Caesar's Hour." He also played the memorable Ernest T. Bass on "The Andy Griffith Show" and has had a long career directing TV shows and doing voices for cartoons.

PAUL PETERSEN *(1945–)* played Jeff Stone on "The Donna Reed Show." He is now involved in counseling child actors.

SOL RADAM *(1913–)* was an agent with the William Morris office.

JOE STEIN was a writer on "Your Show of Shows" and "Caesar's Hour." He later wrote the book for *Fiddler on the Roof, Zorba*, and many other Broadway shows.

DAVID SWIFT *(1929–)* created "Mr. Peepers" and wrote numerous other television shows, including plays for "Philco Television Playhouse" and "Studio One."

JANE WYATT *(1912–)* was a popular film actress (*Lost Horizon*) before she played the role of Margaret Anderson on "Father Knows Best." She has since appeared in many roles on both live and filmed television.

BUD YORKIN *(1926–)* was a stage manager on "The Colgate Comedy Hour." He later produced and directed "The George Gobel Show" and two Fred Astaire specials, and co-produced "All in the Family" with Norman Lear.

ROBERT YOUNG *(1907–)* won Emmys for his role as Jim Anderson in "Father Knows Best" and as Marcus Welby in "Marcus Welby, M.D."

AND NOW THE NEWS

PAUL ALLEY *(1905–1993)* wrote, produced, and edited one of NBC's earliest news programs, "The Camel Newsreel."

HARRY AROUH *(1923–)* began his broadcast career in Columbus, Ohio, in 1946. He then worked in Houston and Little Rock, as a reporter and news director respectively. He joined CBS Network News in 1960 and left in 1970 to teach journalism. He is now retired and spends much of his time painting and working with his son on a rock opera about his family.

MILI LERNER BONSIGNORI *(1918–)* is a film editor who worked on "See It Now" and "CBS Reports."

CHESTER BURGER *(1921–)* worked for CBS News for several years after World War II and now heads his own management consulting firm in communications.

CLAY CASSELL *(1927–)* worked for NBC News on its technical staff from the post–World War II years until his retirement.

HENRY CASSIRER *(1911–)* became a translator and broadcaster for the BBC after fleeing Germany in the 1930s. He was head of CBS Television News from 1945 to 1948. He later joined UNESCO as an adviser on television.

MATTHEW JOSEPH CULLIGAN *(1918–)* worked in the sales department at NBC, where one of his most important projects was the "Today" show. He has since written thirteen books on various subjects.

REUVEN FRANK *(1920–)* joined NBC News as a writer in 1950. He later produced more than a dozen documentaries for NBC. He organized the network's convention coverage in 1956, 1960, and 1964. Mr. Frank was also the executive producer of "The Huntley-Brinkley Report" and from 1968 to 1973 was the president of the news division. He has written an excellent history of NBC-TV news called *Out of Thin Air.*

FRED FRIENDLY *(1915–)* began his career in television news as the producer of the exemplary documentary series "See It Now." He was made president of CBS News in 1964, but resigned two years later in a dispute with the company when CBS decided to broadcast reruns of "I Love Lucy" instead of hearings on the Gulf of Tonkin resolution. He is the author of a book about TV news and CBS called *Due to Circumstances Beyond Our Control.*

GERALD GREEN *(1922–)* joined NBC as a news writer and later became news editor of the "Today" show and a producer of "Wide Wide World." He is now a novelist. His books include *The Last Angry Man* and *Holocaust.*

ANDREW HEISKELL *(1915–)* was the publisher of *Life* when he found himself virtually in charge of NBC's convention coverage in 1948 due to *Life*'s decision to sponsor the broadcasts.

DON HEWITT *(1922–)* was director and then producer of "CBS Evening News" with Douglas Edwards and then executive producer of the program when it was anchored by Walter Cronkite. He was the developer and remains the executive producer of "60 Minutes."

MARTIN HOADE *(1916–)* began his career in broadcasting at NBC radio and later moved into television, producing, directing, and writing public affairs programming. He was producer and director for "The Eternal Light."

ARTHUR HOLCH *(1924–)* was senior editor of "The Camel News Caravan" and later made documentary films.

DONALD HYATT *(1924–)* is a documentary filmmaker who assisted Henry "Pete" Salomon on the landmark NBC project "Victory at Sea." He later produced several segments of the network's "Wisdom Series" and also headed the NBC documentary unit Project XX, which produced a series of historical documentaries that were very successful in prime time.

EUGENE JONES *(1925–)* was already a veteran news cameraman in 1950 when he and his twin brother, Charlie, were sent to Korea by NBC News. They became the network's first cameramen-reporters in Europe and Asia. Gene was later producer of the "Today" show and a producer of "Wide Wide World." He is now a documentary filmmaker and lives in the Los Angeles area.

LARRY LESUEUR *(1909–)* was a reporter for United Press when he was recruited to be a part of Edward R. Murrow's elite team of radio newsmen for CBS before World War II. He later did some work on early television, including hosting his own show on the United Nations.

DAVID LEVY was an executive with Young & Rubicam and later head of programming for NBC. He produced television, shows for Filmways, including "The Addams Family," which he created, based on the cartoons of Charles Addams.

ARTHUR LODGE *(1918–1993)* was the first news writer hired for "The Camel News Caravan." He later formed his own documentary production company.

JAY MCMULLEN *(1921–)* was the reporter on, and producer of, some of CBS's finest documentaries of the 1950s and early 1960s. Later, he became a producer of "CBS Reports."

RICHARD PINKHAM *(1914–)* was a longtime advertising executive who also worked under Pat Weaver at NBC.

LEN SAFIR *(1921–1992)* was a producer on the "Today" show and the man most responsible for bringing J. Fred Muggs into the operation. He later co-wrote several books on language with his brother, William Safire.

JOHN SCHULTZ *(1929–)* is a film editor. He edited CBS's landmark documentary "Harvest of Shame" and many of the "CBS Reports" programs. He later taught for twenty-five years at the Columbia University Graduate School of Journalism.

ROBERT SKEDGELL *(1919–)* was the sole writer on CBS-TV's first regular news broadcast in 1941 and later enjoyed a long career with CBS radio.

ALBERT WASSERMAN *(1921–)* is a documentary film producer whose work has captured nearly all the top awards for both feature and television films. He was the founding producer of "NBC White Paper" and a producer for "60 Minutes." Now retired, he is an artist living in Greenwich Village, New York City.

JOSEPH WERSHBA *(1920–)* was a reporter on "See It Now" and later a producer for "60 Minutes."

PALMER WILLIAMS *(1916–)* was the production manager on "See It Now" and later executive producer of "CBS Reports."

FADE TO BLACK

SAMM SINCLAIR BAKER *(1909–)* spent most of his professional career in advertising. He also has written several books, including one about the advertising business, *The Permissible Lie*.

TOM BOLAN *(1924–)* is a New York City lawyer. He was a partner of Roy M. Cohn for many years and was the defense attorney on the losing side in the landmark blacklisting suit brought by John Henry Faulk against Aware Inc., Vincent Hartnett, and Laurence A. Johnson.

PAUL DRAPER *(1909–)* has danced all over the world. He and mouth-organist Larry Adler were a popular team until they were blacklisted in the 1950s.

MADELINE LEE GILFORD *(1923–)* is an actress and comedienne who has performed on stage, radio, and television. Her husband was the actor Jack Gilford.

LEE GRANT *(1930–)* has had a long, successful career as an actress, director, and producer. In 1975, she won an Academy Award for Best Supporting Actress for her performance in *Shampoo*.

KIM HUNTER *(1922–)* is a veteran stage, screen, and television actress. In 1951, she won an Academy Award for Best Supporting Actress for her performance in *A Streetcar Named Desire*.

ROBERT LEWINE *(1913–1993)* was a senior programming executive with ABC, CBS, and NBC.

HARVEY MATUSOW *(1926–)* was a member of the Communist Party before becoming a paid government informer and an aide to Senator Joseph McCarthy. He later recanted his testimony against various left-wing leaders and wrote a book about his life, *False Witness*. He is now a producer of children's television shows.

ABRAHAM LINCOLN POLONSKY *(1910–)* is a longtime Hollywood screenwriter, director, and novelist. Among his screen credits are *Body and Soul*, *Force of Evil*, and *Tell Them Willie Boy Is Here*. He also wrote numerous scripts for Gertrude Berg's radio programs in the 1930s. He teaches writing at the University of California, Los Angeles.

TOM QUINLIN *(1926–)* was a director of marketing for Revlon, Inc., where he helped create the company's television commercials during the 1950s. He was also an executive with several major advertising agencies and more recently a professor of marketing at Pace University.

BILL ROSS *(1915–1994)* stage-managed about seventy Broadway shows. As a producer, his credits include *Fiddler on the Roof*, *Camelot*, and *No, No, Nanette*.

ROBERT SAUDEK *(1911–)* was a vice president of ABC in the network's early years. He later created and produced the magazine show "Omnibus," which won more than one hundred awards during its nine years on television.

LESLIE SLOTE *(1924–)* is a journalist who worked for the civil service newspaper *The Chief* for many years.

FRANK STANTON *(1908–)* was the president of CBS from 1946 to 1972.

EZRA STONE *(1917–1994)* was a radio actor who played Henry Aldrich on "The Aldrich Family." He later became a producer.

GERALDINE ZORBAUGH *(1905–   )* was an attorney with ABC in the network's earliest years.

SOAPY STUFF

LARRY AUERBACH *(1923–   )* got his start in television at WNBQ in Chicago. He then directed the soap "Love of Life" for twenty-eight years and is still directing daytime television.

DICK DUNNE *(d. 1994)* produced several soap operas in the 1950s. He was later a talent agent on the West Coast.

LARRY HAINES is an actor who was a regular on "Search for Tomorrow" for nearly the entire life of the show.

JOHN HESS *(1918–   )* was a playwright before he created "Love of Life" and wrote the show for many years. He went on to write for other series, most notably "M★A★S★H."

JIMMY LYDON *(1923–   )* is a former child actor who later starred in the early CBS soap opera "The First Hundred Years." He has since acted in many roles on TV and also produced several shows.

AGNES NIXON is regarded as the queen of soap opera writers. With the former queen, Erna Phillips, she co-created "As the World Turns." She also wrote the series "The Guiding Light" for many years and created and wrote "All My Children," "One Life to Live," and "Loving." Although she was interviewed for this book, most of her comments in this chapter come from a series of speeches she gave at the Museum of Television and Radio in 1988.

MARY STUART *(1926–   )* played Joanne Tate on "Search for Tomorrow" for thirty-five years, the entire run of the series.

KIDS' STUFF

DAYTON ALLEN *(1919–   )* starred in many roles on "Howdy Doody." Before that he handled the puppets and voices on "The Adventures of Oky Doky." After his departure from "Howdy Doody," he was a regular on "The Steve Allen Show," and afterward starred in his own syndicated show.

ALEX ANDERSON *(1920–   )* created some of television's most beloved cartoon characters, including Crusader Rabbit and Rags, Rocky and Bullwinkle, and Dudley Do-Right.

LUCILLE BLISS was the voice of Crusader Rabbit and Smurfette. She still does voice-overs on television and radio.

SCOTT BRINKER *(1911–   )* created and built many of the puppets and special effects used on "Howdy Doody," including Flapdoodle and Flub-a-Dub.

BOB COLLEARY *(1929–   )* was the head writer on "Captain Kangaroo" for many years. He later produced and wrote "Benson."

DAVE CONNELL *(1931–1995)* started in television as a clerk with "Captain Kangaroo" and eventually became the show's executive producer. He later moved to the Children's Television Workshop, where he helped create "Sesame Street," "The Electric Company," and other shows.

RICHARD COOGAN *(1919–   )* starred as the original Captain Video on the DuMont network. He was also a star on Broadway and a regular on several other television shows, including "Love of Life" and "The Californians." He is now a golf pro in North Hollywood, California.

HOWARD DAVIS *(1918–   )* was a staff director for the local NBC station in New York before moving to the network with the "Howdy Doody" show, as its director. He also contributed many scripts to the program.

OLGA DRUCE *(1911–   )* directed the radio version of "Superman" before taking over "Captain Video."

WILLIAM HANNA *(1910–   )*, along with Joseph Barbera, created the *Tom and Jerry* cartoons for MGM. When the studio closed down its cartoon division, the two formed a partnership to develop cartoons for television. They created such memorable shows as "The Flintstones" and "The Jetsons" and dozens of cartoon characters, including Huckleberry Hound, Quickdraw McGraw, and Yogi Bear.

CHRIS HAYWARD *(1925–   )* wrote many episodes of "The Bullwinkle Show." He later co-produced "Barney Miller," "Get Smart," and "Alice."

EDDIE KEAN *(1924–   )* was the only writer for the first seven years of "Howdy Doody." He is a professional piano player living in Michigan.

BOB KEESHAN *(1928–   )* first appeared on television as Clarabell the clown on "Howdy Doody," but gained true fame as the genial Captain Kangaroo. Today, he is an advocate for children's issues.

RHODA MANN *(1928–   )* was one of the puppeteers on "Howdy Doody." She later went to WPIX to work with the puppets of Frank Paris, who made the original Howdy Doody.

BOB RIPPEN *(1919–   )* was the director of "Howdy Doody" for three years and later produced the show.

CY SCHNEIDER *(1929–1994)* was in the advertising business for more than forty years. His commercials for Mattel on "The Mickey Mouse Club" changed the way toys were marketed. He later helped found the Nickelodeon network and was the author of the book *Children's Television: The Art, the Business and How It Works.*

ART SCOTT *(1914–   )* was an animator for Disney and later a vice president for production with Hanna-Barbera, where he worked on many of the company's leading cartoon shows.

MARTIN STONE *(1915–   )* was an independent TV producer after World War II. In that capacity he was the co-creator of "Howdy Doody" and the well-regarded talk show "Author Meets the Critics."

GAMES PEOPLE PLAY

ELISE BARRON *(1940–   )* is a pseudonym for a contestant who appeared on the show "Tic Tac Dough."

SHIRLEY BERNSTEIN is the sister of the late Leonard Bernstein and was a producer on "The $64,000 Challenge."

STEVE CARLIN produced "The $64,000 Question" and "The $64,000 Challenge."

GILBERT CATES *(1934–   )* was an associate producer of the nighttime version of "Dotto." He is a producer whose credits include the annual Acadamy Awards show.

FRANK COOPER packaged the game show "Dotto." He is now a talent agent on the West Coast.

ALBERT FREEDMAN *(1926–   )* was a game show producer on radio and television. He now works for General Media.

REV. CHARLES "STONEY" JACKSON *(1913–   )* was a contestant on both "The $64,000 Question" and "The $64,000 Challenge." He is an itinerant minister, currently living in Colorado.

HERBERT STEMPEL *(1926–   )* was a contestant on "Twenty-One." He now works for the city of New York.

BOB STEWART *(1920–   )* created several of television's most successful game shows, including "To Tell the Truth," "The Price Is Right," "Password," and "The $20,000 Pyramid."

JUDGE JOSEPH STONE *(1912–   )* was an assistant district attorney in Manhattan when he investigated and prosecuted the quiz show scandals. He later became a criminal court judge and wrote a book about the scandals, entitled *Prime Time and Misdemeanors.*

MARIE WINN, a writer, is the author of *The Plug-In Drug* and other books. As a student, she was a contestant on "Dotto," which sparked the investigation of the quiz shows.

EXECUTIVE SUITES

EDWARD BERNAYS *(1891–1995)* was one of the fathers of modern public relations and was active in the business well into his nineties.

LARRY BRUFF *(1916–)* was an executive with Liggett & Meyers for many years. He purchased and produced many radio and television shows for the company.

GIRAUD CHESTER is an author and former network programming exective under Pat Weaver. He also worked in the advertising field and is now executive vice president with Mark Goodson Productions.

OSSIE DAVIS *(1917–)* has had a long and varied career as an actor, writer, and activist.

BETTY FURNESS *(1916–1994)* was a stage and screen actress who appeared on the DuMont network before her second career as a spokesperson for the Westinghouse Corp. She later became President Lyndon Johnson's special assistant for consumer affairs and a consumer reporter for NBC television.

HENRY GELLER *(1924–)* is a veteran Washington, D.C., attorney who has spent his entire career in public service, including several years with the Federal Communications Commission.

JUNE GRAHAM *(1925–)* was a TV actress and a popular commercial spokeswoman during the 1950s. She now lives in Colorado.

GEORGE ROY HILL *(1921–)* is a veteran Hollywood director who directed many live television shows for "Kraft Television Theatre." His work on "A Night to Remember" was one of the hallmarks of television's Golden Age.

NICK KEESELY *(1910–)* was a longtime advertising executive and is now retired, living in Florida.

EARTHA KITT *(1928–)* is a singer and actress who has appeared in many television shows, including her own variety show.

MALCOLM "BUD" LAING *(1926–)* was an executive with ABC in the network's earliest years, specializing in affiliate relations and station clearances.

PAUL LASKIN *(1924–)* was counsel to the Dodd Committee, which in 1961 and 1962 investigated televised violence and its effect on young people. He is now writing a book on televised violence.

DONALD LAUNER *(1926–)* was an engineer with ABC from the network's earliest years until his recent retirement.

SHELDON LEONARD *(1907–)* is a longtime actor, director, and producer. His production company was responsible for some of television's most popular sitcoms, including "Make Room for Daddy," "The Andy Griffith Show," "The Dick Van Dyke Show," and many more.

EVAN WILLIAM MANDEL *(1925–)* was a senior vice president with Revlon, Inc., where he helped supervise several of the company's television programs.

EVERARD MEADE *(1910–)* worked with Pat Weaver at Young & Rubicam, where he was vice president. He later taught advertising at the Darden Business School at the University of Virginia. He has also written five novels.

CARL PERIAN *(1929–)* was the chief investigator for the Dodd Committee.

PETER PETERSON *(1929–)* was president of Bell & Howell, where he was instrumental in creating "CBS Reports." He was later the U.S. Secretary of Commerce under Richard Nixon.

JOEL ROSENBLOOM *(1930–)* is an attorney in private practice in Washington, D.C. He served as counsel to the FCC under several chairmen, including Newton Minow.

BERNARD SCHWARTZ *(1923–)* investigated the practices of the FCC for Congress until he was fired after he apparently went too far in exposing the regulatory agency's corruption.

P. J. SIDNEY is a New York actor who has appeared in many television shows.

LOU WEISS is a former president of the William Morris Agency.

BIBLIOGRAPHY

Abramson, Albert. *The History of Television, 1880 to 1941.* Jefferson, N.C.: McFarland, 1987.

Allen, Robert C. *Speaking of Soap Operas.* Chapel Hill: University of North Carolina Press, 1985.

Ambrose, Stephen E. *Nixon, The Education of a Politician, 1913–1962.* Vol. 1. New York: Simon & Schuster, 1987.

Andrews, Bart. *The "I Love Lucy" Book.* New York: Doubleday, 1985.

Baker, Samm Sinclair. *The Permissible Lie, The Inside Truth About Advertising.* Cleveland: World Publishing Co., 1968.

Barber, Red. *The Broadcasters.* New York: Da Capo, 1970.

Barnouw, Erik. *The Golden Web, A History of Broadcasting in the United States, 1933–1953.* New York: Oxford University Press, 1968.

———. *The Image Empire, A History of Broadcasting in the United States From 1953.* New York: Oxford University Press, 1970.

———. *The Sponsor, Notes on a Modern Potentate.* New York: Oxford University Press, 1978.

———. *A Tower in Babel, A History of Broadcasting in the United States to 1933.* New York: Oxford University Press, 1966.

———. *The Television Writer.* New York: Hill & Wang, 1962.

Bean, Orson. *Too Much Is Not Enough.* Secaucus, N.J.: Lyle Stuart, 1988.

Benny, Jack, and Benny, Joan. *Sunday Nights at Seven, The Jack Benny Story.* New York: Warner Books, 1990.

Berle, Milton, with Frankel, Haskell. *An Autobiography.* New York: Delacorte Press, 1974.

Bilby, Kenneth. *The General, David Sarnoff and the Rise of the Communications Industry.* New York: Harper & Row, 1986.

Bliss, Edward, Jr. *Now the News, The Story of Broadcast Journalism.* New York: Columbia University Press, 1991.

Blum, Richard A., and Lindheim, Richard D. *Prime Time Network Television Programming.* Boston: Focal Press, 1987.

Blythe, Cheryl, and Sackett, Susan. *Say Goodnight, Gracie! The Story of George Burns and Gracie Allen*. Rocklin, Calif.: Prima, 1989.

Boyd, James. *Above the Law, The Rise and Fall of Senator Thomas J. Dodd*. New York: New American Library, 1968.

Bretz, Rudy, and Stasheff, Edward. *The Television Program, Its Writing, Direction, and Production*. New York: A. A. Wyn, Inc., 1951.

Brooks, Tim, and Marsh, Earle. *The Complete Directory to Prime Time Network TV Shows, 1946–Present*. New York: Ballantine, 1979.

Broughton, Irv, ed. *Producers on Producing, The Making of Film and Television*. Jefferson, N.C.: McFarland, 1986.

Brown, Lee. *The New York Times Encyclopedia of Television*. New York: Times Books, 1977.

Caesar, Sid, with Davidson, Bill. *Where Have I Been? An Autobiography*. New York: Crown, 1982.

Cassirer, Henry R. *Seeds in the Winds of Change, Through Education and Communication*. Norfolk, England: Peter Francis, 1989.

Chayefsky, Paddy. *Television Plays*. New York: Simon & Schuster, 1955.

Cogley, John. *Report on Blacklisting, Radio–Television*. Vol. 2. New York: The Fund for the Republic, 1956.

Crosby, John. *Out of the Blue, A Book About Radio and Television*. New York: Simon & Schuster, 1952.

Davis, Stephen. *Say, Kids! What Time Is It? Notes from the Peanut Gallery*. Boston: Little, Brown, 1987.

Dunlop, Orrin E., Jr. *The Outlook for Television*. New York: Harper & Row, 1932.

Edmondson, Madeleine, and Rounds, David. *The Soaps, Daytime Serials of Radio and TV*. New York: Stein and Day, 1973.

Erickson, Hal. *Syndicated Television, The First Forty Years, 1947–1987*. Jefferson, N.C.: McFarland, 1989.

Farnsworth, Elma. *Distant Vision, Romance & Discovery on an Invisible Frontier*. Salt Lake City: Pemberlykent, 1989.

Fein, Irving A. *Jack Benny, An Intimate Biography*. New York: G. P. Putnam's Sons, 1976.

Foote, Horton. *A Young Lady of Property, Six Short Plays*. New York: Dramatists Play Service, 1983.

Frank, Reuven. *Out of Thin Air*. New York: Simon & Schuster, 1991.

Friendly, Fred W. *Due to Circumstances Beyond Our Control . . .* London: MacGibbon & Kee, 1967.

Goldenson, Leonard, and Wolf, Marvin J. *Beating the Odds, The Untold Story Behind the Rise of ABC: The Stars, Struggles and Egos That Transformed Network Television*. New York: Scribners, 1991.

Goldmark, Peter C., with Edson, Lee. *Maverick Inventory, My Turbulent Years at CBS*. New York: Saturday Review Press, 1973.

Gross, Benn. *I Looked and Listened, Informal Recollections of Radio and TV*. New York: Random House, 1954.

Grossman, Gary H. *Saturday Morning TV*. New York: Dell, 1981.

Halberstam, David. *The Fifties*. New York: Villard, 1983.

———. *Summer of '49*. New York: Avon Books, 1989.

Hess, Gary Newton. *An Historical Study of the DuMont Television Network.* New York: Arno Press, 1979.

Hubbell, Richard. *4000 Years of Television, The Story of Seeing at a Distance.* New York: G. P. Putnam's Sons, 1942.

Inglis, Andrew F. *Behind the Tube, A History of Broadcasting Technology and Business.* Boston: Focal Press, 1990.

Inman, David, ed. *The TV Encyclopedia.* New York: Perigee, 1991.

Jamieson, Kathleen Hall. *Packing the Presidency, A History and Criticism of Presidential Campaign Advertising.* New York: Oxford University Press, 1992.

Jones, Gerard. *Honey, I'm Home! Sitcoms: Selling the American Dream.* New York: Grove Weidenfeld, 1992.

Kahn, Albert E. *The Matusow Affair, Memoir of a National Scandal.* Mt. Kisco, N.Y.: Moyer Bell, Ltd., 1987.

Kaufman, William I., ed. *The Best Television Plays, 1950–1951.* New York: Merlin Press, 1952.

————, ed. *How to Write for Television.* New York: Hastings House, 1955.

Keeshan, Bob. *Growing Up Happy.* New York: Berkley, 1989.

Kendrick, Alexander. *Prime Time, The Life of Edward R. Murrow.* Boston: Little, Brown, 1969.

Kuney, Jack. *Take One, Television Directors on Directing.* New York: Praeger, 1990.

Lewis, Colby, and Greer, Tom. *The TV Director/Interpreter.* New York: Hastings House, 1968.

Lewis, Marlo, and Lewis, Mina Bess. *Prime Time.* New York: St. Martin's Press, 1979.

Lichty, Lawrence W., and Topping, Malachi C. *American Broadcasting, A Source Book on the History of Radio and Television.* New York: Hastings House, 1975.

Lyons, Eugene. *David Sarnoff.* New York: Harper & Row, 1966.

MacDonald, J. Fred. *One Nation Under Television, The Rise and Decline of Network TV.* New York: Pantheon, 1990.

Matusow, Harvey. *False Witness.* New York: Cameron and Kahn, 1955.

Mayer, Martin. *About Television.* New York: Harper & Row, 1972.

McArthur, Tom, and Waddell, Peter. *Vision Warrior, The Hidden Achievement of John Logie Baird.* Orkney: Scottish Falcon, 1986.

McMahon, Harry Wayne. *The Television Commercial.* New York: Hastings House, 1957.

Metz, Robert. *The "Today" Show.* New York: Playboy Press, 1977.

Miner, Worthington, and Schaffner, Frank J. *Worthington Miner.* Metuchen, N.J.: Scarecrow Press, 1985.

Mosel, Tad. *Other People's Houses, Six Television Plays.* New York: Simon & Schuster, 1956.

Nixon, Agnes. *Seminars at the Museum of Broadcasting.* New York: Museum of Broadcasting, 1988.

O'Connor, John E., ed. *American History/American Television, Interpreting the Video Past.* New York: Ungar, 1983.

Opotowsky, Stan. *TV, The Big Picture.* New York: E. P. Dutton, 1961.

Paley, William. *As It Happened, A Memoir.* Garden City, N.Y.: Doubleday, 1979.

Persico, Joseph E. *Edward R. Murrow, An American Original.* New York: Laurel, 1988.

Red Channels, The Report of Communist Influence in Radio and Television. New York: Counterattack, 1950.

Rhymer, Mary Frances, ed. *Vic and Sade, The Best Radio Plays of Paul Rhymer.* New York: The Seabury Press, 1976.

Rose, Reginald. *Six Television Plays.* New York: Simon & Schuster, 1956.

Schneider, Cy. *Children's Television, the Art, the Business, and How It Works.* Lincolnwood, Ill.: NTC Business Books, 1989.

Schwartz, David; Ryan, Steve; and Wostbrock, Fred. *The Encyclopedia of TV Game Shows.* New York: Zoetrope, 1987.

Seldes, Gilbert. *The Great Audience.* New York: Viking, 1950.

———. *The Public Arts.* New York: Simon & Schuster, 1956.

Sennett, Ted. *Your Show of Shows, The Story of Television's Most Celebrated Comedy Program.* New York: Da Capo, 1977.

Siepmann, Charles. *Radio, Television and Society.* New York: Oxford University Press, 1950.

Skutch, Ira. *I Remember Television: A Memoir.* Metuchen, N.J.: Scarecrow Press, 1989.

Smith, Buffalo Bob, and McCrohan, Donna. *Howdy and Me, Buffalo Bob's Own Story.* New York: Plume, 1990.

Smith, Curt. *Voices of the Game.* South Bend, Ind.: Diamond, 1987.

Smith, Sally Bedell. *In All His Glory, The Life of William S. Paley, The Legendary Tycoon and His Brilliant Circle.* New York: Simon & Schuster, 1990.

Sperber, A. M. *Murrow: His Life and Times.* New York: Bantam, 1986.

Sposa, Louis A. *Television Primer of Production and Direction.* New York: McGraw-Hill, 1947.

Stallings, Penny. *Forbidden Channels, The Truth They Hide from TV Guide.* New York: Harper Perennial, 1991.

Sterling, Christopher H., and Kittross, John M. *Stay Tuned, A Concise History of American Broadcasting.* Belmont, Calif.: Wadsworth, 1990.

Stone, Joseph, and Yohn, Tim. *Prime Time and Misdemeanors, Investigating the 1950s T.V. Quiz Scandal—A D.A.'s Account.* New Brunswick, N.J.: Rutgers University Press, 1992.

Sturcken, Frank. *Live Television, The Golden Age of 1946–1958 in New York.* Jefferson, N.C.: McFarland, 1990.

Terrace, Vincent. *Encyclopedia of Television, Series, Pilots and Specials, 1937–1973.* New York: Zoetrope, 1985.

———. *Encyclopedia of Television, Series, Pilots and Specials, The Index: Who's Who in Television, 1937–1984.* New York: Zoetrope, 1986.

Vidal, Gore, ed. *Best Television Plays.* New York: Ballantine, 1956.

Vision of Ernie Kovacs, The. New York: Museum of Broadcasting, 1986.

Wakeman, Frederic. *The Hucksters.* New York: Rinehart & Co, 1946.

Waldrop, Frank, and Borkin, Joseph. *Television: A Struggle for Power.* New York: William Morrow and Co., 1938.

Walley, David G. *The Ernie Kovacs Phile.* New York: Bolder, 1975.

Wilk, Max. *The Golden Age of Television, Notes from the Survivors.* New York: Delacorte Press, 1976.

Winship, Michael. *Television.* New York: Random House, 1988.

Wooley, Lynn; Malsbary, Robert W.; and Strange, Robert G., Jr., *Warner Bros. Television.* Jefferson, N.C.: McFarland, 1985.

ACKNOWLEDGMENTS

Before I undertook this project, I was a television watcher, not a television writer. I had to do an enormous amount of research and talk to many people (more than four hundred) before I felt I had a handle on the subject, so for the last five years, I've relied on the kindness of friends and strangers. Not everyone I contacted was so agreeable, but it was remarkable how many people were perfectly willing to speak openly with me and go out of their way to offer help, after only the barest of introductions. I was treated to a lot of home-cooked meals, lent precious family photos, and generally treated with more respect than what was called for. Writing a book like this is mostly a lonely, difficult process, but the opportunity of meeting and getting to know gracious people and knowing that one can preserve for the record the good work that they did makes it worthwhile.

So many people helped out. This book was rooted in a phone call I received from Duncan Stalker, asking me to write a Sunday oral-history column for the *New York Post*. Two people I interviewed for the column were TV veterans. Their stories were so good I immediately realized I had the subject for my next book. Duncan is gone now, of AIDS. He was a good guy. It was my agent, Susan Bergholz, who thought an oral history of TV was an idea worth pursuing. Next came Stacy Schiff, who originally signed it, before it eventually wound up with Wendy Wolf at Viking. She saw something in my manuscript even though it was only slightly smaller than the Manhattan phone book. Wendy and Tom Engelhardt did a masterful job of bringing it down to size, although it broke my heart to have to leave out many marvelous voices.

Other people who have played major roles in seeing this to the end include a good friend, Mark Levine, who was really responsible for getting me started in this book business. Bill Barol and Jennifer Cecil and Glynnis O'Connor and Doug Stern opened their homes to me during several trips to California. Because I could then interview so many more people in person, the book is that much better for their hospitality. Generosity runs in the O'Connor family. Dan O'Connor provided me with a list of contacts that became a blueprint for the book. He and his wife, Lenka Peterson, were especially helpful throughout the entire research process.

A number of people reviewed the different versions of this manuscript and offered vital criticisms. They include Bill Barol, Monica Wellington, Sara Hyland, Glynnis O'Connor, and, especially, my father, Samuel Kisseloff. Duncan MacDonald, Red Quinlan, Philip Falcone, John Hollywood, Paul Noble, Fred Wostbrock, Mark Wallace, Bob Morris, Joel Tator, Mrs. Harry Lauter, and Phyliss Smith all offered extra help in locating sources. Laura Wellington, of London town, supplied the book's title.

David Weiss, Isabelle Bruder Smith, and Nancy Urvant saw me through some dark days. Also, lots of aid and encouragement was received from Alan and Nancy Kisseloff, Lil Resnick, Edith Tiger, Peter Gambaccini, Laura Mitgang, and David Goodman. Thanks also to Jane Rosenman for her special efforts on my behalf.

This book is also for my cousin Rose Halpern, who for some mysterious reason has always believed in every crazy thing I've ever done and is always happy to hear from me and see me. Everyone should have a Mama Rosie in their life.

Many of the people who offered to locate sources and run interference for me have been lost to my poor handwriting on endless reams of legal pads. But those names I can recall or that can be deciphered include Art Abrams, Ellen Abrams, Mort Abrams, Eliot Asinof, Sally Baer, Kevin Baker, Joseph Baudino, Orson Bean, Josephine Beaudoin, Margaret Berger, Brad Bessey, Henry Bollinger, Teddy Brenner, Paula Brody, Ward Byron, Syd Cassyd, Ken Chittick, Maura Chistopher, Gerald Clapp, Sheila Colon, Don Dellair, Ann Distelhorst, Paul Doherty, Bruce DuMont, Barbara Dunlop, Dan Einstein, Charles Fagan, the Fischer family, Ron Givens, David Goldstein, Scott Greenhouse, Michael Hardart, Catharine Heinz, Sylvia Hirsch, Alger Hiss, Tony Hiss, Monique James, Brittany, Evan, and Jared Kisseloff, Ed Kowalachuk, Killer Kowalski, Julian Krainin, Barbara Kross, George Maksian, Barney McNulty, Donald Meier, Ira Miller, Friema Norkin, Byron Paul, Sam Perrin, Stanley Quinn, Kim Ronis, Albert Rose, Randy Rubenstein, Phil Ruyter, Angelo Savoldi, Jean Schaffner, Paul Schulman, Harriet Berg Schwartz, Dean Shaffner, Susan Siegrist, Ron Simon, Elliott Sivowich, Tom Smith, John Strauss, Roger Strull, Hermino Travieses, Jim Treyz, Douglas Watkyns, Lydia Wellington, Alberto White, Tim Yohn, Titus Yonker, and Margaret Shue Young. Also, thanks to the helpful library staff at the Museum of Television and Radio, where a lot of research for this book was done.

The following people, all television pioneers, took the time to sit for interviews, but because of my cruel editor, couldn't be included in the final draft. Many of them were terrific. Special apologies to Paul Tripp, whose "Mr. I.

Magination" was one of the best children's shows, Paul Nickell, who directed many of the finest live dramas of the fifties and was always helpful, and Jackie Babbin, Kathi Norris, Korla Pandit, and Curt Gowdy, who were all especially kind.

The others were Larry Adler, Pat Banks, Bill Bogash, Murray Bolen, James Boyd, William Boyett, Tom Bozalsky, Bobby Breen, Herb Browar, Bill Burch, Grace Carney, Carl Caruso, Bernadette Castro, Maureen Christopher, Charles Colledge, Barnaby Conrad, Fielder Cook, Dorothy Cooper, John Cowden, Russ Debaun, Guy Della Cioppa, Don Diamond, Walter Doniger, Hector Dowd, Alex Dreier, Yvonne DuMont, John Dyer, Ronnie Eldridge, Ted Estabrook, Donald Flamm, William Forbes, Arthur Forrest, Cliff Gardner, Dorothy Gardner, Roger Gerry, Marian Glick, Virginia Graham, Ken Graue, Kathy Henderson, Ed Herlihy, Harry Hickox, Richard Hopkins, Wayne Howell, David Huschle, Felix Jackson, Chris Jenkyns, Allan Kalmus, Harold Kihn, Eleanor Kilgallen, Basil Langton, Grey Lockwood, Abby Mann, Kyle McDonnell, Jayne Meadows, Dick Mitchell, Clayton Moore, Jerry Muller, Ann Nelson, Jules Nisenson, Arnie Nocks, Donald Nelson, Ken Osmond, Eddie Palmier, Johnny Parker, Don Pike, Herb Purdim, Larry Racies, Sue Read, Del Reisman, Toby Rutherford, Elroy Schwartz, Bob Short, Danny Simon, John Stagnaro, Wilbur Stark, W. L. States, Cliffy Stone, Walter Stone, Carl Stucke, Bill Stulla, Clarence Thoman, Peggy Webber, Jesse White, Beverly Younger, and Mary "Pocahontas" Youpel.

The first interviews I did after signing my book contract were not successful. Very discouraged and fearing that the project might have to be abandoned, I drove down to Philadelphia to have lunch with two of television's real pioneers, Loren Jones and Ted Smith. Their magnificent stories, and their generosity and good humor, turned everything around for me. As I headed back toward the Lincoln Tunnel, I was sure for the first time that this book could be done.

I kept in touch with them over the years. They were always encouraging, and interested in hearing about my progress. Both were in their late eighties and, I think, anxious to see their stories in print before their time was up. I was as eager as they were. Nothing gave me more pleasure over the course of my research than knowing that I was preserving the legacy of these wonderful people. The idea that one day I would hand them a copy of the book with their words inside propelled me through my tough times.

Well, Ted didn't make it. He'll never see this, but I have every confidence that Loren will, and I hope he sees this book the way it was intended, as a testament to the passion, creativity, and decency of him and Ted and their colleagues who believed that they were bringing something into this world that might make it a better place for us all. Maybe it still can.

INDEX